Between Life & Death

*"Write this for a memorial in book
and rehearse it in the ears of posterity."*
                    Exodus XVIII, 14

Between Life & Death

History of Jewish Life in Wartime Poland
1939-1945

Ben A. Soifer

JANUS PUBLISHING COMPANY
London, England.

First published in Great Britain 1995
by Janus Publishing Company,
Edinburgh House, 19 Nassau Street,
London W1N 7RE

Copyright © Ben A. Soifer 1995

British Library Cataloguing-in-Publication Data.
A catalogue record for this book is available from the
British Library.

ISBN 1 85756 240.2

The right of Ben A. Soifer to be identified as the author of
this work has been asserted by him in accordance with the
Copyright, Designs and Patents Act 1988.

Map by Sue Sharples.
Cover design Linda Wade.
Typeset by Ian Fleming Ltd. Altrincham.
Printed and bound in England by
T J Press (Padstow) Ltd. Padstow, Cornwall.

PREFACE

This book, born of a desire to tell something about the lives and deaths of fellow men in wartime Poland, is a genuine historical study. The events referred to are in the main well documented. But the study is, unconventionally, written as a story.

The intention was to find a superior way of chronicling the unusual reality of those tragic days. It was also necessary to find a form that would enable me to better commune with the Jews there and so to evoke their life to greater depth and with greater immediacy.

Only history as fiction offered a way of reaching and relating matters inside the mind of man; his helplessness and struggles: his humiliation and heroism; the conflicts between his duty and defiance; his solitude amongst buzzing crowds; his fight against loss of humanity and his hope even in the throes of death; his facing urgent moral questions of no immediate answer. At the same time, using the device of a contemporary recording of events allowed me to recoup some of the strength and bluntness lost by distance of time and to overcome, in part, the inhibitions common in current writing about the occurrences of those days.

Fiction also better fitted my purpose of bringing into memory the lives of the victims rather than, as has been the effect of many accounts, immortalising the deeds of their oppressors.

The book mainly uses conversation to discuss even some of the most serious issues of the time; such subjects as theories of race and the causes of war; Polish-Jewish relations and relations between free and captive Jews; the new order of life and institutions imposed by the occupant; or the historical and religious meaning of what has become known inaptly as the holocaust. This style should make the study more agreeable to readers reluctant to read pages of long, dry analyses of necessarily depressing subjects.

Whatever the outward form, the text is always true to fact and deed. But the actual setting is mostly fictional and, with the exception of public figures, such as Ben-Gurion, Churchill, Roosevelt, and Germans connected with the events described, who are mentioned by their true names, all the characters in the book, both Polish and Jewish, are either wholly or partially the creation of the author.

The characters are quite numerous. Some appear throughout the narrative or in several parts, several also symbolize ideas and political beliefs, and nearly all bear foreign names which may sound unfamiliar. Hence, a select dramatis personae is included as well as, at the end of the book, a basic bibliography and index.

My thanks are due to Ms. Ruth Spriggs for her assistance in typing and correcting the English of the manuscript and for her help in preparing it for publication.

And finally my sincerely felt thanks and profound relief for having been able, despite all the adversities of those last years, to complete this study and see its publication. It makes me sometimes think that to survive, one in a hundred, this greatest of Jewish tragedies and to live a long, lonely life thereafter, has not perhaps been quite in vain.

Dramatis personae

Listed in alphabetical order and described by their function or status, if out of the ordinary, and by the beliefs or political orientations which some of the characters symbolize.(P) after the name stands for Pole.

Alter, Berl - master tailor
Antosh (P) - lorry driver
Baruch - orthodox protagonist
Bester, Hugo - intellectual, liberal
Blonder, Reuben (Ruben)
Bodman, Jankel - burial serviceman
Brzostek (P) - Christian Democrat
Buchaj, Samuel - dentist, blasphemer
Chanes - manager
Deker, Asyk - Bundist
Dellmar - super-manager
Dichter - cantor-cobbler, penitent
Erb, Szlamek - messenger
Einhorn, Tunye - pious operatic amateur
Eltes, Bonek - resistance champion
Falban, Henryk - Judenrat chairman
Faulhaupt, Iziek - scribe at camp
Feldmaus, Bubi - camp eldest
Felek - semi-heretic opinions
Flacher, Abe
Freund, Arush - hero of story, mainstream Jewish
Freund family - father Abraham, mother
    Mathilde, brothers Dave and Eli; sisters
    Klara, Gila and Nili
Goldman
Graykowa (P) - Countess
Hausdienst, Sami - radical Zionist-Socialist
Heibaum, Kurt - master tailor
Hilfsreich, Dr - physician
Itzkowicz, Aciek
Jozek (P) - block eldest
Knepel, Lipe - communist
Krel - capo
Krohn, Pineas - camp storekeeper
Krumstein, Maks - JDR deputy chairman
Kwas, Lolek
Laib, Bunim - wealthy upper class
Lander, Maniek - master upholsterer
Lebron - "righteous" woman
Leftof, Maleachi - rabbi
Lewin, Mechil - mystic
Lisko, Perec - master saddler
Maczek, Zenobia (P) - physician
Olkowicz - lawyer, assimilant
Osterman, Wolf - shoe-uppers master
Prater - master cobbler
Rainer, Marek - mechanic
Roter - OD deputy commander
Salit, Adi - OD man
Semmel, Kurt - radio workshop master
Spatz, Shmil - Judenrat Councillor
Srebrny, Mendel - actor-singer
Szinc, Mates - ideal society promoter

Sztok - capo
Teper, Artek - Epicurean
Vadovitzer, Dr Adrian - camp physician
Weltman, Moniek - furrier and shoe-shiner
Wisia (P) - maid
Wróbel, Bolek (P) - patriot
Zauber - ghetto millionaire

Germans
True names of men closely connected with the happenings, described by their functions or SS rank. (C) and (G) stand for civilian and Gestapo, respectively.

Berndt - Untersturmführer
Blache, Hermann - Hauptscharf., ghetto
    commander
Brandt, Oskar - (G)
Brauchitsch, Werner von - General, Wehrmacht
    Commander
Engels, Erich - Hauptsturmf. (G)
Frank, Hans - Governor General (C)
Globocnik, Odilo - Obersturmbannf., head of
    "Aktion Reinhard
Goeth, Amon - Hauptsturmf., camp commander
Grzimek, Josef - Hauptscharf., Lagerf.
Haase, Willy von - Obersturmbannf.
Heydrich, Reinhard - Oberf., chief of security
    police and SD.
Kellermann, Hans - Hauptsturmf., camp
    commander
Kipke, Dr Alfred - SA Oberf. Kreishauptmann
Klause - workshop master (C)
Klipp, Kurt - Untersturmf., camp commander
Kops, Ernst - Oberscharf.
Krueger, Friedrich - Gruppenf. chief SS and Police
    Führer (SSPF) in GG
Madritsch, Julius - business man (C)
Malotky, Paul von (G)
Oppermann, Karl (G)
Pernutz, Dr Karl - deputy Kreishauptmann (C)
Pospiech - Lagerführer
Proschinsky, Hanns - Hauptsturmf.
Rommelmann, Wilhelm - Hauptscharf. (G)
Ruf(f) - camp Raportf.
Saar - Hauptscharf.
Schachner, Hubert (G)
Scheele Freiherr, Werner von - Oberf., base
    commander
Scheidt, Anton - Untersturmf., camp commander
Scherner, Julius - Oberf., district SS and Police
    Führer
Schittli - Hauptsturmf., camp commander
Schrade - Hauptscharf.
Schumacher, Dr - Obersturmbannf., physician
Tann, Freiherr Otto von und zu - Hauptsturmf.
Voss, Bernard - Gruppenf., base commander
Voss, "Brunnhilde" - daughter of Bernard (C)
Zapke - Unterscharf., sanitarian

Contents

PART ONE

Clean up

CHAPTER ONE

It was shortly before dawn when the first suspicious sounds penetrated the silence of the second-floor kitchen, the home of Mathilde Freund and her two remaining sons. The breathless silence was in no way peaceful and the menacingly vibrant sounds came not unexpectedly to the Freunds or to other people in the ghetto of Tarnów. They all knew what was coming - even those who pretended not to know - and they were all on the alert this morning.

For weeks the sky over the narrow confines of the ghetto had been leaden with clouds as black, as inexorable, as death itself. August had somehow gone by, and now on the second morning of September - the fifth September of war - the storm was about to break loose. A glance through the window from behind its covering of black paper towards the Aryan side of the street, confirmed the dismal truth. Men in SS and police uniforms were in position. The ghetto was cordoned off. Another *Aktion*, or *Aussiedlung*, deportation, evacuation - all German euphemisms for the same act of mass destruction - was about to begin.

"Don't lift the curtain," said Mrs Freund. Her firm-soft voice was apprehensive but the warning was superfluous. No one would be so senseless as to do such a thing. Mrs Freund knows this but -as she sees it - it is her duty, her lifelong duty, to warn her children of danger. Even if her children are already young men. She must be, until the end, an example to them. She must preserve calm and by every means avert panic.

Night after night, lying in her narrow folding bed - which, when opened out, took up every bit of space in the room, while the two brothers shared the standing bed - Mathilde Freund had gone over the expected Aktion in every cruel detail. She was prepared for anything, fearing only that the Germans would come unexpectedly, perhaps in the middle of the night, and force them - as they had her husband - at gun point down the stairs to the courtyard. What would happen after that she did not dare to think about. It was too horrifying. Instead the parting occupied her thoughts. What she dreaded most was parting from Eli and Arush, her two sons, but she was determined that when the time came she would not make it harder for them.

They were her two youngest. For some time before they were born, she had thought of having no more children. Had she stuck to her intention, she would have been long alone. Fortunately she had changed her mind. Perhaps they would survive. They are young and healthy. Perhaps too frail for the hard work presently required of Jews, but they are strong in their resolve to endure, strong in character and strong in their faith - even the younger Arush is strong in faith. Her sons - her pride, her only comfort. She herself was no longer young, at 55 considered too old for work by the Germans. Though, how hard she was working now, despite her long illness two years ago. But what matters is not how she feels or what she does, only how the Germans will rate her. For herself she can only expect the worst, but Eli and Arush have a chance. If they would only survive! She would live on through them. And yet, she must decide what to do. From previous experience she knew that people like herself had a better chance in hiding. Those who were not discovered during the hours of storm came safely to dry land. But previous Aktions had been short - a few days at most. How long would this one last? And how long could one survive in hiding? Some people were saying that this time it would be *endgültig* (final) - the ghetto liquidated. But it was no use thinking too much. For her it would still be best to hide. If it worked - good. If not, well we all have to die in the end. Aren't we all doomed, anyway?

Similar thoughts had occupied the minds of most of the people in the ghetto ever since they had heard the rumours of the forthcoming Aktion. After a lot of talk most people had decided that the young and healthy should report as ordered, while the elderly, the sick, infants and mothers with little children would hide. The decision had the blessing of Rabbi Maleachi Leftof, who was generally venerated in the ghetto and who was a close neighbour of the Freund family.

Eli and Arush helped their mother, together with Rabbi Maleachi and his wife, to crawl into the "bunker" (as hiding places were called). They passed in some essential provisions and hesitantly went down the stairs from the attic. Outside the house, too grief-stricken for words, too overcome by emotion, they merely said goodbye to each other and parted, each to join his group.

It was already after six and, like Arush and Eli, men and women, mostly young, were emerging slowly from their houses. They seemed horror-struck but calm. Few spoke, except to greet a friend or neighbour. None were carrying any of their belongings. They had, after all, been told to report for work as usual.

To reach his workplace, the Varnish and Putty Factory, Arush had to cross the Magdeburger Platz. Local people, who remembered it as the town's bus station, still called it by its Polish name - Freedom Square. But to most of its recent users it was known simply as The Platz. It was an appropriately plain name for what had become the daily assembly point for slave labourers leaving for, and returning from, work outside the ghetto. It had also been the mustering ground for the last two Aktions. The cobbled rectangular space, nearly three acres in area, was mostly enclosed. Where there were no buildings, fences had been erected. Gates in the fences, on the eastern and western sides of the Platz, gave access to the outside world. Near the centre the former ticket office had been converted into the headquarters of the *Ordnungsdienst* - the OD or Jewish auxiliary police.

People had only just begun to assemble there, when Arush crossed the Platz from Szpitalna Street, where he lived, to Dembowa Street where he worked. And there were few men in the workshop when he arrived there. But gradually more came in and soon someone told them the startling news that Rabbi Maleachi had left the bunker. One man had seen him joining a working party and later arrivals, some of

4

whom Arush had never seen in the workshop before, said it was true. "Everybody is leaving the bunkers," they said.

At first Arush could not believe this terrifying news. "It's just gossip," he told himself. But, after a while, sensing disaster, he decided, however great the risk, to find out for himself. Passing through the now congested Platz, he overheard fragments of people's conversations. "Rabbi Maleachi left...", "Rabbi Maleachi went..." The news passed from mouth to mouth, raising consternation. It was a clear distress signal. If, people reasoned, the elderly Rabbi Maleachi, indisputedly the most esteemed member of the community, had abandoned his bunker, then someone in the know - a Judenrat councillor or an OD commander - must have advised him to do so. He was clearly forewarned. So it was useless to hide. There could be no more illusions. "It's true," Arush thought, "the last net is being cast and the town is to be made *Judenrein* (free of Jews)."

Before long, the news that the ghetto's guardian angel had left his hiding-place found its way to the most secure bunkers and the people hiding in them began to emerge in their hundreds. As if fleeing from flames, they ran from attics and cellars and streamed into the streets. Unprotected and almost without hope of refuge they crowded into the Platz.

Back at Szpitalna 12, Arush ran up the stairs of the silent house. At the entrance to the attic stood Rabbi Maleachi with two of his followers, a father and son, at his side. His wife and Mrs Freund had already left. Rabbi Maleachi had remained to change his appearance so that he would look less conspicuous. The scene was ineffably touching. The younger of his two followers, Nathan Knobel, wanted to trim his sumptuous moustache. His beard had already been shaved off. But Nathan's hand, in which he held the scissors, was trembling and tears poured from his eyes. This, in turn, brought tears to the large, wise eyes of the rabbi, who otherwise remained composed.

Oh, who could tell the spell of a saintly man's moustache!

In the street, Rabbi Maleachi gave Arush a short "God bless you" and told him to return to his work group. But Arush stopped and, with the two Knobels, who had also been sent away with a blessing, watched from a distance as the sage, alone for the first time outside his home since the war had begun, walked away with slow, measured steps. His back was straight and he still wore his traditional black hat, which was certain to serve as a red rag to any brown-clad German bull. Arush watched the rabbi until he disappeared from sight into the tailors' workshop at which he, his wife and Mrs Freund were registered for work but which none of them had ever before graced with their presence.

Rabbi Maleachi's walk took him along the whole width of the ghetto. Actually this was only about two hundred yards. At this stage in its history, the whole ghetto area was only five times as long as it was wide and included both ghetto A, promoted to *Zwangsarbeitslager* (forced labour camp) at the end of 1942, and ghetto B, housing the unregistered but unregistrable for work.

The street was now full of movement and, it seemed to Arush, becoming busier all the time. It was nearly seven o'clock, the hour at which work normally began. Now it will start, Arush thought. Everyone around him was showing signs of alarm. Arush was not surprised. When he had dashed through the Platz earlier he had already noticed that the mood of the crowd was changing. Now the crowd included children and some of the people, mostly women, carried rucksacks on their backs. Many children were saying goodbye to their parents. Husbands and wives, assigned to different columns, were also bidding one another farewell. The children usually stayed with their mothers. Children or not, everyone was now talking and, although they did so in hushed voices, the sound merged into a veritable roar. Because of the touching farewell scenes, because of the noise of thousands of whispered sounds, because of the imminent hour of deadline, tension was increasing with every breath.

In this tumult Arush became entangled in the throng that filled the Platz. It was so full that he could hardly elbow his way through the crowd and had to push hard against people to pass by. As he did so, he heard lone, desperate cries of people lost in the crush. Mercifully, he was still able to cross the Platz.

At the workshop the atmosphere was not as depressed as he had expected. His workmates looked anxious, but were patiently awaiting what was to happen. Now Arush had arrived the work group was complete.

The workshop was in a solid building named, as were most houses in Tarnow, after its prewar owner. The Englender house was a two-storey building on the corner of Dembowa Street and The Ride, a little square on the far side of the larger passage from the Platz. Upstairs lived the Englender family, with two other families which had been billeted with them. The ground floor housed the once prosperous varnish and putty factory, originally owned by Shie Englender. His oldest son, Leon, had been the manager of the firm since the Germans had put it under so-called commissarial control* in the early days of the war. There was a large courtyard, several outbuildings filled with tools, barrels and sundry garbage and two large workshops. In one, varnish was made. In the other, besides a huge heap of putty in one of its corners, there were several long tables where mousetraps were assembled. Mousetrap production had started in June 1942, when the plant had been taken over by the Higher SS and Police Führer (HSSPF) of Cracow. It had then been accorded the status of *kriegswichtig* (war-important) work.

Tired from his arduous trip across the Platz and from the early start to his day, Arush longed to rest for a while on a bench, but his thoughts gave him no peace and, almost as soon as he sat down, he was joined by a workmate - Bonek Eltes.

"Will we save our necks again this time?" asked Bonek, a lively man in his thirties who, with his wife, but not their children, had evaded all three previous Aktions. People in distress need friendly contact, but not everyone wants to chatter. This was the case with Arush. He half turned towards Bonek and gazed wistfully into his eyes but he did not reply. Not because he refused to answer a painful question, or to reflect upon a forlorn situation, but "what is there to say?" he asked himself. He preferred to stay with his thoughts. And his thoughts were occupied with their dismal prospect. For himself his forebodings were indefi-

*Commissars were called "trustees" set in charge of Jewish property

6

nite, he might survive or he might not. But he was worried about his mother and terrified of what might happen to her and Rabbi Maleachi now they had left the bunker.

Guessing Arush's thoughts, Bonek continued: "People have left the bunkers to be with their families. They always do."

Bonek wanted to talk. It was his way of escaping from his fears and he hoped it would force Arush to answer. His last words were overheard by Jankel Bodman, who came over to them and gave them a good-luck charm. This was a piece of cloth from a garment that had once been worn by a saintly ancestor of a man who had appeared at the workshop for the first time that morning. The man had offered the garment to be cut up and shared among everyone working there.

–"Rabbi Maleachi left so he could share the fate of all the Jews," said Jankel. "He has always said that a man should never separate himself from his people, especially at a time like this."

–"Perhaps even better," commented Bonek. "Perhaps we will be evacuated to a safer place. What do you think?" he asked Arush directly.

–"May it all end well," said Arush, who did not want to increase his companion's distress.

–"That dunce Bornstein says that to flush people out of their bunkers the gallant warriors are threatening to use gas and hand grenades. They're doing all that just to get Bonek to a safer place," said Artek Teper. "The humpy-backed guest there," he pointed to an elderly man with a slightly crooked back, who was sitting on a bench opposite, "he says that in the last Aktion but one he fled with a bullet in his back, only to get another one today. Perhaps he'll...blissfully enough. Ha, ha," Artek was laughing even today.

Bonek was glad to have found in Artek someone willing to chat. "It's too early to draw up a balance sheet," he said. "But sooner or later everything in life repeats itself."

–"Except a bullet in the right place," countered Artek. "The donor of the lucky charms says..."

–"Did you take one?" interrupted Arush.

–"What harm can it do?" replied Artek with another forced laugh. "That self-righteous ascetic over there says he left his bunker because it had become a sinful place."

–"A sinful place?" said Bonek, sounding surprised.

–"Yes. The owner of the bunker refused to admit a woman with a child. He claimed the place was already overcrowded."

–"That's terrible," Bonek cut in indignantly, "when a child is involved. It could be murder."

–"By whom?", asked Artek impatiently.

–"By the man who threw them out. The stronger always pushes out the weaker."

–"Who threw them out? Who pushed them out?" Artek was getting excited. "He just didn't let them in, because there wasn't any more room. What would you have done?"

–"I'd have let in the mother and the child."

7

–"But if there was no more room?"

–"That's no excuse. To deliver a child to its death and the mother to the *Sonderunterbringung* (one of the codewords for murder) is unforgivable. There's always room for two more people."

–"How do you know? If the bunker couldn't support more people, if there's no air and not enough supplies, was he entitled to endanger others? Seventy people could perish for the sake of one child and one mother. Wouldn't that be a crime? Wouldn't that be 'murder'?"

–"No! To avert the danger of uncertain deaths - no matter how many - is no excuse for murder."

–"Whose murder?" asked Artek. "You're talking nonsense. It's all very well to be self-righteous, as long as you're not faced with the problem yourself." And, turning to Arush, he added: "You, Freund, you understand the agony of a decision in such a situation."

Arush had no idea what to say. He was too upset to collect his thoughts. But he felt that Eltes had stretched the argument too far. There are people, he thought, who talk too easily of crime and murder. And Eltes was perhaps speaking from remorse, for he had not hidden his own children during the third Aktion. Instead he and his wife had each taken one child to work with them. Before Arush could answer there was a flurry of activity inside the room. Every few minutes people had been coming into the workshop with rumours. Now someone rushed in to tell them that SS men were marching into the ghetto. They were helmeted, armed and in full battle gear. Their commanders had arrived in droshkies and in cars, which had been left outside the ghetto wall. Among the SS officers was the infamous Hauptsturmführer Amon Goeth - a man whose name alone struck terror in the hearts of the ghetto dwellers. And it was rumoured that he had brought with him a special unit of SS Sonderkommando from Cracow. It was said of Goeth, the legendary commandant of Plaszów concentration camp and the executioner of the Jews of Cracow, that his favourite occupation was to shoot at people just because they got in his way. He was a handsome man, heavily built with a ruddy complexion and glaring, demoniacal blue eyes. He was about 35 years old and had a high opinion of himself as a poet. As if this news was not enough, one of the zeks (lookouts) came in to tell them that the air was reverberating with shots, fired either above the heads of the crowd or into it. Everyone in the workshop stopped talking and listened intently to the sounds from the Platz - sounds that they could scarcely hear above the pounding of their own hearts. It seemed that only now did their fear begin to show, as if they had just realized how close was the danger and how powerless they were to prevent it.

Arush, on the contrary, had become calmer. The imminent sense of danger somehow raised his self-possession and he felt more alive than before. Soon they heard the order: "Varnish and Putty kommando outside! Everybody out!"

The OD man was giving the orders in a voice that was commanding but also defensive. He looked abject and, considering the early hour, strangely exhausted.

Outside the workshop they stood in uneven rows on the pavement, almost oppo-

8

site one of the passages that led to the Platz. They waited in the bright light and warmth of the September morning. Except for themselves, the street was menacingly deserted. But through the passage they could see part of the mass of people crowded into the Platz and they could now hear clearly the frightful noise coming from it. This made the waiting heavy; yet they were waiting in patience, a patience that prolonged hope and deferred doom.

It was the first experience of this kind for Arush, and never before had his endurance been put to such a severe test. After an hour of standing on the pavement with orders not to move, Arush lost all sense of time. In the past he had often speculated about time - how it seems to pass more slowly or more quickly in different situations. Now he did not speculate, but wondered at feeling none of the urgency, the restlessness or the impatience characteristic of waiting for something. Instead, he felt that each passing moment was a gift and he longed for the waiting to go on for ever.

Hardly anyone was talking. Arush did not know whether it was prudence or sorrow that prevented them. It seemed that no one wanted to start a conversation. But Artek, who stood next to Arush, asked him: "Which did you think was more shocking - your first 'evacuation', or your second?"

Arush was not surprised by the question, being aware of Artek's tone of defiant mockery. He also knew how difficult it was to think seriously in their circumstances. Exposed for long to mortal danger, a man's will to survive often prevents him from thinking at all. He himself could not think about anything except the rumour of the town being made Judenrein.

Was it true, or was it just a ploy to get people out of their hiding places? Perhaps it was, after all, better to be out of the bunker. It was no fun to be crowded into a cellar with no air, or to sit for who knows how long in a tiny segment of an attic, cut off from danger by only a thin partition. Your blood freezing at the slightest noise. Creeping out at night, only to return for another day in the same airless, lifeless void.

Arush remembered how, during the second Aktion, the Lebron's baby had started to cry just as the SS men, their heavy footsteps sounding like mortar shells exploding, had come up the stairs. They had been terrified, they felt spasms of agony, every second seemed an hour - yet no one had asked the mother to do the only thing that could have saved them. Their lips remained tight, their hearts throbbing with human feeling - while the baby was crying and crying. The lives of forty innocent people were at stake.

It had been Rabbi Maleachi who had saved the situation. He had had with him a bottle of wine which he had brought to the bunker for the ceremonial blessing on the evening of Rosh Hashana (the Jewish New Year) 5703. The mother had poured some wine into the baby's mouth and the baby had stopped crying instantly. It had seemed like a miracle. The Germans were just outside the bunker. They had shouted "Raus! Raus! We know where you are." The people in the bunker expected shots to be fired through the partition that hid them. But the Germans had gone away.

9

Thinking about it, Arush felt as if it was happening again. The recollection also brought him some comfort. He realized now that, whatever happened, it was for the best; that, with no chance of rescue, it was better that they should stay together. What life was there in solitude, when together they could fulfil their Jewish destiny?

But actually they weren't together. Everyone had gone separately - mother, brother, he himself. What was happening to his mother? Arush saw her as she had looked when young, attractive and elegantly dressed. And, later, as a dignified matron, with a resolute but gentle expression on her bright, round, slightly haughty-looking face. He thought of her motherly love and the warmth and comfort she had bestowed. It was dreadful being separated from her.

He remembered also how calm she had been during the third Aktion, last November. The Germans had already been inside the ghetto. Everyone else in the house had already gone to the bunker, but his mother was straightening the quilt on the bed and putting away the cups and saucers. Unlike other people,who had left their doors unlocked so that the Germans wouldn't break them down, she had double locked the door, as any unsuspecting person would who was going off to work.

He remembered, too, how composed she had been in the days of general agitation before moving to the ghetto, just after the largest massacre, which halved the town's Jewish population in June 1942. It was she who took care of all the preparations and with what looked almost like detachment sorted out the family belongings. This put into the pile, that throw away - she commanded. Take only things that are truly necessary, things that are currency, small and easy to sell. Although this must have offended her sense of order, everything was to be packed not in suitcases but in bundles. They were to be made small and to look shabby and of little value. A hand-cart would be useful, but too risky, she told them; take the bundles to the ghetto one at a time.

Oh, what an unexpected turn things had then taken! How can you express what it feels like to be moving house and carrying bundles the day after your father has been killed? But what could they do? Give up everything? Oh, that incomprehensible, that irresistible temptation to live!

As Arush thus lamented, he suddenly heard a voice behind him shout: "About turn! To the Platz, march!"

The order came from Roter, the deputy commander of the OD. Pretending to be surprised, he shouted angrily: "Why are you still hanging around here?" They could hardly get onto the Platz, which was now filled to the brim. They had to stand in the passage adjoining Dembowa Street, opposite the far end of the Englender House. And Arush stood at the edge of the passage. Nevertheless, he now felt the full ferocity of the *Aussiedlung* (evacuation). For a moment he regretted having exposed himself voluntarily to it when he could have hid in a bunker. But gradually the seething crowd absorbed his mind. The sights and sounds from the Platz made him acutely alert and observant. He could now see as well as hear, the people who made the noise that was plaguing him. He also saw that the Platz was even more crowded than when he had last crossed it. This was because the crowd had apparently been ordered to move back - well away from the OD headquarters, which had now become the command centre of the "evacuation".

At the front of the OD building stood Goeth, who was in command, and next to him stood Sturmbannführer von Haase, who - although higher in rank - had only come to observe the evacuation on behalf of the SS and Polizei Führer of the Cracow district. Around them were their lieutenants, their aides and other SS men. A little way away were the OD commanders and the Judenrat councillors, waiting for their orders. There were also some men in civilian clothes talking briskly with the SS commanders. Among the civilians, one stood out. He was a tall man, wearing a straw hat. Many people on the Platz recognized him as Julius Madritsch, the famous businessman.

Facing the Germans by the command building was the mass of people, dense like a fine-toothed comb. Thousands standing arm to arm, head to head, giving the impression that they were hanging motionless in the air, and yet surging forward. What would happen, thought Arush suddenly, if the whole crowd really surged forward?

Arush knew: instant and total destruction. Weren't they doomed anyway? Perhaps, but they would not bring the house down by their own hands. While they were alive there was still hope. "The curse of hope, the blessing of hope," as his eldest brother Dave had once said. Meanwhile more important things were tormenting Arush, not least the noise that beat into his brain. Had it been an illusion of his, he wondered that the crowd was roaring? Was it a cry of weakness escaping from nine thousand throats? Could death be crying out of their hearts and eyes?

The people did not shout, nor did they speak loudly. But what did they all have to talk about? Arush wondered, himself keeping silent. True, he was alone…Then, catching sight of a man chewing: but how can a man eat in this waste? Teper who, comparing his own disquiet with the peaceful appearance of Arush, had clung to him - offered an explanation.

–"His light sandwich lunch. Thought he's going to work. Now wants to drop load for the outing.

"I warned my wife," he went on. "She tried to saddle me with a packet, too. Oh, how I need a cigarette! What d'you think, should I light one?" Despite his goitre, Teper was a heavy smoker, puffing at a cigarette whenever he could. But now, though squirming, he was afraid to take the risk.

–"Eat the smoke, if you can, or puff it into another chap's trousers."

–"D'you know what they're waiting for?" asked Artek.

–"That's their tactic, so I've heard, to keep people waiting."

–"Clever. Let the victims hope and wear themselves out. Are you tired?"

–"No. It's just the noise…"

–"Would you have preferred it done in silence?"

–"I don't know. It's the first time for me. Perhaps it would be easier to wait in silence."

–"So you aren't as cool as you look?"

11

–"What did you think? Of course I'm not, but there's nothing to rush for."

–"I say, whatever has to happen, let it happen quickly."

–"Rubbish! All because of a cigarette?" Arush, who did not smoke, had never before commented on Teper's addiction. But now he said: "If you can't bear it, lie down and smoke - but spare your breath," - an indirect request for Teper to shut up.

Teper didn't light his cigarette. Instead he pointed to a woman ahead of them.

–"Look at that rucksack on her back," he whispered. "The baby inside it must be suffocating."

Arush strained his ears to hear what the woman with the moving rucksack was saying to a man beside her.

–"What could I do? Tear out with my nails her love for me - or you? The Lord only knows, how I wanted…" Her husband nodded in acknowledgement. "I tried to persuade her. I told her the auntie would be as good to her as I am. I promised her I'd come to take her back. I told her it was only for a day or two. But you know Linka, how it is with her. She clung to my skirt with all her might. She wouldn't let go. She was crying. 'Moma no. Moma don't leave me.' You need a heart of stone. Why haven't I got one? Always weak, hesitant. Call me selfish or whatever you want."

Her husband didn't comment. He just said: "Was the tablet you gave her strong enough?"

Arush's sweet, intelligent nephew, Ami, was suddenly in his mind's eye. When four o'clock in the afternoon came, he would be in the midst of playing the "evacuation game" - Ami himself playing Senft, the most elegant of the OD men and, unofficially, its top officer - but he would drop it all to look out of the window to see if his mother was coming back from work. If her group was late, the child's face would grow pale from fear, and, if no one was watching, he would pray in a corner. On a day she was particularly late, he would throw himself into her arms in full view of the other children. How happy he had felt with her arms around him!

He was hardly seven, but, like the apparently younger Linka, when the question of placing him on the "Aryan side" was broached, Ami told Pnina resolutely, through his tears: "Mama, I don't want to survive the war without you!"

In the end it was Ami's young mother who chose not to survive the war without her son. In the past, when Arush had recalled the same scene, tears had come to his eyes. "Today," he told himself, noting the contrast, "I'm strong - hard as a stone."

Tears came to his eyes, however, as he thought of all the babies. How many rucksacks were there in the crowd? From where he stood he could only see very few, and one cardboard box. But he could see older children, perhaps eight and nine years old, who had been dressed to look like adults. Boys were wearing long trousers and caps. As for girls, Klara Arbed, a nine-year old playmate of Ami, was wearing her mother's high-heeled shoes, while her mother was sporting ski-boots. Oh, how strange the children were! How calm they looked, as if trying to outdo their parents.

One child, dressed as a woman, stood almost in front of Arush. She was gripping the hand of a young, strongly built woman, with dark-blond hair. The woman, who was her mother, sounded agitated and was talking rapidly to lessen her distress.

"I told him to follow my advice," she bellowed at the woman next to her. "Go to Maks and talk to him. What are cousins for? When life is at stake, one must go cap in hand to anyone. Leave no stone unturned. But he? He would never listen to me, no matter how many times I implored him - till my lungs were bursting. But he wouldn't listen. I told him the Aktion was coming and it would be the last one. Now he'll admit it. Now he can see for himself."

She went on, repeating the same complaint, as if all that mattered was to prove that she had been right and her husband to blame.

The other woman tried to calm her.

"He believed you. You know how difficult it is to get in to see Krumstein." (Maks Krumstein was the vice-chairman of the Judenrat.)

"But how else could I save my child?" the woman retorted. And she cried: "Where are you?" turning to the girl who was holding her hand.

As she turned, Arush saw her terrified face, her eyes that were like the eyes of an animal which scents approaching danger but feels defenceless. It was silly to ask what the people found to talk about, Arush had to admit, as he continued to brood over the depth of the problem faced by all the parents who had had to decide what to do with their children. But a voice interrupted his thoughts. It was Eltes who had elbowed his way through the crowd for several yards to join Artek and Arush. Still gasping, and smelling of the frowst that was filling the Platz, he proceeded to hiss out his words.

–"It isn't nearly as bad today as it was in earlier times." He tried to smile with a semblance of bravado, and continued to show off his wealth of experience. "We were on our knees then, or sitting on the ground all cramped up, we weren't allowed to get up or even to move. In the morning everyone had to assemble on the Platz - old, young, people with labour cards, people without. People were dragged out of their bunkers. Some carried trunks or bundles, some came with nothing. Working men were ordered to line up, like today, each with his working group, but no one was allowed to go to work.

"Before it all started - before the orders were given - the ghetto was surrounded by the SS, and there were Ukrainians and some Polish policemen. As soon as the Platz was full, the SS marched in and set up machine-guns. Did you notice, there are no machine-guns in position today. That shows how confident they are."

–"It's not a question of confidence. It has become routine," said Artek. "And, anyway, they'd have a job to find room for their guns today."

–"They would find it, if they wanted to," replied Bonek. "On the second Aktion, there were even more people here than today. But then they were spread over the Platz from one end to the other. You talk of routine. All right, there is some system, but it's not always the same. It's midday already, and the selection hasn't started yet."

–"That's because no one is to remain this time," said Artek.

–"I bet you that isn't so. Some will stay. Otherwise what did Madritsch come for?

13

He's come to pick out the best he can get."

Bonek claimed to know Madritsch. He had worked for him before moving to the Varnish and Putty factory, where he thought his lack of skill would be easier to conceal. But he spoke about Madritsch as if he had been in his confidence.

"He came on business, as he always does. Haase and especially Goeth are his friends. He's hob-nobbing with them and giving them expensive presents. He expects them to return the favour. He wants to take the tailors from his workshops in Tarnow to his workshops in Plaszow. They're his slaves, and he makes five, perhaps ten, Reichsmarks a day profit on each of them. There are more than two thousand of them here. So he's making a fortune. But he treats his slaves well and, behind his friends' backs, boasts that he's their saviour."

–"He may well be today," said Artek. "If the rumours about him are true, he's unique for a German. What do you think, Freund?"

–"Not just unique. A compatriot of Goeth who treats Jews well today, even if they're his slaves - and however greedy he is - maybe you can see him as a righteous man," said Arush, who secretly prayed that Madritsch would succeed in getting all his workers.

Arush had, of course, a private, fateful interest in Madritsch's venture, and he was anxious to ask one of the perspiring OD men, who were moving fussily about the Platz, what were the chances. But they would not say or know.

Though all the OD men were in the prime of life and still bustling, they looked tired and dispirited. They had to exert all their strength in order to squeeze through the dense crowd, which was unwilling to make way for them. Not that there was animosity toward the OD as a whole, or that its members were generally disliked. But today they looked strangely unimportant. They had all sunk in stature, most now hardly distinguishable from the rest of the crowd. Earlier in the morning they had still shouted like bosses, but by noon their orders were mostly faltering.

Several were on duty just where the Varnish and Putty men had been standing. Arush wondered if this was because they wanted to be as far from the command centre as possible. This seemed unlikely, but why did they try so hard to push all the men from the street-passage onto the Platz proper.

The elderly Reb Tunye Einhorn, who in better times was a great chatterer, had asked Gastwirt about this. Gastwirt had once been a journalist and was now a reputedly "disciplined but decent" OD man.

–"Do you think that we do it for pleasure, or to harm you? We keep order, because order must be kept. Not for my sake, but for your own."

Reb Tunye had pretended to cough, as Gastwirt went on: "If we don't do it, someone else will - and more strictly. Only then it wouldn't be so clever for you to cough or to ask questions. You would be lying on the ground with your head smashed in."

–"It's the old story - if I don't do it, then someone else will," Arush whispered.

–"But it really is better if the OD men push us around than if the SS men do it," said Teper. Eltes disagreed. "During the second and third Aktions, the OD escorted people to the Platz, and they were much more efficient than the Germans in finding bunkers."

–"They don't need to find them," Teper objected. "They know where they are. There's an OD man living in every house. Yet, only one or two bunkers were betrayed."

–"That's true, but it's because they all have someone near and dear to them in a bunker."

While Eltes fell silent for a moment Arush heard Teper saying: "So he carries out the orders only to die in harness?"

–"To save himself and his family - so long as there's a chance." Eltes had the answer and he added immediately, "At least today they aren't risking other people's lives to save their own. During the second Aktion they put a table on the Platz and we all had to walk past it, showing our labour cards to Gestapo men. You can imagine what it felt like," Eltes cleared his throat for better effect. "We queued up for the stamp. We knew that anyone who didn't get one would be taken away, and lost without trace. You had to get a new stamp from the Gestapo. The old one didn't count any more.

"Anyone without a stamp who tried to creep away was, if caught, beaten to death. But not by the OD men - this is what I wanted to tell you - the OD men only made sure that people didn't leave their places. They did this, they said, 'for the people's own sake'.

"But if you think that your place of work, or your skill, mattered, you're mistaken. So don't worry that we're in Varnish and Putty. Selection was 'on sight'. Your life depended on the whim of the Gestapo man who inspected you. But no man over fifty-five could hope for the stamp, nor could white-collar workers except those who worked for the Judenrat. And in the end, even a stamp didn't guarantee that you wouldn't be taken away if the quota for evacuation hadn't been filled.

"On the second day, while we went to work, seven or eight thousand people were marched off to the railway station. We'd been a whole day and night on the Platz. Luckily, it was mid-September, warm during the day. But the third Aktion was two months later. Fifteenth November. True that was a short affair, and merely between two and three thousand were evacuated. All the same, nearly nine hours kneeling in the cold..."

Eltes went on describing past Aktions, then suddenly he fell silent. Everyone around them became quiet - a quiet that was strangely animating. The cause of the sudden change was soon obvious. Blache was coming. Conspicuous in his grey-green uniform, he did not need to force a path through the crowd; it was kept free, the people moving aside as if to form a lane. He was accompanied, at some distance, by two OD commanders, shouting *Achtung! Achtung!* and other, unintelligible orders.

Oberscharführer Hermann Blache had come from the general (Waffen) SS to Cracow and after only a couple of days training he had been nominated on 1 January 1943, "commissarial manager" of the Forced Labour Camp, that is ghetto A, of Tarnow. Though of low rank, Blache was subordinate only to Oberführer Julius Scherner, the SSPF of the district of Cracow, who was in too high a position

15

to take part in the killing personally - indeed, as a rule, the higher an officer was placed in the hierarchy, the less he inflicted death with his own hands. A manikin in stature, Blache was supreme master vis-à-vis the Jews. With his appointment, the security services (SD), including the Gestapo, were formally bound to report to him in all matters concerning the Jews in his domain. In practice this meant that the Gestapo informed Blache of the killing of a Jew after the event. Nevertheless, compared with the earlier period of direct Gestapo rule, conditions of life in the ghetto significantly improved: there were fewer killings, less terror, fewer Gestapo "visits", and altogether less oppression.

In general not violent in his behaviour, he allowed the Judenrat to oil his palm with frequent presents, and tried to win the confidence of the ghetto's inhabitants. If only the Jews would work hard and give up the gold and currency still in their possession, he used to say, nothing would happen to them. Not that the Jews were so stupid as to believe his words but, in course of time, as is the way of human nature, they began to be taken in by the appearance of the middle-sized, heavy, forty-year-old man with his full round face and watery, light-blue eyes.

Today, Arush reflected, as he watched the usually slack Blache passing close by; he looked tall, energetic, inflamed. He was stalking, with one hand on the pistol at his belt, ready to shoot instantly. In the other hand he held a whip with a lead-ball at the tip. His eyes flashed with brutality, giving his face a rabid look.

A saw-mill labourer turned SS subaltern, Blache refused with modesty to take command of the Aussiedlung, considering himself unequal to the task. But he was one of its principal captains, and his orders were peremptory. He yelled at the OD commanders as he strode along. Standing among the Varnish and Putty men, he made several, inaudible remarks, giving the impression that he knew who they were, and then crossed the Platz.

–"What did he say?" Arush asked when Blache was too far away to hear him.

– "'Move up. Why are you standing here?'" is what Eltes had heard.

– "'Why are you so close together?'" was Reb Tunye's version.

–"Who'll make the mousetraps now?" said Artek, who had not yet ceased to be himself. And turning to Arush, he added: "Why didn't you ask him?"

It was a logical question, but not meant seriously. There is no point in asking, Arush answered privately. They were resigned to their fate in proud silence. There was no point asking for mercy - the enemy did not know mercy; no crying for help - where could help come from? no sounds of fear - neither the fear of the beast, nor of death; no groaning in pain - the pain was far beyond groaning; not even a display of physical qualities, for qualities of the body no longer counted; no bribes, but one. A bribe which the esteemed physician, Dr Hilfsreich, was to talk about later that evening. "I stood at the front, behind the Judenrat councillors. Opposite, Goeth was crossing the first lines facing us, when suddenly a boy of four, perhaps five, took out of his pocket a round looking-glass and offered it to Goeth. I was stunned. Goeth himself was taken aback. He looked at the little mirror; he looked at the little boy; he hesitated for a few moments. Then he shot the child."

The waiting was becoming less and less bearable. It was slow and immobilizing.

–"It's draining all my strength," Artek complained. Arush was beginning to share his impatience, if not his pessimism and desire for the final hour to come quickly. Neither hungry nor thirsty, yet he was growing weary. They had been on their feet since morning, without food or water, without hope, and without a chance to relieve themselves. They were still bound by the norms of civilized behaviour as well as constrained by unspoken orders forbidding such things in public. Even the children restrained themselves, though nothing definite was known about those in nappies.

Hunger, thirst, tiredness, and confined bowels are all sufferings that require no direct participation by the oppressor. Poland before the war, Arush suddenly recalled, had had in Bereza its one and only concentration camp, with its one and only peculiar torture - the specialité de la maison, as Bochenek had said when relating his experience there. Under pain of punishment, the inmates were forbidden from early morning till late evening to relieve themselves.

No one in the Platz was heard to complain; no one was seen to crack; but some people looked crazed - shocked to the point of losing awareness of what they were doing. A man tried to push ahead screaming; a woman carried openly in her arms a bundle wrapped in a snow-white blanket. Men, women and children lost in the crush, lost in distress, called helplessly to their dearest, within ear-shot of passing SS men. Heartbreaking cries, nerve-racking cries - collective cries of sighing, heaving, gasping people. It seemed to Arush, that there was only noise, cruel noise, around him, and above -oh, Heavens - above him deathly shadows dancing in the air. A portent, it seemed, that he was going out of his mind. You must try to think of something else, he told himself, recall some pleasant event - what about Italy, had it capitulated? Was invasion coming from the west? But there was nothing, nothing but noise. Oh, that noise...

Was it an excuse? Was he giving up? What was there to give up? Nothing. Just mental fog suspended on an empty stomach and a full bladder, between excitement and equanimity, idleness and alertness, between incoherent thinking and presence of mind - all in one breath, in one strange hoop, which you had to go through, to get an idea what it was like.

What more was there to be done here? There's nothing, thought Arush, nothing but noise and confusion. Strangely, Arush felt he would suffocate, but suffocate not because he was out of breath, nor because of the choking smell. No, he would suffocate because of the noise and tightness - a tightness that made his head spin and his eyes swim. No, not swim - this human host seemed to float - a river with no current, or a current without a river. An immense tide of bodies swaying and flowing in the same place, bodies carried high by the flow, stepping motionlessly in the air. And he was a part, a minute, inconspicuous part of this living stream, wedged in its immovable, rhythmic motion, wedged in its rock-like, wave-like tide, still on the surface, head above water, above the black mass, yet slowly, impotently, inexorably drowning in it.

The alarming sense of getting lost, of suffocating in the mess! The masters have

17

us by the throat. How to get out of their clutches? Must slacken the noose, escape the rope.

Though feeling that he was drowning, Arush was not drained of strength. On the contrary, he braced himself to gather all the strength within him. Given the circumstances, he was resourceful - inasmuch as there was still resource of any sort; his senses were sharp - inasmuch as there was still sense at all. There was still a spark, the human spark that kindled in him a strange, inexplicable, inextinguishable passion to live.

They might be doomed, their death inevitable, but not from suffocation here. He must get away from the noise, shut out the clamour, the suffocating clamour that was drowning everything - all will, all sound, all sorrow throughout the Platz. And every minute it became worse. He must do something. He must make his choice sooner rather than later. His experience told him that choice must be made early in the day.

–"Let's go. We must get away from here," he said to Artek in a low, calm voice, but with a determination so sudden, so urgent, that it sounded very solemn, almost compelling.

He expected the answer "You must be out of your mind" - an expression Teper often used.

But Teper said, no less seriously: "But where to?"

–"Back to Englender."   As Arush and Artek turned right and started moving, all the Varnish and Putty men spontaneously followed them in an unbroken chain. Arush was greatly relieved to see this, as it diminished his sense of responsibility for possible consequences. While they were stealing away from the Platz, shouldering and jostling their way back toward Dembowa Street, he kept thinking that there must be in the crowd thousands who were feeling as he did. Thousands craving for direction, for guidance, from wherever it came, even if it came from Arush Freund and Artek Teper.

But just as they were approaching the passage, growing less terrified with every step, Roter appeared as if out of nowhere, and tried to stop them. Striding briskly - with, unusually, a club in his hand - and with more vigour than usual in his bearing, he began shouting imperiously.

–"Halt! Halt right where you are! Who told you to move back?"

–"Blache," said Arush.

The answer was made so quickly, so clearly, so confidently, and without the slightest sign of disobedience from the men, that it could not have sounded other than true to Roter. He was thrown off balance and, apparently struck dumb by the sound of Blache's name, he went away without saying another word.

Arush was amazed by his boldness. He felt he was in good form. But he did not then sense, nor could he imagine, that his spontaneous one-word answer might have crucial significance for the future.

Chased by noise, guided by instinct, driven by a mysterious power within him, and borne along by chance, Arush led the way, at the head of the column.

"There is something special about him," thought Artek. Arush himself was also wondering about the change he had undergone. By nature he was timid; from his earliest school days he had always chosen the back-bench; and his wartime philosophy had been to lie low and behave unassumingly, believing that the higher a Jew rises from obscurity, the more he is exposed to death. Yet now he was walking at the forefront, taking many others with him. But he was not trying to be special, nor was he trying to play the leader. He was still convinced of the wisdom of lying low.

Does it make any difference? The question forced itself into his mind, as, after all the pandemonium, Arush and the Varnish and Putty men relaxed in the long shadow of the factory building, far, it seemed, from the maddened crowd on the Platz. The sky above, he noticed, was not black with cloud. It was radiating an unconcerned tranquillity, only that the cheery, limpid blue of the morning had softened a shade. Shut out, as if by a screen, from the hellish noise, he felt that he and his companions had ceased to be part of the coerced human stream. So when he asked himself, what difference does it make, this referred only to the immediate future. He was no less aware than before how near the end of their lives they might be. By heavenly justice the disaster might start with them. Well, he thought, what difference does it make who goes first?

Similar thoughts were afflicting others in the group, but they did not show for the time being, in their shining eyes and damp faces. As the Varnish and Putty men stood impassively in the relative cool and quiet, they looked like children let out from a teeming hot-house into the fresh air, intent on enjoying every breath, every ray of the setting sun. But it was not long before something disturbed the unseemly calm. Their attention was attracted to some Judenrat councillors and select OD commanders, who were slowly, one by one, emerging into Dembowa Street from the narrow passage opposite The Ride, at an angle to the Englender house. The commanders were soon followed by a host of OD men of other ranks, who immediately formed a human fence, cordoning off the passage from the street.

What all this meant remained for some time hidden from Arush. The mystery was dispelled, however, when he noticed that a few privileged individuals - a doctor, a radio specialist, a droshky driver - were, with the approval of a top Judenrat councillor or OD commander, creeping through the human wall, to head straight for The Ride. So this is it, thought Arush. After all some people are to stay on in Tarnow, and these are the chosen ones. Arush reached this conclusion intuitively but he felt in his bones that it was correct, and he would not allow any doubt to enter his head.

The effect was electrifying. He was jolted out of his indifference - that sad, numbing indifference that became, with the passage of time, common among most "evacuees". His thoughts quickened - every single thought, every single nerve within his brain was now focused desperately on life - his own life and that of his dearest ones. There is still hope, his heart told him, a chance to escape today from the sure, tragic fate facing most of the people around him. And what a chance! Under his nose stretched the boundary of destiny - he, just he, stood one remove from the edge where being and non-being dissolve.

Along with hope, he was seized by fear. Fear of missing the chance, fear of disappointed hope, savagely limited hope. What hope for his mother? What hope for Eli? What hope for...Do they know of the opening at all? How could they - far away, at the other end of this living forest? They must be told! He must tell them!

But how? But how? In silent despair he realized that he was separated from his mother and brother by an immense, impassable space, even though it was a mere hundred yards. Yet he must let them know. He must see to it that they come over here. They are privileged, too. Perhaps they knew? Unlikely. If only he could reach them with the news! But how could he force his way through the throng? Even in the morning, when it was less crowded, he had hardly got through alive. But he had managed. Now you must try again, he told himself. "An errand of grace is its own protection." You must have faith! Make a last superhuman effort! It may be your last chance to be reunited with your mother in this world. What would she not have done for you? Always concerned for her offspring, with her motherly duties. How she had suffered when she saw one of her children in pain! She would have renounced life itself for any of her children. And you? What about you? Hesitating, calculating, weighing risks and chances, forejudging failure, afraid for your own life - practically abandoning her. Even if it means sacrificing your life, is it not your duty to try to save her? But how? Oh Heavens, if only he could save her! And save Eli!

Where Eli is he does not even know. Who knows where the Copernicus-school column stands? Eli is young, he may be sent to a camp. His poor, tender brother! Silently they loved each other so much. In the past year, since the killings had started and their brother and sister had been taken away, they had become even closer than before. In childhood Eli had been his protector, showing an almost paternal affection for him. Once Eli had told him not to cry when he had hurt himself and he would pray to be punished in his place. Now he, Arush does not even know where the Copernicus-school stands! "He may be sent to a camp!" Yet Eli's chance of surviving was not smaller than that of anyone else in this crowd here. But mother! But his mother!

Where is she? She is probably still at the Tailors' Workshop. If not at Szpitalna Street, then somewhere nearby. At least she is not alone, she is with the wife of Rabbi Maleachi, and so with the rabbi. And what will happen to him? Oh mercy! that lovable, saintly sage! Horrified that he could not reach his mother, Arush summoned divine help. Merciful Father! Such a modest request. To cross a hundred yards, to find his mother. He is not even allowed to leave his line, let alone to sneak around rows upon rows of men as hard to pass through as a stone wall. Even if he managed to cross, he would not be able to return. But then they would at least be together, as he always wanted to be. All alone, all alone, without anyone close in the world! Arush was now clearly feeling for the first time that they had perhaps been separated for ever when they had parted that morning. Now he felt more afraid of surviving alone than of not surviving at all.

But how to get there in the first place? And then, somewhat forsaking the idea of dying with his mother, he began to rationalize: even if he succeeded, even if he

20

managed to slip away unnoticed, to avoid all the guards, to dig his way through the pathless thicket, even if he succeeded in conquering all the obstacles and reached there safely, how could his mother and Rabbi Maleachi manage to pick *their* way through the multitude? And before the curtain fell irrevocably. In the morning, there had been no race against time. Now there was. But he must take the risk. He must do something to save them as well. "But you haven't yet saved yourself. Oh, that's easy. I have only to stroll round the corner."

It was just one step, yet he was afraid to take it. What if there was a list of those authorized to stay and the Gestapo were to check it later? They might be watching from a distance, out of sight. What if the precise number of people was fixed? How else could it be? Was that why they were so confident that no one would smuggle themselves through? One false step, Arush reasoned, and you will be hurled into the lower world, with the door of escape shut for ever. Everyone in his group must have been thinking the same. Teper had intimated as much when he whispered: "An animal doesn't think when the door of the cage is ajar." They all waited as if chained to the ground, like bystanders watching a highly exciting, blood-curdling spectacle.

What looked at first like a stir, a fuss, slowly turned into turmoil and bustling, like a battle at the barricades. Desperate men and women, wrestling for their lives, were surging and brawling, beseeching and pushing, all trying to slip through the gate, which was defended with bare hands by rather weakly resisting OD men. Their hoarse, dictatorial shouts of "Get back! Get back!" mingled with the forlorn cries of the charging people, extolling their rights and merits, invoking their ties of blood and friendship, or just trying to outwit the OD men, who, as if retreating before the thrusting mob, stepped back an inch or two.

The hesitancy, the suspense, the sight of some individuals now and then allowed through the gate, suggested to Arush a possible way to save his skin, though the fact that it would be his alone of all his family, made him tense to the point of agony. But time, precious time, was being lost. His brain worked feverishly but he could think of no better idea. Pressure from within was driving him to do something bold, if not actually suicidal, but the pressure was being kept in check by the impossible circumstance and his instinct of self-preservation. He trembled at the thought of yielding to his feeling of impotence and, at the same time, at his determination to brave it. He tried to think of a rational solution and hoped for supernatural help.

He sensed that he was losing his mother and yet he was helpless to preserve her. Again and again he asked himself in distress: What would happen? How could he bring her over to the gate? He saw a glimmer of hope in his black despair. Perhaps the OD men could help her to cross the Platz - and quickly, while the gate was still functioning. Time was running out. He must quickly find an OD man ready to help him - a nervous tremor shook Arush at the improbable thought. He would ask, he would implore a Judenrat councillor - most of them were human, they would surely understand.

No - they would laugh at him. What was his mother to them? One in a thousand mothers. He did not realize that thinking of other people's mothers could be painful! No one would help her, if not himself. But what about Rabbi Maleachi? If his mother was one among a thousand, there was only one Rabbi Maleachi. Who if not he ought to be saved? The blood of all people is equally red only to him who sees red! If some people were to remain in the ghetto, should Rabbi Maleachi not be the first? How all those Judenrat councillors had cultivated him in the past! Let them now give proof of their concern. Let them send for him. Perhaps they had already? They could - they must - bring him through the gate. If Rabbi Maleachi and his wife were sent for, they would not leave his mother behind. The OD would not refuse Rabbi Maleachi. His mother would get through with them. The councillors must send for him. There stands Spatz. Spatz, above all, would help him. It was his duty. Spatz, yes - Arush would approach him.

Shmil Spatz was "number three" in the Judenrat hierarchy. A leading textile merchant of Tarnow before the war, he was head of the Judenrat's "department of commerce and financial affairs". When von Malotky, a noble killer among the local Gestapo men, bought a canary to his home, it was the responsibility of Spatz and his department to take immediate care of its feeding. In his ministration Spatz was unrivalled: he never failed (witness the fact that he was still alive) in finding - even if it were necessary to dig it from the depths of the earth - the most extravagant coverings for furniture newly requisitioned by one of the countless mistresses of Scharführer Wilhelm Rommelmann, who since the spring of 1942 had been the Gestapo official in charge of Jewish matters in Tarnow. Spatz was no less efficient in persuading the local ghetto moguls to surrender part of their paltry, clandestine savings to balance the accounts of his department - and perhaps not his alone. Regarded as wise and trustworthy, Spatz's counsel was greatly valued by his chairman and colleagues. "The brain of the Judenrat," was the popular ghetto opinion of him. Spatz was also said to have remained pious, which he probably was. Anyway, it was he, as a frequent visitor to Rabbi Maleachi who had introduced to the rabbi Henryk Falban, the Judenrat chairman, Krumstein and other councillors, as well as some OD commanders. It had been comic to see Senft, a prewar pimp - and, it was currently rumoured, a confidant of the Gestapo - waiting humbly at the door to pay his respects to the religious sage. Rabbi Maleachi had to accept the visits, and he did so willingly, so that he could help many needy people and exert his influence in religious and welfare matters. Prominent officials, in turn, came to the rabbi, partly to seek his advice and partly to seek an alibi for the future. They held Rabbi Maleachi in high esteem and never refused his modest requests.

Following Spatz with his eyes and plucking up his courage to approach him, Arush also glanced around. One had always to be on one's guard. At the gate there was uproar. Three lines of OD men were now fending off the frantic crowd. If Arush tried to reach his mother, he would be driven off by the sheer weight of this mass of people. They wanted to get at the gate, and he wanted to go in the opposite direction. It would be suicide, he thought, and, tragically, his mother might already be beyond the reach even of the OD men.

He thought of taking quick advantage of the confusion. None of the cohort of

OD men was looking in his direction. But he must first talk to Spatz. It was his holy duty - his last hope. Who could know what lay in wait behind the blind corner? Perhaps Goeth himself, and a bullet. And an end to all hope. And what if Spatz said "No"? He had never spoken to him before, though Spatz would know him, as a close neighbour of Rabbi Maleachi. But he could not - it would be a mistake - accost Spatz in the presence of other councillors or OD commanders. Spatz might feel embarrassed and he might be hurled back to the line he had left without permission. He must wait for the right moment. Would it come? The odds were against him. He was risking his own life and his mother's life. It was hell to bear such tension! No! He could not wait for a lucky chance. But he did - and he knew that everyone in his group was waiting for someone else to take the first, fateful step. This did not encourage action and he persisted in his indecision, weighing all the possible consequences of anything he might, or might not, do.

Yet, by a happy chance, an opportunity did come his way. It happened quite soon, though how soon Arush could not say because of his excitement. Suddenly he saw Spatz standing all alone in the middle of the road, half way between the gate and The Ride, yet only a few yards from Arush. With a furtive glance and risking the worst that could happen, Arush stepped forward. He walked the few yards softly, and, as soon as he was beside Spatz, who, somewhat charitably, did not turn a hair, Arush said to him in a quiet voice: "Reb Shmil" (Spatz still liked to be addressed in this patriarchal way) "what will happen to the rabbi?"

–"I sent Shmil Hules to bring him over," Spatz replied, speaking quietly but faster than Arush.

Hules was Spatz's nephew. He was an OD man but a very gentle one. One of his duties had been to serve as a bodyguard to Rabbi Maleachi on his outings when, each Friday at dawn, the rabbi went to the ghetto's ritual bath. He seemed a natural choice for the present mission.

Arush felt slightly relieved. It was just what he wanted to hear, perhaps even surpassing his expectations. In the circumstances, what more could he ask Spatz to do? Encouraged by his answer and mild manner, Arush dropped his voice even lower and asked: "And can I go there?" intimating the "safe" area behind them.

Without a moment's hesitation, Spatz shot out one word: "Go!"

With the speed of thought Arush concluded that if it were too unsafe, Spatz would not have endangered him - he was not such a reckless man. Arush turned as though returning to his line, but instead ran straight for The Ride.

Having seen Arush take the leap, Teper, Einhorn, Bodman, Eltes and two or three more men of the Varnish and Putty group promptly followed him; they were away before the OD men noticed their escape and with their shouts and bodies blocked others from taking flight.

For some time after Arush reached instant safety, his heart hammered wildly, but this soon gave way to a deep anxiety that lasted for the rest of the day. It was largely the same anxiety as before, and one that was shared by his new set of colleagues: what if there is a list and they come to check? What if they were too many? What was to happen to them now? What and what? Thought chasing thought, despair following despair. He was too frightened to think of the next step.

Not long after Arush's escape, the gate was closed. The *Aufräumung* (Clean Up) quota of three hundred (two men for every woman but no children) had been filled. As the men and women entered "Singer", the sun was already setting, bathing the roof and the windows of the Englender house in a purpled glow. "Singer" was an empty barracks, which not long before had housed a war-important factory, producing cardboard and wooden boxes. It had once been owned by Israel Singer. As they squeezed inside the barracks, by and by night fell, to plunge "Singer" into gloom.

CHAPTER TWO

Deep in the night Arush woke up lying on the bare floor of the barracks. Still only half-conscious of himself or his surroundings, he tried to fall asleep again, but he could not. He felt cramped and was shivering. Against his will he was listening in the darkness.

He was afraid to upset the stillness. Nobody inside the barracks appeared to move. Everyone was lying motionless - as still as the night. Nights were always peaceful, Arush reflected, both in nature and in the ghetto. There were no Aktions at night - in deference to the darkness, he wondered. Soon, however, the stillness was animated by curious, harassing sounds. Even and rhythmic, they reached him from a distance. What was it? Sounds like the tramp of thousands of feet on the march. Then there was a vibrating murmur of whispering crowds. But where were they coming from? Everyone had long since departed; they had been led away before nightfall. The Platz must now be empty. Was it the emptiness that was resounding, sounding louder than the roar of waves? Yet, the faceless voices seemed real. He could hear them. Could he? It was so confusing, so awful. Yet he could not be hearing the sounds. He need not. They were within him. They had penetrated into his mind and heart. They were beating in his brain, the beat of wave, whispers mounting into heaven. He could not still them. He would hear them forever, always like this. An even tread, the strings of his soul moving, tread of feet - the melody of the *Aussiedlung*. A hymn of farewell, a hymn of those departing from this world.

The strange sounds - the cries of his vanished brothers - even if possibly only the echoes of the events of the day, had penetrated Arush to such a depth that, lying face up, he was gradually losing his awareness of his surroundings, as scenes from the day just past and from earlier days unfolded before his closed eyes.

Words of farewell went through his mind. But what farewell? They had parted without a good-bye. Had they not known that they were taking their last leave of each other? Why hadn't he at least kissed his mother good-bye? As always they had controlled themselves, not showing emotion, always avoiding staring into each other's eyes, always careful not to melt into tears, to deceive each other, saying good-bye as if they were parting for a few hours.

It was so with everyone, and it was so every time. Every Aktion snapped a branch off the family tree, every twig was sawn away, leaving only the bare trunk - himself. So far he had escaped. For how long? All the others, all his closest, all his dearest had died, but he somehow continued to live. Just he among the last three hundred. Why did he merit it? He was so much less deserving than Eli. What sort of a man was he who goes on living? Oh, what a day of disaster! In a few hours a world destroyed, every home uprooted, every spring extinct, every sorrow borne, and he was still sticking obstinately, and selfishly, to this merciless, doleful life.

And it had always seemed to him that he could not live without them. As a little child, Arush began recollecting, often while lying awake at night, flanked protectively by Eli and Gila, who slept in beds close by, he had cried his eyes out into the pillow because, sooner or later, his parents would die, whereas he would have to live on. That terrible, unavoidable age difference! That cruel reality! A child is born only to die and suffer. Poor little orphan! Left stranded alone in the world, like Korczak's King Macius on the uninhabited isle. In all his attempts, as a child, to defeat death he could think of no solution other than he and all his beloved ones dying together. To wish to go on living without them would have seemed to him unfeeling, mistaken, absurd.

It was his secret - and a strange thing, he had been as afraid of both darkness and its dispersal, then as he was now. He could remember how once, in the middle of the night, he had been pleased and sorry at the same time when he suddenly heard his father, his loving face bent over him, asking tenderly in a low, singing voice: "Why are you crying, my little child?" But he would not answer, as he did not a few years later, when at the wedding of his eldest sister - during all the festivities, merry-making and dances - he had sat crying his heart out in a far corner of the huge ballroom. He was losing a sister. The home, in which everything had been to him precious and marvellous, the family was breaking up. A portent of eventual dissolution.

The Freund family had been very close-knit, marked by feeling, mutual affection, loyalty and common purpose. With warm and loving parents, the children had been the ground and focus of the family. They had been all the world to each other and to their parents. Growing up in comfortable conditions, in a home that, by Polish standards, was spacious, they had had a happy childhood. It had been a time, as Arush recalled with a sigh, when life had been worth living. He had been the youngest child, the darling of his elder sisters and brothers. But his privileged status had lasted only until the time when equality between the children had become the rule. Then he, like every child of the family, had had to face a degree of competition, above all competition for the approval and favour of their parents. But Arush had the advantage of enjoying his elder siblings' example. Though all gifted intellectually, standards had been set by the child with most ability in each activity or subject.

Even as adults, when they had already developed different characteristics, temperaments and habits of independent thinking, family life took precedence and filled much of each child's time. Individual experiences gained outside the home were shared, as with birds, inside the nest. It had been a family life blessed, not only by social status, stability and established customs, but also by intellect and high ethical values, as demonstrated by the parents. True in practice to what they preached to their children, Arush's father and mother had admired knowledge, and followed religious principles, and this had given shape and direction to the life of

26

the family. A negative side of this awareness of values and spirit was a certain feeling of superiority - a superiority that was not the result of differences of lineage, class, or wealth, but of a contempt for the easy, the cheap, the lax, the life of least resistance. While they refused to see their own parents through the eyes of their friends, as others did, the Freund children judged their friends' families by comparison with their own. Thus, not unexpectedly, the young Freunds kept much to themselves.

In the early years of the war, when everything right and just - home and state, school and synagogue - were destroyed, the Freund family with its old ties, loyalties and values remained largely unchanged. Now, Arush lamented silently, even that, the last scraps were gone. But, in the darkness, they still lived on and he could talk to them jointly and to each of his beloveds separately. And he could see them in various situations from the past, though mostly as they appeared in the "good old days".

He began talking to his mother. He knew it was an illusion, but he wanted to delude himself, and to continue living in this illusion for ever. He told her how much he loved her, what she meant to him and what she had given him - the home, as it once was, the blissful life, its warmth and happiness. He stopped for a while, sighed, and then he went on to speak of his sorrow, what an oppressive burden it was to be left alone, the catastrophe no one could imagine - a whole people annihilated. Despite everything they should have tried to escape; there had been nothing to lose. Together they should have fled while there was still time - before they had seen the first German.

He, himself, had wanted to join the fleeing minority, but more for the adventure of it than out of fear of what might come. He would not, of course, admit to his motives when he had asked: "Please, mother let us leave!" They had all been sitting in the dining-room, discussing the problem thoroughly but, Arush felt, not earnestly. Only a week earlier they had returned from their holidays. The weather was still beautiful, dry and sunny - the whole atmosphere calm, almost indolent, when suddenly news came of the Molotov-Ribbentrop pact, triggering off a general panic. People began talking about war; some even prepared themselves for it, but in a peculiar, half-hearted way.

The panic seized the Freunds as well but, it seemed far less than most people. "People go, people come. They talk of war as if it were at the door, and cause the panic," Arush's father had said.

The day when Arush made his plea it was already getting dark early, and it was no longer hot. Arush was told to close the window to reduce the noise coming from the street - the rumble of hundreds of mobilized soldiers, who were roaming around singing martial songs.

"Bravery begins in the defence of one's home, and in facing up to every misfortune, not in heroic abandonment and flight," said his mother, who had apparently guessed his motives. "And," she added, "where could we go? Who knows where it's safer?" And speaking of endurance: "It's so much easier to suffer under one's own roof." Arush noticed how she put forward her views with little of her usual resolution. In the past none of the children had dared to interrupt her when she was speaking, but on that day she seemed to encourage them to do so, gladly withdrawing from the conversation for long periods.

Arush's father, perhaps already sensing the descendency of the old in relation to the young, which the war would bring about, also had little to say. "Hitler is merely bluffing," he said. "Trying to blackmail anyone who will give in to it. Panic only plays into his hands. His threats of war must be resisted at all costs. We must stand as an example of firmness to the Poles." And he repeated some of the reasons that had been put forward by Jewish leaders - leaders whose good sense he had questioned in the past.

It is strange how the ideas of fanatics can seduce even educated people, even those opposed to them.

Arush knew the arguments from the press, which for months had been commenting on them. Dispersal would be a tragedy. To leave one's home and country, as emigration was rhetorically referred to, was a crime. To desist from struggle at one's place of birth was a betrayal. Just a small sample of the disastrous drivel of the politicians and theorists, with whom the Jews, particularly in Poland, were bounteously blessed.

No one listened to the views of Arush or to those of his sisters and brothers which were hesitantly expressed. Only Dave, Arush's eldest brother, spoke firmly in favour of leaving. "War is imminent," he asserted. "There's no time to waste. Poland couldn't withstand a German attack. The Jews will be at the mercy of the Germans."

–"Well, those who want can flee," Arush's mother told Dave at the end of the discussion. "You're all grown up. Whatever you decide, let God protect you!"

None of them wished to break family ranks. If Dave had suited action to his words, Arush mused, he, and Pnina and Ami with him might still be alive.

The idea of escaping eastwards was not abandoned that evening; it was merely postponed. "There'll be time to flee," was the view that prevailed. Meanwhile it was better to stay and wait at home.

Unfortunately, the Freunds were not the only ones to think like that, expecting, at worst, a long protracted war; similar discussions took place in most Jewish homes in Poland.

The reason that his parents did not want to escape was clearer to Arush now than at the time itself. It was not easy for them to leave everything behind, and at an advanced age "to knock about the world homeless", as his mother put it. Unlike the young, they remembered, and occasionally recounted, episodes of evacuation in the previous war - its disruption of life and the almost revolutionary consequences it had had upon morals and customs at every level of Jewish society. And who could imagine what war might bring? No one expected the Germans to kill. The Jews were accustomed to persecution and suffering. And if one must suffer, then it is easier to endure in one's own town, in the midst of a familiar environment. Cracow was the town where they had lived most of their lives, where they had raised a family, where they were held in esteem, where they had been happy. All this added to the general climate of Jewish opinion, denying the danger of war. And if - a man must not open his mouth to Satan - the war comes, it will blow over quickly with the defeat of Germany.

Four evenings later, immediately after the end of Sabbath, they were again sitting together in the same dining room, this time at blacked-out windows, the panes pasted transversely with white paper strips. That these strips could lessen the impact on the panes from eventual nearby explosions seemed to Arush as curious a thought as that the cotton wool pads for which he had queued in a pharmacy the day before, could protect them from poisoning in the case of a gas attack. The paper strips and the cotton wool pads somehow stuck in his memory as the two vivid symbols of actual warfare.

They had been deliberating more intensely, though half as long as last time. The bad news had not reached them yet. In any case who wished to hear it?

-"What is the point of fleeing, running away from home?" his father asked. "Who can say where west ends and east starts? Bombs might fall in the east before they fall in the west."

-"Aren't the Germans," Dave retorted, "more frightening than their bombs? Flames are sweeping over the land and we just look on."

It was getting late when they all agreed that the sons would leave in the morning. Young men were considered the most vulnerable in the event of occupation. They began preparing some provisions for the journey, and at about midnight mother said that she and father would move as well. She wanted the daughters, who wouldn't leave without their parents, to join their brothers.

But next morning, on the third day of war, the trains were no longer running, and all motor cars, of which even at the best of times there were not many in Poland, had disappeared from the streets of the city, as had all the soldiers. Instead, the streets were full of refugees, arriving in Cracow from the border areas and neighbouring townships. Strangers arriving, local residents fleeing, the former out-numbering the latter. A real migration of people. Altogether confusion, disquiet, no apparent authority in charge.

The hardships of a walking tour were inconceivable for elderly people such as his parents. In the end, the entire family stayed on.

Later, when the people began returning, exhausted physically and mentally, when they told of roads blocked by crowds of fleeing civilians and soldiers, when they described how people had been robbed on the roads and rifled, or rather machine-gunned from the air, had parted with their last possessions for a little water or food, when they spoke of the lightning advance of the German army from all directions - they, the Freunds, were happy that they had remained at home.

When your brother Asher, Arush continued to speak to himself, was relating his particular odyssey, you, mother, mentioned something or other about Pascal and that all man's misfortunes start once he sets off from home. Now, while I am recall-ing this, you are off, "on the way". Oh Heavens, how will she manage the trip? Forgive me, mother, that I lie quietly with my eyes closed and dry, and my heart hardly open to true worry. Something, you know what it is, has died within me. All that is left is a crippled soul. Shall I pray for your death - quick, peaceful death? That you escape the brute's boot and butt? How could I? It is forbidden. "In greatest danger, in your tightest corner, don't cease to pray and hope!" King Hezekiah, you know!*

But some did pray for death. That day once at the market square, on a bright afternoon in the first spring of the war, when two grey-bearded Jews, still wearing traditional garb, were forced to dance, one with a broken umbrella, the other with what had once been a broom, to tunes played by a small military band. The soldiers around roared in boisterous laughter, while passing Jews, compelled to watch, wrung their hands and some, at least, prayed for the speedy death of the two elderly men, so humiliating and morally painful was the sight.

It is all very easy, he knew, to arrange other people's lives, to wish death on a stranger. No, I won't pray, Arush was firm. I must hope and trust! In what could I trust, mother? That we meet again? That you come back? That you'll call my name? My only hope is to lament, lament as long as I live - though no lament of mine can be worthy of you.

His head was splitting and whirling from all that thinking. Just that night when he was so needful of sleep, the sweet, salutary sleep of forgetfulness, he was racked by rare insomnia, which propelled painful memories into his mind.

While you, mother, never thought in terms of your own person and comfort - even on the brink of greatest danger she put the safety and needs of her children and husband first - he thinks of his life ahead, and how far ahead! But what is there he can do? He is powerless to bar his thoughts. Even if his mother, and Eli, and all the departed are now on their way to death, even if it is true that he himself will soon, perhaps this night or next morning, be killed - what should he do? Do the Germans' job for them? To force, as the heathens say, the gods' hand, would be irrational, completely illogical. Should we not spare no pains that "this war would be only a partial success", as Governor General Frank has put it, if some Jews in Europe survive? Perhaps still this night, perhaps next morning, but meanwhile...meanwhile is it a moral weakness to wish to live on? Who would remember us, if their war is a complete success? Mother, who will remember you, when I too no longer exist. Individually we cannot be remembered by strangers. Against the weight of millions, what does a single heart, an unloved heart, count? What a paradox, you may think: to be remembered we have to die; to remember the dead, we have to live. It is true, Arush recalled a saying, the dead *are* alive in us, the living, if we only wish it. Mother, you once said we would survive and continue to exist. "You must live for my sake!" No, he had none of the determination that his mother had shown both now and then.

The last day of the first Aktion leapt to his mind. Practically every second Jew in town had already been evacuated, and mostly "locally evacuated", as the perpetrators referred to extermination on the spot. They, the Freunds, had so far all been spared. Rumours had it that on the last day of the Aktion, June 18th, the evacuators would also scour the Polish district in which scattered Jewish families, including the Freunds, still had their homes.

*Hezekiah didn't stop praying for his life when Isaiah had told him his imminent death had been decreed.

30

Only five of them lived in the flat they shared with its main tenants. Mrs Freund put her husband and Arush in the one-time bathroom with a jib door barricaded by a heavy wardrobe. Eli had a stamp, and Gila was young and pretty and would some- how escape, eventually passing as Eli's wife. She herself? She was a woman, too old for forced labour, and the mother of the stamp-holder. Anyway, someone must greet the devil, should he come.

He did come about noon. Gila must go, they insisted, she has no stamp. Arguing, explaining, cajoling, imploring, invoking special rights, intimating bribes - all to no avail. Gila must go! She, her mother, would go instead. She would explain the mis- take at the police station. They agreed. They were two Polish constables - not the worst devil. She put on a coat quickly, a scarf on her head - Jewish women had not worn hats since the first weeks of war - a handbag under her arm, and off she goes. "Don't worry about me! Take care of yourself! Good-bye!"

With what feelings Eli and Gila watched their mother leaving, Arush could easi- ly imagine. His own heart, hearing everything in the derelict bathroom through the thin wall, was utterly broken. His father was literally trembling with emotion. Never had Arush seen him praying with such fervour.

The unexpected, the incredible, happened. His mother returned home. The only case known in town. At the Polish police station, which was in the same street that the Freunds lived, she somehow convinced the commander, First Lieutenant Wladislaus Laski, of her "right" to stay. What fantastic powers of persuasion! When she spoke earnestly it always seemed as if the majesty of law, or at least the lady of the manor, was addressing you. The imposing figure, the tone of her voice, the dig- nity of her gesture, the ingenuity of her argument, in the past had confused and silenced even the stiffest official, leaving her always the mistress of the situation. Now, Arush despaired, of all this - of all her courage, her sacrifice, and her bewitch- ing grace, nothing remains, "nothing but your calm, melodious voice, Mother, can I hear."

Hules was not the ideal man, too soft and weak, for the exceptionally hard task. Had Spatz sent him at all? Even if he had, he was not surprised that Hules had not managed to get through; he might himself have got stuck in the squalling mire. Arush recalled the much discussed case of Nute Safir, who one day had the golden opportunity to escape in a German car across the border to Hungary. It required his instant decision, without even the possibility of bidding farewell to his wife and daughter. After grievous hesitation, Nute stayed on in the ghetto. Opinions were divided. Some extolled his fidelity; others questioned his sense and motive. "Whoever has the chance to save himself, has the right," a minority even said "the duty, to do it." But Nute, Arush brooded, was not then in immediate danger of death; nor were his wife and daughter. He stayed on to share life with his dear ones, and hoped for another chance. He, Arush, could only have shared death with his dear ones, and hoped for nought.

How do you know? he asked himself. Arush, though young, was often questioning himself, his deeds and motives - and he did it punctiliously. "Probe deep into your heart and seek out," he recalled his father once quoting in response to his present

31

question. He found his conscience clean, but not light.

His soul was loaded down with brooding thoughts of all kinds. He would have liked to take refuge from them in sleep, but this was beyond him. Thus he went on taking stock, more reminiscences and regrets surfacing one after another, when suddenly his mother, as if descended from the clouds, was standing over him, her bright, alert eyes glowing with affection, and with her lucent lips saying conclusively: "That's how I would have done it!"

Not that Arush did not know the provenance of this kind of revelation, but his memories, swarming and flitting in the dark, did not allow him to pause and ponder.

In this war, he continued reflecting, his mother had worked miracles. Who, if not she, fed the family? Without basic means, without servants, without proper supplies - almost nothing on ration cards, almost nothing legal to buy or to stock -and with prices soaring, and resources declining daily. And yet, how she managed to uphold the home and with what patience she assumed the burden! She performed real wonders in the kitchen, where she instructed her daughters in the arcana of wartime culinary art. Of course it was an art - a dozen and more dishes from a potato, boiled, baked, fried, grilled, roasted; from quiches, ravioli, bulva dumplings and cracknels, to wartime pigeons, patties, malai and potato-penitzlech. Initially to lend variety to a uniform diet, then, as times grew harder, with a view to saving fat and fuel, and cutting the waiting time of a hungry child. But potato peelings? - "let *them* eat them," she said after the press reported, already in 1941, that German doctors deemed peelings healthful, nourishing, containing more vitamins than the pome itself. Until the ghetto era, there was normally a second or even a third dish with the potatoes, and their meals, however modest, compared favourably with those of most Jewish households. And until that era, at least one or another traditional Jewish dish elevated the table on the Sabbath and Holy Days.

People were living on coats, sheets, table-cloths; easier, she once said, to live on saccharine, vaccines, and safety razors. Nothing, neither gold or dollars, nor meat nor drugs, not even real coffee, went up in price as much as safety razors. In 1942, a family of five could live for three weeks on a dozen unused blades. Instinct? Foresight? Or the worldly wisdom and experience that life and wars had taught her?

She not only cooked and served the meals, but she also took great care that they were taken regularly, with all the family sitting together at table. In general, she was trying to preserve the prewar order of life at home down to the smallest detail still possible. So, despite all the hardships and trials of war, their former home in Cracow, as long as they could stay in it, was talked about as one of the seven wonders of the world gone mad. "Such floors can be found nowhere else in town," visitors exclaimed with admiration symptomatic of the times. Not without a certain pleasure, Arush recalled how he and his brothers were on alternate days harnessed by their mother to polish up the bright, waxed parquets. Excellent calisthenics, they used to say. The floors sparkled then more than in the housemaids' era, and there were also more floors to polish, as almost as soon as the occupation came, carpets were rolled up and concealed lest they catch the sight of a covetous German eye. Even in the second winter of war shoes had to be removed before one was allowed to set foot in a room; and woe betide the child who, standing up from the table, pushed instead of lifting his or her chair. The order, the discipline, the exemplary tidiness, were, apart from keeping to custom, intended to keep up their spirits, as well as the warmth and charm of life at home.

The splendid cleanliness, preserved in much more modest conditions in exile, had probably saved them, his entire family, from a virulent epidemic of typhus in the winter of 1941/42. How else could one avoid contagion? Although various vaccine samples were on offer on the "free" market, it was impossible for any amount of money to get hold of the legendary Dr Weigl vaccine against typhus. And this dread disease had no respect for person, class or rank. Indeed, it claimed relatively more victims in the better appointed homes of the more affluent. This impudence of typhus was justified by a theory that, in non-epidemic conditions, many of the prewar poor and deprived had passed on the disease without it being properly diagnosed, making them immune for life.

Perhaps for the first time in history, people mumbled sarcastically, the poor had become an object of envy.

Another peril that Mrs Freund had, for a time, thwarted so daringly and ingeniously was potentially no less dangerous than typhus. In February 1940, Jewish males aged 16-25 had been ordered to register with the Judenrat and pass a medical fitness test. The big problem that was nagging almost every Jewish home was how to elude forced labour, to which all Jewish men from the ages of 14 to 60 were already by then formally subjected. After trying this and that, mooting plots and seeking help, Arush's mother went with him to Dr Zenobia Maczek, who shared an X-ray consulting room with another doctor. She would talk to her "mother to mother", though Dr Maczek, it later appeared, had not yet taken marital vows. From the private hour-long conversation, the two women emerged friends, Mrs Freund, in addition, with a medical document attesting to Arush's acutely irritated appendix. Jewish doctors were too frightened to issue such testimonies. Of course, the affair had the assured co-operation of a sympathetic official of the Judenrat, in whose immediate care the organizing of Jewish forced labour then rested.

Later Arush's mother had used the contact to help other dependable youths. "Dear Zenobia! The pale bearer of this letter has a spleen that is clearly visible to the naked eye..."

Always ready with advice and help. A bucket of coal to relieve the congestion of the old Mandelbaums' renal calculi. A heroic dose of real, hot chicken soup for Nomek Meizels, a lonely, bed-ridden young man. "But mother," Gila, who was sent with the soup, remonstrated, "he has TB!" "Well, what of it? Can you plug up the holes in his lungs?" Or, a lot of lemons for Mrs Finkel's jaundice.

No remedy for herself. She recovered from her long-drawn-out illness by the sheer power of her will, founded on faith and love, and also thanks to the uniquely dedicated care of Dr Hilfsreich. A doctor of the "old school", people said of him, meaning a real doctor, one whose life's sole devotion is to healing the sick. At that time, regard for the medical profession as a whole was not at its highest. It was the time when on the other side of the fence, on the soil of the master race, a new species - a doctor-killer - was shooting up.

"You escaped from under the gravedigger's spade." The gentle, good-hearted Dr Hilfsreich had a habit of speaking coarsely to his patients. Was it, Arush often wondered, a sort of mask, or inner defence? Later, it became clear to him that the old-looking doctor, who exuded the authority of both age and medicine, shouted at his patients from sheer despair at being hindered by cruel circumstances from relieving them of their ailments. As the man, seeing people consumed by hungry flames, screams on finding all the taps in the house turned off.

For in his true self, nothing was too hard, too exhausting, too degrading for Dr Hiflsreich, no time of the day too early or too late, when it came to tending to a sick patient - Mrs Freund in particular. Performing massage till the pain went way; taking out faeces with his bare fingers to open exceptionally stubborn bowels; placing cupping glasses for pleurisy; applying leeches to a thrombotic leg. Altogether fourteen weeks, more than a hundred visits. He almost fell in love with Arush's dying mother. "Old wine tastes better," he told Mrs Freund jokingly, after she had recovered enough for such chatter. Arush for his part found himself confirmed in his curious belief that goodness and devotion like that of Dr Hilfsreich would always triumph over disease.

When earlier that evening, Arush had reminded Dr Hilfsreich how he had once cautioned his mother, "if you eat bread, you'll die!" and now she was on that "journey", the doctor kept silent, but his bland, mournful gaze seemed to say, "mad, raving, beyond all words."

CHAPTER THREE

With his eyes closed, Arush did not notice the sunbeams that were shyly darting through the slits of the Singer barracks. Only when the door was opened and a tired, indifferent voice called out: "Get up!" did he realize that it was already day.

Outside, the early morning sky was gaily blue, the air fresh, mildly warm, ringing with distant sounds. "Another day," Arush sighed inwardly. He felt broken, exhausted, not at all braced for the sort of day that could be expected. Not everyone looked like that; some men, those who had perhaps slept through the night, were quietly conversing, guessing, worrying, discussing possible drudgery ahead. Inevitably, Arush was drawn in, listening to the rumours, and wishing, as he had the morning before, that the day's beginning would somehow stay its hand. It won't run away, he kept repeating both to himself and to the men meandering round the barracks.

Of the many uncertainties, the mystery of the vibrant whispering sounds Arush had heard in the night cleared immediately they came out into the open. The Madritsch-chosen, upwards of two thousand men and women, had spent the night on the evacuation arena. It was only after their departure, late in the morning, that the three hundred darlings of Fortune were marched onto the Platz. The *Aufräumung* (Clean Up) began.

As if he were taking his first steps in a strange, lost town, Arush was afraid of what he might see. A littered waste ground was his first impression of the barren square; littered, first and foremost, with corpses. Not that they were numerous by evacuation standards; but the thirty of them, strewn over a space which, although only hours earlier it had contained thousands, looked fairly narrow, seemed to lie everywhere. The contrast with the day before was overwhelming, punctuating the present atmosphere of desertion.

His eyes screwed up like a lynx, Arush zigzagged his way between the corpses, so as not to look at them. If he sensed one lying on the ground, he moved his eyes away.

–"Take care! Mind the body!" softly but urgently called Bodman, who was walking nearby.

As Arush stumbled on the thing under his feet, he bent down by mischance and saw a young, grotesquely disfigured body, arms and legs flung out, sunken cheeks, crooked mouth, whiskers of coagulated blood-trickle under the nose, fixedly staring eyes which seemed to quiver at him. Arush leapt hastily aside with a strangled scream of panic.

–"Assign him to other work! Too queasy for this one here!" It was the voice of

35

Roter, who, brisk and vigorous as always, must have witnessed the scene, and from a short distance gave the order to an OD man accompanying him and to Bodman.

Arush Freund came not only from a privileged family, but from a privileged part of Poland as well. This requires some explanation.

Having overrun Poland in September 1939, the Germans almost immediately incorporated the western part of the country into the Reich. No sooner had this happened than the life of Jews in the incorporated territories became hell on earth: forced labour, starvation, local executions, and above all expulsions; expulsions from one place to another, but in the main, into the remaining German-occupied part of Poland. This was the part which was envisaged as a future Polish state and, by a decree coming into force on October 26, 1939, was designated as the "General Government (GG) for the occupied Polish territories". Initially, the GG was divided administratively into four districts - Cracow, Warsaw, Lublin and Radom - each with a separate governor. Cracow, the Freunds' native town, was named the capital of the GG.

After the first shocks of occupation - the Jews' loss of virtually all rights, scores of prohibitions and restrictions, not least on their freedom of movement, and the plunder of businesses and homes - the situation, particularly in Cracow, eased and a remarkable period of calm set in, engendering false hopes and dangerous illusions. "Little Eretz Israel" was how many Jewish curbstone traders dealing inside the teeming, segregated cafes of Cracow described their illusory comfort in the late winter of 1940, recalling the harassment and physical attacks on Jews in the late nineteen thirties. In short, at the time when Jews of the incorporated territories were already uprooted and ravaged, for most of the first year of war their co-religionists in the GG as a whole thought their lives bearable.

Progressively, though, conditions became tighter and tighter. Cracow, "that German city", and seat of the GG government, must - declared its head, Hans Frank - be stripped of its "Jewish character". In May 1940, the German authorities "advised" the Jews of Cracow to reduce voluntarily their number from 70,000 to a mere 15,000 within three months. This advice was ignored by most local Jews, including the Freunds. When in the following autumn compulsory evacuation was ordered, the Freunds obtained an *Ausweis*, as permission to stay in Cracow was called. But simultaneously they looked around to find a place to move, because of rumours about a ghetto in Cracow. Thus when the rumours proved true and the formation of a separate "Jewish Housing District" (the word "ghetto" was not yet in official use, and its utterance was at that time even punishable) was announced at the beginning of March 1941, the Freunds hastily removed themselves to Tarnow.

About fifty miles east of Cracow, situated on the main west-east railway line, Tarnow was the second largest town in the District of Cracow. It had a population of 65,000, of which in 1939 about one in two were Jews. During the war, Tarnow also gave its name to a *Kreishauptmannschaft* - one of twelve in the District of Cracow - that is, to a regional administration of surrounding urban and rural communities, counting 365,000 people in 1942, with a similar proportion of Jews as the town of Tarnow.

36

The Freunds' choice of Tarnow seemed a fortunate one. True, it had the distinction of being the first town in the GG to force its Jewish inhabitants to wear the Shield of David armband on their clothes, while a couple of days later, in early November 1939, its synagogues had been burnt down; yet in 1941 Tarnow was a relative heaven. While in Cracow the Jews were already secluded and squeezed within the walls of a partly derelict and overcrowded ghetto, the Freunds were able, for a reasonable rent, to share with relatives of relatives a spacious flat in an elegant house in one of the town's smartest streets. Jews in general could live anywhere, except in a small, exclusively German area, and they could move more or less freely in the streets. There were still dozens of Jewish shops, doing business of a sort, with or without "commissarial" supervision; most craftsmen were busy and some workers held paying jobs. The requirements of forced labour could be satisfied by volunteers, who were paid a subsistence wage by the Judenrat. Young people, like young people everywhere, pursued their amorous friendships and attended occasional parties at the homes of submissive parents. And many of the not so young and old alike spent their long evenings playing cards.

Notwithstanding constant anxiety about the future, life went on like this for some fifteen months after the Freunds' arrival in Tarnow; it was disturbed only by two major atrocities. On the morning after the Japanese strike at Pearl Harbour, anticipation of war with the United States cost seventeen Jewish lives and the arrest of another hundred, who were never released. Then, on April 28, 1942, fifty-three Jews were killed. This happened in the course of a so-called hunt for communists, that is for people who had returned without permission from the previously Russian part of Poland, which by then formed the fifth GG District of Galizia. The truth was that nearly all the victims were shot at random in the streets.

Even this crime could be seen as a sign of the relative "softness" of conditions in Tarnow, for in Nowy Sącz, a town in the same district and with less than half the Jewish population of Tarnow, 285 Jews (later rounded up to 300) were killed in a similar atrocity committed on the same day and on the same pretext.

Apart from these two acts of butchery, which naturally disturbed the air deeply (but not for very long), Jewish life in Tarnow continued to be just about supportable until June 11, 1942. On that day the week-long first Aktion began, marking a turning point in the wartime history of the Jews, the beginning of a new era of their rapid extermination.

In many towns of occupied Poland, there never was a ghetto, and in most villages and small townships the Jews never saw a German gendarme until the day of their forcible evacuation. On the other hand, in what had been eastern Poland, extermination of the Jewish inhabitants began immediately following the advance of the German army into the Soviet Union in June 1941.

This divergent course of events, the difference in emphasis and time of persecution, could be one decisive reason why it may never become possible to present a uniform wartime history of the Jews under Nazi occupation - a history that would immortalize the lives and struggles of the victims rather than the deeds of their oppressors.

One of man's foibles is a certain dislike, prejudice, even ill-will on the part of natives towards refugees. This held good, to some extent, with the indigenous Jews of Tarnow in relation to their newly arrived brethren from Cracow. The sentiments of the former were both eased and aggravated by the usual sense of inferiority that people from small towns feel in relation to city-dwellers. But as far as the Freunds were concerned, they did not encounter rejection nor were they rebuffed by local Jews. On the contrary, they were everywhere welcomed and socially sought after. Their good name had gone before them into exile.

It was not the name of Abraham Freund, the wealthy man of affairs that had preceded him; for during the war he was not active in either public or business affairs, nor was he any longer prosperous, even by the reduced standards of wartime. The renown that accompanied him, the head of the expatriate Freund family, on its wanderings, was that of a man of piety and great learning. Arush's father was one of that peculiar breed of men, perhaps less rare among God-fearing Jews than among others, who combined the worldly with the spiritual, a lifelong pursuit of material wealth with an endless quest for knowledge.

Those noble values, the imperishable capital, which, it is said, goes along with man into the other world, brought it about that, despite the loss of all his property, despite the decline of his authority, and despite all the other misfortunes that befell him in old age, Abraham Freund was not shaken in his beliefs, in his sense of self-esteem, nor had he lost that special stamp which is gained only through true modesty and life-long study combined with responsibility before God.

Thanks to these qualities, Mr Freund was also able to preserve, notwithstanding the suffering inflicted on his body and mind, his usual polite, serene, but no longer cheerful manner and a personal decorum that seemed incongruous in the tight circumstances of Tarnow.

At that time, the slim, shortish man, though still in good health, looked rather frail and older than his sixty years. Only his face still retained the old bright, intelligent expression, the large forehead above keen eyes shining from behind gold-rimmed glasses, the thin cheeks overgrown with short, grey, once handsome, but by then thinning beard; a beard that had not been surrendered, even though beards made the Germans see red, and despite the severe penalty threatened for wearing one. Retaining a beard was a rigour Mr Freund and some other, mainly elderly men, imposed upon themselves, for the rabbis had agreed that since the order requiring Jews to shave off their beards stated it was for health reasons, it did not constitute a demand to renounce a principle of faith that would oblige a man to sacrifice his life; the order could, therefore, be complied with.

What made old Mr Freund's company much sought after was not just his polite manner, his reputed wisdom, his engaging conversation, or his wide horizon of thinking; it was also his optimism, which regarding the course of the war verged on the fantastic. While the starkly stationary fronts of the first winter of war were driving every captive Jew to exasperation - to the point of even praying for a German attack, to force the French and English armies to start fighting - Mr Freund was calming his listeners, telling them not to believe what they read in the papers, reminding them how in the last war on every day that the press had followed official communiqués and reported "all quiet on the western front", twenty thousand soldiers were dropping dead.

Two years later, in the autumn of 1941, almost every Jew was plunged into utter despondency as they followed with bated breath the course of the German invasion of Russia, saw the Soviets lose battle after battle, retreating deeper and deeper into the interior, with hundreds of thousands of their soldiers falling into German captivity. Many expected the imminent collapse of Russian defences and an end to the war in the east.

–"An end to the war?" Mr Freund asked rhetorically to counter the gloomy views of the neighbours and his own family who were assembled on one of the long evenings after curfew, in the heated room of the Freunds' flat. "Why, it has only just started.

"True, for us it's difficult to wait, but by now the Russians have already completed their strategy. History is just repeating itself. They have now tricked Hitler deep into Russia, just as they did Napoleon."

–"Like the French have tricked him into Paris," murmured Dave, loudly enough to be heard. He was alluding to something his father had said the day after the fall of Paris in June 1940.

But Abraham Freund would not be put off. He continued as if he had not heard what Dave had said.

–"Real master strokes. The retreats have forced Hitler to stretch out and fight far away from his home-base, while the Russians are concentrating their armies around their own hearth. "Stalin may be 'Marshall Retreat', as you, Mr Laks, say, but he's left Hitler to water the scorched earth and guard the ruins. Don't let yourself be deceived by his stories of daily victories. This is good for his own people. But we should know better.

"Kutuzov's retreat to Moscow drove the French to look for homes, and his retreat from Moscow sent them fleeing home. Remember how the saintly Kozhenitzer Maggid predicted Napoleon's fall to Prince József Poniatowski six months in advance. Nobody would believe it then...But they have really exhausted the German forces, while winning time to muster their own reserves before the decisive battle at the gates of Moscow. And then they'll drive them back to the gates of Berlin."

When Moses Zaler, another neighbour and formally landlord of the house they occupied, had joined in, saying that after the enormous losses the Russians had suffered, they might have hardly any reserves left to muster, Mr Freund told him scornfully: "What's one or two million soldiers to the Russians? Napoleon couldn't sleep at night because half a million children were born every year in Russia. Now eight times as many are added to its population every year."

Convinced or not, the neighbours left after such a discourse with spirits visibly raised, and respectful of the old man's indomitable optimism and breadth of historical knowledge.

Arush respected his father even more than did the strangers with whom they mixed, and even then, on the Platz littered with corpses, he was proud of the name his father had bequeathed to him.

Arush was not without a few qualities of his own. He was blessed by nature as well as by nurture. He was tall and slim, had a high "Freundian" forehead, brownish hair, equally brown, large eyes tipped by very long lashes - altogether a handsome boy, who looked younger than his twenty years. For his age and times, he was well-read, clear-headed, considered a "bright young fellow". The way he spoke, carefully, gently, in a leisurely cultured voice, enhanced both his refinement and the innocent looks of his otherwise sharp-featured face. What made him liked by most was his quiet, slightly shy, outwardly compliant manner; he argued as little with his superiors as he did with his parents, which did not mean that he always obeyed either. Add to all this the fact that, on account of his close relationship with Rabbi Maleachi, he was vaguely associated with the rabbi by the most influential people in the ghetto, and it becomes easy to understand how Arush Freund gained the label of a "better" person.

He was, therefore, not altogether surprised by the consideration that Roter had shown him. Yet, though glad to be released from handling corpses, he was not completely happy about it. He felt genuine remorse, primarily of a religious nature; he belonged to the small minority of men and women whom wartime experiences were driving closer to their fathers' faith. "The highest commandment," he admonished himself. "Coming across deserted corpses," as such dead are called, "it's your holiest duty to attend to them. What is the good of saying that they aren't really deserted? And what if it were your father lying like this? Only yesterday that body there was a father to someone. Have strength to look at them. Remember their faces. To carve their images into granite, to commit them into infinite memory. And you promised yourself," which was a self-reproach of a different kind, "to grow up to your new responsibilities as the last remnant, as a son worthy of your family. Why be an exception? If Bodman and Teper and all the others can do it, why can't you? How can you hope to survive this greatest savagery that man has known, if you won't learn to do everything that has to be done?"

Carefully avoiding the strewn bodies as he tried to slip away from the Platz, Arush also took the precaution of stooping down, as if he were doing some kind of work. It proved a fortunate forethought, for suddenly the unsteady, wild eyes of Gerhard Grunow, one of the most degenerate Gestapo killers, met his own. Insane murder gleamed from those demented eyes, demented as if he were "high" on drugs. The last look, Arush thought as he awaited an instant bullet, and he bent down still lower.

Was it ordained, he could not help wondering later, that a body was lying just at his feet? Whatever it was, under the weight of Grunow's gaze, and of the urgency of the pulses pounding impatiently at his temples, Arush seized the body by its trousers and helped to lift it on the cart that was to take all the piled up corpses for burial at the Jewish cemetery outside the ghetto.

–"You didn't faint at the sight of a dead body, you even touched its clothes,"

40

Arush silently upbraided himself, as he regained composure and the (not too great) confidence that in time he would be inured to handling corpses and every filth under the sun.

Meanwhile, he felt a certain contentment at having taken part in an act of benevolence, as all funebrial activities, however marginal, are considered among Jews.

"May they come to their rest in peace," he silently repeated the traditional blessing, as the cart with the putrid bodies began the journey to their "last resting place".

He sensed how hollow such time-honoured phrases and blessings sounded in their present circumstances, though they evoked nostalgic memories of "normal" funerals. But now was not the time to ponder over such things, or over the way people were dying and reaching the grave. Though, indeed, the changes in this respect charted the vicissitudes in the peoples' conditions at various stages of their captivity.

In the first stage of the occupation, most Jewish deaths were from natural causes, so that there were not many more than immediately before the war. Burial services, held under the control of the Judenrat, were free for all, regardless of residence, and traditional ceremonials, though simplified and circumspect, and increasingly uniform as between class and rank, were still observed. Indeed, simplicity, speed, and caution characterized the ceremonies, as they marked most daily duties at that time.

Gradually, however, funeral processions through the streets, ceased. While they were still possible, strangers were no longer expected to join, even to accompany the cortege for a few steps, as ancient custom required. Numbers of attendant mourners were greatly reduced and in time they began assembling only at the cemetery gates. Box collections of money to the accompaniment of calls of "charity delivers from death" ceased, and soil from the Holy Land, which used to be put under the head of the deceased to accelerate the atonement which the grave provides for sins committed during his lifetime, ran out of stock soon after the war started.

For the rest, the dead were buried with proper rites, administered by members of the Holy Association, as the fraternity for providing burial rites is called. Even funeral orations were still delivered for men of great learning and merit. More important, the cherished desire of every Jew to be buried in the grave of his father or mother could still be fulfilled in the case of long-time residents. But no tombstones were erected, partly because of the shortage of suitable stones, and partly because this category of masonry was not sanctioned by the authorities.

Still, when all is said and done, burial according to traditional rites, with at least family mourners attending, was the order of the day until the beginning of the mass murders.

In the ghetto phase, the desire to have a proper burial was as strong as ever but it could not often be satisfied. Procedures took on a short and pitiable character.

41

Impediments were aggravated by the fact that the Jewish cemetery was located a considerable distance from the ghetto. Corpses had to be transported by horse-drawn carts, rarely in coffins, which became a luxury, and even close relatives of the deceased found it hard to obtain an exit permit to attend the burial, under the guard of an OD man. Attendance was not much less perilous than the burial rites themselves. For although they were never formally prohibited, anyone performing the rites could expect severest punishment if they were seen by a visiting security officer. These officers' occasional visits to the cemetery, and the fact that hardly a day passed without someone being shot dead, were the reason for keeping deep dug graves open, ready for inmates. The diggers knew from experience that they might pay with their lives if they were ever unable to cope with their work at the murderous tempo required by the watching security men.

What wonder, then, that even when no strangers were present at the cemetery, ceremonies were reduced to a minimum. The bodies were, however, cleansed, shrouded in what linen there was, and interred with due respect. Rough, risky, and not a little exacting, the exercise of these duties was, nevertheless, voluntary, and applicants for the job far exceeded the number of men required. For in the ghetto phase the repelling work of a Holy Association member became a greatly privileged occupation. At times of Aktion, the members were among the first to get a stamp for themselves and their families, to exempt them from evacuation. This was no doubt in recognition that they were probably the busiest people in the ghetto. The function also carried with it authorized daily exit outside the walls, and this meant business.

Owing to its screening walls and out-of-the-way location, the cemetery provided a relatively safe site for barter, with access to Polish traders. Thus, the doleful grave-diggers and corpse-bearers ranked high also among the suppliers who smuggled provisions into the ghetto - a function no less vital to the living than the escape from falling prey "unto all the fowls of the air, and unto the beasts of the earth" was to the dead.

Another activity of the Holy Fraternity was neither heroic, nor ultimately of more than casual interest, but was at the time considered important. This was their attempt to record the deaths and mark individual graves for as long as Jews remained in the town, in the vain hope of preserving the records for future generations.

Like the face of death and the grave, so expressions of grief and consolation were changing. In the ever present atmosphere of violent death and the daily struggles to avoid it, grief itself lost its intensity - but that is a different subject.

A third variety of obsequies, extending across both phases, prevailed on days when there were numerous, but not too many, killings. Such as the day of the "communist hunt", or, two months later, the "just for fun" occasion when a passing SS unit took thirty-nine lives, including that of Abraham Freund. The striking feature of this variety of funeral, if this is the right word, was its lightning speed. No sooner was the fury over, than the bodies were picked up and buried in the clothes they wore, without being cleansed, with virtually no religious rites, without the presence of relatives, who were not even notified beforehand. Since speed was imperative, personnel scarce, and, as time went on, space short, despite the expansion of the cemetery area, two corpses were interred in one grave.

Were it not for the unusual circumstances, it would sound strange to mention something so basic and unexceptional as the fact that the Holy Fraternity took pains to separate the sexes, and, then, to couple fitting mates for the same grave. "A man, a Scroll of the Law," was how Bodman, an old-time member of the Fraternity, had reassured Dave about the choice of a grave partner for his father. Whichever of the two partners was considered more meritorious was, as a rule, placed on top.

Those who buried a relative in this way would not precisely say he had been "gathered unto his people", but could still "thank God, he attained a Jewish grave", and that its place was still outlined.

Sui generis were the funerals of people killed in multitudes, as, for instance, on the first day of the first Aktion in Tarnow, when an estimated eight thousand were "locally evacuated". On a day when an incident of that scale took place, a huge pit would be dug at the Jewish cemetery, if there was one "at hand". Into this corpses would be flung indecorously and indiscriminately, men and women, child, young and old, sage, boor, and blind together, layer on layer, pile on pile, face up and face down, headlong and headless, covered with quicklime in between, and with earth to the brim.

These will be buried like those who die in small groups, Arush reflected lugubriously, as he followed the death-cart rumbling over the Platz. Then, at the moment that they neared the curb of the pavement, he jumped into the front door of a house opposite. It was a building that bridged two parallel streets, with entrances in both. It was purpose built, not like the makeshift bridges that people had begun to make soon after the war started, breaking through walls and fences between adjoining houses, in order to walk as little as possible in the open street. Passing quickly through the hallway, Arush found himself at the threshold of Szpitalna Street.

Oh, how strange, how menacing that street looked to him! Not a living person could be seen; not a sound could be heard; a deathlike stillness blew through the empty street. A frightening emptiness filled with terror and destruction. Looking up and down the street, Arush felt as if he were alone in the world. Only yesterday, it struck him, a street full of life, sound and turmoil, today a ghost street. Every inch of its ground, on which day after day thousands of feet had once trod, now marked their disappearance, every inch accusing of murder. Lost in this desert, he was frightened to come out into the street. From every open window, from every door, from every corner the same terrifying emptiness seemed to be crying out to him. How could he start out? How could he move?

Arush had been standing petrified for who knows how long when he noticed a figure or two flitting past the dingy windowpane on the top floor of a building diagonally across from him. He stepped out into the street, skirting the wall, as if this could, in the circumstances, make him less visible. Opposite the building, he ran across the road, climbed the creaking staircase and joined the other men, as he had been told.

On opening the door, Arush found four men in a semi-dark room, partly screened from light. The room was full of sticks of furniture and the everyday belongings of a ghetto family. Some of the things seemed to have been taken out of an open trunk - after all this was Clean Up - the kind of trunk which in these days often served as a wardrobe, kept under the bed. Some chattels were lying on the bed, or rather on bedding, and on a small wooden table; others were strewn on the floor, a shoe here, a pot there. In the mess, Arush, from force of habit, tried to visualize the people who had lived in the room, but he had to give up. Quite common, he told himself as he scanned the things that lay about, with both rich and poor, virtuous and wanton. The mere sight of a bonnet that lay in the trunk evoked a whisper of the woman who, perhaps only yesterday, had worn it.

The men in the room were as grieved and frightened as he was. They were afraid to tread freely, as every step seemed to echo dangerously. What Arush did not know was how much panic he had aroused by the sudden sound of his steps in the house. The man standing *zeks* on the house-landing raised an immediate alarm; another, squatting, was watching through the window of the room. Incidentally, to stand *zeks* in turns, proved to be their main occupation for the rest of the day. Arush soon learned that there were more men in the house, all supervised by a single OD man. When Arush arrived, they had been at a lower floor, searching for food.

His new companions, none of whom he knew, wanted to know what was happening on the Platz, while Arush was concerned to hear what he was to do in this place.

–"I must do some work," he said.

–"Oh, don't take it to heart," one of the four, who was using a sideboard as a chair, told him condescendingly.

As Arush protested, the comrades looked at him with eyes that were half pitying and half saying, "What a fool!"

After a while he heard a man of about forty, an unprepossessing fellow whose name he later learned was Seiden, saying to him: "You're going to be disappointed. Nothing valuable has been left behind."

Arush was offended, as these words implied he had dishonourable intentions. But Seiden continued his tirade:

–"What's the point of checking out the place? The SS were here before you. They ransacked the ground floor and apparently decided not to bother coming upstairs. No money. No jewellery. Food? Not a hope. And this junk" - he pointed at the objects scattered about the room - "what are you going to do with it? This time it's different. You can't be conscious today."

"Conscious" is the literal translation of *przytomny*, which was wartime slang applied to someone who "had eyes in his head", one who knew how to take advantage of circumstances. It referred in particular to the practice of helping oneself to the abandoned possessions of the evacuees. Arush was stung by the spiteful insinuation. To be "conscious" had always been abhorrent to him and to his whole family.

It was definitely not honourable, but whether it was immoral to be "conscious" had been a subject of frequent debate in the ghetto. It is an established social order that the living inherit from the dead. What is wrong, some argued, in taking over the abandoned property of an evacuee? The conscious individual was the one who was first on the scene, acting on the assumption that "someone else will do it, if I don't". Of course, there was always the possibility that there remained in the ghetto a close or distant relative, under almost any law the rightful heir of the evacuee. The conscious would meet this objection with the assurance that, should an heir of the former owner appear, the goods would be returned (something which hardly ever happened), while easing his conscience with the knowledge that he had saved the goods from falling into the hands of the Germans or at least of the OD. "Should everything be left for them to grab?" was not merely a rhetorical question.

Whatever the answer, rightly or wrongly, after every evacuation the conscious grew prosperous and the standard of living of the remaining population rose collaterally. And finally the reason: "One has to live as long as one is alive."

Arush was not impressed by such arguments. Where does being conscious lead to, he wondered, where does it end? He remembered his mother's homily: "Saying someone else will do it anyway, so why shouldn't I, is the first step on the slippery path that leads to crime." He firmly believed this. Madritsch must have asked himself this question, and he may have added: "I at least shall treat them well." But how many did not? How many of the so-called commissars who took over Jewish property justified their actions with this excuse - and then proceeded from plunder to ever greater plunder, and eventually to murder? And the Polish woman telling her Jewish neighbour: "Soon you won't need these things. Leave them to me, your friend, rather than to the Germans. If you return after the war, you can take them back..." And the Jew asking: "Will there be no OD men, if I refuse to become one?" Or indeed, as Gastwirt put it in reply to Reb Tunye: "If we don't do it, someone else will - and more thoroughly..."

The only way to avoid the devilish traps lurking about this path was to resist taking the first step on it. For a number of reasons, in this war the first step was often the decision to be conscious. Only a small minority actually was, but there were many who made excuses for them and still more who were envious. In such conditions, only categorical rejection, avoiding the temptation like the plague, could save one's soul. "Even if it is gold, crying out to be picked up, don't touch it!" - his parents' warning rang in Arush's ears.

It was different when Dave and Pnina were evacuated. Then, the three remaining relatives had moved into their apartment. This was how Mrs Freund and her two younger sons came to live in the kitchen which had once formed part of the flat occupied by Rabbi Maleachi and his wife. What an improvement! What luxury! A kitchen of their own! No more sharing a room with strangers; the full significance of that will become clear a little later.

Theirs was not a unique case; in fact, after every evacuation the housing conditions of the remaining ghetto inmates were improved. For although the ghetto borders were being tightened, the proportion of evacuated population exceeded the proportion of reduced living space.

Now, Arush reflected in the cluttered room of the empty house, their condition was such as they had never known before. No more individual homes, no more private property, no contacts with the outside world to be anticipated. In conditions such as these, who could even think of being conscious! And at him, at him of all people, whom no pretext or persuasive argument could induce to yield to the temptation, at him the slur had been thrown! He nursed his hurt feelings in silence; it would be beneath his dignity to answer a cynic like Seiden.

Arush was roused from his brooding by the men who had come up from downstairs.

–"No food! Not a scrap!" they announced. "Plates, pots, a truss, a wig, prayer-books, but no food."

–"As if the place had been purged for Passover," added one of the newcomers.

Grosser, an amicable OD man who was the leader of the group, held in his hand a pair of glasses with a Hebrew engraving on its gold rim. He showed it to Arush.

–"A good omen," he said.

–"What does it say?"

–"A blessing." The men began jeering but Grosser silenced them.

–"Strange, this is the second today."

Arush wasn't sure if Grosser meant a second blessing or a second good sign. He himself was an enthusiast for omens.

–"Two floors below," Grosser added, "where the SS were on the rampage, the front door is broken. I found a mezuzah attached to the back of the door-post."

–"The things people hide and risk their lives for!" the man who had earlier scoffed at Arush commented sarcastically.

More earthly, urgent needs now demanded their attention. As it turned out, their search for food had not been as fruitless as the men had claimed. Grek, who came up with Grosser, had unearthed some bottled tea labelled "Herbatorium" and, emptying the contents of every primus-stove that they found, produced enough kerosene to fuel a single one.

All seemed to be going well. The primus was burning, the water steaming and the kettle singing, when they heard shots from the street outside. The men dispersed immediately. Arush stayed behind in the room, watching at the window with Seiden. They quickly located where the shooting was taking place. Nothing sensational. Still, it was a sight to behold.

At the intersection of the Platz and Szpitalna Street, near the quondam Tailors Workshop, a truck was parked, its tail-gate lowered. A few steps from the truck, at an angle, stood Goeth with a gun in his hand, and two unidentified SS officers beside him. Men and women were jumping from the truck one after another, at intervals of thirty seconds or so. The firing was measured and unhurried, a display of macabre efficiency such as Arush had never witnessed before; the leaping victims were shot while still in the air, struck in the neck or the head, and were probably dead before they hit the ground. To be on the safe side, one of the SS men kicked his boot into the head of any dubious case. One man, in a transparent but futile "cheat", jumped down with a little child in his arms.

Freund and Seiden agreed that there must have been another officer shooting from the other side of the tail-gate, hidden from view.

"Children found at the railway station and brought back with their parents who were trying to smuggle them out," Arush was told later that evening. About fifty altogether. He also heard that one child had somehow managed to slip away from the intersection. After the shooting was over the toddler crept back to the scene, where his mother lay dead. "Mummy, come home!" he begged her again and again. How heartless of her, he must have thought, to lie unmoved.

In the evening, the three hundred were all billeted in two adjoining houses, both with approaches from the Platz as well as from Szpitalna Street. They were several to a room, the number depending on the size of the room and the status of its inmates. The lodgers in one apartment, and especially those sharing a room, immediately formed a distinctly closed group, a sort of "family". Arush shared his room with former co-idlers from Varnish and Putty.

The two houses were, unlike the one in which he spent his first Clean Up afternoon, well appointed: clean and airy rooms, running water, toilets, and fittings in every flat. Both houses also contained some food, and this was particularly welcome to the men moving in. There was no bread, but there was flour - white wheat flour, with which the civilian population had been forbidden to bake bread since 8 February 1940 - and yeast.

Hungry as they were, they were not yet desperate enough to eat flour. But no one in the apartment which Arush shared with a couple of dozen other men knew how to bake bread, nor was any one of them daring enough to stage the experiment. It was the pitiful state of the elderly among them, who seemed - and none more so than Reb Tunye Einhorn, the oldest inhabitant of the apartment - to be on the point of collapse, that finally tipped the balance. Arush yielded to Reb Tunye's persistent pleas and agreed to try his hand as a baker, on condition that he was not to be held responsible should the experiment fail and the precious communal provisions be wasted.

It was not for him a total leap into the dark. He had often watched his mother baking bread during the days when they lived in a kitchen of their own, a privilege which those uninitiated into ghetto life could never appreciate.

In most places people were forced to move into the prospective ghetto at short notice - in Tarnow it was within seven days following the first Aktion. There, hardly any Aryans were living in the section of town designated for the ghetto. Hence, unlike in most cities, there were no homes to exchange with the Poles. Admittedly, the flats of many families who had been murdered in their entirety, or nearly so, stood vacant. But most of the families rendered homeless by the resettlement had to be absorbed into the dwellings of families already residing in the chosen area.

The responsibility of providing every person with a roof over his head rested with the Judenrat. To accomplish this in an orderly fashion, to allocate shelter equitably, let alone to assign compatible people as neighbours, was an impossible task. Although a housing department at the Judenrat had functioned since its inception, the register of homes and of people inhabiting them was, in the wake of recent events, in a chaotic state. To add to the problems there was the need to distribute necessary basic furniture, as the displaced families were prohibited from moving their own. Those who risked "bootlegging" faced the Herculean task of finding room for their contraband tables or cupboards.

Given the circumstances, people tried to find accommodation with sitting tenants in apartments they owned. Others used force. Most queued outside the Judenrat building, where the scene resembled a fugitive fortress under siege. The turmoil, strife and chaos were indescribable.

It was in such conditions that the Freunds were forced to move, with the added burden of a fresh bereavement. This made them largely indifferent to the choice of new quarters, and following the advice - in the circumstances it seemed more like a will - of their recently murdered father, they opted for the house at 12 Szpitalna, which was made available to them by private agreement with one of the resident families. The house, which had its own tried and "tested" bunker, was in reasonable condition and the family, the prewar owners of the house, of good reputation, its widowed mother even claiming the title of a *tsideikes* or righteous woman - but living space was very tight. The average in this initial period, when overcrowding was at its height, was three or four persons to a room, and a family of this size was eligible for a separate room. The Freunds, four of them, shared a large, partitioned room with the elderly widow Mrs Lebron and her not so young unmarried daughter Hana. In another room of the compulsorily dismembered flat, which included a kitchen, a toilet and a sporadically functioning bathroom, lived Mrs Lebron's youngest son Motel, with his wife Keile and their two children.

While overcrowding itself can be quantified, there can be no statistical recording of the misery arising from it. The difficulty of co-existence between strangers in such congestion may be easily understood; in an atmosphere of permanent tension and fear co-existence becomes very hard. Even were harmony to prevail between neighbours, overcrowding would still lead to noise, insomnia, strain and loss of privacy. This is worse when several families share a single flat, and members of one family are forced to pass through another's room. However considerate your neighbours may be, however quietly they may move about - and they will walk on tiptoe if they need your favour, or your support in their feud with another neighbour - you will still be deprived of your peace. When you would like to sleep, others may be cooking, washing or scrubbing the floors. Your nights are disturbed by the snoring and coughing of strangers, by crying children. You try to rest, but your neighbour behind the flimsy partition wants to talk or chant his prayers out loud. You feel the room is stuffy, you're almost suffocating in the smoke from the kerosene or carbide lamp, but someone else claims it is too cold to open a window, and anyway this is only possible if the window does not overlook the Aryan side. Thus after a hard day's work you face a sleepless night waiting for the day, and during the stress-filled hours of the day you wait for the night.

Bad as the suffering is in overcrowded but harmonious conditions, it becomes incomparably worse when there is feuding in the shared home. The fact that wounds are then inflicted by one Jew upon another makes the situation all the more intolerable. With more than two families in a flat, it is often the third, innocent party who is caught in the cross-fire.

Some people considered their experience with neighbours a special punishment. Indeed, remembering the original cause of their tribulations, it was easy to imagine that the Jews were being crammed into ghettos with the specific purpose of making them torment their neighbours and harass them to death. Aktion was a day or two in hell, conditions in the home were everlasting purgatory. Where strife raged, people could be heard vowing that they would volunteer for deportation rather than endure living with their neighbours. These quarrels were driving people, whose nerves were already strained, into madness. And none of the quarrels, or so it seemed to the Freunds, was as malevolent, as demeaning, displaying as much primitive passion, as that between Mrs Lebron and her daughter-in-law, Keile.

Indeed, the causes of friction in such cases were often normal human emotions - rivalries, antipathies, greed - expressed in attempts to encroach on a neighbour's living space, to cut him out of his due, to cheat on facilities supposed to be shared, such as lighting and heating.

To mediate and pronounce on such matters, to protect in the most general terms the rights of displaced people vis-à-vis host-tenants, to defend the weak and old against the strong and young, was among the responsibilities of the Judenrat. But few chose to avail themselves of this organization's help; to do so was to risk the accusation of "informing" and it might lead, in the last resort, to a person's arrest. Since every arrest had to be reported to the authorities, this could mean delivering a man into the hands of the Gestapo.

Whatever the underlying causes, the flashpoint of the quarrels was mainly the kitchen. The difficulties were real enough where several families lived in the flat: there might not be room for everyone's pot on the hot-plate of the stove (there was no gas or electricity supplied in the ghetto); there would certainly be a queue to bake bread in the the Dutch oven; friction over precious coal and wood might be difficult to avoid; some might wish to put more than one vessel on the hot-plate (without contributing extra fuel); not every housewife's dish would be cooked and ready to eat at the time she required it.

But such exigencies were not unavoidable in the Lebron kitchen. The stove was large enough to accommodate its three claimants; certainly large enough to allow cooking and baking in turns.

This was not, however, the way old Mrs Lebron saw it. She needed the stove all for herself. She had so many pots, pans, tureens, kettles she could not find room for all of them on the stove, never mind those of others. If a neighbour managed to squeeze a pot into a vacant space she would find, on returning to the kitchen, the vessel moved aside, salt or water added to her soup, kerosene mysteriously spilled into the milk, her dough in the Dutch oven ruined, either because the fire, or as once happened to Keile, the dough itself had been doused.

The kitchen was exclusively hers, old Mrs Lebron claimed, and she was determined to keep and defend her property. It was also her kingdom and the symbol of her power. To exercise this, she stayed most of the day in the kitchen in her old-fashioned morning dress, a prim and lanky wig atop her bony, scarecrow figure, keeping silent vigil longer and longer as the confrontation wore on.

Mrs Freund surrendered from the start, against the advice of her daughter whose sense of justice was injured by the iniquity. "What right has she to deny us the kitchen?" she asked indignantly. "Is this Mrs Lebron above justice?"

–"Try defending your rights and you'll make yourself ill," said her mother. "From a woman who pretends to be a tsideikes steer clear as you would from fire."

Not so Keile. She took up the cudgels and with her dogged determination proved perhaps more than a match for her mother-in-law.

–"That priggish old shrew," Keile raged on the day she found her plaited white Sabbath bread floating in a pool of water in the Dutch oven. "Don't you dare touch my dishes again, or I'll throw every one of your pots out the window." Hot-tempered as she was at the best of times, on that Friday morning she did not need to work herself up into a state of seething fury.

–"Don't you dare set foot in my kitchen again. You can cut me up in little pieces, but I won't let you rob me. I'll throw you out of my house!" the haggard old woman squealed back at her, her normally pale, wrinkled face turning bright red.

Whereas the older woman sounded weak and ineffectual as she wailed in her reedy voice, Keile, young, buxom and rustic, roared like a wounded lioness, the cries of her older child, clinging to his mother's skirt, drowned by her own.

–"It's ridiculous!" she yelled. "That rat of a woman wants to starve my kids. Her own grandchildren!"

–"I'll teach you to abuse a pious old woman. Holy Father protect my son and his children from this _reshante_ (wicked woman)," the old woman fumed, her lips trembling.

–"What a good mother! She'd let her eyes be scratched out rather than give away a crumb of bread to her children."

–"She won't even look after her husband. And that damned fool stands by this ghastly woman! A slave to a beggar! We took her in under our roof, penniless, and this is her gratitude! And that a son won't listen to his old mother!..."

Hana did listen to her old mother, as befits a dutiful daughter. But she was visibly pained by the degrading family quarrels. Motel must have suffered even more, mentally that is. Physically, he rather reaped the spoils of the private war.

The Freunds, caught between the two squalling fires at home, bore them stoically. With every passing day Mrs Freund was more convinced of the wisdom of her decision to withdraw from the kitchen, despite the additional inconvenience this had caused. For within the space of their half-room, besides sleeping and eating, they had also to do all the work of the house: cooking on a primus-stove, washing, laundering and sometimes - having found that the string in the bathroom had mysteriously snapped - even drying those articles of clothing unmentionable in the presence of a self-styled righteous woman.

Such conditions shaped patterns of living. Just as lack of privacy induced many women to sleep partly dressed, so cooking on a primus-stove meant that meals consisted of only one dish. Normally this was soup, sometimes a stew. Rising costs increased the hardship. Kerosene was much more expensive - in Poland even before the war - than coal, let alone wood, which in the ghetto was usually available free from wrecked buildings and unwanted furniture. In an undercover economy prices are largely determined by relative risk. As the risk was greater in the case of kerosene than of coal, the price differential was larger inside the ghetto than outside it. Both coal and kerosene were state monopoly products under strict control. That supplies reached the ghetto at all was little short of a miracle. Credit for this was primarily due to the German officials of the General Government, whose capacity for corruption was, fortunately for the subject population, beyond all imagination. What other reason could they have for offering to leave their beloved, victorious, tidy Fatherland and travel to the distant, alien wilderness of the East, if not to make a fortune?

Kerosene and matches were not enough to keep the primus burning. Needles were also required, special primus-needles. The adulterated kerosene was always clogging up the little holes in the burner, filling the room with noxious fumes. As an article in great demand, the production of the needles became a major industry in the ghetto, and Aleks Zupnik, the leading clandestine manufacturer, was said to be a millionaire.

Now it can be better understood what an immense luxury it was to move into a small, but separate kitchen with a stove all to themselves; and not the least benefit of the Freunds' move was that reaped by the new room-mates of the last surviving member of the family.

His baking was a triumph.

CHAPTER FOUR

While they were still waiting hungrily to see how the kneaded flour in the oven would turn out, Arush and his friends began anxiously discussing the prospects of future bread supplies. You can ignore death, but not the means to keep you alive.

The authorized provision of Jews with the necessities of life in this war was never more than minimal. By the spring of 1940, virtually all production in the General Government had come under state control, with every branch of business supervised by a separate office, known as *Bewirtschaftungsstelle*. Without its permission nothing could be put on the market. Foodstuffs had first to be offered for sale by the producers to one of the divisions (*Erfassungsstellen*) of the GG Central Office of Agriculture. Sale of manufactured goods, let alone raw materials, to the civilian population was allowed only by special permission, called *Bezugsschein*. Apart from a few privileged individuals, Jews never obtained a Bezugsschein, if only because none of them was so naive as to apply for one. Thus from the first weeks of the occupation, a Jew could not legally buy even a button.

There was some consolation in the fact that there was, anyway, nothing to be bought over the counter in the shops. As early as 21 January 1940 the authorities had set maximum prices for nearly all commodities, imposing penalties, including death, for both buyers and sellers infringing the regulation. The fixed prices were absurdly low, bearing no relation to real market conditions, and as a result all stocks and trade in general moved underground. The nature of commerce changed entirely, passing from shops to dark street corners, from lawful to illicit venues. In its new undercover setting trade, as some noted not without irony, was decidedly Polonized; an age-old dream of the Polish people had come true. The Poles had from the start of the war shown more aptitude for this style of trade than did the Jews, and the same applied to other aspects of life under occupation. While Jews often grumbled about profiteering and speculation, respectable-looking Poles could be heard saying that after the war a massive monument should be erected to the unknown black marketeer. But the Jews' limited participation in undercover trade was not out of greater scruples, but because of the restrictions placed on their movements and the greater risks in their case. People naturally make a virtue of necessity.

Another reason why the disappearance of goods from the shops was taken lightly was that from the earliest days of the occupation, people showed little concern for provisions other than food and fuel for heating in the winter. There was little effective demand for anything else.

Food was formally rationed, and the Jews were issued with special cards, initially authorising half the food allocation allowed for Poles. The quantity of bread distributed fluctuated over the years; in the case of Jews it fluctuated only one way - downward. A daily ration of 250 grams per head in March 1940 was the highest of the entire war. But it remained at this level for only two months, until the outbreak of fighting on the western front. Products other than bread were barely issued at all to Jews after the first year of war; the bread that was distributed in the ghetto once a week hardly lasted two days. And yet the Jews "lived on" such rations for three years, and those who survived the Aktions for a further year.

As this implied the continued purchase of essentials the Nazi authorities were convinced that, even in 1943, the Jews possessed hidden wealth. There were a few families which still had some liquid assets, a few were engaged in profitable trading, but the majority lived from the sale of furniture, clothing and the like.

In the summer of 1942, shortly after mass extermination had begun, the authorities announced that only Jews whose work was sufficiently important to German interests would be issued with food (i.e. bread) rations. The threat was not taken seriously by the remaining Jews, given the prospect of more evacuation on the one hand, and the experience of surviving for so long virtually without rations, on the other. But it was the memory of that announcement which prompted Reb Tunye to pose the question, "Is *Aufräumung* (Clean Up) sufficiently important?"

–"If they left us here for that purpose, then it must be important enough to them to supply us with bread, so we can go on for the time being," Arush said without conviction. He knew that in this war nothing was rational, except the dying of millions.

–"Four years we have lived and worked for them, without them giving us any food. Why should they start now?" objected Thorn, a former Varnish and Putty employee who always took a more pessimistic view than the others. He went on: "Didn't the Germans know that on the rations they have been providing the Jews with, they couldn't survive for more than a couple of days?"

–"All those years they knew we could buy food on the black market. Now they know this may no longer be possible," replied Arush. The implication of his argument was that once the SS bosses realized that the Jews of the Clean Up could not acquire food illegally, it would be provided lawfully. It was perverse logic but in the illogical setting of life under the legalism of German occupation, it made sense.

Anyway, no one present questioned what Arush had said, perhaps because Reb Tunye changed the subject, asking; "If they knew, and on this point I agree with you, why have they turned a blind eye to it for so long? The most brutal and absolute police state imaginable, and for years it's been tolerating illegal trading, right under its nose?"

The question that he posed was one that puzzled many people in those days. It was a question that Arush himself had often pondered, and now he expressed aloud what had long been his private conviction.

–"They don't tolerate it. They simply can't prevent it. They have issued hundreds

53

of impossible laws, which together add up to a state of lawlessness. To enforce lawlessness is a task beyond the capabilities even of the Germans."

What Arush said was a guess, and probably a sound one, even if he did not know then that, in Tarnow for example, the entire SD (operational SS Intelligence) and Gestapo numbered no more than some thirty officials, including secretaries, telephonists, interpreters and drivers. Of course, besides them were the Order Police (*Ordnungspolizei*) including the Guard Police (*Schützpolizei*), the Security Police (*Sicherheitspolizei*), the Gendarmery and the Criminal Police, and for special operations these could be reinforced by SS commandos, the Standby Police (*Bereitschaftspolizei*) and even units of the regular army. A formidable array of police forces. But its total strength stationed regularly in Tarnow and the surrounding region numbered no more than several hundred men, policing a population nearly a thousand times larger.

Moreover, it was in the main the twenty operative Gestapo and SD men who sowed the death and terror, and thereby held the entire population on a tight rein. Polish policemen, about a hundred of them in Tarnow, made the same effort not to see a Pole trading illegally as did OD men in the case of a Jew.

–"That's what I have always said," remarked Eltes, referring to Arush's assessment. "The risk of a Pole being caught trading is almost zero. That is why they have been willing to trade even over the ghetto fence, and that is why they will continue to supply us."

–"The funny thing is," said Bodman, a man with long experience of hole-and-corner dealing with Poles, "that because he's constantly on his guard, the undercover trader is less likely to be shot or arrested than the innocent Polish passer-by in the street. This is because of the 'terror at random' method which the Germans prefer."

–"That supports my theory," Arush interjected eagerly. "They prefer that method because they can't enforce their laws and punish the guilty."

Seeing that the chances of falling prey to the security forces were fifty-fifty at most and usually less, whether one complied with the law or not, it was small wonder that, given the conditions, many Poles opted to trade and earn a living. To earn a living lawfully was extremely difficult. Asked what he lives on, a witty Pole would answer that one of his adult children was not working. By engaging in petty illicit trade for just a few days in the month, he could earn twice as much as the combined monthly wage of a family of four, all of them legally employed.

Bodman, who knew his trade, was concerned about the prices that the Poles would charge if the risks were to increase again. But he explained it badly, referring to difficulties in supply as to shortage of food. This drew a sarcastic reply from Reb Tunye in a tone of anger.

–"Two days after we were first walled in, a Pole demanded twice as much for his basket of eggs as he had the week before, because, he said, 'there are no eggs'. I told him I couldn't understand this. 'If you pay one Zloty the hen doesn't lay, if you pay two she does?'"

He was right of course; the cause of the price rise was not a sudden shortage of eggs but the increased risk of supplying them into the walled ghetto and the natural, if regrettable tendency of so many people to exploit conditions of hardship and hunger.

Since the earliest days of occupation price movements had been a cause of anxiety to the urban population, and to Jews in particular. In the very first winter of the war, compared with the period immediately preceding it, prices of food were ten times higher, while those of manufactured goods were only three times higher, causing, incidentally, a major and, in Polish terms, unprecedented redistribution of wealth from the towns to the countryside. However, in the later years of the war, as farm production continued to rise and demand for food stabilized, while stocks of manufactured goods dwindled, the price differential narrowed substantially.

Bitterly, Reb Tunye began cursing all grease-bellies and profiteers. But Bodman, Teper and Arush all defended them, pointing out that the Poles who supplied food to the ghetto were, for all their greed, doing a service to the beleaguered Jews. These Poles bore most of the risk of a bargain, endangering their goods and, eventually, their lives. In the early days of barter, when it was "pianos for potatoes and carpets for eggs" the peasants had also to face the risks involved in shifting the bulky bartered goods. In addition there were the long and difficult journeys from the villages to the towns, often in harsh weather conditions.

Hardly had they finished eating, when Teper came close to Arush and confided to him, in a whisper, that he intended to sleep elsewhere that night.

Few things are more sensational than secrets of the bedroom, even a ghetto bedroom, but Arush was not really excited or shocked by the confession. The reason for this was not his depressed emotional state; it was rather that the so-called mating-game was then a common thing. Was it rightly so called? Few were willing to think, let alone talk seriously, about something considered petty, a regrettable yet unimportant temptation. But the subject is part and parcel of the wartime story and although the game was not peculiar to Jews under Nazi occupation, it assumed a special intensity and flavour in their case.

It is apparently true that in times of radical change and confusion, people lose their heads, abandoning principles and moral restraints. Thrown off balance by an upheaval, men and women allow themselves to be driven by impulse.

The upheaval that war and Nazi occupation instantly created, in the lives of Jews in particular, was of dramatic proportions. A Jew's very existence became uncertain and his circumstances precarious, even if this was little in comparison to the trials yet to come. Many people were uprooted, becoming refugees in alien surroundings. Families found themselves separated, men and women without work and livelihood, boys and girls without education but witnessing daily the violence and degradation inflicted by the occupying forces. The inevitable result was an upset in traditional attitudes and habits, particularly among the young, creating a more permissive society. Men and women began forming fleeting relationships, throwing themselves into one another's arms out of boredom or lassitude, seeking release from the emptiness of life.

It was strange perhaps, but surely not fortuitous, that in spite of the burden of restrictions imposed by the Nazi occupier on almost every aspect of Jewish life, he was generous enough to license the continuance of frivolous and potentially licentious entertainment. Theatres closed, cinema admission was denied to Jews, but segregated cabarets, two in Cracow and many more in Warsaw, offering jazz-bands and dancing, flourished with official approval - until curfew of course. Initially these houses were full; they were less so in the course of time, as places of entertainment became favoured venues for rounding-up forced labour.

The same tolerance on the part of the occupier extended inside the ghetto walls, which in the few large towns, including Cracow, were raised more than a year before the period of large-scale extermination. Correspondingly, one of the greatest ironies of life in the ghetto - a tragedy or a re-affirmation of vitality, according to opinion - was that here of all places, in conditions of the utmost deprivation and anxiety, many young people turned their thoughts to pleasure and sought consolation in sexual gratification. The greater the congestion, the narrower the living space, the easier it became to find a willing partner; and the more lonely and scared one felt, the more intense the desire to "forget oneself".

In the vicious squeeze, increasing numbers of young people (how large a proportion it was impossible to know) began living for the hour only. Sexual promiscuity was taken for granted. Gaunt inmates of the ghetto were envious of carnal appetite, at a time of constant hunger for food.

Once embarked upon a lifestyle of pleasure, it was necessary to find the right partner. This was not merely a case of obtaining the highest mutual satisfaction; for a woman, this meant finding a strong and reliable male protector. This explains the powerful sex-appeal wielded by OD men and senior Judenrat officials. In this unstable society, the measure of a man's standing in the ghetto corridors of power depended on having one, or more, attractive mistresses. This came more easily to some than to others. For example, Krumstein, a burly, jovial man of about forty, had such a capacity of bestowing concupiscent affection that people were at a loss to name his extra-marital loves at any given time. By contrast, it was almost comical to watch Falban walking at literally arm's length beside Selma Libeskind, as if unaware of her presence, talking to himself rather than to her. Chairman Falban, not much older than his deputy and of slim build, was a family man by nature. Above all he was devoted to his only daughter, an unattractive girl whom he succeeded in marrying off to a smart and ambitious OD man. In the late spring of 1943, when he began to show himself in public with Selma, an acclaimed beauty of the Tarnow ghetto, Chairman Falban was a bundle of frayed nerves, hardly capable of enjoying human company, to say nothing of keeping a mistress. But Selma, separated from her architect husband, who had volunteered for work in Cracow, found in Falban a formal protector, especially at times of Aktion; in return, she redressed his emasculated reputation, earned as a result of his well-known attachment to his family.

Behaviour and morals began changing well ahead of mass destruction, but as life became more uncertain, incentives to indulge in promiscuity increased. Right from the beginning, there was a marked decline in the overall number of marriages, and a proportional rise of only civil marriages, contracted at the Judenrat offices. Stripped of its traditional and human qualities the ceremony lost all its solemnity, and marriages, in general, tended to become a matter of little importance for the people involved.

Although religious weddings still took place, fewer and fewer of them were solemnized by rabbis, while the ceremony was restricted mainly to the recitation of the prescribed wedding blessings, and the traditional placing by the bridegroom of the ring on the index finger of the bride. Even among practising Jews, the bride was no longer veiled and, frequently, the wedding ceremony was conducted without even the ancient dignity of the traditional canopy. Betrothals and marriage unexceptionally took place at one and the same time. Fasting by the bride and bridegroom until after the nuptials was no longer practised, neither was feasting; even the plain, customary wedding meal was practically dispensed with by the first year of war. As the war progressed, rituals were marked by speed and sadness, and the solemnizing ring was usually of silver or some other metal, not gold. In the ghetto the marriage document (*Ktuba*), if still written, was not read out, and it was seldom possible to seal the traditional espousal benediction over a cup of wine. In days of special panic, the seven wedding benedictions were reduced to the first two.

But generally, during the first phase of occupation weddings were relatively few, except for the natural, ancient form of marriage by co-habitation. Then came the "earth-and-heaven-quaking" first Aktion, and in its shadow a sudden bumper harvest of marital vows. People who hardly knew each other got married. Man or woman eventually married whoever came along first. "Were you, too, left alone?" "Do you have a stamp?"

The life-saving stamp, which provided, temporarily, exemption from evacuation. A husband, a work-privileged husband, whose stamp is shared by his wife. The highest attraction, the overwhelming motive for getting married. Everything else - the partner, the relationship, the consequences, how long it will last - is unimportant. The one important thing is, of course, to live, to survive. This was no time for reflection, no time for courting, romance, emotional involvement, no time for memories, loyalties, fidelities. There was no need for divine sanction - divinity was excluded from most hearts, filled with grief and terror. However, there was still the odd couple who, in addition to registering their liaison at the overworked Judenrat, bothered to get the wedding benedictions recited and the ring placed "according to the laws of Moses and Israel".

A number of marriages were fictitious. Some were between partners who had previously been cohabiting and were, extraordinarily, both still alive. There were also cases of true emotions, at least on the part of one of the two partners. Turteltaub, the unsightly doctor, after years of spurned advances, lived to see the beautiful and once rich Mina Waks, at last giving her hand to him. There was fear of yet unknown loneliness. There was genuine need to care for someone and to be cared for. There were men and women who had been faithful, even loving, husbands and wives taking almost instant consolation in someone new.

This all explains why Teper's confession had not shocked Arush, despite the pain that he had felt for some time over the moral decline of people around him.

Arush Freund did not keep, as it were, abreast of the times. He was one of the few young men, who amid the general demoralization, turned their minds not to earthly pursuits but to the search for spiritual values. Just when all around people were talking of life's futility, Arush began pondering over the meaning of his, and man's existence in general. The great turning point for him was the first Aktion and the trauma of his father's murder. From then on he carried within him the weight of death, and he put away trivial, everyday thoughts - and took life seriously. He found himself rewarded, his life gaining dignity in the face of its overall degradation.

"Today, for tomorrow may be too late!" Arush considered the Epicurean clamour for pleasure of men and women in the later stages of their captivity as shouts of despair. Sex, he thought, would not assuage it. Submission to the caprices of Eros leads to moral decay. It would only drag him down totally. Just because many were getting lost in the panic and just to contradict the popular opinion that in the circumstances man could not live morally, he resolved he would stand firm, and not swim with the tide. On the whole, he succeeded in keeping his head above water, helped by the strength that his parents and family had bestowed on him.

Even if he was not shocked by Teper's news, the speed of his consolation, if that was what it was, took Arush by surprise. In the past, when Teper spoke of his wife, there was always a touch of warmth in his words, and to Arush he did not seem to be the sort of man who would easily lose his head.

While he looked at Teper with tired amazement, Arush wondered what to say. It was not his business to pass judgement upon a a fellow human being in matters of conscience or morals. He would leave that to the self-righteous brothers "at freedom", who were sure that they could put themselves in the place of a man in Teper's circumstances. He, Arush, always resisted being a sort of Momus. He did not enjoy finding fault with others. He strove to understand, even if it stretched his mind to the limit. He knew the savagery of the time they were living in. He knew what profound emotional consequences experiences such as the Aktions had. In the wake of an Aktion, everything changed. Every meaning, every sense, every norm had changed. Funerals, weddings, institutions, beliefs, even the concept of death had changed. How could morals remain the same?

Was the old morality with its rational criteria, rules, practices, rites, appropriate now? Permanent union? Surely the union could not last longer than they might live. They probably believed that they would live long, yet still said: "Tomorrow may be too late." In truth, they were seeking to reduce their suffering, afraid of loneliness - or was it rather of themselves? What was it, this alleged pressure of time that had brought Teper and his new - what shall I call her - together? Was there joy in this casual bed-sharing? The atmosphere of death and fear, their memories and remorses, must kill every true feeling, affection, or even friendship. Nothing is left.

He felt moral superiority over Teper, was grateful for it - but without any sense of smugness. He still thought that he was not moralizing and was determined not to say a critical word to Teper. Even Eli, his saintly brother Eli, would not utter a word of censure, however upset, however pale he was when he told him of Diamant's complaint: "No sooner had I finished with her, than the mother wouldn't let me sleep." Diamant, Eli's pair-labourer at "Copernicus" had been relating his trials of the night before. He had been invited to stay overnight by a girlfriend, who lived with her mother in a small room, with space for just one bed. An egress from Diamant's embarrassing situation might, of course, have been to be resolute and refuse the invitation in the first place. Yet Eli, like many others in those days, was not prepared to blame someone for his lack of faith. After he had finished relating the story, Eli fell into long, eloquent silence.

And all the aged, pious Reb Tunye would comment next morning on Teper's match was: "Whether the bride is a beauty or not is debatable."

Anyone inclined to infer from this remark that Reb Tunye was in a cheerful state of mind would be mistaken. In fact he was going mad with grief, as was evident from his contorted face and the terrifying gaze of his eyes. But sarcasm was part of his exuberant language; he could not easily hold his tongue. If he was not talking, he was singing. It was his life's ambition to become a celebrated singer.

In 1914, like most middle-class Jews of the Austrian province of Galizia, Tunye Einhorn had fled with his family to Vienna before the advancing "Cossacks". Once there, he changed into the clothes of an orthodox Viennese Jew and, it was said, he visited the opera every other evening. By all accounts, he learned by ear to sing all the major operatic parts. He thus considered himself a compeer of his famous cousin Dulitzkaya, whose songs and charming voice captivated the hearts of many, particularly Jewish, song-enthusiasts of that part of Europe in that era. At Varnish and Putty it was never quiet for long with Reb Tunye humming loudly one aria after another, making his workmates clap the putty-pile or tap in mousetrap-hooks to the tunes of Verdi or Puccini.

In those days, Reb Tunye still belonged to the fortunate few who had survived all previous Aktions together with their close families; in his case, a wife and two adult daughters. Not surprisingly, then, he wore his age well, till the troubles of the last two days which were now taking their toll.

On the first evening of the Clean Up, after they had finished eating and most men had already dispersed to go and rest, Reb Tunye began to pour out his heart, becoming the first, if not only, man capable of unburdening himself.

–"In one day...A few moments and one's whole life, everything one lived for destroyed. Just evaporated. Will never see them again. Never, never again - do you understand?

"Do you understand how terrible...what it means to remain alone in old age? How much greater is the grief of an old man, of a father? You're still young..."

He was choking over his words with emotion, as he tried to impress upon Arush how much greater was his bereavement than that of Arush, perhaps also expecting greater sympathy as well. Despite natural age-group solidarity, and despite the common ghetto saying: "He was at least old, he had lived out most of his days" (an attitude that was occasionally reflected in Judenrat policy, namely, that young blood was more valuable than old blood), Arush did not dissent. He agreed sincerely that in old age solitude was harder, life more aimless, and disasters such as they had experienced more trying, than when young. The poor state of Reb Tunye's body compared with his own, seemed to confirm this to him. Yet Arush did not try to comfort him, it was beyond his powers of feeling to do so.

–"What can I expect in life now?" Tunye continued his lament, evoking momentarily images of Jeremiah standing among the smouldering ruins of the Holy City. "What reason for living? All I had, all my affections, everything that filled my life, they have taken away. No one left, no one to look for, no one to meet - until we meet in the next world. What other hope is left, but to meet them soon?"

They were all, all the lone survivors, hoping for the same thing, though not with equal strength. It was a supreme consolation for a number of reasons. It aroused some hope at least. It mitigated grief, which in turn made it easier to endure. If one expects to join the dead soon, what reason is there to mourn those who have already died? What other solace on earth could they find?

But what chance of a reunion?

Well, what stood in its way if one believed in another world, in life after death, in the preservation of one's consciousness after the soul, that inscrutable soul of man, had left the body? Though one could not easily imagine a meeting of souls and it seemed much less attractive than one of bodies.

However, Arush could feel his dearest ones still close to him, in their living past. He had little difficulty in meeting them in this world, and found it easier to arrange in his mind.

–"At least the prospects are good that I won't have to wait for long. So much the better. What am I doing in this world? What is mine end that I should prolong my life? For me the time has come."

While Tunye was thus continuing to vent his sorrow, Arush wondered whether the old man was in his heart really wishing to depart? Like most of us, he told himself, Tunye probably wanted to live and longed to die both at the same time. Expecting this supposition to be confirmed, he asked, as if replying to Tunye's questions: "Shall we not live to see their downfall? The meeting that we all hope for, will take place sooner or later anyway."

But Tunye was in disconsolate mood, likening himself to Job in his trials.

–"For me it could not come too soon. What is my strength, that I should hope? The war will drag on. Whether I live till its end or not, is all the same to me. 'Naked was I born and naked shall I return thither.' Tens of years of life together. We never parted..."

As Tunye went on to recount separately every person dear to him that he had lost during the war, and to specify certain characteristics of his wife and daughters, tears flowed down his cheeks. Arush envied him. Though grieving inwardly, he was too numb to cry. But to curtail Tunye's mourning, and not to show himself less grieved than him, Arush was beginning to detail the dear lives he had lost, when they both cried out simultaneously:

"And Rabbi Maleachi! He was like a father."

–"A veritable father," Tunye repeated.

Arush agreed. One can have, he realized, a second father without any blood ties, without extension of the family, without repudiating the natural father, or diminishing one's love and respect for him. To be accepted as a real though unnatural father, a man must be able to shine as an example to his children, as it were, to arouse their admiration, to offer them protective care, affection and devotion.

Rabbi Maleachi combined admirably all those qualities, and many more. Grace and goodness, great learning and wisdom, and what was perhaps most remarkable about him in those extremely troubled days, was his astonishing peace of mind, a peace that he derived from boundless love of God. Along with all his regard and friendliness for a fellow human being, his ability to engage a man on whatever subject attracted people of all walks of life to his presence, even those without any religious sentiments; whereas his faith and warmth were infectious to the receptive listener.

His influence upon the people was greatest in the inter-Aktion period when, during the exalting sessions between the evening prayers, the congregation were not only seeking guidance and consolation, listening to his learned discourse and animated tales, but also asking questions. Even the aged, devout scholars, "pillars of the faith", occasionally asked questions about what was tormenting everyone's mind. "Why is it happening to us?" "Why are we, His most faithful servants, singled out first and foremost?"

When in the summer of 1942, news from Warsaw reached them of the savage killings of two leading rabbis, a man circumspectly recited the ancient question: "Is this the reward of Torah...?" and the audience lapsed into silence. After a minute or two, visibly hesitating, Rabbi Maleachi replied solemnly, referring to the ancient sage, Rabbi Akiba, that in times of "heavenly decree", "the murder of righteous men is a bad portent for those Jews, who remain living" (that is not a reflection on those who died). There followed yet more silence, grave ominous silence, the listeners apparently pondering uneasily over the harsh uncanny words; but some at least found in those words a meaning to their torments.

Usually, however, Rabbi Maleachi infused strength and courage, arousing hope and faith in his audience. Our fathers facing the sea in front of them, with the advancing Egyptians at their rear, said the *Shira* (song of crossing the Red Sea) in anticipation of their deliverance, and thereupon the sea parted for them. We face a similar situation, with our backs to the wall, and the wicked warriors in front of us. We must remain equally firm in our faith in God, and thanks to this we, too, shall be graced to see our liberation soon.

That was one of numerous similar addresses uttered in that serene, spell-binding manner of his, making his listeners, for at least a short hour, forget all the wretchedness and misery of their uneasy lives. On evenings that were most inspiring they dispersed to their homes satisfied, without needing to have supper - spiritual nourishment stilling their hunger.

Inwardly Arush grieved only a little less for Rabbi Maleachi than for his father.

61

However, recollecting the man and his splendid face had calmed both him and Reb Tunye a little. The latter, even in his dark despair, had managed to gain some glimmer of hope, from the experience.

All things are full of labour, but none is fuller than breathing under the gaze of Goeth, thought Arush, silently transmuting the proverb. The next morning, Arush, and another equally young boy, were picked out by the supreme dispenser of death in person, and ordered to follow him. Should they assume from the mildly uttered order that they were going to be shot? Although half-prepared for departure to the other world, Arush did not feel that his death was imminent. Fortunately they were not allowed much time to ponder over their destiny. Soon they were ordered to move a huge turning-machine from the rear of a lorry to the waiting freight-train carriage, Goeth pointedly warning them not to allow the machine to hit the door of the vehicle. Remarkable, indeed, was Goeth's touching care for this new addition to his country's wealth.

The trouble was, for the hapless boys of course, that the floor-level of the train-carriage was about six inches above that of the lorry, whilst the machine weighed perhaps as much as 600lb. They could never do it, Arush despaired inwardly, in the shadow of Goeth.

He stood a few steps away, his feet wide apart as if they were planted on two detached pinnacles. He was watching them; watching with a whip in his right hand balanced over the left arm to set it going, and a gun tucked in the trouser belt that was shimmering threateningly in the morning sun.

From what depth of their beings did they, two feather-weight boys, raise the strength to make it? Arush later pondered. Well, Goeth's demonic eyes; they fascinated him because of the evil force that emanated from them. Oh, those eyes, their ferociously glistening stare, he would never forget them. He had read somewhere that terrified people can muster several times their normal strength. Yet, it was superhuman; without that mysterious power they could not have made it. A plain miracle. Anyway, to have met the angel of death face-to-face and escaped his claws was a good omen, he told Teper when he joined him in the "intellectual-work" group, to which Arush was allocated later in the day.

Actually he had already met Teper that morning, waiting for the distribution of bread and work. Teper was in a serious mood and seemed to want to bare his soul.

–"Another nice day. Did you have a good night?"

Without waiting for a reply, which was inconsequential anyhow, Teper, straightening his back, went on to say, "I feel rested after a good sleep. Strong again. Fit and light, strangely relieved. Not in fear of anyone. Work or hardship. Glad to be alive, alone."

Perhaps erroneously, but it seemed to Arush that Teper put stress on "alone", so that he waited with a mixture of pleasure and apprehension to hear what Teper might say next.

The pleasure was of the kind a man cannot help feeling when he gets a chance to say "I told you so". "I knew," he was telling himself, "there is nothing in this sort of relationship." No mutual bond or obligation. Neither affection nor friendship, not even friendship of a solely erotic nature. Just nothing, except perhaps guilt, guile and void.

Teper did not seem to guess Arush's thoughts, but he put an end to them by continuing: "Alone, single like you. I need not care. I can chance, decide on my own. I could use my head and hands to save myself. The first opportunity and..."

Arush took the opportunity of passing a hot bowl of coffee-coloured water to move aside, so that he would not need to go on listening. Later he tried, however, to reconsider Teper's words.

He is alone. No doubt about it. He has no one to care for, to fear about. Nor can he lose somebody dear to him any more. He knows by his own experience the horror of the permanent fear of losing a loved person. Since the murder of his father, when death had become his constant companion, that fear of losing another relative dear to him had never left Arush. It was present at all times of the day, it followed him into the night and his sleep. It paralysed all his thoughts and made his life a plague.

Now the worst had happened. All had gone - that terrible losing of one's beloveds had come to an end. "Aren't you feeling relieved?" Arush asked himself. Relieved of that dreadful fear, he was a man who had nothing more to lose. They could no longer take anyone away from him. Quite clearly he now felt less fear of "the black lady". An apparent eclipse of death. Reaped too large harvests. Diminishing returns. Now she can take away only his own life. Well, as Reb Tunye had said, you only spare yourself some suffering, if you go sooner. To be honest, he wanted to live, but the fear of losing his own life was now incomparably less than it had been before when he still had his mother, brother and sister to care for.

Teper, seized by the abandon of a desperate man, talked of feeling relieved, unburdened. Relieved of fear, no doubt, a mixed load of fear and responsibility. Yet he also seemed to think that, as a result, his chances of survival had increased. That was naive, surprisingly undiscerning of him, all that illusion of greater strength, lightness of existence, and the sudden flight of fantasy of escape. On the whole, however, he did understand what Teper was saying. He just expressed himself badly. He was not glad to have got rid of his wife. He was not a bad fellow.

Then they were together again.

CHAPTER FIVE

It may seem strange, as it did to many of their mates at Varnish and Putty, how two such different characters as Artek Teper and Arush Freund could apparently become friends. Apart from a difference in age, the two came from different social backgrounds, confessed to beliefs seemingly at complete variance to one another, and displayed a no less striking disharmony of temperaments. Artek, the cheerful, jocular fellow, told endless funny jokes, and ridiculed all and everything; Arush, the solemn, withdrawn boy, was respectful of a man's spirit and scholarly achievements. The one faithless, devoted to enjoyment, the other devoted to his family and its creed.

However, others saw nothing surprising in a friendship between two young men, whose age differed only by a few years, who were of equal social status (inasmuch as a Jew had status in those days), who ate the same sour bread ration, and who met day after day at a common workshop. Why should it be thought strange that they should seek one another's company?

Matters were, however, not so simple as that. The relationship between Teper and Freund was in fact not a friendship, certainly not in the strict sense of the term. They were not particularly important, or intensely close, to each other. They did not keep to themselves, in seclusion from others. They never met outside their joint place of work. Their relationship could best be described as one of comradeship. The only things needed to encourage it, at least in the circumstances of Varnish and Putty, were a minimum of compatibility, likeableness, and reciprocal satisfaction of certain needs. In a negative sense, they competed in nothing - the only cause of friction, or rather resentment on the part of Arush, was Teper's irreverence, his occasional blasphemous gibes, including a little font of lewd, but comical songs.

Teper's attraction was that he was blessed in those gloomy times with the gift of being able to shake a person out of his depressing thoughts. His peculiar form of humour seemed almost inexhaustible. What had drawn Artek to Arush was the unaffected innocence, intelligence and serious disposition, which made Arush a person worth talking to, someone to whom one could tell the story of one's life.

Although Artek had only been in Tarnow half as long as Arush, he seemed to know everyone in the ghetto and to be well informed about what was supposedly said and done behind even double-locked doors. Through him Arush became party to all the gossip and news concerning the highest ghetto officials - this was an agreeable diversion from dreary idleness, and it enabled him to repeat occasionally useful news to those at home.

No less useful was Artek's help in tapping the little hooks into the wooden base of a trap, making it possible for Arush to deliver his daily quota. For when it came to any kind of craftwork, his fingers were all thumbs. As time went by, Arush became less dependent on Teper's help, but Teper insisted until the very end that lucky would be the mouse that happened to bite into a trap of Arush's making.

What perhaps best explained the comradeship between Artek and Arush was the similarity of their attitudes to matters that were significant to them both. They both were anti-work. This requires some explanation. It was not that the two were lazy or in any sense dedicated to idleness. It was only that they were opposed to the prevailing opinion of fellow Jews about the sense and value of work. In particular, that work improved a Jew's chance of surviving the war.

For the Jews in Poland (and beyond) the ideology of work dated back several decades; from the beginning of the century it had been slowly evolving into a veritable religion, and quickly replacing the traditional one. The Jews, it said, must be re-educated, re-moulded, occupationally re-fashioned after the Polish model (or the model of any other country they lived in), turning them into a nation of peasants and manual workers; their souls would be redeemed by work. The association of Jews with capitalism as the source and cause of anti-Semitism, and the hatred directed at them, had the supreme authority of Karl Marx himself. Socialism would solve a Jew's problem wherever he stayed. So dig in! Fight for the right to work in the country where you live! And in the fine spirit of human fellowship, fight not just for yourself. If everyone had a decent job and bread for the next day's breakfast, what cause on earth would there be for their hating one another, what reason for war and violence?

These ideas, and the political parties propounding them, made particularly great advances in the troubled 1930s. Under German occupation, the work doctrine, reconciling Jews to forced labour, was broadened and also cogently disseminated by the *Gazeta Żydowska* (Jewish Gazette - a German sponsored twice-weekly magazine, which first made its appearance on 23 July 1940). After all, they needed Jewish labour. The Germans were not as mad as to harm their war effort. War required vastly increased production, the Germans were short of manpower, the Jews could partly fill the gap, particularly in skilled labour. Never mind that their skilled workers were mainly tailors, cobblers and capmakers. An artisan is an artisan. Skills can quickly be redirected. A Jew could turn his hand to anything required of him. In the early months of war this reasoning appeared somewhat justified. Later, especially in the ghettos, the "work to survive" party, if it may be called so, received a strong shot in the arm from the first Aktions. Everywhere people with a stamp, that is approved employment and skills, were, together with their families, exempted from evacuation. What better verification of the theory could there be?

At about the same time, the historically controversial distinction between productive and non-productive work, received a new interpretation. Productive work meant, by and large, work considered useful by the Germans and rewarded by the stamp, like a medal. In a still broader sense, productive work became synonymous with hard physical toil.

People began feverishly trying to make themselves "productive", changing their occupations like shirts. Experience seemed to suggest that the greatest security of life was provided by fixed employment in a German establishment, preferably one controlled by the army. Consequently even specialist mechanics and artisans closed down their still lawfully owned workshops, to join the queue at the labour exchange reserved for Jews, in search of a productive job. Foremost in the queue were professional and, so called, mental workers - biologists, botanists, historians, lawyers, librarians, accountants and so on. They were trying by every means, including bribery, to conceal their unproductive callings, and to find an opening in a craft or manual trade. However, acceptable productive work no longer included, as far as Jews thought, watch-making, room-painting, carpentry, let alone needle-work. Skills such as those of a gunsmith or those needed in physical mechanical construction were preferable. Finally, if nothing safer was available, then work as a quarryman, pit-digger or just an ordinary navvy with Brown-Boveri (Germany), Hoch-Tiefbau, or some other renowned slave-employers should be sought.

Arush Freund had from the early days of occupation, when he was still a teenager, questioned the sanity of the "work to survive" theory. Later, reflecting on the first mass evacuations and their possible implications for the future, he developed in his mind a counter-work philosophy, which said: Whether a Jew worked for the Germans or not, he would be equally exposed to their multifarious violence. So why work?

Not that he was unaware of the flaw in this question, as it did not cogently follow from the preceding conclusion. They had frequently debated the matter at home, where Arush was in a minority of one. There was no argument about the exaggeration of the prewar drive into manual work, or about the fact that the occupational characteristics of the Jews had hardly anything to do with the persecution to which they had been subjected in their long history. After the second Aktion, when the "safest" place of employment and stamp no longer provided immunity from evacuation, Arush's family would have also agreed with him that "productivity" was no guarantee of a Jew's life.

Yet the arguments advanced to persuade Arush to go to work were equally incontrovertible. In particular between the Aktions, when it was relatively peaceful, some hope was restored in the ghetto, and most of its inhabitants half-believed the Germans when they said that the latest Aktion was the last one. It was dangerous and nerve-racking to stay at home. What sort of life was it for a young man constantly to fear being caught? "Aren't you in fact a prisoner in your own home?" he was asked more than once. Wasn't it dangerous for someone without a work permit to walk in the street even after working hours?

After the third Aktion the pressure on him increased. Wasn't it better to acquire the right to stay in ghetto "A", where living conditions were so much better, than in ghetto "B", among the old, sick and useless? However little bread is distributed on a ration card, it is not to be spurned. Those who go to work outside the ghetto, don't they bring back essential supplies, and eventually sell them at a profit?

66

Perhaps the most basic argument in favour of working was the one people hesitated to make. The need, as long as one lived, to preserve hope - and what better hope was there, apart from a miracle, than work? "What better alternative to drudgery?" his mother had once asked Arush, after their family had already been reduced to three members.

Hiding in the one-room-home behind the certificates of his mother and brother, Arush was little moved by all that talk. His nerves were strong. His inactivity, which in the past he had found annoying, did not bother him. He read avidly, devouring every book he could get hold of. Like other men in his situation, he used part of the time to broaden his knowledge of traditional Jewish studies. He found this altogether rewarding. To stay at home was safer than going out to work, but this he was careful, for obvious reasons, not to say aloud. Those work schemes were merely nets to catch the unsuspecting victim, and in the meantime work your heart out. People refused to face the facts. He saw things as they were. Yet if that was so, he thought more than once, he could please his mother and brother, without making the slightest difference to his prospects of surviving.

In the end Arush gave in. He could no longer refuse the beseeching entreaties of his mother and Rabbi Maleachi. By the backstairs influence of the latter, he was accepted at Varnish and Putty. A choice place, he was told, and he would hardly get his hands dirty.

When in January 1943, Arush decided to take up his first forced labour post, he reckoned that he would be able to make use of the experience he had gained during several weeks of voluntary, paid employment with a rival Jewish firm, which manufactured varnish and putty under commisarial control. However, Arush was to experience disappointment. He could not have known when he took up his new post that over the coming seven months of his stay at the workshop, varnish would only be made two or three times, and even then in small amounts; or that the privilege of making it the Englenders reserved for themselves. In all that time, putty had not been moulded even once. Only the existing stock had occasionally been sprinkled with oil to freshen it up, in anticipation of one or other inspecting dignitaries.

Anyway, it surprised no one, except himself, that Arush, like most of the men who arrived daily for "work" at the shop, was ordered to join the other section, manufacturing mousetraps.

Inside, the place looked quietly busy, bubbling over with animated talking or singing, some standing, some sitting, since the seats were too narrow to accommodate everyone comfortably. Outside, two men took turns to keep a look out, so that they would not be surprised by any unwelcome visitor. When a visitor did come, announced in advance, the occasion seemed to Arush a rather pleasant diversion: order was restored, the floor and tables were meticulously cleaned, everyone sat silently in his place, only getting up to stand to attention at the shop manager's shout of Achtung! Seconds later they would be sitting down again, after the nod of the inspecting officer and another shout: Weitermachen! (Carry on!). Then the place buzzed solemnly with the sound of rhythmic hammering, putty-ball tapping, and the splashing of varnish. Blache, with the air of a general inspecting his troops,

67

walked slowly along the length and breadth of the hall, a feigned expression of approval on his face. And then the show was over, the men jumped off their seats, and, as if applauding, started to shout and laugh.

To Arush and Artek, however, nothing looked more laughable than the sight of healthy young men playing around day after day with tiny, fragile-looking mouse-traps, as if they were trundling a hoop. It united them in mockery. The little thing was a source of unlimited jokes. "How many mice have you on your conscience today?" "What a formidable industry! And it's kriegswichtig." Varnish and Putty was not an exception. Most of the "war-important" workshops were little more than a deception by both the Germans and, with their connivance, Jews, pretend-ing to do productive work. What induced the Nazi authorities, notably the Higher SSPF, under whose exclusive control the shops were, to participate in this farce, apart from the fact that some shops were a welcome source of bribes and perks for the officers directly concerned with them, a Jew could only guess.

At Varnish and Putty, at least, internal relations were as good as they could be. Solidarity between the forced labourers prevailed at all levels. Unlike in some other workshops, there were no fussy managers, no officious foremen, nor masters-grafters, and, in general, no jealousies, rivalries, or plying for favours. There was nothing to steal either, or anything that it would be possible to produce "on the side". It was also easy to keep the place clean, the all-important requirement of the SS bosses.

Varnish and Putty seemed also to demonstrate better than any other "establish-ment" of a similar kind, the delusion of the "work to survive" postulate.

–"This silly thing," Teper once cried, half angry, half joking, holding up a mouse-trap, "will save our lives. So they say. How could the Germans win the war without these little traps? It's a trap...for all of us loafing here. However easy going, this place is hostile to our breathing.

"You can't even talk about it. Say aloud what I said to you and you're a pessimist, a defeatist and eventually an insurrectionist. It lays you open not only to the anger of the Judenrat, but also to every hard toiling fool as well.

"Don't think that I underrate a job or mind working hard. In normal times work is a blessing, something you can't live without. Unless you contribute something to society by your work, it will discard you like scrap. I struggled to get a job as long as it was paid for. Even after they had stopped paying wages to Jews, I think it was in March 1941, I went on working to keep in touch with Poles and to earn a groschen on the side. But I never deluded myself that my work was an insurance policy against evacuation, departure, resettlement - all those abhorrent code words the Germans have invented."

–"Only a small minority can actually refuse to work, and they can only act as individuals. Don't you agree?"

–"I do. What can be done? We must take things as they are."

–"What d'you mean? Take what?" enquired Arush.

–"That's a philosophy of mine. If life has a meaning at all, then it is to take it as it is. Everything else is bunkum. What is left of all those big words, humanity, morals, perfection, redemption? What is left of man? Pits and ashes, redemption or no redemption. Perhaps not here in town, perhaps a long way from here, but in the end it'll be the pit. And what do you think will be the end of today's killers, who believe they can conquer the world, enslave mankind - war or no war? So why not eat, drink, enjoy life while there's still time? And if the day comes, and it's all over, then all I desire is a little mousetrap put on my grave."

–"What an absolute Epicurean," thought Arush angrily, while Teper laughed himself hoarse, "and what a stupendously ridiculous one. After three Aktions and three and a half years of German occupation, he still speaks of a grave! And he still thinks he's rational!"

That Jews could only refuse to work for the Germans in small numbers and on an individual basis formed part of a much broader conviction shared by Artek and Arush - a conviction which was another element of their special relationship. They were both convinced of the necessity for the captive Jews to remain outwardly obedient, unresisting. They had no doubt whatsoever that, given the circumstances, even passive resistance, such as collective withdrawal of work, would invite the swift, violent death of every single Jew.

Coming from men avowing that the Jews were fated whether they worked or not, such reasoning might seem strange, if not inconsistent. Remember, however, that the Jews had resolved not to die a death of their own making. Perhaps in Germany and elsewhere in the West, Jews were committing suicide, but very few did so in Poland. Looked at from this viewpoint, and knowing the inevitable result of passive, let alone active resistance, to decide against either was quite reasonable. So the difference between Arush and Artek's views and that of the others was more a matter of rhetoric than of reality.

Teper had once indirectly explained the difference to Arush. Referring to his neighbours and to the clusters of young men in almost every workshop in the ghetto, he said: "They all think the same as I do, but they talk ad nauseam about resisting. They remind me of our milkman before the war; all his adult life he was emigrating to America - and every day he had a new excuse for not leaving just yet."

The question of resistance in its various aspects, including escape, hiding, change of identity - all trying existential problems at the time - had been discussed in every Jewish home from the earliest days of war. By 1943, notwithstanding the dramatic changes in the surviving Jews' situation, anything that could be said on that complex question had already been said countless times before. This, however, did not in the least constrain many people from making the broad issue of resistance their daily subject of conversation, habitually confounding words with deeds. The very word "resistance" was mysterious, stirring the imagination, vaguely promising; "conspiracy", in addition to its air of self-importance, raised romantic dreams; "secrecy" gave an illusion of actually living that dream. At the same time, many young Jews began to use strong warlike words, which the Germans spoke with relish.

At Varnish and Putty, the small group of "resisters" centered around Eltes, giving him the opportunity to put on airs and of orating to the top of his bent. He liked to debate with Teper, speaking in a whisper - you know, "walls have ears" - though there was no question of anyone in the workshop informing. People in general were not suspicious of one another. Only Eltes after having disclosed voluntarily what was supposed to be strictly secret, would feel bound to add: "But don't noise this around".

–"We push on as best we can. Zbyszek is back. Brought some news with him", Eltes winked knowingly at the word news, "and he'll be leaving again shortly."

The boy Zbyszek, who in his short 21 years of life had become a legend in the ghetto, was uniquely nimble, endowed with a talent for deception and mimicry, altogether presenting the ideal image of a conspirator. Bold like a bandit, he went over the wall almost every day, on his return telling improbably audacious stories, and cutting a partisan figure in the ghetto, swaggering around with a bulge in his pocket like a gun. Teper considered him a humbug.

–"Why don't you join him?" Teper asked Eltes.

–"One liaison not two. Old conspiracy rule. Easier to foil the scent. Besides, there isn't that much hardware around."

–"Why? You could learn to bulge a pocket as well as he does. And you know a lot more about trafficking goods than Zbyszek. Listen, Freund is a witness, if you, or Zbyszek, or anyone else in the ghetto, will show so much as a tip of a gun, I'll pay you a hundred cigarettes."

–"I don't deny your right to doubt, everyone is entitled to his own opinion. I know what you think. But you'll see." Eltes paused for a few seconds. "There's nothing to lose. We have long ago forfeited our lives as Jews, on the other hand there's everything to gain."

–"Don't be a fool! What can you gain?"

To show his scorn for Eltes, Teper turned to Arush, who was at that moment thinking of the rumours they had heard about Jews rising heroically in Warsaw. The news, provided it was true, had roused him and been given hearty approval. Probably Teper would later feel just the same. But at the time of their discussion he was too full of his argument and went on to develop his point.

"What we can gain is shortened agony. Though for the moment it isn't unbearable. If it only kept on like this...

"To rebel takes much more than brave words. Any act of open defiance would be pure suicide, nothing more. It isn't moral weakness, particularly in our circumstances, to reject the inevitable death of every captive man and woman."

–"Inevitable it is. You're right there." Eltes delighted in distorting the meaning of Teper's words. "If you must die, if you're to be hurled into the pit of hell, you might at least take one of them with you."

–"With what will you take him? With a mousetrap? Or would you just ask him to accompany you? Try to get near one of them without being ordered, and you're dead at the first step you take."

Eltes was unmoved.

–"Yet it's the only course of action. We're determined to fight. We've discussed the strategy exhaustively. It isn't as bad as you think. We've complete operational plans, every fighter at his station with precise battle orders. We'll take them by surprise. But I won't discuss this with you. You'll have to wait. At the right moment, it'll all start rolling, you'll see."

—"He talks like a Pole," Teper turned to Arush again. "They really do have a conspiracy, a huge underground movement, but they've hardly any resistance. What are he," pointing with his finger to Eltes, "and his fledgling rebels prattling about the cage, doing that is so different? Without an underground, without weapons, without guidance or help from abroad, but in permanent 'conspiracy'", and he began to laugh, visibly satisfied with his own wit.

When Teper spoke about the Poles and life on "the other side", Arush always listened intently. He, himself, had no direct access to such news, he lived in isolation. Teper, on the other hand, had been in daily contact with Polish friends in his native Nowy Sącz, and had come from there to Tarnow only the previous autumn. In Nowy Sacz, a town on the escape route to Slovakia, he was foreman of a Jewish brigade labouring at the local railway station. His position had apparently been of sufficient consequence for Teper to be included, together with his wife, among one hundred most deserving men and women selected at the liquidation of the Nowy Sacz ghetto from 23-27 August 1942. The lucky one hundred were made to stand with their hands up, their faces to a wall, for about five hours. During that time, firing squads came and went, orders were given and withdrawn, threats made and renewed, though quite soon Teper and the rest were so crazed by trial and terror that they became indifferent to what was going to happen. In the end, Heinrich Hamann - nomen omen? - the master butcher of the Nowy Sacz Jews, ordered them to be despatched to a nearby saw-mill. Teper told Arush that he had then learnt a lesson that would last him the rest of his life. He lost weight and ambition, he gained light and sapience, finding (not unlike Arush) the longest way to paradise, as he put it, in lying low and working as little as possible. While he was more than willing to talk about that and other episodes in his life, he turned uncharacteristically circumspect when it came to talking about his contacts with Poles. A word dropped by him here and there made Arush wonder if Teper had not once been privy to an underground cell himself.

So when Arush heard Teper say during one of his bantering exchanges with Eltes that, notwithstanding the huge amount of manpower and firepower that the Polish underground commanded, its resistance was merely symbolic, he asked with honest surprise.

—"Are you seriously saying that they aren't fighting?"

—"They're fighting but with each other," he replied, again laughing at his own words.

"The Jews were forced to postpone their inter-party quarrels until better times. But not so the Poles. There are far more political groups represented in the Underground than there were in the Polish parliament at any time before the war."

—"What sense then," Arush asked, "is there in all that underground, conspiracy and talk of resistance?"

Teper was glad to explain, as one usually is to be given the opportunity of lecturing.

71

–"Resistance comes in many shapes and forms and it is not necessarily a matter of confronting the enemy."

–"Then what is it?" asked Arush.

–"It's a matter of self-regard and myth. A means of upholding an alternative community or something independent of the occupying power, of providing guidance to the people on difficult decisions. It generates a sense of national pride while in subjugation, and above all it creates a myth, yes a myth as the most important contribution to national history. For Jews it's of no use; it's too late."

–"Why?" Arush asked in disagreement. "We can't change the course of history - nor can the Poles - but aren't we as much a subject of it as they, or any other people?"

–"We're different. We can't remain alive. No continuity, no history. We can only contribute to the history and pride of our free brothers, who take no pride in us."

–"Pride? You mean take no interest in us?"

–"That's something that has astonished the Poles. One once told me, 'before the war when a single hair of a Jew's head was touched in Poland, what a hullabaloo was raised by the Jews in the West. Now you're being slaughtered in your thousands and not a voice is heard'. The Poles weren't coming to help us anyway. But, given the example of western Jews, how could we expect them to come?"

Arush kept sadly silent, but when Teper again told Eltes that it was much more important for one Jew to remain alive than to kill one, or even a hundred, Germans, he realized how close were their views.

Eltes, however, disagreed, this time with unusual intensity.

–"Even if it were self-slaughter, as you say, it would still be preferable to death at their hands. You're quite inconsistent. One moment you say that we can't remain alive, the next that it's more important for some to remain alive than to die fighting."

–"Understand what I say. As life is so scarce, it's doubly important to preserve it."

Dubner, an ally of Eltes in advocating resistance, and a more enlightened person than he was, joined the debate. He spoke at first vaguely about responsibility, trying to impress both his opponents and confederates by what seemed to him a brave and bright idea. Briefly, this was that along with a man's responsibility towards his family, friends and local society, he had a superior responsibility towards the history of his people, to which he was primarily answerable. Turning to Teper, he said.

–"What entitles you to be so dismissive, stamping everything as suicide?"

–"What entitles you - theoretically speaking, as practically you're harmless - to endanger others by a mere gesture that's bound to fail, whose only result could be to precipitate our wholesale death in who knows what agony?"

–"For you such things as national pride and self-esteem are a mere gesture. All deaths are the same to you. Can't you see the heroic sense of defending one's life, and if not one's life, then at least one's honour? To defy the implacable enemy is the one choice that we still have - to die in a dignified way. Can you think of human dignity? Of personal accountability to posterity, to our people?"

–"I can think of it, and I understand your argument very well. But I doubt if you do - the historical one in particular. To speak heroically as you do is all very well, but words are no substitute for deeds. The fact is there's no defensive action we can take now that would make any sense. And to take senseless action would be historically irresponsible - which is the prime reason why our oppressed people have remained passive. Had they put up resistance, however innocent, they would be providing the Germans with a capital excuse for killing in self-defence. So in the way they choose to die, our people have actually been showing truly heroic responsibilty..."

As Dubner and others angrily interrupted, loudly voicing their disagreement, Teper could still be heard saying: "Particularly in a small ghetto like ours resistance is inconceivable."

–"Why?" asked Eltes angrily.

–"Because with a machine-gun on the roof of that house there," Teper pointed to the tall school-building just opposite the west entrance to the ghetto, "they could mow down every single target inside the walls before you even had time to realize where the fire was coming from.

"What heroism is there in such a mindless act of collective self-annihilation? Is there not greater pride in life and suffering? Is man's survival not more important than national pride? Even the Poles have come to understand this.

"There's more dignity and pride in the way our men, women and children, yes little children, defy death and danger for weeks on end, than in the casual act of firing a bullet - whether it kills or not. How much nobler is the solitary, critical decision of a woman, who is offered life for herself alone, yet chooses to die with her child, than the valour of a one-hour, or even a one-day, armed resister!"

Arush was touched to the heart by Teper's last remark, which was like a carbon copy of what had happened to Pnina and Ami. "And so Dave too, chose to join them," Arush cried inwardly. Reflecting how many women had done the same, he declared somewhat didactically.

–"I agree that dignity is our prime duty. But there's disagreement about what form of dignity is more dignified. I'm all for dignity of a human kind, which is, I think the noblest form of resistance. That's just what the Jews have chosen to do. We have nothing to be ashamed of. On the contrary, violent defiance is immeasurably inferior to the proud and silent submission the Jews have been displaying in their acceptance of suffering and death."

Later, Arush questioned Teper's view about the feasibility of Jewish resistance in the early stages of occupation, asking what made him think that to resist before the establishment of the ghettos would have been more sensible that it was after.

Teper partially retracted, explaining that he was speaking solely of passive resistance. Then, drawing analogies with the Poles, he outlined the sort of resistance he had in mind. "The Poles," he said, "were gathering intelligence, occasionally performing an act of sabotage, or what's broadly called subversion."

This surprised Arush, who pointed out that the analogy with the Poles was quite erroneous. Unlike the Poles, the Jews had been singled out from the early weeks of occupation; long before the ghetto era their movement had been severely restrict-ed, and they could not easily vanish and hide. Besides, the acts of resistance he mentioned were futile and of no consequence for the course of war. The one activi-ty of this sort which the Jews had undertaken, and in which they had yielded to no Pole, had been propaganda "warfare", and its results had been disastrous. Finally, if the main task was, as they both agreed, to preserve lives, how could subversion and the like contribute towards this aim?

Teper retreated further, conceding that until the first Aktion it had not been unreasonable for a Jew to expect to survive the war. And yet, he argued, it was not certain how the Germans would have reacted to passive resistance in the first or second year of war.

Arush strongly disputed this suggestion. He claimed that the people knew instinctively what they could expect for open defiance, and their later experiences could leave no doubt what the German response would have been. The fact that the occupied Jewish (and other) people had not tried to confront the Germans was sufficient proof that they had all considered even passive resistance impracticable and undesirable.

What could the Jews have achieved if they refused to work? At no time were the Germans unable to get along without Jewish work.

Incidentally Arush refuted the view suggested by Dubner and his friends that the passivity of the people was indicative of a mood of resignation and social disintegra-tion. In Arush's opinion, it manifested the social and moral responsibility of the people and their trust that they would endure the suffering.

Teper did not contend this. Yet when the Germans announced that they were going to herd the Jews into ghettos, it was not difficult to guess what the ultimate consequence would be. He was at that time in Warsaw and could convince himself that it was still possible not to move into the ghetto - come what may.

–"The wise thing to do was somehow to submerge. It was the one chance worth taking."

–"Was it as simple to disappear as you seem to think?" asked Arush disapprov-ingly.

Well, in one respect it was, at least it appeared so to them from the distance of time. It was a fact that in the first months of Nazi occupation - long before the ghettoization of Jews in the General Government - it was possible to take flight. The authorities actually encouraged Jews to emigrate to any neutral country; they certainly did not place special impediments in the way of people willing to cross the new, provisional frontier with Russia.

Prohibition of the Jews' departure from the GG was formally decreed as late as October 25, 1940. In practice, illegal crossing of the frontier had become fraught with danger several months earlier. But at least until spring 1940, tens of thousands of Jews and Poles had moved back and forth across the border, under the eyes of Soviet and German guards, who, mystifying everyone, impassively folded their arms. For a Jew this was a splendid and, as it turned out, the last opportunity to escape extinction.

This much was agreed in retrospect: as to why the overwhelming majority of Jews missed that opportunity opinions varied, not least between Teper and Freund. They did, however, agree that the Jews had never accepted the Stalin-Hitler Pact as genuine, and that, as Teper had once said, it made little sense to flee to the east, when the Russians were coming to the west. This assertion might sound crazy, not to say absurd (as it really was) to people who, unlike Arush and Artek, were fortunate enough not to have experienced those events at close range; and for those happy generations of men and women the wonder needs to be explained.

It is doubtful whether people will ever comprehend, even be capable of comprehending, the part dissemination of freakish rumours played in the wartime life of the Jews, and to what degree this contributed to the tragedy that befell them. The phenomenon is historically not unknown, nor limited to one people or area of the world. In the case of Jews under Nazi rule in Poland, it was an extension of the unbridled propaganda in which their press, their local and international leaders had indulged in the years immediately preceding the war. Though self-defeating, the campaign was motivated by fear of the West's, and in particular Poland's, surrender to Nazi Germany, and it was aimed at dismissing the danger of war. So in the course of the operation, Hitler was remorselessly presented as a bluffer, Germany as frightened and weak, both economically and militarily, and the Nazi regime as strongly opposed at home. But however wild and foolish the prewar stories were, they were cautious, sober, short in every sense of the word, when compared with those that were spread during the occupation. Particularly in the first year of war the rumours industry reached astounding dimensions. It would be difficult to say who were the more productive rumour-manufacturers, the Jews or the Poles, though the self-deception of the former went deeper, lasted longer, and consequently was much more self-damaging. Anyway, that so many people were willing to accept, or to pretend to accept, the most fantastic stories as true raises questions about the human mind, which may be as difficult to answer as why a normal man suddenly starts calling day night. Bad news was passed off as rumour, denied in the teeth of all evidence. Truth was that which was desirable and pleasant. To the unpleasant, ears were stopped and eyes shut.

A not insignificant plant of this curious genus was the expectation of war between Germany and the Soviet Union from the day they had partitioned Poland; in the meantime clashes were said to be taking place daily between units of the two armies, the Russian one, of course, invariably crossing the new Rubicon that separated them. And there were always people around who had actually seen this occurring. Not just disreputable simpletons, but serious, respectable people as well.

Arush told Artek how one day in early November 1939, he and his father were walking down a long corridor connecting two houses, when they met a friend of his father, a former senator. "They're coming. In a few days at most," he began, unable to catch proper breath in his excess of zeal. "Russian troops are in Jaroslaw (a town on the German side of the then border). I assure you, it's true. Absolutely trustworthy people have seen them. They arrived today in Cracow, fleeing to escape the fighting."

Artek in turn recalled his experience from the days when he had lived in Warsaw as a room-mate of a gymnasium professor (the title of a secondary school teacher in Poland). He used to come home every day with a different story. Shortly after New Years Day, 1940, it was very cold and there was no coal at home, so the good Mr Szwach, as he was called, was warming us up with information he had obtained from a prominent Polish acquaintance, 'in strict confidence'. "There's soon to be an exchange of territory with the Russians. Warsaw and its region to them, for Lwów and eastern Galizia to the General Government."

There was a historical background to this invented exchange of territory. Before 1914, Congress Poland, including Warsaw, was Russian, while eastern Galizia was a province of Austria, in 1939 itself part of Germany. After Germany's victory over the Allies in France, when the prospects for a quick end to the war had dismally diminished, the people of Cracow and of remaining Galizia discarded that historical bond. Germany, they said, was to cede the whole of the General Government to Russia without any territorial quid pro quo, though still granting it some unspecified economic and military concessions.

Even though the German victories were declared useless and the Allied defeats held up as something that had been carefully foreseen and planned, the events of May 1940 forced the captive "planners" to do some urgent reshaping of the rumours industry. Earlier, when the fierce fighting said to have taken place on the western front since the beginning of the war, and the continuous advance of Allied armies into Germany did not produce the desired effect, it had been adjudged that the road from the French border to Berlin was a bit too long. In the winter of 1940 the Allies were said to be taking the shorter route to Poland from the Balkans. With the gravely distressing military engagements of the following spring, the bombardment of German cities and destruction of her industry had intensified - vivid proof was, the thousands of German families evacuated into the GG (actually arriving to take over the administration and economy of the country); and then there was the mounting dissatisfaction with conditions inside Germany, leading everywhere to the formation of rebellious soldiers' councils, which were precipitated by the enormous losses in men and material - a million soldiers alone in the break through Belgium; altogether a hopeless situation. So how could the war last much longer?

For all that, in early summer it had become somewhat obvious that poor, lonely England could not do the trick by herself. Powerful allies were urgently sought for her. Apart from the Soviet Union, whose significance went up sharply after the debacle in France, the United States were joining the war almost daily, and thus assuring its rapid end.

Perhaps it is now easier to understand Teper's scornful remark about the Russians' coming to the West.

However, Arush was not convinced that this rumour was the main, let alone only, reason why the Jews of the GG did not avail themselves of the opportunity to save their lives by crossing the border to Russia, while this was still within fairly easy reach. He explained his doubts to Teper.

– "Rumours were no doubt important in shaping Jewish attitudes. But they are

76

only part of our lives. And life is more complicated by far. There were old people, and mothers with little children, for whom it wasn't simple at all to walk for miles on foot, to steal across forests and rivers, even if they are frozen. There was also the problem of family ties - a very human consideration. And then the vexed question of money; not many people had enough money to risk the trip.

"Then into this shilly shally situation stepped the returnees with their selective, dispiriting, exaggerated stories of exhausted and disillusioned men."

–"Most disillusioned of all were the prewar drawing-room communists and other Jewish marxists," interrupted Teper gleefully, guffawing at his remark. When he had stopped laughing, he said calmly: "But they're a most unrepresentative minority."

Arush, instead of indulging in this interesting subject, preferred to follow up his argument.

–"Aversion to the regime on the other side was shared by most of our people. Even the poor were reluctant to move of their own choice to live under the dreaded and dreary communists, at a time when most Jews were confident that they could hold out under the Nazis until their defeat; and, last but not least, at a time when the inevitable hardships, to which everyone was resigned, appeared easier to endure at one's own home on the German side of occupation, where food and fuel were less scarce - according to the word spread by the returnees - than on the Russian side."

At first Teper was hesitant, saying that people often give serious consideration to things that should not be considered at all. But then he cast doubt on Arush's whole argument. "The fact that people believed the rumours hopefully expecting the coming of the Russians as if by invitation, confutes your elaborate explanation." He only wondered what made the people believe every sort of trash so readily.

–"But did they believe?" asked Arush.

–"By all appearances they did. What makes you doubt it?"

–"Men believe and at the same time disbelieve. It's a complex mechanism that works inside our heads. It's a device that blindly regulates which messages are admitted and which excluded from human consciousness, creating a sort of no mind's land which borders between certainty and uncertainty, belief and disbelief, self-deception and self-assurance, something resembling a state of mind between dream and reality.

"Despair threatened to crumble our people. It's difficult to live without hope, and rumours spread hope."

While professing to understand, Teper wondered how people could be so wilfully credulous as not to distinguish the probable from the improbable? How long could they go on accepting, and diffusing, increasingly fantastic rumours?

Disappointed at Teper's lack of better insight into the matter, Arush replied in a detached way, using metaphor and analogy.

–"Rumours grow like any plant and gain currency. And who could check them? This is how life looks in times of utter confusion and disaster. This is how life is without direction, without leadership - and excepting the Judenrats imposed by the

Germans the Jews were leaderless from the first day of war - without modern means of communication. We can now easily imagine how people lived in the Middle Ages, when news was spread only by word of mouth and, consequently, legend and myth swept the land. We have returned to those ancient days in this war. Rumours have replaced media of modern times."

Teper was unconvinced, objecting that this was the twentieth century, and the Jews, as educated people, should have known better. Moreover, people were listening clandestinely to foreign radio, and could read the German press, which however full of lies and hateful propaganda, offered to a sober reader the means to winnow grain from chaff.

–"Very few people listened to foreign broadcasts," countered Arush, "and as for the German press the only news that the Jews were prepared to believe, was that which was not written in it."

–"Not quite true," Teper suppressed a smile. "I remember, when in May 1940 obituary notices began to appear in the *Warschauer Zeitung*, they were believed. 'Just a little too short,' people were heard commenting. The daily column was limited to twenty-five notices."

–"But even that was seen as proof of the enormity of German losses. It's part of the amazing technique of newspaper reading, and a good example of the hugger-mugger news production. And it appeared impolitic to deny the 'news'."

Thus Arush and Artek, sitting at a table playing with a mousetrap, were almost daily discussing various topical issues, their thoughts wandering back to the past, from which they thought that they had also learned worldly wisdom about the untoward future. Their discussions usually took the same course. At first strongly at odds, discovering some common ground as they talked, only to find their views, on the whole, close in the end. Their argument about the Jews' failure to go into hiding when the formation of the first ghettos in the large towns was announced took a slightly different path.

Artek's reasoning on the matter was probably less sound than on the broader argument concerning passive resistance. Yet there must have been something peculiar about the suggestion of going into hiding in 1940/41, as it was proposed by many rash and guilt-ridden critics which the time had engendered.

–"Everyone knew that it wasn't good to go into the ghetto." Arush tried, as he often did, to disarm his opponent by first conceding part of his case. "But where else could they go?"

This seemed a silly question to Teper, who seized on it.

–"Anywhere. Just to stay out - while there was still time and it was still relatively easy to hide."

Arush did not say aloud that to the ship-wrecked, death-crazed men everything seems retrospectively easy. Convinced of the puerility of Teper's reply, he only asked softly. "But how many could hide? Hide just by themselves? With no outside help, no preparation, no 'friendly forests' yet, no partisans yet?"

–"We weren't yet placed at the mercy of others," replied Teper. "You could still get away on your own then."

—"Suppose you could - but without sufficient means? Who would have hidden you without payment?"

—"Some Poles would. They weren't then so infested with the money-bug. Anti-Semitic feelings and seeking of favour with the Germans began rising only just about the time the ghetto was first on the cards. Anyway, you didn't need so much money then and plenty of people had enough of it to hide themselves."

—"For how long? Some folk went into hiding, stayed on for several months or even longer, then ran out of money, and ran for shelter inside the ghetto."

—"That's true, the longer you had to stay in hiding, the higher were the costs, the more money was needed, with rising prices, rising risks, rising penalties for sheltering a Jew."

—"Of course rising - as long as the Jews hadn't tried to hide, there could be no penalty for hiding them," said Arush with some animation, "and no blackmailers, for that matter," he added. But the stakes were always high. Registration and all that. Road blocks. Police check-ups. The sense of being pursued like an animal.

Teper persisted in his view, which began to annoy Arush. He pointed out that, but for a small minority, the choice was strictly circumscribed, that conditions were getting comparatively tighter and nastier outside the ghetto, if only by dint of the ever greater scarcity of hide-outs and fake documents; and he questioned whether the fact that people didn't go into hiding wasn't proof enough that they had considered it unavailing and, by the same token, life on the Aryan side impossible? He further asked Teper if he thought that everyone could put on a new face, so to speak and pretend to be a Pole and Christian?

Thus they were drawn into discussion of the ever present question of so-called Aryan papers - an intricate question which, in those days, thrust itself on your mind however much you tried to avoid it. "If only," Arush sighed, "other aspects of Jewish life under Nazi occupation would just once receive as much attention as the hollow problem of life on Aryan papers, or the wider, perhaps not so hollow, problem of resistance!"

They talked about the general difficulties in human relations; the sense of isolation and apprehension of a man in disguise; the mysteries of appearance, physical features and manners; the expertness of Poles in detecting a Jew; poor knowledge of the catechism (or even of the Polish language) by some of the "Aryans".

Among the considerations, qualms, misgivings that were inhibiting Jews from braving life on the Aryan side, there was, for a small minority, a religious inhibition. Fearful that he would arouse the scorn of a man with Teper's opinions, Arush had hesitated to tell him of the stand Rabbi Maleachi had taken on this question.

In matters of ritual or minor substance, Rabbi Maleachi did not persist in dogmatic strictness; his great concern for man had moved him to ease the wartime hardships of all his brethren, and of those who came to seek his advice and comfort in particular.

Take the odd case of the religiously unobservant commander of the Ordnungsdienst in Nowy Sacz. Standing, along with Teper, with his face to the wall awaiting execution, he had vowed to fast every Monday and Thursday for the rest of his days, if he were spared his life. When his wife, a first time visitor to the rabbi, had come to enquire about the vow, Rabbi Maleachi told her with great sympathy and regrets that it could not be annulled because of the circumstances in which the vow had been made. But, he added, it could be suspended for the duration of wartime hard labour, though her husband might care to eat a little less than usual on those days.

Or, when in the summer of 1942, the eminent Rabbi of Koziglów enquired by letter, if a man had not only a morsel, but literally not a crumb of bread, yet he still had a boiled potato, was it right for him to say the Sabbath benediction on it, or not? Rabbi Maleachi made a truly unprecedented concession, replying that it was right.

But there could be no yielding, not an iota, when it came to fundamentals. "What sense does it make," Rabbi Maleachi asked a man who contemplated moving out to live on Aryan papers, "to expose your life to needless risk?" For if asked: "are you a Jew?" and he or she was most likely to be asked, "you must not abnegate it." "Die and don't deny you're a Jew," says the Law. Life is not an end in itself; there are obligations and principles which come before it.

Still, if someone already living on the Aryan side did slip into the ghetto for a short visit and come to see Rabbi Maleachi, the man or woman would not leave without his blessing.

Arush was pleased to see that Teper reacted to the story better than he had expected. When Arush had finished, Teper became pensive, and as if in sequel to Arush's story, he began telling about a young woman, already widowed, and her little boy of four, his close neighbours at Nowy Sacz.

–"For any mother, you realize, to give away her child must be one of the most cruel decisions on earth to make. But for a pious Jewish mother," Teper sighed as he tried to find the right scale of words, "a thousandfold more cruel. And if the decision is about giving the child away to heresy - don't ask me!

"What shall I say? Why, I don't know. Perhaps because they're more egotistic, love their own self more intensely? Perhaps religious fervour heightens their passion, their pang, their sensitivity to grief? Perhaps because of special conditioning from generation to generation they treasure their offspring particularly strongly? Or perhaps because they put the worth of human identity above all other considerations? I don't know. But I can tell you, it was a shattering scene to watch.

"One evening, not long before the end," Teper meant the liquidation of the ghetto in his home town, "she went into a frenzy of melancholy. Pacing up and down the room her features distorted by spasms of anguish," Teper himself spoke with a lump in his throat as he pictured the scene, "tears running down her cheeks and a torrent of words flowing from her mouth. 'Oh,' she cried nervously, looking at the child, 'my little Berele will be left alone, left without a mother. My little one will be torn away from me for ever, for ever, for ever'. She was right in this. She could not preserve her Berele in the ghetto. The only safe place she could find for him was outside. And she did find one, the safest place she could offer him. They'll save

Berele, but not Berele the Jew; they'll save his still 'innocent soul'. Either way he'll be left alone among strangers, he'll cease to be a Jew - either way lost forever. And so on and so forth.

"All that time the little boy remained amazingly quiet. He didn't weep, he had not even uttered a whine. He looked shyly at his mother, leaning his head against hers whenever he could. I had the impression that he sensed he would be losing his mother.

"The woman was clearly heart-broken in her dilemma, crying for help, but not asking for it openly. Anyway, she didn't stop crying and lamenting. The neighbours tried to calm her. At last she took our advice, ran out of the room to cool down, and returned collected. But soon, with the child again in her arms, she was once more overwhelmed by emotion and torment.

"Only now she was crying not because Berele would be left alone, not because the child, separated from her, would grieve and wilt, though this must have been in her mind; now she was lamenting that he would wither afar off his ancestral soil, she was lamenting the sale of his soul. This was something she dared not do.

"What'll I say," Teper went on, "said the woman, still weeping, if I'm asked in heaven: 'What did you do with Berele? What had become of him? A goy?' How will I look my parents and my husband in the face?

"Have you heard anything like it? People try to get rid of their Jewish identity, pay pots of money for a fake one, curse their Jewish origins, and there she was, bewailing the fact that her child would cease to be a Jew! Can you believe it?"

Arush was not inclined to argue, even to make a retort, but he said.

–"I can. There are things in life which you Artek may never be able to understand."

–"What, for instance?"

–"That there can be, even these days, someone who doesn't wish not to be a Jew. And there are more such people than you imagine."

–"I know that so I do understand it. But to make a tragedy of it? To prize identity to the point of weighing a child's life against it?"

–"What's life without identity? What's a man without origins? Isn't identity the past, the whole precious past, that we carry within us? To throw away thousands of years? I told you there are aspects of life which you may be unable to understand - that mysterious spark in man which gives meaning to his being in the universe, which differentiates him from other individuals, which guides him in this terrible darkness on earth. Even now, in the midst of this graveyard of ours, would you wish to live with consciousness of yourself discontinued?"

Phrased carelessly, this was a mischievous question. Teper possibly didn't quite understand it, for without giving it a thought, he replied.

–"Yes, I would; and there are, you know very well, many men and women who would wish to live in a completely new fashion. Yes, discarding all loyalty to ancient ways. Deserting, just as you said, thousands of years. That's thousands of years of being persecuted, massacred, martyred, and of deriving morbid pleasure from recollecting past sufferings. It's enough!

81

"What's religion? Do not all religions consist of men, women, children? Do they not come first? To renounce a child's Jewish identity a sacrifice! A sacrifice for hardly anybody knows what?"

It was enough for Arush. "A pity to waste words," he fulminated inwardly. "Teper would never understand a man who's more than flesh. Perpetuating oneself - the fundamental desire of man - wishing to eternalize through a descendant - these things are all alien to him. If her son ceased to be what she was, a Jew, how could she survive in his memory? It would be not just physical death, but her total extinction. What would be left? Nothingness, absolute nothingness hereafter."

Concealing his annoyance, Arush interrupted to ask almost gently.

–"Did she hide the child away?"

–"No. Procrastination. Jews always have time. Then, a few days later, the final Aktion came. The poor woman probably wanted it to end so. The child was too small to say. She may at least have felt in her last moments the satisfaction of a religious sacrifice. A heroic act!"

–"Heroism, inasmuch as there's heroism in it, can you say whose is greater, the mother's who, under stress, parts voluntarily with her child, or the one who holds on to it?"

–"It's a question of the heart."

–"I'd say of eyes - of the eyes with which one sees things."

CHAPTER SIX

On that morning, after he had emerged safe and sound from his close encounter with Goeth, Arush returned to report for duty in a slightly brighter frame of mind. He no longer felt the stifling indifference that had consumed him in the last two days. He also detected, or so at least it seemed to him, some signs of life returning to the dead neighbourhood. Stepping into Szpitalna Street, he saw all along it men walking, singly or in small groups, talking, busying themselves about something, or at least pretending to. He sensed in the air, apart from excitement, the scent of smoke, the source of which he had yet to discover. The whole street-scene was reminiscent of a travelling fair preparing to pitch their tents.

Everything was to be cleaned up, and Szpitalna Street was given pride of place, and, as it turned out later, centrality of place as well. All sorts of things were already on display, as it were, in the street. The Cleaner-Uppers were bringing them out of the homes, which were standing wide open, all scheduled to be cleared of every last object. Suitcases full of junk, beds dismantled and folded, cupboards and tables in good condition and falling out in pieces, rusted iron ovens, piles of pots and crockery here and there embellished with scraps of dried up food. Everything, now the property of the conquerors, was to be carefully sorted, graded, wrapped up and loaded onto lorries, to be sent for re-distribution to the *Heimat* (fatherland).

Things tattered to the very limit, mattresses sunken beyond repair, family portraits, feather beds, rubbish were dragged outside into the dusky courtyards at the back of every house, and burned to a cinder. God forbid that anything that could still be of use should be committed to the flames. In case of doubt, like, for example, that of the thoroughly foot-worn bed-side rug, said to be Persian, the opinion of Krumstein himself was sought.

A feather in the air could prove more pernicious than pestilent insects. Yet because the masters wanted only bedticks, they had to be stripped of down and feathers. Preventing the feathers from oozing out of the apartments into the street became a life-and-death struggle, however helpful in keeping the masters, or even their servants (all anxious not be be spotted by the white locust) from peering into the dim interiors of the emptied homes, which had already been searched by SS officers. In addition to chattels, corpses were carried out of some homes, usually from attics and cellars, where they had remained in condition that told plainly how their incarnate owners had met their deaths. The corpses lay on the pavement, waiting to be collected by Bodman and his brotherhood. Though they were not many, the sight of the bodies marred the impression of a busy flea market.

83

On reaching his new commando, Arush was greeted with no little surprise. None of the fellows had believed they would ever see him again alive. After some complimenting and patting on the back, they explained how the Clean Up orders related to their domain: they were in charge of books. Hence the "intellectual" sobriquet attached to the work-group. Arush saw his assignment to this group as another proof of the special regard paid to him. The work was considered light and clean, and coming under the direct orders of the local SD commander, it proved to be privileged in other respects as well. Directly answerable to him for the sixteen man-strong commando was its nominated leader, a doctor of medicine and amateur man of letters. It was intellectuality all along the line.

In keeping with the master-cremators' humour, the same privileges held good for the bonfire itself which, as another prerogative of intellect, was permitted to flame away in the street. The orders issued to the commando were as plain as a pikestaff. All manuscripts and one copy of every book, regardless of its content and the language in which it was printed, were to be preserved; all the rest were to be burned at the stake.

Arush set about the job in earnest. To him it was at once a loathsome charge and a duty - a duty both sacred and sacrilegious, distressing and heartening. To watch him standing intently by the fire and pulling out from the flames this or that book was truly disarming in its unaffected quixotic simplicity.

To some, however, the sight was apparently an incitement, as it must have been to Samuel Buchaj. As a dentist he was in a commando allocated to removing latches, unscrewing door-handles, separating stairway railings, and extracting nails from walls. Passing by the bonfire on one of his errands, and seeing Arush retrieving a copy of the "Vision of Nahum" from the fire (a book which was roaming about the street in countless numbers) Buchaj flew into real rage. He began swearing loudly, picked up a copy of the same book, then another one, and, as if taking revenge, hurled them both vehemently into the flames, at the same time defiantly shouting a challenge to the Heavens.

At first Arush was staggered by the fury with which Buchaj, a devotee of reason and education, was reviling and slinging the books into the fire. But then, without being capable at the time of conceiving why, he felt somewhat consoled. Telling himself that this behaviour was too contemptible to rebuke, Arush switched his attention back to the awful picture of books mounting to the sky in coils of smoke.

To him the books turned into living images. It was the first time in his life that he had felt about books like this, and perhaps it was just because they were now being annihilated. They became images that were not only living but speaking. He could, as it were, hear their voices. And through them, he soon realized, spoke first of all his father. To drag a book from the fire acquired a vital, though mysterious meaning to him. The books assumed an aura of immortality, arousing affection that he could not bestow on any living person.

Teper, unlike Buchaj and a few other men, did not burn religious books with a particular vengeance. He treated them all indiscriminatingly, as if the entire performance were a crazy sport. Seeing how exhilarated Arush was by the operation, he pleaded with him compassionately: "But Arush, this is only paper. Books can be revived. At a time when man..." Arush hardly heard what Teper was saying. He was staring dimly at the burning stake, lost in thought. The flames appeared to him ageless, as if it were rising from a distant, unknown place or time. It had all happened before, in the dark Middle Ages. Now it was a thousandfold darker. Now it was his turn to uphold the torch, to watch over the flame. Seven hundred and one years ago in Paris (Arush had a memory for dates and names), Rabbi Meir of Rothenburg had witnessed the burning of not many fewer books, and all Hebrew ones at that, than he was witnessing today. Hardly two hundred years had passed since the Baalshemtov stood at the market place in Kamieniec Poldolski and watched, as he now watched, copies of the Talmud being put slowly, one by one, on the burning pile. On that occasion the local bishop, under whose command the spectacle was taking place, was suddenly seized by a fit of myo-clonic spasms, and the assembled crowd had dispersed in panic. Maybe it was this or similar folk memories, that made Arush, after all a sensible young man, persist doggedly in his quite hopeless attempt of salvaging a few books from the flames. They were, of course, all awaiting a miracle, including Buchaj, even if he would probably have called it "unpredictability of fate". At least, Arush extracted something positive from this tragi-comic struggle against fire. For a few hours he considered himself a very important person in the world - a man carrying responsibilities, acting, if you wish, as champion for his people and visited by the ghosts of immortality.

Then came the less painful part of the operation: sorting and packing of the surviving copies and manuscripts. In a fortnight it was all over, and the group dissolved.

So they were making history, as they used to say, the tiny, insignificant, yet uncommon history of Clean Up. In practice this meant little else but work from dawn to dusk, the unattractive time limit set with regard to the quickly shortening daylight. Day after day, house after house was turned inside out. Some fixtures were pulled down, certain objects taken to pieces, others put together. In general, anything that could be moved was transported, within the walled district, to buildings or homes that had been assigned as storehouses. There, separated by kind of booty - furniture, clothing and bed-clothes, kitchen and table utensils - they were cleaned and sorted, mainly by female prisoners. Gradually the houses which stood empty of their evacuated occupants were also emptied of their contents.

It required no particular discernment on the part of the prisoners to perceive that were they to go earnestly about their job, it would soon be finished, and they would become dispensable. So they were in no haste; yet, it must be said, nor were they hastened. As Teper and Arush quickly observed, a familiar situation was repeating itself with both the Jewish prisoners and their German jailers pretending that real work was being done. What they actually did for most of the day was to settle in small groups in an apartment, talking, reading, if there was something to read, cooking, if there was something to cook, always with some work ready at hand, always with one man on the lookout, so that they would not be caught napping. It would, however, be untrue to say that the men complained about their days passing monotonously, or that the way they passed set their minds at rest.

During the first days of Clean Up no one brooded too much on his situation. Others had gone, they were still there, and Clean Up was the reason. But as the last Aktion grew more distant and the numbness of their minds eased, they began to think again. From then on a single question superseded all else in their musings and discussions: What next?

–"There's no telling what next," argued Teper.

Arush objected.

–"Are we different from the others?" he asked. "Can we expect a better deal? The question is only, how long?" How long would the SS keep the Clean Up business going?

Agreeing that the worst was inevitable, yet various conclusions to their destiny possible, they were once more in accord. At least, Arush noted with little comfort, no one now tried to avoid thinking of his immediate future.

Admittedly, they had not felt their lives were secure before, in the old ghetto days. But now that they were fewer and, at the same time, more closely watched, the chances of being killed at any day or hour, indeed at any minute of the day, had incomparably increased. Not a day passed without someone being killed. The local hangmen's lust to kill had, it seemed, reached its highest pitch.

Of all the changes the most striking one concerned Blache. This was, no doubt, because in previous days he had skilfully worn a mask, concealing his true self. During the Clean Up he took the lead in killing. It seemed, he was also aiming to surpass his colleagues-rivals from the Gestapo in brutality. In one incident he was seen treading on the neck of a child to save a bullet. In another, he enjoined his son, who could not have been more than fifteen years, to shoot a man.

Well, the next generation must be inducted into the trade of their fathers, Arush commented silently after the incident. He was not in the least surprised, for he recalled a story brought from Cracow, about a boy of only six years who, watching his SS officer father, performing his apparently daily routine, implored him: *"Vati noch diesen!"* (Daddy, this one too!)

Of experiences with less serious consequences, the most excruciating were the bodily searches held from time to time to find items stolen from the Clean Up inheritance. On one occasion, Blache ordered the people to be stripped to their skins and to wait naked for his arrival. But with regard to food, Arush's hard logic proved correct. Bread was distributed regularly, and the daily rations were larger than before. The Poles, too, came without fail to exchange food for goods over the fence. Wares of all kind were plentiful and the hard pressed Jews offered them dirt-cheap. Once-in-a-lifetime bargains changed hands, like the painting by a first-class Polish artist which was bartered for a chicken.

Surprising and inconsistent with his general demeanor, was that Blache winked at the continuously rising ranks of people in the Clean-Up brigade. The total number of men and women at the end was at least a third larger than at the beginning, not counting replacements for those who were murdered or escaped. It did not seem enough to attribute Blache's tacit acquiescence in this cover-up manoeuvre to bribery alone; but enlarging his domain and prolonging its existence may have neatly squared with his self-interest. Yet only a minority of individuals - those wise enough to reappear singly or those with contacts to someone in the highest ghetto hierarchy - could hope to reach the heaven of Clean Up ranks.

All the other people who emerged from hiding were invariably trying to surrender to OD men rather than to the Germans or their Ukrainian helpers. If they succeeded they could avoid being beaten or shot on the spot, and so to preserve some hope of perhaps mere despatch to a concentration camp. After their surrender, the people were put in a new, makeshift prison which was located in the basement-cum-cellar of a house with grilled windows which opened onto the Platz. There, they were held at the disposal of Blache or, in his absence, of the Gestapo.

Why did they come out? asked some of the lucky fellows who were legally in the Clean Up brigade. Eltes had told one of those who gave themselves up: "You should have stayed on." The man replied defensively: "For how long can thirty living persons hold out in a narrow cavity, dark as a grave, with no air, little food and water, and in constant fear of being discovered? My wife and I couldn't bear it any more."

And what were their prospects? Arush asked himself, partly to console his mind for his mother's abandoning of her hiding place on the morning of the last Aktion. As it later turned out, it made little sense to stay on in hiding, as the Nazis ordered the demolition of the whole ghetto in the following winter.

Among one of the larger groups that had emerged from hiding, Arush noticed through the prison window Reb Mechil Lewin. Seeing him was, for Arush, like being struck by lightning, and instantly summoned into his mind a wealth of memories. It was all the more startling because of superstitious belief in Mechil Lewin's invincibility, a superstition such as people form as a joke or through some grotesque way of thinking and then come to believe. How else could you explain the fact of an old man who remained fit in body and mind although he had been shot several times? The first time had been as early as the first Monday in December 1939.

It had still been deep dark when they were suddenly wakened by a barrage of automatic fire, Arush remembered, recalling in some detail the circumstance of the Grand Search, as the event came to be known later. The gun-play, inexplicable initially, was intended to inspire terror and warn the Jews not to leave their homes, or even to come near a window. Later a special German commando was to pay domiciliary visits to every Jewish home in Cracow, to "collect" foreign currency, jewels, and anything made of gold and silver.

Must one have silver cutlery? Was it worth risking who knows what penalty for this or that? Arush remembered the feverish discussions that took place at home while they hid away everything truly valuable, leaving only a few things ready at hand, "to stuff their mugs, if they come", as his mother had said.

They had no food at home, and no one knew how long the curfew would last. Some said only one more day, others said till the end of the week. But next day, December 5, at 11 a.m. the whole thing was suddenly called off. An hour later,

Maxim Litvinov, Stalin's special emissary, had arrived in Cracow on his way to Berlin, to be received by the General Governor Frank at the Wawel castle. What a lark! What a disgrace! The author of the Nuremberg Laws was himself to entertain a Jew, and with what affected cordiality! And - greatest irony of all - just when the homes of other Jews in the town were being plundered! Arush's brother Dave had maintained against all the rest that it was more scandalous of Litvinov to visit Frank than of Frank to receive Litvinov. Their father laughed at this, saying that Litvinov felt as much about being a Jew as a pike feels his days of fry. If he knew about the search and that it would be cancelled because of his visit, he would have postponed the visit.

When on that morning the fusillade had started, Mechil Lewin was on his way to ablutions at the communal bath. The bullet he caught made him bed-ridden but for only two months. The second time he was shot he was already in Tarnow. Carrying food under his coat, Reb Mechil thought it would be safer to raise his hat, as many uniformed Germans required of Jews, to greet the passing police office on the other side of the narrow street. That officer - a stranger and a particularly surly type - took the greeting as insolent familiarity and fired at poor Mechil Lewin. The bullet went right through his back but he recovered again. At the height of the first Aktion, "when the angel of death was given free reign", as Reb Mechil described it later, he, among others, was lying flat, face on the ground of the attic in the house where he had lived. The place was dark and dusty, piled up to the ceiling with all kinds of junk. The SS men who came up to search were either frightened or too lazy to proceed inside, and simply sprayed the attic with bullets from the entrance. Although some were wounded, the fugitives kept quiet and were not discovered. As for Reb Mechil, he lay unconscious from sheer fear, while a bullet scratched his buttocks. At all other Aktions he was in hiding, and in between he hardly ever ventured outside the little room which he occupied with a fellow inmate of his own age. "Can he escape again?" Arush asked himself in true concern, glancing furtively through the prison window. And how could he help? For he had built up a good deal of sentiment for this man.

"Thy brother's blood cries out to me from the earth." With these words Mechil Lewin had greeted Arush when he came to visit him in his hiding place after the death of Arush's father. When he had heard of his death, Lewin asked that at least one of the Freund brothers should come up to see him, so that he could express his condolences. He wouldn't go out at that particularly tense time. "I loved your father with eternal love," Reb Mechil went on, trembling and weeping as he spoke. It was a love of admiration, love of a charitable nature, enhanced perhaps by gratitude. Reb Mechil didn't need much for his upkeep, as he was one of those men who lived by the Word rather than by bread. He was very proud of being a Levite. Levitical heritage, he claimed on the authority of a certain rabbi, "sprouts" from the lines of a man's hands. Arush's eyes were not good enough to see this, but it had always seemed to him that a childish innocence and kindliness shone through the finely seamed lines of Reb Mechil's face - a face that was partly overgrown by a short, thinning white beard which he used to finger as he talked.

This made Arush all the more surprised at what Lewin said next, and the words were now ringing in his ears like a warning-bell. "So shalt thou put away the guilt of innocent blood from among you." Was he serious? Who was to feel guilty of the innocent blood shed "in our midst"? And if they felt, how could they, the kindred of the slain, put away the guilt of innocent blood? Lewin claimed that unless the blood of the slain were redeemed, his soul could not rest in peace. So it is written. As it is of the two thin threads by which flows the richness of spirit reaching the sphere where the soul cleaves to its Creator. Whom would you expect to feel more strongly about humanity and the sanctity of life than a man of such beliefs? Yet he insisted that, after the war, Arush was duty bound to avenge the murder of his father. Nothing seemed to Arush more incongruous than such a plea coming from the mouth of Mechil Lewin. Lewin could not hurt a fly, Arush was quite sure; he was more likely to free it from the fly-paper. Arush could easily visualize being killed himself, but both then in the small, stuffy room and now in the open air opposite the prison window, he could not imagine himself killing others. He wanted to tell Reb Mechil that this was not the way of expiation. Blood-redeeming - fine, but by all means other than blood-shedding. Otherwise, blood would fill our planet as the waters cover the seas, the roar of its waves deafening those who hear the cries of innocent blood that rise from the earth. But Arush felt constrained to agree.

Now Arush felt guilty as he furtively watched the tall, erect figure, standing there in the cellar, a black plush hat - which he had not worn during the war, but had apparently taken with him into the bunker - covering his head, a sash around his hips, facing the wall and praying continually. Guilty on account of his helplessness, guilty to think "I may still live on, he'll certainly not". What could he do? The question bothered him persistently. He could perhaps give some encouragement, but this was the most difficult thing to impart. He dropped a loaf of bread through the window, simultaneously shouting out: "Reb Mechil!" The man did not even turn his head. He was engrossed in turning his soul to Eternity. What interest could he still have in bread, in anything earthly? As he peeked at him out of the corner of his eye, it seemed to Arush, that Lewin might already have severed his bonds with the living. His religious fervour was probably reducing his suffering, perhaps also assuaging his fear. For him, Arush mused, giving himself faint comfort in his own anguish, death was certainly not all that important; the important thing was how one died, the passage from this world to the other one, for which Mechil Lewin was so obviously preparing himself.

To tell the truth, all the men and women inside the prison were indifferent to everything around them, at least they looked so to Arush. None of them expended any emotion over their situation, although, or perhaps because, they knew pretty well what to await.

Yet Arush continued to ask himself, what will be? What will happen to them? That night he woke up several times with the same question immediately on his mind. The answer soon presented itself to him in a telling form. When first thing next morning he went to see how the men were getting on, the prison-cellar was empty.

That day Smolensk fell, or the news of its abandonment by the Germans, reached the Clean Up prisoners.

–"Have you heard, Smolensk was taken?" Arush asked Tunye Einhorn in the evening, expecting to re-awaken his passion for analyzing political-military news.

–"Yes," was all he answered, curiously cool. After a minute he added: "Too late. It's been obvious for some time that the Germans have lost the war, but it will be too late for us. How can we endure to see their end?" Einhorn's reply summarized the general mood and response to events of nearly all the other prisoners. It was a fact, a sad change, which Arush had been noticing for some days, that the good news from the battlefields no longer aroused the same expectations in him as before.

That eventful summer of 1943, eventful in matters of war, the remaining Jews were still rejoicing at the encouraging tidings that were reaching them in the ghetto. It was the first war-summer that news was truly good. Oh, how exciting, how magical, were all those names of battles and German defeats! Arush sighed as he ran through those fairly recent, yet oddly remote days, in his mind. It had started with the news of the Russian offensive in July. The battle of Kursk, the great breakthrough, the fall of Orel in the following month; Germany's evasive admissions of retreats. They had "removed (*abgesetzt*)" themselves from the enemy, they were applying "rubber-rope-tactic (*Gummiseiltaktik*)" - with what rapt attention they imbibed this new vocabulary from the German war communiques and press comments. The most striking news, news that was almost too good to believe, was of Mussolini's replacement by Badoglio, five weeks before the last Aktion. That wasn't just good news, but an intimation of the enemy's ultimate collapse, a harbinger of the war's end. Even the usually cautious Rabbi Maleachi had said so.

Now, only a few weeks later, Arush observed, those inmates of the ghetto who were still alive were wary of all news, often seeing it as mere rumour. Just as the German victories of 1940 and 1941 had at the time been reduced to insignificance so the German defeats were now minimized. While the Jews of Poland made Italy declare war on Germany back in February 1940, and three months later, in view of the crumbling Allied defences, had them bribing the Italians to come to France's help with promises of Tunis, Dschibutti, part or full ownership of the Suez Canal; so now, when, at the beginning of October 1943, Italy did actually declare war on Germany, the poor Clean Up men first refused to believe it and then denied, not quite wrongly, its great importance. They were similarly dismissive of the fact that the last Aktion had coincided with British-American landings in Italy, whereas only a few days earlier everyone in the ghetto had expected an immediate Allied invasion in the West. Salerno, Tarranto, Volturno, all those beautiful, evocative, but distant names, what relevance did they have to their survival? Smolensk, Vitebsk, the Dniepr, so much more familiar to their ears, so much nearer home, had carried a promise of deliverance - but when? In July many had still optimistically expected the war to be over before the end of the year; two, three months later, they doubted the war would ever end - for them.

While no less sceptical than others, Arush nevertheless felt that the good news with which they had recently been blessed almost every day, made it easier for him to continue suffering. On the other hand, his, and probably other fellows' pessimism was increased by the changing scenery of the skies. The fine summer was over. Even if for a few weeks more, the sun still shone brightly, the days were growing short and cool. Then clouds, rain, starless nights had loudly signalled autumn - though what their life would be in the nearing wintry season they didn't think. It was preposterous for them to think so far ahead.

Just as the season was moving onward with a bad grace, so the Clean Up proceeded unwillingly towards its inevitable end. That it could not last interminably they knew from the beginning. By mid-October they understood that it could not go on for much longer. What then? Rumours of every sort were circulating, but hardened by experience they gave little credence to any of them. They were apprehensive of what would come, but not of death. Fear of death had quite inexplicably, if not absurdly, declined, as had fear of punishment, including Divine punishment - of which Samuel Buchaj was only one manifestation. Theirs was a feeling of suspense - the by now familiar limbo between life and death. Bodman's admission that he found some peace at the cemetery illustrates how great was nervous tension within the Clean Up area. True, cemeteries afford rest and the only peaceful spot in most modern towns. But Bodman called at the cemetery on duty, and he had disclosed in confidence to Arush that several hundred bodies had been buried since the beginning of the Clean Up.

To Arush Freund, the somewhat dainty boy, not yet delivered, as it was commonly said, of the sensibilities of the past, even minor outrages, regarded by most as trifling, caused anguish. One such indignity was a scene involving a mare, a cow, if you forgive the term, and their driver. One sunny morning, half-way through their Clean Up term, a droshky driven by Froim Reles, personal cabman to the "Forced Labour Camp" commander, rushed through the gates and pulled up in the centre of the Platz. Getting out quickly from the back seat of the cab, Frau Blache squatted, lifting her dress, and pissed. The mare switched its tail in embarrassment; Froim Reles, by virtue of his professional function one of the most influential Jews in the ghetto, remained seated at the dicky as stiff as the whip in the holder beside him; while the panic-seized prisoners around, scattered from the Platz like pigeons fluttering from a bounding dog.

It did not seem to Arush that he would ever feel humiliated by whatever a German would say or do to him. Every Jew had felt the same from the early weeks of occupation. Yet this tiny example of the new Abendland civilization displayed by one of its matronly traegers (carriers), aroused in Arush a deep sense of shame. It made him forcibly aware that he, and his fellows, were not considered to be humans. When Arush told Teper of the sensation the scene aroused in him, he laughed, though this time not very sincerely.

—"Is that something new to you? Anyway, who could feel ashamed in front of creatures on the verge of slaughter - particularly over a trifle that even kings perform standing up?"

Even Teper was plunged in gloom, Arush noted silently. To expect the worst was for them the right philosophy of life - a life that became every day more difficult to bear. The indignities, the cruelties, the killings - would there be an end to them here? they asked themselves and sometimes each other. You needed nerves of steel to take all this. Anything would be better than this life in Clean Up conditions, they thought in careless resignation, adding to comfort themselves: sooner or later it'll end anyway. So that when it began to be rumoured, at first in whispers, and then with official encouragement, that they were moving to a camp they were glad, come what may. They had had enough of uncertainty. They had had enough of constant insecurity. They wanted change - change without knowing what to expect, without real hope of any improvement in their situation.

No wonder, then, that when, precisely eight weeks after the first day of the last Aktion, they were waiting lined up in the Platz with their belongings, which consisted of not much more than the clothes they wore and a ration of bread, their feelings were a mixture of relief and dread. But as they continued to wait, the feeling of relief quickly receded and suspense of a familiar kind returned, bringing back an awareness that worse times probably lay ahead, and doubt - were they really being removed to a camp?

In the end, many of the prisoners standing in the lines began to envy the selected hundred or so who, it was said, were to stay behind for a little longer with Krumstein and Roter in command, to clean up after Clean Up.

What the men and women, in their separate lines, waited for, they did not ask. It was standard practice, they knew by then. So that they would not grow impatient, they were repeatedly searched and counted, and redeployed: four lines deep, then three, then four again. Then the rearrangement completed, they were checked to dress the ranks, and inspected, like troops on parade. Not for nothing had they been occasionally drilled over the past few weeks.

The day was sombre, mist in the air, the sky grievous - and the heart of Arush heavy beyond bearing. He could imagine what he must look like from the appearance of Milek Walach, who stood next to him in line. Milek was a tall, dark-haired boy of no less tender looks than Arush, and at nineteen was the youngest in the Clean Up brigade. On that morning he stood a bit hunched, despondent, inclining to one side or the other as if he were seeking to huddle against a warm human arm to give some vigour to his body. Similarity of appearance, reflecting inward agony, may also have explained the extraordinary civility extended to both Arush and Milek.

At one of his inspections of ranks, no less a person than Chairman Falban had stopped for a while to speak just to the two boys. And how gently he spoke! He almost embraced Milek. Though he didn't say much - "Don't worry! It'll be good. You'll see. Don't fear!" - the great wonder was that he spoke to them at all. Not that Falban was proud or unfeeling, only that because of his "nerves" he was said to be no longer accustomed to talking to people unless he was forced to. And yet here he was stopping and speaking to two insignificant, humble youngsters, confounding the impression people had formed of him.

It was not the first time that Arush had heard Falban speaking to him; it had happened once before, but that encounter had been of an entirely different character. In the early days of Clean Up, Arush was passing during work-hours through the passageway connecting The Platz with Szpitalna Street when he met Falban, walking in the opposite direction. Falban stopped Arush and gave him quite a talking-to, sounding not unlike a headmaster, whom in fact he resembled in his general appearance. What was he doing there at that time of day? Didn't he know the consequences? He was warning him for the last time, and so on. He was right, Arush conceded silently, and since to answer back would have been unwise given the circumstances, he stood to attention and put on a remorseful face. It worked well; for, without uttering another word, the Chairman turned round in a way he must have acquired in his youth at the Polish Military College, and moved away visibly disarmed - his look possibly expressing regret for having shouted at the boy.

Arush had known a different Falban as well. One particularly sunny day (it had been sunny all that Clean Up September), Arush was squinting at the Platz through the window of a flat he was supposed to be working in. The Platz was completely deserted except for three men near the entrance to the OD police station. Rommelmann who had returned from performing a not too sizeable execution in a side street, had apparently sustained a misadventure; one or two, perhaps even more, drops of the victims' blood had bespattered his immaculate beige-coloured summer suit. The scene unfolded before Arush's eyes as if in slow motion. At first he saw Rommelmann standing, head leant forward, examining his suit. Near him on one side stood Lerer, the supreme OD commander, bent double, gazing intently at the disaster area; on the other side, Falban, in a squatting position, held a small bottle, apparently of benzine, and a white handkerchief ready to apply to the offending spots. But Rommelmann declined the offered help. He took the bottle and handkerchief from Falban, and after scrutinizing it from all sides, stretched one leg forward like a dancer, and began with studious delicacy to clean the suit. All that time, the two master-slaves held their positions, the one squatting, the other bent over, both staring at Rommelmann's tenderly sliding hands with the kind of adoration normally reserved for a masterpiece by a Rembrandt. The cleaning completed, Rommelmann left visibly pleased, declaiming blithely a poem which, if Lerer got even the few words right, went:

> wolan, wolan, es ist gleich gut,
> (how nice, how nice, it's equally good)
> auslassen dem Jud das böse Blut.
> (to relieve the Jew of his evil blood.)

All things considered, Falban was basically a quiet, meek man, not a bad person, but in the last year or so, not surprisingly he had become so nervous that he occasionally lost his way. He certainly did not give the impression of a man drunk with his "power" or enthusiastic about his job. Yet, to have survived for so long, he must have known very well how to handle his Gestapo bosses, who included some of the wildest criminals to be found even among that singular species.

93

No one doubted, however, that Falban could speak if he wished to, and Arush's surprise that Falban had spoken to him and Milek was not the amazement of someone seeing the lips of a statue moving, especially of a god who might have already sensed the pedestal being removed from under his feet. Rather it was the surprise of a child lost in a dim alley who suddenly hears its name called softly by a stranger.

Falban did not say anything extraordinary or particularly reassuring. Nevertheless Arush felt grateful. It was nice of him, he thought. Perhaps a good omen, too? Didn't Isaiah say "The tongue of the dumb shall sing", on the day "God will come and save you?"

In any case, Falban's few words had somewhat shortened for Arush the waiting, the heart-grinding waiting for a journey into a terrifying unknown.

PART TWO

A Good Deed is not Lost

CHAPTER SEVEN

It was late evening when the Tarnow transport reached its destination. In the darkness, the prisoners could see only the bare outlines of the camp. For their visual encounter with its horrifying details they would have to wait till morning, though the grim quality of the place was felt immediately.

At what was benignly called reception, there followed a routine procedure. The new entrants are marched inside to line up before the so-called guard-block, which is a well-lit and properly equipped barrack room; another check of numerical strength; an order to put down, on penalty of death, all one's possessions; and then, one by one, the men, who have been separated from the women, enter the block, where jack-in-office prisoners, seated at bright desks, write down the newcomers' personal details. That finished, the prisoners turn their pockets inside out, some being frisked by Ukrainian or German guards. They then leave the room by a door at the other end. Outside, the prisoners are drawn up in new lines, while at the front of the barracks the ground has been carefully cleared of their belongings - now transformed into state property. When the last man comes out of "registration", a final count is taken.

On that memorable evening of 28 October 1943, everything passed quickly and uneventfully. All the two hundred or so men were led by their new OD men into one, completely dark barrack room, already overcrowded with sleeping prisoners. Just as there is no head that cannot shelter more lice, so there is no prison into which more inmates cannot be squeezed. Groping in the dark, the newcomers climb up to the bunks and, like the rest without undressing, they lie down sideways, eight men cramped together across the adjoining bunks.

The barrack room, as seen in daylight, was a wooden structure, forty meters by nine, originally designed to lodge two dozen horses, but now containing on either side of a gangway a continuous row of three-tier wooden bunks covered with straw, in sacks or loose, in which at night sleep six hundred men. The floor of the windowless barrack room was not boarded, nor had the entrance a door, but through the gap the sun could penetrate only a short way during the day, while at night a single kerosene lamp, hung on a wall, relieved the stale, dark depth of the place.

As he lay motionless on his bunk, huddled between two strangers, Arush listened to the whistle of wind and rustle of straw. He felt the darkness more distressing than anything else. Electricity abandoned, houses abandoned, beds abandoned, it felt like returning to cave-dwelling. And yet, he said to himself, thank God that you are not spending the chilly night in the open. Nor is it as bad as we had feared. Selection, exhaustion, senseless beating. People somehow manage to live here.

97

Perhaps it's for this night only. Perhaps tomorrow we'll move into a better barracks. Oh, how good it was in Tarnow! But, however much he tried, Arush was too tired to recall scenes of his earlier life, to think of what lay in store for him, or indeed to think of anything at all.

Szebnie was but one tiny jewel in the Nazi crown of nine hundred concentration camps. It took its unassuming name from a remote little village at the southern tip of the General Government, close to the border with Slovakia. There, on the road leading from Krosno to Jaslo, the Germans had built, as a staging point for their army, about a dozen barracks, which were later enlarged and surrounded by barbed wire as a camp for Soviet prisoners of war, who were kept there between October 1941 and October 1942.

Later the site was turned into a concentration camp for Jews and Poles. The first pioneer consignment of about seventy Jewish prisoners arrived at Szebnie in March 1943. More prisoners followed, mostly men, but including some women, who had been seized at round-ups, or "resettled" from other camps and from the few ghettos which at that time still remained. At this early stage, work in the camp consisted mainly of redeveloping it, for it was said that it was to become a large centre for production of German war needs. Yet, to be sure, labour was not a prominent feature of Szebnie.

During the summer months, several thousand Jewish and Polish prisoners arrived at the gates of the camp. The young and fit were admitted, the remainder, a large majority, were driven into the nearby woods of Warzyce, where they were shot and their bodies burnt. The unconsumed bones were thrown into a nearby river, and the execution ground ploughed over to erase all traces of the slaughter.

In October, after a visit to Szebnie by a commission of high-ranking SS officers, frenzied extension-work started with a view to speeding up production. At that time, in a fine display of co-ordinated planning, the remnants of the last four ghettos in the General Government - Bochnia (from which town workshops were also brought), Rzeszów, Przemyśl and, finally, Tarnow, all in the District of Cracow, arrived at Szebnie, bringing the number of Jewish prisoners there to a peak of well over 4,500 men and women, plus a few children.

The camp was severely overcrowded. It occupied altogether twenty-six acres, and consisted of three parts. Near the gates were the administrative and living quarters of the SS and the Ukrainian guards - elegant barracks, luxuriously equipped with furniture and the facilities of urban living. To the west, behind a taut wire fence, was the Jewish camp, deprived of almost everything to do with civilized living, with a man's section strictly separated from the women's section. Still further to the west was the Polish camp, which was even more strictly isolated, and hardly visible, from the Jewish one.

Who could imagine the dread the place inspired in Arush as he paced through the Jewish part of the camp on his first, pale-grey morning in Szebnie? Everything struck him as grey. The whole atmosphere, even the light of the day seemed to have the same quality as the inside of the barracks. The only difference he was aware of was that outside the sky was a little brighter, and the air cooler and less stale. On the dark, rough surface of the ground, splashed with scattered pools of mud, that made up the Szebnie "street", were hundreds of grave-faced people. They came out of their barracks, in which they were forbidden to stay during the day, and moved around idly like spivs, always on the watch, always with an air of danger in their eyes. Overhead one dark-grey cloud stood for the sky, while the whole horizon was turned into a greyish wall by the mist of autumn, which smells so strange in open space - confined space which mercifully diminished the oppressive presence of the barracks, the sentry-towers, and wire entanglements. Well, nature remains true to the place, Arush said to himself. Does the sun ever come out here?

The grey air, it seemed to Arush, who was always thinking ahead, could not augur well. What a calamity, he thought, everything has been turned upside down within a few hours! It is unbelievable. It was even worse than he imagined. Everything familiar had vanished, every normal way of life turned into dust, everything connected with home irretrievably gone.

The ghetto a home: was he idealizing the past, so soon? No, but the grace of the name - it was such a big word - home. Only someone who has lost it can appreciate what it means. A family, living together, the warmth and comfort of a habitable nook, a bed and a pot of one's own.

The ghetto was essentially a concentration camp, a more or less short-lived staging-post on the tortuous death-trek of people who had survived the bullets. Yet isolated from it only by a fence, only a few steps away, men lived, breathed and walked freely, creating a constant illusion of possible escape. And, after all, the ghetto had had some semblance of home. The familiar streets that remembered happier days, the same houses were occupied mostly by the same people. There had been water, toilets, windows, doors - all now things of the past. In the ghetto one was living; in camp one was sitting, as people say in both Polish and Yiddish. How could one live here? At best a few months. Oh Arush, what is with you? Try to regain your balance. Put aside your own suffering. Then you may do some good. If only I could! The degrading bodily conditions stifle the spirit. In the ghetto there was still a glimmer of hope. Italians were capitulating, Kharkov falling, Mińsk abandoned, the English bursting out of Salerno. All this encouraged dreams of freedom. A refuge from the unbearable - the war would after all, not last very much longer. Here in this sub-human, dead and alive bog - do people outside even know that such a place as this exists? - here no news ever surfaces. Here, even war seems unreal. How can you see an end to it? What is there to expect here? Even in dreams there is no getting away from here. How to hope under such a grey sky? In this greyness you can expect nothing but misfortune - you could not even hope for a miracle.

Completely lost in his melancholy thoughts, Arush suddenly heard a passer-by stop opposite him and speak his name.

–"Freund - what are you doing here?"

It was Moniek Weltman. Arush recognized him immediately, but was so dejected he did not answer immediately.

–"Hello, hello," Weltman said, warmly shaking his hand.

99

–"I arrived yesterday evening," Arush said at last. He did not need to elaborate.
–"Alone?"

Arush understood and he nodded. No one in those days expressed words of sympathy (which at least did away with a common form of insincerity), but it was clear what Weltman was feeling.

–"I'm glad you're here. Never mind. You'll be all right, I can tell you!"

Weltman - it flashed through Arush's mind - what a nice surprise that he is alive. Arush recalled the day when, answering a quiet knock on the door, he had seen a young, dark-haired man of middle height, his face pale with exhaustion and his eyes expressing quiet despair, asking if he could have something to eat. He came from the ghetto of Cracow, the man had said.

Weltman had been a famous name in Cracow before the war. It had been the name of what was probably the largest women's fashion store in the town. The display windows had stretched over the whole floor of a large building at the corner of Grodzka street and Dominikańska street. From above, a huge, proud signboard had declared simply - WELTMAN. The raglan coat which Nili, Arush's sister, had worn years ago had been bought at Weltman's. Arush recollected vividly how his mother had taken him, still a little boy, to the shop, and how he had enjoyed the scene. The large, brightly lit room full of people and garments, from simple outerwear to expensive furs. He remembered how, of all things, his greatest pleasure had been to watch his sister trying on coat after coat. He imagined now her delight, turning round and round before a large wall mirror, touching here and there, adjusting this and that, until finally her choice fell on the raglan. Dear, beloved Nili, with her graceful figure, her small, oval face, delicate chin, narrow, neatly curved mouth, slightly upturned nose and golden hair. Arush enjoyed recalling her face, had been hungry to feel her presence, as she stood before him in that grey-green, loose, tweed-like coat, the tall, upstanding collar fastened by a leather strap, while he listened to Weltman's words on the Szebnie street.

The rugged and slightly dirty man in his twenties who had knocked on the door and asked Arush for something to eat had been the son of one of the Weltman brothers, the store owners. Inviting him to lunch with them, Arush's mother had given Weltman a second hunk of bread, sighing sympathetically as he told her his story.

When on March 13 and 14, 1943, the ghetto of Cracow was being liquidated, Weltman had stood with other Jews on the historic Zgody (Harmony) square waiting for the "evacuation". He had seen how at one corner of the square older children were being shot, while younger ones were being loaded into baskets and on to lorries to be driven away. In the late afternoon, Weltman had taken advantage of a guard's momentary inattention and had dashed into the entrance of a nearby house that had already been searched by the SS. At night he jumped over the ghetto wall, and then for several days, he had made his way, mostly through fields and woods, until he arrived in the ghetto of Tarnow.

Arush's mother had taken a jacket from a hanger, and brushed it to give it to Weltman. At that time, the Freunds had still been rich, with three spare suits in the wardrobe. The jacket had belonged to Dave, who had "gone" in the previous November. When Weltman had arrived at the Freunds he had been wearing only a shirt and trousers. His jacket had been bartered for food on his way. Mrs Freund had held out the jacket, saying: "Put it on, Mr Weltman. It's still March; it's cool outside. And please come, if you can, every day for lunch. It's very modest as you have seen. But what we're eating, you'll eat with us."

Mrs Freund did not exaggerate. Their meals, like those of most people in the ghetto consisted only of soup and a hunk of dark rye-bread - every day the same. What a feast - Arush reflected, facing Weltman at Szebnie in his elegant short jacket and shiny boots - potato soup as his mother had cooked it, with browned flour and butter!

Weltman had become a daily visitor for lunch at the Freunds, until one day in May he failed to turn up. Neither did he come the day after, or ever again. The Freunds knew that something must have happened to him. People in the ghetto talked vaguely about a round-up on the day Weltman had first missed lunch with the Freunds. It was sufficient reason to worry, but nothing to wonder about in those days, when no Jew knew where he or she would be an hour later.

But listening to Weltman's reassuring words on that first morning in Szebnie, Arush *did* wonder about the man and what he was saying.

–"We're going to be here for some time to come. So we must come to terms with it and do the best we can. It will be winter soon. November is already at hand. The first thing - to get through the winter - is not to work in the open. This afternoon all you new arrivals will be assigned to work. Say you're a furrier, then you'll pass the winter in a warm barracks."

–"But how," Arush protested, "I haven't the slightest idea what a furrier does. I don't know how to hold a needle in my hand. I may..."

Weltman did not let Arush finish.

–"That's my business. Rely on me. There's nothing simpler in the world than a furrier's work. I'll teach you. In eight days you'll have learnt the craft. Do as I tell you, and don't worry. Let it be my responsibility."

Arush was a little baffled and he didn't know what to think about what he had just heard. He knew Weltman to be a modest, serious man, who was not given to bragging or lying. But what he was now saying made Arush suspicious and he wondered whether Weltman was on the level. Perhaps Szebnie had changed him, perhaps it had even turned him into one of those shady characters of which every camp had its fair share. The first thing prudence requires, Arush reasoned, is to be cautious and find out a little more information from Weltman. He tried to do it gently, speaking half in fun and half in innuendo.

–"Oh, thank you. Responsibility - a great thing. Someone must take it. Thank goodness that you're...saying that." Weltman understood what Arush was driving at and he probably also noticed the suspicion in his face. So little by little he explained his position in Szebnie. He described his experiences from the day he had arrived, but without losing himself in too many details.

–"Compared with what it was when I came here in May, Szebnie is now gold."

What kind of gold! Arush thought, but he did not interrupt Weltman, not so much out of politeness or true deference, as out of genuine interest in what the man was saying.

—"Barracks and roads had to be built. I was digging ditches. Others were clearing woods. Anyone who couldn't keep up the murderous pace was beaten dreadfully - sometimes to death. There wasn't a day when at least one person didn't die like that. And each day brought something new. The camp commandant then was Anton Scheidt, a middle-aged brute, who had been a building contractor before the war. His only ambition, he told his men, was to be one up on Amon Goeth, the commandant of Plaszów, who you must have heard about. Terror was applied by every sort of brutality. I was getting weaker and weaker, and I considered all the ways of escaping. But they were all futile. From the first day I came in, I thought, here life will be short.

"Every day at six before work, and at six after work there was a roll-call. Sometimes it lasted for two or three hours. Anyone who tottered was shot dead or, even worse, was set upon by dogs that attacked him and gnawed him to the bones. The Lagerführer Pospiech - a son-of-a-bitch from Danzig who spoke better Polish than German - had a special passion for flogging. For this purpose he designed a novel wooden horse. If, after fifty lashes, which the victim himself had to count, the man was too battered to get up, a dog or a bullet would finish him off. The days followed one another - all the same - until unexpectedly one day things began to change.

Light seemed to bore its way into Arush's mind. That would explain, he thought, certain things Weltman had mentioned earlier, and his outward appearance, which did not fit in with the conditions he was describing. Arush went on listening with undiminished interest, asking no questions.

"There was less terror, more food, easier work and short, irregular roll-calls. No one knows to this day what brought about this change. Only one thing has become known to us all. Scheidt - people say because he was lining his own purse too much - was replaced by Hauptsturmführer Hans Kellermann, who moved into Scheidt's place in the castle. And that's where I'm assigned for duty."

This excited Arush so much that he was unable to suppress his curiosity. "What castle?...What duty?" he asked.

Weltman didn't give a straight answer. Instead he started to explain that all the surrounding land, including the village of Szebnie and the ground on which the camp stood, belonged to a Countess Graykowa (born Princess Jabłonki) but Scheidt had forced her out of her castle, as it was called for short. The abbreviation, Arush later learned, was made by dropping "gut" from the compound word *Schlossgut* (manor-house), leaving simply *Schloss* (castle). Scheidt had also seized the best of her furniture, and had allowed her only two back rooms on the upper floor, in which she now lived with a single maid, a nice woman called Wisia. It was through these two women, though mainly through the countess, as Wisia was not too bright, that Weltman learned about the social life and off-duty happenings at the castle.

—"Kellermann," Weltman continued in his quiet, conversational tone, "is a handsome, well-mannered man in his forties. He has an intelligent face and a passion for music. He plays the piano himself. The Hauptsturmführer was switched to the SS from the Wehrmacht. He told the countess, with whom from the first day he became friendly, that he was compelled to do so. But Countess Graykowa believes that what brought Kellermann to Szebnie is the good living, which is his sole and only interest in life. She might have added that it was a good alternative to sniffing gunpowder on the eastern front. Anyway, when with time they became better acquainted, Kellermann also confided to the countess that he was not the right man for what he called the things that are done here. But, he told her, life was pretty tough at the front and the orders had come directly from Berlin, so he had to obey."

—"You, too, seem to be on friendly terms with the countess," blurted out Arush, disappointed not to hear what he was hoping to hear.

—"She is a good woman and she is friendly to me. Apart from Wisia and, in great secrecy, myself, she has no one she can speak freely to and she wants us - the prisoners - to know where she stands. Graykowa is a wise woman, and she has probably got it right about the lagercommandant's motives, for he hardly takes any interest in the camp itself. He pops in rarely, just signs the papers, and leaves everything else to Lagerführer Grzimek. The name sounds Polish, but he is a German, and - take my advice - avoid coming near him or Rolf, his dog."

The name electrified Arush. Why do they all call their dogs Rolf? The question sprang to his mind as he recalled how the pious Gestapo man, Karl Oppermann, who boasted that he "always got up and went to bed with Herrgott," once beat a Jewish attendant in Tarnow to a jelly for having addressed his black-spotted, white hound as just Rolf, without the prefix "Herr". Another time Oppermann had hit an OD man in the face for holding out a bowl of water to the dog, assuming thereby that Herr Rolf was allowed to drink from the hands of a Jew.

Remembering these incidents, Arush missed a remark about Grzimek's Rolf. But he was soon listening carefully to Weltman again, as he gave an oddly accurate description of the castle, clearly contrasting its picturesque features with the desolate landscape of the camp.

—"Behind the house there is a garden - not large but, in season, full of roses, lillies and scarlet pelargoniums. The garden merges into a green glade bordered by a wall of willows. On the other side of the stone-paved path there stretches what from a distance looks like - I never came near it - an avenue of poplars. Halfway between the edges of the glade there is a pond with a fountain in it. Ducks and a single swan glide on its surface, and reeds grow on the far bank.

"For Hauptsturmführer Kellermann's guests the place is like an exclusive summer resort. They have been coming for weekends with their families, wandering around in swimming costumes and sun-bathing. The children play in the pond, trying to catch minnows with nets - while their villainous fathers shoot at birds, or at prisoners if they come into their sights.

"These are just glimpses of the luxurious social life that began blooming after

Kellermann took up residence at the castle. Almost every night there's feasting and dancing. For every ball scores of guests arrive. They come from Cracow, from Tarnow, from all the other county-towns, from Plaszow, from Mielec, and from other concentration camps - all that bunch of skunks in charge of murder. Honouring the castle with their presence are Hauptstürmfuhrer Goeth, Sturmbannführer von Haase, and such high personages as Oberführer Scherner, the district SS and Police Commander of Cracow. Even such big shots as the successive commanders of the entire Security Service in the district of Cracow, Dr Hahn and Dr Max Grosskopf have attended one or another of Kellermann's country house parties. And many distinguished civilians such as Dr Alfred Kipke, the Kreishauptmann of Tarnow and his deputy Dr Karl Pernutz, of whom you must have heard, have been there too.

"To entertain these important guests there's a band. It was put together on the order of Kellermann from among prisoner-musicians, and it's led by the violinist Leon Kantor, who used to play with the Radio String Quartet. They play dance music and concert music. Kellermann sometimes accompanies Kantor on the piano, while Ratzówna, the star-singer of Cracow shortly before the war, appears in a gala evening dress and does her best to raise the *Stimmung* (mood) of this grand society with her beautiful voice. And what food is served! They want for nothing. Local peasants compete to supply them. Every morning they queue up at the approach to the castle with their produce. They're keen to barter it for clothes and other things recently looted from their vanished owners. And Kellermann is very generous, you know. The finest meat dishes - pheasant, venison, fried quail - are prepared by a dozen cooks, including some chefs transferred at Kellermann's request from Plaszow. Day and night professional confectioners bake all sorts of pastries, patties and giant cakes coated with cream, icing and sugar flowers. Choice cakes are packed in boxes for the most honoured guests to take away. Every day all sorts of desserts, fresh ice-cream, souffles, mousses, meringues, stewed fruit. The countess says she is sure that even at royal courts such magnificent feasts took place only on special occasions. And if she says royal she knows what it means. One of her ancestors was made a prince by the Emperor Karl VII of Austria. Kellermann, incidentally, is terrifically impressed by this.

"Certainly at no royal court, she says, were such amounts of alcohol consumed as at Szebnie castle. Every one of their parties ends with everyone completely drunk - and don't underestimate their capacity for drink. When they get sufficiently ecstatic in their Dionysian devotions, the guests start roaring with tipsy laughter and song; they dance until the plaster of the corridor ceilings below comes off; they rave so the whole house shakes, until at last, in the morning, reeking with sweat and spirits, they fall dead-drunk on a bed, sofa, or armchair. The countess is reticent about one thing, understandably restrained in talking to a man - girls. But Wisia, who is less prudish, and has a rustic fondness for metaphor, once remarked: 'plenty of young, chirpy titmice. German and not a few of our own hatching'."

As Weltman's account of conviviality at the castle progressed, Arush's interest flagged. By then it seemed to him transparently plain what the "duties" performed at the castle were. But why, he asked himself, do they need a furrier? Discreetly pondering, and tepid about the sodden pleasures he had just heard about, a casual remark escaped his lips.

–"Quite a place, snug to snare."

Anxious to complete his lengthy tale, and not understanding the quip, Weltman assumed it was a reproach. "It can't compare with the dread and misery of the camp," he said. "But there's nothing to envy her for. It's no bliss to lie in bed and listen to all those wild goings on night after night, never certain that one or another of the drunkards won't pay her a visit.

"Even when there's no sinful party, Kellermann, as Graykowa put it, is sinning against music. When he's alone, he plays solo late into the night, wreaking his diabolic force upon the piano keys. It makes the sparks fly! Hit after hit. After which he bursts forth into sentimentality and takes revenge on Schubert - apparently he has all the scores. The countess, who, it seems from what she says, is a connoisseur of music, says that Kellermann even ventures to perform Schubert's Impromptus, and such pieces as the Wanderer Fantasy, but without any insight into the music at all.

"All in all - sleepless nights for her. Wisia is a tiny bit deaf. But why am I telling you all this? Especially since I must go. I could miss the guards. They leave at one for the castle. Do as I tell you, and fear nothing!"

Arush feared very much, but thought it pointless to say so, particularly as in the abrupt haste, more pressing thoughts came into his mind.

–"Will you be there when I first report to work?"

–"Yes - as soon as the furrier-shop is opened. Until then hang around among the tailors, and don't talk to anyone. I'll talk to the head manager. If they ask you - you work for me."

To Arush it all seemed quaint, doubtful and risky, but at the same time so guileless and irresistible that it was senseless to question. Yet to reduce his qualms he quickly enquired, "Where will I find you if I need to?"

–"I'm out. But in almost every day. I'll seek you out. Only now I really must go."

–"I won't keep you. Aren't you assigned to a barracks?"

–"Yes and no. I'll come to the workshop. Don't worry. Everything will be OK. You're in my care. Keep well!"

–"Thank you. Good-bye," was the last Arush said, as Weltman walked away quickly, almost running.

Arush's fears remained with him. He could not dispel them. But somehow his harrowing feeling of depression was palpably less. A ray of light flitted in the thick of darkness. An awareness of having a close soul in this bottomless solitude, someone who cared for him. And a man of importance. A reminder of former life. Renewed lure of the future; at the edge of doom, something to look forward to again. Perhaps he really could learn furriery in a couple of days? All things in life are possible. Fortune's wheel turns round. What a difference, to dig ditches, build roads, lay cables, or to sit ensconced at a machine, sheltered from frost and wind. And he would use up fewer calories, need less food. No black market here, no extra rations for hard workers. What other way was there to scrape through even a short, mild winter? Ha, don't envy her. Why does she stay there? How splendid! Peasants supply pheasants. No chance of anything of that kind happening...

Pacing ahead on Szebnie street with his slightly disordered thoughts, Arush decided he would have no soup. Not worth going. Turnip water, smelling of carrion. First day in camp; he had no appetite. He would do better to get to know the camp through and through. Though he had no wish to look at the expanding panorama of barracks. Nothing but murk and dumps, he kept repeating. If he watched anything at all, it was the men passing by. Actually his mind was preoccupied with Weltman, but only half-consciously. How beautiful that there is still charity to one's fellow man, and from someone who has himself tasted the deepest of earthly sorrows. "Would I have been such a caring friend to him," Arush was melting into tears. "Take an example! Suppose it is in your power to help another of God's creatures. We have no brothers of the same parent so we must be brothers of the same heart. Isn't your dejection an excuse, a defence from battling? No, definitely not. It is honest, natural, uncontrolled. But Arush mustered his moral defences. What if I do nothing, but despair? he asked. Will this exculpate me at the bar of judgement? This man Weltman doesn't care much for the ultimate, afterworldly scales, yet he cares and feels responsible for me. But what am I to him?"

Arush was roused from this conversation with himself by the dry voice of an undersized, but robust and swaggering, OD man, asking him loudly: "You're new?"

Without waiting for an answer, he added: "At two o'clock in the Labour-*Zuweisungsbarracke* (admission barracks). You must register! Barrack 6!"

In outward appearance the Szebnie OD men hardly differed from those in Tarnow. The same riding breeches, the same smart, belted, three-quarter-length coats, and the same caps with yellow hatbands - the shirts still cravated. Only the officer-boots, it seemed, had a bit less shine. More carried a cane, but none a rubber-quirt. In camp, prisoners were no longer required to wear the shield of David armband.

The OD strength was no greater than one hundred men, formed mostly from the elite of the ghetto officers. Coming from several towns, competition for the job - which assured, among other benefits, better accommodation and food rations - was incomparably tougher in Szebnie than in Tarnow, where, perhaps uncharacteristically, recruitment to the force required, for most of the time, a certain amount of publicity.

The ordinary prisoners, too, Arush had already noticed in the morning, did not strike a contrast. Yet he sensed, in his afflicted mind, that the men in Szebnie, for all their sameness in appearance, and the kinship one immediately felt with them, were strangers. In the ghetto, he innerly lamented, everyone knew one another, daily contact and common experience had forged a collective to which one consciously belonged. There was none of that closeness and familiarity here, where one was thrown together by coincidence with people neither you nor your fathers had known. Cosmopolis, the chic word, was on the tip of his tongue.

Although, with time still on his hands, Arush was wandering about slowly, the approaching interview was making him increasingly apprehensive. You are walking a tightrope, he told himself. If they find out, as they undoubtedly will, that you've been lying, you may discover yourself ensconced in the arms of the wooden horse, counting strokes. Rolf will make a cutlet of you, licking his lips at his choice morsel before you give out your last sinful sigh. At best they will send you to a penal column. Arush could see himself standing half-sunk in deep, icy water, pulling cable under the sting of hunger and pickets' clubs. Tell the truth humbly and you may get some easy work inside the camp. All officials, not excluding the biggest shots - he recalled how even Falban had comforted him before the departure for Szebnie - have always shown you consideration.

It would seem that Arush was forcing himself to make up his mind, weighing up the consequences. In fact, he did not seriously contemplate ignoring Weltman's advice - not so much out of much trust in it, or heedless adventurism, as out of deadly resignation. Making decisions is often a matter of mood. In his mood there was no room for earnest deliberation. He was playing for life. The question that in those days never left his mind was "what is there to lose or gain?"

Perhaps to free himself from this upsetting thought, Arush asked the man he saw coming towards him: "D'you know where barrack 6 is?"

–"Just behind you, on the left. Are you also after a job?"

The barracks was like those for prisoners' living quarters, only it was devoid of any fixtures. In a two-deep column people were already queueing, waiting for the registration to start. Arush joined the line, standing with the man he had just met, who was eager for conversation.

–"What are you?" he asked.

–"Everyone is something."

The man was not discouraged and continued as if nothing had happened.

–"I'm actually good at making stamps. But I don't know if it's wise to mention that here."

The man went on to explain how one day he had discovered he had a talent for imitating, as he put it, stamps, seals, signatures. Then, by dint of frequent practice, his talent grew into mastery. He became a saviour to those who fancied clearing out from the ghetto of Przemysl, where in a small office-room at the Judenrat, he served both his private customers and public employers. On his arrival in Szebnie, he had fallen ill immediately. That was why he had not been assigned work till now. He was full of praise for the doctors and nurses at the hospital, from which he, however, got out alive "only by a miracle". Lagerführer Grzimek had come one afternoon for an inspection. Patients and doctors alike expected the worst. But instead he enquired about their state of health and wished them quick recovery, as their labour was urgently wanted in the workshops. Earlier that day, he told Arush, Grzimek had commanded a routine execution of people outside the camp.

A plain, unpainted table was brought in and placed right at the centre of the barracks. It was generally regarded as a sign that registration would start shortly. A stir went through the ranks of the waiting men, but this did not restrain Arush's neighbour from continuing to talk.

107

–"You know who Grzimek is! The greatest monster under the sun. The heroic commander of the ghetto of Lwów, at its last stage, when everyone was in barracks. Legends are told about his feats there and the handy 'evacuation' of the place. As a reward he was transferred to Szebnie, which is renowned for its amusements. Star choppers feel as snug as a bug in a rug here. Grzimek replaced a man called Pospiech. He was suspected, not of theft exactly, but of misappropriating state booty. He carried things too far when in the absence of Kellermann - that's our camp commandant - he shot his dog. It got him clinked in Montelupich (a famous prison at Cracow).

"Yet it's not for his solid exploits in Lwow that Grzimek will go down in history but for having invented a little game, called by him fondly 'the match', perhaps inspired by the story of 'The Little Match-Girl'. Grzimek may have wished to improve on its author's imagination. The harmless, petty game is just this: A man with a wooden pole (that's the match) weighing a hundredweight on his shoulders, must run five times round the camp street, altogether six kilometres. You're not allowed to cheat, that is to slow down, to trip, or to fall, as this could spoil the funny spectacle, which the Ukrainian and German pickets watch groaning with laughter. The victim doesn't find the game so amusing. But one man, though he was in his final stretch, writhing in agony, with the skin hanging in shreds about his neck, laughed in their faces. So Grzimek let loose his straining, snarling killer-dog on him. I'd better not tell you what happened next. I can only assure you that I tried to rid myself of the dog part of the game, but I couldn't for many days and nights."

Everything was suddenly still. Accompanied by two OD men, a tall, hatless, but well-dressed, man of about thirty entered the barracks. He immediately arrested the attention of the waiting lines by the way he walked and held himself erect, by the air of his entire person. Even the Przemysl master of a singular craft, lapsed into silence.

Arush could not take his eyes off the man, who unceremoniously took his stand at the far side of the table and set about his job. Fine-figured, nice dark hair, high forehead, a distinctly interesting face - everything about him was handsome. What impressed Arush even more than the man's striking physiognomy, was his superior yet natural manner, his smiling reserve, his dignity, yet modesty, all of which were visible in his composure. A man of class, Arush adjudged silently, at the same time admiring how patiently the man spoke in his sonorous, cultured German.

The neighbour from Przemysl had all the vital information: "His name is Dellmar, some say Tellmar. He was among the first to come to Szebnie. Goeth personally picked him out in Plaszow to organize the workshops here. Now Dellmar is what one would call 'on freedom' head manager of a complex industrial plant." What a position! Arush thought, and he nodded in agreement when his companion said: "He comes from Berlin. But not one of those German Jews who regard their presence in ghettos and camps as a grand terrible misunderstanding, and who keep saying that Hitler means the Ostjuden only.

–"A decent man. But is it safe to confide in him?" the master counterfeiter unburdened himself of his problem.

–"What sense now?" Arush replied, after a moment of reflection, continuing to watch the job allocation closely - and not relishing what he saw.

In rapid procession, one man after another approached the table, stating his name and then his craft - mostly tailor, carpenter, brush-maker, locksmith, baker. A few said plumber, cobbler, engineer, or watchmaker. Dellmar, in his agreeable way of dealing with people while discreetly marking the names off a prepared list, spoke to everyone more or less briefly, but always with courtesy and understanding - yet with no change in his earnest expression.

As the line ahead of Arush grew shorter and shorter, he remained calm. He thanked heaven that his heart was not pounding. Nor was he dithering or changing colour. He merely kept telling himself that to have any effect he must quickly put on a wise and innocent look.

In his assessment, the prospects seemed not too bright. But when his turn came at last, it was a relief to face the man across the table. He bowed slightly, then stood to attention. Looking Dellmar straight in the eyes, Arush found him even more attractive - a face to remember, he told himself.

–"What is your profession?" In his engaging manner, Dellmar used the respectful *Sie* form of address, and on hearing the instant and resolute answer, "Furrier", his face brightened up like that of a man who, listening to a dull story, suddenly hears something unusual.

–"Furrier," Dellmar repeated, half with disbelief and half with pleasant surprise.

–"Do you know *zwetschen?*"

–"Of course."

–"And *tretzen?*"

–"Oh yes," Arush spoke in the same confident tone. Finally Dellmar told Freund that he would have the opportunity to put his indispensable skills into practice, and that he should report next morning to tailor-workshop B.

CHAPTER EIGHT

Back on Szebnie street, Arush at first felt relief and satisfaction. "Arush Freund the indispensable craftsman," he could not help chuckling to himself. Then he felt some remorse: "Such a nice man and you pulled the wool over his eyes."

"But what harm did I do to him?" the other part of him countered. If he had harmed anyone, it was himself. "What a fix I'm in!" he began to worry. "Everything now depends on Weltman. Did he say zwetschen, or quetschen? Perhaps tretschen? And that other sinister word. I must find out discreetly before I get into an even worse tangle. Weltman will certainly know."

When Arush Freund turned up at Workshop B next morning, the first thing the person in charge asked him, was: "Are you a tailor?"

–"A tailor? I'm a furrier."

The official, and who professed to be a *Leiter* (manager), was no stranger to Arush, nor was Arush unknown, probably, to the official. Arush knew the man well by sight, as well as by hearsay. Iziek Faulhaupt had been five years ahead of Arush at the same school in Cracow. When the ghetto there was to be established, he moved to Bochnia, from where, as Arush learned later, he had arrived with the workshop in Szebnie.

The Faulhaupts were rated a "good" family. Iziek's father, an observant Jew, was one of the largest lamp-sellers in Cracow. But it was a rating that, for personal reasons, Arush could not concede them. He remembered clearly the sunny day in May when, aged ten years, he had passed by the Faulhaupt shop on a detour home from school. Having been fascinated for some time by the large variety of fancy lamps displayed in the shop windows, he decided to pay a visit to the shop with the most honourable intention of surveying the glittering collection. But almost as soon as he went in, a shop assistant chased him out. Since then Arush had borne a grudge against the Faulhaupts. He disliked the name, and Iziek in person. In the opinion of Arush and his colleagues, he was arrogant and conceited.

Arush was careful not to let any of these sentiments surface during the fateful encounter with the Herr Leiter. But since the man conducted himself as if he had never seen or heard of Arush Freund, our hero was too proud to act any differently, even though admission to the workshop seemed to him a matter of continued existence.

Faulhaupt greeted Arush's answer with undisguised scorn. "This is a tailor's workshop, isn't it?"

The question and the tone in which is was made, though vexing, did not disturb Arush's tranquillity. He said nothing, hoping to appease Faulhaupt by his reticence and self-effacement. But the latter, heedless of getting no answer to one question, followed briskly with another.

–"And you came to this shop to work? Am I right?"

–"Yes," Arush changed tactics. "Till a furrier's shop is opened - presumably some time this week."

The two embarked upon a rather lengthy, waspish wrangle, centred around the singular question, whether or not every furrier is a tailor as well. Faulhaupt, who made this assertion, was bent upon making Arush admit that he was not a furrier. Again and again he asked, why be chary of telling the truth? But Arush, by then thoroughly piqued, would not give in. This Iziek behaves as if this were his own shop, he fumed inwardly, as if it's his to lord it over.

–"There are furriers who do not know how to tailor," Arush insisted, though with enough restraint not to mention himself as an example. "We live in times that require maximum specialization in every craft. In a decent furrier's atelier, what one man makes, another does not. The utmost division of labour. How otherwise could a man survive in trade, in the break-neck competition there was before the war?"

Despite Faulhaupt's interruptions, urging him, among other things, to stop talking as if he were delivering a set speech, Arush continued unabashed.

–"Do I know how to work a sewing-machine?" he repeated Faulhaupt's harassing question. "Certainly, I do. But even ignoring that one sewing-machine is unlike another, a machine will not make a fur coat, or any other garment for that matter, without two skilled hands to operate it. And that I have two such hands in furriery is well know to *Oberleiter* (super-manager) Weltman."

–"Who is that? A spook?" Faulthaupt asked. "I have never heard of a man of that name in Szebnie. Someone must have spoofed you, Freund." He sounded as if he could not help laughing, but at the same time was in earnest. "If a furrier's shop were to be opened I would be the first to know about it."

That this was a boast, Arush had no doubt, but he was truly worried that a man in Izieks's position seemed to have really never heard of the man on whom he pinned all his hope for the near future. But he did not lose his countenance.

–"Would Dellmar, who is responsible for all skilled work at the camp, have sent me to this shop if I were not a furrier?"

The logic of the question could not fail to impress Faulhaupt. Although he was convinced that Arush was inventing his skills, he was more amazed than amused by the cheek of this young refuge-seeker.

A bit more haggling, and Faulhaupt realized that it was time to finish the argument, not least because he felt that it would be degrading for him to speak for so long to a common prisoner. In order to assert his superiority, he again told Arush not to talk so much, and then finally pointed to an empty chair in a far corner of the room, saying peremptorily, but without malice: "Sit down there! Work will be brought to you!"

The chair stood at the wall by a window, affording a good view of one side of the camp street. Arush appraised the position. This will reduce the boredom and will provide a look-out against approaching danger. This thought slightly gladdened his heart which had been rather cast down by the seat he had been allotted. That it was not at a sewing-machine was not so bad, because sitting at a machine, he noticed, was the privilege of only a small minority of his new co-workers. But his chair, unlike nearly all the others in the huge room, was not placed at a table, even though there were empty spaces at several of them.

The barracks itself looked new, bright - though electrically lit because of the ashen day - well aired, yet not cold. How merciful! Arush was comparing it with the living barracks. At least he could spend the day-time here tolerably, and perhaps, with time, he could hide somewhere for the night. And considering future expansion of production, after a good day's work, he might even be able to do a little more on the crook. He was interrupted from his dreaming by a young man - an *Unterleiter* (sub-manager), he wondered - who placed a pack of sacks on the floor near his chair. He gave Arush the necessary sewing utensils and instructed him to mend the holes in the sacks. "This is for the day," he said, and went away.

When the same official returned in the evening shortly before *Feierabend* (clocking off time) to collect the sacks, and looked at the patches Arush had put on, he undid the stitches without any fuss and told Arush, "Tomorrow just keep a sack and a threaded needle in your hand, and don't do any mending!"

Everything was not so calamitous. To have a good-natured, intelligent and sensible boy such as Aciek Itzkowicz for one's nearest neighbour was a piece of good fortune. At least Arush regarded it to be so. They drew their chairs a little closer to each other and agreed to share the duty of lookout at their vantage point at the window. Aciek told Arush in a whisper - as to speak was formally forbidden during work - that none of the sixty men working in this room was a tailor. Some knew how to use a sewing machine and most to botch a hole in a sack. The real tailors were working in other rooms which were out of bounds for non-insiders. There work went on in full swing, and everything was made to measure exclusively for the benefit of Kellermann, his high-ranking SS friends and their women. Producing goods for the army, the alleged purpose of the workshops, had not yet begun; hence the substitution of the sacks, which it wouldn't normally be worth the cost of repairing. No one knew who was the manager of the workshops. According to Itzkowicz, Faulhaupt had no right to refuse Arush admittance to the workshop, or indeed anyone else, who was sent by Dellmar or the camp *Arbeitsamt* (labour exchange). "Faulhaupt's a decent chap, only a *Schwitzer* (fuss-pot) of the first order. He is one of those people who believe that, whatever the circumstances, they have a divine right to command others. His true assignment is that of a scribe. As the other bureaucrats and foremen are too bored to give a damn what happens to the sacks, and they spend all day long the deuce knows where, Faulhaupt took over the care of this barracks and grabbed all the paper-work."

If conditions were not calamitous for Arush, there was nothing to soothe him either. Venturing outdoors during the day was, cautioned Aciek, fraught with danger. Indoors, Arush tried to gather his idle thoughts, as he sat, half-squinting helplessly at the window, and half-herringboning or, more accurately, scalloping round and square rectangular patches on rags that once he wouldn't even have used to make a ball - however much a luxury rubber balls had been in the nineteen thirties. Your first day in a new workplace, Arush repeated to himself, as if in a trance. He began mending with an appearance of seriousness and competence.

–"Will this be our work?" his neighbour muttered sadly.

That there is little to do, Arush thought, is no cause to worry. He had never trusted in work as a means of surviving the war. Yet he could not escape an eerie feeling of unreality in the place.

He inspected his first patch. Not exactly a work of art, he simpered to himself, but a start at least. You learned how to make varnish, putty, and in the end even to make a poor mousetrap. You'll master needlework as well. "Will I?" Arush sighed heavily. If Weltman turned up, everything would work out for the best. He could not forget himself in this work! But what did he expect? It was quiet, warm, with no hustling, and he was not even getting his fingers dirty. Aciek Itzkowicz found life here less terrifying than in the ghetto.

But then Aciek had the tantalizing experience, if that was the right name for it, of an interim American nationality.

–"Bolivia? Guatemala?" Arush asked as soon as Aciek began telling him about it.

–"No, Paraguayan."

The Itzkowiczs had obtained the "American papers" - another of the ghetto idioms - from a caring relative in Zurich. He had exchanged the papers for a pretty sum of Francs from a Jewish philanthropist of locally high standing and wide acquaintance, who secured them from a no less high-standing philanthropist friend with first rate connections in South-American diplomatic circles in Switzerland. It was thanks to these precious contacts that the man succeeded - within the context of relief work for Jews languishing in German captivity - in procuring South American naturalization for tens of his oppressed brethren, and in getting their adoption documented in passport-simulating certificates.

A drop in the ocean - still a few saved. Let the world know that someone cared for them!

The Itzkowiczs did not know how many charitable hands their relative's monies passed through. But it seemed to them fairly plain that ultimately it must have found sanctuary in the safe pockets of one of those diplomats who clearly deemed his potentially risky tenderness and humanity deserving due consideration.

There was vaccillating, and discussions went on for several weeks, as people weighed up the risks and chances, and considered every possibility. Finally, "the Gellers registered and the Sterns" - it was example, even more than rumour that played a major part in people's decisions - and the whole family Itzkowicz, father, mother, a sister and Aciek himself, called at the Judenrat to register their foreign citizenship with the proper authorities. But, like all the other neutral nationals, they did not dare to move outside the ghetto limits, for no one would tell them if they were entitled to, or not.

"One evening last March," Aciek related tearfully, "the Gestapo swooped simul-taneously on the homes of all the neutral Americans living in the ghetto of Bochnia. Those arrested, about fifty people, were driven in trucks to Plaszow, where all were shot dead the next day." That woeful evening Aciek had been with a detachment working outside. The news of what happened reached him in time for him to go into hiding. For several weeks he changed places almost every day, furtively stalking through the streets. When nothing more was heard of the "foreign-papers" affair, he surfaced under an assumed name. Formally a secret, his true identity was, of course, known to the Judenrat and the Ordungsdienst. He lived, consequently, in a condition of constant nervous terror, which his delicately ashen, skinny face, and his large, restless eyes still revealed. He longed to get out, and merge with another locked-up crowd, not least in order to stay away from the place where his family had lived.

Arush felt at once pleasantly and self-reprovingly surprised to hear this gentle Cracovian boy trembling with emotion as he talked about the loss of his family - for in those days no one did, or was even capable of talking about such things. It was even more difficult to administer comfort. As Aciek finished his story, Arush brought himself with a great effort to say in a soothing tone: "Ah, your family went for American papers." That was how people used to speak in those days. One went with the *Aussiedlung*, or evacuation, with the children's transport, on the sick list, for a mother, accidentally. "Went" was so expressive of how things changed in a few minutes: a life, one's whole past "went" with the speed of wind.

–"At least they were spared living here," Aciek said after a while. "Anyhow, soon we all will be gone."

This was something Arush recognized. In order with the times. Ultimate solace!

They both remained silent for quite a time. From the interior of the room whispers reached their ears, occasionally drowned by the rattle of a sewing-machine. Everything appeared sluggish and dull and Arush discovered that he had been sitting for at least three hours on his chair, botching one rag. The scene from the window seemed as slothful and somnolent as the atmosphere inside the shop. The weather has not changed, he observed; sunrays that have managed to filter through the clouds were of the same colour as his sacks; the same misty, damp, windy air. None the less he felt like going out for a change.

–"Let's go to the latrine," he broke the silence.

Aciek gave a shrug of his shoulders for an answer. He preferred the weariness of the warm barracks to the cool lure of a hard walk through the camp street. Nor was he expecting to meet anyone of interest to him.

–"Sit on your bottom, if it does you good," was his advice. "You can see everything that's going on in the street from here."

Arush had no wish to make the excursion all alone. To break his sickness and unrest at heart, he asked, expecting a positive reply, if Aciek had heard of a co-prisoner from Cracow, named Weltman?

–"The Putz-y-boot?" asked Aciek?

The word is authentic, a cross-breed of German and Polish, the spelling anglicized. Its meaning is much wider than shoe-shine-boy, its usual rendering. Far from denoting a slight, or a mean sort of service, it was much more: for, as Itzkowicz explained, "Weltman was the camp commandant's putz-y-boot. A job," he added, "coveted by hundreds of able-bodied, intelligent men - would you believe it?"

The reason Aciek put forward was convincing. Apart from releasing its holder from other compulsory "duties", a post at the castle meant getting enough food to eat and comparatively better sleeping conditions at night.

These were the main criteria for ranking occupations at Szebnie. In some respects they differed from those in the ghetto. Leading functionaries of the camp administration and the OD men may still have stood at the top of the social ladder, but they were not much better off than common prisoners with regard to food and, especially, accommodation. Master craftsmen enjoyed special consideration also at Szebnie, but compared with the ghetto a more limited range of skills was now in demand. Clearly downgraded were the many physicians, who nearly all survived till the end of the ghettos, where their calling was of highest standing, but of whom only two or three were assigned to work at the camp hospital. Among common prisoners there was in general much less differentiation as at Szebnie the distinction between "essential" and other work largely disappeared.

–"Weltman is indeed a very important person," Aciek explained. "Even top camp brass reckon with him. He has no doubt a good bite to dispense. At the castle they have..."

Arush was no longer listening to what his neighbour was saying. He was sunk in his own thoughts, asking himself, "but is he important enough to drag me out of the slough I've got myself bogged down in?" If he has such a coveted job, why should he wish to abandon it for a Leiter of furriers? A silly question, he snapped back at himself. It could be safer and more rewarding. Everyone wants to be in his trade. And there may be other advantages. Itzkowicz may not know everything.

It had not yet occurred to Arush that people might seek status and "power" even in a concentration camp.

Glancing out of the window, he noticed that the street was strangely empty; only at the far end a few men were scampering, apparently for cover. He also noticed that Aciek, who could see out of the window from another angle, was overcome with fear; he had stopped talking and was trying to look intently at his sewing. Arush also noticed that all over the room men had fallen silent and, as if at an arranged signal, all the machines were set in motion; a handful of Leiters emerged, as if from underground, and began moving excitedly between the tables, pretending to be inspecting work in progress. Then Arush caught sight of an SS man walking leisurely along and leading a dog that was straining at the leash. As the SS man was strolling away, with his back to Arush, he was less perturbed than his neighbour at the sight of Grzimek - for that it was him was an easy guess.

Actually, the day before Arush had already had a glimpse of the broad-shouldered, middle-sized and - not having seen his face, he would say - middle-aged man, and of his darkish grey Alsatian. The panic they caused then was similar to today's.

It had happened when Arush was walking back from registration. His companion from Przemyśl, who earlier had introduced himself as Raizeles, was freely outlining his plan for making use of his skills at Szebnie, when they suddenly saw men in the street taking to their heels - and so they instantly hid in the nearest barracks.

Inside there were other terrified prisoners - Arush could not say how many. The *blokowy*, as the prisoner responsible for the barracks was called, was brave enough to let them stay, though it was forbidden to enter a strange barracks. He only urged them to be quiet, while himself never ceased to talk. He also looked less frightened than the other men, who were lying flat on their faces at the back of the barracks.

–"He lets off at anyone who gets in his way," Raizeles, apparently unable to keep quiet for long, whispered into Arush's ear. But he was outdone by the blokowy. The man had been among the first to come to Szebnie from Plaszow, and, evidently fond of making comparisons, was telling everyone of his experiences.

–"In Plaszow, if Goeth found a single straw on the road, the block eldest, or the prisoner who was that day assigned to sweep that section of the road, was immediately sentenced to whipping. Grzimek is different. He shoots at once, or lets loose his hound at the victim. True," he went on, "at the mention of Ralf and Rolf, the chief representatives of the camp kennel, every prisoner in Plaszow counted his bones. But Goeth didn't often send his dogs into action, though they were trained to rip a prisoner's flesh off him. For Grzimek, to let his hound cut a man to pieces is more fun than shooting or flogging - to him it's a sort of sport, practised daily, as a means of relaxing and mood improvement."

Raizeles ventured to interrupt the blokowy, suggesting that Grzimek's dog had acquired a preference for human flesh, and his master only tried to let him have his favourite lunch.

Seizing the point, another man lying outstretched on the ground remarked in Yiddish: "And impudent as this dog is, he never has enough," while Arush recalled the passage in Himmler's speech, which he read in a newspaper that had been smuggled in only two days before his departure from Tarnow: "We Germans are the only people in the world to adopt a decent attitude toward animals."

As if he were finishing a verse, the man speaking in Yiddish, added after a few seconds: "And his shepherd is most caring."

–"It isn't a daily occurence," the blokowy said, and he made another comparison.

–"In Plaszow neither Goeth nor his aides used to comb the streets looking for stubble, but Grzimek sets out almost daily on an inspection, searching, it would seem with a magnifying glass, after a husk of straw. It's an obsession with him."

–"If there's no straw, then a bunk wasn't made properly. It comes to the same thing," Raizeles demurred.

But the blokowy stuck to his form.

–"Goeth and Grzimek," he said without disclosing the source of his information, "have both graduated from the Jagdkommando" - a sort of college for perfect cruelty and murder. "And in Szebnie Grzimek isn't yet showing all the learning he acquired; at Lwow's Janowska camp in Grzimek's days they used to axe a living man into halves; to sink stomachs like wells with wooden drills; men were hanged in every fashion, pattern and shape. You wouldn't believe in how many positions a single man can be hanged.

"And what an important man he is. Gzimek is one, perhaps the only one alive, of the SS men who, wearing Polish uniforms, feigned an attack on a German border post in the early hours of 1 September 1939. For this deed after the war he's been promised one of the highest rewards from Hitler himself."

Who cared whether it were true or not, Arush commented in silence. All this left him cold.

Yesterday afternoon Grzimek had only been crossing the street on his way to the Polish camp, and as soon as he faded from sight people streamed out of the barracks. This morning Grzimek was on his routine hunt. For the time being, however, Arush and his friends entertained a short spell of suspense and uncertainty - perhaps not today? Another discreet look through the window revealed nothing. The street was deserted of all life. "Am I looking in the right direction?" Arush was asking himself when he suddenly noticed Grzimek emerging from a barracks. Just as Arush quickly turned away his head, so as not to be seen looking out of the window, blood curdling shrieks filled the air. A man must have been screaming at the top of his voice - was he trying to escape the claws of Rolf? Arush wondered - since it had penetrated through closed windows from a hundred yards distance.

–"Stand away from the window," a fidgety, bowed-down Leiter shouted in a muffled voice.

The shrieks grew louder. Then amidst the yells, there came a shot. At last, delivered from the powers of the animal. Then only the savage growls and barks of a dog were heard. And then silence fell again.

However frightened, however horrified, curiosity made Arush take another look through the window. Mercifully, the distance was too great for him to see the body clearly. It lay there under the grey sky in a no less dark, glistening puddle. Soon a small surging group of men was seen moving towards the spot. A minute later all was clear again.

For a long time after, people in the workshop kept still, sitting as if nailed to their seats. Arush summoned all his energy to pluck his neighbour by the sleeve and to ask in a whisper: "What do we do now?"

–"Nothing. What's there to do?"

–"Let's go to the latrine."

Arush didn't mean it this time. It was just something to say.

As before, Aciek's answer was a shrug. After a while, Arush heard him muttering under his breath. "Good they didn't live to see it." Then a little louder: "Every day one or two men die like that. He bore his fate relatively well."

Arush did not understand why, but he told himself that he was not yet acquainted with local custom; there must still be much to learn.

However, pausing briefly, Aciek began to relate various episodes which explained the reasons for his assertion.

And Arush learned something else that he found truly disturbing. The Szebnie prisoners, it appeared, could think of little else than Grzimek's dog and its ever present threat. The subject loomed large even at the unique feast that was celebrated that Sunday evening.

After supper, Arush managed to fetch a glass of hot water for Reb Tunye Einhorn.

Reb Tunye was completely overwhelmed by the deep calamity of Szebnie. Arush realized how much less of a shock it apparently was to himself. Reb Tunye did not go to take soup. He seemed to have lost interest in all earthly and mortal things. He was too weak, he said, to walk. He did not feel well. It could not be untrue. It seemed to be written on his face. After all, he was counting the seventh decade of his life, the time pious Jews before the war called bonus-years.

When Arush brought the water, the men who had gathered around Reb Tunye's bunk proposed a muted "*Lechayim! Lechayim!*" (Cheers!)

"A real feast," a voice remarked. "Better than *yash*, better than any strong drink of old."

An ironic truth - not a frivolity. Indeed, though most of the men were unemotional, the heart-sickness of all present was almost palpable.

It would really have been more fitting for this occasion, if all those taking part had been sitting on the ground, with dust, even if it were of maledict straw, cast upon their heads. Heads, faces invisible in the faint light of a kerosene lamp, blinking blearily at some distance. The names that were mentioned, apart from that of Bunim Laib, of the famous Laib textile manufacturing family of Cieszyń, meant nothing to Arush. He was, in any case, thinking of matters far, far beyond the barracks of Szebnie. He stood there starry-eyed recalling long evenings, wonderful evenings by the light of an oil-lamp. Oh, how charming were those evenings when the electricity was disrupted! When did a train of chairs and broomsticks tied together look more genuine? When, if not in semi-darkness, could playing robbers be more fun? Yes, it was! All these snatches from an irretrievable world of marvel.

Then again, after the electricity was switched off in Jewish homes during the war, the twinkling winter evenings, their length shortened by the need to save precious lighting fuel. At times stinking carbide-lamps substituted for very scarce paraffin, or costly candles. They could still afford candlelight. Candlelight that lent a peculiar warmth. The wondrous warmth of home - all around one table, drawing nearer the flame to read; moving around the house with a light in your hand; waiting in darkness for mother's return from the kitchen. Now everything, childhood, wartime home, the Szebnie barracks, so distant in time and space, were merging in the awestruck shade of the flickering wick - turned in his dreamlike vision into a ghostly memorial light.

They were still standing and talking, in undertones, without seeing each other's faces. Only Reb Tunye, all sighs and moans, was lying restlessly on his bunk. For a long time he said nothing. All of a sudden, he cautiously started up a little, lifted his stifled voice and said: "I know why he so dreads a single straw. He knows what stands written." He quoted by heart: "'And the house of Jacob shall be a fire, and the house of Joseph a flame, and the house of Esau stubble'. That, with God's help, will be their end!"

Arush had considerable doubts, which he kept to himself, whether Grzimek had ever read, or even heard of, Obadiah. He was not even sure if Grzimek's dog was really the one of the four havoc-playing families of Jeremiah's prophecy, as another of the participants in the feast, addressed as Reb Luzer, maintained. However, he listened intently when the same man - not of the first youth by the sound of his voice - began to speak of the Tsadik of Rhuzin, the ninety-third anniversary of whose soul's return to heaven they were celebrating.

Yes celebrating, for the commemoration of a righteous man is no occasion for sorrow, not even in the most gloomy circumstances that man could imagine. Arush could not help thinking of the improbable contrast between their present surroundings and the splendour of the Tsadik's palace, which was the envy, and object of imitation, of many a prince in Europe.

−"When he came out of the Tsar's prison after nearly two years," Reb Luzer, who was not particularly good at telling a story, related, "the Rhuziner, may his memory be for a blessing, was asked by his closest followers to tell them something about his days in jail. He only said this. It says: 'I will not fear evil, for thou art with me'. 'I fear only,' the Rhuziner paraphrased, 'for thou art with me! And for Him I prayed'."

Arush was fascinated. God in prison! Praying for His release! As if guessing the question Arush was about to ask, Reb Luzer continued a little ecstatically. "Yes, here in Szebnie, here in this thousand times worse prison as well, here in this dark barracks, here amidst most wretched despair. He is everywhere. And in His boundless mercy, we'll live to see and rejoice in His salvation."

−"Yes, fear of God," said the man who stood behind Reb Luzer, "made him fearless of man. Let his merit shield us!"

The feast was over and it was shortly *Lagerschluss*. The men started to disperse, saying by way of farewell: "Let his merit shield us and all of Israel!"

Not a shield of iron, they meant, be sure, nor a sort of safety vest. Theirs was the indestructible armour of faith, the trust in what was good and righteous; a belief in another world, a world of grace and hope, to which they turned their thoughts and affections.

On his bunk, curled up and squeezed between fellow-occupants, Arush continued to reflect on what the men had said at the feast. The short flight from grim, lurid matter into higher spheres, as it were, made him, for the second time in Szebnie, feel a little uplifted and satisfied. But this was a higher emotion, more inspiring, than the one he had experienced when Weltman had shown him his unselfish consideration. The lesson which followed from the story he had heard was that even extreme adversity cannot make a virtuous man lose faith and feel abject. The momentous, consequential thing was to be virtuous. If you were, Arush chided himself, silly questions such as the one Reb Luzer guessed you were going to ask, wouldn't even come into your mind. Nor would you, the sole reluctant survivor, be thinking only of yourself. And it would be so much more rewarding to turn your mind to former life, its lost beauty and charm. What if not a commemoration of the good and the beautiful was this anniversary-feast about? In these dark days of all and everything lost, only memories remained. Go on remembering and you'll feel human - even in this inhuman place. Yes, and now sleep!

CHAPTER NINE

He was at his sacks again in the morning. Nothing had changed; neither the morning nor the sacks. He was holding one, dutifully, on his knees, and a needle in his hand, telling himself not to prick the needle into the sack, an urge towards repression he had not practised before.

Enviously, he watched the man at the nearest table quietly pushing the coarse, folded hem of a patch under the thread of a whirring sewing-machine. "And you'll sit like this, dawdling away the whole day long, watching other people work. And the same day after day. Oh, what a delight it must be to do a fair day's work, as the men in the outer room do. For the Germans? Nonsense!" his answer was instinctive, as in part his question had been.

But the question took him aback. It induced him to try to exercise his increasingly torpid brain. "What better time to think," he asked himself, "than on a morning like this after a long, if tortuous, night's sleep, and with an even longer, blank day ahead?"

Was it really a moral issue? Was it wrong to work for the Germans in our circumstances? Not just now, but during the past four years as well? Arush began recalling the early days of war, when the issue had first arisen. Not exactly the wider question of working for the enemy. This was never seriously asked, for, given the circumstances, it did not occur to anyone that it deserved consideration. Almost anything performed outside one's home indirectly served the occupying authorities. And a little away from home one could see the Poles actively volunteering their services to the enemy. For all Jews to refuse to work appeared senseless and hopeless. Arush recalled how he and Teper had agreed upon the reasons for the impracticability of such opposition and recognized its predictable consequences. Actually no one had ever suggested communal passive resistance, let alone tried to organize it.

But if collectively it was impossible to refuse work, individually it was not only possible, but also widely practised. It required neither fortitude nor special intelligence. For at no time, not even in the ghetto days, was local German demand for Jewish forced labour nearly as large as its voluntary supply. Strangely, it was the fact that many Jews escaped forced labour, while others did not, that gave rise to recurrent controversy over the complex, and seemingly moral, problems involved.

In particular Arush remembered one evening at home in the winter of 1940, when discussion of the matter had raised temperatures to near boiling-point. The men of the family were sitting in the dining-room with visiting neighbours, including two brothers, Manes and Dudek Abramski, who lived a floor below. Everyone was chatting about the war, discussing new regulations, coal shortages, who had been arrested, and the like, when Manes, a middle-aged intellectual and the elder of the two brothers, burst out excitedly.

–"The poor are, of course, forced to work. Those who have money bribe their way out."

At this, Arush's father, who had listened quietly to the debate for some time, intervened to calm the man.

–"They force us all to work. They have made us all poor. But the day will soon come when they'll pay for these crimes."

This was not entirely accurate. The Freunds were not actually obliged to buy their exemption from forced labour. The Cracow Judenrat of that time was apparently anxious to spare or, as some said, to bribe the select families of the community. Unsolicited *protektia*, to use the Polish word for favouritism.

But Manes Abramski was not pacified. He snapped back:

–"Mr. Freund, I don't mean you, God forbid, or your family, but when it comes to compensation, the rich will be the first to push their claim. Now they stand back, and let the poor toil."

Dave, also now becoming flustered, began to speak angrily, saying the same thing over and over again but in a different way. Though it was forced labour, he argued, the men did it voluntarily. So far there had been no need to force anyone to work. "Get up early in the morning," he said turning to Manes, "and watch the crowds that are queueing to get a day's work."

This was common knowledge. Manes Abramski did not really refute it. What he grumbled at were secondary objections to his basic one. It was immoral, he argued, for the Judenrat, or any Jew for that matter, to act as broker of such business. Then he added, "The poor toil for a hunger-wage, that the rich get their exemption cheaply."

Going back to that time in his thoughts, Arush now found Manes Abramski's strictures priggish, typical of the grumbler that he was, and of the kind of people who thrived on the iniquities that war and occupation had engendered. But Arush also realized that his brother Dave's reply, though correct at the time, had since lost its soundness. In the ghettos there had always been enough men willing to work locally. But very few went of their own volition to work in labour camps. Selection was often, though not exclusively, made with regard to a person's financial standing.

Has there ever been a society without discrimination, without class or occupational differences? Rich and poor, leisure and drudgery, equity and injustice? What a bunch of bigoted dreamers were those "progressives-moralists", who just in the most debased of human conditions, when all civilized norms of law and justice lay trampled under feet, sought - and would be seeking after the war - a just and morally perfect society! Given the conditions, Arush thought, instances of social injustice were, even in the ghettos, comparatively mild.

But old Mr. Freund went on to pacify Manes Abramski, explaining to him, as if to an outsider, that not only did the German authorities pay nothing for Jewish labour, they also demanded every day all sorts of things, as gifts, bribes, fines, or simply cash. Altogether plain, daylight robbery. The Judenrat ran a special "Provisions" department to meet these various demands. Part of the income from labour-exemption fees paid for them. The more the occupier demanded, the less would remain to pay the workers.

–"Unparalleled conditions. We no longer know what is right for us to do as individuals, still less what we should do collectively as a community. We have our Commandments which are eternally valid, but we must pray that we interpret them rightly in these unprecedented conditions."

Not put out by the dry, sceptical faces of his guests, Arush's father went on to ask.

–"Would it be better, if the man who clears the snow from the roads were not assigned to it by the Judenrat, but taken by force to do it by the Germans? As it is, the unfortunate man at least gets paid. Not much, as you say a hunger-wage. Still something - enough to buy the minimum food necessary for him and his family to live on. And this is the most important thing of all, Mr. Abramski, to live on. Another day, another week, another month - the war will not last very much longer. Spring will come, and the delayed Franco-English offensive will finally begin. One big push through the Siegfried line and ..."

"Oh, father and his optimism," sighed Arush.

It was Dudek Abramski who had then interrupted Mr. Freund with a comment that seemed to confirm the ambivalence of his views, or rather of his emotions.

–"You're right. As the German demands must be met anyway, it's better to slave for pay than without it. Many people who are seized in the street by a soldier or an SS man really do a full day's work without any recompense - without even food during the long day. But the wage would be much better if Judenrat officials didn't take part of the labour-exemption money for themselves."

Everyone agreed that regrettably there was corruption. "But when wasn't there?" asked Dave.

Corruption was indeed common before this war, and had been still more common before the first World War; though it was less so within Jewish communal institutions than within state ones. What people could not yet understand at the time of the debate that Arush re-lived in the Szebnie barracks, was that social life under Nazi occupation was one big corruption. The system of government was based on corruption; the entire economy, all growth and progress, all activity took place within this framework. A corrupt state of affairs from first to last. In particular it was not then understood - and will it ever be? - that in a community under siege, even in one less tightly, less oppressively beleaguered than the Jews during the war years, corruption boils and bubbles till, to borrow from Shakespeare, it overruns the stew. It's no more possible to prevent it than it is to prevent infectious diseases from spreading in conditions of feverous overcrowding, undernourishment and exposure to filth and fear.

"To live on," Arush repeated at heart and, returning to the original question which had started these memories, he added silently, "it's work for oneself."

All over the world people were working. They could not exist without work.

What a man's object was in working was a question that had bothered him in quieter times. It suddenly dawned on him that it was easier to define the motive now than it had been when they were free - they worked in order to live on. And to work was to keep himself sane. For how long could he go on like this? Sitting and looking at the ceiling - catching flies? He could not hold it against Weltman. He would have come if he could. Would he, though? Well - if Weltman did not turn up today, he would abandon the whole thing. He could not hang on to the lie for ever. He must act before it was too late. He could get into no end of trouble. He could not live in constant fear.

Oh, don't panic! You have learned for years to live in constant fear. What has changed, Arush?

He knew the answer. He also knew that he would not take any precipitate action, or probably any action at all. What could he do? Was there a better alternative? Was there a better hope than Weltman?

What Arush knew equally well was that all this turning over of his situation in his mind, was a way of despairing, mixed finely with his immanent belief, or rather self-deception, in his capacity to decide his own destiny. No one likes, especially when they are young, to think that is not so.

He believed, however, honestly, as did all Jews in those gruesome years, that he was working, inasmuch as he ever did any work, for his own purposes, and that the question he had asked himself had no ethical weight.

None at all? Even work of substance for the German war effort?

All right, suppose it is a moral situation. Is there a way out of it? Do not circumstances, coercion, modify a situation completely? We know what's wrong - he went on debating within himself - at least we know what's wrong in the view of moralists of the Manes Abramski persuasion. It's wrong to work and it's wrong to be exempted from work. But what's morally right? How can one do the right thing without knowing what is right? Why don't they tell us? All that swaggering swarm of our inter-war leaders? And our brave and free moralist-brothers? Why don't they come and tell us? They will. After the war.

Oh, I know without them telling me, he thought. Cease living: that's the only moral way out. The one right thing for us to do. And one that should have been done in the early days of the war. That way no moral stain would remain for the living - now or in the future.

Dash it - so many people work and don't wish to die. From the Volga to the Atlantic everyone works for them. What is making mousetraps and mending sacks compared with tilling the soil, running trains, constructing machines? What about the millions of skilled men and women all over occupied Europe who...

He would have continued to think out the matter to the end, or endlessly, had he not been distracted by Iziek Faulhaupt, who was slowly moving along the tables with a sheet of paper and a pen in his hand. He came straight to Arush.

-"You're a furrier?"

Receiving a curt "yes" in reply, he went on to ask Arush about his age, if he had any family or if he was alone in Szebnie?

From the end of the room, where Arush was sitting, Faulhaupt moved on to put similar questions to others, making up his list mainly from the youngest men, those least trained in tailoring.

Arush, persisting in his coolness and aversion towards Faulhaupt, did not ask him what it was all about but others who did question him received only an evasive answer.

Various rumours began to circulate - all mere conjecture. No ordinary prisoner in the whole tailor-barracks knew the real purpose of the list. Arush, too, joined in the dispiriting guess-work, becoming increasingly intrigued, but otherwise not disquieted. He was already in a state of nervous suspense and did not intend to disturb himself over a vaguely sinister list.

However already during the lunch-break, his attitude changed somewhat. Walking in the street, he joined a group of quietly arguing prisoners from other workshops, in which a similar picking and choosing of names had taken place. Some of the men, particularly one whose name was Klacki, insisted they knew the secret of the list. It consisted, Klacki maintained, of a hundred and twenty skilled workmen, all skilled in their respective crafts, required for transfer to Pustków.

A terrifying name. Even for camp veterans the name was frightening. Pustkow was the first Nazi camp in Poland Arush had heard of. As early as spring 1940, Jews from Cracow had been sent to Pustkow. At the beginning, some had been volunteers, attracted by promises from the Judenrat of a decent wage and other privileges. But very soon only force could induce people to go. The assignment was said to be for merely three months, but in practice only those of the abducted men whose families were able to pay a large ransom, would eventually be released.

The people who did return from Pustkow after a sufficiently long stay there, came back, it was said, tuberculous, frostbitten, prostrated, maimed - human wrecks at the end of their tether. These men told terribly bizarre stories of roll-calls - to most people a novelty at the time - and drills and exertions, and races and beatings - hard, frightful beatings, which, it was said, they had not had the heart to describe in detail. Driven to work at five in the morning, they had toiled in hunger and cold until late in the evening, building roads and houses, erecting a large, new town on muddy land where villages had been razed to the ground, with training facilities for SS troops, and a prison camp for themselves. In the meantime, they lived in old sties, slept on bare floor boards, crowded together like the lice and fleas which plagued them till they were decimated by disease. Word of these spine-chilling occurrences was spreading ever wider and this at a time when most Jews in Cracow still lived relatively undisturbed in their own homes.

Arush had never met any of those unfortunate men who came back to Cracow, but his conception of Pustkow and of forced-labour camps in general had been formed by the stories that were attributed to them. Later, in Tarnow, he had heard many other accounts of Pustkow, admittedly incompatible with the earlier ones, and thus confounding him. But now in Szebnie he blocked the later stories from his mind. They were somehow not permitted to blur his initial imaginings of the place.

As soon as he heard on the Szebnie street about a "list for Pustkow", Arush began

124

comparing his present warm workshop, where the days passed without a stir or sting, with the terrifying vision of the camp to which they wanted to send him.

What a prospect! What a calamity! He must avert it, was his immediate resolve. He must do everything conceivable to get off the list. He felt a sudden challenge, a clear, identifiable object to strive for. Strangely, the new danger - or was it excitement? - caused him to lose something of the poignancy of his general dejection. His thoughts quickened, and the problem of how to wriggle out of the Pustkow net went ceaselessly round and round in his head.

"What am I so anxious about?" Arush was once again meditating "at work". Is it his desire of escaping Pustkow, or of remaining in Szebnie? Well, a cold and hungry place Pustkow undoubtedly was, but if craftsmen are required thither, then people must somehow manage to live there. He had to admit that he knew little about Pustkow at the present time. Was it just that he didn't like the idea of moving to an unknown place? And after all, who does? During this war in particular, people were horrified when they had to change quarters. Everyone considered a wrong compulsory removal. Quite clearly Arush had been wronged. But who had not been? Who could nowadays go anywhere of his own free choice? Still...So what is it? Funk? Fear of increased suffering? Not inconceivable. Yet, if he could only be sure that Pustkow didn't mean the end of all his sufferings, he would not hesitate to go there. His concern was to survive. He must do something about Pustkow.

The first man Arush approached to discuss this matter was Bunim Laib. He was an acquaintance of only a day, but on account of the special circumstance at which the acquaintanceship was struck, he was already a friend in whom, Arush felt, he could confide. It turned out that Bernard Laib, as he was formally named, was another *Leiter* at the tailor-workshop. Bernard assured Arush that he would do all he could to get him off the list. He would talk to Faulhaupt.

Laib had not promised much, but Arush sensed the man's sincerity and that he was on his side. Let him talk to Faulhaupt. Arush himself would not.

During the encounter, Arush also asked Laib, whose first language was German, if he knew what Dellmar had wanted of him. The first word, which had sounded to Arush like *zwetschen* was, Laib was certain, *zwecken*. What "to tack" meant, however, Arush thought it too much to ask. The other sinister word, Laib could only guess was *besatzen*, or trimming.

Laib, for his part, told Arush movingly of the personal tragedy that had befallen him not long ago in Szebnie. The story was too shocking, and Arush too absorbed with himself, to think of it then. Though he admitted to himself that his current trials were only a pale shadow of Laib's recent experiences.

The sense of injustice done to him rankled even more strongly in Arush's heart, next day in the workshop. Two or three out of a hundred had to move and they had to pick him. Just because he was alone, the sole remaining spokesman for his family. What a strange kind of justice! Surely it couldn't be the Germans who were showing all this concern not to break up families?

"And where is your sense of justice?" he asked himself. Didn't he want to save his

125

own skin at the expense of another fellow's bones? No, that wasn't true. They could cut down the list. Wouldn't a hundred and nineteen men be sufficient? Whoever could save himself had the right to do so. "Your own life comes first!" Arush suddenly recalled this ancient double-edged maxim, and the circumstances in which he had heard it discussed.

In June 1942, Sianka Raiwicz stood with her younger sister, Esta, at the extreme end of a crowd of captive people destined for "evacuation". Schachner, of the Gestapo of Tarnow, recognized them for they had a corset shop where his wife was a gratis patron. Then, at random, he ordered two other women to join the group which the Raiwicz sisters had left incomplete.

There wasn't a single person among those who knew all the details and circumstances of the case, who did not exonerate the two sisters of any blame - except perhaps Sianka and Esta Raiwicz themselves. Judging from their frequent and minutely detailed descriptions of the event, they must have suffered qualms of conscience, asking themselves if they had not contributed to the other two women's death. Even Michal Kuter, the most indignant of the self-righteous moralists, whose judgements of people caught up in arduous moral situations were the most pitiless that Arush could remember - even he pronounced the Raiwicz sisters guiltless. They didn't know the consequences to others of their changing groups, he said, and they had certainly not consciously done anything to cause the other two women to take their place. What could they have done? Should they have asked to go back, when they saw that other women were forced to replace them? That would have been impracticable, and of most doubtful effect. It had all happened so quickly, almost in a flash. Yes, in this sort of situation, Arush knew from what he heard, that decisions required spontaneity. In seconds, all possibility of redress, by deed or word, was gone.

A neighbour of the Raiwicz sisters, Zalman Herc, an acknowledged Talmudic scholar, whose opinion the two women especially valued, went so far as to tell them that even had they known the consequences of their action it would still have been right for them to change groups, as long as they did nothing themselves to select anyone else to replace them. It was for such circumstances, Zalman Herc said, that the ancient code, "Your own life comes first" was proposed, and it still held good.

Wasn't it like the case of the Nazi doctor who was told by his bishop that immoral orders, in his case selecting people for murder, must not be executed, though of course this did not mean he had to put his own life at risk. No, Arush quickly corrected himself, it was nothing of the kind. Quite apart from the fact that the doctor's life was not at risk if he refused to kill, and that, unlike the Raiwicz sisters, he had the power to choose an alternative course of action, in the doctor's case, he carried out the order by a physical act of his own. Oh, pondered Arush indignantly, that's a formula that could be stretched infinitely; if it were followed where would the killing stop? Who could not tell himself, his life was at risk? That bishop's rule would indeed make killing a religiously and morally admissible act.

But his own situation was similar to that of the Raiwicz sisters. Was it? Did their story illuminate his own problem? Arush was so absorbed with the analysis of the two cases and, in general, with the grisly Pustkow list, that he did not notice the needle slip from his hand.

The Raiwicz sisters had not been in the least instrumental in what happened. But for him the choice whether or not to try to get off the Pustkow list, was his alone. On the other hand, this was not a case between one group destined for life and one for death, but between two concentration camps. And the Germans had not asked for him personally. Did this matter? It did - though he wasn't too certain why. Well, he asked himself, weren't all those list-compilers acting as involuntary agents of the devil? Moreover, the Germans couldn't have meant him, since they required craftsmen. This exposed him to greater danger than it would a truly skilled work-man. If they found out, as they soon would, in a place such as Pustkow that he had sold them a pup - well, it was too frightful to think what would happen to him.

And he would only have himself to thank for it. Incredible, to have all this brought down on him by his own fault. By a silly fib. No, he had lied like a conjur-er. It served him right! And he told himself to get out of the falsehood while there was still time. Ah, Weltman! Weltman could get him off the hook. He would reclaim him. He would go to Dellmar. If only he would appear! Arush sighed.

To go himself to Dellmar or Faulhaupt and admit the lies was an idea unworthy of serious consideration. They would send him to Pustkow all the same, just to pun-ish him - even though this would make them culpable of the cheat involved.

It seems proper to explain our hero's moral compunction, which may give the impression that he was being rather hypocritical. A lie was a trifle in those depraved circumstances. And Arush Freund was certainly not a saint. No decent person considered it to be in the least wrong to lie to the Germans or to any of their hapless handy men. Yet the truth was that Arush still had a bad conscience about having deceived Dellmar - just him who was such a nice man. Inwardly, he also felt that lying was sinful, injurious to one's soul, and that in the long run it dis-torted one's personality. Now he had clear, demonstrable proof of what a lie did; the fact that he was on the list for Pustkow was an immediate retribution. Was it any wonder that he felt remorseful?

Did this mean that he ought to prefer his own greater danger? But that wasn't the question, Arush quickly retorted to himself. The question was not his own escape from going to Pustkow, but the possibility that he might cause another man to take his place, and someone who was not much more of a craftsman than he was. Yes, he had got it all muddled up. It was altogether too much for a man under such a strain. But he didn't give up. He couldn't; the thoughts connected with his problem were jamming his brain. He did, however, notice one immediate advantage of being put on the list. He wasn't ordered to sweep and scrub the floor of the work-shop at the end of the day. Nor were any of the other men on the list. This made him painfully aware that he really was moving to Pustkow. He felt crushed. Woebegone.

Arush emerged rebellious from the embrace of night. He had slept badly, waking up a number of times. Just before reveille he had a dream. The "get up" shouts put an abrupt end to it. In the dream, he was all set for departure, when he found himself running out of money for a train journey to some vaguely familiar but unidentified place. A tall, gentle lady, her face blurred, dressed in a dark grey overcoat with a towering, black astrakhan-fur collar, resembling one worn years ago by his mother, asked him if he wanted to borrow from her. In the morning he was mystified, his spirit agitated. His mother had insisted that every time her dead mother appeared to her in a dream before a day of crucial decision or crisis, everything later turned out well. Was it a good omen for him? He couldn't tell, he had no precedent to judge by. Two months and one day ago his mother was still alive. He had not dreamt of her since. He wasn't even sure if the woman who offered him a loan was his mother.

Unaffected by the uncertain interpretation of his dream, he decided in the end that in a situation like his, when a man did not know what was the right thing to do, he should follow his instincts. He did not wish to go to Pustkow and, listening to the voices of his heart, he felt no scruples about trying to elude the list. It's no disgrace to follow the dictates of one's heart, he told himself, nor to have the will to survive.

Later, continuing the debate in his mind - while no longer even touching a needle, in defiance or perhaps in the knowledge that, as a chosen evacuee, he would be overlooked - uncertainty and doubt crept in. Would his life be more unsafe, or any worse in Pustkow than it was in Szebnie? He was trying to escape transfer to another camp, but would such an escape really be good for him? He did not know. One never knew what action would in the long term be to one's advantage. Aciek Itzkowicz, who as a young and solitary prisoner, probably escaped the list because his barracks-senior had commandeered him to do some rough work in the camp when it was drawn up the day before, said that he wouldn't mind going to Pustkow. Arush did not doubt his sincerity, or suspect that he was only saying this because he was not being sent there; for he already knew that Aciek was eager for any change, and that Leser Szlaifstein, who was on the list, said the same. In the queue for bread that morning he had heard Baicz, from the carpenters' workshop, saying that he was glad to be leaving Szebnie. Arush understood that it required heavenly mercy to arrange that what a man wished and did turned out to be right for him.

However confused he was, Arush could not fail to notice that his attitude to his fellow prisoners was strangely changed. Aciek, whom he had found so agreeable at the beginning of the week, now bored him. "Keep quiet!" he snapped at him once. And he was impatient not only with him but with almost everyone else in the workroom. A gulf now seemed to separate him from the men who were to stay on in Szebnie. He felt amongst them like a spectator invited to a private gathering. And yet, when he asked himself why he was so anxious not to move to Pustkow, his first and foremost thought, apart from a vague fear of change, was that he "lived" among men like himself, people with whom he had so much in common - people, he had not forgotten, with whom he had been thrown together by coincidence only last week. What did it matter? Today they were congenial to him. In

Pustkow no one would give a damn about him. Here he had scores of nodding acquaintances, and closer ones, men who still had some consideration for Arush Freund; and, last not least, there were Laib and Weltman, his influential friends.

Weltman still had not shown up, five days since they had met, and Arush had already lost almost all hope of him. Yet strangely, whether because he liked his invention, or because he instinctively believed in Weltman's sincerity and devotion to him, not even once had Arush blamed him for his misfortune.

"I must not rely too much on my instincts," Arush admonished himself slightly, "nor put unreasonable trust in men." Yet he must look out for other influential connections. The next man Arush approached was Chanes. Chanes - what a surprise! He, too, turned out to be a Leiter, and by all appearances a top one; he was hardly ever seen in the common tailors' shop, spoke haughtily, and, the most obvious sign of supremacy, he wore a dark-blue, custom-made suit in which he looked strikingly elegant. So it appeared to Arush quite understandable that Chanes returned his greeting with marked reserve, but not without propriety.

Chanes! - he was from another world, Arush couldn't help reflecting. Memories crowded into his mind. It was four years since he had last seen him. Even then, circumstances had been so different from those of their initial encounter.

At home Arush had been the first to go out to work, and this he did entirely on his own initiative. The habit of wage-earning outside the family was neither long-established nor too widespread in Poland. To begin with, jobs were scarce, especially for Jews, in those years. For a person not desperate to earn a wage to seek employment was, to say the least, not in vogue. It was unseemly, if not wasteful, in a family like the Freunds. The daughters, having completed grammar school, continued taking private lessons - foreign languages, literature, history of the arts - visiting exhibitions, travelling abroad This they did for several years until they found a worthy, loving husband. Finding a husband wasn't difficult for them - more or less beautiful as they were, intelligent, witty, modest, from a "good home", and, last but not least, with a good dowry. Father Freund had enough to provide every one of his children with a sparkling piece of property when they married and left home. Ever since his middle years, it had been his pride and hope to be able to provide suitably for his sons and daughters. Hence, sons were not to work, they would study - education above all - with emphasis in their case on the traditional Jewish curriculum. In their early twenties they were expected to marry, and with a wife under their tutelary authority, to enter business on their own. An old beaten track.

But new winds were blowing in the 1930s. Arush could sense them perhaps less well than his older kin, but more resolutely. In the last spring of peace, he asked his uncle, the owner of a large firm in Cracow, to let him work at his business during the coming summer holidays. His uncle agreed.

It was on arrival for work at the shop that he first met Chanes. He remembered him standing behind a counter in a long, black, salesman's linen coat, a cap on his red head - the proprietor was orthodox - very deftly packing parcels. Oh, how neatly he cut the thick string with a swish of his fingers. Arush never exactly learned the trick. But he quickly learned many other things, and as the nephew of

129

the proprietor and an office worker, was treated with noticeable deference by the shop employees. A person of status. Even as a schoolboy.

The Jews of Cracow were shown special consideration by the German occupying forces. Two and a half months before other Jews in the General Government, they were ordered to mark their shops with a Star of David hung in windows. The order, which was issued through the intermediary offices of the prewar Polish deputy mayor, came into effect on the eighth of September, barely two days after Cracow had fallen to the German army. The same day all shops in town were ordered to open - though without the pretence of "business as usual".

The following week, Arush decided to "pop in" at the shop where he had worked for nearly two months in the summer. The owner and his family had fled, as had most of their employees, to the eastern part of Poland, which was soon to be occupied by the Soviets. Only one porter and two salesmen remained. They attended to the shop together with their young wives, who had tiny scissors hanging on a ribbon attached to their velvet sales uniforms, a memento of their previous work at a haberdasher's. On account of seniority, Chanes was the new, self-promoted manager.

The morning Arush came in, he was greeted by a loud chorus: "The fatherland is saved." This was not simply because he would help behind the counter, while people were literally besieging the shop (as they were almost every other shop in town) - but much more. Here at last was someone who would know where to find a letter or an invoice, know to calculate a price, at a time when prices were rising day after day, but when to charge a German customer much more than the prewar purchase cost was fraught with danger. One-off sales to a Jew were severely restricted; Germans, like many Polish customers, could wish to buy as much as there was to sell, but a Jew was forbidden to hold at any time more than two thousand Zloties, a commercially insignificant amount of money. How could they cope with all this? And how could they communicate with a German, who did not understand Yiddish? To the firm's present staff, Arush was their one hope, the man who could relieve them of these problems.

It was fairly late in October, when stocks of everything were almost exhausted, that a well-behaved major of the Wehrmacht came into the shop to snap up any commodity obtainable - coffee above all. He would have bought, and sent home to Dresden, hundredweights of it, but was offered only a few pounds. In the course of his ensuing bargaining with the softly spoken German officer - a manner of speaking which the Jews in their wishful thinking immediately took as a sign of resistance to Hitler - Chanes was effusively relating to him that, in short, the sacks he had found on inspection, contained coffee polluted during their passage at sea.

–"Perhaps it could be blended with the good coffee?" inquired the officer.

–"No, *Herr Major*, if you mix this coffee with this coffee, you'll *hargenen ab* both coffees." Chanes could murder coffee as well as a language, but the Dresdener had understood him.

Now, four years later, Chanes was interspersing his conversation with *stutzig*, with *derbes Luder*, with *schweingehabt*. How quickly people change! Only his hair, it seemed, remained red, but that mid-day on the Szebnie street, it was arranged with an undulatory care Arush had not noticed in earlier years.

When Arush made his request, Chanes reacted with affected anger.

–"Just you they want to send to Pustkow! Who put you on the list?"

–"Faulhaupt."

–"That Schwitzer! That bungler! Who does he think he is? I'll show him! I'll clip his wings! Did he have no one else but you? I'll grow hair here," Chanes pointed his right index finger into his left palm, "before you go to Pustkow."

It was reason enough for Arush to thank him profusely, but not to be too trustful.

In the evening, Arush went to see Zauber. Zauber who was the legendary wartime upstart of Tarnow, one of those moneyed men thanks to whom the JOINT (American Jewish Joint Distribution Committee) was able to dispense financial aid, reaching in the years 1940-1941 on average, the equivalent of five U.S. cents for every Jew living in the General Government. Believe it or not, five cents per soul!

Arush had no qualms about asking Zauber's help. It didn't bother him that Zauber had not enjoyed a particularly good reputation - indeed he was branded as a nouveau-riche, a man of "formerly no-substance".

To "make" money in those ruinous years - what a disgrace! How could it not invite suspicion? The man must be a rogue, a spoiler; only through thievery and plunder could he become rich. Well, in every socialist manual, especially the Yiddish editions, you could read that; no one came to riches by honest means.

It would be foolish to think that Zauber's money was a triumph of knightly purity. Early in the war, when most Jews were being swiftly dispossessed, he had the impudence to start a new manufacturing business. Together with a partner, he opened a factory, producing marmalade, under German control of course. Ersatz marmalade - yet a rarity, a luxury, in conditions of food shortage. The product, requisitioned by the provisions authority, was distributed on Polish ration cards. Nothing sensational, so far plain business. Less plain was his ability to produce from carrots, beetroot and sweeteners acquired on the side, more marmalade than the prescribed quantity, and to sell this surplus through that formidable institution, known as the black market; an institution on which millions of people had so far survived the occupation, and on which the Jews at least depended for virtually all their essential provisions.

Still - profiteering, black-marketeering, feeding on the misery of others, stirred other peoples' narrow emotions; the received social sense of probity suffered; moral censure inevitably followed. But was it honest? Who in this war was not a black-marketeer? A speculator, as anyone engaged in any kind of gainful initiative was popularly called. Who had not lived outside the law? Could anyone, especially a Jew, live otherwise?

Not everyone, only a few of course, made fortunes, and it was this that was pilloried, and will be surely criticized even more strongly from a distance and in the abstract. When all are poor, it's a crime to be rich; when people are starving it's offensive to be sated; when men grow thin it's revolting to gain weight.

Was it really wrong, Arush asked himself, to be affluent in the midst of penury? He wasn't fastidious about men-of-formerly-no-substance either. He pondered how far back Jews "of-formerly-substance" dated in Poland? Seventy-five years ago, he was taught, there wasn't a bank where one could hold an account - the essence of "substance". He had heard that the progenitors of our brave and mighty brothers, the would-be censors of wartime Jewish money-makers, reached the shores of America and Palestine devoid of all substance. He was, of course, well aware of Zauber's slight grossness. He remembered how he had heard him guffawing in the face of Rabbi Maleachi, before whom, out of reverence, most people were afraid to utter a sound. Zauber would know who he, Arush Freund, was. A river-bed doesn't dry up completely, even in a desert like Szebnie. He must still have money, which means influence. And he was a first cousin of Falban, who had himself only last week shown Arush compassion. No one had seen Falban since his arrival in Szebnie. He kept himself isolated in the sanctum of the high-command-prisoners' barracks. But his cousin would be able to reach him.

An orderly agreed to pass a message to Zauber. He came out from the darkness of the barracks into the black night, where Arush was waiting. He told Zauber pathetically why he had called him and humbly asked for his help.

A man of about fifty, Zauber spoke to Arush in a fatherly manner, with unexpected tenderness.

–"Yes my child. But you see, tomorrow there's to be a roll-call. If this passes safely, I'll do everything I can to release you from going to Pustkow."

–"Oh what a fool you are," Arush reproved himself on the way back. "Everyone except you has heard of the roll-call." He then realized that in his six days in Szebnie, there had not been a roll-call. It's this, he reasoned, that apparently makes tomorrow's roll-call suspicious, and why Zauber was so visibly worried.

Where could he go now? The camp was plunged in total darkness. For reasons unknown to common prisoners, all the lights had gone out. Only, at long intervals, a makeshift searchlight gleamed through the night, making it possible for a while, to tell earth from sky, a barracks from empty space.

"There's nothing I can do now," Arush thought. Nor, on such a night, would he even bother about Pustkow. His only concern was to reach his barracks, and while he was trying to feel his way, he predicted silently that next day rumours would claim an attempted mutiny, which for unforeseeable, or unknown, reasons had failed. Once, he grumbled in silence, when the powder-magazine had exploded in Cracow on the eve of Pentecost, it was, people said, because that spring of his childhood, the town was short of cheese for the festival; and only the last summer before the war, when the Warsaw railway station had burnt down (probably arson by German saboteurs) the public attributed the disaster to sacrilege committed at a nearby church a couple of days earlier. Nowadays, in more war-like spirit, when the electricity went out, or a train was cancelled, it was immediately a revolt, an uprising.

He was of course angry - angry at himself, at his helplessness, his preoccupation

132

with what suddenly seemed to him trifles, angry at the crippling darkness, angry against the whole accursed place - and, deep inside, apprehensive about what the morning would bring.

But when at last he was up on his bunk, he asked himself: "Will there be no roll-call, or will it be any shorter, if I don't sleep?"

CHAPTER TEN

At five, in the dead of night, the day began - Thursday. Shrieking shouts: *"Auf! Auf!"* Not just one, as on normal mornings, but several OD men yell out together: *Auf!* Up! All up! *Appel!* (roll-call!) They sound menacing today, and today they flail their sticks.

"Schnell (quick) *Schnell, Appel, schnell!"* Today they shout only in German, louder and louder, as if they wish to outshout one another.

Some prisoners have risen earlier. Arush is sound asleep when the uproar starts. He has to get up in haste, and is shaking with cold.

–"Will there be coffee?"

–"No!" bellows the OD man to whom the question was addressed by a prisoner who knew him well.

A new wave of clamour. *"Raus! Raus! Aber raus* (but out)!" Shouting their hollow threats the OD begin to drive the men out of the barracks.

"Everyone to his workshop! Take everything with you!"

They move hurriedly, searching the barracks, every bunk and nook, with their electric torches - more a token of superiority than a means of intimidation - shining them in the faces of prisoners, increasing their distraction.

"Out, onto Appelplatz! Everybody line up with his barracks! Leave your belongings!"

Conflicting orders. Confusion, chaos, which perhaps the clamour and haste are intended to conceal. Nobody seeks an explanation.

Excitement rises gradually, and in the midst of the turmoil, in the thick of the jostling and hustling crowd, Arush feels lonely, completely forsaken. The ordinary inmates remain silent in their agitation, mute in pain. Nobody speaks of his forebodings, nobody dares to speak. But it is Arush's first roll-call and he would like to know what its routine will be. He finds the courage to ask Lipschitz who arrived in Szebnie in September.

–"Nobody knows. One thing is certain: it'll take hours... In any case be prepared!"

–"Be prepared," Arush repeats to himself. "Prepare yourself. You must be strong." And he utters a short, fervid prayer.

On the sodden ground outside, in the tumult and hurry-scurry shouts that mingled with the murmur of hundreds of thrilling voices, and shrilling whistles, anxiety was still greater. It was also wet and chilly, the air smelled foul, there was no light in heaven - and on earth a few yellow glowing lamps turned the black of night into greyish darkness.

Orders blared in authentic hard, but not too harsh, German from an indiscernible loud-speaker, were echoed obstreperously by OD men. *"Achtung!"* *Achtung!"* resounded from all sides. The huge space of the Appelplatz, normally the camp street, was completely packed with human creatures, terrified and seemingly unruly men who were rumbling through the darkness, driven on, here and there, by no less confused and frightened orderlies, shouting at the top of their voices.

"Form lines! Five abreast! Silence! Silence! *Achtung!* To attention!" At last they were standing in deep columns, face to neck in front, arranged according to barracks, separated from each other by ample space, through which the OD men continued to race as if possessed by demons.

"Don't move! *Achtung!* Look straight ahead!"

At the far end of his barracks, which formed the back of the column, stood Arush, erect, still, and watchful.

Not certain at first of what he was seeing, he suddenly made out disconnected shapes rising out of the misty darkness. He could only steal glances sideways, and for a while he thought that it was a delusion, the nocturnal vision of a sleep-dazed mind. But then, there was no more room for doubt. Dim figures were moving continually, a silent procession of ghosts.

It was alarming, so alarming that Arush was at once covered with goose-flesh.

The images were marching stiffly, in measured steps, looking straight ahead, with horizontally held machine-guns in their hands, finger on trigger. An air of calamity descending in their wake.

On and on they moved in single file until they had unobtrusively surrounded the prisoners waiting at attention. Then they turned on the square, their faces, stony and swarthy, like the muzzles of the automatic guns they directed at the encircled columns. From then on they stood firm and motionless in place, twenty paces from one another. Wherever you turned, a fence of dark, lifeless beasts faced you. Behind them, yet another fence of thick, barbed-wire. And above them watch-towers, on which sentries kept guard, their machine-guns pointed at the same stationary target.

Stationary they were indeed, the poor men, who remained standing impassively, looking straight in front of them, as they had been ordered. What else could they do? Start moving and shouting? What sense would it make? No, their fate might be sealed, but they would await it calmly. Inside their bodies, though, they were burning, burning to do something, and shuddering. The pre-dawn cold was hard on them. This overcast November morning was chilly and wet. Snow flakes, lazily melting in the drizzling rain, soaked into the grim and grimy ground of the Appelplatz. It seemed as if the leaden, lightless skies were in silent league against the hapless men. Arush Freund, for one, could not stop shivering.

Immediately he perceived the deployment of armed guards, Arush realized its true, baneful meaning. He could see they were doomed. "It's the end," he repeated over and over in his mind. As soon as the encirclement was completed, he awaited wild shooting - as it happened at the start of every Aktion - to inspire terror. But they did not shoot.

Numbers were to be checked at the roll-call, but they did not do that, either. What was the point? People's pockets will be checked instead, came an announcement

"Money and gold, all objects of value, hand them in!" the loud-speaker roared. "Under strict penalty of the code!"

The OD men moved around with baskets, like those - an image rose before Arush's eyes - in which laundry used to be carried to and from the mangle. Men threw everything out of their pockets with curious eagerness, almost with malicious enjoyment. Spoons, pens, combs, mugs clanged into the baskets. Arush didn't stir, he had nothing, and his fingers were too numb to turn out his pockets. "Search, if you wish," he said to the OD man who approached him.

–"Watch out, and keep your mouth shut! For your own good!"

But discipline was temporarily relaxed, and in their deep anxiety some prisoners asked the OD men what was going to happen?

–"You'll get personal notification," was one sarcastic answer, which was also intended to pretend that the OD was in the know.

–"Achtung! Achtung! Stand to attention! Look straight ahead of you!"

The collection was over.

The roll-call went on. The men continued to stand still and grow cold.

Arush felt the cold was atrocious. He was thinking that the frost had set in, and that he was not dressed for it - and, dammit, it was all through his own folly. From almost the first weeks of war it had been the fashion to sport spencer-jackets. To wear a normal long overcoat was considered slow, clumsy, dronish, middle-class. In a short overcoat one looked smart, agile, diligent, workman-like. The day before the roll-call, as he was resignedly preparing himself for despatch to Pustkow, Arush had been to the Bekleidungsbarracke (clothing barracks) to exchange his heavy, double-quilted, winter overcoat for a stout jacket. In the dim light of the barracks, he could not see what he had chosen. He tried on blindly a number of short coats and took the one in which he felt comfortable. It was only at the roll-call that he had seen what he was wearing: a light-woollen ladies' jacket, with high turn-up cuffs and choice buttons - it must have been a very tall, but not big, woman, dressing with some taste, Arush thought. "You fat-head! You transvestite!" Mourning his warm overcoat, he swore at his damned silliness which made him now, on the Appelplatz, more exposed to frost. Oh, that the earth would open under his feet and swallow the whole horrid place! It was all one to him. He had no regrets at losing his direful life. And the thought of losing it in grand biblical style gave him a strange touch of comfort, almost a feeling of a happy ending.

"What are they waiting for?" was the question that was constantly on his lips, as it must have been on the lips of all the quietly shivering prisoners. Nothing was happening. No activity, no movement, no sign of the roll-call coming to an end. Only the OD men roamed about, aggressively urging the waiting rows of prisoners not to talk, or to look sideways - they were considered to be standing to attention. The still dog-like servility of the OD men must have appeared distasteful to others as well as to Arush. But they hurt no one. Probably nobody ordered them to.

Yet it seemed sheer madness for them to assume anything other than the end. At least Arush did not deceive himself about what concerned him personally. It was useless and stupid; in the last moments of one's life simply disgraceful. If the Germans knew what they were waiting for, he and his fellow-prisoners standing stock still in the biting cold, were just awaiting whatever was to come upon them. He could not wait any longer. It was pointless. Weariness overwhelmed him. He couldn't stir a toe. With leaden legs, fastened to the ground, he was turning into a pillar of ice.

His thoughts were suddenly diverted, though not for long. Grzimek came swaggering between the petrified columns. He appeared satisfied, and abnormally, was without Rolf. "Too cold for dogs to stroll," Arush observed mutely. The Lagerführer even accosted a prisoner or two, and spoke to them quietly - with a sarcasm that was not instantly recognized. All the men were wet. The rain, blown spasmodically by wind fell sideways, collecting in a rivulet of water that trickled down a prisoner's face. Grzimek - so the whispers had it, comforted the man: "You'll dry your face and clothes after the roll-call is over."

Hope? Satanic guile?

Futile questions to ask, when there was no shelter, no refuge from cold, when you couldn't escape the dripping rain, nor the overpowering weariness.

Arush felt the cold piercing to the marrow of his bones, dragging heavily on the heart. He had the sensation of imminent subsidence. His body seemed to crumble away. With the waiting, torpid, hopeless waiting, he felt his defences falling apart. His spirit of not yielding to death was progressively disappearing; his interest in being was almost lost.

He was still sufficiently aware to notice when the light of dawn came through the fence of clouds and haze. The sun did not. It wouldn't come out, it would never shine on this place. So, he reasoned, it must already be at least eight o'clock. Nearly three hours. Unlike Arush and his fellows, time was not standing still, after all.

Daylight did not diminish the terror that darkness had seemed to increase. It became more dangerous to turn one's eyes or head, and what now became visible was not reassuring. None the less, the arrival of day, however grey and misty, brought some good as well. A prisoner could now watch his breath, giving him something to do, and, no less important, further strategic positions came into view. The loud-speaker, from which the orders came, was located, along with a field telephone and a heavy machine-gun pointed straight at the columns, on the roof of the guard-block - the same one at which registration had taken place a week ago, but which today had apparently been turned into operational headquarters.

At its base, about sixty yards from the first line of prisoners, there could be seen Sturmbannführer Willy von Haase, flanked by Amon Goeth and Hans Kellermann. Later in the day Oberführer Scherner himself would arrive. Around them gathered the whole caboodle of lesser rank SS death-heads. But there was remarkably little fussing about.

As the day passes, they will be making a few speeches. Von Haase, who is in command, will speak first, followed, at some intervals, by his two second-in-command. Oh, how they all relish making speeches! Even Grzimek, as the Lagerführer, will not be denied the pleasure of addressing the prisoners. With apparent gusto, he tells them how sorry he is that Szebnie could not furnish them with work appropriate to their skills. But in the camp they have been assigned to by the German leadership, everyone will have the opportunity to do the work which suits him best.

Arush could not be fooled by all this oratory, least of all by Grzimek's. He hardly listened to it, or to anything other than the silent voice of his own thoughts. Indifference and apathy had been steadily gaining on him. He was feeling desperately faint. Hacking hunger, though reminding him of his existence, sharpened the sensation of cold and weakness. He could not feel his flesh or his bones. His whole body was crying out in a single howl of pain. He had reached the point of wishing to die.

Simply to cease suffering. No other motive. Just a natural desire to find refuge from unbearable torment; nothing but a sensible longing to be released of all sorrow on earth. By late morning, he had hardly a thought for anything but how to end his suffering. No lust for living, once so boundless in him. Not a tremor at the thought of his death; the cold and the weariness were stronger than all fear. Not even the other world, which had so often preoccupied him in the past, came now earnestly into his mind. His must have been the feeling of people committing suicide.

What can you expect in such a state of body and mind? What can you imagine that he, that any of them can do? As it is, you wait quietly - because you are reconciled to your fate. You show no fear because you have none. You stay serene for you desire the end. You keep silent for this is the peculiar privilege of death. Anyway it's so much more dignifying. You do not resist, because you are convulsed, exhausted and overwhelmed by the display of their sheer fire power; but because they don't shoot at you, there's still that crippling uncertainty, confused with hope. Whether there's hope or not, is a matter decided by your individual belief. And just in order that you stand still, do not move, do not jump at them - they don't shoot.

Oh, they never shoot at you when you want them to, they may even miss, Arush concluded in dull submission.

There was still one question that preoccupied him: how to die quickly? Quick death is definitely preferable to slow death - like the one he is dying. Why prolong the suffering if it can be cut short? No, his life is so bitter that death could not come too quickly. And with this wish, which overcame the usual fear of death, he began thinking of the way the wish could be granted - of the shot which would bring his existence to an end.

He was standing most auspiciously in the last row, his back to the guards positioned behind him. No prisoner, no obstacle, between their line and his, nothing to shield him from them. Where would the bullet hit him? In the head, preferably. No! Usually they do it, neatly, in the neck. Stretch your neck! Expose it! A single shot would do it. Amazing, one bullet and a whole life is extinguished. How insignificant is man! Years of learning and wisdom, riches and power, of life begetting and life sustaining, and here comes one little bullet and ends it all. Yet a bullet was what he wished. Just a nick. A painless, instant death, without even knowing if and when.

He started to imagine the bullet and, then, what it would be like to be dead. He saw himself lying on the ground in a pool of blood. The blood was hot, however icy cold he was when alive. Steam was mounting, and so was the temperature, making his lifeless limbs warm again. He could almost feel the marvellous sensation of spreading warmth. Oh, what bliss to be lying tranquil and warm! No longer to have to stand motionless and frozen. To be free from this terrible suffering. No more feeling of cold and pain. No more feeling alone in the world.

What comes later? The great mystery would not bother him now. He was not obliged, he reasoned with considerable relief, and too tired, to think at all, let alone of what he would do as a dead man. Anyway, the experience was not transmissible. Of course, it would be nice to capture the entirety of his life, this side and beyond, his short mournful passage through raging streams of blood and tears; to embrace it all, not to miss a single detail, and to hand it down. He is reconciled to the inevitable. No point in regrets. With God's help the House of Jacob will not die out with Arush Freund.

While Arush's thoughts were thus, for some time, fixed on death, becoming increasingly giddy as he brooded over the futility of his existence and the delights of lifelessness, he missed a sudden stir on the hitherto still and stale Appelplatz. But somehow the noise from the loud-speaker cut through the blank wall of his brain. He then perceived that, at short intervals, names of prisoners were being called out and that those called were running speedily from all directions towards new assembly lines at the far-right of where he was standing.

"Szlaifstein, Leser!"

Did he hear correctly?

Then several names later: "Popper, Naftali!"

That's the childish-looking boy, who, like him, had not been required to clean up the workshop on Tuesday evening. Pustkow? No, he couldn't believe it at first. Yet the possibility of it being true, kindled in him a flicker of hope, an instant gleam of life.

"Baicz, Gimpel!" beamed through the air.

"Oh, mother! What have I done? What'll now happen?" Arush whispered anxiously under his breath. On hearing the latest name, his doubts began to vanish. The chance of yet another, however temporary, escape and of leaving Szebnie electrified him, shaking him out of his lethargy. To his amazement, he soon realized that what he really wished was not to die, but to live, as strongly as before. Suddenly he felt some strength and youth within him again.

Yet as soon as his first doubts receded - particularly after hearing over the loud-speaker the name of Klacki, the carpenter from whom he had first learned the purpose of the list - others took hold of him. First, what if his name had already been called out before he, in his demented blackout, had begun listening to what was going on?

No! This could not have happened, he felt certain, because the OD men were watching to make sure that after each name was called out, a man started running. But still he had not heard his own name, and it was among the first to be taken - at least in his workshop. Had they acceeded to his entreaties? Were his prayers granted? "What have I done?" was his recurring self-reproach. "Terrible, what a damned fool I am! The greatest dolt on earth."

With every new name that was called, but not his, Arush's agony rose. Minutes, or strictly speaking, names dividing life from death, were literally running out before his eyes. He began feverishly to weigh the chances of still being, or not being, on the list.

Zauber could not have interceded yet on his behalf. Chanes, who knows? He had only half a day to act, and he had not shown much interest, let alone enthusiasm, for pleading for him. But Bunim Laib! He had been sympathetic and compassionate. He was willing to help him. He may have succeeded. He must have done.

Had he? Laib wasn't too influential a Leiter, and was trying not to call attention to himself. How he had trembled on that morning of Grzimek's stroll through the camp street and Rolf's subsequent banquet! Nor was Laib persuasive enough to have swayed Faulhaupt, let alone his superiors, to get him off the list, once he was on it. But is he still on it? "Oh, merciful God help me! With your help everything is still possible!"

There was a longer interval in the roll-calling. For two or three minutes it seemed as if it had come to an end. Arush was desperate. Time was for him balanced on a knife-edge. In the silence he could hear the loud alarm of his heart-beat, undampened by the murmur of dropping rain and the sobs of wind.

Another spate of names - but not his. "Just my luck! Bad-luck always pursued me." Arush was preparing himself for the worst, so as not to be killed by sheer anguish - self-inflicted at that.

As more names followed, he calculated that there must have already been a hundred and twenty. It was useless to deceive himself anymore. Other people resist their destruction, he obstructed his survival. Hoist with his own petard. At least he, the blockhead, would have proved that a man's destiny rests upon his own actions.

Again a name, and another one, was called - that must surely be all? It can't go on any longer. Good-bye Pustkow! Good-bye to you, and your silly life!

But then, after a few more names, it reverberated like a thunderclap:"Freund, Arush!"

He began to run as fast as he could. He knew by then that his earlier feeling of total exhaustion was a matter of feeble spirit rather than of feeble body. Nevertheless the surge of power within him that made him race ahead so quickly, came as a genuine surprise, for frozen and numb he certainly was.

Arush reached the new column to fill the last row of five men. Perhaps no one else had had to cover such a long distance as he. So he could not tell for certain if his name had been the last one called.

Another check and another count, every one of the guards satisfying himself separately, and at last the column of a hundred and twenty men was marched away from the battle-field strewn with standing corpses.

Midday must have been well past, when the men of the Pustkow contingent entered the clothing-barracks, the same one in which Arush had only yesterday exchanged his overcoat. They were locked up inside and strictly forbidden to lean out of the windows; unless you did, the Appelplatz, some fifty yards to the left, could not be seen from the barracks.

Yes, this barracks had proper windows, with panes, and doors, and a wooden floor. It was of course unheated. But who could relate the blissful sensation of warm comfort that the half-frozen and inhumanly tired men experienced when they lay down on the floor. To make room, the clothes scattered all around were heaped onto one side. Bolder men would later dare to substitute them for pillows. Meanwhile, it was strangely quiet; no one uttered a superfluous word, whether from fatigue, heavily leaden limbs and hearts, or as a token of deep sentiment for the men still standing outside. What other manifestation of solidarity was left?

Before very long, darkness descended over the earth - a measure of the time they had spent on the Appelplatz - and everyone in the barracks fell, some sooner some later, asleep.

The initial delight of the men who were temporarily reprieved was irrepressible, and even after more sombre thoughts returned next day, the feeling of relief at having avoided death remained with them all. But Arush also felt genuinely uneasy in his reflections.

"I was lucky," he repeated again and again in his mind. "Strangely, this time I didn't believe I would escape it. All the same it wasn't today; as for the morrow, I'm still alive; and as long as one lives there's hope. The most important thing now is to get away from here." To worry about Pustkow, about going there as a qualified furrier - the reason for his miraculous escape - was at the time simply impossible - incompatible with human nature. What he pondered over remorsefully, as he lay on the floor of the dark barracks, was his calm, his egoistic apathy, in face of his fellows' doom. "All that matters is that it's not you.

"Well, and what if it were you too?" he asked himself. But he could find no better answer than, "Nothing".

Just a thought.

Upon awakening, Arush felt restored; sleep healed, made events more distant than in time alone - a prisoner's best friend. And soon breakfast came.

They were let out of the barracks, and allowed to stay around it. The prisoners who brought the breakfast, and the OD men who accompanied them, were unusually gentle, their eyes glittering respect, an expression of homage to the good fortune of men chosen to leave Szebnie. But they were curiously reticent; no spare word was spoken, no question answered.

A hush began to spread among the waiting group as well. It was difficult to talk. A glimpse at the Appelplatz revealed that it was empty - an emptiness filled with wreck and ashes. The sight weighed them down by its void, overwhelmed them by its depth.

Arush withdrew into the quiet of the barracks. He tried, but was unable to think of anything but the surroundings. The memories of yesterday shut out everything else from his mind. While his elation over yesterday's miraculous escape had not yet completely cleared, heavy-heartedness re-imprisoned him. He had lost his reason to die, but had not regained a reason to live. He was insensate, yet deeply affected. He felt as though he were two men at the same time. Strange? Well, to feel a little as he felt, you must really experience what he had just undergone.

At times he was not sure if it was all true - a dream or reality? One thing was certain, that grief and remorse must be postponed till later. He would worry again, when he reached Pustkow. Now all he wanted was to get away from Szebnie. To start a new life. Yes, to leave this place was like beginning a whole new existence.

As the hours passed by, he became more and more overcome by melancholy, made worse by waiting, boredom and recurring doubt. Would they ever leave?

Next morning brought no change, no announcement, no news. But with the men who brought soup at noon, Weltman slipped in. Arush was delighted to see him. This time it was he who shook Weltman's hand more warmly. But they did not smile, nor did they talk. Oh, how difficult it was to talk! They just stood impassively and looked at each other, as if dumb.

At last Weltman blurted out: "I couldn't come."

Arush wanted to speak, but only gestured that he understood.

–"Monday morning, Kellermann ordered us not to leave the compound of the castle. 'For your own good,' he warned, 'let no one try to steal through to the camp.' We worked during the day. At night some of us slept in the garage, some in the stable."

He fell silent once more.

After a while he began again, in short, broken phrases.

–"I had to come. I wondered...I hoped you were perhaps here."

"They stood on the Platz till 10.30. Then, in groups of five hundred, they were ordered to march. Two miles to Moderówka railway station. Surrounded all the way by extra guards. Whole battalions. Along both sides of the road, lorries with blazing headlights. And heavy machine-guns on the lorries. Every hundred yards floodlight projectors. Full daylight. In the silence of night, we could hear the awful sound of the tread of hundreds of feet and the hum of human voices. It was so terrifying...Nothing we could do...

"At the station, according to Gicher, the OD man who was there on duty, before mounting the train came the order: Shoes off! Coats off! Jackets, sweaters, ties..."

–"Because of the cold?" Arush interrupted to ask.

–"Not just that. *Hauptstelle* (head office) standing orders. Not to strip off the dead. It's easier and more economical to strip the living. *Werterfassung*."

–"What is this?" Arush heard this term for the first time.

–"All that business of plunder and enrichment. Besides, they can take the cream of the cake for themselves. It's either here or there, where the prey is going to. Why leave the share-out to others?

"I'm telling this badly," Weltman felt it necessary to excuse himself for his dryness and sarcasm, which he feared might be misinterpreted, "it's just a pale shadow of what really took place."

Arush nodded approvingly, thinking at the same time that any story a Jew could tell of wartime life would only be a shadow of reality.

—"About five hundred - including us working at the castle, all the top functionaries, OD men, most of the doctors, nurses, cooks, master-craftsmen, largely with their families - remained. Left to clean up the camp. All the rest went..."

He paused a few moments for breath, then continued, speaking more rapidly and more vigorously.

—"The job at the station over, they arrived to celebrate at the castle as Kellermann's guests. Countess Graykowa says the revelry that followed surpassed anything in the past, in loudness and disturbance. She couldn't imagine that such pandemonium and rowdyism were possible. Shouts, riotous laughter and music mixed with the sound of shattered glass, broken fittings, and gun-play. An almost continuous fusillade. Victory all the way..."

Arush listened stoically, suppressing his disgust, prudently allowing Weltman to conclude his tale.

—"At one stage, Kellermann, with undeniable flair, rode into the drawing-room on his horse. This must have won wide applause from the audience, for it became the rage of the party. The mare, apparently scared witless, peed - as pools of urine, next to larger puddles of vomit, indicated hours later - and thus raised the orgiastic frenzy to a climax. The most honoured company roared orders at Kellermann, egging him on and on, but the countess wouldn't say to do what.

"But at half-past nine in the morning, even the highest-ranking guests were already rested, polished up, and, after breakfast, stuffed their elegant suitcases into their limousines and drove away.

"When they had gone, Kellermann summoned the countess for help, and she said, if she hadn't seen the havoc with her own eyes, she would never have believed it. Window panes, crystal glass, chandeliers crushed to tiny pieces. Every single piece of furniture smashed. Locks, door-handles pulled out. Countless bullet holes in walls, in doors, and in ceilings. The floor covered with plaster and litter. Everywhere soiled. Everywhere muck.

"Legions of workers, masons, decorators, carpenters, glaziers, electricians, were quickly mobilized from Jasło and Krosno, to put the house straight. Kellermann, unable to stand the sight of his home's devastation, has fled to the camp. He hasn't returned yet. That's how I managed to slip away today."

Weltman suddenly looked around, added quickly, "Keep well," and was off. Arush watched him running, merely able to follow him with his eyes and thoughts, as he vanished over the horizon.

The soup-barrel-bearers had long gone.

Still that afternoon, before the sun hid completely, the hundred and twenty prisoners departed.

It was much later in Pustkow that Arush learned through a chain of Polish prison-

143

er-contacts what had happened to his former fellow inmates of Szebnie.

Of the four thousand or so men, women and a few children who were sent off by train, two thirds were on arrival in Auschwitz immediately despatched to death.

On the Monday following the departure of Arush and his group, another selection took place at Szebnie. Kellermann was severely reprimanded by his superiors for having left so many prisoners in *Aufräumung,* and was ordered to reduce their number to a hundred. Four hundred men and women were killed about noon. Later that evening, from among the remaining one hundred, all who had worked at the castle, and hence were privy to the goings-on there, were personally picked out by Kellermann, and shot dead. This he did, rumour had it, on specific orders, suggesting that his superiors were deeply displeased with his conduct.

Before the year's end, Commandant Kellermann was himself arrested. Some said it was because on that memorable victory-night he refused orders to make love to his mare. Another rumour attributed his misfortune to a suspicion that, in return for a mint of money, he had turned a blind eye to the escape from Szebnie of a group of prisoners (including Zauber and Falban). However others, more reliably, maintained that Kellermann was charged with misappropriation of "state property". What was right for Oberführer Scherner, or even a Sturmbannführer von Haase wasn't right for Kellermann, a mere Hauptsturmführer. Still others gave broader reasons for his arrest. Kellermann, they explained, was not liked by his bosses, who felt that he didn't quite fit into their pack.

It is said that the wicked do not repent even at the gates of hell - but some perhaps do inside the gates of prison?

Poor Hans Kellermann. He came from afar to Szebnie, where, on the quiet graveyard of thousands, he hoped for nothing but sweet, good life, and found a cup of sour wine.

PART THREE

Oasis in Evil

CHAPTER ELEVEN

The journey was over. The convoy halted. The prisoners agape; the great unknown before them. Through the half-open rear of the lorry the camp came into partial view as dark shapes of structures rising above the ground.

It was evening, a cool, wet November evening. For two weeks the weather had been wretched. Yet the air was mysteriously calm, the place strangely whispering calm, it seemed to Arush. What sort of place would it be? They had arrived almost without any sensation of dread, curiously, even without that usual fear of change. After the shock and turmoil of the last days, nothing could frighten them, and it had dawned on Arush Freund that this might be why the place seemed calm.

However, their admission to camp was relatively calm, too, and short. There were none of the usual attentions connected with such occasions; no selection, no guards with guns or dogs, no smell of blood and death. Not even, surprisingly, searchlights trained from towers to disperse darkness. It all took place in the pale light that was gleaming through the doors and windows of the barracks. The mustering SS men, their faces hardly visible, were anything but gentle, but they displayed neither brutality nor unusual bustle. If anyone was bustling, it was their aides from among the local prisoners, men of unknown identity and status, who sounded firm and resolute, but not frightening. The only frightening things were some shadowy, lean figures walking by with slow, swaying gait and equally slow movements.

The counting over, the orders issued, the new arrivals were led straight from the roll-call into a nearby barracks, from which moments earlier the last of the walking shadows had been hurried away.

The large room into which they were brought added to the mystery of the place. Windowless, faintly though electrically lit, it was completely empty, with two parallel rows of holes, spaced a yard apart, in the middle of the clean, green concrete floor. Arush was quite baffled by it. A gym-hall? But what were the holes for? What did the masters intend to do with them? As he had held back since noon, he thought of urinating into one of the holes, but was frightened. The holes aroused inexplicable awe in him. When minutes later he saw others urinating in them without hesitation, and understood what the holes were for, Arush laughed inwardly. He suddenly recalled a funny story about the peasant prime minister, who, as he was spitting on the floor of a Warsaw restaurant, had a spittoon placed beside him, and said to the waiter: "If you don't take that thing away, I'll spit into it." This anecdote (spread by right-wing opponents of the man) generated another memory. But he was prevented from diving further into the past, by voices of the present, faceless voices of human ghosts, who yet spoke normally, even energetically, and in defiance of orders just issued to them.

Countless questions flew through the wall. Where have you come from? What news from Tarnów? Rzeszów? Cracow? When did it happen? And so on.

The men inside the barracks asked in turn: what sort of camp is it? How long have you been here? What kind of work is there?

They did not ask about food.

Among the urgent questions and answers a choice morsel of news filtered through: "Kiev has fallen!"

All were elated, possibly thinking, with Arush, that a camp where news like this was circulating could not be such a bad place.

– "Quite propitious," Arush said to Baicz, who stood next to him. "To arrive at a new camp on the day Kiev is re-taken is undoubtedly a good omen."

Baicz remarked that although the men looked drained of bodily strength, they spoke quite normally, adding: "How soon will we look like them?"

Arush nodded, signifying that he had already asked himself this question. But he was not inclined to worry about it in advance. Not after Szebnie. He did not even intend to worry about his supposed craft, though this problem had begun to intrude into his mind ever since they had set out on the journey. Baicz had acquired some knowledge of ironwork and seemed quite at ease on that score.

From behind the wall they heard voices calling: *Lagerschluss*, camp closure (the particular meaning of which Arush was to learn later), and the shadowy prisoners outside rushed into their barracks. Inside the one with holes in the floor, which so blatantly contradicted a human dwelling, all the hundred and twenty men settled to sleep on the cold concrete.

The day, that is camp day, had hardly begun before they were driven out of the latrine. In the mornings there had always been a little crush inside, but the stink was not too bad. Formally still forbidden to communicate with the other prisoners, the newcomers were held together in isolation, and then made to stand in lines as on the evening before.

In daylight they had their first sight of the place. The camp lay in open barren country - somewhat fitting one's imagination, as Pustków means waste and solitude - closed off on all sides with thick rows of barbed wire. In its narrow, just visible confines, the camp enclosure formed a rectangle, measuring nearly two hundred yards in length and about a third less in width. The first things to catch the eye were dark-brown smartly built wooden barracks, each with an entrance door and wide windows opening onto the camp square. The two on the east side, one behind the other, were the prisoners' dwelling barracks. Several yards further to the east, a threefold wire fence divided the Jewish camp from the Polish one.

At the northern side of the rectangle stood a barracks with separate entrances to the latrine, washroom, and the kitchen, all three divided by an inner wall. To the right a much smaller barracks housed the camp infirmary. To the west, was an open space and on a clear day one could see, well over a mile away, the dark shapes of a wood. At the north-west and south-west corners of the compound were two gates, one leading to the Polish camp and further on to the guards' quarters and camp-command building; the other, at the southern corner, led to the workshop extension of the camp. Above that gate rose a solid watch-tower, on which, day and night, stood a guard with a machine-gun. There were, of course, more watch-towers, but they were not visible from the Jewish camp area. The remainder of this enclosure was just bare earth, called the camp square, where roll-calls and exercises took place and which connected the various barracks with one another.

The following morning, which was the first work-day, the newcomers were taken to disinfection. The way led outside the camp through open fields, bare of all greenery in mid-autumn. The weather was cold and limpid, the ground hard after the night frost. Marching along in silence, Arush, like most prisoners, had time to reflect. He did not like the purpose of their walk. Disinfection - who knew what this might mean? It was hard not to be suspicious. Besides, the term evoked memories which could not inspire confidence. As early as the first year of war, many affluent Jewish homes had been threatened with disinfection. Anyone who did not pay up had his home "disinfected" of all its valuable contents. Of what could they rob him now? Yet certain memories are not easy to shake off. Apart from their anxious reflections, they marched soberly, flanked by SS guards, and with that energetic Jewish orderly at the rear, none of whom were particularly harassing them. They barked their commands in hard menacing voices, but not too often and not without any reason. At the head of the guards walked the same SS man who took the roll-calls and who had admitted them to the camp. He bore no badge of rank but was, they managed to learn, Unterscharführer Ruf (who knows if it was spelt with one or two "f"s), the jailer in actual charge of the Jewish camp, formally its *Rapportführer*. The man was about thirty, robustly built, very strong looking and with a face that showed brutality but strangely mingled with traits of fairness. "We'll see," Arush told himself. He had already learned not to pass judgement on people by their facial features.

On the whole Arush enjoyed the two-mile walk. The disinfection works was in a two-storeyed brick building, near the Kochanowka rail-station, an extension from the main east-west railway line, purpose-built for the use of the SS base. Approaching the building, the prisoners started sniffing at the air. It stank of gas. They became apprehensive. The smell filled the whole ground floor of the house. Behind the half-closed door of the cloakroom, it was choking. Yet they were ordered to undress, bind their clothes into bundles, put them into the disinfection chamber, and then take showers in another gas-stinking room. They were deathly afraid both of complying, and of not complying with the order. Yet the energetic Jewish orderly urged them to undress, saying there was nothing to fear.

It took only seconds to throw in the bundle of clothes, but to find and retrieve it an hour later, could take several minutes. Yet one minute inside the disinfecting chamber, even after its door had been opened, was enough for a man to come out semi-poisoned. Many had to be carried out into the fresh air and resuscitated, which the SS men did not interfere with. All were saved, except one boy of about twenty. Because of its unique circumstance, it was more terrible than usual to witness his death - a strange, hardly solemn death that took place before his comrades' eyes. Worse, before the eyes of his father. The one and only father and son in the camp. When, in Szebnie, they had put the fifty-year-old Goldman on the list for Pustkow, his son had asked to be allowed to join him. "What a peculiar stroke of fate!" Arush could not help thinking. "The first death since our arrival; and how many more to come?"

It saddened all the prisoners and they walked back in mournful silence. At camp, they queued up for "lodgings". The two barracks into which they were distributed each had five rooms and a corridor. From the corridor, doors opened into three rooms, from two of which, on the right-hand and left-hand sides, doors led to two other rooms. Arush Freund was sent to the last room on the right-hand side of Barrrack One - the socially privileged one, as it turned out later.

It was a two-windowed room, quite large and bright - electrically lit at night - with wooden bunks at two levels. The bunks stood in pairs against opposite walls with enough space between them to turn round. At the centre of the room stood a little tin stove with a pipe extending through an opening in the roof. There was no other furniture in the room; the bunks were the only place to sit. Each of the arrivals was given the same bedding as the old inmates, two blankets and plenty of clean straw to fill up a sack-mattress. They were instructed how to make the "beds" in the uniform fashion strictly prescribed by camp regulations. Arush was to share his room with about fifty men, out of some four hundred and sixty-five prisoners, all males, in the entire Jewish camp.

In the evening, after work, Arush could see that, contrary to his first impression, not all the old-timers were nothing but skin and bones. Though with some it was not an exaggeration to call them walking skeletons, others looked less ascetic, and even the thinnest were far from being altogether drained of life force. Only a newcomer could notice the generally miserable appearance of the men: the old-time prisoners were accustomed to seeing them.

The majority of both the veteran and new prisoners were from Tarnow, Rzeszów (Pustkow lay halfway between the two) with Cracow a poor third. This furthered their mutual attraction. Because of the relative lengths of their incarceration, and the social reasons that lay behind this, the newcomers were on average better educated than the old-timers. The latter could, however, lay claim to respect not only on account of their seniority at camp, but also on account of seniority in age, which on average was significantly higher than that of the newcomers.

Allocated a top level bunk at the far corner of the room, Arush found that by chance his nearest bunk neighbour on the same level was to be a Cracovian boy, hardly two years older than himself. His name was Marek Rainer. In the beginning they didn't take to each other and on the first evening barely exchanged a few words. Marek was determined to assert his superiority over Arush immediately and in no uncertain terms, and not only because of his seniority in the camp.

150

There were more important things to worry about, Arush thought as he lay on his bunk that evening. He tried to comfort himself by remembering that he was no novice to barrack life and already knew what a concentration camp was. Nothing could frighten him; yet he trembled at the haunting vision of his furrier vocation. All sorts of answers crossed his mind, but none satisfied him. He lay scheming and scheming till salutary sleep overcame him. But as soon as he woke up the oppressive thought was back on his mind. Queueing in the cold - it was already very cold in the mornings before the sun came out - he asked himself again and again: what should he say? Admit everything? And what about the consequences? He had cheated the SS; cheated his way into the camp as a craftsman. A nice craftsman who knew no trade. Was there anything he could do to be of some use here? But he must say he knew something. But what?

He was delivered from this predicament by the energetic orderly whose ubiquitous and commanding presence Arush had noticed before. By that morning, he already knew who he was: the camp eldest, named Bubi Feldmaus, but to everyone just Bubi. The title of eldest seemed strangely inappropriate for him. Because Bubi was a young man, not much older than Arush. He spoke a quick, stentorian German, trying here and there, though not very aptly, to throw in a word in Yiddish. Not tall but well built, he had a ruddy face, his whole body glowing with health. His clothes were also conspicuous: dark-grey riding breeches set in fashionable black knee-boots, a blue three-quarter length coat and a ski-cap of the same colour. The only other men dressed like this were the two camp capos - a strange word the newcomers had never heard before - who were assisting Bubi that morning. When it was Arush's turn to be interviewed, Bubi, speaking in a firm but friendly manner, told him straight out: "Look, we know that many of the men who are sent here aren't the craftsmen they're supposed to be. Are you a furrier?"

As bluntly as he had been asked, but in a much lower voice, Arush admitted the truth.

– "Sorry, I'm not."

– "What can you do?"

The fight to live had made Arush inventive and on the spur of the moment he told Bubi a thumping lie, which had not occurred to him in all his earlier ruminations.

– "I studied law, but I haven't finished. I'd only done three years, when the war broke out."

In a twinkle Arush had calculated that he could not have had more than three years of university studies, since he had replied to an earlier question that his age was twenty-five. Could anybody disprove it? He was playing a hazardous game, at least it seemed so to him at the time.

– "Can you keep accounts?"

– "Yes. Actually I worked as a book-keeper during the war, and even before..."H e was not allowed to finish for Bubi cut in curtly.

– "Step aside and wait!"

Arush was beside himself with momentary joy. He could have hugged Bubi. He

151

could hardly stem the fullness of his heart, and at the same time he somehow wanted to humble himself before Bubi. The latter also seemed to take a liking to Arush. In this, as in getting his assignment, he may have been helped by his ability to speak correct German, Bubi's native and only language. Of all the hundred and nineteen arrivals from Szebnie, only one other beside Arush was given office work and he was a man of nearly sixty years.

After he had finished his part in the job distribution, Bubi accompanied Arush to his new post at the tailors' workshop, where he introduced him to his future superiors.

The so-called *Industriehof* (industrial estate, a term that seems to be an SS contribution to the German vocabulary) was situated between the inner and outer wire fences of the camp. It consisted of five large and solid wooden barracks, some including forecourts in their work area. From the inside they were variably equipped and hence looked different. The interior of the tailors' workshop surprised Arush rather pleasantly; not because of its inner decor, but because of the inner atmosphere. The principal shop-floor was the *Flickstube* (patchwork room), in which about forty men were employed, each sitting at a new-looking "Pfaff" sewing-machine. The custom-tailoring room was much smaller, with only a few highly qualified tailors working there. A door led from the tailors to the saddlers, who were far fewer, and from them to the cobblers. The three workshops could also be entered from a common corridor. Together they comprised the *Bekleidungsbarracke* (clothing-barracks).

Arush was given a separate table of medium proportions, placed in the large room at the corner of the doorless entrance to the custom-tailors. Sitting with his back to the window, facing the men at their machines, he was in a "strategic" position of vantage, from which he would be able to observe almost anything that happened in the entire workshop.

A rare smile of bliss brightened Arush's face as he sat down at the table, a pen in his hand and an account-book in front of him. What heartened him most was the warmth that seemed to radiate from those humble, mostly gaunt and hollow-cheeked men with whom he was to share the days of misery ahead. His instinct told him to be glad at having landed in their midst and not having been driven to rougher shores.

Internally, the master of all tailors was Berl Alter, a prewar gentlemen's tailor of Tarnow; ladies' fashions were in the care of Kurt Heibaum, a real sartorial artist formerly of Katowice, who even in Pustkow treated his work as an art. But immediately responsible for the Flickstube was Sami Hausdienst, a tall, handsome, and, at first impression, likeable man in his mid-twenties. He attracted Arush's attention also by his dress, as, alone among all the non-capo prisoners, he too was wearing black knee-boots, though they were, like the rest of his clothes, less elegant; and also his cheeks were less ruddy than those of the capos. As his job of supervisor required him to keep an eye on everything in the room, he was also the only one in the workshop without a permanent seat.

It was he who first entered into conversation with Arush, explaining to him his duties and the general rules of the shop. This was soon dealt with, however; in the main he asked Arush about life outside - ghettos, camps, the fate of the remnant Jews, all questions which Arush would have to answer again and again to his other work mates. Hausdienst, who said he came from Będzin and had spent the last summer of peace at a nearby *Hachshara* (preparatory training farm) of the radical Zionist-Socialist party, suddenly asked if Arush had heard of the Laibs. Yet when Arush said he had, and began telling how he had met a man of that name at Szebnie, Hausdienst growled out "relative", and moved away.

A chain of look-outs signalled "Saar is coming." When the sleepy-eyed Hauptscharführer, a middle-aged six-footer with a wizened face, came in, the sounds of conversation in the Flickstube fell silent, leaving only the resounding clatter of the machines. Saar quickly cast his eyes over the enlarged crew of the workshop, and after apparently similar inspections of the saddlers and cobblers, returned to the custom-tailors. They were the ones who were truly busy and his interest lay in orders made for local custom, although repair-work for the troops was supposed to be the raison d'etre not only of the Bekleidung workshop but of the whole Industriehof.

Nearest to Arush, almost parallel to his table, sat two men, who both came from Tarnow. The older one, thirty odd years of age, had fiery red hair and a friendly, though true workman's face. When he smiled or opened his mouth, only eye-teeth were visible on the upper jaw. Lipe Knepel, as he was called, was said to have lost his teeth with tailoring. Before the war, he had been a trouser tailor, working for as many hours a day as his employer would accept, sometimes as much as sixteen at a stretch. The garment industry, almost entirely Jewish owned, operated on the principle of maximum time-saving division of labour. There were sewers, cutters, pressers, finishers, button sewers and buttonhole makers and so on; one worker carried out only one particular part of the manufacturing process. In his earlier years, Knepel had seam-sewed single trouser legs; later, he worked himself up to sewing two legs together. Reputed to be a stakhanovite in the Tarnow garment industry, Knepel, who did not know hand-sewing, could complete forty trouser legs in an hour. Combining piece-work (there was no other rate of pay) with overtime, he could, in the season, earn up to ten Zloties a day, enough to buy ten kilos of granulated sugar, or, for two days' wage, a standard pair of shoes. But his was a seasonal industry, the season lasting at most eighteen weeks a year; during the remaining slack period of the year he was idle. Still, from the wage he earned, Knepel managed to maintain not only himself, but also his elderly mother and unemployed sister the whole year round. He was indeed the object of envy to his fellow tailors, for there were at least two tailors anxious for each available job, and the employment situation in other trades was not much better. There are always grounds for envy, but Arush, listening to his story, thought that in such labour conditions, it was not surprising that, however delusive the promise, Knepel had been a communist. Though, as a clever man, devoted to his family, he had officially been a member of the overground Jewish marxist-socialist Bund party. What did astonish Arush was the man's wit and sense of humour, which he had not lost even in Pustkow.

In this respect he was a striking contrast to Asyk Deker, the other man sitting nearest to Arush. Asyk had a sullen temper, which made him look middle-aged, though he was not yet thirty. His outward appearance, too, was not particularly attractive. Rather short and scraggy, he had a large head - had it lengthened from hunger? Arush wondered - elongated still more by a curiously pointed skull. Although he had acquired the skill of machine-sewing, Deker was not a tailor. Up to the war, he had held the job of political organizer with the local Bund party, to which, again in contrast with Knepel, he was devoted body and soul. There was not much love between the two men, though, as Deker once averred, there were no significant differences between ordinary supporters of the Bund and Jewish communists; serious ideological and tactical differences only began at leadership levels, despite both parties embodying revolutionary change in their programmes.

As Arush was shortly to discover, red was indeed the atmosphere of the workshop, most men being politically minded and, though first generation proletarians, having a well developed class consciousness. Together with the other Bekleidung workers, they were closely representative of the former Jewish working class, which in the main consisted of tailors and shoemakers, with in addition some capmakers. A variety of factors determines the character of a working class; in this particular case the responsiveness of Jews to domestic demands was the dominant factor. Insofar as the ordinary man in Poland was left with any money after buying his food, he next tried to satisfy his need of shoes and clothes. The Jewish shoemakers and tailors of those days were better organized and more dedicated to socialism than factory workers. The craftsmen were no less dedicated. Though conscious of their status, they did not belong to the middle classes; and in terms of earnings they were no better off than labourers in gainful employment. The sense of injustice which both craftsmen and labourers felt, forged strong solidarity between them; there was full social intercourse between these two kinds of workers; and craftsmen formed the largest single group in the separate Jewish trades unions. Berl Alter was no less committed to socialism than was Lipe Knepel.

Notwithstanding the circumstances, Arush had the uneasy feeling of being an intruder among the brotherhood at his new place of work. They too immediately felt him to be a stranger, a man not of their own kind. (The word "class" would sound ludicrous given the conditions.) Hausdienst, coming to talk to Arush, had first looked, quite unmistakably, at his hands. Arush, for his part, had also quickly recognized the problem that he would have to face. He had never lived the life of these people. He understood that it would be wise for him to adapt, to seek out everything they had in common and try to be accepted as one of them. As far as Knepel, Deker and Alter were concerned, the fact that he was from the ghetto of Tarnow stood him in good stead. No less important an asset was his fluent Yiddish, for Yiddish was the common, if not exclusive, language of the tailors and, by and large, of the Jewish working class in Poland; hence of the majority of Pustkow inmates.

In marked contrast, many of Arush's neighbours in his living room, including Marek Rainer, spoke Polish; they were also, on average, better educated than the

154

tailors. There was a fair number of skilled workers among his room-mates, the most elevated being Maniek Lander of Myślenice near Cracow. A young man of 23, he had an excellent character, and was the master-craftsman of the upholstery workshop. The barracks eldest was Capo Krel, a healthy, good-looking, but not likeable fellow of about 25, who lived in another room - "luckily", as almost every man in Arush's room hastened to add.

His bunk neighbour, Marek, must have once been very handsome, as he was tall, blond-haired and had a round pleasant face with lively green eyes. But now he looked pretty gaunt. He, too, proved to be a very decent young man, perhaps a bit dull and inclined to disbelieve almost anything, which gave him a pessimistic outlook on things. The differences in their upbringing were not insignificant, but these did not seriously impede their relations.

Marek was the only son of his parents. His father was a manufactuer of kitchen utensils. The home was "progressive". The parents attended synagogue only on the High Jewish Festivals. On those days his father also closed the business, but made up production by working night-shift on the following Sabbath. Although the family was affluent, Marek had not received the customary secondary education. His parents were of the minority who took very seriously the Jewish leaders' exhortations on the need for Jewish youth to re-adapt vocationally and to acquire a trade. As a result, they sent Marek to a Jewish crafts school which had opened several years before the war in Cracow. He completed a two-year course in mechanics, for which he had shown some talent. Marek had been taken by force to Pustkow at the end of 1940. There he was given a job in which he could make good use of his acquired skills so that when several months later he was offered conditions of work that were reasonable for those days, and considering that, in the meantime, a ghetto had been established in Cracow, he had stayed on in Pustkow voluntarily. At the time when Arush arrived there, Marek was working at the *Autohof*, a barracks for the repair of motor vehicles, along with three other more or less qualified mechanics. This being the age of motors, Marek, though not a "master", belonged to the elite of Pustkow prisoners by virtue of his job. It was on this account that he considered himself superior and expected Arush to acknowledge it. This source of initial friction had as time went on gradually subsided, and, telling each other in the long hours they spent together the chief events of their still young lives, Arush and Marek had become friends.

Day began at six in the morning, when Ruf, or an occasional substitute, came to open the barracks, which he had locked from the outside at seven the evening before. This was the *Lagerschluss*. At "get up", the prisoners tumbled down from their bunks and ran out of the warm barracks, stripped to the waist, with usually a towel thrown over the shoulders, to catch a "seat" at the latrine; then on to the washroom, which was fitted with several large stone bowls with multiple taps from which, when turned on, cold water flowed plentifully.

Back at the barrracks they had to make the bunk flawlessly and to dress quickly. There was something to put on. The outer clothes of a prisoner were what he had happened to be wearing on arrival at the camp, or, in the case of the old-time and privileged prisoners, what they had managed to have sewn either by themselves or by a tailor-friend. The cloth for these came, ostensibly, from scraps, but in fact was misappropriated. In order not to stab the SS men's blind-turned eyes, materials were turned inside out, with linings on the outside and with different fabrics sewn together to make the garment look as if it was made of patches. Shirts and underwear were changed but not too often, so the prisoners laundered them drying them overnight in the barracks. Feet, wrapped in military cloth, were nearly all properly shod; shoes, like jackets or trousers, being repaired stealthily at the workshop. Everyone was thus differently dressed, the only common items being the personal number each prisoner was compelled to sew onto his outer garment. This was, however more for reasons of discipline than identification, as men were addressed by their surnames or the jobs they performed at camp.

Once the room had been put in order, the men queued up for so-called coffee and bread, if there was any distributed. When it was very cold, much below freezing point, or pouring with rain or snow outside, gruel was dealt out in the barracks corridor. Everyone had a red enamel bowl and a spoon (some also had knives made illegally from scrap metal), and each man was responsible for leaving his own washed clean. At seven came roll-call, one of two - the other, in the evening, together the most important event of the day. Roll-calls took place on the square outside in all kinds of weather. But at Arush's time in Pustkow, they were usually short affairs. The prisoners were well drilled, knew how to dress a line quickly, how to stand stiffly at attention, and when ordered "*Mützen ab!*" to remove their caps all together with one rhythmic movement of the right hand. Then Bubi reported attendance to Ruf, who quickly checked the lines and strength. A final announcement "*Mützen auf!*" and the columns marched out, everyone to his workshop. There was no outside work except for occasional repairs or cleaning, for which men were borrowed from the shops. Working hours were from 7 to 12 in the morning and from 1 to 6 in the afternoon, six days a week. The break for lunch at noon was spent at the dwelling barracks. Sunday was a formal rest day, and the most boring and doleful day of the week, with nothing to do except all the cleaning and washing "at home". In the evenings in their dormitories, the prisoners were more or less free to do whatever they could with their time, at least until formal "lights out" at 10. But there was little they could do; physically enervated and hungry, most were too tired to enter into more than fragmentary conversation, leaving more comprehensive discussions for the long hours at work.

Something out of the ordinary, if not unique, was the cinema which entertained them on some evenings or at lunch breaks. The "cinema" was a grim-looking, sunken-faced man of thirty, called Waicholc, who had a photographic memory. Years after he had seen it, he would narrate the story of a movie, scene after scene, even repeating, apparently word for word, the long dialogue between Greta Garbo, as Anna Karenina, and Vronsky, on their last days together. Arush was less interested in the stories than in the phenomenon of a man being able to retell them so colourfully after many years. He tried to cultivate Waicholc's acquaintance so that he could make him recount past events that interested him, lamenting that such a brain stored only a very narrow range of information.

Another, much shorter diversion, and only for a few, was prayer. In the evenings, preferably in a shadowed corner of the room, one could pray at his leisure. It was much harder in the mornings, as there was very little time before the roll-call, and phylacteries had to be shared. Pressure was so great that often prayers had to be deferred until lunch-time.

Immediately in the first week, Bubi suddenly noticed Arush at prayer. In his surprise he made a highly derogative remark, but without malice in his voice. A petty insult to Arush, this minor confrontation nonetheless put an end to the friendship, if it ever was one, between the two. How else? Arush's showy reputation floundered in a flash. He did not greatly regret the change, because he had felt instinctively that Bubi was too high-flying a bird for him to catch up. Later, when he knew Bubi better, he thought it safer to avoid closer relations with him. There was nothing shameful about praying, and comparatively little hostility to religion in Pustkow, but it reduced a man's social standing. What a backward thing it is to pray, most men thought, in particular after what had happened to Jews most recently. "How do you explain the present state of Jews in terms of prayer?" Marek asked Arush when they were a little better acquainted.

The story of a day in Pustkow shortly after Arush's arrival would be incomplete without mentioning that here and there, before the day came to an end, someone, and often more than one, was beaten up. Not at work, that would be quite exceptional, but in the morning rush, while gathering at roll-call, or most commonly at the distribution of food. It was the capos who dispensed the blows. No sticks or whips were used, just fists. While Krel and Sztok, the eldest of barracks 2, may have been a little more liberal in exercising their power than Bubi, he had far greater strength in his arms. Well-nigh every stroke of his that made contact with any part of a semi-emaciated man was a near knock-out. With such force in his fists, almost all his fellow prisoners were of the opinion that he had certainly missed a brilliant boxing career. Yet his and the other capos' thrashings were nothing like the savagery a Jew often experienced in this war. They exercised restraint, while preserving discipline and, as apologists rightly argued, their blows forestalled a perhaps worse trouncing from Ruf and his companions. These latter struck only if a prisoner allowed himself to be caught at some mischief, such as loitering in the dwelling barracks during working hours, or failing to raise his cap. But these were not daily occurrences. Generally speaking, the beatings were more frequent and harder during the autumn and early winter of Arush's stay in Pustkow than later, for reasons that were subsequently to become clear to him.

Little more than two weeks in Pustkow had been long enough for Arush not only to assimilate the local daily routine, but also to absorb the specific climate of the place. And they left him pondering, pondering over the changes, over the new mystifying circumstances, and over the effect they were having on him as a person.

Above all, how quietly his life flowed on here! What a contrast with Szebnie, with all the dreadful camps he had heard of, or with the Tarnow ghetto in the last year or so! Most amazing, simply unbelievable, was the fact that he was once more

157

breathing air clear of permanent violence, let alone death. Lately he had become used to living from day to day, from disaster to disaster, expecting a new one every hour. Here death did not lie in wait at every step. Here death, if it came, would either come abruptly, on orders from above, or slowly, progressively, unobtrusively, a long protracted death of hunger and disease. He was not ill yet, and only beginning to suffer real hunger. For the time being, sentence was once more deferred, and life was not unbearable. True, the days that passed were not much to wait for. But they held a promise. And as he told Marek, he wanted to be no prophet of their precise fate.

Meanwhile, it was not only that the smell of death had faded away; gone also were the soul-crushing tension and the desperate fight for life that had characterized the Clean Up and the Szebnie days. After the turmoil and shock of those laborious times, the tranquillity and pattern of life at Pustkow had strange emotional consequences. The air of calm that blew in and about this place was balm to his racked nerves, somewhat soothing Arush's woeful soul. He could feel how, as a result, his numbness was easing away, so that he was slowly recovering his even serenity of mind. What a pleasant surprise it was to be able to grieve again. One evening, reflecting on these things in a dark corner of his barrack-room, he found for the first time, after long tearless weeks, that he was crying. And when he began to weep it was as if a dam had broken inside his heart, as if the legendary celestial gates of tears had irreparably been breached. During all those months of blocked emotions he had promised himself that he would cry like this after the war, if he survived. Now the calm weather was rapidly melting the icy mass in his heart. Never in his life had he released such a torrent of tears. These were no tears of commiseration, no tears of self-pity, or of purgation from the storms of youth. It was simply that all the pent-up grief inside him, all the deaths that he carried in his heart, all the sorrows of life that filled his soul, streamed out in a mountain waterfall of tears. He was relieved, glad that he could weep, feeling a different person, only afraid that the weeping was causing him joy. But he could not stop it, however much he exhorted himself to try harder. After an hour, perhaps longer, he at last managed to dry his eyes, and to lie down on the bunk, imagining a new beginning, while sighing that he would never be able to cry as much again.

When one night in his dormitory, Arush heard a room-mate sighing for bread, he replied in his mind that he was not afraid of hunger. Not very long after, he realized how rash this was. Gone were the days when Arush felt uneasy at the sight of the skinny, sunken-faced men. Feeling hungry himself now day after day, countless times every day, he could only see his own hunger reflected in the other men's faces. It might not yet be a precisely accurate reflection. But make no mistake, he was losing flesh and consequently it seemed to him that he could also feel his strength draining out of him. It was a strange fear, one he had never before experienced, this fear of losing his strength. When no one could see him, he began literally to test his muscles. He concluded that they were softening, though he wondered if he was not taking too much notice of what other people were saying. It may have only seemed to him that his movements, like theirs, were slowing down progressively. But certainly, like all the others, he became subdued, and rather apathetic, a state which at the same time damaged his newly regained normal human reactions, and brought back a greater sense of reality to his life.

Reality was, broadly, a vision of hunger; narrowly, it was a daily ration of eight or nine ounces of limy, chestnut-coloured bread made of anything but grainflour, a pint of black, bitter, warm water passed off as tea or coffee, and a bowl of soup usually prepared from boiled potato peelings. Arush somehow managed to swallow the almost indigestible bread, but no matter how hungry he was, he could not eat the soup. It was such an abomination that after tasting it a few times, he always had an agonizing heart-burn and felt sick. How long could one live on such a diet?

Dr Vadovitzer had said that prisoners were getting less than a thousand calories a day, but no ordinary man knew how much or how little this was. "Let him stuff himself with calories, I want bread to eat," said Zukber, one of the oldest drudges in the Flickstube. But at the beginning of December, that is one month after the prisoners had arrived from Szebnie, Dr Vadovitzer was widely reported to have said that with no improvement in the diet, men would be swelling with malnutrition in six weeks at the latest.

Dr Adrian Vadovitzer was a fully qualified and reputedly experienced medical practitioner. He was the doctor of the Jewish camp, who had been recruited from Dębica in 1941, and had since passed luckily through all the vicissitudes of the Pustkow wilderness. He was middle-sized, aged about forty, with a round bespectacled face and neatly arranged hair. He was portly, ruddy, and another feature that contrasted with everyone else, could sometimes be seen smiling. He walked in a stiffened, snow-white doctor's coat, with his hands clasped behind to add to his air of authority. He was the overlord of the infirmary, except that lording over him was Unterscharführer Zapke, if that is his real name, the SS sanitarian in charge of health matters in both the Polish and Jewish camps.

It was the first time that Arush had heard of people swelling with hunger and at first it seemed to him inconsistent. Then he conceded silently that it was not the only thing that mystified him about the functioning of the human body and that the story was not an invention. But it appeared to him unreal, the likelihood of bloating remote, and he began to reason - the mind's self-defence against dismal prospects - that it would take much longer than six weeks for him to swell up. And for years now they had been living on borrowed time.

Meanwhile the body took less notice of hunger than the mind. People seemed unable to think of almost anything other than food. Whether in the evening at the barracks, or during the day at work, conversation centred on eating, the men debating, for example, what was more filling, soup or bread and what were their relative nutritional values. Many sat silently calculating the best position to take up in the soup queue, although they knew that there was nothing in it. Watching the men at food distribution it seemed to Arush that some were as if hypnotized by the sight of it - not surprisingly, the few who had more and better food ate it as far away from the others as possible to avoid the envying eyes staring into their mouths - and most were convinced that their neighbours received a larger ration of bread and thicker soup than they did. Though many understood that these calculations only increased their hunger and fought the impulse. Some delighted in describing what they used to eat at home, others talked mainly of what they would eat after the war, often salivating at the mention of it. The food of most men's dreams was frankly modest, causing Arush to recall Crazy Shimen in pre-war times wishing himself death by drowning in a barrelful of hot potato soup. Oh, Arush sighed ruefully, how little concern one showed for the poor in the old days!

Every day the same conversations were repeated, only that as he grew more depressed, a man's mind became more and more indifferent to everything other than food. This was one of the main reasons why some men were maltreated by the capos and why the beatings mainly occurred at food distribution time. The least heinous sin was to jump the queue, the next to complain about one's allegedly unjust portion, asking the soup dealer "Why haven't you dipped the ladle deeper?", or the like. There were, of course, men who tried to get a second helping of soup. This wasn't quite as bad as pretending that you hadn't received your due, or storming the drum to lick it clean. Some men took risks, heedless of the lashes falling on their bodies. Szainowitz was a particularly tall, once broad-shouldered man in his twenties. Because of his large frame and village origins - peasants in general endured hunger worse than townsmen - his need for food was probably greater, and inner restraints possibly weaker, than those of others. He was certainly beaten more often than any other prisoner. He simply ignored the capos, rarely answered back, and in spite of the strokes that rained down on his head, neck, back and bottom, continued to lick off the soup, making no attempt to shield himself. Such disobedience - which like tardiness in executing orders, caused by generally slowed movement, was seen to smack of passive resistance - made the capos furious and led to still harder beatings.

With Arush, things never went this far and he thanked God for his body's lessened need of food. But he felt disgusted by his mind's preoccupation with eating. He must not think of it, he told himself repeatedly, it makes life not worth living, it is soul-destroying. And yet he could not rid himself of the trivial thoughts. He recalled once reading of a saintly man who craved God with every part of his body separately; Arush, mocking himself, craved bread with every part of his body separately. When he once confessed his suffering at the workshop, Hausdienst, with curious piquancy told him: "You don't really know what hunger is, do you?" And with an old-timer's fondness for telling their experiences to newcomers, he began describing the hunger he had seen in the not so distant past.

–"When I arrived in Pustkow in 1940, there was nothing, neither a base nor a camp. Who do you think built it? Who if not us built the roads, the buildings, the homes, and training facilities? In six months we cleared a forest five miles long, and raised a town there for twenty-five thousand SS men and their families."

Knepel interrupted to correct Hausdienst.

–"It took more than six months to complete lodgings for twenty-five thousand. But by the time the war with Russia broke out, living quarters for thirty-five thousand troops and officers with their families were ready."

Though visibly angered, Hausdienst continued unabashed.

–"Whatever you say," he countered disparagingly. "Well, we were labouring under enormous pressure. And we were only a few hundred men in those days. Later, more people began arriving and the number of Jewish workers went up to more than a thousand, perhaps even to two thousand."

–"There was a time when there were more than two thousand Jews in Pustkow. The number of workers depends on the time one is talking about," Knepel again intervened.

–"But in the meantime," Hausdienst went on, "we also began building, though not us Jews alone, extensive training ranges for infantry, artillery, and special service troops.

"At that time Pustkow was a labour camp, living conditions varied from good to bad, but on the whole were fairly bearable. Hell started for most of us in mid-1941, when a man named Ernst Kops became commander of the Jewish camp. In March 1942, they divided Jewish prisoners into two categories. Some went on to live in a so-called A-camp ("A" standing for *Arbeit*, labour), where life was peaceful. The work was mainly craft production and there was fairly wide freedom of movement."

–"Within the camp?" Arush asked as a matter of course.

–"The camp had no fixed borders. Some of the men," Hausdienst continued, "enjoyed various other freedoms. But the majority was placed in a newly created Z-camp ("Z" for *Zwang*, forced, i.e. a forced labour camp). There, the inmates were isolated within a narrow compound, forbidden contact even with the A-camp workers. Conditions in the Z-camp were terrible. It wasn't hard work alone that broke your back. The beating was harder, pitiless, indeed so cruel that men's bodies turned blue with it. Some of the victims became so black with bruises that it was said "they were beaten to a Negro". Oberscharführer Kops himself frequently tied prisoners to tree trunks, keeping them in this position until they fainted, when he started to beat them, continuing for as long as they showed any signs of life. And you had to work on an empty stomach. Oh no, you don't really know what a camp is yet," Hausdienst was delighting in the eloquence of his memories, while Arush was slowly beginning to understand why he had heard such diverse and conflicting stories about Pustkow in the past.

"Food was as scarce as it is today. The same daily rations, though soup and especially bread wasn't as bad as it is now. People used to eat wild plants and leaves, whatever they could find and swallow. Long, countless days with nothing to wait for but hard work and beatings, soup at noon and a slice of bread in the evening. Always hungry, always tired, finding release only in sleep - and death of course."

Szpunt, chief assistant to Kurt Heibaum, could not hold back and jumped from his seat at the custom-tailors to add his story.

–"There was little to lose, life was no prize. You know what I did one day? I stole out of camp to go begging bread at the nearest village. Hunger was stronger than the fear of being caught. It was a cold windy night in December. There was no moon and hardly any stars. The path led through the forest. I knew the track since

161

we had often seen the village in the distance as we marched to work at the shooting-range. It's only a few kilometres away, but that night it seemed to lie at the other end of the world.

"I must have lost direction, I wanted at least to find the way back to camp. But I couldn't. My feet were sinking in the snow, and after a time I stumbled and fell. I couldn't get up and there was no one to call for help. God alone knows how I dragged myself out of the snow. I walked on only to go further astray, moving now up, now down in the snow, like a boat on the waves. I couldn't feel my toes, the wind was buffeting me, and I was hungry. Nothing but snow to eat. I thought that I would freeze to death. Just when I had lost every hope of salvation, all of a sudden a stray dog joined me. It was a big animal, nearly as tall as I was, a thoroughbred of some kind. At first I was terrified, fearing the beast would eat me up. But then I told myself, better to fall into the clutches of an animal than of SS men. Soon I calmed down, for the dog was walking quietly along beside me, leading the way. And I let myself be guided by the dog. After a few minutes, I sensed he was a friend. We walked in silence through the forest for nearly an hour, then the dog halted and, as suddenly as he had joined me, discreetly turned away. Later I realized why. For when I looked up after a while, I caught a glimpse of a clearing in the darkness, and shortly after, the shapes of village huts came dimly into view. I was afraid that I might cause a disturbance, but not a dog moved his tongue. On both sides of the snow-covered village road stretched log huts, their windows closed with shutters made of rags or boards. No light showed outside. With my heart going pit-a-pat, I knocked haphazardly on the door of a plain hut and asked if I could have something to eat. The door opened to let me in. In the very pale light, the little cabin looked dark and old, the roof propped up with poles. Close to the stove an elderly, bearded peasant was filling his morning pipe, while an equally old-looking woman in a kerchief was busying herself about the home. There was compassion in their faces. Without asking any questions, she laid a plateful of warm thick gruel and a big slice of bread on the table in front of me. And to take away they gave me a large loaf cut in half. Warmed up and with new strength in my feet, I rushed through the forest to get back before sunrise."

Hausdienst did not allow him to continue.

–"He was exceptionally lucky. Others only got into trouble and failed."

Szpunt grimaced, but gave way to Hausdienst, who took up his own story where it had been interrupted.

–"At that time work and starvation reduced most - not all - men to 40kg weight, and yet their bodies were swelling up. That's one of the tricksy things about it. Several maladies are caused by food deficiency. Because your body resistance is lowered, infectious diseases, of the skin in particular, cling to you. I've heard about men getting holes in their cheeks, though I haven't seen them myself. Yet the most common disease is plain swelling. The Germans called it, strangely, water sickness, and they spoke, perhaps jokingly, of an epidemic. The body fills up with water as a result, it is said, of insufficient protein being taken into the blood. People grow progressively weaker and their shapes and looks change. Faces become dimmer, the skin hardens, turning a greenish-grey. Then, depending on how long they have been starving, larger or smaller swellings appear. The sick men had to work as usual even in this state and they often died either on the way to work, as their bloated legs failed to carry them, or later actually at work. Anyway, anyone who was visibly sick and weak had their clothes marked with chalk by Kops as they went through the camp gate on their way to work. This was a sign for the guards to shoot them in the forest or wherever they were working at the time."

Deker couldn't forebear remarking: "In other ways it's an easy death. When you are all swollen up, you don't feel hungry any more and death comes imperceptibly, as if in sleep. But don't think that everyone was pinched up by hunger. Hundreds were, but others weren't. These were said to be 'cheating', in fact they became the object of envy and suspicion because they had somehow managed to get extra food."

Was this a dig at Hausdienst's present condition, Arush wondered, while Hausdienst, taking up Deker's remark about dying, went on to say, "No! The queer thing about the swellings is that the part of the body that inflates more or inflates less, depends on the time of day. In the morning a man's face is more bloated, in the evening it's his legs. What does Vadovitzer know about this? He talks of six weeks. But some men swell slowly, others quickly. With some the swelling comes first, with others it's preceded by other disorders, diarrhoea for instance. Diarrhoea, as you must know, is a serious disease in camp conditions. Dysentery used to rack many hungry bowels, sucking any remaining strength from a man's body, but in those days there was no medication for it in the camp. People tried to make charcoal by secretly burning wood; some prisoners even burned bread to make charcoal. This gave us a new definition of a 'millionaire'."

Arush, who had been plagued by diarrhoea for two days, was trying not to betray his absorbing interest in Hausdienst's tale and warning. Yet he was more than reluctant to call at the infirmary. What made him hesitate was not the fear of selection for "special treatment" because of sickness. Unlike its equivalents in other camps, the Pustkow inifirmary was not a killing facility. Nor was it a place where one was prescribed a laxative for an infectious disease. Nothing of the kind. The infirmary in Pustkow was well provided with tablets against diarrhoea, besides offering the possibility of a dietetic cure. Around that time, many prisoners considered it a piece of good fortune to be hospitalized for at least a day or two. And prisoners who had stayed at the infirmary bore witness to what an extraordinary favour it was. They told of the relatively cosy conditions there, as well as a clean, warm bed, various games, and even rice pudding for supper.

Arush was averse to visiting the infirmary for a particular reason of which he was well aware. He disliked Dr Vadovitzer perhaps more than most other prisoners did. The doctor's name was in those days frequently on their lips.

Marek Rainer argued one evening: "It isn't a crime to be fit and fat just because others are not. Perhaps he only looks plump because we're so thin?"

–"I thought of that and I share your view," replied Arush. "But don't you agree that it's very stupid of him to promenade up and down the square every day in full view of all us starving, emaciated men, trying to lose weight?"

–"It's unthinking of him. But why should he care? How many of the rich felt self-conscious because of their affluence when they were at liberty? But I'm sure he'd like you. You speak good Polish, could carry on a conversation with him, and you play chess. He admits Herszkowicz, his chosen partner, every other week to the infirmary. Only don't let him find you praying."

The same prisoners who left the infirmary talking of the "luxuries" there, also reported that Dr Vadovitzer destroyed any sacred article that came to his notice. True, he was responsible for the infirmary and everything that came to be there. Jewish devotional items were highly offensive to SS men, and if found, might have attracted severe punishment. But their possession was not formally prohibited; nor was prayer. No Nazi decree had ever been published that forbade Jews to pray. Shortly after the occupation of Poland, all synagogues were ordered to close, some were destroyed, and Jews were forbidden to congregate for any purpose. The Nazi authorities, of course, knew that the Jews flouted this prohibition. As early in wartime history as the first Passover festival, Oskar Brandt, at that time head of the Jewish department of the Gestapo at Cracow, ordered all the local Judenrat members to spend Seder night in the open as a punishment for not having prevented the Jews from praying. But at the very same time, Jewish services were being publicly performed at various places under German occupation; and even much later, in 1942, synagogue services were held in some closed ghettos with German sanction. In the strictly disciplined Nazi camps, where dehumanizing tactics were in force prior to extermination, prayer, though still not formally forbidden, took on a broader and more dangerous dimension. Even individual prayer was regarded by the SS as inner resistance, as defiance of SS designs. Amon Goeth, commander of the camp at Plaszow, used to walk around the prisoners' barracks on certain nights, and if he suspected that Jews might be praying in the dark, would shoot indiscriminately through the window panes into the dormitories. But in Pustkow in its Industriehof era, that type of reaction to prayer was unlikely. At that time in Pustkow prisoners had some minor latitude in arranging their "free" time; there were no obvious attempts at dehumanizing or destroying a prisoner's personality; nor were prisoners, apart from being starved, specifically abused or tortured. All that was likely to happen to a Jewish prisoner caught at prayer was that he would get a couple of black eyes and perhaps a broken rib as well. Nothing worse.

But Marek again disagreed.

"Zapke is quite unpredictable. You've no idea what a mad sadist he is. Not long ago Dr Vadovitzer was called to remove the appendix of a Pole, as the doctors in the Polish camp didn't know anything at all about surgery. Zapke watched the operation, which was performed without anaesthetics. Witnesses say that, while the poor man lay strapped onto a kitchen table screaming in pain with all his might, Zapke was beside himself with joy, laughing as if it were the happiest day of his life."

–"But he's not mad when he's with Vadovitzer. I heard that Vadovitzer has Zapke in his pocket. All the good things in the infirmary come through him."

–"That may or may not be true. There's no doubt that Zapke treats Vadovitzer with special regard. He has a weakness for him, or rather for medicine. He's mad enough to want to step into his shoes - no that's the wrong phrase - to put on his doctor's coat. Every time he comes to the infirmary, he swamps Vadovitzer with medical questions. Vadovitzer must report every patient's case history to him, he has to explain the illness in theory and practice, touching upon matters which go far beyond the actual treatment required. Zapke thus has the illusion of studying medicine privately, with Dr Vadovitzer as his tutor. Even so, if Zapke found a man praying, or came across devotional aids, at the infirmary, no one knows how he would react. Such things may look innocuous to you, but punishment could be severe.

"So Dr Vadovitzer flings the confiscated phylacteries and prayer books into the burning stove as if they were intended for just this purpose."

Arush chose not to go to the infirmary, at least not for as long as he could possibly avoid it. But how long could he hold out? He must not risk his life. He must do something about this diarrhoea. It wrung him more severely every day. But what could he do to stop it?

As he wondered despairingly what to do, Arush recalled that at home, when he, or another child, had an upset tummy and was defecating excessively, their mother used to tell them to starve for a day or two, on a diet of rusks and camomile tea, perhaps later with some oatmeal porridge made with water, which was said to be binding. Well, in his circumstances, rusks, oats, even camomile were an unattainable dream. The only part of her advice he could follow was "to starve". He ceased taking all food, which, in any case, came out the other end as soon as he had swallowed it. In the mornings he rinsed his mouth with the "tea" for freshness, otherwise nothing.

After a week on this "diet", Arush risked a few sips of the warm liquid, to see what would happen.

What a grand surprise! It stayed in!

He was lucky. Still, he wondered in the ample time that followed, what was it that had made him recover? Was it just a matter of his body's power of resistance, or was it some inner force that helped him to endure this fantastic trial? Whatever it was, he was very glad to have recovered on his own.

And there was a lesson in it for him to learn.

CHAPTER TWELVE

While food was the men's main preoccupation, it was not their only subject of conversation. All the prisoners were keenly interested in the current war situation and not much less so in the political one. The then almost daily good news from the battlefields was distributed and discussed fervently, raising the men's subdued spirits. News thus became an important element of their efforts to survive. It surprised Arush that news reached them at such speed, sometimes arriving the same day it happened, while they were still at work. More important was the fact that he could on many occasions convince himself of the veracity of the news. Rumours, a constant plague of the Jews in earlier years of war, hardly circulated at all, and no one would dare to invent them, in Pustkow. But for weeks the source of the news remained a secret from Arush; the few men in the know would not share it with him.

However, this ignorance of the source did not in the least prevent him from making optimistic commentaries on the news, including "strategic" analyses, which found well disposed listeners. Another thing that Arush knew from his experience at home was how to impart his views, at the same time safeguarding his vulnerable position by not contradicting the opinions of men who mattered. Yet he had also known for a long time that in order to gain a hearing it was essential to sound different from them - while still saying something his listeners wanted to hear. With his largely unsophisticated audience, Arush was particularly good at such things as calculating their true distance from the front, making good use of his liking at school for studying distances between various towns.

If, about the turn of 1943, the front line was along the Dniepr, then in a straight line, Fastóv was 400km from Lwow, from there to Rzeszow was 150km, and another 20km to the west was Pustkow itself. When in early January 1944, the Russians managed to advance 35km westwards from Winnitza in one day, Arush commented that they were not more than about 265km from Lwow, and at even half that pace the Russians could be in Pustkow in four weeks, give or take a little. Of course to sound plausible, he added a caution, "if they are not delayed," but the important thing was that he was conjuring up the promise of imminent liberation. Anyway, after a war that was in its fifth year, who would not excuse a short delay? On hearing that at the Conference in Teheran, which ended on 1 December 1943, the Big Three had discussed plans for speeding up the defeat of the Third Reich, and for Germany's post-war future as a country, Arush was not slow in drawing up his own plan for ending the war quickly. But to his surprise he found that the centrepiece of his detailed plan, the immediate opening of a second front in the West, was received with much less enthusiasm by Knepel, Deker and a few other comrades, than he had expected. More popular was his way of poking fun at the misleading language the German High Command used when announcing their defeats; the familiar shortening of lines, elastic movements, and a new trick phrase: the *Zwickmühle* (morris dance, figuratively, a dilemma). "What a fretful fix: how can they stop dancing to the Russian tune?" Arush wagged his head in derision. He also remembered to tell a few political jokes from the ghetto.

Before long Arush had established a reputation as a leading, well-seasoned commentator, whose views and, better still, whose company, was sought after, and by not just anybody. By the highest class, the most senior master- craftsmen.

He liked this attention, apparently thinking that it could be of use to him. Remembering his conviction that in this war it was wise to stay low, certainly never to push oneself forward voluntarily, his new-found willingness to gain prominence, may seem strange. The more so since it had arisen at a time when continuous starvation made his survival more questionable every day.

As a matter of fact he still believed his old view was right, but as often happens, the environment changes one's attitudes. His new environment, in particular at the workshop, required him, in his appraisal of the situation, to re-adapt himself, to become sociable, acceptable, a man of consequence. Two particular, unconnected circumstances affected his thinking. Watching the daily routine of their lives, he gradually realized that the camp was largely run by the prisoners themselves. Overall discipline and order were under the control of Bubi and his aides, while inside the workshops, management and most other arrangements were in practice the responsibility of the few masters and even fewer overseers. Simultaneously Arush realized that at camp, as in the ghetto, the prisoner had his own private life apart from his strictly regulated pattern of daily existence. And, at least in Pustkow, this private life was more comprehensive and absorbing than the public one. This was, of course, liable to create a distorted sense of reality and with many prisoners it did so.

Then, to say that he did not feel quite himself at his workshop would be an understatement. The graded social structure, the various differences, which imprisonment and hunger failed to level out, were quite evident. To Arush the class consciousness of his fellow prisoners was a marvel. But he quite soon recognized that the social divisions were not so much those of class as of cultural background and above all, of skills. Skills he had none, except perhaps his intelligence and relative eloquence. What was certainly exceptional about him was his job. He was the only one at his workshop - and almost the only one in the entire camp - who was not doing manual work. He was thus already by force of circumstances conspicuous. While work was a socializing force for others, binding them together, it failed to do so in his case. Was there any good reason to begrudge him his job? It certainly did not carry with it a crumb of extra food - the thing that really mattered. Nor did it offer the reassurance of daily work. Yet, he did arouse envy, at least in some. The very singularity of his work assignment, emphasized his middle-class status. This made him look superior to some eyes, and perhaps worthy of dislike. Hausdienst once remarked to him: "Times have changed. Now everyone has to work." And on another occasion, more insidiously, with barely hidden implications for Arush: "He who works hard must eat." Knepel, more sincerely and without any malice, but with the wholehearted approval of Berl Alter and also of Mates Szinc, who was emerging as the social conscience of the tailors, made known his conviction that integrity was proved by hard physical work. Less hard working men were less honest. And Hausdienst, too, lectured him on the dignity of manual work although Arush suspected that he had not been a manual worker before the war, and would certainly not become one after it, should he survive. Among the others, Arush noticed that Berl Alter, certainly Kurt Heibaum, and Wolf Osterman, a genius shoe-upper-maker, if they did not exactly take pride in their work, did at least show a proper love for it. "A true cause for envy," thought Arush.

What was Arush's attitude to his work? If only it were work! To his sincere disappointment, it very soon turned out that his job was a sham. He had a book, but nothing to keep in it. There was one entry to make when work was delivered for repair, recording the number of pieces, another on its return. But this was at best a once-a-week affair. Made-to-measure orders were not entered in the book, understandably enough. Though Arush could recall reading about a crook who had meticulously recorded all his frauds. Still, Arush was a book-keeper and this was his formal position. And, however strange it may sound, the job was considered a privileged one. Stranger still, its main advantage was the status it carried. Other advantages were partly real: it was a leisurely job in, given the circumstances, pleasant surroundings. Arush was not so much anxious to keep his position, as afraid of losing it. What was the alternative? In Pustkow all work was, blissfully, skilled. But what skill could he exercise? Either way, he felt insecure and fearful of the consequences of his inactivity. Not that many of his fellow workers were much more active than he was himself. When Saar, or another SS man came in, Arush kept his head bent low over the ledger book, giving the impression of great mental absorption in his work; his mates also kept their heads bent low over the sewing machines, but from these came a busy clatter of activity. What a devil of a difference, his simulated work was completely still, and yet so conspicuous. How he wished he could change places with them, even if it meant working hard.

He still did not believe that their lives ultimately depended on work. But meanwhile, work meant a lot; for some, it meant additional food and standing at camp; for others, at least a degree of psychological ease. Arush was afraid of being sent, because of his idleness, to do other chores. "On loan" from the workshop. To work outside in winter, without food, without strength in one's body, could be fatal. And for how long could one only pretend to be doing real work? For how long would the SS bosses close their eyes to it? One way or another, idlers would be the first to be disposed of. Arush vaguely calculated that the combined influence of friendly master craftsmen could perhaps save him from this fate. His new bearing, his quest for attention and prestige were nothing else than a shift in his private struggle for survival, of which almost everything attempted at camp was a part.

And so he manipulated the situation all day long. In the long hours of idleness, Arush tried to explain to himself what was going on in Pustkow. The fiction of work common to most prisoners, truly baffled him. For here, unlike in many other camps, the fiction was not something invented to work them to death. That kind of cover-up was familiar enough in the ghetto. But in a concentration camp specifically intended for forced labour - he was looking at the long rows of machines on the shop floor - one would expect every prisoner to work, to perform a useful service to the SS. For what other purpose did the Germans keep them here? More curiously, why else had they brought them here from Szebnie?

Arush repeatedly raised this question in conversation with his fellows. The usual answer was the kind one wishes would come true: the shortage of work was temporary, large orders for repair work would start coming again soon. This implied, and many of the old-time prisoners said as much explicitly, that work had been more abundant in the past. But when pressed further, most would admit that this was debatable.

Arush's questions had somewhat shaken Knepel in his belief - a belief that was indeed shared by most of the men. This was that after all the losses suffered at the fronts Germany was short of able bodied men. At the beginning of 1944, that seemed a reasonable assumption and Arush did not question it. Knepel, however, went further, arguing that the military defeats of the Germans, resulting in the necessity to rebuild army strength on the one hand, and increase arms production on the other, had increased their industries' demand for manpower in general, and labour force in the concentration camps, in particular. "You (meaning the newcomers from Szebnie) were brought here because of the victories of the Red Army."

–"Increased demand for labourers there may be, but not, it would seem for labour," Arush quipped. And he went on to press his point. "Isn't the reduced demand for work in Pustkow a result of the beatings the Germans receive at the fronts?"

Developing the argument, Arush put forward a formula, needless to say an unproven one, which nevertheless received the unqualified approval of his friends, namely, that the worse the German military situation was, the better were the prisoners in the concentration camps.

His friend Marek, drawing on his experience at work, took a more realistic view. He did not expect the amount of work in Pustkow to increase. "They have fewer motor vehicles and they can't retreat with all of them, so they can't bring them for repair. And spare parts are no longer so plentiful. I can see it. Once this or that SS boss used to take parts with him to Rzeszow and return with a stuffed wallet and other good things in the boot of his car. Now they go there less and less frequently."

–"But will they keep us here without work? Just rear 'parasites'?"

–"You worry too much. Suppose you had work, what would you expect to get for it? Why use more energy than is necessary?"

It was easy for Marek to talk, as the mechanics still had work, and he was not living on the official ration alone. But Arush let it pass, sticking to his point.

—"Still thinking logically, why did they bring us here from Szebnie? To have us swatting idly at flies?"

—"This isn't the only strange, illogical thing about the way they play with us. You think yourself wise and want to unravel every mystery. But you have no idea what a tangled corner Pustkow is."

Arush had in fact been trying to learn everything he could about Pustkow ever since he had arrived there. He listened to everyone. He plied the old-timers with many questions, collecting their replies, adding them to his own minor observations and analysing them all, but he never found it easy to pierce through the crust of the things that puzzled him.

So far he had managed to establish that although a camp, with forced Jewish labourers, and partly skilled workers, had existed in Pustkow since the end of 1939, the era of the Industriehof had only started in the autumn of 1942. The most essential thing about the local camps, whatever their formal designation, was that they were at all times part of the huge SS military base, which its workers and prisoners called Pustkow. The formal name in German was initially SS Truppenubungsplatz Ost-Polen (SS Military Training Base East-Poland). Later, "East-Poland" was replaced by Debica, the name of the nearest town and, later still, Debica was substituted by "Heidelager" (heath camp). This was not just any base. It was the largest SS base outside Germany, at least in the East. It covered a 230 square mile (625km) quadrangle of land between Tarnow and Rzeszow in southern Poland. Thousands of acres of forest had been cleared for its construction and numerous villages eradicated, including the village of Pustkow. At any one time, ten thousand men could be trained at the base facilities which included areas for distant and close combat, shooting ranges for a wide variety of weapons, as well as secret installations, the nature of which Jewish prisoners could only guess.

The starting-point of the base was the confiscated site of a large prewar munition works on the outskirts of Debica. After the extensive building programme, which Hausdienst had already briefly described, the base consisted principally of five so-called accommodation Rings (circles). These were, in fact, roads on both sides of which were built barracks, garages for all sorts of motor vehicles, and other buildings. The roads were circular (except Ring 5, near the Kochanówka rail station) and linked to other roads, which lead to the various training places. All these structures and roads were built mainly but not exclusively by Jewish slave labour, in conditions varying in the degree of death, brutality and suffering. Also involved in the construction were so-called free Poles as well as German craftsmen and overseers, all of whom were more or less paid for their work.

For a time government of the entire base was under the exclusive orders of its commander, who in turn received his orders from the SS-Command-Head-Office (SS-Fuhrungshauptamt) in Berlin. The first commander of the Pustkow base was SS Oberführer Werner Freiherr (baron) von Scheele, who was replaced in 1941 by SS Standartenführer Paul von Nostiz; its last commander, during almost the entire

Industriehof era, was SS Gruppenführer Bernard Voss. Their deputy commanders were SS Standartenführer von Paris, SS Obersturmbannführer Bernd von Steuben and SS Führer von Baudissin. The brotherhood at camp did not know the rank of the last one. However some of the tailors, Deker in particular, called attention to the fact that most of the top SS commanders had "von" before their names, indicating nobility, and tried to draw from this far-reaching, and perhaps unwarranted, conclusions about the hierarchical class structure of that criminal organization.

The pattern of command at the base underwent a change, probably in 1941, when administration of the base was separated from the Kommandatur, its overall command, and put in the hands of an independent body, the *Standortverwaltung* (base administration). From then on the base commander's powers were restricted to his own staff, certain units permanently stationed at Pustkow, and to prisoners of war brought there. The command reorganization was the result, as Waicholc, who remembered the details and names of the various commanders, kindly put it, of "minor irregularities". But they could not have been so minor, since they led to the arrest of Commander von Nostiz and some of his staff officers, and were followed by legal proceedings against them. So perhaps the corruption they were now witnessing, Arush privately wondered, was only the tip of an iceberg.

One of several departments at the Standortverwaltung was the *Unterkunftstelle* (accommodation office), which was in charge of all economic matters, including employment of slave labour. So that, at least since the reorganization, the workshops in which the Jewish prisoners toiled were the responsibility of the Standortverwaltung, which was again subordinated to the SS-Wirtschafts-Verwaltungshauptamt (SS Economic and Administrative Head Office) in Berlin. But what about the camp and its SS supervisors, who seemed to form a separate - perhaps also independent - command unit? Not even Waicholc could tell.

Of the various units permanently stationed in Pustkow, special mention deserves to be made here of the SS-Guards-Battalion (*Wachbataillon*), which was under the authority of the base commander. Among the duties of this battalion were, in the first place, training recruits and guarding the military base. This guard duty included guarding Jewish and Polish workers as well as prisoners of war held at the base. These were the SS men to whom Hausdienst had referred in his tale of the beatings and killings of the Z-camp prisoners. This SS-Guards-battalion was also the one that had participated in the first Aktion in Tarnow and Rzeszow, and which had covered itself with glory by its indiscriminate murder of thousands of men, women and children. At the time of the first Aktion in Tarnow, the commander of the battalion was SS Hauptsturmführer (later Sturmbannführer) Otto Freiherr von und zu der Tann.

The batallion was dissolved at the end of 1942. The newly formed SS *Schützmannschafts-bataillon* (Guard Battalion), mainly manned by Ukrainians, took over the functions of its predecessor. Hence, Arush concluded, the SS men who stood guard at the towers and watched him were probably Ukrainians - fortunately, however, under the orders of their local German commanders.

Indirectly related to Jewish captives in Pustkow was the presence of prisoners of war, whose fate was a story the old-timers never tired of relating. The first prisoners of war brought to Pustkow were Frenchmen. They were employed at the same construction sites as the forced labourers, sometimes working alongside them. But in December 1940, after only four months, the French p.o.ws were evacuated from Pustkow to a destination unknown to the other prisoners.

The first transport of Russian p.o.ws arrived in Pustkow in October 1941. The Jewish old-timers' estimates of their numbers varied widely. But they all agreed that these Russian p.o.ws were encamped in the open, without shelter, south-west of Hill 218 as it was officially called. Surrounded by barbed wire and by SS men of the Guards Battalion under the command of Hauptsturmführer von und zu der Tann, the Russians lay motionless on the ground, in the cold snow, with almost no food, "dying like flies", to quote Hausdienst. He once saw how one of the otherwise quiescent Russians caught a squirrel, strangled it in his hands, and gobbled it up. The SS men who witnessed the incident, watched it calmly, having been instructed that this was no infraction of the law. Eating human flesh was a different matter.

One day the chief medical officer at Pustkow, SS Obersturmbannführer Dr Schuhmacher was watching a group of p.o.ws through field glasses from a considerable distance. He was flanked by his colleagues, Drs Altenhausen and Meckel, both SS officers, while a few yards behind them stood Dr Judel, a Jew, then working at the camp hospital. After a few minutes of watching, Dr Schuhmacher told his colleagues: "Look now they're already cutting the corpse and getting at his intestines." Thereupon he beckoned his SS orderlies and told them to take the culprits away. These Russians had to be taught manners, they could not behave like barbarians in a German camp! The men were summarily "tried", found guilty of cannibalism, and executed.

When Arush heard the story for the first time he interrupted at this point to ask why just doctors bothered? His friend Marek said: "Doctors regard cannibalism and death, in particular unusual death, to be a medical problem."

Yet other Russian p.o.ws, who apparently arrived later, had barracks built by themselves, and were also sent out to work, mainly to clear forests and build roads. Occasionally, a Jewish worker succeeded in snatching a word with a Russian p.o.w. One of them told Seibald, a cobbler, who came from Przemysl and so knew Ukrainian well, that three thousand men from his transport had died on their way to Pustkow.

Death from exhaustion, disease and maltreatment also decimated the working p.o.ws in 1942. In the early summer of that year, their camp was liquidated, as only a few dozen, all highly skilled men, remained alive. How many of the Russian p.o.ws lost their lives in Pustkow no one could tell precisely. Berl Alter put the number at five thousand, Hausdienst at three times that figure. There were estimates in between the two; to Arush Freund, Alter seemed the more reliable witness.

In one other way the Russian p.o.ws affected the Jewish prisoners' lives, or rather affected them after their lives had been taken away from them. Until close to the end of 1941, all victims who died in Pustkow were buried in a huge common ditch -

172

Russians, Jews, Poles all together. At the end of 1941, the Germans began to cremate the Russian p.o.ws and from then on this procedure was extended to other captive peoples. On Hill 218, which the SS men liked to call sportingly "Queens' Hill", and Polish as well as Jewish prisoners referred to by a name that would be unprintable in translation, a grate was fixed, staked with wooden pyres on which the dead were burnt. In the following months, the old-timers reported, smoke rose day and night from Hill 218 into the empyrean heavens.

Below on earth, there were roads, Rings, and rifle-ranges. In the main, it was in 1940 and throughout 1941 that Jews from all over Poland were forcibly brought to Pustkow. At that time, there was another category of Jews there: men who had enlisted voluntarily through the intermediary of the Judenrats in towns near Pustkow. Many of the volunteers were refugees, mostly from Germany. But there were not only refugees. The Judenrats, themselves under pressure from their German superiors, urged young Jews, especially skilled workmen, to enlist, offering them additional emoluments as well as certain privileges for their families.

Additional advantages because in the first two years, Jewish voluntary workers were paid proper wages in Pustkow. Even as late as the beginning of 1941 they were also allowed home leave at weekends, though not every week, and even, in certain circumstances, a short holiday. Many of these workers could also receive visitors from outside. The range and duration of these privileges depended on the SS unit for which the men worked.

As good employers, the prisoners remembered in particular the Kommandatur, whose workers were spoken of as the "aristocrats" among the Jewish prisoners, on account of their general labour conditions; the Unterkunftstelle, whose head until the end of November 1942, Hauptsturmführer Gerstmeyer, had treated the workers fairly well; and the SS Communications Unit, whose telephone and other connecting lines were laid by Jewish labourers. The commanding officer of that unit, Hauptsturmführer Thom - the old-timers recalled with appreciation - had resisted orders for his unit to participate in the "evacuation" of Jews from towns in 1942. When his protests were overrruled by the Pustkow base commander, Thom appealed successfully to a higher SS office (which one, the prisoners did not know) in Berlin. He was not forced to comply, nor removed from the command of his unit.

Among the bad employers, however great the savagery of the various firms employing Jewish workers, their treatment depended even more on the SS commanders of the sites at which they toiled. The most notorious site was the shooting range; for the brutality of its commanding officer, Hauptsturmführer Hanns Proschinsky, the old-timers could find no fitting words.

No less important in determining a Jew's fate than the employer and the officer commanding the unit of the site at which he worked, was the kind of work he performed. Work for the Kommandatur and the Unterkunftstelle consisted of labour at depots, at maintenance, and above all at various, initially decentralized, craft-workshops. The men involved came largely from among those who had enlisted voluntarily. On the other hand, labour with the bad employers meant, except for a small minority, hard physical drudgery at forest commands and various building sites. The Jewish labourers at these commands had nearly all been brought forcibly to Pustkow. Even without the beatings and shootings that took place at work, their general living conditions were mainly such that there was little chance of them surviving for long.

In the first two years, however, exchange of workers was still possible. The SS officers-employers at the base would usually agree to release sick and exhausted prisoners, if they could replace them with healthy, and perhaps also better skilled, ones. This incidentally explained how it was possible, through the intermediary of a Judenrat, to buy out forced labourers from Pustkow - for a tidy sum.

During that early phase, 1940-1941, when there were relatively many Jews in Pustkow, it, too, was given a Judenrat. And Bubi Feldmaus, hardly twenty years old in 1940, was one of its "departmental" heads. To rid themselves of the work-load caused by the simultaneous presence of between one thousand and three thousand Jewish workers, the SS command of the base was glad to allow the Judenrat to take over a large part of its administration in matters concerning its dependants. The local Judenrat maintained contacts with its counterparts in the towns, was instrumental in procuring the workmen wanted by its SS bosses, and endeavoured to get outside funds for the needs of men already ensnared in Pustkow. The Judenrat also took pains to provide limited social services, in particular a health service operated by several Jewish doctors, who were answerable to the SS medical officers at the base. And as long as the Jewish workers were paid wages, their food supply was also the responsibility of the Judenrat. Later, the Standortverwaltung paid directly for the provisions supplied to Jews.

A Jewish labour camp was first established in Pustkow on the enclosure of the Kommandatur in November 1940. Before that, and in the case of some groups of skilled workers even later on, the Jews lived scattered in quarters provided by the SS units that employed them. This meant, for example, that a Jewish groom slept in the same stable with the horses in his care. In times of stringent camp rules and in particular of the Z-camp, this would be a privileged abode. In general, accommodation at the base outside the camp was no better than inside the camp, but it gave the selected men a sense of freedom of movement.

For the majority of Jews a drastic change for the worse took place in June 1941, when the notorious Oberscharführer Kops replaced Unterscharführer Schmidt as commander of their camp. In the autumn of that year, the Jewish camp was moved to a site near the Kochanowka railway station in the so-called Ring 5. It was not only camp frontiers that changed, so also did the frontiers of human torment. While these were continuously being pushed to new limits, a truly tragic reality came into being with the division of the camp into two segregated parts in March 1942. In the A-camp, containing mostly skilled workers, life was still bearable. In the Z-camp, which was surrounded by an electrically charged wire, conditions were as bad as in any of the most ill-famed concentration camps. Kops arranged a special chamber there for hanging prisoners, assisted in this by his deputy, Unterscharführer Kleindienst and other SS men, notably Hamann and Harke. In particular those Jews who were exhausted and, hence, no longer able to work were bound by their throats to bunks and strangled. Kleindienst, who liked to lasso his victims, used to kill them with bayonet stabs in their throats.

At the time the Z-camp was founded, hundreds of Jews from Mielec were evacuated to Pustkow, on foot, a distance of about twelve miles. On their arrival, they were shot by SS men, on the orders of Hauptsturmführer Wawrzik. Still, about eight hundred of the Mielec arrivals were allowed into the Z-camp.

Worse was to come.

By August 1942, all Jews working in Pustkow were concentrated in the camp in Ring 5, bringing the overall number of inmates to nearly two thousand, on the eve of September 16, 1942. On that day, the camp was "evacuated" under the command of Sturmbannführer Albrecht. About 1,300 men were sent to the extermination camp at Bełżec; the sick and the weak were shot dead locally; about 215 prisoners, all specialist craftsmen and those with other required skills, were left in Pustkow. These were the "old-timers" of later days.

The Jews who remained were to work for the Kommandatur in workshops which were also moved to Ring 5, and then renamed collectively - Industriehof.

The evacuated Jews were immediately replaced at the shooting-range and other building sites by Polish workers. A more sadly dramatic consequence of this was that the Poles, who until then had been "free", that is civilian workers, were turned into forced labourers, and imprisoned in the camp which the p.o.ws had vacated three months earlier. Later, the Jews were also moved there. The Germans began to send into the Polish camp men who had been arrested or just rounded-up for forced labour; among those arrested were some politically motivated patriots. Pustkow became an important camp for Poles.

Not long after the evacuation of the Jews, Kops was arrested for alleged sexual offences, and Haupsturmführer Schittli, previously commander of the Russian p.o.w camp, was nominated to command both the Polish and Jewish camps.

On June 13, 1943, the Jewish forced labour camp was officially turned into a concentration camp (K.Z.). The Germans had accorded more than a dozen different names to their camps. While, as regards Jews, the purpose of all was the same, it would be wrong to think that all camps meant the same to the Jews who were held in them. But in the case of Pustkow, the prisoners could not tell what difference the change in name made. There was perhaps an eventual effect for the better, as later experience suggests. In the short-run, a follow-up to the renaming was the almost immediate replacement of Hauptsturmführer Schittli by Untersturmführer Kurt Klipp. A tall, skinny, slightly stooped man of about forty with a waddling gait (hence the Jewish prisoners nicknamed him *Bruchkraut - Hernia*), Klipp was a member of the special death-head KZ squad of the SS, and had a horrific reputation.

Shortly after the new shop-sign followed the interior refit. The SS masters decided to buiild a new Industriehof next door, as it were, to the Jewish camp south-west of Hill 218. The new workshops, together with living quarters, were erected by Jewish prisoners, carrying barracks parts and some equipment a distance of two miles from Ring 5. The workshops were ready to start production in August. From then on the Industriehof extended its pretentious name to the Jewish prisoners' dwelling barracks as well.

The SS commanders must have been entertaining great hopes for the future of the Industriehof, as no sooner was it functioning, than its workforce was increased by about 130 slave labourers from Biesiadka. This was the name, derived from the nearest village, of a forced labour camp, and in the popular language of its Jewish prisoners who arrived in Pustkow, it included two neighbouring forced labour camps at Huta Komorowska and Dęba (near the site of a Wehrmacht military base that was even larger than Pustkow). All three villages were only about 10-15 miles away from Pustkow. These camps, to which Jewish forced labourers were brought from all over the General Government but mainly from the Mielec area, existed probably from the winter 1941/42 till September 1943. The Jewish prisoners worked there as tree fellers, sawyers and woodcutters. They were guarded by civilian German foresters and Poles turned *Volksdeutsche*, who both treated the Jewish prisoners no better than the worst SS guards in Pustkow. On average, there were several hundred Jewish workers at any one time in these three camps; about two thousand over the whole period. The 130 men who arrived in Pustkow, were apparently the sole survivors.

The next, and last, reinforcements to the Industriehof in Pustkow, were the men who arrived from Szebnie in November 1943.

Before he realized it, Arush had been in Pustkow for two months. Two months of unremitting, ravaging hunger. It seemed there would be no end to it, other than starving to death. It was only a matter of time. He would not have thought that he could survive for even that long starving.

And yet. Rescue, like ruin, strikes suddenly. About a week after Arush had "celebrated" his two months in Pustkow, and just as Dr Vadovitzer's six weeks were running out, provisions improved. Not only was the bread ration doubled, rising to 500 grams a day, but its quality improved. Real bread from grain flour, though of course not of high quality. And there was a dollop of margarine or marmalade to go with the bread. Still more palpably improved was the soup which would sometimes contain vegetables, potatoes, fat, flour, and occasionally a scrap of meat. Even "coffee" and "tea" improved; they tasted good and were slightly sweetened. No change, it seemed could be as abrupt and as momentous as this change in their daily fare. On this diet, estimated at 1,700 calories a day, a man not doing hard manual labour could live several months.

Initially the men were distrustful of the change, doubting its durability. Marek Rainer suspected that it was a prank. On the first evening following the improved provisions, he recalled that at Ring 5, the SS command had once similarly increased the rations, only to reduce them again a couple of days later.

As time went on, doubts receded, and after Bubi was heard saying on the authority of Ruf that the new food rations were to stay, the brotherhood began to speculate on what lay behind the change.

—"If anyone had told me that such a change would happen, I would have laughed in his face," Hausdienst exclaimed two weeks after the event.

Knepel, who took pleasure in contradicting Hausdienst whenever he could, maintained that the change did not surprise him. Speaking to Arush, but with an eye on Hausdienst, he said.

—"Now you see that they need our labour. Didn't I tell you so? That's why they're giving us more bread."

—"Who gives the bread?" asked Arush. "The workshops are the business of the Standortverwaltung. Do they reward us with more food for less work?"

Hausdienst seized on Arush's question to refute Knepel, and asked: "If our camp is the ultimate responsibility of our local bosses and is intended for work, why have they turned it into a KZ?"

This in turn gave Arush the opportunity to display his experience of life under occupation and to rebuff Hausdienst.

—"That isn't a good question. In July 1942 Himmler ordered that no Jew should remain alive outside a camp by the end of the year; well, a couple of days before the deadline, the SS and Police authorities in the General Government simply promoted the ghettos in the towns, including Tarnow, which still harboured Jews, to forced labour camps. That made everyone happy."

But Hausdienst did not give in, asking: "If we're a KZ, then orders for better or worse come from Bruchkraut's superiors on the outside."

Arush adopted the view of Waicholc who the evening before had told him some interesting news. First, and this information, if true, could only have come through Bubi from a German, that the improvement in food rations, as well as in other aspects of a prisoner's life - including, apparently, orders prohibiting the killing of a prisoner without the prior sanction of superiors in Berlin - was simultaneous to all concentration camps, and was implemented on orders of the department in control of all KZs at the Reich Security Head Office. Second, that as they were KZ inmates, orders concerning their existence came from the outside; nevertheless, because the camp was situated inside the Pustkow SS base, Klipp, who was of so much lower rank than Voss, must be taking the latter's wishes into consideration. Pustkow, Waicholc further claimed, proved manifestly that how prisoners are treated at a camp, or in the ghetto for that matter, depended largely on its local commanders. Arush repeated this view, but went on to qualify it.

—"However, it's unlikely that the Standortverwaltung would spend more money to raise our rations. But it should not prevent them from sending out reports telling how busy the Industriefhof is, how hard we're toiling, and perhaps requesting still more workers. Why not, if another authority is to pay for it? If GG state agencies on the outside are snatching merchandise that's scarce on the black market from one another, why shouldn't the same thing go on inside the confines of a military base, with Jews as the scarce commodity - for that's what we are now?"

In the end they all agreed, though it was no more than a presumption, that authority for matters concerning their work rested with the Unterkunftstelle, its workshops division, headed by Obersturmführer Klerk (who, camp rumour rashly claimed, was a relative of Dr Goebbels); everything else about their lives, including their ultimate fate, depended on the orders of Klipp's superiors.

They were also at one in their estimation of the mute, puny part they were playing in this tragic life-comedy, or, as Marek put it; "helpless pawns in a charade to which the clue is corruption."

This fully accorded with Arush's view but Marek's particular reference to corruption provided him with another opportunity to draw on his experience of earlier, pre-camp years.

He explained to Marek, as he did to the other mates whenever the subject came up for discussion, that, at least from the occupied people's point of view, corruption in this war had gained a different quality. He told them of the sheer dimension of the phenomenon. That corruption, built up into a major social institution, actually enabled millions of the oppressed people, especially the Jews until their extermination, to provide themselves with the necessities of life. He delighted in stressing the amazing way in which corruption had bridged the abyss between people who breathed hatred of one another, by creating a common interest. "Don't you see," Arush asked Marek, "that they need pawns to make a game worthwhile? Poisonous but profitable pawns. Mutually profitable, too, for the greed and corruption of SS officials have for many months prolonged the life of Jews in the ghettos. That some of us came here and are still breathing is also indirectly the merit of corruption."

Though essentially true, Arush was aware that in the last instance he might have been exaggerating, as he was when he said at the conclusion of his discourse that, helpless pawns though they were, and constantly just a hairsbreadth away from death, larger peoples than the Jews under occupation only survived at the whim of the Germans.

CHAPTER THIRTEEN

As distrustful as his mates, even if he hid his fears from others, Arush Freund none the less at once sensed the significance of the improvement in their diet, its revival of hope and its raising, somewhat remotely, of the expectancy that they might live.

Certain changes were noticeable very soon. Their narrow sphere of existence appeared to be broadening, so much so that, compared with the monotony of the immediate past, each day that followed the change seemed to Arush to bring something new. It was not a complete illusion. To begin with, his thoughts commenced to wander a little faster, to embrace a wider scope of things, and his power of imagination was increasing. This experience was apparently not his alone, as the broadening and deepening subjects of their conversations suggested. One obvious change was that more and more men began to talk about their past lives, when they were free. And looking back brought some comfort, at least to Arush. Even their food discussions took on a different complexion. There surfaced a new type of amateur practitioner, self-appointed food heralds, who announced every day before noon the taste of the soup, and if it was thick or thin. The message of highest excellence being that the "spoon stands". At the Bekleidungsbarracks the news was brought by Cetel, a young cobbler, who had the extra assignment of soup distributor. Apart from drawing satisfaction from this function, his reward was a ladleful of the thickest soup from the bottom of the drum.

A common theme that had arisen with the improvement of bread was what to do with it: to eat it at once or to put it away? One school of thought, the so-called pessimists, favoured eating their rations on the spot. The reason was not fear that it would be stolen, for this happened very rarely in Pustkow - only once did a bread ration disappear in the tailors' shop without its owner's participation - but because "you couldn't be sure of the next moment". The optimists, on the other hand, hid away their bread "against a rainy day". This school of thought also maintained that to have a piece of bread in reserve made one less hungry. Some of the same school also held that the gratification derived from bread consumption varied with the time of the day and the surroundings; namely, that the pleasure of eating the bread was greatest before sleep, while lying quietly on the bunk. But a major reason for putting away bread was the possibility of barter, of exchanging bread for tobacco or cigarettes. These, along with unrationed food, were provided by some SS men, including Saar, given mainly to the masters, as a reward for work done for them. There were not a few prisoners who exchanged their bread rations for tobacco, despite the grave hunger that was still common.

Arush always ate up his bread at the first sitting, for the one and only reason that it made him think less about it. He was aware that bread entered one's consciousness, not just through the belly, but even before it had reached the mouth.

Was he rewarded by a dream of distributing bread freely, in unidentifiable circumstances, certainly in freedom?

Eating mends everyone's mood, let alone that of hungry people. The collective mood of the Pustkow brotherhood had indeed been slowly improving since the change in their daily fare. But what affected it more than anything else was the ever better news from the fronts. And as a consequence, the improved mood increased the amount and raised the quality of comment, not least that of Arush Freund.

On the first anniversary of the victory at Stalingrad, he tried to recapture for his mates the sentiments this event had aroused among the Jews in the ghetto, and to review its effects, gleaned from news heard since that time. The great battle between the rivers Don and Volga, he ventured, ended with the greatest single defeat in modern German history. The Germans lost about one and a half million soldiers in dead, wounded, and men taken prisoners, besides huge material losses. To the Russians, the victory was of even greater consequence, a true landmark. It enabled them to establish a strategic initiative and to go over to the attack on all fronts. Since then, he said, they had been rolling irresistibly forward. And yet, Arush - knowing well how to link various events that would pleasantly excite his listeners - also claimed that the failure of the Germans to take Moscow was more decisive for the outcome of the war than their defeat at Stalingrad. Delighted to expand, Arush explained how at the end of October 1941, after only four months of war - and to the Jews' despair - the Germans were merely 30 kilometres away from Moscow. It looked as if they would take it any day. The Russians had already left the Kremlin, were preparing to evacuate the population, and building defences in the city that only days before had been the nerve centre of Russian public life. The Germans threw everything into the Moscow battle scale. Their failure to tip it in their favour was their first strategic defeat in the war, and was of paramount political and military significance. It shattered the *Blitzkrieg* myth, and demonstrated to allies and foes alike that the German army was not invincible. After halting the offensive, the Red Army proved they were still capable of striking back: on the 6th of December they began a counter-attack that pushed the enemy back and exhausted his thrusting power for some time. Meanwhile, Arush concluded, an immediate effect of the German debacle before Moscow was that in the occupied territories captive Jews were ordered to hand over their furs, felts, sheepskins, skis, until the end of December.

Not everyone agreed with his interpretation, in particular his attaching greater significance to the victory before Moscow than to the one at Stalingrad. Knepel and Hausdienst pointed out that Arush actually labelled both battles as turning points in the war. However Arush was able to explain this away and somehow managed to connect both victories to the military situation at the time of their debate.

In February 1944, they heard only a day or two after the event, that the Russians had reached the towns of Dubno, Łuck, and stood before Kowel. These names acted upon them like narcotics. These were not some strange, distant towns in Italy, where military operations looked ever more irrelevant, not only to their own fortunes, but to the fortunes of the Allied cause. These were familiar names of towns, built on the same land on which they had grown up, and Arush quickly calculated the distance between themselves and the nearest of the towns mentioned. It seemed persuasive at that period of their bondage to think of liberation in terms of the Russian advance. Arush had consequently been planning new Russian campaigns, offensives, battles, and unfolding them to his mates. Yet in moments of sober reflection he self-deridingly appraised his plans as perhaps too quick for Stalin's generals. The mockery was not unrelated to the fact that after moving forward rapidly during the winter, the Red Army had bogged down to the boundless chagrin of all the Pustkow inmates. They felt betrayed.

–"But they haven't advanced for more than two weeks! Why?" Marek asked in a mixture of frustration and spite towards Arush, as if his opinion really mattered.

–"The winter came to an end. They don't attack at a temperature above minus five centigrade." Arush felt his flesh creep as he spoke, not so much at the implication for their future of what he had said, because he was half-joking, but at the thought of living in trenches in the freezing cold. He started to curse the war and its cruelty, which was another of his popular comments.

At the workshop, along with more debating there was more singing. As far as singing is concerned, the connection with improved food rations was more evident than it was with discussions of politics and strategy. Tailors are probably more fond of music than other craftsmen. Performing a quiet trade, at least in pre-machine days, tailors were accustomed to humming melodies during their long hours of drudgery. The words of many Yiddish songs are about tailors. Anyway in Pustkow, they were the patrons of vocal music. Since the brighter days, Berl Alter or one of his deputies occasionally offered a chunk of bread or a handful of tobacco to a guest performer. The concerts, if one may call them that, took place in the tailors' room, and needless to say, during work-time. Actually there was only a single "professional" performer, though a very eager one. Mendel Srebrny was said to have been a street-singer in his native Warsaw before the war, and had been seized there during a razzia and brought to Pustkow in the winter of 1940/41. A middle-sized man in his twenties, Srebrny had a strange boxer's nose, was bald (not just because his head had been shaved), looked thinner than most prisoners, but he managed to sing in a strong baritone voice.

There was a better singer than Srebrny at the Bekleidungsbarracks, but he was reluctant to perform. This man's name was Dichter. He also came from Warsaw, where he had once held the venerable position of cantor at the Nozhik synagogue. Dichter liked to come to the tailors for a chat, in particular with Arush. He took pride not in his former calling, but in presenting himself as a communist. Telling

181

how he had been converted to communism was the one major enjoyment left to him. Dichter had led a quiet life in the bosom of his family, enjoying his music, until the day in the summer of 1931, when he was given notice of instant dismissal. It was the time of the worst economic depression, he told Arush: "I suddenly found myself without a job, without savings, without redundancy pay, or entitlement to unemployment relief. Without means to live, but with a wife and five children, the sixth on the way. I was desperate. After a few months, grown shabby and down at heel, I began as a cobbler at my home, and clandestinely joined a cell of the Communist Party.

"When I was still a cantor, I wondered about much that I had seen around, I used to ask myself why the wealthy well dressed *balebatim* (philistines, bourgeois) always sat at the east wall of the synagogue, while the poor, the truly pious men, were assigned to a back seat or not offered one at all. Is a pure coat more valued in heaven than a pure heart? But I kept silent. I had my job, and did what I was required to do. But when I found myself on the street, I started asking where is God and where is His justice?"

Until the war, Dichter had not shaved off his beard and earlocks, nor did he take off his strictly orthodox outfit. The reason, he explained to Arush, was not one of safety, to disguise the fact that he was a communist - but one of not unfounded fear that, living in a pious neighbourhood, he would be avoided by potential customers if he changed his outward appearance. Arush was not surprised at what Dichter told him, because it was well known before the war that quite a lot of Jews who dressed in the traditional way, were not really observant.

Though Dichter no doubt knew many secular Yiddish songs, his specialities were prayer melodies and hymns, which he was often heard crooning under his breath, but was reluctant to sing aloud. He could not be enticed by a piece of bread, because as a senior cobbler, he did not live on the standard ration alone - indeed, he had a relatively full, and quite pleasant, face.

If the songs they sang in the workshop had words, they would be in Yiddish. This naturally strengthened the position of Yiddish among the men, and, in particular, for the Jewish workers in Poland. Yiddish was not just a language but an ideology as well. In everyday singing, their repertoire ranged from military marches, the Marseillaise and the International, all sung without words, through the old sentimental songs such as "Rosinkes and Mandeln," "Oifn Pripetsil", "A Yiddishe Mame" - which had a special poignancy to it, as they had all recently lost their mothers - to the lately popularized "Es brent", whose words alluded to the Jews' destruction and called on them "to quench the flames" that threatened to envelop all their homes. Srebrny introduced some new songs from Warsaw, such as "Wie ahin soll ich gehn", hammering home the prewar situation of Jews struggling to emigrate, "wenn ale toiren sind vermacht" (while all the gates are closed). But his showpiece was the very melodious "Matushka Russeya", which was popular with most prisoners.

"Matushka Russeya
(Mammie Russia)
wie stark ich benq nuch dir
(how strongly I long for you)
nuch dem khatkale dem kleinen
(for the little hut)
un nuch dem grinen dorf."
(and for the green village.) and so on.

When Arush, feeling his position at the tailors' more secure, once risked suggesting that they sing the "Hatikva" (Zionist anthem), he met with grim silence. But his mates did not object, when on another occasion he began singing a verse made popular shortly before the war by a leading Polish-Jewish cantatrice, Hanka Ordonowna. The melancholic words went something like this:

O jej, jak tam pieknie
(Oh my! How beautiful it is there)
Gdy bialy Telaviv lsni w poludnie
(When white Telaviv shines at noon)
O jej, jak tam cudnie
(Oh my! How marvellous it is there)
Gdy tutaj pada snieg
(When here it's snowing)
Tam jest Maj
(There it's May)
Zeby móc tak ujrzec
(If only one could see)
Ten raj.
(That paradise.)

The fact that Arush was allowed to sing this, and in Polish too, convinced him, if he had been in doubt before, that even Deker, Knepel and the other influential tailors, who were ideologically hostile to Zionism, would not mind being in Palestine. But that was a dream; in reality they were in Pustkow, entrenched in their Marxist-Socialist past, and bound to a future, if they lived to see it, with the Soviets.

Who wants to sing out of tune?

The singing occasionally overflowed into theatre. Yiddish theatre, of course. Not in the way of acting, but in the manner of plain discussion, and yet not precisely discussion either, rather, I would say, lectures by one man Asyk Deker. Yiddish theatre was his favourite indulgence and he was easily tempted into tall talk. He was really conversant with the subject, though to his mostly unenlightened listeners in Pustkow, it seemed - as it usually does in situations like this - that his knowledge was much greater than it really was.

Plays, he maintained, were far superior to other forms of prose narrative; Yiddish has been the means through which the life of a Jew took shape and in Yiddish drama it reached the highest form of specific meaning. Universally, embracing the whole of mankind, it presents actual life in its dramatic purpose.

"Avrum Goldfaden, the father of the Yiddish theatre, at once succeeded in adapting his drama to dramatic intention, simultaneously exalting the souls of his folk-audience by melody and spark."

"Itzik Leib Peretz, a legend in his own lifetime. The writer who brought Yiddish drama to the highest world standard."

"Peretz at once the great romantic and realist, satirist and tragedian. The genius painter of social and moral problems in dramatic form."

"Peretz the inspired teacher of socialism and humanity's path to liberation."

"Shulem Aleichem the genius of Yiddish humour. In him humour reached its highest peaks. The specifically Yiddish humour fusing the comic and the tragic, self-mockery and pride, invariably ingenious and pungent."

"Shulem Aleichem, the great creator of eternal Jewish characters and of artistic settings."

"Shulem Asch, the prodigious Yiddish writer of literary masterpieces, capturing Jewish folk-life on a giant artistic canvas."

"With Shulem Asch the Yiddish novel climbed to the uppermost rungs of written prose. This attained an even greater intensity of action, a higher sense of folk community and artistic elan, in dramatized form."

A tiny anthology of Asyk Deker's didactic reviews. Hardly anyone ever tried to dispute them with him. Though, after one of those lectures Hugo Bester (about whom more later) said privately to Arush: "What a fuss! All about inconsequential, second-rate literature."

"Second-rate, I agree, but not inconsequential. The best proof of that is Deker himself. Try to understand what he is bemoaning."

What did once attract argument, especially from Hausdienst, was when Deker, in the course of stretching the cult of Yiddish, said that Hebrew was a non-organic language, incapable of creative expression. Even if it were, he said, there in Palestine a new tribe was being formed, cut off from the cultural family roots and hostile to them. And in America, the immigrants were striving so mightily to be absorbed into the new environment, that they were becoming ever more estranged from their Yiddish past, in so far as the Jews in America had still any time for such luxuries as the past or ancestral heritage.

With the extinction of the Jewish folk in eastern Europe it was not only the grand and uniquely rich Yiddish civilization that had disappeared; even the prospects of it resurrecting itself, or of finding people curious about it in the future, had vanished.

For once Deker's grief was unaffected.

Although the theatre lectures did not attract a great audience, the concerts and the frequent comments on the news often brought extra listeners to the tailors' room. Several times, to avoid hazardous overcrowding, some lesser mortals had to be asked to come another time. A frequent visitor, and prominent supporter of Arush Freund, was Wolf Osterman. As well as sharing some memories from Tarnow, Osterman, considering the great length of his imprisonment and lack of education, took an unusual interest in political matters. Arush was attracted to him as well, not only as to one of the most influential and still relatively young master-craftsmen, but because he sensed in him an artist of a sort. That he raised the making of shoe-uppers to an art, Arush did not question. The Germans seemed to agree, rewarding him accordingly, and thanks to his genius - well, one can be a genius in anything - even low ranking SS men in Pustkow, such as Saar or Klipp, wore probably the most chic riding-boots in the whole German Reich. Arush admired how Osterman managed with a few strokes of the pencil to draw not just a boot but a man neatly wearing it. At the same time, the master-artist hardly knew how to write more than his own name and had only a smattering of Polish. Yet Osterman liked to emphasize what was, in the circumstances, an "avant garde" taste in clothing. He wore nonchalantly a type of slip-on shoes, even in winter, an open-necked flannel shirt and a bright blue, woollen pullover - and, when no SS man was present, a pipe in his mouth. More suprising to Arush were some of his observations that bore a social or political stamp. Talking of his background, and referring to a debate earlier that day, during which the radical tailors had said that the war would end with the demise of capitalism, Osterman told Arush: "Capitalism or no capitalism, socialism or no socialism the bootmaker must return to his last." But, then, Osterman had no wish to change from a bootmaker to a commissar or a politician. Another time, in response to Deker and Knepel, who had argued with great excitement that the triumph of Soviet arms signified the victory of the working class, with the consequential elimination of all distinction between men and peoples, Osterman said (and unlike Arush he was not afraid to say it loudly) that the war would end with the victory of Soviet Russia but not of the workers, the true working man. "Things have never gone that way", he added.

Another, strange and less frequent visitor to the tailors was the master saddler and harness maker, Perec Lisko, who came mainly to have a chat with Arush. One of the oldest prisoners, at fifty he looked older than he was, with an expression of wear and dullness on his face, only a few teeth in his mouth, jaded hands with fingers brown from tobacco stains. Lisko had behind him a hard life which he had spent in Warsaw, until he came to Pustkow in 1941. He had very few interests except one that went back to the great, and perhaps sole, passion of his youth. This, believe it or not, was the famous Beilis trial of 1913. By a curious chance, Arush, who was born long after that trial, knew a little about it. At their home a few newspaper copies from the time had been preserved, containing pictures that were imprinted on his memory. The fact that Arush could describe the house in which Mendel Beilis lived before he was arrested and, alone of all the Pustkow prisoners, could relate a few other details, in particular names, connected with the trial, won Lisko's heart and raised Arush in his eyes.

–"So you remember the trial?" Lisko repeated eagerly.

–"Only from what I have heard and read."

–"Then you don't really know what it was like. Several thousand spectators in the courtroom every day of the trial. Newspaper correspondents from every civilized country in the world. What a spectacle! What excitement! New revelations every day. Pictures of large, horse-drawn carriages, carrying volumes of the Talmud and other Hebrew books to the courtroom. It wasn't the trial of a single man. All Jews were tragically on trial."

–"What stays in the memory is a satire, though a macabre one," Arush threw in.

–"A nice satire, I must say! People were overwhelmed. I couldn't eat. For over a month, newspapers were my meat and drink. I'd get up early in the morning to buy one. Everywhere you'd find Jews not working but reading the papers and discussing the proceedings deliriously.

"So much stir, and the jury just twelve plain peasants. Not that I was afraid they wouldn't understand what was at issue. But they are just the people to believe a blood libel. Every time I realized what was at stake, I came out in a cold sweat. I wept like a child when I read that Beilis was found not guilty."

–"With Szmakow, the private prosecution counsel, declaring, 'A terrible blow for Russia'", Arush again interposed.

–"D'you remember that?" Lisko asked rhetorically, quite delighted. "I didn't believe he would be acquitted. Those terrible pogrom speeches by the experts for the prosecution, 'If the earth was to give up its dead, everyone could see how many Christian children had been murdered by the Jews.' And he himself a converted Jew, turned monk. We almost lost heart completely. Hardly to raise spirits because the only Jewish witness admitted to the trial, Rabbi Maze, came to court 'not to defend the truth, but to proclaim the truth.' And then the chief prosecutor's speech, don't remember his name."

–"Czaplinsky."

–"Yes, Czaplinsky saying that they must avenge the blood of the poor child shed by Beilis. It was so distressing. I had no wish to live. And last of all, the summing up by the presiding judge..." Lisko fumbled for the name.

–"Bolderko."

–"How you remember the names," though Arush would not swear to its authenticity.

"He was impartial of course, he had said so in his introduction. But then he told the jury not to take into consideration anything that was said in the defence of the accused. To consider only that a Christian child had been murdered."

Even though Arush did not believe that the judge had said what Lisko ascribed to him, he agreed: "Yes, the verdict was a miracle."

–"But until this day, I can't understand, why a man like Oscar Gruzenberg, who wasn't particularly pious, should conclude his speech for the defence with the words: 'Beilis if ever you're convicted, proclaim loudly: Shema Yisruel (Hear, O Israel, the first words of a basic Jewish doxology avowing the Kingdom of God).

This made Arush reflect that in the present war many "non-pious" Jews must have uttered the same prayer in their last moments of life, when all hope had vanished. But he said nothing. He was bored, and considered that having listened for so long to Lisko, he had humoured him enough, even if he was a master-craftsman, a person not to be treated with disregard, let alone to be despised.

Things at the workshop were not as difficult for Arush as this would suggest. The class and political differences between him and the tailors, between the "old" and "new" prisoners in general, were slowly becoming blunted. The longer they were acquainted, the more tolerant the men became of one another. Even the debates were probably more unifying than divisive, while the common singing advanced their sense of togetherness. As in normal life, frequent association mutually influenced opinions, while the plain, indisputable fact that the harbinger of their eventual liberation was the Red Army could not fail to affect everyone's thinking, including that of Arush. Even so, and despite the need to ingratiate himself with his superior fellow prisoners, he succeeded in retaining his independence of mind - in remaining himself.

More significant than ideological or even class affinity were personal relations. There was little love discernible between Deker and Knepel, but Arush had come to like Knepel, and perhaps also to be liked in return; it was difficult not to become fond of Knepel's radical humour, openness and goodness. In general, shared concerns and circumstances - the common enemy, the common danger, the common aim of survival, the common anxiety about current camp conditions, the common sorrow and suffering - drew human beings to one another.

Even his difficulties with Sami Hausdienst had diminished since their memorable talk, which had soothed one of Sami's old but rankling wounds. What a small world, people often declare in genuine or affected amazement, and Arush could not help repeating it, when, one evening towards the end of winter, Hausdienst confessed to him that his father and the father of Bunim Laib were brothers, but on the spear side only. Their common grandfather, Nuhim Laib, Arush quickly grasped, had apparently not married his second wife at the registry, so that his children with her were in the eyes of the law "out of wedlock" and bore her family name. Consequently, Bunim's father was a Laib, while Sami's father bore the undistinguished name of Hausdienst. This would not have been so painful, if the Hausdiensts had not also been poor. For reasons not clear to Arush, Nuhim Laib had made over his wealth to the sons of his first wife before he married the second time "in the autumn of his life", as Sami put it, tongue in cheek.

"You know, they," referring to the Laibs and the rich in general, "made their fortunes with their heads and their two hands. To them, others who had not, were just lazy and shlimazels (duffers). To take them into the family business, well, business and family don't mix well. What good is a poor family? The only thing they know is to sponge off their rich relatives. Can you imagine the injustice? How the rich are exploited by the poor? Instead of feeling guilty and working hard, they ask for more help.

"They, the rich, certainly work hard. Answering a customer's phone, calling a supplier, and between a visit to a banker and a chat with a broker, working with tooth and claw at lunch."

These were the finer points of a long story. Although Arush had his doubts about its exactitude, and asked himself if Hausdienst were taking revenge on him, he kept his mouth shut and did not interrupt. But Arush did intervene when Hausdienst went on to rail, though not by name, at Bunim and his other semi-relatives, saying: "That fairytale world of theirs is gone, the world of rich merchants' sons, of mothers' darlings and idlers. They've had a chance lately to learn what it means to be poor and to work hard." At this, Arush had recounted to Hausdienst the tragic tale that Bunim Laib had broken-heartedly told him in Szebnie.

In Plaszow, Goeth had selected Bunim Laib as one of the managers to set up tailor workshops in Szebnie, and his wife Hedwa, a nurse, to assist a doctor in organizing a "hospital" there. They were exceptionally allowed to take with them their two little sons aged six and four. Several months later, in September 1943, a Jewish prisoner, a driver to SS bosses, took a car to repair in Jaslo, and escaped in it over the border with Slovakia. When this was discovered, Kellermann, the camp commander, let it be known that if the man did not surrender, ten Jewish prisoners would be executed. Next day, all the inmates were lined up for a half-day-long roll-call. So that Kellermann's threat could be carried out, five men and five women were picked out to die, including Hedwa Laib. Her unmarried sister, Rachel Kirsz, implored the SS officer in charge - Berndt was his name - to shoot her instead of her sister, in order not to orphan her children. The SS man readily agreed. From a distance of ten yards, he aimed straight into Rachel's face as she stood proudly upright; only after the second bullet hit her brow did she fall to the ground. Then Berndt, of course, shot Hedwa dead as well. Bunim was also standing at the roll-call, separated from his children, and watched the execution. When finally the two little boys were led to the firing place, the older one held his brother by the hand, and was heard comforting him: "Chaimku, hold me firmly by the hand, for we're going to Mamie."

Hausdienst heard out the story in silence, visibly moved. He never spoke to Arush again about Bunim Laib or his other relatives.

The private troubles of Arush at the workshop, or the sneers of Hausdienst that he bore so meekly, were, however, not yet all in the past. The idleness that he had to endure was enough to try the patience of angels. He endured it but impatiently, drowning in constant fear. While everything they did there was slave-work, to do no work was a much greater slavery, Arush philosophized self-pityingly.

Though it was hardly a consolation, the fact that everyone now had progressively less and less to do improved his own position somewhat. They were also witnessing something rather unusual at the tailors' - the beginning of a "social experiment", or, as Arush slightingly described it to his bunk neighbour, a microcosm of an ideal society. None the less, he felt guilt in relation to his mates, who were really working. So much so that, however much it pricked his pride, he was glad towards the end of the day to scrub the shop-floor, a distinction which Hausdienst and Alter conferred on him in the name of justice.

Hardest of all was the time when a German came to the workshop. The most frequent, almost daily visitor was Hauptscharführer Saar. But he, luckily for Arush, never gave him so much as a glance. Indeed Arush soon realized that although choleric, often shouting until he was foaming at the mouth, Saar, for the uniform he

188

wore, was not a bad man. But there was Rapportführer Ruf, and Arush had no doubt that he was fully informed about the situation. As if that were not enough, towards the end of February, a civilian German master, Herr Klause, started daily coming and goings. He was a slim, slack, small-sized man of about forty. A civilian, but one who wore a brown shirt and black tie with a swastika-badge pinned to it, a slightly larger one in the jacket lapel, and quite a large swastika arm-band on one sleeve. However, the most striking thing about the man was his unhealthy pallor. This seemed to explain to Arush his long absence, which had started well before the arrival of the labour reinforcement from Szebnie. The old-timers who had known him for years maintained that Klause was not a dangerous Nazi. But, unlike Saar, he did look at Arush and, to his horror, quite piercingly at times, yet without saying a word to him. No one actually knew what Klause was supposed to do all day long. But he was a German and boss to the prisoners. And a permanent thorn in Arush's pants.

Driven by the terror of idleness, after more than three months of daily contact, Arush asked Hausdienst to give him some tailoring work. At first he met with a stark refusal. But after turning down repeated requests, Hausdienst, being in a gay mood, one day formally obliged.

–"If I were you, I wouldn't try a new trade. All jobs have their advantages and drawbacks. It comes to the same, whether you know how to sew, or not. But since your fingers itch to do some sewing, I'll train you as a tailor."

What Arush really desired was a seat at a sewing-machine, but to this Hausdienst would not agree, however much Arush asked. Alter also voiced his opposition.

–"To sew on a machine one has to be a tailor," explained Hausdienst. "You cannot jump the gun. You must start from the beginning. I began, and every learner does, with basting and then removing the stitches."

All-right, let it be basting.

Visibly disappointed that Arush managed to thread the needle at the first attempt and began pricking it into the cloth, Hausdienst stopped him.

–"You must use the thimble, to push against the needle."

–"But I do it better without. The thimble is to protect the finger. I don't hurt mine."

–"You must learn to use the thimble. Every tailor does."

Trying to push the needle through the cloth was painful. He went on pricking his fingers, growing increasingly annoyed, not least because of the sneer behind Hausdienst's instructions. He realized, as he had often before in this war, that there were no limits to torture. No need for iron chains, a tiny, silly thimble would do it. At last he told himself: "If I must suffer, let it be for something and not at Hausdienst's hands."

His apprenticeship was over.

"Work co-operation", "comradeship", "a new social order", Arush had muttered under his breath somewhat sourly as he pricked his finger and listened to the discussions. "Fine, brave words. We'll see what will come of it when one of these comrades is required to make some personal sacrifice."

189

Though self-critical as he had been, he was pained at the thought of how trifling were his personal anxieties and endeavours against the depth and gravity of their past and present conditions. But, then, he had been percipient enough to notice from his earliest days in Pustkow that at camp, unlike most people in the ghetto, they were doomed to worry about themselves alone. Hugo Bester was, therefore, a pleasant exception for, apart from himself, he had someone to worry about on the outside. Arush found it refreshing to listen to someone of his own age expressing concern about a person dear to him. It opened his eyes to a different world from his own. Though Hugo was not a particularly endearing fellow. He was easily excitable and petulant, which showed strangely in his shining dark eyes and small round face, with cheeks which, though of late normally pale, instantly reddened once he became agitated. Whether by disposition or upbringing, he was generally pessimistic about human nature and motivation, which made him require absolute morality in a man; in particular, he was inclined to grumble at the Jewish wartime institutions and leadership, enormously exaggerating the magnitude and even more so the significance of Jewish collaboration. Fond of talking big and of boasting of his courage, Hugo often mentioned that he was prepared to die - as if his permission were required - but used to reprove all his Pustkow mates, because they, like any Jew, were not concerned about the death of another Jew - implying that he was.

With Arush, Hugo also liked to play the intellectual, and a liberated one of what he called dubious morality. Reciting book titles and the names of spicy authors, such as Courts-Mahler or Pitigrilli, he pretended that their libertine views were his own, which matched oddly with his own claim to asceticism. Arush listened to all this in splendid silence not only because he was a stranger to the authors and their genre of books, but mainly because he could not help laughing inwardly at the posturing of Hugo, who, Arush had no doubt, was really an innocent, decent fellow.

Hugo came from a culturally assimilated Jewish family of Katowice. His only sister, Ludka, had married exogamously in 1937; her husband was a Polish mining engineer. Since their flight eastwards at the start of the war, she had lived with her husband in Cracow as an Aryan. Hugo completed his grammar-school education in 1939. For the last three years, he had attended a bilingual school together with many pupils of German nationality, and he spoke German as flawlessly as Polish. While most Jews were expelled in 1939 from the territories incorporated into the Reich, which included the formerly Polish part of Upper Silesia, Albert Bester, as a senior manager at one of the largest collieries in the neighbourhood, was given permission to stay on with his wife and son, Hugo. But in the spring of 1941, the family was ordered to leave their home near Katowice for the General Government, taking with them only one piece of hand-luggage each. They decided to move to a small town near where the daughter lived, but after only four months landed in the ghetto of Cracow. Shortly before Christmas 1941, Roman, Hugo's brother-in-law - whose family name he was careful not to mention in Pustkow even to Arush - arrived with Ludka at her parents' one-room home in the ghetto, declaring that he was in financial straits and that if they did not lend him five thousand

Złoties, he would be forced, with great regrets, to leave their daughter with them and return alone to the "other side".

Five thousand Złoties was at that time a fairly large sum of money, on which, at the average standard of living in the ghetto, a family of three could subsist for nearly a year. Hugo's parents did not have the money, and asked Roman to wait a day or two. They sold what they could - two coats, linen, wedding-rings - to scrape together the required sum of money and gave it to Roman, begging him to take good care of Ludka.

Three months later, Hugo responded positively to a notice at the Judenrat, offering work at comparatively reasonable terms in Pustkow. But he denied having volunteered - a moot point - because he had been forced to offer himself as a result of the tight conditions in the ghetto. Recalling those events two years later, Hugo told Arush in tortuously roundabout language, that he did not expect to see his parents again, but that he hoped his sister remained alive in hiding, and that he would thus after the war have a relative and a home, if he survived. In saying this, he touched a tender nerve not just of Arush but of all his co-prisoners. Which of them did not constantly ask himself, though seldom aloud, who would await them if they returned "home"? Though used to suppressing this thought, talk of a living sister, plans for the future, life on the outside, carried Arush, too, into a daydream away from prison into a fairytale world.

At the Industriehof, Hugo was store-keeper of the Bekleidung shops. His duties comprised receiving goods, storing them properly, and dealing them out, against authorized orders, to the tailors, cobblers and saddlers. This did not require much more real work than Arush put into keeping his books. But it was much easier for Hugo than for Arush to simulate work, by moving materials from one shelf to another, or by taking stock whenever a distasteful SS man was expected. Moreover, his store was in a separate room with an entrance only from the corridor, and his work thus was inconspicuous to wicked and envious eyes alike.

Officially, Hugo had over him a civilian German store-keeper. He was known by his nick-name Wry-face, as he really had a badly contorted mouth, which seriously impaired his speech. Although he was of combatant age, his disability apparently made him exempt from active service and he was able to take shelter from war at an SS training base, in a non-job job. He, too, had a swastika pinned to his tie and jacket-lapel, but otherwise wore civilian clothes. Like Arush and Hugo, Wry-face loafed his time away, though unlike them, he absented himself from his office for hours or even days at a time.

Apart from chatting, Arush liked to visit Hugo for another reason. To keep its accounts the store had a separate book-keeper, named Belfer. He was the other Szebnie arrival who had been given an office job. But he took his idleness quite calmly, if not light-heartedly. Admittedly, Belfer was three times the age of Arush, and thus did not offend "natural justice" by being a penpusher. Nevertheless he was a comrade in play, if one may say so, of Arush, though not as comforting a one as Hugo. For Hugo lived in constant terror of a kind exclusive to him, worrying day and night that he would be held responsible for the shortfall in stocks which resulted from the supply of goods on irregular orders issued by SS men, and from Wry-face's occasional thefts. Mercifully for Hugo, the materials were mostly stolen by the men who were in charge of the store and the workshops, so that no official stock control ever took place.

The terror of Hugo and the calm of Belfer made Arush ponder whether he was not too sensitve and fearful. It could not fail to affect him. He began gradually to quake less in his shoes.

At the store-room one could also pick up the latest news before it reached the tailors' shop. It was Hugo who, assuming that Arush was in the know, disclosed to him in the course of a faltering conversation, the source of the news that circulated among the prisoners. One of the production barracks was the so-called *Bildstelle* (photo service) though it also contained workshops for the repair of radios, electrical appliances and certain musical instruments. Master-prisoner of these workshops was Kurt Semmel, an intelligent and gifted man in his late twenties, who came from Kassel in northern Germany. His talents were many-sided. Apart from the skills required in the technical workshops, he could carve very nice things out of wood, and even constructed a violin at camp.

"It's quite simple," perhaps it was for Hugo, certainly not for Arush. "Semmel uses radio parts that are stored over there for repairs and puts together the ones he needs to make a wireless receiver. As soon as the broadcast is over, or if an alarm warning is raised, Semmel quickly disconnects the various parts. No trace of a radio set."

Semmel and his associates usually listened to news bulletins, including foreign ones, as soon as they came to work in the morning. It was the safest time, as the man in charge of the Bildstelle, Hauptscharführer Schrade, or any other SS man, did not arrive at the workshop so early. In any case, there were always men on the lookout, who at the mere appearance of an SS man in the distance immediately signalled, giving Semmel enough time to cover up his tracks.

Arush wondered if after so many months Schrade had not nosed out what was going on? Hugo was categorical that he had not. Marek, to whom Arush put the same question, thought that Schrade might vaguely know, but that he was the sort of chap who did not care. From Schrade's own occasional indiscreet remarks it seemed likely that he was himself listening to foreign radio stations, which Germans were also forbidden to do.

Arush learned the secret of the wireless when Hugo brought news from the latrine that the Russians had crossed the rivers Prut and Dniestr. After days with no advance, Arush wished to impart the good news to the tailors'. But he found Hauptscharführer Saar at the shop and the atmosphere a little excited.

–"Where have you been?" Hausdienst, uncommonly, reproached Arush. "An important visit is expected and you're off gadding about somewhere. Everyone must be at their seats and showing maximum attention."

The tables and the floor had already been swept clean, and the distribution of additional material was almost complete. Minutes later no less a dignitary than the base commander, Gruppenführer Bernard Voss, arrived. He was greeted with due respect inside the custom-tailors' room by Hauptscharführer Saar. The purpose of the commander's coming was plain: dissatisfied with previous fittings made by Saar at his office, he had come to try on the military uniform which Berl Alter and his helpers had sewn for him.

Such a din had never been heard before, as all the machines whirred frantically to produce as much clack and clatter as possible. The whole place was bristling with activity, the men bending their heads lower than at any similar performance in the past. Arush, too, was exerting all his energy, concentrating both body and brain on the task of recopying all the entries in his book, while at the same time glancing furtively into the other room where the visitor put on his act.

Gruppenführer Voss was not a particularly tall man, square-framed, but not corpulent, and fairly spry for his build and age. He seemed to be about fifty-five, had greyish blond hair, and a face which looked as though radishes had been grown on it. A large scar above his right eye heightened his brutish look.

He stood erect in the new uniform, the jacket fitting like a glove, not a single wrinkle, not a ruck showing in the large mirror, which Saar moved around him; Alter, though all the time standing bolt upright, stretched up more stiffly to attention when he was addressed by the commander or spoke himself. Voss raised his arms, threw them about, put fingers under the armpits; he was comfortable and satisfied. But then he sat down, and what a calamity! And what a show (for Arush)! The trousers, which while he was standing had stretched smoothly, the cloth moulding to his hips and calves as he wanted, creased and crumpled at the groin when he sat on the chair. This should not be. Herr Gruppenführer was visibly displeased. He had not expected such a fault. He would not stand for it. You may be inclined to think this is fiction or at least a gross exaggeration, but it is all true, just as it is told. He wants trousers that will not rumple at the groin when he sits down. Saar tries to apologize, to persuade, to appease him, but to no avail. Trousers must not crease! Let them use starch. But that will only make things worse, explain Saar and Alter. Then iron them stiffer. All right, Alter irons the trousers under wet linen, smoothing and patting the cloth with the wooden back of a large brush. Then pressing them once more and then again. But the trousers show no mercy; they wrinkle, they fall into folds as soon as Herr Gruppenführer sits down.

Arush began to sweat, imagining himself in Alter's situation. Saar, clearly tired and ruffled, also seemed to be sweating, though, remarkably, not foaming at the mouth. The tailors, too, were not amused. They had not expected such a long visit, their feet ached from continuous pedalling and might soon cease to obey; the clatter was indeed clearly weakening. Finally, after repeated ironing, smoothing and stretching, and more re-enacting of the sitting scene, the Gruppenführer resignedly accepted Saar's suggestion that he wait and see if the trousers would not set smoothly in walking; if not, a new pair would be sewn.

After Voss had left, Arush asked himself whether the SS brigadier would have been as fastidious about his attire if he were serving at the front; and besides, how long did this rogue expect to wear that uniform? Saar, more joyous and relieved than anyone in the shop, may have been asking himself the same question; for returning from seeing Voss off, frowning and winking at Alter, he seemed to say: a cranky guy, what to do?

In the week of the great visit, and almost two months to the day after the improvement in the daily food rations, something equally unexpected happened in the life of the prisoners. The news came like a thunderbolt. Bubi, assisted by barracks orderlies, brought seven sacks full of bread from the Polish camp. The treasure was to be distributed together with soup at supper time. To most of the men it seemed too good to be true. A similar sensation to theirs must have come to the Children of Israel on hearing that manna was to drop from heaven. When the news proved true in the evening, it was still met with general disbelief and suspicion. Who knew what lay behind it? A sweet pill before the bitter end? Perhaps not? Perhaps just once, today? But there was more two days later, and then two or three times a week for the rest of their stay in Pustkow.

So what were the reasons? Were the SS men concerned merely trying to stir up the Polish prisoners' hatred against the Jewish ones? Unlikely, given the local camp conditions. It was much more likely to be meant as a punishment to the Poles - the sacks were carried so that as many Poles as possible could see them - who were undisciplined, some caused trouble a few even attempted to hide and escape. There was also a class of Jewish prisoners who saw in the sacks a reward for work done by them and others. Similarly, opinions were divided about who was to be credited with the provision order: the officers in command of the camp or those of the base at large?

When the bread sacks arrived more than once, Arush, among others, had expressed his not wholly serious scruples about feeding at the Poles' grieving expense. Though the food was taken forcibly from them by the Germans, which was the main justification for relishing the spoil.

Marek Rainer advanced another explanation as an excuse.

–"The bread isn't taken away from prisoners. It comes from the RGO (initial letters for the Social Care Council sanctioned by the Nazi authorities). They're known to have included Pustkow in their care."

"Pustkow may be," retorted Arush. "But not our camp. You know very well that the RGO is an agency for aid to Poles. They aren't allowed to help Jews."

"But JUS, its Jewish equivalent."

"Even if it's still operating, JUS couldn't possibly reach Pustkow. Besides, the food itself speaks against you. The bread is mostly home-baked, of a sort that no Polish charity, let alone JUS, could either arrange or afford to provide."

Indeed the sacks included not only bread of a quality that was not on sale in the market, but also some cakes and pastries.

Thus, notwithstanding the unvarying scenery and the monotony of colour, the days in Pustkow were not entirely devoid of change. Even more shifting were the ways of the prisoners. As their mood began to improve, so their attitude to life began to mend. In short, as hunger diminished, hope increased; hope of more life;

hope, the fount of life itself; hope, the stimulus of the human mind.

Already in the winter, as Arush was slowly recovering both mentally and physically, there re-awakened in him the desire not just to live on, but to live meaningfully. And his habit of introspection and self-criticism revived with his strength of body and mind. He began once more to admonish himself to set aside his private sufferings and needs, and to turn his mind to the immaterial qualities of life, to look at it in the context of events that had befallen his people and to which he had been witness. The re-awakened spirit, the force deep inside him, was driving him anew to do something deserving and durable, something that would justify him being alive when almost all the Jews around had died, something that would be worthy of their unsurpassed tragedy. In his waking dreams this aspiration usually crystallized in a lasting desire "to tell"; to tell, in however small a part, something about the lives and deaths of his fellow men.

No less, no more. What an ambition! And what an impotence of talent and skill! The feeling overwhelmed him. There was no want of subject matter, as all the war years had passed, at various times, before his eyes, though passing in broken order, with actors and scenes changing. But how could he arrange so much memory? How turn memory into story? So much history, so much detail and content, only made things worse. How could he put them into form and frame? It was beyond his power; better not to try. He did not. But the idea would not let him go. It grew within him into a heavy load, making him live permanently in a state of mental pain, which did not lessen with the inertly passing days.

He received no encouragement either. His friend Marek, to whom Arush had divulged his plan, and his private doubts, asked him: "D'you want to bring the dead back to life?"

–"In a sense yes. To recapture, if only a scrap, of their lives these last years. The problem is how to do it?"

–"No one can do it. It's a hopeless task. Better to be dumb than to produce drivel. The silence of the dead is more telling than the words of any number of poor pen-men."

He refrained, kindly enough, from referring to Arush directly.

Another time Marek said to him: "You want to describe something that can neither be described nor explained in words understandable to strangers to these things."

–"Words could be found to at least give a feeling of what happened."

–"Suppose so. But for whom would you write it? Who would be willing to read these tales?"

–"Some will. There'll come a time. The dust will settle over the graves. The cloud will lift off the dust. Guilt and contention will subside, the voices will rise, and the sounds will be listened to by offspring of the present age. Even them, those brothers of ours who watch from a distance, unwilling to listen, even them we must impel to hear."

–"You'll just be throwing words to the wind."

–"Only few have ever been ready to listen. Jeremiah had to flee to foreign lands before his countrymen, partly because he was telling them the bleeding truth. And yet his laments have survived millenia."

–"Now I understand. You, too, want to write a lament that will survive millenia."

The scorn and discouragement made Arush regret having confided in Marek but it did not put him off from pursuing his purpose. Pursuing it, that is, in his heart. The whole design remained as it was, a wishful thought. He could not gather the required energy to come out of his passivity, to overcome the hesitation and the cramping self-distrust. The emotion was weakening in procrastination.

But after the Polish bread became an accepted occurrence, there surged in him an even stronger will to forge something positive out of what they called briefly, the tragedy. The inner drive to leave a shade of it in written words had evolved from a call of duty, a kind of repentance for being alive and not hungry, into a force that broke all his previous restraints. It is no great feat for one blessed by talent. He must try, inept as he was, to do all he possibly could, and do it as soon as he could - whether words were short or not. Marek might be right that it would be well to wait, to let the years of tragedy come into focus, to let the memories crystallize, even though they might lose their punch and edge, even though old-time feelings lose their bluntness and strength. But could he wait? Would tomorrow for him not be too late?

Writing his story from a wraith of memories turned into material notes, recorded at once in mind and skin, committed to paper by who knows what wondrous means, as peculiar a type of a story as were its times themselves, at once mysterious and plain, fiction and fact, always truthful to deed and act. A story that leaves volumes on its theme still unwritten.

CHAPTER FOURTEEN

Spring is filtering through the wires. Though not a single pre-vernal plant is yet in sight, the air is unmistakably breathing the peculiar scent of spring. The evenings are still and dull, provoking welcome reminiscences and sadness, sadness perhaps of the same kind - I was reflecting later at night - that has from times immemorial seized man watching the setting sun. The mornings are wet with dew and still cool. Later it warms up enough to sit at open windows and to listen with all one's ears to the mysterious, now louder, buzzing in the air. There is something disturbing, though unreal, about these sounds, coming from nowhere, perhaps from the sky.

Marek Rainer says that in the beginning he thought that we had brought the rumble with us from Szebnie, as it started the day after our arrival. Only the buzz is heard, there's nothing to see, either in the air or on the ground; some say that a white cloud of steam tints the sky, but there is no evidence of it. Perhaps it is only an illusion, as sometimes I am inclined to think? Perhaps it is, as almost everyone discerns, by which sense I do not know, the German secret weapon.

Do they really have one? And if they have, what does this mean for the future course of the war? For our own future? Last September, while still in Tarnow, I remember reading in the newspaper that in six months they would have a secret weapon which would fundamentally change the military situation and assure them ultimate victory. We did not take this threat seriously then. But now we may be fortuitous witnesses to the weapon's existence. Oh, it is so disquieting! Let us hope they are still only experimenting. And perhaps, after all, the buzzing has other, atmospheric, causes? But what if it is a decisive weapon in German hands? We can do nothing about it. How absolutely nothing we count for in this world!

In any case, what our western Allies are waiting for is almost beyond explanation. For us even the Russians are advancing too slowly, and lately southwards rather than westwards, heading for the Bukovine and, it would seem the Black Sea. The western Allies are just doing nothing and taking a great risk, not least by continuing only to watch how the Russians forge ahead.

The subject is a recurrent theme of our debates at the workshop. When Lipe Knepel said the other day that the Allies were still waiting for the sea blockade to force Germany into submission, he did it of course with his tongue in his cheek. But one could hardly disagree with him, when he somewhat triumphantly asked: "After all the beatings that the Germans have had from the Red Army, I can't understand why the Americans and the English won't have a go at them? What are they waiting for?"

Even that was not a sincere question. For Knepel's view, which incidentally explains his coolness when I first mentioned the matter, is that although Stalin has accepted a promise from Churchill and Roosevelt that they will open a second front in western Europe and every so often castigates and cajoles them to carry it out, it is actually the last thing that he wants them to do. "By now the Russians can defeat the Germans by themselves. To end the war with the victory of the working class alone," as he put it.

The Poles are openly critical of the Allies' conduct of the war. It is they, unlike us, who have still much to lose. At the time the Germans were setting their hopes on the secret weapon, the Poles - inevitably my reporting is second hand - were voicing their apprehensions that, without some dramatic action by the Allies, Poland would be overrun by the Bolsheviks by the turn of the year, that is last year. Now the Russians are on Polish soil. Having lost patience with the perennial rumours of a second front, and having long recognized the naivety of expecting a quick decisive victory from the landings in Italy, the Poles at once view the Allies' inactivity with bitter irony, yet are piously hopeful that they will liberate Poland from the air. It's all quite familiar to me, as not so long ago, when we still had some family and shreds of a home, Jews nourished similar fancies.

Our impatience and bitterness found vent in humour. Racking my brain for a sensible explanation for what is, in our eyes, the unpardonable dilatoriness of the Allies it was a relief to recall some fine Polish jokes. There's the one, for example, where Churchill explains in parliament that victory requires manpower, material-power, and patience. "The Russians will provide the manpower, the Americans the material-power, and we'll provide the patience." The joke certainly expressed the impatience of its makers, but it also gave a glimpse of the popular image of the main combatants in the war. The phlegmatic but steadfast English soldier always has time, but once he starts moving, he proceeds on securely to reach the target. The American soldier carries a pillow and, in winter, a hot-water-bottle as part of his combat equipment. The Red Army man, untiring and insensitive, warmed by vodka, feels no cold and speeds at minus twenty degrees centigrade on the bonnet of a car rather than inside one. The German, the only soldier of the four who has actually been seen, is virile, mechanized and superbly professional. I make use of these funny stories to pronounce my weighty opinion that in war it is martial skills that count. The Allies have been inferior in this respect. They started seriously training, re-arming and planning their strategy significantly later than the Germans; they are perhaps justified in feeling that they do not yet match up to them in skills. They are led by democratically elected leaders, who, unlike dictators, must show concern for the lives of their people. Hence, all together, the doubting, delay and dodging of attack until they feel they can meet the Germans' superior skills with a crushing demonstration of superior firepower. But start to fight in earnest they will, and very soon the second front will begin. And to end on a novel, not just an optimistic note: "This waiting is a mistake which the Allied leaders may come to regret, for the attack may now require of them more, not less, sacrifice than a year ago." No one asked me to explain, but if challenged, I was prepared: the enemy is now better fortified, his logistic difficulties are smaller, the distance between the eastern front line and the French coast hundreds of miles shorter.

Not that I am by now always on the defensive, though I am still careful to be unoffensive. Now that the surroundings appear, through habit, less menacing, and my position at the workshop reasonably settled, I have become bolder in occasionally hitting back at my mates. As when I asked how was it that we, the oppressed and repressed all knew of Hitler's impending attack on Russia, but Stalin let himself be taken by surprise, as his army's defeat, retreats, and enormous losses in the first months of war suggest?

At the beginning of March 1941, German troops and armour began rolling eastwards day and night. Before long the ominous movement became the main talking point among the fearful, watching, captive people. Tarnow lies on the main, and probably only road from Cracow to Lwow that is passable to motor vehicles and by extension, the only usable road from southern Germany to the Ukraine. And this road passed across the principal streets of Tarnow, from one end of the town to the other. People living near the railway line, which runs through the outskirts of the town, counted the number of troop-trains and carriages, later arguing about the estimated number of men per carriage. Travellers arriving from Warsaw told of similar, even greater one-way traffic. In mid-May, shortly before this movement drastically declined, a Viennese Wehrmacht major was living in a requisitioned flat which, by force of authority he shared with a pretty Jewish grass-widow. One of the most pacific of his kind (and even suspected of having an affair with the widow), he replied when she asked him what he thought of all the transport, that considering its dimension, he would not like to be in Russian skin. It could not even be said that the attack on Russia was an open secret; it was open knowledge to every one of us; the only thing we didn't know was the date on which it would start.

Knepel, however, parried my question by asking sneeringly and with feigned disdain: "So you say that you, and cleverish boys like you, knew, and Stalin did not?"

–"Yes. Because I saw it, and he didn't. His aides who did know kept the news from him, in case they were suspected of opposing Stalin's pet policy of friendship with Hitler and ended up a head shorter.

"If Stalin did know, why did he go on providing Germany with precious war-materials up to the last minute? If he did know, why did Molotov ask the German ambassador when he delivered Germany's declaration of war, 'What have we done to deserve this?'"

The transitional friendship between Stalin and Hitler was the most vulnerable spot of the Knepels of this world, driving them into agonizing and ill-concealed embarrassment. It was also the one question on which Knepel and Deker fundamentally differed. Deker, though he preferred not to talk too much about it, unequivocally condemned the Molotov-Ribbentrop pact of late August 1939, which in practice had allied the Soviet Union with Nazi Germany. It was, he said, "a betrayal of all working men in the world." Knepel maintained - with what conviction and personal qualms one could only guess - that in the circumstances (later

199

explained as France and England intending to stand aside and watch Russia bleeding and exhausting itself in a war with Germany) it was wise and politic of Stalin to sow discord between the capitalists and force them into fighting one another. My laughter at his words was drowned by a chorus of loud disapproval at the workshop. But when Knepel more soberly, and perhaps truthfully, said that Stalin had not been taken by surprise and that he had reverted to anti-Napoleonic tactics, I kept silent in deference to a precious memory.

How trivial I am with all this rose-coloured commentary of mine! Father had to uphold an almost mystical faith in victory against a background of constant defeat and despair. Now the task is so easy, with victory clearly in sight - the only question is, shall we live to see it?

6 April 1944

One, unforeseen advantage of spring weather is the expansion of our little universe. It is not forbidden, provided not too many do it, to lie down on the ground during the lunch-break. If you are resolute, you can choose a patch of ground several yards away from either side of the wire dividing the two camps. Lying down behind the last barracks you are invisible to the guards on the towers, neither can they hear you although you can talk loud enough to make yourself audible to your partner lying twenty yards away on the Polish side. From this position, you could even, if need be, smuggle through a written message. There is the risk of Ruf or another SS man suddenly appearing out of nowhere, but this is small. From Bubi, or one of the other capos, there is nothing worse to expect, if you are caught, than a verbal dressing-down, with perhaps a kick in the bottom in addition, depending on who the offender was. And so a tenuous link with the Poles has been established.

Besides letters from home, which do not tell anything except personal news, the Poles receive a constant, however intermittent, flow of information from the new prisoners who arrive in their camp. Brzostek is a brave man with a bent for conspiracy like so many Polish people. Maniek Lander knows him from the old days, and today Brzostek told him over the "wire telephone" that a man arrived from a prison in Cracow this morning, and related, among other things, that there are about twelve thousand Jews in the camp at Plaszow - which strangely brought a joyous tear to my eyes, at the possibility that so many of our people are still alive.

To widen contacts, to talk, is a great support to every prisoner. Too much talk, however, may become tiresome, and I find listening to Perec Lisko more and more tedious, especially since I now once more value solitude. But today he surprised me, with a thought-provoking question.

–"How is it that in Russia, considered a boorish backward country, thousands of men have endangered their safety and positions for the sake of truth - certainly it was thanks to the four prominent Russian counsels and many more non-Jewish witnesses, who wanted only to see justice done, that Beilis owed his acquittal; but that in Germany, considered cultured and refined, 'a nation of thinkers and philosophers,' not a single man rose to protest at what was done to us?"

–"Inside Germany. Once out, many did," I said.

–"And in the civilized West?" continued Lisko. "What a flood of protest they showered over the trial and persecution of one man, even if he symbolized all of his creed - but they watch in silence the persecution and murder of millions."

–"Perhaps the fate of a single man does arouse emotion, but not the fate of millions of people? That may be too much to comprehend. Some may not even believe that it did, or could, happen."

–"Always the same disbelief. Then we were all saying 'how could such a trial happen in the twentieth century!' Now they must be saying the same in the West with even greater disbelief at this incomparably larger blood-accusation. Because, you see, I think of Hitler's fanatic charge against Jews in those terms. But after all these years what makes our enemies, then as now, pick on the blood canard to charge us with?"

–"You think it specious. But in fact it's a proven, brilliant choice of charge. There's nothing as dramatic as blood, nothing as strong as blood ties, nothing as emotive as this red substance - you defend your blood, you fight to its last drop, you redeem yourself with blood, you remake mankind with new blood. Blood calls, boils, cools, curdles; some never dries, is eventually washed clean with repentance and conversion. The mystique of blood is incomparable in its power over man; it has never failed to inspire him, to arouse his deepest passion, to deceive him in the neatest way. With blood you can paint the blackest lie red."

No one has understood this as well as Hitler and no one has exploited this mystique more fully than he. If this required genius, only a churl could deny it to Hitler. To be sure, his blood theory has been more than a mystique. It has ultimately become the basic, most forced, yet most forceful, element of his ideology and world design. To execute it, he had first to win the support and then the obedience of his people. To this end, he sensed, the blood theory offered the most promising means. He understood very well the cogency of the human blood relationship, the affinity between blood and nationalism, the historical propinquity and property of blood as a symbol of domination and supremacy. He decided to utilize this propensity of blood for the purpose of arrogating and asseverating German supremacy - a supremacy to be expressed in blood.

The operation required a distinction between blood and blood. It was in this respect that the blood mystique was so helpful, as the distinction is part of the mystique itself. Blood is pure or muddy, blue or dark, noble or common, good or evil, and, a late Nazi contribution, Aryan or Jewish. With enough skill and effort, you can always fool at least some of your people that their blood is superior, and that of others inferior, and fool them in such a manner that they believe the other blood is no longer that of a man, a human being, but just an obstacle to your own blood - an enemy to be subdued. Then the road to mass murder is open.

Once elected to power at home, Hitler was able to put his blood theory into practice in Germany. At first only against its Jews. Unlike many of his bewildered observers, he had long perceived that common hatred, or friendship for that matter, must be directed to a common object, and that the Jews provided the most obvious and perfect choice. They were a small, internationally scattered, yet significant minority - both in Germany and in the world at large; small enough to be helpless and significant enough to cause a scare. Jews were the easiest of all peoples to depict as carriers of the bad qualities of blood, threatening to contaminate good Aryan blood, as there was ample historical precedence for it, particularly in German theological tradition. Germany was the country of Martin Luther and his assertion that next to the devil the Jew is the greatest enemy, would require little effort to revive, if indeed it has ever been forgotten. To incite hatred and persecution of the Jews would be a force integrating the German people at home, while winning them popularity and solidarity abroad. It was a force that Hitler credited with enough potency to transform sentiments and standards in the whole world.

The blood theory had more attractions for the German people. It stipulated, as the nation's main task, a commitment to breed an elite German race. To secure its victorious path, to advance the superior Aryan blood, to protect it from Jewish obstruction, was to become the prime duty of the Nazi state, a duty to which everything else was to be subordinated. You can find all this inscribed in Hitler's *Mein Kampf* or in one of his recorded speeches and table talks. Some of it was half-openly brought under the umbrella of the Law for the Protection of German Blood and Honour - for do not forget that blood "is" honour as well.

In the process of "breeding", a new, top genus of man, who was *deutschblütig* (of German blood) - as opposed to *fremdblütig* (of alien blood, mainly Jew) - was fashioned. Thus at the stroke of the pen, and thanks to the blood theory, even the humblest deutschblütig man could, and mostly did, feel like an aristocrat, compared with men of alien breed. And so the *Neuadel aus Blut und Boden* (new nobility of blood and land) also came about. To qualify for the Herr status, a German no longer needed to be of noble birth; thanks to the blood supremacy claim, all Germans became Herren; together they formed the *Herrenvolk* (master nation), and the purity of blood became the expression of the German peoples' *Herrschaftsanspruch* (aspiration to empire). This was, in due course, to be satisfied by other means and enjoyed in full after the conquest of foreign lands, whose defeated inhabitants were to be made serfs to German masters.

Well, who does not like to be master? What greater joy and pride is there than in one's own blood? What is more important than its triumph? This is why the blood theory was so attractive to its Aryan breed, and why it was accorded supreme place in Nazi ideology, something that Hitler had correctly foreseen and instigated. This is also why his success with the German people, measured in terms of popularity and devotion, has reached heights unprecedented in their history.

Blood and land, the pairing was neither accidental nor entirely original. "Blood and land are the fate of nations", was the German patriotic cry long before Hitler. At about the same time as Hitler published *Mein Kampf*, Oswald Spengler was writing in "The Decline of the West" of a struggle between *Blut und Boden* (was it resolved in the *Neuadel?*). Nor was clothing nationalism in the mantle of blood and land entirely new. Land as "soil dewed by the blood of fathers" is not unfamiliar, while Volk (people, nation) and blood are tacitly, but closely, related in the general notion of family. And war as an instrument of nationalist statecraft was not so tacitly expressed in the famous phrase of "blood and iron policy" coined by Bismarck, one of Hitler's idols. What was new in Hitler's formulation of nationalism was its actual foundation on blood; hence a decisively anti-Semitic nationalism with, at least as far as its choice of phrase is concerned, new objectives and duties, tasks and solutions. Once the Jews were regarded as a national enemy, the crusade against them was turned into a struggle for national survival, requiring a *völkische* ("national" Germanized) solution. Thus presented, the extermination of the Jews has become a national duty, an act of self-defence of the German people and their Aryan blood - a vital and laudable act.

The war provided the pretext. In times of war, generally speaking, people designated as enemies are permissibly and patriotically killed. And in a so-called (by the Nazis) total war, no concept of crime is conceivable. In origin, however, the murder of the Jews in this war was essentially inspired by Hitler's blood theory and its, by and large, enthusiastic adoption by his people.

Why waste so many words on a subject that has been so extensively discussed that I could hardly add anything new to it? I was surprised to find how little this subject, which we often debate at the workshop, is understood and taken seriously. It is deemed irrational, and people want a rational explanation for Hitler's, and his followers', hatred and subsequent murder of Jews. As if emotions such as hatred, or love for that matter, were rational phenomena, or as if man, in general, were a rational creature, even if this is what we are taught and compelled to read in various textbooks. What is rational about killing, or war, or about extreme nationalism, fanaticism?

The objection that it's all irrational is many-sided. Hugo Bester, who in this instance wishes to establish his claim to intellect, has put forward a few basic arguments, which summarized sound like this. First, the racial doctrine, a phrase he prefers to "blood", was born out of mysticism and as such is of a metaphysical order; it cannot, therefore, be explained in secular ways. Second, given the extravagance of the doctrine, and notwithstanding all that has been said about the dynamic motives of its propagation, its overwhelming success with the German people, its supremacy and inviolability, and its calamitous consequences, are a mystery beyond human reason. And so is - the obverse aspect of the same argument - the understanding of what there was about the Jews that aroused in Hitler and his followers such a sanguinary wrath against them, as to call for their mass murder?

What is it about all these pretentious intellects? Are they unwilling, or too ignorant to understand that what counts in matters of the mind is not what there is, but what one believes there is, about something? And believe Hitler did in all those things he attributed to the Jews. In the first place, he did believe in a Jewish plot to dominate the world, a plot specifically directed against Germany, aimed at causing its disintegration into a collection of small states. He believed that the Jews really caused all that he detested: the democratic revolutions which took place in Europe in the eighteenth and nineteenth centuries, the Bolshevik revolution of 1917, and that they actually organized the abortive mini-revolutions of the winter 1918/1919 in Germany; that they were the fathers of the Weimar Constitution; that they invented capitalism and founded socialism, created the proletarian movement and a Jewish-Marxist stock exchange press; that indeed the Jews were Bolsheviks and at the same time capitalists in control of international finance. This, incidentally, explains how the alliance between bolshevik Russia and capitalist America and England came about, as one could read almost daily in the Nazi press for the past three years. The Jews, Hitler believed, bring about war, and bring about defeatist peace. What is worse, they were responsible for every German defeat in history. He even believed that if Germany had in good time submitted to poison gas twelve or fifteen thousand of the Jews who were, in his view, corrupting the German nation, she would not have lost the First World War; nor if she had not then treated her enemies so softly. Read him, or read what's written about him by his chums, if you have doubts about all this.

Precisely when Hitler began to believe in all these things is difficult to know, but it was early enough to draw his conclusion logically that his task was to take upon himself the "historic mission of liberating" first Germany, then Europe and the rest of the world from the Jews. As a good anti-Semite himself, he knew that all true Jew-haters wish to, and will, believe those same things. And he set about making them believe.

He was quite clear and decisive about means. First, he must dupe and daze his people. His appearances, parades and speeches made an unique impression on them. Indeed the extraordinary spell of Hitler upon the Germans - which still seems largely to last - resembles mass psychosis. The masses, he said, follow their leader only when they become fanatic. A zealot himself, he knew how to stir up fanaticism in others, exalting and coaxing his Aryan people relentlessly till they turned into a thoughtless instrument of his policies. This he accomplished mainly through intensive propaganda, of which the blood theory and its promises were the sharpest weapon in his armoury. By repeating something often enough, he claimed, you can make people believe even that heaven is hell and misery is bliss. A lonely man, given to fantasies and indulging in his emotions - anti-Semitism the strongest among them - Hitler, by the time he wrote *Mein Kampf*, must have repeated in his mind all the things in the book so many times that he already believed them to be true.

What is, I ask, metaphysical about all that? And why does it defy analysis and understanding?

The exact time when Hitler decided to wipe out the Jews is, like the time when he decided to wage war, not known. Both were probably on his mind from the very beginning of his political career. His book, his speeches, and the testimonies of his early associates dispel any doubt that at least his homicidal intentions with regard to Jews dated back to long before he came to power. Though not yet worked out in detail, his general intentions were clear. His approach was to be radical and "bio-logical" - one of the euphemisms he used at an internal National Socialist assembly, as the dramatist Alfred Herzog, an early deserter from the party, disclosed in

1931. Hitler would not commit the same mistake as many before him. In all the long history of suffering mankind many have attempted to save the world from the Jews - what is, ergo, so special about killing Jews? - but they did it in a ridiculously half-hearted manner. Plenty of such attempts had been undertaken in Germany itself. Wilhelm II, who was one of those who did not want to accept the guilt of the Jews, (was this why a few years later the Führer put the ex-Kaiser off with a promise of the return of monarchy in Germany but only after the solution of the Jewish problem and victory in war?) could be excused because his Chancellor, Prince Bülow, was a devotee of the Jews. But no one was going to fool or dissuade him, Hitler. His solution would be a once-for-all, biological solution. Could this have meant something other than mass murder? No. But how the Jews laughed when they read this! What does he mean by "biological solution", they asked in feigned amusement? He was a raving madman, they decided. Why wonder, then, at the incredulity of the Jews in Poland, if this was the reaction of the Jews most directly concerned - the German Jews.

Yet at that time Hitler's plan for the Jews was not ripe for action. He knew that this, his prime mission, was incidental to his life's other mission - war and conquest. Once, however, the opportunity arrived and a country was conquered, the fate of its Jews was sealed. Their mass murder was only a matter of time.

In the light of all this, when Hitler actually first ordered the annihilation of the Jews is irrelevant. Yet - notwithstanding the usually coded language - there are pointers to the date. The first clear instruction was the now famous "Commissar Order" issued on 6 June 1941, but already prepared in March 1941 on the orders of Hitler, who repeated its contents in a speech to his generals delivered on the penultimate day of that month. This was an order that, on the advance of German armed forces into Russia, which materialized shortly afterwards, selected categories of people, including Bolshevik commissars and Jews, should be killed. While this document could still be interpreted as ordering the murder of Jews for "political" and not "racial" reasons, another order issued apparently a few days after the start of the war against Russia, decreed the extermination of all Jews in the occupied eastern territories who were not indispensable.

A significantly earlier indication is provided by the so-called *Schnellbrief* (urgent circular letter) of 21 September 1939, sent by SS Gruppenführer Reinhard Heydrich, Chief of Security Police and the SD, to the chiefs of all the SS *Einsatzgruppen* (special SS and police units) operating in occupied Poland. The Schnellbrief outlines the measures to be adopted against the Jews, which were to form part of the general strategy of their ultimate destruction - the *Endziel* (final aim) of the letter. Such an elaborate and carefully worked out plan of action was unlikely to have been prepared in the few days that separated its despatch from the start of hostilities.

Nine days earlier, on 12 September, in Hitler's special military train, four men discussed a plan to exterminate the Jews, as if it were a foregone conclusion. They were Foreign Minister von Ribbentrop, Generals Keitel and Jodl, and Admiral Canaris (the latter somewhat critically inclined). And nine days before the invasion of Poland, Hitler, in a speech to the High Command of the Army told his top generals that one aim of the war was to eliminate the enemy's "vital forces", which was why he had ordered his "Death Head" formations to follow the army into Poland. He further urged his audience: "Don't know mercy, be brutal..." Well, the "vital forces" killed in the following weeks, were mostly Jews. This order clearly preceded the war.

Nothing had aroused greater controversy in our debates on this issue than my particular views on the connection between the war and the extinction of Jews. Lipe Knepel, while not denying that Hitler had to wait for war to put his planned slaughter into operation, nevertheless insisted that it was wrong to separate the two, for they were part of a single plan, the war against the Jews was a mini-target of Germany's larger aim of war.

Only the other day Knepel said: "Germany's principal war aim was to gain territory in the East. The purpose of the campaign against the Jews was merely to provide an ideological justification for the conquest of Russia, then Europe, and ultimately the whole world. Your reasoning is typically illogical - it lacks methodical understanding. This can be provided only by a scientific approach to historical analysis."

What is the scientific approach? Not that I did not understand the euphemism. Indeed Knepel, with Deker's support, had explained it on more than one occasion.

"The blood theory, as the root of the Jewish tragedy, is fundamentally wrong, because it ignores the class roots of racialism which sprout from imperialism. Imperialism as the late stage of monopolistic capitalism has, in alliance with junker-militarist circles, produced in Germany the special kind of capitalism that is fascism. That is why racialism and the mass murder of the Jews are intrinsically bound up with the whole question of German fascism and aggression, culminating in the present war."

While saying roughly the same, Deker, as I understand it, tried somewhat to mollify and simplify Knepel's scientific expertise.

"The class origins of racialism and its use as an excuse for Germany's fascist aggression are beyond question. Who except perhaps Freund could question that imperialism was born out of economic considerations? Or, who could overlook the economic interests of the ruling capitalist classes in Germany, including the interests of the newly arisen SS economic empire, in the destruction of the Jews? First to loot their property, then to use them as slave labour, whether in towns or camps, and finally to fill the space left when they'd been cleared with Germans or Germanized Slavs."

Knepel, however, found fault even with this exposition, and anyway he would not allow Deker to have the last word.

"That comes at the end. What imperialism aims at in the first place is markets for exports, cheap raw-materials, and still cheaper labour. This is where racialism, conquest, Aryan supremacy and the suppression of the Jews merge. Only then comes expansion to the east and its Germanization - the real aim of this war.

"But however close the connection between the Nazi policy of depopulation and the biological solution of, among others, the Jewish problem this policy did not originate in Hitler's blood theory, but the other way round. The *Lebensraum* (living space) theory having come into the world at the time when monopolistic capital formation began, towards the end of the nineteenth century, is much older than Hitler."

While hardly suspected of sympathy for the "scientific approach", Hugo, who happened to be at the tailors when this exchange took place, threw in a remark that unwittingly supported Knepel.

–"In the German school I attended, suggested reading for upper form students included the book by Hans Grimm *Volk ohne Raum* (nation without space) which, it was said, gave a poetic expression to the German colonial idea."

At this, Berl Alter interrupted to ask: "What actually is this Lebensraum ideology?"

Knepel was only too pleased to explain.

–"It's a widely held opinion in Germany that its territory is too small for the size of its population and that this is the source of the scarcities and privation from which the country suffers. In other words, there's not enough living space for its people. In fact, this was a smokescreen for Germany's aggressive intentions. Hitler seized upon this idea from his very beginnings and produced a remedy: Not enough territory at home? Help yourself to territory abroad. This was to be found in the East, in the vast expanses of Russia."

Hugo once more wished to flaunt his familiarity with the subject by remarking that, ironically, twenty-five years ago it was Clemenceau who complained that it cost too much space to have sixty million Germans in the centre of Europe. To which Hausdienst reacted: "Costs, profits, greed and grab - that's the real cause of this bloody war."

But Knepel could not accept such crudity. He continued:

"Of course territory depopulated of men. *Lebensraum* for Germans, *Todesraum* (dying space) for others."

To elaborate and improve on Knepel, Deker added:

"In his speech to the General Command of the army before the attack on Poland, Hitler declared openly that only in this way - by war and depopulation - could they get the living space they needed. Then came the time to prove it. The Jews were the first, but next to meet the same fate were the Poles, the Russians, and other inferior races."

There were many voices raised in this argument, so I shall summarize the replies I and others made to all this on various days. There is room, we said, for differing approaches to understanding the war and the concurrent Jewish tragedy. As for my own views they make no claim for a scientific approach, nor shall I poach on its preserves, which make assumptions that are no less dogmatic than some of the Nazi theories. To say that imperialism gave rise to class division is merely imprecise and unscientific, but that "class" is at the bottom of Hitler's blood theory, and that hence his extermination of the Jews stems from class, is not a serious proposition. It is also contradicted by my comrades' admission that the mass of ordinary German people gave blind support to Hitler's policies and that without their active help he could not have committed his crimes. In any case, it's irrelevant to the main issues of our present concern. As against this, the nexus between war and the mass murder of Jews is incontrovertible and its recognition is indispensible for the proper understanding (and to forestall the allegedly "analysis defying" explanations) of the Jewish catastrophe. War has not only provided Hitler with an outlet for his aggression and an excuse for murder, it has also been politically and practically, a prior condition to satisfying his life's greatest passion and purpose, the physical destruction of the Jews. But to maintain that this dastardly war against Jews has merely been a part of his mammoth war against well-armed nations is completely wrong; even if it were right, the extermination of the Jews could not be, as Knepel argued, a justification for the wider war. If anything, however unthinkable a suggestion it is for Knepel to make, the ideological war against the Jews may have been the ultimate reason why Hitler decided to risk the aggressive war against Russia, and later to declare war on America, a decision of which even some of his close aides have been critical. Only if one accepts this motive of Hitler's aggression against Russia, could this war and the one against the Jews eventually be seen as one.

This argument would, admittedly, be inconsistent with the one that considers conquest of territories in the East as the main reason for war with Russia, which indeed is doubtful. And so, even more, are economic reasons as an explanation for the extirpation of Jews. It cannot be denied that the Germans had an economic interest in the oppression of Jews. But, after having dispossessed them of everything they owned, what economic advantage was there in their biological extinction? On the contrary, by this they dispossessed themselves of a virtually costless labour force. It would be superfluous to cite more inconsistencies in the economic motivation argument, were it not also made by my comrades with regard to the war in the east. Surely the supposed German interest in acquiring markets for their exports and cheap labour to improve their competitiveness, is at odds with the alleged intent to depopulate the conquered territories?

This is not to ignore the significance, over the past decades, of the Lebensraum theory in German thinking about a solution to their economic difficulties. Less than twenty years ago, there were even some prominent German Jews, deemed liberals at that, who shared this view, commonly held in their country. But that the German war against the Jews, or possibly even against Russia, was for living space in the East is a weird, untenable suggestion. If the living space theory was a smokescreen for aggression, as it may well have been, it could not at the same time be a motive for it. If territory free of men in the East was the aim of war against the Jews, why murder those living in the West? The fact is, as we could see with our own eyes in the towns of Poland, that the relatively small space cleared of Jews was filled not by Germans but by Poles, except for the best Jewish homes, which comprised a tiny proportion of the whole. Indeed the Jews made up such a small minority of the peoples occupied by the Germans that the space gained by their murder could hardly have provided room for the present day "surplus" Germans, let alone for its expected increase in the future. And finally, it may or may not be true that, after the war, Hitler envisages for the Poles and other "inferior" races the same fate as the Jews; as it is, the only people in his reach who have actually been murdered wholesale were Jews. It is, therefore, inappropriate to ascribe their uprooting to a presupposed biological depopulation of the East to gain living space; the extermination of the Jews is a singular and distinct case. What makes it so distinct is not just the completeness and ferocity of their murder, extending to every corner of the continent within the sway of German power, but equally the fact that the victims were defenceless non-combatants, killed as a specific Jewish race.

I admit that my "unscientific approach" puts emphasis on Hitler, as the person responsible for unleashing the war against the world in general and the Jews in particular, but it is not true that by this I am clearing the Wehrmacht, or many other of his people, of the guilt of participating in the war crimes - which was another criticism made by Knepel and Deker. The involvement of the Wehrmacht in the crimes has often been mentioned in our discussions. I know that, while many officers and other ranks behaved correctly, at least half the murders of Jews in the first months of war were committed by members of the Wehrmacht. For much of that time, that is until 26 October, 1939, the day Hitler's decree transferred powers to the newly established General Government, the administration of the occupied territories was in the hands of the Wehrmacht, deriving from a proclamation signed by its commander-in-chief, von Brauchitsch, on 11 September, 1939. The SS Einsatzgruppen had operated at the rear of the Wehrmacht units advancing into Russia, and were formally subordinated to it. And some orders issued by top Wehrmacht commanders, as for example the one by Fieldmarshal Erich von Mannstein on 20 November 1941 echoed the "Commissar Order", by telling the armies under his command that the Jewish-Bolshevik system must be exterminated once and for all. As for the mass of ordinary Germans, civilians and soldiers alike, their continuing obedience in executing every order, however atrocious, is - in view of the devastating defeats and retreats that were taking place - simply amazing. Nevertheless, looked at dispassionately, Hitler must be seen as the moving force behind the war and the extermination of the Jews. It was his feral aggressiveness, his fanatical ideology and his hatred of Jews that set the course for these events. Even before the war he alone had been the source of all laws in Germany. Without him, no man could lift a hand or a foot in any of the countries under his control. It was Hitler who raised the idea of, and later aimed at, creating a great German empire of a thousand years' duration. There is nothing to laugh at in this: all he needed to realize his aim, the climax of his dreams, was one small thing - to win the war. This we, fortunately, already know that he will not do.

In one respect we all agree, refusing the psychological approach to the phenomenon of Hitler and historical events in general; in particular rejecting as absurd all explanation of his aggressiveness or hatred of Jews to be the result of some imagined experiences of his early childhood. Our unanimity, unlike other exchanges on this subject, produces moments of hilarity. Here, too, Hugo tried to show off his learning, though this time in a humorous way.

"The barbaric features of Hitler's super-ego, you know what I mean, and his pathological *Weltanschauung*, were just incarnations of his distress as a baby. All the fault of Oedipus. Hitler has turned the Jewish doctor, who treated his mother, into his father, poisoning her."

Berl Alter interrupted to ask half-seriously: "Was this Oedipus an anti-Semite?"

–"No, but his complex may be," I said.

–"His oedipal complex," Hugo continued, "not only remained unresolved, but was re-activated at a later stage of Hitler's life with such great intensity that it forced his anti-Jewish feelings to break into the open. To free himself of the incestuous fixation of his libido, which troubled him most of his life, he displaced the psycho-sexual aggression of his infancy onto the Jews."

But Knepel was not satisfied with Hugo's complex exposition and, showing his own fine sense of humour, declared solemnly that all this bloodshed and destruction was because the infant Hitler could not get an easy grip on his mother's nipple.

Yet, despite my misgivings about projecting personality to great historical events such as war and the murder of nations, and despite the risk of Hugo's taunt that I, too, was trying to apply some Greek legend to Hitler's private parts, I thought that we could perhaps seek a clue to these events in Hitler's psychology if we were to go back to Homer and his age of heroic killing. If we were to accept that Hitler's main concern had been his own everlasting fame and grandeur; that for him a life other than that of power and glory was not worth living. It had to be either world conquest or defeat - his own and that of his simple-minded, technically talented, crudely submissive people. For him, as for Homer's heroes, war and killing were the most glorious things in the world. Like them he was waging war and killing to exalt his Aryan people and his own godlike person - Wotan, the god of the dead and of war, the Führer of the Wild Hunt, surrounded by wolves, the master of the world residing in Valhalla. Hitler is neither the first, nor, I fear, the last man in history who has sought in killing compensation for the vanity of life and, at the same time, the immortality that arises from millions of graves, now enhanced by his palm-bearing creation of gas chambers and pyrotic halls.

Once more my mates complained that, like those enthusiasts who admire Hitler or attach importance to his personality, I was immortalizing him. That may be, in the same way that Amalek, Goliath and Haman of the Scriptures are immortalized. But far more significant, I replied, was that, by making the Jews his prime enemy, and slaughtering them in their millions, Hitler had put them at the centre of current world history. And as the Jews who were out of his reach would survive and, I hoped, persevere with Jewish community life, Hitler might have unwittingly, and exactly contrary to what he had intended, contributed to immortalizing his most detested foes - the killed and the living alike.

CHAPTER FIFTEEN

10 April 1944

"With you I would like to go into partnership after the war," Herr Klause said the day before yesterday as he caught me wandering in the corridor during work-time. He then went on his way, and I, of course, answered nothing. Even in normal times it was futile to protest against our reputation of shrewd traders. Let it be so, we said. The poor Germans, they are such bad businessmen, the very image of Aryan innocence in money matters. Let him go to hell, I thought.

It is a bit worrying, for he appears to have an accurate view of my mental immersion (in his presence) in the accounts book. But did I really doubt it? Hardly more significant, and yet heartening, is that this shabby German master is already speaking of going into business after the war with a Jew - a Jew held in a concentration camp! Oh my Lord could he be truthfully seeing ahead? Would we see liberation?

When I told my friend Marek about the encounter with Klause, I added that his predication was a good omen. Marek got a bit irritated, as he usually does on such occasions. Then, more indulgently, he asked: "What's the omen?"

To tell Marek that Klause made his business proposition on the thirty-two-hundred and fifty-sixth anniversary of our ancestors' release from pharoic Egypt, seemed too tantalizing. I did not want to annoy him. My reverting to good omens was a way of raising hope and faith in survival. However Marek dislikes bold, abstruse expressions of hope and faith. Thus instead of answering his question, I asked him: "Have you heard, Odessa was re-taken?"

"So what? They're moving farther away from us. In fact, the Russians too, have stopped advancing.

"All right, so Klause already wonders what he'll do after the war; all the Germans must be thinking of their future. Can we think of ours? Can you imagine the end of war?"

It was hard, and Marek was perhaps unaware why. To think of the future fills us with fear. And our future extends emotionally into our recent past, stirring up mournful memories and strained, painful feelings. Our true inner-selves are a vast stream of sadness and frozen tears, a burdened conscience urging us to punish the flesh and to grieve in dust and ashes. On the outside we are calm and composed, we know we must be sensible and useful. Reason advises us to defer our sorrow until after the war - anyway, how can one mourn for others, while facing constant uncertainty for one's own life? And although we know that this is neither the right time nor place for sadness and tears, we also know in our hearts that after the war we shall not be able to retrieve the intensity of our present feelings, the depth of the more immediate sorrow - distress and pain slowly losing its poignancy. What a fearful future! For Hausdienst it's not a cause for worry. "Sighs and tears aren't a virtue, but signs of weakness. We must be hard and cool like all the other people," he said the other day. Lately the feelings of remorse have "put on weight", because we are not hungry, physically feel fairly well, we are laughing. When last evening in the barracks, Capo Krel warned a fellow with the already worn-out witticism, "this is not a sanatorium", the midget Kulik, the camp youngest, snapped back: "Isn't it?"

We have stopped asking the reason for this extra food and good treatment, as if it were something normal. But it's a strange thing - strange in terms of human nature - now that we are not hungry nor ailing, we worry much more about the future than before. Life has become more attractive and has brought back potent longing - a longing that seems unattainable to those of us who consider themselves to be "thinking realistically". This I think lies behind Marek's gloomy questions and complaints about all and sundry, including the Red Army.

–"It's difficult to imagine something you have not experienced," I answered. "Can you think of life after us? Though some people do."

–"That's something different. To me our existence often looks like life at old age: expecting death, and yet hoping to live on."

–"What we actually expect to happen controls the shape things take in our minds. The trouble with you, and with me, is that we expect too much and, therefore, aren't satisfied. People never are. Think of the time behind us. How long is it since we were sure of dying of hunger? Think of the contrast with other camps, with life in the ghetto. There we said, 'just let us be certain of their defeat before we die'. Now their defeat is certain, we want more, and feel discontented."

–"What people say is not necessarily what they think and desire. The Germans have indeed lost, but what about us? Isn't that what we're thinking? Can we hope to be spared?"

–"It isn't beyond the bounds of possibility. Now, in Pustkow we have hope, some say high hope."

–"They're silly. They live in a fool's paradise, cherishing vain hopes. They naively believe, most of us do, that the Russians want to liberate us, that they're planning, racking their brains, how to surprise the Germans, in order to prevent them disposing of us at the last minute. But this is just wishful thinking. We mean absolutely nothing to the Russians or to the western Allies. And yet most of us believe that we do."

I could not deny that Marek was right this time, even for the sake of argument. His words reminded me of conversations we'd had at home; how the Jews had counted on the Allies to save them before and, in particular, after the mass killings had started; how they had talked about the conscience of the "free world" and its leaders, and how they had appealed to it in the most rousing words, which were, however, never heard outside the walls of the room in which they were uttered. I remembered Father once telling an audience of neighbours and family that the

Allies would certainly do everything to help us. After all it was their moral obligation. They must do it. This was what they were fighting for. Wasn't it? Didn't they
go to war against Hitler to foil his ideology and criminal designs? Wasn't the racial
issue fundamental to this ideological confrontation? Wasn't the defence of the
weaker and helpless people against the stronger at the root of this cruel war? If they
did not come to the rescue of Jews, this would mean they had capitulated to Hitler,
allowing his barbaric creed to triumph. They must save us!

I also recalled Dave modestly replying that whatever the Allies' war aims, and
however strong their opposition to Nazism, neither their political leaders nor their
peoples cared about Jews. They would pursue their own war objectives and
restricted national interests. There was no morality in politics. To count on their
consciences and help was no less naive than to count on those of our free Jewish
brothers and leaders.

I answered Marek with another remark of Dave's.

–"Suppose the Allies care and want to help us, how could they do it?"

–"That's hard for us, prisoners in a camp, to answer. There must have been ways
they could have helped us, otherwise they wouldn't have hidden the news of the
atrocities, whilst we were being finished off. Such rescue action requires brains,
planners, experts, courage. If the Allies, as a matter of policy, decided to do nothing
to help us, then there's nothing they could do.

"Their dilatory war conduct, their comparative inaction until now, indicate how
little we, and all the other people who suffer under German occupation, mean to
them."

–"But this could be interpreted in a different way. That their comparative inaction and war that they're waging at a distance from the enemy, indeed show that
they could not have helped us."

–"But not their comparative silence, their indifference, their cynicism, which are
only equalled by those of our free Jewish leaders - though I often wonder of the two,
whose indifference and cynicism is more merciless?"

However exasperating these conversations about the indifference of the Allies
and of our free Jewish brothers, about German aggression and our own defenceless-
ness have been, they have helped us at all stages of our ordeal to carry on, by providing an outlet for our frustration and bitterness. Now, as camp prisoners, they
help to pass the time and to harden our determination to survive. At the workshop
these conversations are fairly frequent, and are on a similar, but broader plane than
the one just reported between Marek and myself.

The discussions refer to the past as well as to the present and include almost the
entire range of criticisms, reproaches, pretensions, that have been voiced by our
people over the war years. Talk is mostly disorderly and indiscriminate, making no
distinction between social and national groups, confusing people with their leaders,
the Allied Powers and the western Jews, all sometimes put together under a
generic, distant "free world". But for the sake of greater clarity, this requires separating.

One of the most painful experiences of Jewish life under German occupation was the feeling of being completely forsaken at what the Jews in Poland rightly sensed were the most tragic hours of their long history. What made it particularly hard was the striking change of relations with the Jewish communities abroad. Only yesterday, as it were, there were close, lively contacts with them, visits from their leaders, whether to collect money for joint national purposes, to inspect one or other institution, or to participate at some political function, but always ready to give advice and to meddle in internal Polish-Jewish affairs. But, then, from the first day of the war, the same foreign and free Jews lost all interest in the lives of the now captive Polish Jews, leaving them adrift in silence.

All of us at camp agree that all contacts and help were more important in the first, relatively tolerable, period before, rather than after, the ghettoization of the people. But how could the Jews abroad help us? This was perhaps the most frequent and controversial question asked. Material help, though admittedly of secondary importance, understandably figured in any reply. Until December 1941, the United States were not at war, its citizens, including Jewish ones, were considered neutral by Germany, as were citizens of many European and other countries.

–"Transferring money," Hausdienst argued, "was no problem. The Germans were only too willing to obtain foreign currency or even food parcels."

Hugo nodded in assent, and then said.

–"I remember how at the beginning of 1940, the American Express Company advertised in the local rags that they had resumed money transfers into Poland. And shortly after, representatives of the United States Red Cross and the Quakers arrived in Warsaw to supervise aid for the Polish population. So why couldn't American-Jewish institutions and other neutral Jews do the same? The whole argument that help couldn't be advanced because of US government objections that it would assist the German war effort is a poor excuse. It was the Jews, not the US government, who prevented transfer of funds."

Did they? I wondered at heart. Did they have funds to transfer?

The question of material aid was frequently stretched in our discussions to include the elusive question of buying us out for money. This referred to popular talk in the first year of war about negotiations for the release of Jews for ransom. Starting in the winter of 1940, it was for many months a favourite rumour, according to which various missions - including Jewish Council leaders from both the General Government and the territories annexed to the Reich - were in Berlin negotiating the freedom of the captive Polish Jews. The rumour included details of the way the Jews would be evacuated, the sums of money demanded for every person released, and other conditions of exchange.

Though weakened, the rumours have not died out, and when one day some doubts about the matter were raised, Osterman, Alter and others asserted their beliefs.

–"It's a fact," Osterman insisted unusually loudly, "that for the first twelve months of the war, and perhaps even longer, the Germans were prepared to let the Jews leave, and even encouraged their emigration. It was all a question of money."

This time I felt sufficiently stirred to reply.

–"What you say may be true. But the whole idea of bailing us out for money has never been more than a phantasm of ours. No negotiations about this have ever taken place. Besides, it's not only that the money - hundreds of millions - necessary for such a venture wasn't to be found, not to mention means and safety of passage, but there wasn't a country in the world that would take us in large numbers. And you can't blame the Jews abroad for that."

This, however, prompted even more protests, Knepel and Deker shouting: "Three hundred thousand escaped to Russia. And many more could."

–"That's a different matter. Quite different circumstances. Neither exit nor entry visas were necessary to get into the eastern part of Poland, then occupied by Russia. And very little money.

"I think that much of our sense of disappointment about the lack of financial help during the war comes at least partly from the false notions we had about the amount of foreign aid received in earlier years. Even here in Poland, most of us were victims of skilful propaganda by our brothers of, mainly, the philanthropic institutions in the United States, who implied that our survival in prewar years was due to their fraternal help. In fact, they weren't sending us much more than they had in the first two years of war - a few US cents annually for every living Jew in Poland. In the hardest years of depression, they actually took back what they had given in preceding years.

"That's why our expectations were disappointed."

–"Suppose they did pretend. Why?" asked Hugo. "Weren't all those philanthropists rich?"

"The philanthropists, both the real and imaginary ones, were rich. But the philanthropic institutions, such as the JOINT for instance, didn't have a cent to bless themselves with. During the war they probably had no more than they had shortly before it. Hence the pretence, which goes on and will probably go on after the war.

"But let's not lose sight of reality and exaggerate what material help could have done for us. Money could not have altered our ultimate fate. It could have alleviated the suffering of the poorest section of the population, but it couldn't have saved its lives. No more than transferring foreign funds to occupied Poland could have put the lives of Allied soldiers at risk."

Again this assessment of the significance of foreign aid was hotly disputed. Provision of foreign passports and visas was repeatedly mentioned, even though we all agreed about the lack of sufficient gates to freedom. Yet the one undeniably sound element of this criticism was that in the first stage of war, when help could have reached us, escape was still possible.

–"As long as opportunities to flee from, or even hide within, the General Government existed, funds were vital. Money and proper guidance could then have saved many lives," argued Hugo.

–"What do you mean by guidance?" I asked.

–"Just telling us what to do. Providing us with information. Guidelines for collective behaviour. Awakening the people to the dangers ahead. Simply telling us: run for your life; go into hiding; go underground - if underground it must be."

Osterman, who was not unsympathetic to Hugo's view of our free brethren, nevertheless interrupted him to ask: "Why did they have to do this, why couldn't we do it ourselves?"

Hugo did not explain beyond saying that the Jews in Poland were constrained in their movements, isolated, disorientated, plunged into a social vacuum. And he went on:

"Regardless of taking flight, people needed guidance on how to adapt to the new conditions of daily life, to tell them what were the right and what the wrong things to do, to form a sort of underground society - like the one the Poles formed - not for active resistance, but as a parallel society to the one imposed on us by the Germans and the Judenrats they appointed.

"That's what the Polish government-in-exile did for its countrymen in Poland. Our Jewish leaders abroad failed to do the same. They didn't even ask the Polish government to extend its care to the Jews, to keep us informed as well as the Poles, and to pass through its channels the funds needed to organize all this. And it was just as important to request the government to urge its nationals inside Poland to help the Jews; there might have been enough Poles with whom this would have touched the right chord. I have no doubt that the Polish government-in-exile would have responded positively to such a request. Of all the Allied governments and its agencies, none did as much to help Polish Jews, as the Sikorski government in London, however little help this proved in practice."

There was much truth in his words. From the first day of war the Jews in Poland were leaderless; their numerous chiefs had either escaped or were lying low, preparing to flee. The old established authority gone and daily routine shattered, the people faced a political and social void. They were forced to lead a new pattern of life, without knowing how to react to the different laws, standards, and unaccustomed circumstances. It was of prime importance to create, at least territorially, a new framework of internal organization, separate from the one imposed by the Germans, one that would be motivated by Jewish interests, and which would institute a pattern of action in the exclusive self-concern of Jews, with saving lives as its leading objective. Particularly pertinent were Hugo's remarks about the importance of providing the people clandestinely with information. For someone who has not witnessed it, it is hard to realize the isolation from all forms of communication into which the Jews were thrust almost overnight, especially in the small towns and villages. In the large towns, German media, for all its misinformation, still provided some news and one could read more between the lines, or occasionally, at the risk of one's life, listen to the radio. Though even this ceased almost completely once the people were ghettoized. The condition was not without its paradox. The forced restraints brought people closer, with the tenants of one house becoming like a large family, but at the same time made them more distant, almost beyond the reach of anyone outside their immediate commune. A network of at least regionally disseminated information was vital to tell the people what was happening in other localities, to explain to them the occupier's policies and his extraordinary moves, and thereby to draw a picture of their common destiny. Hugo was probably also right that in the state of isolation and tyranny in which the occupied Jews were forced to live, all those tasks -initiating a news distribution service, establishing institutional organizations that could mobilize the people and be accepted by them - required help, including material resources, from the outside were indispensable. The help of a free, dedicated, centrally organized authority, with the Polish government-in-exile as the obvious go-between.

But could all that variety of help have significantly changed the Jews' fate? Perhaps, after all. If it had been provided in the first years of war, thousands more might eventually have escaped, and be alive now. But Hugo was no doubt exaggerating the effect that outside help, both organizational and material, could have had in saving lives.

He also seemed inconsistent. On the one hand he accused Jewish leaders in the West of lordliness in relation to Polish leaders, claiming that they believed they were so superior, and the Poles' anti-Semitism so fanatical that it was a waste of time talking to them. But at the same time he said that this was merely an excuse made by the Jewish western leaders for their generally negative attitude towards helping the Jews of Poland, an attitude which went back to the nineteen thirties. Others said that there was no contradiction between the two.

But the criticisms that Hugo had raised were not the only ones that were pertinent to the matter of outside help. There were the additional non-material issues, such as breaking the isolation of the condemned, the sympathy and solidarity that help implied, its spirit-lifting capacity, and the moral issue anent the free Jews: to succour or not.

However the sharpest comment was reserved for what Hugo called "negative help", that is the attitude of the free Jewish communities in the later stage of the war, from the time mass extermination began in 1942.

–"Having deserted us as soon as the war broke out, the western Jews, including the Palestinian ones, grew dumb and deaf to our fate as it was sealed. They lost all feelings of brotherhood, all warmth in their hearts, or willingness to save the lives of people who were, after all, officially their co-religionists. Instead, their leaders raised a wall of secrecy around what was happening to us. It looks like a planned conspiracy of silence, which only helped to preserve the silence of the Allies."

–"Why do you pick out the western Jews?" asked Hausdienst, not to question Hugo but, as it turned out, to agree with him. "Our own, Polish-Jewish leaders, who happened to be in the West, didn't breathe a word until 1942, when it was too late.

"And simply inexplicable is the response (or rather non-response) of the Jews in Palestine. Telling us 'you're lucky' that war has broken out, was probably well meant. Many Jews in Poland, and elsewhere, said the same, believing that the Anglo-French Alliance would quickly defeat Hitler. And telling us, when we were forced into labour camps in 1940, that 'our youngsters' regard it as a *hakhshara*, may have only been the ranting of an exceptionally loose-tongued politician, perhaps still mindful of the humiliation he had once suffered from his Jewish constituents in

217

Poland. But the community as a whole? At least two out of five Palestinian Jews are from Poland. Mostly first generation immigrants. They must have had, before the carnage, close relatives - parents, a brother or sister, or even a child - in Poland, and yet they kept quiet."

–"Hard indeed to explain," seconded Deker. "Our western Jewish leaders expected us, trapped in Nazi Europe, to disappear before it actually came to pass, and yet they sat quietly doing nothing."

–"There's been a failure of leadership all along the line," Hugo returned to his argument. "Not just by a few individuals. The whole unholy partnership, almost without exception. Hence, I say, it's a conspiracy. They all agreed among themselves to keep silent."

–"Did it matter?" I asked, more to enliven the discussion than in quest of an answer.

–"What do you mean?"

–"What if they had not kept silent? What if they'd screamed loud and long?"

–"I know your view. Nothing could be done. No amount of screaming could help. Yet to keep silent meant to suffer the crime, if not to become quiet accessories to it. Surely, you'll agree that silence and secrecy could hardly spur the Allied Powers into remedial action, and so contain the magnitude of the disaster?"

–"Not sure. What could the Allies do to help us?"

This question had drawn, as on similar occasions in the past, a hail of dissenting voices from my comrades, but none was incontrovertible.

–"They, not the Jews, had the power to check the Germans. But they did nothing to stop the slaughter. They practically acquiesced in it. I don't say, they could have saved all, or most of us, but thousands, perhaps tens of thousands," Hugo shouted loudest of all.

"Won't you agree that they could at least have warned the Germans? Why not threaten them with retaliation? Retaliation wouldn't have helped us, you say. But this could only be proved, if they had tried," Osterman added more calmly.

–"All right, they couldn't reach us, to stop the Aktions and the death-camps but they could reach Germany," Deker spoke curiously imprecisely. But as he continued it became clear what he meant: reprisals from the air. He thought wrongly that the western Allies could not reach Poland from the air in 1942, when the extermination work was in full swing.

The bombing of German cities and targets connected with the mass murder in occupied Poland, was the favourite among the "shake-heaven-and-earth" measures, which the desperate Jews, survivors of the first Aktions, and waiting for the next ones, used to call for to save them. "Only reprisals could be effective," was Deker's view, though it was most doubtful if retaliatory bombing of the Germans would have deterred their leaders from finishing off the Jews before the end of the war. Other suggestions which the prisoners of Pustkow voiced were all familiar from the ghetto days. Threaten all Germans with retaliation, including those living in Allied countries. Inform the German people by every means of what is being done to Jews (as if they did not know), make them exercise pressure on their government to stop the slaughter, in order to avoid retribution later on. Arouse public opinion in the world to the crimes, and many similar suggestions. It was hardly surprising that the Allies' refusal to accept any of these suggestions had aroused nearly as much bitterness and scorn among the men awaiting annihilation in Pustkow as it had earlier among those in the towns.

"It would make a cat laugh," Deker continued, "to hear the Allies say that they can't bomb the Germans to prevent them totally destroying the Jews, because only air attacks on military targets are admissible."

It was mockery by the Allies, he argued, as many had before him, to deny in public that the war had anything to do with Jews; or to say that they were scared of helping the doomed Jews under German occupation, because this would increase anti-Semitism in their own countries. "Is it any wonder that Hitler keeps chaffing the Allies that they aren't at all displeased with his liquidation of the Jews."

As usual, Knepel tried to go one better, saying that the Allied leaders were careful not to mention Jews in their speeches or broadcasts to Germany, because if they did, this could cause more persecution. "As if," he added in a mixture of laughter and anger, "we could be killed twice."

However neither he, nor Deker, denied, when challenged, that the Soviets do not mention Jews at all in their declarations and denunciations of German atrocities. While Deker tried to explain this as their reluctance on principle to regard Jews as a separate people, Knepel showed perhaps more insight. Millions of people, he said, have been killed in the war, many of them Soviet civilians; as a result human life has become relatively less precious in Russia (it was so in earlier years as well, he might have added). Hence the Soviet leaders' scant interest in the particular fate of the Jews, on the one hand, and their overriding concern with the military operation, on the other. For the present, they promise retribution against the perpetrators of the crimes in the future, after victory.

This is actually not very different from what the western Allies are saying, even though they do occasionally mention the Jews publicly as the prime victims of Nazi crimes. They, too, believe that there is no other way to help "the poor Jews" than to defeat the Germans militarily, and then to call to account those responsible for the atrocities. The Jewish leaders in the West are apparently quite satisfied with such policy statements though they must understand that the promise of "help" contained in them will not restore to life those who are meanwhile being murdered. This is one of the opinions which we all, whether in the ghettos or in Pustkow, share. About whether there was really no other way to "help the poor Jews", opinions always varied.

Yet on this, as on almost any other subject, our sentiments in Pustkow, however caustic, are far less passionate than they had once been at home. At camp, and in our singular conditions especially, we somehow feel less desperate than in the ghetto, probably because virtually every one of us has nothing more to lose than his own, tenuously held life. Teper's feeling of the lightened burden of being.

Opinions however vary with circumstances and with a person's emotions. And Hugo, speaking once quietly and intimately, conceded that until 1944 the Allies

219

could not do much to help the Jews. Continental Europe was under the undisputed domination of Hitler's armies. The year 1942, during which most of the murdered Jews ended their days, was particularly critical for the Allies, who were on the retreat for the better part of the year. While the situation greatly improved in 1943, most of Europe still remained in the grip of German power. During those years, the western Allies could issue declarations, warnings and threats, which they occasionally did, but they were probably careful not to overdo it, in order not to diminish their effect, and provide Hitler with the opportunity of calling their bluff with scorn.

Still, the Allies turned down the drastic measures which the Polish Jews had appealed for, and which the Jewish leaders in the West were too timid to repeat. As they also turned down the similar requests made by some of the governments-in-exile on behalf of their people living under Nazi terror. While it was true that, as the desperate remnant Jews had maintained, only Allied reprisals from the air could in those years have had any effect, it was very doubtful if such action would have stopped the slaughter of the Jews. Their extermination was of such high priority among Hitler's war aims, that nothing except crushing military force could have prevented him from accomplishing it. The Allies could, of course, have shown a token of help, could have heartened the living, consoled the dying, made the crimes more widely known, by broadcasting news about them more frequently both to Germany, and to occupied Europe, appealing to its people to help the Jews.

Reflecting upon these matters in the spring of 1944, long after the tide of war had turned, Germany's defeat was certain, and threats by the Allies had acquired substance, we all sense that if they would warn Germany's allied governments and peoples now about the consequences of acquiescing, let alone participating in the German crimes against the Jews, this could not fail to impress them; though it could eventually help only the remnant fraction of European Jews who are still alive in the satellite countries. All in all, the Allies' wartime response to the distant calls for help was muted; they failed to do most of the things that could be done to support the oppressed Jews. But in this respect the failure of the free Jews comes first.

–"The failure of the free Jews comes first," Marek repeated. "What d'you think, why have they been silent? Didn't they know what was happening?"

–"They certainly did. Perhaps initially they didn't believe it. But they did know. Even if some didn't, this wouldn't make them innocent. The silence was deliberate."

–"This is just what I'm asking, why?"

Maniek Lander, who occasionally joined our evening discussions, climbing up onto my, or Marek's bunk, interrupted to ask: "Why talk about it?"

–"We must be truthful," I hastened to answer. "We must speak not only of what's pleasant. To avoid the unpleasant is to distort history. Its lessons must be learned. We must be truthful. Should speak the truth, anyway.

"Though, as I've said before, I personally doubt whether in terms of life-saving it would have mattered much to us, if our free brothers had raised their voices. But

220

they didn't keep silent or actually suppress the news of the murders out of ineptitude or shattered nerves. Nor out of ill will, even it it was deliberate."

—"So what is it?" Marek asked impatiently. Like many of us, he was more interested in the internal Jewish aspects of our great tragedy than in the external aspects, including what the Germans did to us.

—"Probably a mixture of indecision, indifference, inconvenience and stupidity. Hugo Bester says that politicians in general aren't the most courageous of men. In support of his claim he cites the authority of Disraeli, a politician himself."

—"Did one need courage to inform the public in the West? To awaken its conscience, its sense of responsibility towards innocent human creatures?"

—"This wasn't just a question of informing the public in the West and hoping it would exert the necessary pressure on the various governments. It was more a matter of exerting pressure by direct action so that the Allies would be forced to take the 'earth-and-heaven-shaking' measures that would hopefully save some of the doomed Jewish lives. The Allied officials maintained that any public protest would disturb its war efforts. It required some courage to deny this; to say that the measures that were needed couldn't seriously affect Allied military preparedness, and that extending help to the oppressed Jews and other occupied peoples wasn't incompatible with the Allies' war aims."

—"Brzostek says that a recently organized group of patriotic Poles issued a protest about the 'stubborn silence' of international Jewry concerning the slaughter of their co-religionists in Poland," Maniek again interposed. His words reminded me instantly of Teper and his Pole's taunts.

"The Poles are also astonished," Maniek continued, "that the western public persists in disbelieving the things that the Germans did in Poland."

However Marek turned the conversation to enquire about another feature of inter-Jewish relations, which is also of general relevance.

—"Why is it that we're mainly blaming the leaders? Don't they reflect the attitudes of the communities they represent?"

—"In general I agree with you: it's the community that 'makes' its leaders, not the other way round - even though Jewish leaders in the West, except perhaps those in Palestine, aren't democratically appointed. Yet to jolt a community out of its apathy, to mobilize it for protest and action is the responsibility of the leadership. This responsibility of a leader for his flock has deep Jewish roots, if you want to know, dating back to Moses and the Children of Israel.

"Another evening, Marek asked straight out: "Did they wish us to die?" He meant the free Jews in the West, and their leaders in particular.

—"I don't know. What makes you ask me such a serious question? I have never said that they wished us to die."

—"Suppose they didn't, how do you explain their negative attitude to rescuing us - you did say that?"

—"That attitude goes back to prewar years. Policies of the past shape attitudes of the present. But that attitude doesn't mean they wish us to die."

–"Maybe you're right. Perhaps watching a man drowning and not jumping to his help is no proof of wishing his death. But then, how would you explain why they are so reluctant to come to our help?"

–"I told you once why they kept silent. Besides, in America and England, the Jews believe they must be more patriotic than the rest of the population. The first way of proving this is to look on Jews from other countries as aliens. And in times of war, it seems to them unpatriotic to mention specifically Jewish concerns. The Jews, especially those in the United States, have also been perhaps unduly afraid of domestic anti-Semitism, of being accused of so-called dual loyalty and the like. Moreover, political and personal strife, which was internally aggravating, must have unnerved the rivalling Jewish notables in the United States. The situation hasn't been so very different in Palestine, where the community is anxious to endear itself to the British authorities, and the leadership is deeply absorbed with plans for the future. In short, the Jews in all those countries have their own priorities and preoccupations, as the Allied Powers have theirs; and rescuing European Jews from German hands comes very low on the list."

–"Yet saying 'don't know' means that you don't exclude the possibility."

As I did not reply, he repeated what he had said more emphatically.

"What makes you suspect that fellow Jews could wish us to die?"

–"That's very saddening," I said to give myself time to work out my answer. "You, Marek, may think nothing of our sages of old. But they were wise men. And they said that if a man doesn't visit a sick relative or friend, he does not wish him, or her, to live, though neither to die. All right, I admit that our free brethren couldn't have saved us, but they could have sent a word of sympathy, moral comfort to the dying, a simple 'I'm with you'. The other leaders exiled in London or elsewhere did send such messages to their peoples, who were suffering much less than the Jews under German occupation. It's improbable that the western Allies would not have allowed the Jews in their countries to go on the air and do the same if they'd been asked. That's how this awful suspicion steals into the mind."

–"That could be just a moral low. And your quotation from the sages isn't quite logical. Can you think of some rational explanation?"

–"What's irrational in wishing not to be disturbed in caring for one's own vineyard? What's irrational in not wanting to accept responsibility for a remote community of strangers? And then, if your conscience is troubled, you tell yourself 'there's nothing that could be done to help them', and you sleep quietly at nights."

–"This I understand, also what you may be implicitly saying. I myself often wondered whether our expectations of help, our pretentions, don't come from an illusory belief in general brotherhood between Jews of various climes. This may have been true in earlier days, when earnest attachment to religion made Jews brothers in faith and so inspired a feeling of oneness. Times have changed. Nowadays most Jews are religious in name only. They have, moreover, adopted the cultures and ways of life of the peoples in the midst of whom they live; and so they differ from country to country. Difference bears indifference. For most of the others, the brotherhood is disposable, or at least suspensible, in times of hardship and crisis. But this is not enough to explain why Jews of either of the two convictions should wish the death of other Jews?"

–"It seems a logical question, but it's only superficially logical. It isn't uncommon for a man to wish the death of a fellow man or relative. I told you once how some Jewish passers-by wished the death of two fellow Jews, who were being forced by German soldiers to dance humiliatingly in the street. Here you have a wish born from moral qualms, a humanitarian wish for death. It's so easy to talk oneself into a humanitarian motive. You're also exaggerating the importance of devoutness in this regard."

–"Certainly not of modern western Jews. And I'm still waiting to hear a rational, convincing reason why they should want us to die.

"For myself I was thinking of their negative attitude to our emigration from Poland. Their not being willing to have us, asking themselves, as you once said of many Allied officials: 'What if they get out? Where will they go?' But there never was a question of us getting out in more than trifling numbers during the war."

–"Quite right. Where Jews wanted us to come, to Palestine, the gates had been shut, or almost shut. As we couldn't leave, and since the outbreak of war have also ceased to be a source of support, financially and politically - worse, we've become contenders for the scarce funds - our brethren in Palestine, too, almsot instantly lost all interest in us.

"You know Hugo, the warehouseman at the Bekleidungsbarracks. He referred the other day to Gogol. Hugo called his idea of turning dead souls into a source of wealth extraordinarily imaginative and, somewhat contradictorily, 'just perceptive'. When I remarked that it was only after Tchitchikoff had turned the dead souls into living men that he made money out of them - implying that it's living men who produce wealth, and that no one is likely, anyway, to imitate Tchitchikoff in our case - Hugo retorted quickly that I'm wrong. 'Wait, if we survive you'll see that you're wrong.' He's convinced that the wiles are under way while we're here.

"When Hugo was still on the outside, it used to be said that some goody-goodies involved in helping people in hiding and in the camps, exaggerated their numbers, including on the lists names of people who had died years before, to get a little more money out of the rich. The point of the story is, Hugo concluded, and I couldn't make out if he was being ironic or not, that poor survivors - much poorer than the serfs in Russia a hundred years ago - are nothing but a burden and create far greater problems than the dead.

"Be that as it may, you people who seek only rational solutions without looking at facts, must admit that the dead have truly settled a serious problem. The Jewish problem in eastern Europe. Not that its disappearance gladdens our free brethren as much as it does our non-Jewish neighbours in Poland and the countries around. Certainly not. But they see matters differently from us. And their leaders, like the wise strategists they consider themselves, must think in world-wide terms, embracing the Jewish people as a whole, thinking in terms of overall strength, resources, and the days ahead.

"The Jews in eastern Europe, relatively poor, unwanted, constantly under attack,

223

have on balance been a source of weakness in the whole. If, as a result of their demise, the hub of Jewish vitality is transferred to the rich and liberal West, it would modernize and strengthen those who remain. They must extract something positive from this catastrophe, the founts of revival, the wings of the proverbial phoenix rising out of ashes, as he has risen before in the course of Jewish history. The past cannot be undone. They must think of the future. So, they are certainly absorbed, and have been throughout the worst days of the tragedy, in planning for after the war. Especially in Palestine.

"There, the trying is hard, the stakes very high. The Jews and their leaders, who claim to represent the nation, are on trial before the court of history. They must not fail. They must not miss this opportunity for it will not come again soon. They must concentrate on the single task. Even if that means turning their backs on the dying millions. In the long night of exile, Jews more credible and nobler than they have been prepared to sacrifice one half of the people in order to redeem the other half. But is it necessary? Are the two mutually exclusive? To forsake millions of still flickering flames in order to raise a single giant torch? I doubt it. It's wrong. Egocentricity? Hardness of heart? Strain? Or, simply too great a load for their little shoulders to bear both at once? The responsibility is, admittedly, heavy. The difficulties formidable. They must hold out. Theirs is the great hope. Perhaps the emerging phoenix himself. They must not fail! For us, the forlorn in ashes, it would be much easier to lie in peace if we knew they had not failed."

CHAPTER SIXTEEN

17 April 1944

It may be true that each spring the same flowers blossom, but that not every spring festival blooms the same. If I ever had any doubt of this, Pustkow dispelled it once for all. Passover at a Nazi concentration camp! What an improbability! And yet...It is now forty-eight hours since the eight-day festival came to an end. I decided, for the record, to relate how it was celebrated. Not a tale of a tub; everything happened exactly as it is narrated.

It all started with a sigh, as every one of our days starts and ends. Sighs at the approach of the solemn festival with its once glorious rites, and our inability to honour it now. But, then, a few days before the festival started, an odd rumour whispered that those prisoners who wished to observe Passover, could forego their daily bread ration, and would then get flour to bake *matzot*, unleavened bread for themselves. There would also be a separate Passover "kitchen", that is ritually prepared soup and tea. A mere rumour? A joke? Risking no more than exposure to ridicule, I registered my interest. Two days before the festival, everyone in our barracks who had declared their interest received about two pounds of white flour between them. In the evening, after Lagerschluss, my room was turned into a bakery for an hour or so. Though heating is no longer allowed, the two tin stoves in the room were set burning with saw-dust smuggled in from the workshops and other combustible waste. Sparks escaping through the flue into the night sky. And on the red-glowing surface of the stove-plate, little, round matzot, the size of a pocket-watch and weighing about five grams each, were baked in quick succession. Everyone enlisted was preparing stocks of sixteen pieces for the eight-day duration of the festival.

Next morning, the eve of Passover, reveille was at a quarter to five, instead of at six, for those who are observant. They were to peel potatoes for three days in advance. The kitchen would not hold so many men; two sacks of potatoes and a thoroughly scrubbed, long unused, cooking cauldron were put out into the square by a prisoner called Piler, whose face is so wasted by his experiences that he looks sixty-five, though he has hardly turned fifty. He is one of the cooks, and was to be in charge of the Passover "kitchen". Work was brisk, the peeler-knives swinging quickly, everyone was hurrying: it was for their own bellies, and the whole operation must be finished before 6 a.m. So undoubtedly it was an occasion full of both exaltation and anxiety.

Not long after the performance had started, Bubi, wearing only slippers, riding-breeches and a shirt, though it was still cold so early in the morning, comes outside to reconnoitre the scene. The knowledge of what may be going on has apparently kept him awake. He looks on for a while and seems dismayed. The sight is indeed quite extraordinary. Forty men standing in the middle of the roll-call ground before day has officially started, peeling potatoes under the eyes of SS guardsmen on the towers. Where, when, who has seen or heard of such a thing? Where do they think they are? This is a concentration camp on an SS training base. Who, if not Bubi himself, is answerable for this daft extravagance? What is all this Passover madness? A Passover diet from an SS kitchen! Bubi flies into a rage. He shouts, curses, threatens. But he has only himself to blame for this. He has authorized it. Had he not, this folly would not be taking place. Yes, but to picture a misdeed is not the same as actually witnessing it. Does he regret it? Yes and no. I do not know, but taking a peep at him, he looked genuinely scared. Everything rests on his shoulders. What if Ruf comes ahead of time to "start the day"? What will he tell him? And even if Ruf does not come earlier, what if he gets word of it? The news may even reach Klipp? He, Bubi, will be held responsible. He may lose his job, be "reduced to the ranks". He may even get a few days solitary in the bunker. Oh, what the hell did he do? Why has he given his consent? He fumes. "Finish this straight away!" "You *Speckjägers!*" (literally, bacon hunters). "You *Kartoffelwänste!*" (potato bellies). He will overturn the cooking pot and spill all this *Dreck* (filth) out. He will make us roll in it. He will do this and that. It's not very serious. He has given his permission beforehand. The men go on peeling. Yet the air is tense, and it is not at all pleasant to see Bubi in such a state. Piler comes forward to assure him that however great a quantity of potatoes is peeled, he will see to it that the place is cleaned and cleared by a quarter to six. No, Bubi roars even louder. "Halt it at once!" He kicks the cooking pot. The men stop work and begin cleaning. "In five minutes the place must be cleared!" and, slightly chilled, Bubi returns to the barracks. Not to come out again until the work is finished at fifteen minutes to six.

Well, what was behind all this? It was a man, whose name is Krohn. He is an old-timer and one of the oldest prisoners, aged over fifty, with grey hair and a serene, plump face. He is the camp storekeeper. His duties include the delivery of provisions to the kitchen and its supervision, as well as the overall distribution of food rations to the prisoners. By virtue of this post, his standing informally equals that of the capos, who may even ask favours from him. Krohn lives in one room, together with Bubi and only one other prominent prisoner. But the room also serves as the rations storehouse. Krohn and Bubi came from the same town in Germany. Theirs is a special relationship; Krohn is said to have Bubi's ear in almost everything, and Bubi looks on Krohn as a father-figure. Krohn is an observant man; while several prisoners own phylacteries, only Krohn also has a prayer-shawl, which he brought with him to Pustkow when he arrived there on his own decision for work nearly four years ago.

The Passover venture was not only his brain-child from start to finish, but he also obtained Bubi's consent to it. However, everyone says Bubi would have been unlikely to give his consent merely at the prompting of Krohn, no matter how "special" their relations are. One does not take such a risk - and the risk was substantial - without inner conviction. Bubi, it seems to me, must come from a religious background. Rather than out of regard for the fatherly image of an elderly man, he is more likely to have done this in memory of his true father and of Passover at his home.

In the evening, there was to be a collective Seder, a ceremonial service, in which everyone would participate, although most of the men are indifferent, if not opposed, to all ritual. I was sceptical, indeed sure that such a common "table" could not succeed and will only divest the ceremony of all piety and emotional grace. So it was. Following the initial blessing on the matza, in lieu of wine, there was immediate uproar. Five minutes later, amid shouts, laughter and ribaldry, the party was over.

It was only then that it started for me, in a setting which I had planned from the outset. In a darkish corner of the room, in communion with myself, I solemnly recited the *Haggadah*. Never before had I felt so poignantly the meaning of words such as "this bread of affliction which our ancestors ate in the land of Egypt," or wept at the mention of their sighing and lamenting "by reason of bondage". Of course, the tears, in which these words were swimming, were not shed for the lives of our ancestors in Egypt, but for events nearer in time and space, stirred by the sight of that once blissful, ecstatic night that carried all the warmth of a family table at home, though I was really sitting in the dim, dull corner of my barrack room.

There were forty-three men who undertook not to eat bread but to live on the Passover food. They made up nearly ten per cent of all prisoners; a similar proportion of inmates of the ghetto had still been observant on the verge of its liquidation, nearly three years into the war. But ten men opted out in the intervening days of the festival, not so much, I think, because of hunger, which all of them had suffered for much longer in the past, but because of the attraction of an alternative - a nice portion of bread.

On the last day, the soup was sour and uneatable, as it had been cooked a day or two before. For how can you cook kosher food on a Sabbath! So, except for the last five-gram matza and a few gulps of water in the morning, the remaining men had to endure until nightfall, as on *Yom Kippur*, the day appointed for fasting. Krohn had seen to it that the loyal group of thirty three still had the day's bread ration and hot "tea" out of hours.

Later, already on his bunk before sleep, Marek declared sententiously: "An accomplished act of defiance." His approving comment intimated why the Passover practice was generally well received by the majority of prisoners, while other religious manifestations were usually met with jibes or even derisive invective.

−"I never felt that I was being defiant during these eight days," I replied, "but I felt great. To feel pure and proper in this degrading, evil place made me feel good, human, a Jew. Besides, to me holding to ritual and tradition, as tokens of faith, gives sense to existence.

227

This same Pineas Krohn, who master-minded the Passover in Pustkow, does not speak to his co-believers, or to other Polish-Jewish fellow prisoners. Strange? Yes, but not surprising. At least not to me. Not just because I am aware of the notorious Jewish self-hatred, that is, the mutual dislike and estrangement, that exists in varying degrees between Jews of different ethnic and religious colouring. In Krohn's case, there is also the wide divergence in age between him and most of his co-believers, as well as the weight of his personality. Krohn gives the impression of being a reticent, withdrawn person. I am also aware of the fairly common practice of emphasizing one's own superiority by keeping one's distance from those considered inferior; and aware that our camp community, like probably any other in the world, is not egalitarian - only that in our peculiar society, a prisoner's function replaces property qualifications in determining his status. In our case, status is, however, decided almost as much by language, namely proficiency in German. Krohn combines both advantages.

The German Jews of Pustkow were a species of fairly recent Germanic pedigree. Jews long established in Germany were not discharged by the Nazis into the southern part of Poland. When their removal began in 1942, they were sent, if not directly to an extermination camp, then to one of the large ghettos in the once Russian part of Poland or farther to the east. The same was the case with Jews who were stateless or German by naturalization, only that their evacuation took place earlier in 1941. The Jews who arrived in the southern, formerly Austrian, part of Poland, including those now in Pustkow, were mostly the so-called Zbąszyń expelees.

When a year before the war the Polish government issued a decree aimed at withdrawing passports from Jews living abroad, Germany expelled about fifteen thousand Jews, holding Polish citizenship on October 28, 1938, a day before the decree was to come into force. The expelees were kept, for periods ranging from a few days to several weeks, in the "no-man's land" between the two countries, or at hastily set up camps at the Polish frontier point of Zbaszyn. Hence, the collective designation of this group of refugees. And the name was loosely extended to include Jews who sought earlier refuge from Nazi Germany in Poland.

It seems fairly safe to assume that these Zbaszyn expelees were mostly first generation German, born from at least a Polish-Jewish father, some from German-Christian mothers (though none of this category is known to be in Pustkow), and not a few of the older folk, had been born in Poland, and still had close relations there.

It is equally easy to perceive that these family origins reduced the diversity between the Zbaszyn expelees and the Jews in the country of their arrival; also that they differed in many respects from the majority of the Jews in the country they had left. They were culturally less deracinated from their Jewish origins, and less attached to their recent German past; and very few of them expected to resume their lives in Germany. Even fewer blamed east European Jews for the misfortunes that befell them, and those who did, probably spoke without conviction, in anger. On the whole, they were not less sensitive to the overall Jewish catastrophe than the Jews of Poland.

The Zbaszyn expelees were mostly young and came from a fairly ordinary background; none of them had upper class origins, or were intellectuals. They did not speak Polish, but had no difficulty in communicating with the indigenous Jews, many of whom spoke German more or less well, and some of the expelees knew Yiddish. For all that, they were strangers in their new surroundings, and although not resentful, they felt alienated. They had hardly any "good" connections - which particularly in wartime conditions were so important in gaining advantages - and no source of income other than from selling personal belongings and, eventually, valuables smuggled out of Germany.

Given those circumstances, it was understandable that these people tried to take advantage of their natural knowledge of German, once it had become the first official language under Nazi occupation. Knowledge of German was of great help in finding employment, even when this required no direct contact with German officials. All this explains why, when a disciplinary Jewish police was organized on the orders of the German authorities, the proportion of OD men recruited from among the German Jews was significantly higher than the proportion from a local community. But most of them were decent men, behaved no worse and no better, than other OD men, and at least in Tarnow, none of the German Jews was counted among the Gestapo informers. Taken altogether, the general impoverishment and oppression under German occupation had levelled out the earlier differences between the expelees and native Jews, and once all of them were forced into the ghetto, the former adapted to life in it no worse than the latter.

For the reasons I have already given, the percentage of Zbaszyn expelees who volunteered for work in Pustków was much higher than their percentage in the total number of Jews in Tarnów, Rzeszów and Dębica, from where nearly all the volunteers had come. Hence the relatively high proportion of German Jews now in Pustkow, especially among the old-timers and holders of privileged positions. Also, while these German Jews have, at least now, no different perception of the nature and aims of the SS from their Polish-Jewish fellow prisoners, they nevertheless feel - and certainly felt during the first two years of the war - comparatively less remote from Germans in general. This is the usual rapport that a common language occasions even between adversaries. This and the almost daily contacts over many months, would account for the relatively greater trust SS men have in their German-Jewish prisoners, on the one hand, and these prisoners' relatively smaller distrust of SS men on the other. They regard the Pustkow SS men, including the camp warders, to be of an exceptional kind, who if left to themselves would let us live - a belief that has passed to many other prisoners, old-timers in particular - and they occasionally defend them, and Germans in general, to the Polish-Jewish men. "Do you think that all SS men are murderers?" Or, "You must admit that not all Germans are Nazis." "Most Germans don't know about the crimes," and similar inanities. It seems to me that this doubtful apology for the Germans was said out of pique, or in a sort of self-defence, as they feel personally tarnished by the deeds of people from the country they came from and of which they once felt a part. This

229

uneasiness, I believe, is also reflected in the German Jews' disposition to talk about every SS man who ever did anything good in the past, while reminding us of the various misdeeds committed by Poles and, in general, railing at the treatment of Jews in prewar Poland. Along with this, they are more inclined to believe that the circumstance of speaking proper German and performing skilled work - and the German Jews are, on average, better skilled than the other prisoners - will save their lives.

Among themselves, the German-Jewish prisoners form a sort of closed circle, on the whole keeping their distance from the Polish-Jewish prisoners. But even if they are somewhat patronizing, there is no question of their abusing, let alone bullying the others. Though not a large group, the German Jews are not of one status, nor of one variety; in fact, they differ widely in their attachment to Judaism and in their attitudes both to Germans and to other prisoners. At one extreme Krohn stands out as probably the only one of his group who is still observant in Pustkow, while at the other, there are a few men who do not even consider themselves Jewish. In between there is, for example, Biegel, a prisoner nestled in the job of senior cook, even though he is rather a late-comer to Pustkow.

Biegel, still unmarried despite his thirty years of age, entered the ghetto of Rzeszow together with his mother and sister. When three weeks later, on 10 January 1942, the ghetto was closed, he was stilll able to go out daily with a work-ing party and bring some food back home. His forebodings of disaster and his description of his shock at finding himself caged inside a narrow space, surrounded by enemy police, is quite familiar. At the first Aktion, which began on 7 July 1942, he was separated from his family. On account of his "important war work" as a mechanical excavator at a Wehrmacht building-site, he was allowed to stay in Rzeszow. But on the fourth and last day of this Aktion, which was the 19th of July, his "stamp" was ignored and, together with hundreds of mostly elderly men, not so elderly women, and children, he was made to climb onto a lorry and driven a few miles to what turned out to be an execution site in the forests of Glogow. There, apparently due to executions on the earlier Aktion days, a huge mass grave, partly filled with corpses covered with quicklime, was already waiting, so that the killing started immediately on their arrival. It was late indeed, daylight was already fading, and there were no lights to illuminate the place. The killers had to hurry, making the shooting so continuous that it had never really stopped until all the prey were believed to be dead. Some of the victims were shot first and then thrown into the grave, others were first forced to lie down in the grave and then shot. But this was not without consequence, Biegel explained. For having been selected for the sec-ond kind of treatment, that is, clubbed into the ditch while still alive, he was hit by a bullet in the back and not killed. He feigned dead, lying fully conscious among the really dead and wounded, whose groans were deadened by the sound of shots and the dreary thud of the falling bodies. A child, hurled into the ditch like a bag of rubbish, hit him in the face, leaving marks Biegel proudly shows in Pustkow. Meanwhile in the ditch he lay protected by another body for about half an hour till the shooting had stopped. Late at night, despite the pain of his wounds, he found the strength to scramble out from among the corpses and managed to escape into the forest. The next night, keeping off the highroad to avoid human beings, he trailed back into the ghetto, helped in finding his way by the corpses that still lay on the ground. Altogether during that Aktion, two thousand were shot in the forest, twenty thousand sent to Belzec, and four thousand left, for the time being, in the ghetto.

Back in Rzeszow, after having recovered from his wound, which was secretly tended by a doctor, Biegel took up the offer of going to Pustkow to work as a mechanic.

Once when I was listening to him, I said, perhaps thoughtlessly, that there are thousands of stories like his. Biegel became angry and since then does not speak to me - though not to me alone. Eager to emphasize his superiority and proud of his refined German speech - unvaryingly referring to Reichshof, as Rzeszow was renamed by the occupying power in February 1941 - he at the same time curses all Germans and speaks of revenge - as many do in camp though, in my view, they don't really mean it. He proposes as the ultimate retribution to put Hitler on show after the war, driving him all around Germany in a cage. Biegel is not unexpectedly, but uncharacteristically for those in his linguistic gorup, quite pessimistic about the chances of surviving.

Probably not too fond of his fellow German Jews, and feeling inwardly closer to Polish Jews, is Meyer Zirels, who works in the tailors' patching room. Meyer was born in Frankfurt-am-Main to parents who had immigrated from Poland. At the beginning of the school term in the autumn of 1935, he arrived at his new school, which was affiliated to the orthodox Breuer community in Frankfurt. Next day all the other children of his form stayed at home. In the afternoon, the headmaster and the secretary of the school came to see Meyer's parents to say how sorry they were and how much they disapproved of this conduct. But what could they do? Should they close the school? They asked the Zirels, despite everything, for their consideration and to withdraw their son from school. Meyer's parents had wisely agreed, and several weeks later the boy, their only son, then approaching the age of *Bar-Mitzva*, arrived at the home of his mother's sister, who was living with her husband and two little children in Rzeszow. There, Meyer, who was a rather bright boy with, at least now, large shining eyes and quite a neat face despite his rather long nose, continued to receive traditional education until the war. His parents, having become stateless, were not expelled in October 1938. They corresponded during the war, the last letter from them arriving towards the end of 1941. Since then Meyer has not heard from them again. During the first Aktion in July 1942, he was in hiding together with his relatives. His problems started later. He had no "stamp", hence was a fugitive of enemy justice. When he tried to legalize his stay in the ghetto, applying at the Judenrat for an assignment to work, he was told that he must go to Pustkow.

At the tailors', Zirels usually listens quietly to the debates, even if a theme is of particular interest to him. But when it comes to practical matters, he takes, plainly, advantage of speaking German in a natural way, and will not answer in Yiddish, which he can speak well, unless he is sure that no unwanted person will hear him.

At the other, far-end of this line is Hans Hirom, who comes from Bremen. For the first two years in Pustkow, he maintained contact with his parents in Rzeszow through one of the SS men on duty at the Kommandatur, where Hirom then worked. When in the late summer of 1942 the SS man brought him the news of his parents' deportation, Hirom is said to have spontaneously reacted: "It serves them right. After all they're Jews."

I was not in Pustkow then, and do not know if this rather incredible story is true. But my friend Marek says that it is, adding, more to make the words comprehensible than in Hirom's defence, that he was a silly boy of eighteen at the time.

Hirom and a few of his fellow German Jews are not the only ones who do not feel Jewish, who ask themselves why they are in Pustkow, who may even hate themselves for being forced to stay there as Jews. How much easier it is to suffer for something one knows and holds dear! That it must be difficult to accept punishment for no other sin than just being declared a Jew, I can understand. But in the present circumstances to rebel against being born a Jew seems to me as foolish as to rebel against being born a woman, or born to poor parents - which probably lies at the root of Hausdienst's radical views.

Yet none of those who rebel against their Jewishness is to be found among the tailors or cobblers. The rebels descend from different spheres. One of them is Olkowicz, a middle-aged lawyer and author of no-one knows what writings. Nor is it known what precisely his function in camp is, except that of adviser to Bubi, which means his protegé. Olkowicz does not, of course, mix with ordinary prisoners, let alone enter into conversation with them. Hugo Bester, who is an exception, did not contradict others when they said that Olkowicz persists in rejecting his Jewishness. Yet he is enslaved by the Jews' destiny and, forced to stay with them in camp, is resigned to endure them.

Hugo himself initially had similar difficulties but he accepted the inevitable and now acknowledges his Jewish bonds. However he suffers from a complaint which I would diagnose as a religious ache. He was brought up in a spirit of faith, which however was not Jewish. Now that he feels a full Jew, he has lost his faith. He would like to believe, but he cannot, experiencing the sort of inner crisis that afflicts most modern men. Because of his upbringing, Hugo, unlike many former votaries of Jewish tradition, is not rebelling against God. But he tries to make out of the present tragedy a case against Jewish religion. He keeps saying that so many Jews have turned their backs on the ancestral creed in this war, not so much in order to survive, as in order to free themselves from its oppressive hold on a man's life. Then, although only the other day he was arguing that the present persecutions of Jews resist all rational explanation, he still keeps asking how I explain these happenings in terms of the Jewish religion. This question, in varying forms, is one a man has had to face every so often these evil times.

That the Jews of Poland were losing their piety (both real and assumed) at an almost unprecedented pace in this war was undeniable. But this is an old historical process which, at least in Poland, dates from the second half of the nineteenth century. It started with a number of coincidental social changes. Mass migration from backward, dormant villages into towns; occupational transformation in the wake of industrialization; the spread of secular education combined with a pervading spirit of modernism and liberalism, and the rise of Jewish nationalist-political parties. The trend was quickened by the upheavals of the first World War - conscription into the armies of the three partitioning Powers, mass displacement of Jews following each military retreat and advance, resulting in disruption of family life and loosening of morals. In independent Poland, free and compulsory elementary education, the increasing misery of the people, and the onslaught of modern Jewish nationalism, besides other revolutionary ideas, together led to the abandonment of orthodoxy, if not religion, at a then perplexing speed, halving its strength between 1919 and 1939. It declined - it would seem - again by half within three years of the present war.

But the decline of observance during those three years was neither the result of rebellion against Jewish religion, nor of the sense of incredulity at holding on to its rites in view of what was happening, or indeed of much introspective contemplation. It was brought about by the almost complete breakdown of organized religious life, by being forced to desecrate basic religious laws, and, also to change one's outward appearance - while perceiving as this happened that the sky did not fall.

–"Why should we try to explain it just in terms of Jewish religion?" I asked Hugo. "This time the object of the hunt isn't religion, but blood. This time the converted, their children, Christians who didn't even know before that they had Jewish blood in their veins, are put together with full-blooded Jews, the devout and the godless alike. Don't you see that this time the hunters aren't after our souls, but after our bodies?"

–"Just so. Just because this time we weren't offered the alternative of escape by conversion, and yet Jews still massively abandoned their religion, proves that they're doing this not to preserve their bodies but to free themselves from constraints of the Jewish creed."

–"What you call oppression, others may regard as inspiration. You're inconsistent if you claim that the war and persecution have nothing to do with the Jews' abandoning religious practice, and then ascribe a religious motive to the tragedy.

"I should think that the quality of the present tragedy is, above all, a fatal blow to those uprooted Jews, like Olkowicz, who belong nowhere, to all those who maintained that the only important thing is not to be identified as Jews, those who found their Messiah in losing themselves in the nation where they were living."

–"I can see that in the present war, as you say, the religious and non-religious alike are chased. But why should this be more of a blow to Olkowicz than to you, and especially to all those pious Jews who were singled out for special pursuit?"

–"Because it proves to Olkowicz and his like that there's no escape from one's Jewishness, and because they die and suffer for something they don't feel and cannot sacrifice."

–"No one can sacrifice something he doesn't have. Can you? What sacrifice have you in mind? Innocence? Faith? Admit, there's no alternative. If there was one, everyone would have taken it up."

"Many say, 'fortunately there wasn't an alternative.' But since the enemy is after our bodies not our souls, preserving one's life is the prime, even one's religious duty. And leave remorse for not dying heroically to the bigots."

–"D'you really think that our brothers who are safe, and those few of us who may survive in hiding or elsewhere, will learn the lesson you prescribe for them?"

–"I don't know. Lessons are soon forgotten. But in essence, it was instructive."

–"In reality the lesson could prove to be just the opposite of what you think. It may prompt many to speed up their desertion of the Jewish trap.

"And indeed, tell me, can you honestly envisage Jewish religion recovering from the calamity it has suffered in recent days?"

It really is very hard to imagine. No one expects religion to regain after the war the place it earlier held in the life of Jews. But I did not wish to admit this to Hugo.

–"One can say nothing with certainty. The message from the past is reassuring. Every steep fall has been followed by an upward rise.

"And the lack of any alternative has another facet as well. Once, against the narrowness, dullness and constraint of the ghetto, there dangled the promise of freedom, the wide world and a blossoming culture. Today what we see outside is a different brand of culture. And that the lecturing comes from Germany - where the promise of Menschheit and Brüderlichkeit (humanity and brotherhood) was preached first of all to the Olkowiczes of all lands - surely makes the blow doubly hard to them.

"You also overlook the element of spite: those alive clinging to the creed and ideas of their fathers; persisting in the memory of all that has vanished; and procreating to rebuild lost numbers."

Hugo was gazing in front of him, a suggestion of doubt in his eyes, but he made no reply.

Unlike Hugo, my comrades at the tailor-workshop have never been bothered by these problems. They were not anxious to shed the burden of Jewishness. Revolution, "that historical imperative", they say, would not differentiate between peoples or creeds; it would demolish the barriers that separate man from man. Since God had had no place in their lives, they would not rage against, let alone defame, Him - and it was only when I heard that Olkowicz had been doing just that, that I was suddenly aware why I had not been upset when Samuel Buchaj started cursing in front of the burning books in Tarnow. By blaspheming God, he was actually affirming the Deity that he pretended to be denying.

The tailors were not so unreasonable. Considering, as they did, Judaism to be, like any other religion, a mere superstition, they did not seek to take revenge on it, or to blame it for the recent Jewish misfortunes. But they used it as a springboard for the usual invective against the rich, and the thing to blame for the penury of the "masses". They believed this in earnest and used to repeat to the point of boredom that religion leads people to idleness instead of to toil, to seek charity in place of productivity.

–"The manufacturers and merchants throw the poor a crust of bread and exhort them to resist temptation, and to pray. They grow fat on the prayers of the workers."

Deker, by force of habit, tried to correct Knepel, mingling his words with a show of erudition in Yiddish literature and adoration for its acclaimed "father".

"Itzik Leib Peretz was all for spiritual riches and accepted them as compensation for material poverty. But he championed work, progress, and fought for world justice and affirmation of life.

"Of course you're right. If one is poor one's time is taken up with prayer. The rich don't need to pray. But as Shulem Asch said, if there was only a farthing above every word in the *sidder* (prayer book), the rich would grab it for themselves, brutally preventing the poor from praying."

Neither did the tailors and cobblers grumble about circumcision, although this was a frequent subject of discussion among Jews even before the ghetto was closed. Indeed, as the war dragged on for much too long, it became fashionable in certain sections of the Jewish intelligentsia to single out the ancient practice of circumcision for hearty, vindictive swearing at the Jewish religion. Circumcision, unlike prayer, was blamed for many deaths, because it allegedly prevented Jewish males from living on Aryan papers. To listen to these idle and spiteful charges was a little irritating and in the end boring. The liberated, or shall I say self-hating Jews, repeated the whole arsenal of their arguments against it, and were answered no less profusely by the faithful traditionalists.

–"An obnoxious custom, to mutilate the body of a child with a senseless tribal mark."

–"The mark of Jewish loyalty. The seal on his flesh of the covenant between God and Jew."

–"A thoughtless action of communal self-destruction in making themselves distinct and different."

–"We survived for centuries by remaining distinct and different, not by imitating other nations."

–"The circumcised and the uncircumcised are treated alike."

–"Why do Jews condemn themselves to death? If I survive the war, I'll never allow this to be done to my son!"

When the other day, I heard Hugo issuing the familiar sigh: "Oh, if only I weren't snipped!" it instantly reminded me of the story of my colleague Abe Flacher of Tarnow.

Abe was a tall, fair-haired boy of the same age as I, and a neighbour before we moved into the ghetto. Shortly after the third Aktion, which left him the sole survivor of his entire family, Abe escaped to live on Aryan papers in Cracow. There he eventually found a job as mate to Antosh, a Polish long-distance coal-lorry driver. Antosh, a burly coarse sort of a fellow, suspected a Jew in this son of a school-master, whose demeanor and manner of speaking, however carefully adapted, did not match particularly well with his situation. Before long, Antosh started bullying and threatening him, while Abe firmly denied the suspicion.

"Well," one day Antosh said: "show me your prick!"

It was winter, evening, dark, and they agreed to wait until the next day. Abe was desperate, but that sleepless night he saw no alternative to surrendering to the odd gamble of an examination.

Before he turned up for work in the morning, Abe jogged some four miles. Not that he expected this would make his foreskin regrow, but he hoped that the flesh at the symbolic region might become sufficiently mortified not to reveal the scar around the prepuce.

Antosh arrived with an accomplice who was equipped with a magnifying glass and said to have considerable experience of such matters. All three went into an empty room at the railway goods station, where the two examiners dragged Abe's trousers and pants down, while he lay on the floor. It happened to be a grim, misty morning outside, and inside the room electric light was, for reasons of economy, a bit wan. Antosh and his expert colleague looked and looked, touched and touched, palpating with their fingers as one feels a hen for eggs, and arrived at a negative conclusion. "No, not cut," they said to one another.

Insulting as this slightly unexpected opinion was, Abe forgave them the slander, considering the circumstance. What he found unpardonable, however, were some remarks of Antosh, which gave him reason to believe that the finding of the two judges was not irrevocable, and his nerves not being made of iron, Abe took temporary refuge in the ghetto two days later.

CHAPTER SEVENTEEN

25 April 1944

It is time to try to sketch the methodically repressed and paralysed course of Jewish life under German occupation in Poland - inasmuch as this is possible. And it may not be possible, at least in a uniform, point by point order. First, because of the different dates of conquest and the different political status of various parts of the occupied country, second because the timing of measures and conditions of life varied from region to region and from town to town.

Besides, the Jews in Poland were virtually outlawed from the first day of occupation, unlike their brothers in Germany proper, where at least until the outbreak of war, their legal, and hence material, situation can be deduced from legislation relating to them. In occupied Poland the Jews had no rights of any kind. Their lives were from the beginning determined by the Nazi design to eliminate them. All the published laws and orders concerning the Jews were secondary to that design.

Concerning the design itself, surely one of the earliest and most revealing documents that has become known is the one already mentioned, the *Schnellbrief* of 21 September 1939, sent by the SS Chief of Security Police (SP) and Security Service (SD), and deputy of Himmler, Reinhard Heydrich, to the SS Einsatzgruppen operating in Poland. Copies of this Schnellbrief, which primarily outlined stage by stage the plan to exterminate the Jews, were also sent to various government ministers in Germany and to the High Command of the Army, for their "*Verständnis*" (consideration).

The plan distinguishes between the *Endziel* (final aim, a cover-name later changed to *Endlösung*, final solution) and earlier successive stages, which should be short. As the first preparatory measure to the final aim, Jews from the country should be quickly concentrated in the larger towns. But distinction should be made between two areas, one including Danzig, western Prussia, Poznań and Upper Silesia (which were all incorporated into the Reich seventeen days later), the other comprising the remaining occupied territory. The first area is to be made free of Jews; in the second, Jews should be concentrated in only a few places and preferably in towns near a railway line or at least one where a line passes nearby.

In every Jewish community there is to be established a Council of Elders (later the name was changed to Judenrat, Jewish Council) made up of authoritative personages and rabbis; the number of elders depending on the size of the community. The elders are to be made fully and personally responsible for strict and prompt execution of orders given to them. It thus becomes clear that the Jewish councillors were from the outset envisaged as an ancillary instrument of the occupying power, as well as its hostages.

Next, Jews should be marked, counted, registered, removed from economic life, forced to labour, put into ghettos - besides other measures that would accelerate their intended extinction. Indeed the process of actual destruction exactly followed the instructions contained in the Schnellbrief, except for one deviation: in many towns, particularly the small ones, the "final aim" preceded ghettoization.

The final solution itself was discussed and settled in detail at the so-called Wannsee-Conference on 20 January 1942. Its purpose was to inform important departmental officials of the worked out plan of extermination, and to discuss specific questions of organization. The measures endorsed were decimation through mass executions, starvation, disease, and forced labour; for the particularly resistant section of the Jewish people, gassing. At the time of the conference, mass gassing was already taking place at Chelmno (Kulmhof), while "test-gassing" had begun at Auschwitz four months earlier, in September 1941.

As to the starting date of the whole thing, oppression of the Jews began in almost every town on the day of its occupation. In a different context, the Germans refer to an eighteen-days-*Feldzug* (military campaign), that ended a day after the Russians crossed the eastern border of Poland. But most of the country's territory had been conquered by the German army between one and two weeks earlier, and immediately put under the military rule of the Wehrmacht. Indeed, the looting, beating, seizure for work and the killing of thousands of Jews in the first weeks of occupation was partly carried out by Wehrmacht soldiers and only partly by special SS units. Worst affected were Jews (as well as Poles) in western and north-western Poland. These regions, including Gdansk, were by a decree of Hitler of October 8, 1939, incorporated into the Reich, as the new Gaus (provinces) of Danzig-West Prussia and Wartheland, while Upper Silesia was administratively merged with the formerly German part of Silesia. Hardly a month later, the mass expulsion of Jews from these territories began, in conditions arousing visions of ancient migrations of peoples, as men, women and children with their bundles, trudged on and on further eastwards. Most of Wartheland was cleared of Jews before the end of the year. Other Jews who had not yet been expelled were for the time being moved to a few larger towns. In the largest, Łódz, a ghetto was formed as early as February 8, 1940; the walls closed three months later.

Following another decree of Hitler issued on October 12, 1939, in the part of occupied Poland which was not incorporated into the Reich the so-called General Government (GG) came into being two weeks later. This nominally independent polity of limited autonomy, was granted a civil administration of its own, at the head of which stood a General Governor, in the person of Dr Hans Frank, a former *Reichsminister*. The GG, of which the highest authority was officially a government of twelve departments, was divided into four districts, each headed by a district governor and administratively sub-divided into *Kreishauptmannschaften* (sub-districts) and *Stadthauptmannschaften* (municipalities), within whose ambits care of Jewish affairs technically lay. The sub-districts were again sub-divided into urban and rural commissionships, to whom the mainly Polish township-burgomasters and village bailiffs were subordinated.

When on August 1, 1941, a part of the formerly Russian-occupied territory was administratively merged to form a fifth district of Galizia, the boundaries of the GG stretched over nearly 150,000 square kilometres, with a population of about 18 million, of whom some 2.5 million were Jews. It is with these Jews, GG "citizens", and with the related GG legislation that the rest of this chapter is concerned.

But along with a civil administration, the GG had also a political, or rather a police administration. The GG Nazis were very proud of their creation. For the first time in history, they boasted, a foreign territory conquered at war had been given a civil administration of its own kind instead of the usual form of military rule. The political administration was of special importance to Jews, and its existence partly explains the difference referred to earlier, in the legal situation of Jews in the "old" Reich and in the "new" occupied territory. The "political" administration, the head of which was the Higher (Chief) SS and Police Führer (HSSPF), a Himmler nominee, was similarly divided into district SSPFs, under whose orders came the commanders of all the manifold police forces at central and regional levels.

By Hitler's original decree which created the GG, the SS and police forces were to be subordinated to the General Governor and his government, but this was never the case. The HSSPF, SS Gruppenführer Friedrich Krueger, a former school teacher, then general of the police and of the Waffen SS, took his orders directly from Himmler, or from the SS chief office in Berlin, particularly in matters of "special importance", which included the solution of the Jewish problem. The HSSPF thus established a position independent of the General Governor, which led to considerable tension between the two and to much of the notorious muddle that characterized the running of the GG. The conflict was ultimately settled by a decree of Hitler dated May 7, 1942, in favour of the HSSPF, nominating him deputy General Governor and Secretary of State for security matters in the GG, and, in this capacity, putting him officially under the direct orders of Himmler. Following that decree, Frank transferred all duties concerned with security and policing, including "Jewish matters" to the exclusive competence of the Secretary of State. With the offices of HSSPF and Secretary of State combined in one person, the HSSPF thus became completely independent of the General Governor and the real holder of power in the GG. It was the HSSPF and the district SSPFs who were in charge of the annihilation of the Jews in the GG. In this they were assisted by a variety of German police forces, units of the Waffen SS and of the Wehrmacht; next by the various auxiliary Polish, Ukrainian, etc. police formations; and, lastly, in certain matters, by the German civil administrators of the regions, whom the SS and police commanders were, for their own reasons, interested to involve in the commission of crimes. It was probably not accidental that Frank's decree, transferring, among other things, authority in Jewish matters to the HSSPF, was issued on June 3, 1942. On that day the systematic "evacuations" of Jews began in the "old" GG, though in a few places in the district of Lublin mass murder of Jews had started a little earlier.

Prior to this final stage, there was still Jewish life, differing in duration and quality between the regions and towns. Looking back, this first phase of war against the Jews was characterized by legislation which marked out the path to destruction. Though the published decrees and orders are admittedly marginal to that aim. They were at once deliberately deceptive - a form of psychological warfare - intimidating, malicious and dispiriting, without exception restrictive, tightening the breath. Some laws were evaded, others, probably most, published after the event. (Thus, for example, while the ghetto in Warsaw was closed on November 1, 1940, the order concerning the formation of a Jewish *Wohnbezirk* (residential quarter) in Warsaw is dated April 1941. The peak of cynicism in this respect was a similar order, relating to other parts of the country, which mentioned for the first time the word ghetto, and is dated October 28, 1942, that is, after about two-thirds of the mostly ghettoized Jewish population had already been murdered. Very few "police decrees" which the HSSPF was empowered to issue, are, as regards Jews, on record. Orders of greatest importance to the life of Jews were never documented; if deemed desirable, they were given orally to the Judenrats. The Jews learned of them with their hearts, with the blood of their loved ones. For all that, for all the overall lawlessness, the published regulations cast enough light on the preparatory lines of the Nazi design, its pace of execution, and the atmosphere of Jewish life prior to its extinction, to be worth chronicling here.

Perhaps because of respect for property and the likely involvement of Aryans, most of that legislation related to the dispossession of Jews. Looting took place well in advance of murder, though the two also went hand in hand; at the end of the day the spoil was minor.

Already on September 6, 1939, an order issued by the chief of civilian management (which at that time could only mean an army officer clad in civilian clothes) prohibited the transfer and sale of Jewish property. This supports the assertion that oppression started on the first day of occupation, as, for instance, Cracow only fell on the 6th of September. Two days later, the Jews of Cracow were ordered to mark their shops. This was merely a "temporary" order, for the decree of the General Governor requiring Jewish shops to be marked with a Star of David in a way visible from the street was only published on November 23, 1939. Jewish physicians and men of other professions were ordered to mark their sign-boards in a similar way about a year later. The decree of November 20, 1939, about "securing Jewish property", and several supplements to it, introduced countless restrictions that were mostly already in force. All Jewish bank accounts were blocked, so that their owners could only draw a tiny amount of money per week. Jews were not allowed to keep more than 2000 Złoty outside the blocked account, nor were they allowed to accept payment of more than 500 Złoty per month, all relatively trivial amounts of money. The order of January 24, 1940, requiring Jews to register all their property gave many people headaches, but was of little practical consequence. By then, Jewish property had been confiscated either physically or practically, inasmuch as the owners were severely restricted in its disposal. From the earliest days of occupa-

240

tion, so-called trustees, who were Aryans, usually Germans, were put into all but the smallest Jewish enterprises, including rental houses. More hurtful were the evictions of Jews from their homes, and at a later stage, the issue of separate ration cards, allowing Jews much less food, compared with the remaining population. Many Jews were seriously affected by exclusion from all kinds of social benefits, including old-age pensions. In the field of labour law, Jews were excluded very early on from the generally held norms, and from March 1941 no wages needed to be paid by German employers to their Jewish employees.

In addition there were prohibitions and restrictions which applied to the entire population. On October 13, 1939, Goering ordered his subordinates in Poland to remove everything really valuable from the occupied territories to Germany. The following spring, in meticulous fulfilment of the order, all over the country squads began collecting metals, such as brass, copper, iron, even stripping house-gates or garden railings. Though the decree of December 27, 1941, ordering furs to be surrendered was directed only to Jews, the one issued four days later required all non-Germans to give up skis and ski-boots. For the plundered people all such chattels were treasures exchangeable for the food they needed to survive.

Restrictions of movement and communication were also economically disabling. Though primarily these were restrictions on personal freedoms intended to isolate, humiliate and bring the Jews to bay. The new identity cards, which were introduced on the day the GG came into being, were a different colour from those of other people. In November 1939, a separate population census for Jews took place. From December 1, 1939, all Jews from the age of 10 had to wear on their right sleeve a band, at least ten centimetres wide, with the Star of David on it. Who was to be considered a Jew in the GG was only determined by a law published eight months later (July 24, 1940): all persons with even one parent born of Jewish parents. From December 1, 1939, special curfew hours applied to Jews. From 1 January, 1940, a police decree forbade the Jews to change their present place of living or to "wander" outside it without special permission. From 26 January, 1940, Jews were forbidden to use trains, without special permission. Though a major restriction of free movement, its effect was, like many other restrictions, mercifully abated by the downright corruptibility of German officials. At varying times in various towns, this restriction was extended to local means of communication, to the use by Jews of certain streets, squares, etc., or even to walking on one side of a street or the other. But, curiously enough, emigration was not legally forbidden until October 25, 1940.

Two legal bills, dated February 19, 1940, passed the administration of criminal justice into the competence of "Special Courts" (while in civil matters they established separate courts for Poles and Germans, but said nothing of Jews). Though from the end of 1941, an offending Jew if caught by an SS man or German policeman was commonly, and illegally under the existing law, punished by shooting on the spot. This practice was sanctioned in 1942 by Himmler, who ruled that a German was basically not to be punished for shooting a Jew even without an order or authorization, if the perpetrator acted out of purely political motives and not for reasons of personal gain.

Education of Jews was said to be regulated by a decree of August 31, 1940, according to which Jews could only attend schools maintained by a Judenrat. This might give the impression that such schools really existed. In fact, since all Jewish schools had been closed by an order issued on December 11, 1939, Jewish children were barred from getting any schooling officially, though some continued to attend the clandestine lessons that were held in private homes. Religious practice was restricted even earlier. Like the introduction of forced labour, ritual slaughter was prohibited on the day the GG was proclaimed. By then, synagogues in the whole of occupied Poland had already been ordered to close for "police-security" reasons. Though later within the walls of large ghettos, such as Warsaw, one or two synagogues were re-opened with Nazi permission. Orders to shave off beards and earlocks were among the first issued. In the first phase of occupation, orthodox Jews were singled out for persecution, which also found its expression in the Nazi's specific insistence upon Jews working on their holy days.

No laws specifically referring to the provision of health services for Jews were published. During the first two or so years of war, those Jews who were not yet living in ghettos could, if they had enough money, obtain treatment in general hospitals as private patients. But the overwhelming majority of the Jewish population was left to depend on Jewish hospitals, which existed only in some of the larger towns.

Perhaps the most whimsical oddity of the GG Nazis is the case of social care for Jews. During the long years of total dispossession and deprivation, even during the period of mass slaughter and afterwards, the Germans provided, indirectly, funds for the social welfare of Jews, and the institution in charge of it, the so-called Jewish Social Selfhelp (JSS), was the most favoured of all Jewish institutions; it is enough to mention that its chairman, Dr Michael Weichert, was allowed to live in Cracow long after all Jews had disappeared, and on the Aryan side at that. (A probable explanation to this mystery is a desire by some SSPF commanders to establish a secluded address under their exclusive control, for the receipt of food parcels from abroad, which some naive Jews were still sending even in 1944.)

The JSS was founded in 1940 within the framework of the Supreme Social Care Council (NRO), which had Polish (RGO), Ukrainian and Jewish sections. The NRO was subordinated to the Department of Social Welfare at the GG, which endowed the NRO with budgetary funds. These were distributed between the three sections, including the JSS, in proportion to the size of population. The JSS also received some grants from the Joint (AJDC) representatives in the GG, as well as occasional assistance in kind from Jewish charities in neutral European countries. The JSS activities, which were confined mainly to providing peoples' kitchens and aid to hospitals, extended over the whole GG; at its peak it was functioning in some 400 places, with Cracow as its main seat. Towards the end of 1942, the Germans suspended the functioning of the JSS, but after changing its name to Jewish Help Agency (JUS) they re-activated it the following spring, at a time when the ghettos of Cracow and Warsaw were being finally obliterated. The name change is said to have been necessitated because in the former acronym the letter J rubbed shoulders with SS. After the liquidation of all the ghettos, the JUS sporadically provided some alimentary and medicinal help to Jews held in several concentration camps in the GG, until the summer of 1944.

Jewish labour was only second to property in its interest to the Nazis, not so much for its value as a cheap human resource, but as a means of subjugation, capable of accelerating the intended exhaustion of the victims. Simultaneously with the formation of the GG (October 26, 1939) a decree was issued which introduced forced labour (*Arbeitszwang*) for Jews and obligatory labour (*Arbeitspflicht*) for Poles. This was much more than a nice semantic distinction, the most important difference being that obligatory labour was to be governed by the Department of Labour in the GG, whereas forced labour was put in the charge of the HSSPF. Subsequent enactments concerning the operation of the law specified various details and penalties, and an order of the HSSPF issued on December 12, 1939, made all Jews from the age of 14 to 60 subject to forced labour for two years. The duration could be extended if by the end of the two years the educative purpose of the exercise had not yet been achieved. In the following weeks, registration of Jews eligible for forced labour was ordered in most towns. Some of the eligible men found a way to extricate themselves or to do the work locally, which was not yet so bad, but many were taken for "re-education" at camps of various degrees of severity.

In retrospect it can be seen how all the laws recorded here, ostensibly civilian in character, fitted into the planned gradual run-up to the final aim. Yet however cruel, the regulations still concerned the functional activity of the Jews. It is interesting to look at how the people existed in conditions shaped by those regulations and by the ensuing events. Psychologically, or morally, perhaps the worst times were the first weeks of occupation. Apart from the unusual killings - even if they were sporadic outside the annexed territories in the west - it was the sudden jump from measured life to unprecedented confusion that was overwhelming.

As soon as the occupation started, the people were faced with a series of assaults, though not all Jews suffered individually in the same way or to the same degree. Supplies were requisitioned, with food from abroad being the first to go; jewellery, money and valuables were plundered; families were evicted from their homes, forced to leave all their possessions behind; bearded men were dragged to a barber or forcibly clipped in the street; women were pushed and humiliated, especially those wearing hats. From early evening there was curfew; from early morning queuing for food; and every day the phenomenon of random abductions from the street. Not just for labour, but also for various humiliating spectacles, such as being forced to march through the main streets, shouting "we wanted the war, we wanted the war" while Germans assiduously photographed them, some expressing indignation: "because Jews wanted war, Germans had to die." Such experiences were still painful then. Later, the insults and jeers of the Germans meant less to Jews than a fly on the nose.

As time went by, all that had become part of daily life, and the initial sensation of shock and humiliation faded away. For want of any alternative, people became temporarily reconciled with their new conditions, believing that the war would end soon - and everyone really believed this until the collapse of France. Having adapted, many felt a renewed will to struggle for existence and were able to ignore the oppressor, as if he were not at war with them. Spurred by necessity, they began to invent means of evasion, of income, and, in self defence, ways of expressing their contempt and derision. With others, indifference and resignation set in, the disparity in reaction to the situation depending on the depth of a man's suffering. In general, the elderly people and solid businessmen, who now became impoverished, adapted least well; the poor were not made poorer, at this stage. What made it easier to come to terms with misery and ruin was that the painful plague of daily raids largely subsided, due to voluntary enlistment of men to work for wages, and to a change in the German demand for labour. Similar adjustments took place in business. Reconciled to the loss of their enterprises, their expropriated owners started managing them for more or less low salaries, supplemented by earnings on the side - often reaching an understanding with the inexperienced Aryan trustees, to their mutual benefit. While many lived by work or trade, others lived off their coats or carpets. Evictions from home also came to a virtual stop, as most Jews had already either been removed from houses outside the Jewish quarters of a town, or were sharing their flats with German "sub-tenants" who had been forced upon them but who, for the time being, protected the Jewish owners from total ejection. In short, for one reason or another the Germans temporarily relaxed their oppressive grip. This at once misled the Jewish objects of oppression and raised their hopes of enduring the war. Overall, as it was under Nazi occupation, life in the GG during the first 12-15 months of war seemed not intolerable.

Even later in the ghettos - in those which had been established in the pre-hellish phase - after the initial horror of being encircled by a fence subsided, the mood improved. This was particularly true of those ghettos into which only a part of a town's Jewish population was squeezed, usually consisting of the young and active members. But even where conditions were very hard, where hunger and disease affected many, people in general bore up at that period; the Jews could not bring themselves to believe that they would be annihilated.

Meanwhile, by the summer of 1941, annihilation was, so to say, under way. In the east it had actually arrived. In the territories conquered from Russia, the SS Einsatzgruppen of the Security Police began to murder Jews by shooting as soon as active combat in a locality was over. By secret orders of the Supreme Command of the Wehrmacht of March 26, 1941 and April 28, 1941, the SS Einsatzgruppen were authorized to operate in the rear of the fighting army units, and to carry out "police-security" duties, including "justified" measures against the civilian population. The Commissar Order reached the Einsatzkommandos in the field immediately after the attack on Russia had started. But another order directed to the SS Einsatzgruppen towards the end of July 1941, ordered them to exterminate the entire, non-working and hence dispensable, Jewish population in the newly occupied territories in the east - already for no other reason than for being Jewish. Thus, the fifth district of Galizia - like the rest of former eastern Poland, which was either included into the new entity called Reichkommissariat Ostland, or annexed to the Reich - did not have a pre-hellish phase. There, mass murder started with the occupation. There, under cover of his advancing army, screened, as it were, by the vastness and remoteness of that corner of Europe, Hitler decided to create hell without delay.

With regard to Jews in the original GG (and indeed in the rest of Europe under Nazi power), at about the time of the July order to the Einsatzgruppen, Goering ordered the SP and SD Chief Heydrich on July 31, 1941, to make all preparations, with the participation of other authorities, for the final solution of the Jewish problem within the area of German influence. A little later that summer, Himmler ordered the SSPF of Lublin, Obersturmbannführer (later Gruppenführer) Odilo Globocnik to solve the Jewish problem in the GG finally. Upon this, Globocnik, armed with the necessary special powers, built up an intricate organization for the extermination of Jews, under the cover-name of "Aktion Reinhard". Its first task was the building and then running of the death camps. Next, and concurrently with the overseeing of the camps, it was to control the so-called evacuations, which it was the duty of every SSPF in his district to carry out, and to deliver the prey to a death camp.

General Governor Frank hinted at the secret preparations by declaring in a speech delivered on October 9, 1941, that the Jews must be "done in" one way or another. On December 16, 1941, the whole plan and the state of preparations were discussed at a meeting of the GG cabinet.

Not long after the death camp in Bełżec had been made ready in March 1942, transports with "evacuees" from nearby and then from the whole of southern, formerly Austrian, Poland began to arrive there. Jews living in central and eastern, formerly Russian, Poland met their deaths in the camps of Treblinka (completed about July 1, 1942), Sobibor (from the beginning of May 1942) and Majdanek (where mass gassing started in November 1942). In 1943, the remnant Jews were mostly being transported to Auschwitz (a place of mass extermination of Jews from March 1942).

The Aktions, as Jews who survived them preferred to call the "evacuations", all had a set pattern, exemplified by those in Tarnow. The ghetto, or Jewish quarters of a town, were surrounded by a solid chain of armed guards; the people inside were ordered to fall in at an assembly square; commands were shouted, bullets whistled down the streets, stones stained with blood; some people panicking with horror, others, a large majority, remarkably calm. Special police and SS squads searched flats, cellars, attics; people found hidden, or arriving late for assembly, were mostly shot. Selection to stay on was made from among workers waiting at the square, the rest were either "locally evacuated" (mainly the very old and the very young) at the Jewish cemetery or in a nearby wood, or marched in heavily guarded columns to the railway station, to climb onto the waiting goods-trains. To paint a full picture of what happened during those Aktions, and afterwards in trains and camps, the dead would have to be resurrected and persuaded to talk of their experiences.

Between the Aktions - the intervals varying in length - contraction of the ghetto, new "frontiers", new homes, new neighbours, old misery and torment. People working, people not working, people hiding, all hunting for food. All asking what, or rather when, next? Hoping against hope, expectations rising the longer the lull.

All illusion. On July 19, 1942, Himmler ordered Globocnik to complete the "resettlement" of Jews in the GG by the end of the year. The only residual interest the Nazis had in the remaining Jews was their "evacuation". Hardly any more regulations about them were published. The last one that mentions Jews is a police decree of November 10, 1942. Jews are no longer the subject of GG law; they hardly exist at all. On November 4, 1943, Globocnik reported back to Himmler: Aktion Reinhard completed. The balance - about one and three quarters of a million "evacuees". In the four "old" districts of the GG alone.

CHAPTER EIGHTEEN

2 May 1944

This first fine morning in the month of May, radiating cool, sunny light, brought a seasonable surprise. A visit of high moment is announced; a visit of quite a singular kind. It has instantly thrown the whole workshop into turbulent bustle. Every corner is made to look spotless. These days there are not many scraps lying on the floor, and only ragged garments to put on the machine-tables. Before long the flurried room is filled with the sounds of trotting hooves, growing gradually louder. Many of us hurry to the half-opened windows, to be met by wild shouts from the overseers, ordering us to return to our seats. But I managed a long look, long enough to catch a bewitching sight before the trotting died down.

A lovely young woman, her unbraided golden hair streaming in the air, was riding on a reddish-brown mare. "Like the mythical Brunhilde" struck my mind. Though this one was not riding into battle, but into the Jewish prisoners' camp. Surely a She-warrior of some kind, yet without armour or weapon, and dressed in modern riding array. Having invaded the camp, she was greeted in the forecourt by officers of rank, and two of the lowest took away the mare, as soon as she had jumped nimbly off its back. "Brunhilde" is the daughter of the base commander, Gruppenführer Voss, and so goddess to his SS inferiors. She lives in her father's residence at Ring One, and had ridden all the way from there. Not in pursuit of adventure or games, this time, very prosaically, in pursuit of a new jacket.

Saluted with knightly respect at the barrack-vestibule by Hauptscharführer Saar, her arrival in the custom-tailors' room was heralded by the preconcerted noise of clattering sewing-machines. No less deafening is the noise than that produced in honour of her father; and no less low over their machines do the patch-tailors bow their heads. But, my curiosity whetted by the memorable visit of Kommandant Voss and by the latest vision through the window, I have this time shed my reverential fear and begun insolently watching the scene and the actors in the other room. "Brunhilde" is no less handsome close to, than from a distance through the window-pane. Her sulky, oblong face is still flushed pink from the wind, her eyes blue or green, and she stands uppishly erect in her grey riding-habit, her jodhpurs tucked into shining riding-boots - an unmistakable product of Wolf Osterman's skill. To a prisoner's eyes, too long accustomed to tatters, she looks fabulously dressed, though anyone might call her really chic.

It is a new jacket of best SS-grey-green cloth, sewn for her by Kurt Heibaum, that she has come to try on. Under-the-counter cloth - this prim Hitler-Maiden alumna has apparently no qualms about this. Coming out of the improvised changing cubicle, she looks in the mirror that Saar is holding for her. It is also Saar who chalks or pins the cloth where Kurt tells him; she is not to be touched by a Jew. Nor will she address Heibaum directly, unlike her father, who did speak to Berl Alter. Indeed the father, considering the situation, seemed not inimical, nor could one discern in his look animosity towards his wretched slaves. But in the face of this Nazi female, pride breathes plain hatred, as if poisoned arrows were shooting from her eyes. Saar himself looks more in awe of her than of her father. He may be the base commander, but this iron girl of twenty, brought up and trained in villainy and horsemanship, might be in command of him. Yet unlike him, she strikes no grotesque postures, makes no crotchets about creases, is not cranky at all. And her visit is relatively short, all over in twenty minutes.

No sooner had she left, than our fellows rushed to the window. It is difficult to describe the curiosity that her appearance aroused among us. As Berl Alter, who is nearing the fourth anniversary of his stay in Pustkow, later asked in wry jest: "Does such a species still exist on earth?" It was probably not only I who had been painfully reminded of a different, seductive life, of youth that is young not in years alone. Kulik and Kichel stood with their noses glued to the window panes, uttering loud cries of enchantment: "Have you seen her this? Her that?"

Kulik, who is fourteen, came to camp at the age of ten. Kichel, two years older, also landed at camp in 1940. They both arrived as children, and reached puberty in camp. Hence their sense of discovery, which was interesting to watch. The exceptional character of their initiation into maturity has not failed to shape an out-of-the-ordinary relationship between them. They are clearly fond of each other, neighbours at night, intimate during the day, often scuffling, as it were, altogether suggestive of a distinct, yet unconsummated, homosexual liaison.

Another similar friendship in our midst, equally susceptible to queer interpretation, aroused discussion about defining homosexuality. Benish Dombil is a nice boy in his early twenties and already a master cap maker, a craft he has mastered entirely in Pustkow. Chamul Furen, ten years older than Dombil, was said to be a tailor, but unemployed. During the war he was living off "table money", commission gained for setting up games of cards in the shadowy flat in which he lived with his bed-ridden mother. Remarkably unmolested for nearly three years, he arrived in Pustkow in the summer of 1942. Dombil and Furen are both from Tarnow, and of the same social-cultural level, but they first met in Pustkow. With time they have become very close friends, a friendship which a small camp like ours and daily work at the same shop, helps to further. They walk with their arms around one another's neck, gazing affectionately at each other, always full of secrets which they share exclusively, like the bread and other luxuries, which Dombil earns for the caps he makes "privately" for SS men, from top commanders to ordinary guards. Their relation probably does not go any farther than this sharing of enjoyments. Yet by displaying their mutual affection, they lay themselves open to lightly whispered suspicion - which I suspect mostly arises out of envy for the pair's close friendship in our unfriendly world.

248

Ours is also an ascetic world. Women are seldom mentioned in our talks, except mothers, wives, tenderly remembered friends, but without a tinge of sexuality. Indeed, in great contrast with life in freedom, sexuality has no place in our day-dreaming efforts to escape reality. Hugo says that people do not speak of things that are purely imaginary. Marek maintains that our personal trials and hunger have emasculated us. This seems unfounded. For weeks now we have not been hungry, our food intake is more than necessary to keep men physically potent. It's rather that our extended abstinence has made all desire disappear; we have no desire because we want none. Chastity and modesty are products of the human will, and our experience possibly suggests that it may not be too difficult to repress one's desires, if a person really wills it, let alone enjoys doing so. That we, in Pustkow, do will it manifests itself in the way everyone, except perhaps the capos, says they are glad that our camp is unisexual. This is in recognition of the fact that life is less hard, because it is less corrupt, in single-sex camps. As Hausdienst once said in his mordant way: "The greed for a woman's body is no different from other types of material greed that make capitalist societies corrupt." However ideologically bigoted, he may have made a valid point if he meant to say that every society provides the motives of its members' moral conduct, and if he was attributing crime in modern societies mostly to sexual motivation. He may have even been referring to the specific conditions in the ghetto, where conquest of woman lay behind many of the not so virtuous deeds committed by some of its inmates.

11 May 1944

Ours is also an ideal world! You may think that I am mad. Perhaps I am, but my remark merely refers back to earlier talk of our "social experiment", now to be discussed in a less dismissive manner. Our ideal miniature world is not a new system of ideas; it is based on rather old, if not pristine, ideas put into practice, at least theoretically, by Mates Szinc and a handful of his co-builders of a perfect society in Pustkow. This apparently is how they see themselves in their first endeavour.

Their programme, if it may be called so, is very simple. The introduction of new laws of camp life based on the highest possible (even if yet historically unattained) moral standards. In pursuit of this, to create a social environment dominated by the principle of value of a person's work and ethical conduct. What this would mean in particular is comradeship in personal relations, solidarity at work, care for the weaker prisoners, in short, the epitome of proletarian brotherhood and equality of men in the best socialist tradition. The undeclared, yet often discussed, aim behind this attempt at a sublime social order is to prove that an ergatocracy must be possible in the larger world, if it can be effected by worker-prisoners in the microcosm of a concentration camp. As Hausdienst the other day concluded at the end of a lengthy discussion: "Once the cult of money as the basis of social order has disappeared (replaced by the cult of soup? I thought of interrupting but on second thoughts considered it wiser not to), full equality of men and the satisfaction of everyone according to his needs, will become possible." And so we are experimenting with the dawn of a new ideal world.

Not quite, because our circumstances somewhat thwart an all-round trial of the perfect state. If only because, to quote Szinc's sapient saw, "the dream of living by the sweat of one's brow" becomes every day more difficult to realize, as work contracts continuously. Hausdienst badly misses "ennobling work on the land". When I raised my unsweating brow at this, he told me solemnly; "Martin Buber, you won't deny, is a very wise man, and it was he who said that he 'pins his hope for the future of Jews only as agriculturists, as peasant folk.'"

–"When did he say this?"

–"Not long before the war."

While, in general, exposition and exaltation of the programme is coupled with memories of past grievances and social injustice, it is also tinged, especially by Deker, with quotations and examples from Yiddish literature. He indeed confirms me in my belief that writers such as Peretz, Asch, Mendele, have converted more Jews to socialism than all its theorists, including Marx and Engels. It is probably the influence of that largely extravagant fiction, at once folk and didactic literature, dominated by a spirit of radicalism, and dramatizing almost exclusively the material side of Jewish life, which inspired our little experiment of remaking the universe. Otherwise it is inexplicable, because my tailor-champions of the experiment often show themselves to be realists, without illusions about life and society.

At first I was sceptical about the men's sincerity, when they spoke of brotherhood, equality, and so on, and I considered the whole thing to be childish play by adult but naive enthusiasts. "Provide them with good life, money, let alone power," I told Marek, "and they'll abandon their ideals." At best, I thought, the men are seeking a sort of escape, or recompense for the poverty and drabness of their lives. This may still be the case, but with time I have been forced to modify my view about the consequence of the experiment itself.

There is still little charity toward one's fellows; if help, in the form of bread, soup or tobacco, is extended by a "rich" prisoner, it is not to the "poor", namely the weakest inmates, but to one's closest mate, usually by virtue of occupational ties. Yet, although after three months of continuous exaltation, very little of the new moral qualities are visible in positive terms, much is noticeable in negative terms, that is in the general decline of not so perfect behaviour. The line of conduct has markedly shifted, first of all among the tailors, the pioneers of the experiment, and it has spilled over to other groups, affecting their social attitudes and behaviour for the better. Many men, including the leading prisoners, though not the capos, take the trouble to be comradely, at least outwardly. And I reap the benefit of it.

Slowly inter-prisoner relations have visibly improved. There was no violence in the camp before (always excluding the capos) but influential prisoners now less often take advantage of ordinary prisoners. Men speak relatively kindly, certainly not coarsely. (The best example of this is Jakubek, a prewar porter, whom I remember waiting for clients by his handcart in the street, or in winter, standing at an improvised street-stove, waving his arms about to warm himself up, shouting and cursing - and how quietly, almost gently, he now speaks at camp!) Nor do men betray one another in Pustkow, and there is little scheming against a fellow inmate.

And virtually no one steals from another prisoner (stealing from the SS is not regarded as immoral); irreverently and pointedly enough, the only theft of bread in the tailor-workshop, was from Szinc. While raging inwardly, and even though suspicion fell on an "intellectual", Szinc forced himself to grin and bear it, in order not to disclaim too plainly what he preaches.

Admittedly, the prisoners here did not behave badly even before the experiment started, and the relatively mild camp conditions have made it easier to preserve one's humanity. It's also unquestionable that the improvement in diet, with which the launching of the experiment roughly coincided, generally improved the men's behaviour. And unlike in other camps, the population in Pustkow is stable. One lies down to sleep every night with the same neighbour, and one sits during the day with the same people at the same work place. This naturally fosters the faculty of making friends. Nevertheless, I have no doubt that the experiment has positively affected the conduct of most men, in particular the tailors. Moreover, while camp conditions generally demoralize its inmates, as was equally true of the ghetto - mentally perhaps the harshest of all camps - the moral stance of the prisoners in Pustkow is remarkably fair. And consciousness of this, has raised the men's respect for themselves and for others.

15 May 1944

Speaking of morals, I should have mentioned an event which happened in our midst two months ago. I haven't said anything about it earlier because the event was a suicide and that evoked in me memories at once too precious and too insignificant to share readily with others. Memories of distant happy days of childhood, one little delight of which was cream-cakes at "Rubinfeld's". If not treated to one at home, I used to stand myself one or two out of my pocket-money. When Klara, my eldest sister, entertained her girlfriends she had cakes from "Maurizio", just for their appearance and the elegant paper cases in which they were sold. But the cakes were not as good as Rubinfeld's. No cream-cakes tasted as delicious as Rubinfeld's. And those cream-cakes were distributed to shops in a tray balanced on the head of a very tall boy, named Szlamek Erb.

In those cheery prewar years, Szlamek's father was paralysed, his mother busy with children and home. As the eldest son, Szlamek was, perhaps already in partnership with a younger sibling, supporting the whole family.

Lately in Pustkow, Erb, an old-timer, was messenger. It was quite a privileged function. For, although in winter he had to stay for hours in the open at the outer camp-gate, the job was potentially, and actually, rewarding. SS men, let alone Wehrmacht soldiers, who brought implements for repair, were not allowed to enter the prisoners' camp. It was the duty of the messenger to receive the consignment and, with the help of other prisoners, to transport it to the appropriate workshop; and similarly after its repair to deliver the stuff back. On the side, Erb also acted as intermediary between the soldiers and masters in arranging private, that is unauthorized, work. For this the soldiers, even some SS men, paid with food and tobacco, which the messenger shared with the masters, and indirectly with Bubi. So that

Erb, a young man in his twenties, was a "rich" prisoner, and looked, even in the worst hunger-ridden days, healthy and handsome.

But one day in mid-March, he was caught red-handed by Ruf with the contraband, or was it perhaps Bruchkraut himself? Ordered to return to camp, he entered his barrack-room, took off his shirt, fastened it to the bunk and his throat and strangled himself. The second death in Pustkow in my time.

I was moved almost to tears by the incident. Even more I was surprised - and so were many other prisoners, as subsequent discussions have revealed - because suicide was rare among the Jews of Poland, even during the most tragic days of this war. Throughout their history, Jews in general have had a very low suicide rate, probably lower than any other urban people. This notwithstanding, Yiddish novelists and publicists, often made a story more dramatic by embellishing it with suicide to illustrate the non plus ultra blackness of Jewish conditions.

Hugo Bester correctly observed that Durkheim, an authority on the subject of suicide, was wrong in the case of Jews for he maintained that there was an inverse relationship between murder and suicide in communities.

The rarity of suicide among Jews probably has its roots in their perception of life and death, as well as in their religion, which declares suicide to be sinful, even homicidal. Accordingly men who commit suicide have been regarded after death as outcasts, to be denied customary funeral rites, though not burial at a cemetery, even if it has to be apart from other dead. Since in recent years not many Jews were still pious, the main reason for the amazingly few suicides of Polish Jews during this war, was probably rather their ready adaptability to life's conditions and their long tradition of suffering. Religious Jews are duty-bound to accept suffering "with love", others might have found in it who knows what meaning, but to most it looked like something normal. Virtually all, to be sure, spurned the Greek and Roman pagan claim that a man has the right to destroy himself.

–"What was he afraid of?" With his question, Knepel was aptly implying that fear and anxiety are probably the most immediately potent forces to induce suicide.

Yet Hugo interrupted to ask: "What makes taking one's own life so exceptional and graceless?"

–"Life's sacredness," I said.

–"These days? What is the reason for living?"

As he must have noticed the disdain of my silence, Hugo went on to ask: "Haven't you ever entertained the thought of suicide?"

–"No! And could you take your life?"

But Osterman somewhat strangely seconded Knepel by asking:

–"And to commit an act of sabotage?"

This has become the standard Jewish wartime quip, used whenever you hear that someone has died of natural causes.

All were agreed that Erb was unlikely to have killed himself because he feared the beating and "bunker" that were awaiting him. The "bunker" was the four foot square cell, to which a prisoner was confined for several days without food, in extreme punishment. Equally everyone agreed, that he was probably more afraid of cracking under torture, and giving away his co-delinquents. But we could only guess who the Jewish master and the German involved were; for the men firmly believed that Erb was anxious to protect both the fellow prisoner and the soldier, or SS man, implicated in the conspiracy.

Hugo, who regretted that he was incapable of taking his life, wanted to know if in the circumstances and despair that led Erb to kill himself, I regarded suicide as murder?

–"No, definitely not! No sensible man would," I replied, at the same time recalling father once saying that a man should never sink into despair, the parental cause of all sin. Mingling with this memory was my admiration for Erb's deed, which I was sure that I would never be able to imitate. So I asked Hugo again: "Would you, in his place, have done it? How?"

After a thoughtful delay, he replied: "I was thinking of it."

The final epitaph was given by Hausdienst, who solemnly declared that Erb disproved all those pessimistic philosophers, who maintain that there is no crime that a man will not commit to save himself.

The morning after the suicide, it was very sad to see through the window smoke rising to heaven from Hill 218.

18 May 1944

From smoke into smother, as the saying goes. And from form to matter. Evaporating in fumes, a body is visible from a great distance; in solid substance its outlines evanesce much closer. This reflection thrust itself into my mind this morning, while I was looking into the Polish camp. How merciful, I thought, for even the blurred sight was quite revolting. A tall wooden scaffold from which a dark frame hangs suspended in the air - a human corpse, I had no doubt. Confirmation with details came later from Brzostek.

Polish prisoners go to work daily outside the camp. Now and then, especially since the snows have melted, one or two prisoners do not come back. Not because they have been killed, but because they have managed to escape. Many more attempt to, but few are successful. If even one man escapes, the Germans make the entire camp responsible. Punishment was quite familiar: long roll-calls, repeated during the night, withholding of parcels and letters from home, harder work, and the like. As the attempts to escape are increasing in spite of all this, so are the German reprisals. Stricter discipline has been imposed at camp, dutifully carried out by Swietlik - the camp eldest - who, according to Brzostek, has a death sentence, passed by his co-prisoners, hanging over his head.

As the Germans now realize that punishment does not deter prisoners from attempting to escape, they have resorted to a new method of reprisal. This is *Sippenhaft* - collective family responsibility. When last week another chap escaped, the Germans arrested his elderly parents and brought them to Pustkow. Inside the camp they were paraded before the eyes of all the prisoners, while outside the camp, in the neighbouring villages and townships, placards were posted announcing the arrest of the escaped prisoner's parents and their prospective punishment, should he not surrender. The escapee was far away and safe, but freedom at the price of the torture and possibly even death of his parents? He gave himself up. It was his body that was left hanging high up in the air, so that all would see and digest the lesson. The new method is certain to succeed, says Brzostek; there is a price which no decent man is likely to pay to buy his freedom.

–"They can't arrest our families," cried Knepel. It was not clear whether he meant to point to the difference in situation between us and the Polish prisoners, or whether, in a moment of forgetfulness, he was reproaching his Jewish fellow-prisoners, none of whom tries to escape. Alter apparently had the same doubts, because he remarked spontaneously: "But we aren't let out beyond the gate."

Thus started a lengthy debate, not the first one, nor, I am sure, the last, on the many-sided subject of escape. To me it is also an endless subject, with exhausting discussions at home, with Teper and the other chaps at Varnish and Putty, still fresh in my mind. But it is not so to my present workmates, who left their homes early in the war, never lived in a ghetto, and so are incapable of assessing for themselves the reality of conditions there. To them it seems that escape is just a matter of personal courage and determination: to some it is a quixotic dream of the life of daring, to others it forms part of the fantasy of armed (yet armless) resistance against the truly and fully armed Germans. It is entertaining to watch Hausdienst, Knepel, Deker squabbling about who is to bear the palm of heroic resistance, which unavoidably results in magnifying and extolling the merits of the thing. What a pity that beau sabreurs of the Revisionist-Right, who take no less pride in revolt, are not also represented in our workshop! Perhaps it gives one a foretaste of the debating delicacies of the future. But by now I feel already tired of the whole subject of resistance, including escape, hiding and other methods of disguise. For that reason I hardly participate any more in my mates' discussions and shall confine my recording of it to what seems to me still new and worth mentioning.

Alter's remark was not much to the point, as others simultaneously noticed; for there *were* times when Jewish prisoners worked outside the camp. The reason why they had not tried to escape was, according to Osterman, the same as the one now faced by the Poles; fear of collective responsibility, in particular of reprisals against one's family. "They had our names and addresses at home. Would have come to search and if they couldn't find us, they would have killed our relatives and friends instead."

Hugo threw in a general, philosophical question: "Is one morally entitled to endanger another person in order to save one's own life?"

In reply to both, Knepel said: "But Jews, unlike Poles, were being killed anyway."

–"In the Z-camp, Jews were shot almost every day, even without trying to escape," seconded Hausdienst.

But in Osterman's view, for Jews all ways of escape have long been cut off. "Where could we escape to?" he asked. This question switched the discussion from the adventurous world of dreams into more realistic tracks, as it had often done before.

Alter agreed with Osterman. "We have no place to live, but in camp," he said.

–"But we had before. I wasn't so difficult to escape from town as it is from camp. In the ghettos the people were neither numbered not known by their names, except for the few prominent men." Thus Knepel widened his criticism to embrace the Jews in the towns.

Osterman retorted, not quite appositely, that in the ghetto all inmates were hostages, and only a few people could escape anyway. A successful escape was not only a matter of finding people ready to hide you, but also of avoiding people ready to expose you.

With the raising of the ghetto walls, it had become a matter fraught with danger to reach a hiding place on the outside, let alone to hide one's true identity for long, while trying to move around as an Aryan. The danger did not arise so much from expected police-checks here and there or from casual identification by Germans, because they did not know how to recognize a Jew in disguise from a non-Jew. The danger came from Poles who could spot a Jew from quite a distance, be it by his, or her frightened face, gestures, physiognomy, or gait. I, too, would have had little difficulty in recognizing a Jewish person in this way. But the professional Jew-hunters claim to have spotted other signs of which neither I nor anyone of us here was aware before. Those Poles claim that Jewish women have a distinctly protruding collar-bone and that their ears are a slightly different shape from other women's. These expert manhunters operate in almost every larger town, positioning themselves on busy streets and at central points, in particular at railway and bus stations, knowing a fugitive's need to move from place to place. The hunter having spotted his prey, sometimes mistakenly, the Jew is first blackmailed for his possessions - "either you pay me off or come with me to the police". The ransom paid, the hunter will either release his prey or transfer it to a fellow hunter for further blackmail, or, more often than not, hand the Jew over to the Germans for the reward. While these human-hyenas form a tiny proportion of the Polish population and are condemned by most Poles for their actions, they are sufficiently numerous to be the scourge of, and a serious deterrent to potential Jewish runaways. There is, it seems, no limit to the amount of blood one such head-hunter could spill.

Given the formidable difficulties first of finding a decent hideout, then the terror of being spotted by a blackmailer, or given away by the "rescuer", on the one hand, and fear of reprisals at home, in the ghetto, on the other, what wonder that so very few Jews attempted to escape, preferring to stay with their families? At a time when almost every social bond that once formed a man's life had disappeared, family was the one attachment that remained.

Notwithstanding their dreams of impossible escapes, the tailors and cobblers of Pustkow are, in general, more realistic about it than the people on the outside. This may partly follow from their personal experiences, learnt the hard way. They, for instance, know very well how significant money is in finding a place to hide. Though Hausdienst, not without some justification, asserts that a runaway Jew without money had a better chance of getting a safe refuge than one with money. A Pole who was helping from pure motives, he said, that is, one prepared to risk hiding a Jew without payment, was the most reliable one. Many of those who did it for money were, experience had shown, likely to act both as saviour and betrayer; namely, to take away the escapee's possessions and then either turn him out or hand him over to the Germans. The danger increases with the size of the fugitive's wealth. If it is great enough, the urge of a poor, and not so poor, Pole to "inherit" it is almost irresistible. In the ghetto, there were people who seriously contended that to deposit valuables with a Pole for the duration of the war, was to turn him unwittingly into a potential criminal. Some of the Polish "friends" were straightforward: "I wish you well, as I always did. But these possessions will soon be of no use to you." The predatory greed of peasants and urban "rabble" in falling on "post-Jewish" property, after the owners' evacuation seems almost incredible.

On the other side of the same escape question were the substantial material enticements offered by the Germans as reward for denouncing a Jew in hiding. According to information Hausdienst received from a Pole after the mass evacuation of Jews in 1942, in Debica and the villages around Pustkow, posters warning of penalties for hiding or helping a Jew promised 10 kilos of sugar and 5 litres of vodka for every Jew turned over. Hugo maintained that the prize offered in Cracow was much more generous, and included money. Lisko and other Varsovians said that thereabouts the reward was 100 kilos of grain and half the possessions of the denounced Jew. The block eldest of Szebnie with whom I spent some terrifying minutes in hiding, related that the Nazis in Lwow were so eager to make sure that no single Jew survived, that they promised his entire property, in addition to 8,000 Zloties, 10-20 litres of vodka and 1,000 cigarettes per Jewish head. A fantastically high prize, but he vouched for its veracity, adding that to popularize the cause with ordinary people, the Nazis made a Polish couple walk along under a suitable banner, with their reward, two sausages and the heads of two Jewish children, whose meat stuffed the saveloy.

When Osterman repeated his question borrowing the refrain of the Yiddish song, "Wie ahin soll ich gehn?" (Where could a Jew go?) Knepel instantly retorted:

–"To the partisans! I know of all the difficulties, but, despite all the risks, there's more chance in escaping than in staying on."

"Partisans" were Knepel's pet hobbyhorse. He was aware that his comrades on the outside approved wholeheartedly of armed struggle with the Germans and had accorded it a central place in their party's redrawn political objectives and their contest for power with their adversaries on the right. "A tactic", as even Deker once charged him. This policy was also in line with the intent and requirements of the Soviet Union, engaged in the gigantic war effort, towards which partisans fighting at the rear of the enemy provided welcome, if minor assistance.

Knepel's rejoinder had drawn replies from all corners, the most vigorous from Hugo who called it an illogical suggestion. He subsequently explained why he had thought so. First, because only a very few young males were suitable for partisan warfare. "What about the rest, the old and the children?" he asked.

–"And indeed all the women?" Osterman threw in eagerly.

Secondly, Hugo said, because there were no partisan units a Jew could join. And without weapons, Jews could not form partisan units of their own.

–"And where could they form them? In the hostile woods?" Alter unexpectedly intervened to question the partisan option. His woods were "hostile" because they were controlled by the mainstream Polish underground forces and the nearby population.

–"You know very well," Alter went on to answer Knepel, "that the AK didn't admit Jews, except for the specialists they needed, and even they had to assume false identities.". (AK were the Polish initials for "Home Army", the main and by far the largest underground military organization in Poland during the Nazi occupation. The AK was officially subordinated to the Supreme Commander of the Polish Army and government-in-exile in London. Actually at home, in Poland, it had a separate, largely independent command. The AK reconstituted itself from elite cadres into a mass military organization only in 1942.)

Understandably enough, Alter kept silent about the underground army which did accept, even welcomed, Jews. So that Hugo quickly interrupted him to continue his own point.

–"As for the AL, how long has it been active? Even the scanty units, whose total strength counted in hundreds, all right, let it be thousands," he corrected himself, seeing the disapproving expression on Knepel's face, "which were later incorporated into the AL were not in the field before the autumn of 1942. A bit too late for the Jews, don't you agree?" (AL were the Polish initials of "People's Army", called to life on January 1, 1944, by decree of the newly born "National Home Council" formed several hours before. This, intended as a counterforce to the parties behind the government-in-exile, was founded by the Communist Party of Poland, in conjunction with other small closely allied factions.)

Strangely, no one mentioned that it was only after the Russians had pushed the war-front back past the former Polish eastern border, that partisans became active inside the country. Though Osterman did say, rather awkwardly, that all the underground armies, not just those of Poland, only started making themselves heard months after "Stalingrad". The Nazis did not wait that long to exterminate the Jews.

Knepel however held to his view that many young men, even women - and it was only the young he had in mind - could and should have tried to join the partisans. "It's the only way of deliverance, and never too late." But he did not venture to talk about the partisans' location, their record, where they were during the Jews' "evacuation", or how to reach them. According to Knepel, the reason why the surviving Jews did not try to escape after the first massacres was much the same as the reason they had not tried, while there was still time, to fall over the border into the safety of the wide open Russian arms.

–"People believed the German lies. Every gossip, every rumour, be it of the most disingenuous kind. Above all they listened to the malicious prattle of disgruntled men who came back from the other side seeking comfort and enjoyment on the German side, deluding themselves that the war wouldn't last long."

Escape to Russia was another theme particularly close to Knepel's heart. To me this echoed endless similar talks from the past and I was tempted to repeat Teper's view that the most disgruntled of all were the enlightened Jewish marxists, so-called *Geist* proletarians. But I wanted to do this with circumspection. I started by saying that we should remember that so many Jews, even the common men, simply did not like the Soviet system, and then intended to give the other reasons why people stayed at home. But I was glad to give up when Deker interrupted me.

–"The most discouraging and disparaging stories were given out by Poles. Most of them, returnees or not, regarded living under Nazi occupation as the lesser evil."

This reminded me of Gila quoting her former teacher, whom she went to visit on his return from Lwow in October 1939: "If I have to receive a slap in the face," he said, "I prefer to get it from a German than from a Russian." He might have changed his mind barely three weeks later, when he was arrested along with many other Cracow university professors. But there was no point in telling this then, especially to Deker, who is said to have returned, like Szinc, from the Russian side after only three months. Though he related earnestly that, unlike under the Germans, in the Russian zone synagogues were open and kosher meat was sold, Deker was certainly far from sharing Knepel's apparent enthusiasm for the Soviet experience, any more than he shared his arguable advocacy of the partisan option.

Hugo said, in short, that no one, neither Poles nor Jews, could foresee the future. As for German deceptions, they would have never succeeded, in as much as one can speak of success, if the Jews had not been willing to be deceived. Nor were they really deceived, only that people do not believe in the worst before the worst has happened.

Thus all views turned against Knepel, or at best were neutral. But did he honestly believe all he said? I have my doubts. While to many people escape seems to be within the grasp of captive men, Knepel seems to me, despite his dreary life, to be a sort of romantic, who adores the spirit of risk and valour. What excitement is there in passive existence? So resist in your mind and in your words, if you can not in action.

On one thing we are all agreed in camp, unlike in the ghetto where opinions differed: that it is more important for any one of us to remain alive than to take the worthless life of our blood-stained captors.

CHAPTER NINETEEN

–"It's unbearable! We must do something! We can't just look on like this."

What's unbearable is the ominous buzz which leaves us in no more doubt about its origin. Since the days have become truly bright and translucent, the vibrations are more frequent, last longer and sound louder. It often seems that the rumbling mystery is trailing over our heads. But to the annoyance of everyone, we can see nothing. This makes us all the more anxious. Some of our men say that it is an invisible bomb which drives itself; others maintain the sound is of "blind" flying dishes; still others claim that these are rockets flying too high to be seen by the human eye. Whatever the differences of opinion about the nature of the some-thing, we all now agree that it is the secret weapon, and that it is being launched not far from our camp, probably within the compound of the Pustkow SS base. We, of course, do not know if these are only test-flights, or if by now - which makes the experience even more terrifying - the Germans are already firing the weapon over-land across very long distance towards targets in Russia, or England - or both.

–"What can you do?" was Marek's rejoinder to my worried outburst.

–"Must talk to Maniek and make sure he contacts Brzostek."

–"What for?"

–"He would know. Then he can convey urgently the message out of the camp and his friends on the outside can inform the Russians."

But Maniek, when we went to talk to him, said that Brzostek told him some days ago that his friends of the AK know more about the thing than we do. He also told Maniek that his friends on the outside had transmitted the news to the government in London, to pass it on to the British. His friends would not inform the Soviets.

–"But it's only the Russians who can bomb and destroy the launching site. The British can't do it."

"Yes," said Maniek, "but Brzostek and his friends won't co-operate with the Russians. They don't view them as allies and friends. They fear them almost as much as the Germans."

–"But this is too important a matter to indulge in such petty sentiments. The fate of the war may hang on it.

–"It isn't a petty sentiment to Brzostek and his friends. Only the other day, lamenting the long path of suffering and sacrifice, Brzostek finished saying bitterly: "And at the end of the road the prospect of a red flag."

Yes, there lies the difference. We, whatever our political preferences, are con-cerned just to remain alive and see the defeat of Germany. The Poles are not being killed wholesale. Their lives are in the main not in danger. They are sure of surviving, individually and as a nation. So they think about their future state, where their borders will be, what kind of freedom they will have. Of course among them, too, opinions and expectations broadly differ, in particular regarding the strength of sentiments towards the Soviet Union, which, with the approach of the eastern front, has become the prime Polish preoccupation. Their sentiments towards the Jews differ nearly as widely and on roughly similar lines, for the Jews have not ceased to absorb Polish minds.

–"Isn't this obsession strange, almost unbelievable, in view of what has happened?" Marek asked, more to air his frustration than to seek an answer.

To explain this truly astounding fact, not just to Marek, but to many other people, I must here go back a little in time.

The long-standing dislike of Jews by the majority Polish population sharply increased in the tense, precarious nineteen thirties. It assumed the force of a rising tide, which at times looked as if it would wash away the fine, age-old premises of the Jews in Poland. The menacing waters subsided with the change of weather brought about by the clouds of war, and the subsequent need to mobilize all forces to resist the common Nazi threat. On the eve of armed hostilities and during their short duration the attitude of the Poles towards the Jews changed so distinctly for the better that to many Jews the longed for rapprochement and fraternal co-existence between the two peoples seemed at last to have come true. This state of relations continued for some time, in the days of "common woe and chains", under German occupation. There were, of course, exceptions. Polish officers in POW camps demanded to be separated from officers who were Jewish and, as Hausdienst remarked, after only three months of occupation plaques with the word "Aryan" began appearing on Polish homes and businesses (as both "Polish" and "Christian", in fashion before the war, were unacceptable to the German rulers). Yet this was still the action of only a small minority of the people and could have been, optimistically, put down to fear by the faint-hearted, anxious to avoid the harassments to which their Jewish neighbours were already being subjected.

In general, the common fate, as it seemed then, and hostility towards the occupying power promoted a sense of solidarity and identity of purpose. Indications of Polish sympathy for fellow Jews were in those days still visible in the street. As well as privately condemning the barbaric measures taken by the invader from the very beginning of the occupation, Polish townsmen at that time spoke more impetuously than the Jews of retribution after the war, which everyone, Poles and Jews alike, then expected to end shortly, with the defeat of Germany.

But as the war was neither ending - in fact was rather extending territorially - nor Germany defeated, but on the contrary recording formidable victories in the spring of 1940, the attitude of many Poles began to change; the first decisive change, a real turning point, was in the opposite direction from the Jews'. After the fall of Paris many Poles thought that Great Britain would not hold out against Germany. Hence they began saying that one must learn to live with the Nazis. As time went on more and more Poles tried to jump on the victorious bandwagon and to win favour with the Germans. For the Germans the touchstone of reliability and loyalty was identification with Nazi racial policy. So anti-Semitism began quickly to revive and spread onto a road now wide open to collaboration. Collaboration, rooted in the expectation of German victory, motivated, mainly, by economic advantage, was negotiated by men and women individually, not as members of a political or ideological group, with the object of future power-sharing.

In this war, collaboration with the Germans is a problem common to all the occupied countries. It is also a nationally painful problem; the Poles are not the only ones who prefer not to talk about it, and wish to keep the subject out of history books. They naturally prefer to speak of things that can be regarded as a source of national pride and honour; to raise the fact that Poland was the first country to take up arms in its defence against Nazi aggression, an attempt that admittedly did not last long, but was rehabilitated in the eyes of many Poles when France, a great power, did not hold out much longer; to mention with pride the many Poles gallantly fighting on the side of the western Allies - "An army of 115,000 men at war", as Brzostek rather emotionally put it - but they keep mostly silent about those fighting on the side of the Red army; above all, they love to speak about their popular underground army. They tend to do this in a way that gives the impression of an entire nation united in a relentless struggle against the enemy over the long years of occupation. This is how history is made and national myths created.

Anyhow this is not a subject for me to explore, beyond remarking that the main, non-communist underground organization now unites a spectrum of political opinion, divided into perhaps as many as fifty parties and factions, ranging from the extreme Right - which more or less openly hails the extermination of Jews as an event in the national interest of Poland - to the democratic-socialist Left, which voices sympathy for the Jews and provides its hidden survivors with a minimum of humanitarian help. Nor is it my business to trouble my head with collaboration in Poland, with its definition as something essentially applying to German-naturalized Poles, be it as *Reichsdeutsche* (full status Germans), *Volksdeutsche* (of German nationality) or *Deutschstämmige* (of German descent), plus persons serving the Germans in a way particularly harmful to the Polish people; or to inquire into the precise number of such collaborators - some talk of three million including dependants - because, firstly, so many of them reside in the territories incorporated into the Reich (where Poles have been subjected to considerable pressure) from which nearly all Jews were expelled in the first months of war; and secondly, because these so-called *Koniunkturdeutsche* (opportunist Germans), being evident, privileged and pragmatic have been less of a plague to the Jews than their supposedly non-collaborationist tormentors.

From the point of view of possible Jewish refuge, the most important segment of the Polish population were the peasants. People acquainted with the Polish countryside - its remoteness, its seclusion, its partial inaccessibility for several months every year - must be thinking it an almost ideal place to hide. Yet much as the strength of commitment to the Underground and the attitude to Jews varied between different social strata, so did it differ between various parts of Poland. Nor

261

were the German invaders received with the same feeling throughout the country, especially in the rural areas. Remembering their prewar poverty, suffering and semi-serfdom, to many peasants Poland was not much of a motherland - at best it was a stepmother. So in certain parts of the countryside the Germans were initially greeted with relief bordering on delight. Soon the invaders were seen by many peasants as liberators from hunger. In contrast with the townsmen, villagers were getting "rich" quickly; only three months into the occupation it was said that the peasants could decorate the bleak walls of their wooden huts with banknotes.

This aroused the curiosity of my workshop mates, Alter asking outright: "How did the Germans manage to do this, and in such a short time, too?"

–"By plain robbery," I answered. This drew laughter and disbelief, though perhaps only great curiosity.

–"But seriously, how did it happen?"

–"I'll explain it to you step by step, and you'll see that I wasn't joking.

"First came the Wehrmacht or some other German authority which bought produce from the GG peasants. For this they agreed prices which were very much higher than before the war, and paid with a piece of paper, saying 'IOU'. The peasant then took this voucher to one of the few banks that were allowed to operate in the GG and exchanged it for cash. The bank in turn presented the IOU to the GG 'central' bank. In order to pay the commercial bank, the central bank issued new money. 'Cover' against this newly printed money was the IOU, which the central bank had to deposit with a so-called clearing office in Germany; the original IOU thus became the GG's financial claim on the German Reich. And so, you see, the accounts of the 'central' bank were balanced, the Germans got their products without paying a groschen for them and the Polish GG peasant got plenty of good money - and as prices of manufactured goods were increasing far less than prices of foodstuffs, they were getting 'rich' quickly."

–"Old colonial method," was Hausdienst's comment, when I finished.

–"Well, colonial. But the British have partly paid and will probably repay their debts after the war. Even the French may one day repay theirs. But will Germany, after a lost war and all its probable consequences?"

–"How large would the accumulated surplus of 'financial claims' of the GG be?" Hugo wanted to know.

–"Who knows. Several billion Reichsmark, I'd guess."

What worried Hugo was that as these funds are nowhere recorded in the statistics: "Would they ever be regarded as part of Germany's financing of the war?"

–"Those who'll live will see."

But back in the first autumn and winter of war, the immediately visible improvement in the peasants' fortune brought praise and respect for the Germans, though there was still animosity among many peasants. With the economic betterment came improved social status, not merely vis-a-vis the condescending and historically much less poor townsmen, but even in relation to the much hated class of large landowners, in particular the liege lords - whom the Germans were now humbling. While in the past the peasant had always tried to keep in the good graces of

262

those socially superior classes of men, those same social superiors now had to seek favour of the peasants, providers of the increasingly scarce food supplies. Ironically enough, it seems that for all the bitter legacy of the German occupation, they may have done away for good with the last vestiges of feudalism in the Polish country-side.

However that may be, the actual feeling of relief from hunger and shame in a matter of weeks went so deep, that some peasants openly voiced their distinct lack of enthusiasm for the restoration of an independent Polish state; "The devil him-self's rule," they said, would be better than a return to prewar conditions. Anyway, given the changed circumstances, it was not difficult for the Germans, perhaps even easier than in the towns, to find villagers prepared to serve their interests.

As the occupation continued, and the Germans resorted to increasingly harsh measures, including the murder of civilian Poles, the sentiment of most peasants towards the occupiers began to change gradually into one of deep revulsion and fear.

–"Fortunately! Now we may say, the Nazis couldn't help baring their claws," Hugo remarked while we were talking about this. His point was that had the Germans adopted a policy of benevolence towards the occupied peoples, they might have won the support of Ukrainians, many Poles, Russians and other east European nations, with who knows what consequence for the outcome of the war, in the East at least.

To the Germans, however, these people were racially inferior, sub-human, and the Polish peasant, *inter alia*, good for nothing but to furnish the food quota and do forced labour in Germany. When this became clear to the peasants, the Germans had already firmly established their authority over the Polish countryside, made up as it was of thousands of tiny and partly inaccessible hamlets. This they did largely thanks to the support of country people of real and assumed German descent, who had lived in the villages from earlier times. Besides these local followers, there were peasant-settlers newly expelled from the territories incorporated into the Reich. These were men with no community ties, without land or income, and therefore dependent on almost any work that was within their reach; and as most of them knew a little German, they were favoured by the occupiers. From among those elements and the naturalized Volksdeutsche village gendarmes were recruited who could be relied on to look after "law and order" in the rural communities - without the Germans having to police it with their own nationals.

Local rural administration in the old GG (i.e. excluding the district of Galizia, which was populated largely by Ukrainian villagers), the Germans chose to leave, by and large, in the hands of the prewar Polish village bailiffs. As in the towns, hardly any of these officials refused the post, and knowing of many candidates eager to step into their shoes, they tried to please their German masters. The Germans in turn allowed the village heads to reap the substantial benefits that went with the job. For the Germans and the villagers alike, the most important duties of the vil-lage bailiffs were to allocate local compulsory food quotas, then to collect them, and to select the people for, equally compulsory, work in Germany. The bailiff was also made responsible for the whole village - thus becoming at once servant and hostage.

Yet within the local community, the village heads assumed great importance, although, unlike their urban counterparts, they did not provide any real effective services. They derived their importance from the powers assigned to them, which they used for their own advantage, accepting bribes in cash and kind. By these means, individual farmers tried to secure exemptions from quotas and forced labour. The only service the village heads actually provided was to obtain, through costly gifts, concessions from their German superiors for the whole community. As a result a situation developed where people thought "bribes could do everything, but nothing could be done without them". Compared with prewar times, village life has become more demoralized than urban life - greed increasing with rising prosperity, as is usually the case with humans.

In general conclusion, because of the conditions created by occupation, based on terror, exploitation and corruption, village life which for centuries was quiet and closely knit, has become susceptible to internal divisions and hostility. This hostility was directed in particular towards the now feared and hated village heads and their auxiliaries; mutual suspicion and mistrust, heightened by local informers which the Gestapo commonly succeeded in finding, set the villagers apart and in cases of personal and pecuniary feuds, they occasionally resorted, though less readily than fellow townsmen, to denouncing their antagonists, openly or anonymously, to the German authorities.

Little wonder, then, that in those circumstances the peasants, who still live in a relatively tight and intimate community in which everyone knows everyone, on the whole refused refuge to Jews when the murdering started, even though they are the least anti-Semitic class in Poland. It was not easy to keep someone hiding a secret from a neighbour, or, though less so, from the village head, who was likely to inform the Germans. So the risk was serious, the eventual penalty severe - the entire family of the hider likely to be punished with death. None the less, there were a few individual peasants who did take the risk and hid Jews. That they mostly did it for money or other favours, should not be counted against the act itself.

Meanwhile, in the towns, the dispossession of the Jews and their separation from the rest of the population was continuing. The formation of the first large ghettos - welcomed by the Polish Right, in spite of apprehension on its fringes that the ghettos could become dangerous enclaves of bolshevik power - was the second major turning point in Polish attitudes towards their Jewish neighbours.

To the long-standing religious, economic and political differences were added new conflicts of interest, including elements unknown before. Most critical was the question of housing, which set the two peoples literally as well as metaphorically on opposite sides of the barrier; in a state of acute shortage of decent housing, the Poles were anxious to have the frontiers of the ghettos pushed back as far as the occasionally petitioned Germans would agree to; then came "inheritance" of the abandoned Jewish homes, especially the better ones, with any of the contents that could not be moved, and of the remaining businesses outside the new boundaries fixed for the Jews. The opportunity to "grow rich on the Jews" has undoubtedly been the main contributing factor to the wartime intensification of anti-Semitism in Poland. It's equally certain that those Polish people who benefited from this "enrichment" became the most vehemently opposed to the Jews. These are also the people who, apart from the formal collaborators, have most to lose from a German defeat, and this has accordingly shaped their political preferences. They are apprehensive about the loss of their acquired property not just if there is a Soviet sponsored government in postwar Poland, but also if the constitutional Polish government returns. Now exiled in London, this government has publicly committed itself to revoking all laws passed during the occupation, including transfer of property under the jurisdiction of those laws. "A real predicament," as Marek sardonically remarked.

–"A real strain, I would say, for future relations between Poles and Jews, who might survive the war in Poland," was Hugo's comment.

The beginning of the mass murder of Jews, which took the Poles as much by surprise as the victims themselves, marked the next and most decisive turning point in Polish attitudes. Until then, the Jews, as viewed by most Polish eyes, though they were crushed and ineffably humiliated, presented a hungry mass of desperate paupers, who, caged tightly in the centre of cities, could pose a greater problem after the war than they had as free and gainfully active people before the war. Now the Germans are solving this problem radically, once for all. They are thus fulfilling a historic mission for Poland. True, the murderers are the same people who are making Poles suffer and treading them under their feet, but the Germans will leave sooner rather than later, while Poland will be left for the Poles alone. This is another subject Poles consider unbecoming for decent people to talk about. Of the less than decent, some, not many, assisted and delighted in the murder, and some, even fewer, complained of being inconvenienced by it (as for example people living next to the railway tracks who complained that their sleep was disturbed at nights by the noise of passing trains carrying Jews to the death camps). Many said they were horrified by the murder, which they undoubtedly were for a number of reasons; but most have kept "neutrally" silent, probably struck dumb by the perplexity of conflicting humane and nationalist feelings.

Attentive as ever, Hugo hastened to remark understandingly that we must remember that nationalism is a most compelling force in the life of modern man.

–"Besides, what could the Poles do? Could they stop the Germans from killing us? How?"

Looked at liberally he was right. But Hausdienst utterly disagrees.

–"They could help; they could rise against the Germans; give us arms; at least provide shelter and refuge."

From Knepel's reaction it would seem that even he has some doubts about this.

–"They could express solidarity. They could extend symbolic help. The Jews have always fought for Poland. Thirty thousand of the hundred and twenty thousand defenders who died in September 1939, were Jews. Two and a half times their proportion in Poland's population. "

Knepel may be right, though he did not reveal his sources. But curiously Brzostek, according to Maniek, holds views which are not far removed from Knepel's. He acknowledges that it was the moral duty of every Pole to come to the help of his Jewish compatriots, regardless of the risk to his life. Regrettably, he says philosophically but with a touch of bitterness, people in general do not rise to such high moral standards. He invokes and laments the bad example of the Germans, the influence it had on loosening morals in general. It is unbelievable, he says, how many people rightly regarded as respectable before the war, have lost their moral bearings during the occupation. Good, stolid men and women, by tradition scornful of worldly goods, were reduced by war to chasing money. Seeking to assert their superiority over fellow-men still more degraded than themselves. In strange contrast to normal times, the lowest people show the highest spirit. Social outcasts and the low orders of people, heedless of dangers and hardened by suffering, are the most likely to take risks and help Jews. It is horrifying to think how many rogues, renegades, blackmailers, denouncers this war has produced from among the not-so-lowly people. One must not forget, of course, that they denounce far more of their fellow-Poles than Jews, sowing the seeds of death.

–"Yes, they do of course," commented Osterman. "It was because the Poles weren't unsympathetic to the extermination of Jews that the Germans selected Poland as their execution-site. And where wood is being chopped, splinters fall."

This is not true, says Brzostek with startling composure, even though some Poles say the same out of spite. He explains that Poland was chosen, because it was where by far the largest number of future Jewish victims lived - which sounds persuasive enough. With the same calm he also readily admits, pouring scorn on opinions to the contrary, that the deaths of the two peoples are in no way comparable, either in human scale or meaning, and he disdains as most stupid of all, the view that the Jewish deaths are merely an integral part of Poland's losses. Equally he decries as sanctimonious bigots those who "discern" in the Jews' massacre a divine judgement on them, and upbraids even more strongly those of his fellow countrymen who allegedly wish to convert Jews, as the last salutary service they could do for them, before the end of their lives. For all that, Brzostek does not deny the motive of national interest in the overwhelmingly equivocal Polish attitudes towards the extinction of the Jews, and - however painful it is for him to say it - in the even deeper silence of the clergy, who could be expected to be the first to practise what they preach - love thy neighbour. And everywhere, in every country, the same priorities, the same motives, the same dilemma.

"But opinions and relations will change once this nightmare is over. There is not a single decent Pole who has not suffered from the common enemy. This will alter the people. Hatred will disappear. The Jews who survive will be brothers in a free Poland."

–"And what about in the meantime?" Marek asked in a mixture of sarcasm and boredom.

–"In the meantime," said Maniek, "as I understood him, for all his well-meaning words and avowed moral duty to help the Jews, Brzostek is a realist. The Poles could not have significantly eased the lot of Jews by fighting the Germans, while German vengeance on the Polish people and towns for helping the Jews would have been out of all proportion to the relief Polish armed resistance could have brought to them."

–"He seems to be an honest man," I said in reply to a question Maniek addressed to me, "and a lot of what he said is true. But his painting of a rosy future in a free Poland, or of people undergoing a metamorphosis when the war is over, wasn't genuine. He doesn't seem silly enough to believe in that."

As to his argument about armed assistance to Jews and German retribution, this essentially tallies with the official policy of the democratic parties of the Left. While their "hearts go out to the martyred Jews", declare the socialists and their friends, there are higher Polish national aims, which take precedence. Even the Jews must understand this.

Do you agree? Does it comfort you? These and similar nagging questions were thrown especially in Deker's face.

–"D'you still insist that the Jewish underground is part of the Polish underground?" Hausdienst inquired mercilessly, as this was the political line of the Bund party.

"Can't you see how unwise it was to link the policies of the Jews (meaning the Bund) with those of the Poles (meaning the Polish Socialist Party), when our and their situation and respective aims are so completely different?"

Poor Deker usually keeps silent when he is being hectored like this. Though once he said quietly: "But we're Poles too. Aren't we?"

Knepel is proud that his fellows on the outside have pledged support for the hounded Jews, and pleased by their view that the extermination of the Jews is a preliminary to the extermination of the Poles. But as Hugo aptly remarked, the communists' declared patronage of the Jews in 1942/43 was a doubtful blessing as it drew a quick response from the entire Right: "What better proof is there, that the Jews are communists?"

Most altered of all is the position of the patriotic Polish Right, the National democrats and their allies. It is easy to understand why. Their dilemma, originating in the conflict between the National Socialists of Germany and Poland, has been lately, and depressingly, deepening. Initially declaring "war on two fronts" and hoping for the simultaneous defeat of Germany and the Soviet Union, their strategy since "Stalingrad" has switched to praying for the holding of the one front that militarily still matters, the Eastern one. Politically, the Right's new policy, and last hope, is summed up neatly by its slogan: "Death to Hitler! Long live Pétain!"

Not unrelatedly, though curiously, the so-called Delegate (in Poland of the government-in-exile, a sort of prime minister of the Underground) has only recently urged his peers in London to tone down their official statements sympathetic to the Jews - please understand "the country doesn't like Jews" - of whom, apart from the remnants still breathing in concentration camps, only a few thousands are left hiding in Poland.

–"How d'you explain this?" Marek asked humbly.

–"The coalition that makes up the government is engaged in a life-and-death battle with adversaries on both the Left and the Right. The latter still regards anti-Semitism as a very useful political weapon, in view of the prevailing sentiments shared by the majority of ordinary people.

"And so you can now see, why the Jews have not ceased to occupy Polish minds."

–"Will they, then, ever cease? Even with no Jews around?" he asked sighing.

–"Can you really worry about that now?" asked Maniek. "And anyway, after all we have lived through, whom could their charitably malevolent kicks still hurt?

"You remind me of the Jew, who, in the third year of occupation, suddenly noticed the once so familiar catch-phrase 'Bij Żyda!' (Hit the Yid) and tenderly embraced the post on which it was scratched, crying: 'Oh, my beloved Poland!'"

CHAPTER TWENTY

Nothing has, however, incited among us such passionate debates as the subject of wartime Jewish Councils, usually referred to by their German name of *Judenrats* (JDRs).

–"Collaborators from the outset, at the end delivering their own brethren to the Germans, to certain death," shouted Hugo, waving his arms in the air, during one of our most memorable discussions. "The Germans could never have exterminated all the Jews without the assistance of the JDRs and the *Ordnungsdienst* (OD) auxiliaries under their orders." And raising his voice still more: "They betrayed millions of fellow Jews, sharing responsibility for their murder, to save their own and their families' lives."

Deker, displaying all his political prejudices, joined in, determined not to be outshone by Hugo.

–"To save a few, they sacrificed many. Because of that bourgeois-Zionist-Orthodox clique of unelected leaders, the Jews will be seen in the eyes of history as having participated in their own destruction. The very formation of the JDRs must be condemned, and the memory of its councillors obliterated.

"Can you deny that by deceiving the Jews in their charge, the Judenrats facilitated their murder?"

This time there was no need for me to answer, because Knepel was ahead of me, protesting with ill-disguised relish: "The reactionaries have never had any regard for the masses, in this war they became its oppressors.

"The only way to save at least some of the Jews was through armed struggle, and it was just this that the JDRs and the OD men opposed and frustrated. This was their greatest crime."

–"Growing rich and powerful themselves, while making the poor and the weak work like slaves," was Hausdienst's contribution to the litany of JDR evils. "Utilizing selections for slave labour and then for deportations to extort money from those who could still pay."

Even the usually not too eloquent Szinc put in a damning question: "Can there be any doubt that the JDRs and the OD helped the Germans in their bloody job?"

It would be difficult, almost impossible, to write down everything the JDRs, their hapless councillors - the Judenraete - or the OD men were being accused of by the not so preternatural alliance of the Jewish hard Left with that unique Jewish species, the self-haters. But having quoted the heaviest of their accusations it is not absolutely necessary to recite the lighter charges, though I will go into some of those when the opportunity arises.

Apart from the personal prejudices of the accusers, their grave imputations against the institutions and men implicated were prompted by old party political divisions, which, even at camp, stirred up ideological differences, that otherwise had been gradually subsiding. At times, my mates directed their charges against the JDRs at me, either because I somehow personified to them all those social elements which, in their squint-eyed view made up the JDRs, or because it suited them to substitute, by a peculiar process of transference, a living person for the vanished objects of their hatred. Even so, they showed some regard for me, or rather for my opinions, perhaps because at heart they recognized the monstrous nature of their accusations. Even Deker may have understood this, notwithstanding that criticism of the JDRs had become a fundamental Bundist dogma, on which its surviving followers might hope to restore their shattered fortunes after the war. But perhaps this consideration for me was a way of expressing gratitude for relieving their boredom by the debates which my opposition brought to life.

In the workshop I could not unfold my arguments other than in snatches, or in broad terms, because among the debaters at the workshop, unlike in the entire camp, the accusers of the JDRs were many, and their only defence counsel, excepting occasional intervention by Osterman or Lisko, was myself. But in the solitude of Hugo's store-room, face to face with him - the prime abuser of the JDRs - I was able to set out my views in the full and, I hope, reasoned terms, that this emotional and complex question requires. Hugo, too, with only myself for audience, was less vehement in his pronouncements than he was at the shop.

What were the JDRs? The question must be asked because the JDRs performed, within a relatively short time, a variety of partly erratic functions and, therefore, are not easy to define. Certainly, they meant something very different to the Jews and the Germans. In creating the JDRs, the Germans purported to be granting the occupied Jewish population a representative body of their own, or, as they initially claimed, a sort of internal autonomy. But in fact, the purpose of establishing the JDRs was broadly to create a tool by which to exert control over the entire Jewish population with a minimum of German personnel. This was, however, not immediately understood either by ordinary Jews, or by most of the Judenraete. Curiously, in the early days of occupation, the bulk of the Jewish population regarded the JDRs in the deceptive German light.

Even much later, many Jews considered the JDRs to be Jewish bodies, reflecting the people's overwhelming, though involuntary approval. But, in reality, the JDRs were as much a German institution - even if not hostile to Jews - as the municipalities which operated on the Polish side. On this, however, the opinions of the JDR accusers were neither uniform nor sufficiently explicit, and Hugo merely asked critically why the people had so readily approved of something that was a German institution.

Not that he did not know the reason, which was that, however displeasing and objectionable, the JDRs were a necessity. But Hugo reverted, as he had before, to the well-known fact that in many towns, particularly the larger ones, the Jews were

270

told by one boss or another to re-activate their prewar Communities.

–"You must have heard about Cracow," he said, "where hardly a week into the occupation, the Polish vice-burgomaster, in the absence of the presiding officer, instructed some prominent local Jews to resume the functions of the *Kehila* (Jewish Community). Isn't that sufficient evidence that the JDRs were an extension of the prewar Jewish Communities?"

–"No! That's perhaps the most hateful of all Deker's calumnies."

As Hugo was my interlocutor, it was politic not to charge him but to lay the blame at Deker's door. Actually, in prewar Poland, the truly assimilated Jews hated the Jewish Communities as much as the Bundists did and, along with the Jewish communists, refused to recognize them. This was understandable enough, for to become a member of a Kehila would have meant to affirm one's Jewishness, which these individuals wanted to shed. The Bundists did formally recognize the Kehilot, but tried to subvert them as institutions because they accused them of being socially retrograde and politically inimical to the people. When, however, the popularity and, hence, the political fortunes of the Bund began to soar in the 1930s, its leaders changed tactics, starting to contend for the domination of the Communities - but with little success. For although in municipal elections held about that time the Bund obtained, with the support of communists, the absolute majority of Jewish votes in most of the largest towns, at elections to the Jewish Communities, the Bund received only enough strength to paralyse them - though for this the Bund was not the only party to be blamed.

To give the JDRs the belated compliment of being an extension of the prewar Kehilot had been the ultimate revenge of the Bund and their allies on an institution that they had detested and fought against for decades.

–"It's true," I told Hugo, "that in Cracow the Jews were initially ordered to reconstitute the Kehila, but only a few days later, the Germans announced the formation of a new body - the Judenrat. They also nominated its chairman and councillors, as they did in every other town. Though respectable, if little known citizens, these were nevertheless German nominees, whereas councillors of the prewar Kehilot were elected democratically by its members."

I also pointed out to him many other differences between the two bodies, of which functionally the most important was that while the prewar Communities were constrained by law from extending other than religious and social welfare services, the JDRs were required to assume most functions that are normally undertaken by local government; though just religious services, as they were unofficially banned, were removed from among their duties.

–"But," I ended, "among all that multitude of duties, the JDRs were never given - as you once quoted Olkowicz saying - that of extermination."

–"Officially?" asked Hugo.

–"Also practically - except perhaps in some instances which would require verification. Because you know," I wanted both to cajole and caution him, "that people talk and write hearsay, others pure nonsense or malice. But even those who tried to be objective, to speak and write critically about themselves, the events and the

271

people around them, could not do so because their view was strictly circumscribed. There were more than 200 JDRs in Poland with probably over 3,000 councillors in all. How, I ask you, could a man shut up in a ghetto, sealed off from events of the living world within the walls of a hide-out, know what happened in all the other places?"

–"But there are big places. One, two or more men may know enough about them to have an accurate view."

–"Even if this were so, the comparative importance of the big place is with regard to the number of common people affected, not with regard to JDR councillors; because the difference in their number as between a big place and a small place was at most a dozen men or so.

"Anyway, there's no continuity whatsoever between the prewar Communities and the wartime JDRs, except that in many towns the buildings, offices, and some employees of the two were the same. What does it mean to say, as Deker does, that they worked on the same principle? That bureaucracy is bureaucracy?"

–"What he means is that they both had the same immoral motives."

–"But that's just part of his wholesale vilification of both. And he's even more absurd when he puts on his sanctimonious airs of Yiddish patriotism to accuse the JDRs of promoting assimilation because they conducted business in German and Polish - as their masters ordered them to.

"And as far as the motives of the Judenraete in accepting and performing their duties are concerned, there's no reason to believe that, at least initially, they weren't honourable, even if not quite altruistic. But does one become a state president or minister out of 'quite' altruistic motives?

"Whether they accepted their nominations out of a sense of duty and responsibility to the community, or from personal reasons and timidity, the Judenraete weren't, and probably could not be, in the early days of occupation, clear in their minds about the intricacy of the work they were taking on. But the reasons for assuming it appeared compelling, whatever the misgivings which at least some of them must have had. Have you ever heard of any example of a fairly large and advanced community living without some administrative, controlling authority? Or one continuing to exist for long without the most elementary, and, in the circumstances, most urgently needed services? But the JDRs were the only authority that could provide them. This was, of course, because the Germans wanted it that way; so supplying the community with the services it needed inevitably meant co-operating with the occupiers. This dilemma emerged early on and no councillor, indeed no Jew, knew how to solve it.

Hugo was clearly discontented, narrowing his eyes, but he allowed me to continue.

–"You may say now: 'There's a simple solution: don't accept the job in the first place'. But then, to a responsible man, taking the rights and wrongs of the situation into account, the urgent needs of the people outweighed all other considerations."

–"Why?" asked Hugo with a vehemence that emphasized the strength of his disagreement.

–"Because the very existence of the community, at least the poorer half of it, was at stake. Leaving aside the question of organizing some sort of orderly life, take food first."

One by one I reminded him of the most vital services the JDRs provided. Ration cards for Jews were to be issued only through the JDRs. Later they were also responsible for distributing the essential bread and supervising its Jewish bakers. And from the beginning of the occupation, many people were thrown on the bread of charity. In addition to the existing poor, thousands of men and women everywhere lost their livelihoods as a result of the vicissitudes of war and occupation. Worst affected were the refugees, who continued to stream in, in ever greater numbers with the expulsions from the Reich. Who was to provide social relief and a minimum of subsistence to these most unfortunate of all people? I asked Hugo. Who was to organize public kitchens and the like? Who was to provide the crowd of refugees with a roof over their heads?

The JDRs formed housing departments. They instituted health departments to take care of sanitary conditions, to prevent epidemics. In Cracow, where there had been a Jewish hospital before the war, the JDR quickly re-opened it, adding various out-patient clinics, and distributing basic medicines which were otherwise hardly obtainable. Later, when epidemic diseases began to spread, a special hospital was opened. But also in smaller towns the JDRs provided some care, in time the only care, for the health of the people. Whether voluntarily or not, the JDRs also took upon themselves to organize production and to tackle the problem of labour.

–"You must not forget," I told Hugo, "that in the dreadful conditions of privation and economic disruption with many thousands of men out of work, employment was a privilege - and what a privilege! I see the scoffing smile on your face, you're probably itching to ask: 'And what about forced labour? What about the JDRs' direction of people to labour camps?' First, labour camps only came into the picture later on, they weren't around in the early days of the occupation. Second, they're part of a problem which later had much wider and more significant connotations, so my answer can wait till later as well."

–"What d'you mean?"

–"The question whether, given the circumstance, it was right or wrong, good or bad for the people, that the JDRs acted as intermediaries in procuring - to use Deker's deprecating word - Jews for the labour camps, instead of the Germans taking them forcibly themselves."

–"Oh yes, I see, 'the lesser evil' claim, which all collaborators argue so expertly."

–"Where the rule is terror, some people's co-operation with evil is the unavoidable consequence. And this the overwhelming majority of the Jews understood."

–"Understood what?"

–"That their affairs must be managed. People were relieved and thankful when by organizing teams of willing and paid workers the JDRs nearly put a stop to the Germans' daily practice of abducting men from their homes."

–"But at what cost? Was it desirable? Didn't compliance with the occupier's wishes, appeasement, the striving for normality, for an ordinary, reassuring way of life, contribute to a much worse disaster later? You're too clever not to know that in the reality of this world catastrophes, in particular of the kind that has befallen the Jews, don't come over from the Beyond. They're brought about by men, and frequently brought upon one's own house."

–"That's a heinous charge to make, that the Jews, notably the JDRs, contributed to their own destruction. The people themselves provided the answer to your questions. Has anyone ever asked for the JDRs' services to be abandoned? Have any normal men or women desired anything but the return of normality and an orderly life? If anything, people wanted more and better services. If there was criticism of the JDRs - and where has there ever been a bureaucracy without critics, an authority without opposition? - it was with a view to improving the services. Though far from loving the JDRs, the public's attitude to them was, as I have already said, that to a basically unwelcome yet vital necessity. For, as a result of all the different functions the JDRs fulfilled, the lives of Jews became to a large extent dependent on them - much more so than the lives of Poles were dependent on their municipalities. From the beginning of the occupation, the Jews were forbidden to approach any Polish, let alone any German, institution directly, except through the agency of a JDR. If you didn't want to have your water, electricity or gas cut off, you had to pay the bills at the JDRs. The same with taxes, old and new, which had to be settled within a matter of days of receiving the account, on pain of exacting penalties. And in circumstances where restrictions were the rule and rights a rare exception, every licence or permission, for example to perform a craft, or travel by train, could be obtained only through the JDRs."

–"Obtained by bribes, by taking advantage of the restrictions, growing rich on the misery of the people."

–"You're magnifying things beyond all limits of truth. Though you don't go as far as Deker and Hausdienst, who say that corruption created a community of interests between the Gestapo and the JDRs. It's very easy to be moral at other people's expense. Surely if there was bribe taking this was by council employees and not, or only very rarely, by the councillors themselves?"

–"Good to know that you don't deny that there was corruption."

–"But when was there not? Not just in Poland, where, particularly if you were a Jew in the nineteen thirties, you could hardly have got fair treatment in matters of real import, without a consideration. Indeed I doubt if corruption, nepotism, or chicanery at the JDRs were greater than in public affairs of the country generally before the war. And yet in that state of moral rottenness that the Germans spread around, in a state that, as you well know, has made corruption the basis of their administration, you require absolute purity of the unhappy JDR servants. They, captive men, were probably more vulnerable than human beings generally are; and the chosen few who were important enough to be oiled, however sad it is to say, accepted bribes in cases where most people would probably show no greater rectitude.

"But with regard to all the trumpery social criticism that is being blustered about in the workshop, let me tell you that an overwhelming majority of the employees, as well as councillors, of the JDRs were men of integrity, devotedly serving the community. In places that I know, and where conditions were probably not very different from others, they tried to evade German orders as much as possible, were generally helpful and not excessively bureaucratic."

Indeed, the limited bureaucracy and, in general, the way the JDRs discharged their duties was a surprise to many observers, when it was considered that they were required to perform, in exceptionally difficult and "dynamic" circumstances, functions of which the JDR officials had no previous experience.

Likewise, there was in the ghettos no "social ferment" - another ambiguity of Deker, who had never tasted life in a ghetto personally. There was, of course, inequality, but naturally much less than before the war, because in the ghetto nearly all people were objectively poor. Anyway, less inequality could hardly have significantly improved the welfare of the community at large. And while there was occasionally some of the usual and inevitable strain between bureaucrats and the public, relations, in general, were not tense. Quite the contrary. But Deker would even have the people in Tarnow fighting their OD men, which was a lie. While Knepel, in his crazy addiction to armed resistance, invented a Jewish uprising during the last Aktion there; though he doesn't even know the precise date when this took place. I told Hugo that I shuddered at the thought of what might be told after the war about what people did or did not do before they died.

–"It must have struck you as well, that while Deker and Hausdienst are inclined to shower the JDRs so generously with abuse and condemn their very existence, they vindicate, almost glorify, the activities of the Jewish Social Self-Help (JSS). Of course, I understand why; their political friends were eagerly involved in the JSSs, but had difficulty in joining, or even working at, the JDRs. Much of the criticism of the JDRs sprang from this difficulty and the rivalry between these two. But you, who have no particular liking for either, can you tell me why membership of the one was right and of the other wrong? Were they not both appointed and controlled by the Germans?"

–"They were. But you know the difference. The JSS were engaged only in social welfare, whereas the JDRs carried out other tasks, for which they're damned."

–"But the JDRs are damned by you even for providing social welfare.

"Isn't it true that for the first two or three years, just before and after the JSS were established in May 1940, JDR activities were largely confined to social care? Moreover during that period the two institutions shared some of the same leaders.

"Whatever the differences between the two organizations may have been, the reason why friends of Deker and Hausdienst were plentifully represented in the one and not in the other was simply because for membership of the JDRs the Germans designated prominent middle-class citizens - originally they intended to include rabbis everywhere, but for one reason or another this didn't materialize - but almost completely omitted common people of other classes, let alone known communists. Together with other prominent people, most Bund leaders had escaped to the East when the war broke out. Of those who stayed behind, or fell later into German clutches, many did indeed join the JDRs if they were required to, as, for example, the councillor in Lwow who was perhaps the most eminent criminal lawyer in Poland before the war."

–"D'you really think that it's because their leaders ran away that Deker and his friends keep so curiously silent about the Bund's crushing electoral victories before the war?"

–"I'm glad that you have noticed that as well. It's quite remarkable. Especially by contrast to the way they trumpeted those victories in the weeks and months preceding the outbreak of war. And they were truly imposing victories. Probably never in history had socialists received such a large percentage of votes in free elections as the percentage of Jewish ballots cast on the combined socialist lists in Warsaw, Lodz or Vilna at the end of 1938. But I don't think Deker and his friends keep quiet about it because their leaders fled - which was a wise thing for them to do, even if it was not very courageous to leave their supporters leaderless and lost in confusion. But since Deker, Knepel, and indeed yourself, seem to consider instant dissolution right - disorder, disintegration, all going down together like Samson with the Philistines' temple - then the disarray caused by the flight of the Bund, and other leaders, could not be a reason for shame or reproach.

"No! that's not the reason. They keep silent about those electoral victories because in this way everything they condemn - the alleged moral decline, the 'Jewish response', its meekness, lack of dignity, non-resistance, and hence the Jews' self-destruction - they feel able to blame all this on the heads of Jews, who, they say, were fifty per cent orthodox - quintuplicating their true proportion - and nearly all the rest middle-class, Zionist, capitalist, obscurantist. If it were spread around that those Jews were ordinary, overwhelmingly non-observant, 'liberated' men and women, who bestowed their confidence upon the Bund and other socialist parties, what a crisscross that would make, what a foil to their plans, what a spike in their mud-throwing guns!

"Would it then still be possible to claim moral superiority over 'the Jews' and their wartime JDRs? Would the claim not lose its avantgarde quality?"

–"It would lose nothing. You try to overdo the significance of those elections, to talk down the invariably valid indictment of the JDRs. The people, just as you say, the ordinary, non-religious men and women, have themselves voiced their disapproval of and hostility to this harmful institution. And nothing you have said can change my mind or alter the fact of that hostility."

–"I may not change your mind, but even in the deportation phase there was no hostility expressed towards the JDRs - excepting of course by politically prejudiced Pecksniffs, such as Deker, or people with personal grudges - and this was because of all those vital services which the JDRs provided and because of the public's generally correct perception of the situation.

"Best proof of this is the strenuous efforts thousands of common people made to get work at the JDR offices. At first this was just to earn a wage, as the JDRs were not only one of the largest wartime employers for Jews, but also paid relatively well, though not by prewar standards. Later, after the first Aktion, when it had been established everywhere that work at the JDRs shielded the employee and his close

276

family from deportation, people were literally besieging JDR buildings, investigating all sorts of connections, and paying kickbacks, to get a job there. Can you seriously maintain that if all those honest men and women had considered the JDR a hostile institution, let alone, as you have implied more than once, a criminal institution, they would have tried so hard to work for it?"

–"That's wrong from the outset, fraught with disastrous consequences."

–"But what's the alternative, 'at the outset' in particular?"

–"Not to work for the JDRs. To repudiate their German-derived authority. To reject them as leaders. To refuse all those self-abusing and self-oppressing services you have mentioned."

–"D'you realize what that would have meant? That what you're suggesting meant immediate disintegration of life, total chaos? Would that have been better?"

–"Yes! The result would indeed have been chaos, but that wouldn't have been as bad as what happened later. We know where compliance with orders led. If, on the contrary, German authority had been ignored, they couldn't have killed all the Jews. Tens of thousands could have escaped, simply disappeared in the chaos."

–"That's just supposition. Quite unwarranted. Even if it were not, you are drawing on the benefit of hindsight. Who 'at the outset', during the whole first phase of war, expected the calamity that descended upon us later? Why, then, should they have decided upon collective suicide, for that's what a recusant attitude such as you suggest would have meant. And that's assuming merely for the sake of argument, that it was realistic at all. "But I have noticed that you're actually shifting the alleged guilt of complicity with the German extermination of Jews from the JDRs to their humble subjects."

–"Where do you get that from?" there was genuine, slightly indignant surprise in Hugo's voice.

–"It's the logical conclusion one must draw from your gravest accusation of the Judenraete. If they assisted the Germans in the destruction of Jews, then the ordinary folk who, in your view, accepted them as leaders and carried out their instructions were as much, if not more, responsible for their own destruction.

"I really suspect that all the vicious assaults on the JDRs, the deliberate focus on them, ostensibly explained away by interest in the internal aspects of our present tragedy, displays - apart from the sheer boastfulness of some 'resistance fighters' - a new facet of the old Jewish sickness of self-hatred; and the arrows are in fact aimed at the totality of the Jews concerned. For the more intelligent of the accusers understand that what ultimately mattered was not that the JDRs complied with German orders but that the public at large did so."

–"That's not true. I have never thought in those terms. The role of the JDRs is the central issue of the internal aspect of the catastrophe, and so it's only natural to concentrate on it."

When I reminded Hugo that the JDRs are only one of many "internal aspects" - which interest me, too, more than what the Germans did to us - and that to focus on the JDRs to the exclusion of almost all other internal matters is, therefore, suspect, he denied this and counter-charged.

277

—"Actually, it's you who, in your attempt at all-out defence of the JDRs, drags ordinary people into the mud. It's the JDRs, and not the ordinary people, their subjects, who stand in the dock."

—"But in the final analysis, it was the ordinary people, their resolve, that mattered. Suppose, however unrealistic this is, that all the JDR nominees had refused to serve. And so had the second batch, and the third, and so on. There would have been no JDRs. But there would still have been German orders. Whether they were carried out or not, would have depended on the totality of the common people who received the orders. This didn't change because there were JDRs; compliance with the orders still depended on the people as a whole."

—"But the Judenraete were their leaders."

—"That isn't true," I interrupted him angrily. "It's absurd to regard them as our wartime leaders."

—"What were they then?" asked Hugo, just as angrily.

—"A hierarchy imposed by the Germans. Their helpless victims. Undeclared hostages, if that isn't disagreeable to you. Yes, hostages in the clutches of a mighty enemy."

—"Whatever you call them, hierarchy, superiors, chiefs, or any other name, they were leaders and they delivered the orders. That these weren't rejected, but complied with by the masses, was the JDRs bidding - an attribute of all leadership - and they bear sole responsibility for it."

—"For what, precisely?"

—"For transmitting the orders, and so doing the Germans' work for them."

—"We come back to where we started. You can't avoid the temptation of hindsight if you maintain that the Judenraete shouldn't have accepted any functions in the first place because of the tragic happenings years later. Then I suppose you'll say that they should have resigned when they realized that they were assisting the Germans against the Jewish people. And so should have let anarchy rule, which would have served as a signal for the people to 'run away' and disappear.

"But who wanted anarchy? The people, without exception, wanted to live. Anarchy could only lead to certain death. And I ask you again, for heaven's sake why should the Jews have opted for collective suicide during the first phase of war, when their lives didn't seem to be in mortal danger, living conditions though hard weren't unbearable, and all were hoping, however naively, for the quick disintegration of the Third Reich?"

—"But it's discipline and obedience, not anarchy, that led to the death of us all. Instead of opposing the Germans, instead of resigning and warning the people, the JDRs stepped onto the road that led to the disaster."

—"Suppose they had resigned, and by this, according to you, had warned the people. Then what? Warned them of what? Of mass extinction? Years, or even only months, before the event? The JDRs certainly couldn't warn of that, because, unlike their critics, they weren't clairvoyant. Of course anarchy did not lead to extinction, because there was no anarchy, but if there had been, it would have led to extinction 'at the outset', not years later. That truly large numbers of people

278

could hide and survive is a delusion, big but empty words. We've often discussed why this was so and I don't need to explain it again. The only alternative to complying with orders was resistance. But you're exaggerating as wildly as Knepel the possibility of the captive Jews offering active resistance, given the circumstances they faced. Even the few men and women who proposed armed struggle envisaged it only as a last ditch venture. Until the 'last minute', namely till it became sufficiently clear that all the Jews who were still alive faced immediate 'evacuation' - how was the attitude of the resistance champions any different from that of the rest of the people, including the JDR councillors? And indeed who of all the occupied people of Europe - besides perhaps the Jews - thought of actively resisting the Germans, before they began to retreat and be defeated?

"And let me repeat that the consequence of anarchy, protest, or resistance in any other form, could only be the death of all, whilst there was actually still great hope of survival. Both the Judenraete and the ordinary Jews believed that the 'strategy' of formal submission to orders, that is to circumvent but not oppose them, was the least harmful to the interest of the people. They were both convinced that by carrying out orders that couldn't be evaded, they were avoiding something worse; and while the JDRs were trying to mitigate the orders, the public at large definitely preferred - a crucial point - to get them from Jews rather than directly from the Germans."

–"That's questionable. In any case, not to tell the people, not to warn them about the orders' real purport and its potential effects, but to entice innocent folk into blindly submitting to them, was to betray hundreds of thousands of their brethren. Why be chary of calling things by their names?"

–"But what is the name? Was it betrayal? Did the people blindly submit, or did they act in conscious belief of doing the best they possibly could? How did the Poles respond to orders they got?"

To be sure, the municipalities in the GG were, like their Jewish counterparts, the JDRs, operating under German orders. Similarly, the Polish people understood as well, if not better than the Jews, that chaos would be disastrous, that man could not live without essential organization and services, and that this requires co-operation in its daily administration. Because of the services the municipalities extended, the Poles regarded them in the circumstances, as a welcome necessity, indeed as institutions that benefited the nation. This, and the fact that they were overwhelmingly staffed by Polish personnel, might possibly have made many people forget that these were none the less local authorities under German command.

Thus the question I posed to Hugo referred first of all to the Polish heads of the municipalities, who worked most immediately under the orders of their German superiors. Then I asked him some questions about circumstances that had, regrettably, no parallel on the Jewish side, and of which Hugo might not have heard before.

–"Aren't the Polish heads of municipalities, in particular of the largest ones, performing their functions with the approval of the highest authority of the Underground? Before every difficult decision, don't they consult that same authority, which represents the government-in-exile inside the country?"

–"This they're right to do."

–"Of course they are. But what advice do they get? Not to recognize the authority of the occupier? No! To resign? No! To carry on with their tasks? Yes! To provide the population with the best and broadest services they can; to expand employment in the municipalities by as much as the Germans would allow - which was quite a lot, as the inexperienced German supervisors could easily be fooled - and in particular to make the municipalities a refuge for the most exposed sections of the population, the intelligentsia and professional men; for municipal employment, especially in an 'expert' capacity, usually shielded a man from arrest and forced labour. And this advice was given notwithstanding the fact that all prewar civil servants who became employees in the GG public services, including members of the Underground, had to renounce their earlier oath of loyalty to the Polish state authority, and take, along with other public employees, a new oath of obedience and fidelity to the GG authority. This, at least, the Germans didn't require of Jews."

Incidentally, I thought that it would not be surprising if as a result of the stratagem of creating dud jobs, there were more Poles employed in the central and local government recently than there had been in equivalent public services on the territory of the GG in independent Poland. This was certainly the case with the railways, which are now employing perhaps twice as many people as before the war, though in this instance it was also due to increased demand for labour. The railwaymen weren't, of course, told by the Underground to withdraw their labour from this truly vital service to Germany's war effort. Not even those railwaymen who carried Polish, not to mention Jewish, prisoners to the concentration camps. They were in fact told to carry on and, the trusted ones, to work at the same time for the Underground.

–"A patriotic duty," I stressed to Hugo, "was to help people to survive and to protect as many as possible from German harm; and this was, of course, equally true of the Jewish population."

Hugo wanted to say something, but in the end he agreed to continue listening.

–"You may perhaps have heard that when the Germans appointed two Poles to serve as governor and deputy governor of the GG 'central' bank, the two men consulted Cardinal Sapieha, the highest Church, and hence moral, authority then in the country, whether they should accept or not. They weren't told by him to refuse from 'the outset', but to accept. And they still serve. Neither they, nor the heads of municipalities, or other Poles in high executive positions are accused of treason or collaboration as you, Deker, and other Jewish critics, accuse the wretched Judenraete."

–"There's a basic difference of which you can't be unaware. The Poles weren't being exterminated, whereas the Jews have been."

–"One could argue the other side. But I won't. What I would say is that extermination, or the circumstances of the second - terminal as far as Jews were concerned - phase of the war don't change the conclusions on the functioning and nature of the JDRs in the first phase."

And so our discussion reached the phase of war that was most important of all for the assessment of the JDRs.

Replying to my last remark, Hugo asked in assumed indignation:

–"How can you say that? Millions have been murdered and the JDRs concealed from the people what was going on. They prepared lists for deportation, selected the victims, assisted in their 'evacuation'. Without that assistance the Germans could never have succeeded in murdering as many as they did, and you say that extermination changed nothing in the nature or function of the JDRs."

–"Let's take your accusations one by one, because they're so involved and heavy that truth will not easily extricate itself from under their weight. What I meant when I said that extermination had changed nothing is that the JDRs continued to be considered as indispensable as before; they still provided the same vital services, organization and discipline; they still reduced the harshness of treatment; and for all those reasons, the surviving people still wished, perhaps even more than before the Aktions, to get their orders through the JDRs rather than directly from the Germans."

–"This I must emphatically refute once again. Do you seriously maintain that the people did not resent the JDRs assisting the Germans in the Aktions?"

–"'Assisting' is an ambiguous word. Opinions were admittedly divided on whether it would be better or not, if the Germans carried out the Aktions without the 'assistance' of Jews. But even the minority who thought that it would be better admitted that the outcome in numerical terms, that is in the number of dead, would have been broadly the same, while in terms of suffering it would have been worse. You overlook also the obvious, namely that it's impossible to have no JDRs on the day or two of an Aktion, and yet to have them on all the other days, before and after the Aktions, when the people wanted the councils for all the reasons I've already mentioned. It remains a fact, however much you may wish to refute it, that the survivors of each Aktion still rejected anarchy and suicide."

–"You keep saying things which are controversial and which you can't prove. First, had the Judenraete refused collaboration, there wouldn't have been any JDRs either on days of Aktion or thereafter. Second, whether the suffering of the people was greater or not, the number of survivors would certainly have been larger. The Germans had not sufficient means to reap such a rich harvest by themselves.

"It makes you squirm I see."

–"Yes. You sound as if the captive Jews couldn't be murdered without the existence of JDRs. That's nonsense. Don't you really know, for it's a well-known fact, that in many parts of Europe, notably in Russia, mass extermination took place without JDRs having been established there? That's negative proof, if other evidence doesn't really satisfy you, that the massacre would have happened just as it did, even if JDRs had not existed at all. That the public realized this is confirmed by the fact that, even during the phase of Aktions, no one asked for the JDRs to be dismantled. Was it any wonder that the councillors did not resign? But if they had, it would only have changed things for the worse, given the circumstances of unlimited German will; and JDRs would undoubtedly still have existed with much less worthy councillors in business.

"Had there been no JDRs you could not condemn them for not telling the public the truth, not warning it of danger ahead. But did the inmates of the ghettos need to be warned? The truth is that the public knew of the impending Aktions only a day or two later than its JDR councillors. The news was always leaked from inside the JDRs - besides one or another German. And what 'evacuation' means, ordinary ghetto inmates knew as well as the councillors did.

"Admit that we all knew, at least from mid-autumn 1941, when all those refugees from the formerly Russian occupied part of Poland began to arrive, telling that the Jews there were being murdered wholesale. But we brushed the news aside, as if it didn't concern us. 'There, it was Russia, Communists, Ukrainians, instant reaction to enemy occupation, special circumstances. It won't happen here. They won't dare, will restrain themselves. The war will be over before that.' Though what was the alternative? What could 'knowing' have changed in circumstances without choice?"

–"Was it really without choice?"

–"Yes, except the choice to die by oneself. But this choice all rejected."

–"I know your views. To run away wasn't a choice, because there was nowhere to run and it was fraught with danger. Though some, you must admit, could and did hide. To resist wasn't a choice, because of lack of arms, because of collective responsibility, because it would mean collective suicide. So all one could do was to obey orders and wait for the next Aktion. But this, too, was a choice, wasn't it?"

–"No! It really wasn't. It was the given, the regular, the set pace, which one was powerless to alter."

–"Still there apparently remained one choice: to give this man, and not that one; to deceive, to play for time, to serve and slave in order to save the chosen few, and oneself in the first place. Was that a justifiable, I won't say choice, but policy?"

–"But was it a policy? You're mistaken. At best it was a tactic; actually an instinctive response, common to all men. Everyone believed in the necessity and justness of 'playing for time'. Since, for one reason or another, the Germans decided upon our destruction by instalments, to take advantage of this and delay death for as long as possible, was a matter of self-preservation. It was also a testimony to the continuing hope to survive. If there is Jewish deceit in it at all, this was tacit and by everyone of himself. Similarly, with regard to the most critical and most agonizing of all decisions, the task of trying to preserve at least those who, it seemed, could perhaps be saved, those who had some chance to survive, while leaving others to their fate. This, too, was a natural response, a dictate of reason, if not of the heart as well, and this, too, had almost general approval, even from most of those who were deemed to be past help. It's calumnious of you to insinuate that the Judenraete were motivated in this policy - as you wrongly call it - solely by their desire to preserve their own and their families' lives. Of course, they thought of themselves as well, and probably first of all. But who doesn't? You demand of the hapless Jewish wartime councillors, who were living under unprecedented tyranny, the behaviour of saints

- if saints behave beyond all selfish thought. Listening to you, one could think that these councillors were immune to all danger and led a life of ease in the midst of extreme hardship. You appear to ignore the fact that though they enjoyed exemption from forced labour and a high standard of living compared to the vast majority of their subjects, JDR councillors were of all Jews the most exposed to terror, and nearly all were murdered in the end. Indeed, you leave terror out of your considerations altogether, its effect on human behaviour and on people's inclination to obey orders.

"D'you know how Rommelmann introduced himself to the JDR in Tarnow? He came into the offices shouting and shooting, and demanded to see the chairman, Henryk Falban. When told that he was out, the Hauptscharführer ordered them to produce him within five minutes, otherwise 'they would see'. Meanwhile he set about destroying the typewriters, overturning the tables, smashing the windows. When Falban arrived in his office, he was greeted by a round of shots aimed a few inches above his head, and only then did Rommelmann tell him of his appointment as the new head in charge of Jewish affairs at the local Gestapo. Then he ordered Falban to furnish his flat and that of a mistress, as well as to provide various other supplies, within twenty-four hours, 'or else...'. And so it was almost every day: a visit from Rommelmann, and often from more than one Gestapo man per day, who were usually playing with their guns all the time they were talking to a JDR or OD man, intimidating and humiliating them in some studied way.

"And you envy them!"

–"That's all the more reason to resign their posts. Since they didn't, it can't have been so bad, the terror and the humiliation must have been worth suffering when weighed against the advantages of the job.

"But let us forget this inference, while remembering all the terror, tension and trial; can you justify - answer me straight - the personal involvement of the JDRs in the Aktions? To have known its meaning, and to urge people to obey orders, to turn up and join transports? And this assistance - even if they did not select the people themselves - you call ambiguous?"

–"Yes I do, and I have explained why.

"On a personal basis, to do any of the things you mentioned must have been the most harrowing decision for any man of conscience - one that should never be experienced by anyone. But whether they did it or not, you, to make your all-damning accusations, are selecting certain occurrences regardless of the awful predicament of the hour, and without trying to see the facts in the wider perspective of the tragedy.

"By the time the Aktions started, it was too late to resign."

–"Why?" Hugo interrupted impatiently.

–"Because it would have changed nothing and because it would have inescapably meant renouncing one's own life. Some of course did just this, either in the most direct way, by killing themselves, as for example the top JDR of Warsaw did, or by joining the 'evacuees', like the chairman of the council in Cracow, or by just refusing to comply, and thus inviting death, like the council chairman in Lwow. And that's what most did choose. You would understand why, if you were open-minded about these men. Some of them were not given time or opportunity to take one of the two other options; others felt incapable of making away with themselves, which isn't an easy thing to do; you must remember that killing oneself often required murdering others first: one's children, sometimes one's parents, perhaps one's wife."

–"This I know. But what about the overwhelming majority of Judenraete who took neither course? Who chose to comply and 'live on'?"

–"Whether it's an overwhelming majority is debatable, and neither I nor you know. There were certainly some who, though honest remorseful men, were too weak to take a firm stand, which, after all, required considerable courage. But most, undoubtedly, believed that to give up would be irresponsible, that what they did was right, in the best interest of their communities. To act accordingly, required no less courage than to resign."

–"Once they had carried out the atrocious business, it was immaterial what they believed, or whether they acted out of good or bad intentions. What difference did it make to the millions of victims?"

–"What difference did it make to the victims whether they were murdered by the Germans with or without the 'assistance' of others? But to hold that the intentions of men were judicially or morally immaterial is an astounding assumption, flying in the face of all human feeling and practice."

–"It's immaterial because in either case it fitted into the Germans' scheme, it was part of their overall plan; to fall in with it led to the murder of fellow Jews.

"Anyhow, what's the responsibility you say they believed they bore?"

–"The responsibility of man for his fellow. They believed that some people could and would be spared. Hence, responsibility to act so as to save what it was possible to save. Precious human lives were involved, and it would be irresponsible, they believed, not to try to limit their deaths. But if you equate 'assistance' for the sake of avoiding worse, with that of causing worse, then you can't, of course, understand the moral dilemma they faced. From a distance, you and Deker reduce its human scale to miniature; it's mere meretricious casuistry."

–"Wasn't the moral dilemma they faced either to die themselves or to select others to die? Am I trying to miniaturize the problem, or are you turning the argument upside down? That entire baneful 'strategy' of saving some while sacrificing others was from first to last mistaken, mischievous and naturally doomed to failure."

–"By no means. Your difficulty is you are so opposed to them you can't admit that the Judenraete could have been honourably motivated, torn by doubt, overwhelmed by the burden of their responsibility. Try to put yourself in the place of the chief councillor in Lwow. The Judenrat building is suddenly, though not unexpectedly, surrounded by scores of armed SS men. They take up positions at all the gates and office doors. Into the chairman's room comes Hauptsturmführer Erich Engels, the officer in charge of Jewish affairs at the local Gestapo, and commander at all the Aktions in Lwow. He is accompanied by equally highly-placed officials and demands people for 'evacuation', using the most accomplished intimidation and threats. To no avail. So Hauptsturmführer Engels changes his tactics. He begins to appeal to the chairman's reason, his sense of duty, and pleads with him to listen to his conscience. German orders, he says, are unalterable, there is no force in the world that can withstand them - a routine formula used by Engels' equivalents in every other town. 'Well, Mr Chairman, you're allowed to risk your own head, but as president of the Jewish community, are you also allowed to risk so lightly the heads of all your subjects? If you persist in your refusal to hand over the half I ask for, we shan't recoil from any necessary steps, even if they cost the lives of all Jews in Lemberg (Lwow). Your duty, Mr Chairman, before taking a hasty decision, is to ask yourself what would the community at large want you to decide. Will they forgive you if you sacrifice all their lives? Listen to your conscience before you fling caution to the wind!' The chairman in Lwow had previous experience of Aktions and was not a fool. He understood that if Engels wanted to 'evacuate' the whole community, nothing could stop him; that Engels wanted one half now and the rest later; and that he was to pay with his life for his stand - as he did a few hours later - but this did not frighten him.

"But can't you imagine that someone less experienced and less confident in his judgement than he, might have, in similar circumstances, asked himself: 'Have I not a duty to postpone, if I can, the demise of all and to limit the extent of the killing now? Would I be right to refuse one half and so bring down the rest? Would I not be responsible for their deaths, if I did so? Perhaps, after all, the Germans won't kill the rest? Perhaps they need young men and women to work for them? Perhaps the war will end before it happens?' You apparently can't understand that such questions, on the answer to which fateful decisions about people's lives depended, were, or even could be, asked honestly; let alone that the men put to the test could have concluded that it would be wrong, humanly inexcusable, not to rescue what was possible, even if that required surrendering those whom it was impossible to save."

–"If they were 'good' men, acting honestly, I can't really understand how they could bring themselves to do the Germans' work for them? Whether they were deceived or not, whether they collaborated out of good or bad intentions, they sacrificed the people on their lists, and thus caused many to die who might have not been murdered. How can you, on moral grounds, justify all that fatal 'strategy' of delivering Jack to die, in order to perhaps save John from dying?"

–"Few could indeed rise to your moral level, whilst you fail to see that, judged by different standards, your stand might not be moral at all."

–"To choose this man to die and not another one, is quite a moral problem. Isn't it?"

–"It is, but it's a problem which has different answers at different times. The simple truth is that in a large majority of places, 'evacuation' was accomplished without selection-lists prepared by JDRs, simply because they weren't ordered to prepare them. But where they were, the Germans only did it either for sadistic reasons - like choosing particularly pious men to desecrate Holy Scriptures - to torment the JDR officials, or to make Jews their accomplices. Best proof of this was that where they were supplied with lists, the Germans in command of the 'evacuation' usually ignored them, carrying out selections by themselves, or they picked up men at random. The plain truth is that the Germans didn't need any Jewish 'assistance' whatsoever. Had the JDRs refused it, had the JDRs not existed at all, the number of Jews murdered would be no smaller than it actually is. In a few cases, this man would have died instead of another. But not fewer people; whereas there are good reasons to believe that without JDR 'assistance' fewer people would live now, some of whom may even live to see the end of war.

"Take Tarnow for an example. With no 'assistance', more people might have hidden in bunkers and probably survived the first, second and third Aktions. But during the last one, the town was to become Judenrein, all Jews removed. Even if many had hidden, even if they could have endured long periods without fresh supplies of water and bread - which it is unrealistic to assume - they would have all been killed five months later, when the ghetto was razed to the ground - no doubt to make sure that a Jew or two who might still be hidden did not get away. On the other hand, because of the JDRs 'assistance', and the public's compliance with orders, more than a quarter of the people who assembled on the Platz for 'evacuation' at the last Aktion were sent to other camps. A few of them, and perhaps even more than a few, may survive the war. Had the people resisted, had the JDR not 'assisted', all would have died there on the Platz."

-"So, you owe the fact that you are here to the JDR?"

-"No! That I'm here is the result of many a coincidence. But I certainly wouldn't be here had the JDR not 'assisted'. The one absolute test of its activities at any place is to enquire, if the Judenraete did, or did not, do anything on their own - that is not on precise German orders - which contributed to the death or suffering of the Jews under their care. The answer beyond any doubt is that, excepting a few individuals, they did not."

-"That's debatable, as is your basic assertion that had there been no JDRs, or had they not 'assisted', no fewer Jews would have been killed. But on the moral plane, to decide who is, and who is not, to die was, even if done under orders, culpable from all points of view."

-"The decision was inevitable, humanly defensible, and required personal courage. In these days of unprecedented happenings and the unthinkable depravity of the enemy, old established morality has to be suspended. But I wonder what 'all points of view' you have in mind? I hope you aren't, like Deker and Hausdienst, calling Maimonides to help beat the downtrodden JDR councillors?"

Deker and his fellows had somehow learned of a ruling by the twelfth century Jewish scholar and codifier, Maimonides, which says, in short, that if heathens demand of Israelites: Surrender to us one of your numbers, not a named individual, they should all suffer death rather than hand over a single Jew. Either the learned tailors did not know that this rule had much older origins than Maimonides, or, rather, they preferred to quote him because his authority as a philosopher and rationalist appeared to them more impressive than that of the rabbis of the *Mishna*, who lived eleven centuries before him.

Ignoring the abstract circumstances of this now famous ruling, the reason for

Maimonides endorsing it was the divine command to sanctify the Lord's name. Can you think of greater hypocrisy than of men, who don't believe in God themselves, condemning others because they haven't sanctified His name? Is there greater cant on earth than of men, who confess to no religion, or rather to anti-religion, yet censure the morality of others by reason of religious laws, which form the sole basis of Jewish traditional ethics? They even censure the rabbis, who, when consulted in the matter by some Judenraete, virtually all ruled against Maimonides.

By way of comment I repeated what I had told Hugo earlier. "The recent persecution has no religious quality; its aim is simply physical destruction. Hence it's not the sanctification of the Lord's name, but of human life that is the highest order of the day; and thus it is a duty to save as many Jewish lives as possible."

What would Rabbi Maleachi have ruled? I asked myself on reflection. There is no record of a decision by him because, selection-lists not being demanded in Tarnow, the question was not put to him by JDR councillors. There can, however, be no doubt what his answer would have been, considering in particular that eighty-six years before, one of his venerable ancestors accepted, not for the first time in our history, the voluntary death of a follower in lieu of himself. Having made his choice, the young and healthy man became ill the following day, and died two days later, whilst the mortally sick rabbi recovered and lived on for twenty-five more years.

–"And so everything is discarded, time-honoured morality, sacred laws, tradition," Hugo thus tried to show his ill-feigned despair. "One life is more precious than another; it would seem to be even more moral to surrender, than not to surrender, the one, in order to save the other. At least in the case of Judenraete. But if there's still any morality left, what entitles a man to cause the certain death of one person, in the hope of saving another?"

–"You exaggerate. You must admit, if you don't prize falsehood, that every society values some lives more than others. The general and the private soldier, or the proverbial prince and beggar. Equally in 'sacred law and tradition', which you chose to single out. The maxim of our ancient sages: 'Who can say that your blood is redder than his' was meant to apply to equals; as if any two men were entirely equal. In fact, the same sages, who propounded that egalitarian formula, set forth various criteria by which to value human life; to mention only one, the extent of a person's bounden duty to fulfil Divine commandments. So, for instance - sorry if what I say makes your blood boil - the precedence in theory of man's over woman's life. Those criteria weren't ordained for the sake of the JDRs, as you seem to imply when you wail over its councillors' decisions. Theirs was a unique case, acting as they did in special circumstances, which called for special morality. In their circumstances it might indeed have been more moral 'to give one, to save another', than not to give. While I agree that it's uncertain if the 'other' would be saved, it's far less uncertain that he wouldn't be saved if the 'one' weren't given. As well as inevitable, it was also morally compelling to judge who had and who had not a chance to survive, and to try to save exceptionally scarce lives. A septuagenarian cripple or an iron-bending youth, a famous artist or a notorious criminal - corresponding to the universal division of society into superiors and inferiors.

"I understand that you don't care much about rabbinical morality. You may not know what Christian morality dictates in similar circumstances. But you must know something about general secular morality, so what was the right thing to do by those standards? To give the one who couldn't be saved, in order to protect another who might be saved; or to let fall prey to the beast also the one who had a chance to live, when this required surrendering the other who had no chance?"

–"I don't think that by not giving the one, you're even indirectly responsible for the eventual murder of the other, while by surrendering the 'one' you're directly assisting in his murder. The circumstances, as you say, were indeed quite special, but human life still remained the most precious thing."

–"On this I agree with you. But then two lives surely are more precious than one life? And if so, your cardinal stricture that it's *fundamentally* wrong to surrender one, to save another, falls to pieces."

–"I doubt that. But if you agree with me in the other case, then you must admit that to give two, to save, perhaps, one, was wrong. Isn't it a fact that the Germans demanded to be given many, most ghetto inmates, while there was only a chance to save relatively few?"

–"I must repeat that these were unique circumstances and that to rescue what it was possible to rescue, was the prime duty of everyone with whom the possibility of rescue rested."

–"While committed to rescue, actually rescuing - as you would have it - their fellow Jews, in the meantime they were rounding them up, dragging them out of their hiding places, helping to send them away, seeing them loaded into the trains."

–"That's not true. the Judenraete weren't doing all that."

–"Only their executive arm, the Ordnungsdienst men."

–"Ignoring your exaggeration of their functions, if you really think that the OD was part of or an agent of the JDRs, then you're quite mistaken. True, officially they were subordinated to them, in particular to the head of the JDR, but in practice the JDR head, let alone his councillors, were subsidiary to the OD commanders, mistrustful and afraid of them. To an observer on the sidelines, it looked as if the OD were enforcing JDR 'authority', but in fact the OD were taking their orders directly from the Gestapo."

–"But so were the JDR."

–"Yes, in a sense, as was every captive Jew. But between the two the JDRs and the OD, a wide demarcation line must be drawn.

Initially it was the JDRs who, as early as mid-1940, were given "permission" to found a Jewish local police force, and to recruit its members. Consequently, at that stage, the modest force was made up of young men, who were nearly all of acknowledged civility. Both the recruits and the recruiters believed that they were performing an essential service for the community. "Where was there a commonwealth without a police? So much better to have one made up of one's own kin," most Jews said at the time. The approved name of the unarmed force, Ordungsdienst (literally

Order-Service), was persuasive enough to reassure a great many doubters, and indeed the OD's functions, on its foundation, were to keep order in the broad sense of the term, including control of traffic, tidiness, and discipline in public places, especially on JDR premises. To this was, however, soon added the gathering of taxes and fines, and more painful, of men selected for forced labour. Still, the community at large was convinced that this was inevitable and preferable to having the things enforced directly by German security forces, or the auxiliary Polish policemen. But before very long, even more objectionable functions were added to OD duties, such as, for example, arresting people on behalf of the Germans. By that time, the OD, acting already on direct orders of the Gestapo, had, as I've said, made themselves independent of the JDRs, and when ordered to recruit additional men, they did it by themselves. This led to the inclusion of men who, in the belief of acquiring a greater chance to survive, paid large sums of money or utilized "connections" to get themselves into the service, and also some less deserving individuals. In this respect, it is not irrelevant that the enlargement of the OD mainly took place in the second phase, that of mass destruction. Thus in Tarnow, for example, shortly before the first Aktion, when the Jewish population of the not yet ghettoized town numbered about 40,000, the strength of the OD was about fifty men. Immediately before the last Aktion, with the population reduced to no more than 9,000, there were nearly a hundred and fifty OD men. In the ghettos, the OD had the additional duties of guarding walls or fences, escorting complements to work, imprisoning offenders while at the same time acting as their judges, to avoid, if possible, delivering them to German "justice". And during the Aktions, everything that Hugo had mentioned.

But all this they did with no bad intent, rather being distressed and horrified at what they found themselves doing; though a few had enjoyed the "power", the elegance of uniform, and other substantial benefits that went with the job. From the public's standpoint, there were also many positive sides to the OD's functions, in particular between the Aktions, when life seemed temporarily settled. The people's mind was then split in assessing the merits and demerits of the service. Hugo was not unaware of this, but reluctant to admit it, and chose to question the existence of divided views on this subject.

–"Whether the OD men enjoyed or detested the work they were doing is beside the point. While I'm not saying that without the OD, Aktions would not have taken place, there was no disagreement about OD participation in them. They weren't carrying off strangers but their own brothers, knowing full well where they were being taken, and they did this to perfection. All the talk of keeping order for the people's sake, or of there being any advantage to the victims from having the Aktions carried out by Jews rather than by Germans, is merely the OD making excuses for their own criminal cause, supported by a small minority of well-intentioned but mistaken people, such as you. Anyway, what is it that made their participation desirable?"

–"As if you didn't know. While they were implementing German orders, but no more, the OD were reducing the suffering that accompanied the orders' fulfilment.

Most OD men showed compassion for the victims, were approachable and considerate. The entire grievous enormity wasn't as brutal and physically hard, as it would have been if the Germans or their allied helpers had done it with their own hands. True, OD men had better knowledge than foreigners of the ghetto, its nooks and corners, the layout of its houses, and so were much better at unearthing 'bunkers'; while some did this, others warned the hidden people not to come out yet, and supplied them with food. But the greatest advantage of being policed by Jews was felt during the weeks and months of respite. After all, the Aktions lasted altogether only a couple of days. D'you realize what it would have meant to have strangers, even only Poles, permanently stationed in the ghetto? Life inside supervised by them? During those long periods between the Aktions the OD were helpful, perhaps the most helpful category of inmates, in preserving life in the ghetto. They would look away from infractions of the rules, circumvent them themselves, and warn their fellow prisoners of an impending or current German visit to the ghetto, and of similar dangers. The significance of this can only be understood if you remember that almost everything a Jew did to survive was illegal."

–"You're trying to bleach the OD's dirty linen so much that you blur the dividing line between it and the JDRs. No doubt there were some decent fellows among OD men, but equally, some were confidantes of the Gestapo. You can't seriously maintain that the Gestapo didn't know what was happening inside the ghetto. They just didn't care as long as it suited them. That's well known. Whether it would have made a difference to the inmates' lives, if the ghetto had not been policed by Jews, but by malefactors of some other nationality, isn't at all certain. You're trying to play down the gravity of the crimes committed collectively by the OD, as if they did not share responsibility for the deaths of their fellow Jews."

–"They weren't responsible. The Germans would have 'deported' the Jews just as they did, without OD assistance. In the East within six months of the invasion of the Soviet Union nearly a million Jews had been murdered, before the OD had come into existence in most of the area. All the talk that without Jewish collaboration, the Germans lacked the manpower to exterminate, especially so totally exterminate, the Jews, is shallow, malicious babble. They had more than enough men to carry it out. Had they needed more Germans for the task, they could easily have mobilized SS and police units from other duties. And the number of Ukrainians, Lithuanians and other nationalities, including auxiliary Polish policemen, who were willing to help, and indeed participated, in the extermination of Jews, was many times greater than the number of men required for it.

"Of course the Germans in charge of the ghettos knew something of what was going on inside. But that's not the same as having detailed information and a constant watch. The difference to Jewish lives between having the OD or an alien force policing the ghetto was like the one between in-laws living together in one flat, or separately in different parts of the town. It's impossible to deny this. Though, whether the OD's intention in doing their job was, as some of them have claimed, to prevent strangers from performing it, is, in your own phrase, beside the point. Nor was their function at the Aktions merely marginal. But as a whole the

OD wasn't a criminal organization. It lacked some of the essential elements that would qualify it as criminal: it performed under duress and force; it had no hurtful intent; its members ultimately suffered an identical fate with other Jews. What so distinguishes the OD from the JDR was that, unlike the latter, the OD actively, with their own hands, participated in the 'evacuations' of their brethren.

"And yet everything would have happened as it did, had the OD not taken part. I must stress again the flimsiness of the charge that without Jewish assistance, the Germans couldn't have exterminated so many Jews. Had the OD not existed, no more Jews would have survived, but the suffering of the victims would have been greater. And for that reason most, if not all, of them preferred to be 'evacuated' by OD men rather than by non-Jewish policemen.

"By itself, it was no offence to be an OD man; what mattered was the man's personal behaviour, his actions, if not just his intentions, and on this basis alone each one of them must be judged individually."

–"You defend the OD so forcefully that I'm impelled to ask you, would you have wanted to be one of them?"

This question touched off a train of memories, the best part of which I was not prepared to share with Hugo.

Back in Tarnow, in the depths of winter, at home with the last of my beloved ones, and the long hours, now such cherished hours, of pressure brought to bear on me to go out to work. On one of those occasions, in January 1943 - Oh Heavens it is only little more than a year ago - Rabbi Maleachi Leftof sombrely mused over my joining the OD, quoting the various existentially important advantages of OD membership. I kept silent, I dared not speak. Not even when he touched the most sensitive chord: as an OD man I could perhaps safeguard my mother as well as myself from deportation. There was nothing more precious to me than my mother, and I wanted nothing in the world more than to save her, if I could. But I knew that I could not. I knew that by becoming an OD man I could not save my own life, let alone that of my mother. She herself had never during the long, tender-hearted pleading with me to go to work, even so much as intimated that I become an OD man. She probably understood as well as I did that none of us could be saved, except by a miracle. We knew what the Germans' ultimate target for Jews was. Apart from knowing that to be an OD man, or any other "dignitary" under the Germans was anything but a blessing, I also knew that the supposed greater chance of OD men surviving was an illusion; that they would be disposed of like other Jews, as soon as they became dispensable; that they were merely gaining the prospect of becoming the "last ditchers". I knew other things that the saintly Rabbi Maleachi did not know on this unholy subject. It was painful, this only time, not to meet his possible wish.

Earlier in the discussion Rabbi Maleachi mentioned that one could be an OD man "like Mechil Blumenblat".

Mechil Blumenblat, a tall, bespectacled, diffident Jew of thirty, was the first OD man I came to know. Shortly after my arrival in Tarnow, I was walking inattentively through one of the main streets, when suddenly an OD man had approached me and said: "Forgive me bothering you, but please do me a favour and cross over to the other side." Have you ever heard of a policeman talking like that? Indeed I laughed heartily at him. This was, I think, the first week that a German order had been in force forbidding Jews to use the "right-hand" side of principal streets. Mechil Blumenblat was by then already a legend among the Jews of Tarnow. It would take volumes to relate all the stories about his fear of God, his acts of charity, his help to people in distress, and I was never sufficiently interested to explore their authenticity. But what had been unquestionably true was that Blumenblat's position did not deprive him of his humility and kindness to fellow humans; and, equally true, that goods and men crossed almost unhindered, when he stood on guard at one of the ghetto gates.

Though none equalled Blumenblat in good reputation, there were other similarly unblemished OD men. At the other end, there was a, probably smaller, number of tarnished officers, whilst the large majority were normal, decent men. Indeed, Rabbi Maleachi's scantly spoken opinion of the OD might be proof of the good reputation the service as a whole enjoyed and of the near-harmonious relations between it and the public in Tarnow. But I knew that the moral dangers of the service would be hard to avoid, and I was not sure that even Mechil Blumenblat had escaped them. Anyway, I felt that he was an exception and that no one else should expect to be granted similar indulgence by the service. The OD was certainly not an order dedicated to the advancement of mercy. The moral pitfalls, or all the demands of the service, could not be known to Rabbi Maleachi, who stayed all day in his room and was dependent on information fed to him by visitors; and, as a being of angelic qualities himself, he had little understanding of the works of a neoteric devil. He did not even know of one such little work which ensnared a man of his close entourage.

In 1942, Adi Salit, a man of nearly fifty summers, was living in Tarnow. A refugee from the border zone, he had managed to escape with substantial financial means. This enabled him to stay in business, the varied illegal wartime kind of business, and as a pious, charitable man, he paid a tithe of all his earnings to Rabbi Maleachi for further distribution among the needy. Otherwise, he avoided ostentation which presented no difficulty to him, as he was a modest, quietly-spoken person, in striking contrast to his brother Gedali, who, when asked once at the Judenrat offices if he would mind not speaking so loud, replied: "Sorry, in 'the old days' I was accustomed to shouting orders down long factory halls."

Adi's wife Helen was also unlike him. Born, just as he was, into a family of manufacturers, related to the Laibs, she had been brought up in luxury and relished the rich style of life. On her way back from summer holidays often spent at Monte Carlo, she used to leave a little more money with fashion houses in Paris. Helen liked to exhibit some of the new look couture of only two-three years ago at a sort of fashion show for certain visitors to her home, apologizing ironically that most of the gowns had become démodé, because there was no demand for them. Apparently the nouveau riche peasant women were quite unappreciative of a sequined evening dress or even of one in black rayon with reasonable back décolletage, and other Chanel or Poiret creations. On those occasions she also liked to recall brighter episodes from her "old" life, while inhaling deeply a cigarette fitted into an amber holder which was so long that the cigarette tip almost reached the person sitting opposite across the coffee table.

Their eldest son, Munish, born in 1918, was zealously religious. Freddie, his younger brother by seven years, resembled their father in temperament. In between was the beautiful Ila, who took after her mother.

On September 11, 1942, the second day of the second Aktion, this lovely family had already been standing waiting for thirty-six hours among those privileged to remain, except for the father, who was on duty. Eleven days later, on the holy Day of Atonement, Adi Salit - who had bought his way into the OD during the intermediate days of the first Aktion in order to get the "stamp" for himself and his family - volunteered a sort of confession.

Life had not yet returned to "normal" in the then newly closed ghetto. SS men were still raiding the place daily, carrying off booty; life inside was very tense. Rabbi Maleachi was permitted only one room of his flat, which had been sealed while he was in hiding. In this room the prayers on the Day of Atonement were conducted, with attendance restricted to a bare forum of ten men, for security reasons. During intermission at noon, sitting ashy pale and quivering in a quiet corner, Adi opened his heart in a whisper, to my brother Eli.

"It was already late afternoon, hardly two hours before the start of the New Year. The day before, I had been on duty inside the guard-house or at the gate. The second day, to get out of the wicked ones' eyes, I was meandering along side streets, sheltering in houses for hours, ready to pretend, if caught, that I was searching for hidden people. As evening was drawing near, I hoped the thing would soon be over, and I would get away. I didn't know that the Germans were still short of a few people to make up their quota. And thus, roving about in a side street, I stumbled into Rommelmann. 'Halt,' he shouted, and then coming near: 'OD man 222 (Salit's identification number) 'report within half an hour with two dodgers! If you don't comply, you and your family will go instead!'

"I suddenly saw the precipice outstretched at my feet. Black despair seized me. What could I do? Never mind myself, but my whole family! I was horrified. I was going mad. I didn't know what I was doing. I walked hither and thither up and down the same street, unable to think clearly. Only one thing was clear to me, that I would not surrender two people. Not for a moment had I thought of doing this. Well, no one lives forever, I told myself. I was preparing myself to die. But I might also be causing the death of my wife and children. Well, that's uncertain, perhaps God would help them? Even if I wanted to deliver two people, where would I take them? But not for a second did I think of surrendering any one. Upon my word, I swear by all that I hold dear. I was ever more desperate. What should I do? Oh, if I could drop dead where I stood! I felt such a longing for my family, it filled my whole soul. I saw myself taking leave of my wife and children. Would they at least know? I couldn't show up at the Platz. God help them. I must die.

"The half hour was running out and I was completely running out of my senses.

And while I was walking so aimlessly round the street, I suddenly saw from some distance away two people coming out of the doorway of a house close to the passage connecting Szpitalna Street with the Platz. I caught up with them. An old man, nearly seventy, and his daughter. I asked them gently: 'Where are you going?' 'To present ourselves. We have had enough!' I swear to you, this is what they said. So I told them quietly: 'Then please come with me.' We walked together like companions. At the Platz I reported with them to Rommelmann. Oh, Almighty God, what have I done! It's the whole truth, what I have told you. I swear to you. They were going in the direction of the Platz and when I asked where they were going, they answered, to present themselves. I swear by this day of Yom Kippur, that is what they said. But what does it matter? I should have told them not to surrender. To go back and hide. Instead I accompanied them onto the Platz and handed them over. I'm guilty of their death. I led them to death. Oh, my God what have I done! It's so much better to die, as I wanted. Oh, Judge of all the earth, what shall I answer at the day of judgement? What shall I say when brought before thy Court?"

–"What did your brother tell him?" Hugo wanted to know.

–"I didn't ask him. Knowing his sensibility and subtlety, I was certain he said nothing.

"They'll say something, our free brothers, who have never experienced situations like that, who have never known Aktion. They'll sit in judgement and pass sentence."

CHAPTER TWENTY-ONE

–"Now it won't last much longer," in so many words Hauptscharführer Schrade greeted Kurt Semmel on his arrival at the Bildstelle yesterday morning. The matter-of-course manner in which Schrade thus referred to the Allied invasion of France finally decided in favour of those prisoners who in the past have maintained that he knew about the radio. Indeed, we heard of "D-day" two hours before Schrade came to the workshop at ten in the morning. The news spread with the impact of a thunderbolt. Some men were howling with joy, others abandoned their seats, as if the hour of going home had struck. But later in the day we calmed down to a mood of solemn delight.

On the other side Schrade was in a mood that urged him to confide his thoughts to somebody, and he made Semmel listen for more than an hour to an extemporaneous, yet apparently privately rehearsed soliloquy. According to Semmel's summary, Schrade's reaction to the invasion was practically that of "At long last". He kept repeating in different words the magic formula "the war will now end soon". However the main proposition of his monologue was that the fighting no longer makes sense. The war was lost a long time ago, the landing in France merely brings the fact home dramatically, demonstrating the hopeless military situation. To continue fighting now, to sacrifice the lives of countless people (German people he means of course) in a futile war is madness. To deny defeat, still to expect a reversal, to speak of victory, when this merely endangers the future of the nation, one must have a screw loose - Schrade was thus, in Semmel's understanding, imputing madness namelessly but unmistakably, to the Führer. It would be the height of madness to dissipate forces by continuing to fight on two fronts, now that the landing in Normandy makes surrender to the western Allies practicable (which would probably explain his "at long last" attitude). It is false to talk of "a road of no return" and that "1918 won't happen again", which is the official propaganda line.

They should now, he maintains, hold the front against Soviet Russia with all their forces, and allow the Anglo-Americans to occupy all German territory. Though the Western leaders make this regrettably difficult by insisting on unconditional surrender. This is stupid of them. It will only result in delivering most of Europe to communist rule. Yet, as defeat is certain, to fight to the last (even against the Russians apparently) only means to prolong senseless bloodshed and risk total disaster. The future of the nation requires that what can still be saved must be salvaged from the wreckage - national heritage, the towns, the population, the maximum number of both soldiers' and civlians' lives (his fellow countrymen).

When towards what proved to be the end of this outpouring, Semmel ventured during one of Schrade's longer pauses to ask him: "What'll happen to us?" the SS man, not wanting to spell out the worst nor to be deceitful in raising false hopes, replied hesitatingly: "I don't know what the orders will say." Upon this, Semmel asked him boldly: "Will you, Herr Hauptscharführer, shoot me if the orders say fire?" Schrade did not think long before answering in the way his kind speak, though in a lowered, plaintive voice: "*Mensch, Mensch* (man, man), d'you know what an order is?"

So here you have an SS man who is not a fanatic (not any longer at least) and who admits that the Germans are beaten; who does not fully share the indifference to human lives and suffering of the troop whose uniform he wears; who does not even consider the killing of Jews a patriotic duty; and yet he would obey every order, to kill, probably not just foes, but his compatriots as well, if the "order says so".

Marek Rainer suggested that SS men are formed, like monsters from another world, of a compound all their own and are therefore inscrutable to ordinary men. While I would not claim to grasp fully the chemistry of SS men's minds, the truth requires me to say that this dismal business of executing every order is not the monopoly of the SS - though probably no other body of men has anywhere near such a large share of it. While the thought occupies our minds completely, we have little illusion about what the orders will say, or that "our" Pustkow SS men, who do not kill or even torture on their own initiative, will finish us off, if they are ordered to. But there is a brighter side to Schrade's confidential profession of political faith, and we prefer to talk about this at the camp.

After all, he belongs to the vanguard of the Nazi movement, for whom whatever the Führer did or said was eternally right and sacred; Schrade personally must once have been seduced into taking the oath of absolute loyalty. Now this recently most faithful servant of the Führer has failed him, suggesting that he is mad to endanger the German nation; and he says that to continue the war and to shed blood is senseless. Probably millions of like-minded Nazis, soldiers and ordinary Germans, all of whom once blindly and proudly backed the Führer as their greatest leader in history, must now, as things go not so well and military disaster follows upon military disaster, be sharing Schrade's view and national programme; but they cannot find a Jew, a KZ inmate at that, to tell and thus cannot show Schrade's courage.

All this, it would be perfidious to deny, is a little encouraging to us; while Hitler would, of course, consider all those millions of his faithless countrymen unworthy of him and his ideals. But he would not include among them his generals. For they, no less heel-clicking before him than his death-head-capped warriors, continue, unlike Schrade, under the spell of their Führer, and remain indifferent to the senseless bloodshed and destruction, though they know as well as Schrade that the war is irreversibly lost for them.

Listening patiently to this evaluation, Marek broke his silence to ask in his usual pessimistic way: "And if they, too, did bolt? Would that do us any good?"

–"Yes, it would. It's certainly the most hopeful turn of events one could imagine. Orders refused. All bloodshed ceased, including the butcher's war against the Jews."

–"Not to finish it?"

–"Of course that's not certain - nothing is certain. But surely it's the great moment we are waiting for?"

–"Reasonably?" Having failed to elicit an immediate answer, Marek continued: "Of course one feels better for the knowledge of their break up. But to us, will it bring liberty or death?"

This was the big question and one which I was not inclined to answer; being myself not too sanguine about the outcome, though unwilling to admit it to Marek, I changed the subject: "We'll see, at least now that things have started moving in the West, it can't take much longer."

Aware of the emotions the invasion in France has aroused in nearly all of us, and of how near and dear the Allied armies are to our hearts, although they are so far away in space, I expected Marek to accept my prevarication with good grace. But he did not.

–"You're not your usual self, the reputed 'strategist'. You know, the invasion can't help us."

I did. I know that we can be liberated only by the Russians. This certainty probably prompted Knepel's response to the invasion for he repeated that the Russians can beat the Germans all by themselves. Some Poles' reaction, according to Brzostek, is that, to overcome the distance problem, the Allies will now land a million-strong army from the air. As for myself, although my mind rejects this as wishful thinking, I keep the belief in the recesses of my heart, sustaining it with signs and tokens. It is amazing how hope and energy are stirred by such fantasies. In this vein, I told Marek; "There's a good omen."

This drew an unexpectedly angry reply from him today.

–"You'll send a man into the grave with your good omens." He was so annoyed that he did not want to know what the omen was.

By a peculiar sense of caution - or was it tact? - birds would not even so much as stray into the space of the camp, as they never did into that of the ghetto. Yesterday during the lunch-break, I saw for the first time in two years - not a dream I assure you - a little bird freely and proudly fluttering its wings high above our cage.

To do Marek justice, there are times when he completely forgets to be pessimistic, and the frailty that engenders this amnesia is something I like best in him. Strictly speaking, it is nothing more than a nostalgic memory - the memory of a girl, which has left an apparently indelible imprint on his imagination. It is a reverie that comes round again and again in his mind. In favourable conditions for dreaming he likes to talk of her, without overtly expending any emotion.

He always speaks of her in the present tense, as of someone absent or lost, not

297

deceased. She may not be, for all he knows, but rather only in the dream; an inessential part of it. For, by dint of dreaming, his Jasia has lived all this time inside him, while he finds, as most of us do in different ways, precious moments of refuge from the years of oppressive loneliness.

11 June 1944

One becomes hardened to facts, however menacing, and does not take them seriously. This is how I explain to myself our coolness about the state of business at the Industriehof. To say that there is less to do every day would no longer be true, because there is now so little to do as to make any lessening undiscernible. And yet we are unconcerned, insolently unconcerned. Gone are the days of qualms and fear and of the self-pity I felt because of my chronic idleness. How stupid now seems the thought of justifying my stay at camp by work! True, I still consider it prudent to be on my guard at the workshop. But it is now Klause and Saar and the other SS masters who pretend not to see that we do not work; while we have strangely stopped asking whether they will keep us here for nothing. It could almost be really true that our Pustkow bosses need us more than we need them, as Maniek Lander remarked jokingly at our bridge game the other day. My friend Marek, who, until recently used to be fully employed and able to earn perks, grumbles at the holiday atmosphere, as he calls it, which, he says, is dangerous; it allows us to be carried away by good news and brilliant weather, instead of being watchful. I told him that our lives do not, never did, depend on our watchfulness or mood, but on the Russians' coming. At the workshop, Knepel insists that the front is too near to make repair work necessary. But Hausdienst casts the blame for the lack of work on inactivity at the fronts, which reduces wear and tear. Any explanation is good enough for me, and the best is that the Germans are falling to pieces.

But the general idleness undeniably also has negative effects. Boredom has tangibly increased, while the frequency, and in particular the level, of our debates has declined. But I hope that I am not overdoing it if I say that the gravest consequence of the scandalous lack of repair-work is hygienic. There is no cloth for a patch, not a decent clout, to wrap round our feet. And remember summer is almost here. More than this. As the days have become fairly hot, Bubi announced that every night before sleep a foot inspection would be carried out either by him or by the barracks capo. Between Lagerschluss, when access to water ends, and "lights off" there are three hours during which enough vapour could form on miserly wrapped feet to provide Bubi or Krel with the opportunity to scold anyone they wished to pick on. The matter, however, aroused a major conflict of powers. As soon as he heard of the new injunction, Dr Vadovitzer vigorously protested that all matters of bodily hygiene lay within his sovereign competence - which claim Unterscharführer Zapke readily confirmed. Thus Bubi and his aides were forced to give in, and since Dr Vadovitzer has not the slightest interest in men's legs, especially in a nocturnal setting, the inspections ceased after only two nights. That is, except those incidental to the so-called *Schwanzparade*.

From the end of winter, at about monthly intervals, regularly on Sundays, we have to assemble at the infirmary for review of our naked bodies, with particular study of the hindmost private part. Since it has become warm, we march undressed in procession from the accommodation barracks to queue up outside the *Krankenstube* (infirmary), under the command of a capo. "Tails up!", bellows Krel, pleased with the quip's double entendre. There is nothing sinister, let alone lascivious, in the drill, but it is pretty humbling and gives ample opportunity for personal humiliation. This is not so much from Dr Vadovitzer, who can not be bothered to muster the naked parade. Though he does occasionally pop in, mainly to instil in us some respect for the place.

–"Don't you know where you are?"

Caught talking, Baicz, who had not met the doctor since his arrival from Szebnie, was too abashed to answer.

–"Is it your first visit to the infirmary?"

–"Yes, Herr Doctor."

–"So you haven't had it so bad here?" meaning Pustkow.

When an orderly drew his attention to a man's red pimples, Vadovitzer rebuffed: "He'll not die of it." Though he later ordered the man to be smeared with a sort of "balsam".

The chief abuser of the "parading" men, is the prisoner variably called hygienist, nurse, medic, but rarely by his family name of Chires, who is in actual charge of the assembly. Keen to assert his superiority, or occasionally to take revenge on a somewhat privileged mate - not a master, for they are excused the whole parade - Chires would take a tuft of cotton wool, dip it in alcohol and rub the arm of a prisoner with it to show that the cotton turned a shade of grey.

"How long since you last washed?"

–"Since this morning."

–"Whom are you trying to fool? We may have to give you a 'bath'."

Or someone whom the hygienist dislikes a little more, he will refer to the express attention of the barber's blunt clipper, adding in farewell: "You haven't had a 'haircut' for a long time. D'you want to get crab-lice?"

Most men pull a face at the taunts, yet are content to acquiesce. "None of this will matter, if we come out alive and can tell of it in joy," they say.

12 June 1944

As a matter of fact, Hauptscharführer Schrade is not the only SS man in Pustkow, who talks to Jewish prisoners confidentially, that is, not in the presence of another German. But the other SS men I hear about are much less eloquent and sophisticated than Schrade, and don't bother their heads about politics or strategy.

They have enough to worry about. With the war, as it seems, all but over, they are apprehensive of the future, above all of what they can expect of the Russians. Many must also have come to realize that they are now reduced, and if not now, then they shortly will be, to the status of beggars; and they give voice to this feeling by words and deeds - which arouse in us a feeling of even greater contempt for them. They all now beg if they want some more or less expensive thievish job to be done for them. While the camp-guards still pass their requests to the master-prisoners through Bubi and retain their tough, rude attitude, there are exceptions. SS Rottenführer Kaczorowski is one, and a peculiar case at that. A Polish miner in Belgium when the Germans occupied that country in 1940, he apparently calculated that life would be easier for him as a guard at a fresh air camp than digging coal in a dusty pit underground, so he joined the SS death squads. Now, his boats to Poland burnt, and wishing to burn those to Germany himself, this stooping SS man with the face of a troglodyte, is apparently so stupid as to put faith in a "Jewish future". You should see this killer's honeyed politeness when he now asks a prisoner if there is something he could do for him actually meaning would the prisoner, especially if it's a master, do something for him.

With the SS men of the Standortverwaltung the case is straightforward. They now offer guerdons of various kinds first, to barter for more valuable returns later, often asking what more they can do. None is more forthcoming than the SS Scharführer called by the prisoners derogatively Kune Lemel, the epithet for a misfit in the title of a play by Goldfaden. I do not know if Kune Lemel in the SS uniform is a misfit, but he is so misshapen that he strikes a comic figure. At least he also behaved tamely in the past, and, as he holds in the upholstery workshop a position parallel to Saar's at the tailors, he has neatly provided Maniek with provisions in return for the stolen materials he received from him. Lately, Kune Lemel does not know what bribe to invent, and two weeks ago brought Maniek a pack of cards.

So that when I mentioned yesterday that Maniek said something "at the bridge game", this was not a joke. It really sounds absurd, so much so that I had misgivings about recording it, were I not committed to telling the truth. "Is this really a concentration camp?" I have been asking myself lately. My friend Marek, in his disheartening encouragement of my memorizing, told me: "By writing about Pustkow you could only hand down an unreal, distorted picture of German camps." He is right, of course. The Pustkow of my days is entirely unrepresentative of the KZ culture. But I replied that exceptions prove the rule; also that the first thing is to be able to tell about the camps at all and then to have qualms about having survived. This requires the good luck of "enjoying" a camp like Pustkow, or, though others may not wish to admit it, exceptional Pustkow-like conditions at one of the deadly camps. Otherwise how could its inmates, especially a Jew, survive them?

Bridge itself is not such a delight as it might seem. Sitting slightly crooked on the bunk, legs hanging down, and waiting for the laggard Herszkowicz to play, makes one lose patience. And there is the scruple of playing cards in our circumstances. But, apart from killing boredom, which, to put it extravagantly, helps one to survive - oh, one can always find excuses - we are the only four in the whole barracks who know the game, on which Maniek Lander is very keen. No less tempting is the status that goes with the game. And how gratifying it is to watch the grudging-grievous face of Krel on seeing an ordinary prisoner like me playing cards! He is constrained to say nothing, because the game is put down entirely to the account of Maniek who is a master, and one who from time to time throws Krel a titbit, at that. Thus, since the beginning of the month, we play bridge almost every other evening after Lagerschluss.

15 June 1944

Among the things with which the SS men reward their elite prisoners, there is something which is plainly corrupting. I mean the cheap novels and magazines which are the staple "literature" of those SS men. "Cheap" in this instance is a rather generous rating. For these are stereotyped stories, of no literary merit, dealing with savage crime and pornography of the most sordid kind, potent enough to fuel lewd, sadistic desires. This is what they read; this is what they are willing to share with their chosen slaves, in the sincere belief that they are doing them a great favour. As they, the powerful bosses, suffer from boredom themselves, they rightly judge that the prisoners must be similarly afflicted. But what they misjudge, as it is probably unthinkable to them - the "bearers of culture" - is that most of their contemned captives would not allow themselves to be corrupted by the "literature" bestowed on them. Maniek Lander and Olek Platnik, the head mechanic, either return the filth after a few days untouched, or after they have in the meantime relent it to Krel. Indeed the capos, who as the idlest of the privileged prisoners are most bored, have been the principal readers of this stuff along with some of the intellectuals, such as Olkowicz. Bubi in particular is showered with it by Ruf and other guards, incidentally, in breach of camp orders. Also Zapke takes good care to provide Dr Vadovitzer with this mental pabulum, but whether he consumes it or not I do not know.

If what our SS bosses read is an abuse of language, what they speak is its advanced degeneration. And because of its personal impact, it is potentially more corrupting. The spoken word has always been more persuasive than the written one. The language a man uses is naturally bound up with his inner life and is circumscribed by the range of his thinking. This, first, shows up in those SS men's strikingly limited vocabulary. Their dialogue consists, it would seem, of only a few dozen words, by far the most frequent of which is *los*. This word of many senses, foremost an interjection but employed by them as injunction, is apparently sufficiently expressive of their consciousness and with some supplementary gestures, is enough to convey everything they mean to say. With one exception, which is the second distinctive feature of their language. This is the stock of swear words, the wealth of which is in such contrast to the poverty of their total vocabulary. My friend Marek observed the other day that it sometimes seems to him that "in their language, apart from *los*, all one can do is curse." And, it appears to me, the whole language of theirs is geared to power - above all power over us.

All this would not matter a farthing to me, were it not for the infectious nature of this language that we are condemned to listen to. It manifests itself in the speech of our capos, through whom more often than directly from the jailers most of us learn the whole glossal glibness of that language. They, too, enjoy the power that comes from cursing. Particularly now that our living conditions are such that there is hardly any opportunity for the physical manifestation of power. More remarkable, however, than the imitating of this language, is our resistance to it. Apart from a few prisoners, such as the mentally immature Kulik and Kichel, to whom apeing the capos is attractive, there is a strange moderation in our use of words; the overwhelming majority do not employ coarse language, not even those who, as I've said before, did speak coarsely before the war. I have never heard any of the workshop masters throw a curse at a fellow prisoner. Since the days that hunger began to retreat and the fronts to advance, attempts to achieve status by speaking German have become less and less common. Biegel oddly denies he speaks the same language as the SS men; his is, he says, the unpolluted German tongue. Even Hugo avoids speaking German, if he does not have to, because of his disgust for the language the bosses speak. Marek, musing the other evening over brutality latent in speech, asked obscurely if the best thing were not to speak at all?

This is not the answer; there are other ways of self-defence from this cursedness and general degradation of our lives at camp. I found one in a little book quite dissimilar to theirs. It was brought to Pustkow from Biesiadka by Sender Pintel, a teenage boy who occupies a bunk next but one to mine. Not long after my arrival, during the worst period of our stay here, I suggested to him that instead of my borrowing his phylacteries and prayer-book every day, he could borrow them from me and for the transfer of tenure get two days' bread ration. It was the best bargain I have ever made. I also correctly estimated from close observation of his daily progress at camp that quite soon he would not feel the need to borrow them at all. It is a small sized prayer-book, but it contains the Psalms and Pirkei Aboth (Ethics of the Fathers), just plain text without any commentary. It has become my daily practice to read short parts of these gems during lunch break and for about thirty minutes almost every evening. What a treasure! What a different world from ours! What a relief it is to think of other things than our personal miseries! By now, I have learned the whole of the "Ethics" and half of the Psalms by heart. When I mentioned this to Marek, he inquired jokingly if I will want to leave Pustkow before I know all the Psalms by heart?

–"This would be the one thing worth having been here for. But seriously, I wonder about this ability to memorize so quickly here. It's like regaining the powers of childhood."

–"Perhaps - it often occurs to me that you imagine things like a small child."

–"Imagination or not, this ability could be the result of living for so long without having anything to read. Returning partially to the age of exclusive oral communication when human memory was, compared with our times, so prodigious."

–"Does it make you exult? I mean, because it might help you to memorize the things you want to immortalize?"

–"If I were you I would wait to prove that I was wrong before rejoicing."

16 June 1944

"Today theatre and perhaps tomorrow the pit," shouted Marek in doubtful indignation. His present outcry was in reaction to the news I brought him yesterday that there was a theatrical performance later in the evening. This sounds crazy, but I am in my right mind. The news was true.

How the idea was conceived - at the tailors' of course - and kept secret for days, is not important; how it was turned into fact may be interesting enough to narrate. Even though I have not personally been to the show. While rebutting Marek's strictures by pointing out that everyone tries to deaden unpleasant reality, I myself had an unsavoury feeling about the matter. Theatre at the scene of recent mass murder? But why not? Is it so very different from playing bridge? Perhaps both are morally wrong, but are they inexcusably wrong? It is done not at the jailers' command - like the compulsorily attended concerts performed by inmates at Grzimek's orders in the JULAG of Lwow - but on the contrary, it is carried out clandestinely under their noses. Has it not the same defiant quality as praying or remaining loyal to our past and customs?

No, these were not the true reasons why I have not been to the performance, nor was it because it took place in the other barracks - as the capos exceptionally winked at someone who changed his quarters that night. The reason was a certain distaste for the programme. To listen for the umpteenth time to Srebrny's melodic nostalgia for Mamie Russia? Or to listen to his artistic ardour, as Yekl Tshapshovitz, the brothel owner, taking vengeance on God for the seduction of his daughter by a client, in a scene from "Got of Nekume"?

The rest of the repertoire included the central scene from "Yoshe Kalb" and a fragment from "Bei Nacht oifn alten Markt". In the musical part, classical delights such as "Di Mechitunim gehn", "Oifn Pripetsil", or "Motke der Marviche" were sung. The cast, apart from Srebrny, included Froim Fessel, a former member of a dramatic circle of the Zukunft youth organization, and three or four other, less accomplished amateur actors. Dichter, bowing to the insistent requests of his workshop masters, agreed to sing some songs, other than hymns, that were close to his heart.

On stage, the actors appeared without make-up, though in a sort of costume made from linen sheets, which Krohn, apparently with no dissent from Bubi, lent for the occasion. Decor was furnished by blankets hung up neatly from bunks, which also formed the side stays of the stage. The stage itself was built from boards smuggled in from the workshop. Carpenters, tailors, upholsterers, etc., all gave a helping hand to stage the show. It was performed to the maximum standing capacity of the largest room, causing not a bit of a squash. The curtain fell, it is said, to the general applause of two hundred spectators. Today I regret that I was not one of them, so that I could tell you more of this extraordinary theatrical event.

20 June 1944

Aeroplanes are entering the bounds of our perception and from this many of us tend to infer that the battle fronts are moving nearer. We can hear the planes but only rarely see their shapes on the clear horizon. These are probably German planes, but we prefer to think they are Russian. Brzostek, however, says, from sources he at least considers trustworthy, that from about the beginning of this month the Western Allies have had permission to fly over Soviet air space and land at one of its air bases. Simultaneously he also passed on the information that trains full of Jews are again arriving day and night at the death camps in Poland. The coincidence of this news with the noise from the sky has provided us with a new subject, which although not directly related to our present or past lives has, nevertheless, occasioned excited discussion. There was no disputing that the Jews, whose sad turn had now come, were from Germany's satellite countries. It was equally uncontroversial that, despite their military set-backs, the Germans can still afford the luxury of diverting so many trains to transporting Jews, which must present quite a logistical problem. But this surprises no one since the destruction of the Jews is one of the supreme war aims of Hitler and his Hunnish chums. The question we debated was, in a nutshell: can Jews within the German power orbit, who are still alive, be saved? Or their death at least delayed? There is no need to explain that the question referred to our Western Allies, who now, unlike in earlier years, have undisputed supremacy in the air over the retreating, nearly defeated Germans, and the range of whose planes now extends far enough to reach Poland or indeed any other part of Europe easily. The question did not include the Soviets, who are much nearer to Poland, not out of regard for Knepel and his fellow sympathisers, but because it did not occur to any one of us that Stalin would undertake military operations for the sake of Jews, or perhaps for any other group of people, if this was not in the direct interest of his state or party. With regard to the Western Allies, most of us, like most of the Jews in the outside world, have not yet shed our illusions. So it was with genuine misapprehension that Berl Alter asked: " How could the Americans and the English save them?"

Osterman who joined the discussion early on answered with unusual discernment:

–"First, they could destroy the railway lines leading to the death camps; second, they could destroy the camps themselves."

–"With the inmates?" asked Hugo provocatively.

"They're doomed to die anyway," rejoined Hausdienst.

But Osterman corrected himself, to explain that he meant the camps' killing machinery.

–"But would that prevent the death of the Jews involved?"

It was this contentious question of Hugo's which really sparked off the controversy. Most of the mates answered the question in the affirmative but that does not necessarily mean that they were in the right.

Firstly, taking Osterman's points in order - the bombing of railways. This, the supporters claimed, could put the lines out of action, and, since it would take plenty of time to put them back in order, would considerably retard the transporting part of the murderous undertaking. This reasoning was vigorously disputed by Hugo, who quoted in his own support facts, which no one could prove or refute, allegedly confirming that tracks near the front lines, which were frequently bombed, were repaired within a day. And, he asked, could one seriously expect the Allies to divert their air forces from active war for long enough to keep the railways carrying the death trains permanently disrupted? When Alter in turn asked with unaffected innocence, if in the chaos following the bombing of the trains the "passengers" could not escape to safety, everyone burst out laughing, however disrespectful this was to the workshop master. They were probably expressing their hardwon knowledge that but for a lucky few, escape had no chance of succeeding. Or, as Dichter, trying to be witty, put it: "As if the dead needed to flee for safety." However when Hugo suggested that a far more practical and effective way of disruption than bombing would be the withdrawal of work by the railwaymen running the death trains, all curiously remained silent; though this was just as fanciful an idea as Alter's, since it tacitly called for open rebellion, which none of the occupied, let alone satellite, nations were more inclined to risk than the Allies were to bomb the railways.

The second suggestion, to bomb the death installations inside the camps, had drawn more varied questions. Apart from the obvious difficulty of locating the installations and precision-bombing them from the air, there was the objection that Hugo Bester's provocative question had already raised, the poignancy of which Hausdienst's rejoinder had not diminished. Hugo later reinforced his argument by saying that the Allied Command was understandably reluctant to participate in the possible killing of camp inmates; not just Jews, who, in his view, form our only concern, but many non-Jews, who have a good chance of surviving the war. And they might well be killed because, as Hugo rightly noted, the camps are now largely populated by nationals other than Jews, while it was Jews alone of all the people arriving there who are being exterminated.

This argument, however, carried little conviction with most of the debaters. They countered that the Allied Army Command don't care a damn about prisoners in these camps; what they care about is their own possible losses in men and material, which is why they do not try to destroy the deadly apparatus inside the camps; besides, bombing the camps could be seen as proof that they are raiding civilian targets, which, despite the razed German towns, the Allies deny doing. However, the debaters also claimed that if they did destroy the death installations, rebuilding them would take some time, during which the process of extermination would at least temporarily be slowed down, and thus many lives be saved. And who knows, perhaps it would not be possible to reconstruct the installations with all their apparatus before the end of the war?

During all this discussion I listened quietly, but when Osterman asked why the Germans had built such costly, intricate structures and why they used gas to kill, I was stirred to answer, incidentally touching upon the earlier debate. Yet I was forestalled by Deker, who asserted that the installations were just a function of fascist power. "The machinery is part of what is termed technological progress. And that the most reprehensible kind of murder is committed with it shows what modern technology can be used for in the hands of powerful barbarians."

Knepel as usual tried to improve on Deker: "The German fascists just want to commit a new, more spectacular kind of murder, and to do it at maximum speed. They're in a hurry, you can't deny that."

However, Hugo maintained that the only reason for constructing this machinery of death was the Germans' desire to keep the killings as secret as possible. "It could be that it's done more quickly by these means and also that it's technologically innovative. But its main purpose is to do the murders unobserved and so to reduce to a minimum the number of men involved in it, on the one hand, and on the other, minimize the sickness they might feel at performing the butchery."

When at last it was my turn to put in a word, I first referred to Hugo's remark. "The desire for secrecy implies in this case scruples and shame. They aren't ashamed of what they're doing. On the contrary, they're proud of it." And, recalling a speech of Himmler's which I had read during the Clean Up, I added: "They consider the killings an unwritten page of glory. And the use of technology and gas makes it more glorious. They feel no disgust in doing the job - they delight in it. There may be some exceptions - the master-killer, Himmler, is himself said to faint at the sight of blood - but such individuals can always excuse themselves from the job. Anyway, the technology and its trappings provide the Germans with an excellent opportunity of displaying their organizational talent and proverbial efficiency, of which they are as pleased as punch.

"There's no denying that they're in a hurry to finish the job thoroughly. But whether killing by gas is the quickest method, or the most reprehensible, is doubtful." And I went on to argue my case in detail.

I began by saying that there are good reasons to believe - though firm evidence will only be found in German archives after the war - that Hitler and his advisers on the subject of extermination initially intended to carry it out by other means than gas. I called it "the p.o.w. method". This was a reference to the story told by the mates in Pustkow of the way the Russian p.o.ws were destroyed. What the master-killers intended was, as soon as the war in the East started, to round up all the Jews under German power, to herd them onto trains, and, travelling under the protection of the quickly advancing army, to transport them deep into the Soviet Union. There, in the remote regions of the country, in its vast empty, uninhabited expanses, the Jews were to be unloaded and held without food and water, perhaps stripped of their clothes, in an open space, surrounded by a fence and SS guards. Men who were strong enough might still have been forced to do some work outside the fence. But even the strongest could not survive in those conditions for more than a few months in the summer, and a few weeks in the freezing cold of winter, before dying from disease and starvation.

That we have been mercifully spared death by this most horrible method, we of course owe to the upset in the war against Russia, for the German advance was practically halted, after only four months, at a relatively small distance inside the prewar borders of the Soviet Union. To support this view, I mentioned the fact, that it was only after the German leaders realized that their plans had gone wrong, that they introduced the first gassing in vans at Chelmno. This was before the end of 1941; and simultaneously they embarked on the construction of the deadly installations at various camps in Poland, although the decision to exterminate the Jews had been taken years before.

This long exposition drew lively objections from most of the mates, who reproached me for inconsistency.

–"Surely if they intended to kill the Jews deep in Russia, away from human habitation, then this was precisely because it secured maximum secrecy and the minimum number of butchers to carry out the job," shouted Hugo triumphantly.

–"You admit the speed motive,"Knepel accused me, "but to carry out the job in the way you have described, to transport millions of victims hundreds of miles, would have required vast numbers of scarce rolling-stock, and thus made the whole job last for who knows how long. Certainly longer than using the gas method."

This criticism did not perturb me. I felt that in this instance I could afford to be both right and wrong in the same argument. Besides, I had a reply up my sleeve.

–"This isn't a matter of perspective, with you seeing it differently from me. The plan of moving the victims to die deep in the Soviet Union doesn't prove either a wish for secrecy or consideration for the sentiments of the killers. The great advantage of the p.o.w. method over other methods was its low cost, low effort and, probably decisive, high potential for deception."

Turning to Knepel, I said: "If speed was really so important, there's the 'Siller method'."

–"What's that?" several voices cried out in unison.

–"It's in honour of an SS man. I don't know his Christian name, nor do I know his rank, but his family name is Siller. He may have established a world record. On Monday, 24th May, 1943, during the Aktion in Lwow, he personally shot two thousand seven hundred people."

Seeing expressions of disbelief on their faces, I continued:

–"I know, you think it incredible, and I'm inclined to think it incredible, too. But I must tell you, sadly, it's true; the information came from an utterly reliable source.

"On that scale of murder - speed aside - a mere hundred men armed with machine guns...work it out for yourself. They applied this method elsewhere but mostly with fewer than a hundred 'Sillers' in battle position. Take Kiev for an example, thirty-four thousand were shot in just two days. Nearer home, on the first day of the first Aktion in Tarnow, Rommelmann is said to have killed about eight hundred people with his own hands. When, towards the end, he ran out of ammunition, he used an iron pipe that happened to be handy to complete his task on schedule.

"I mention all this here to make you understand how spurious, if not grotesque, is the idea that bombing the railway lines to the death camps, or the installations inside them, could stop, or at least delay significantly, the murder of Jews from the satellite countries. In anger, in despair, it's natural for people to clutch at straws, and to extend the blame for one's misfortunes to others. Now, in 1944, that the Allies are triumphant, if they urged the satellite nations and their leaders to protect the Jews in their countries from the Germans, this might have some positive results. But bombing?

"And if the railways and the gas installations were disrupted, there is nothing to prevent the Germans from re-adjusting quickly to the situation and adopting a mixture of the Siller and p.o.w. methods. And thus probably completing their job in even less time.

307

"After all, you should know by now, that of all the murdered Jews, about two million were killed by the Siller method - well, to be precise, killed by the special commando units of the SS and Security Police, which were operating in the territories conquered during the Eastern campaign.

—"So why did they switch to gas?" asked Osterman.

—"Perhaps because Hitler and company were not sufficiently aware of their men's potentials to rely entirely on the Siller method. Perhaps because, as Knepel said, the thing was so spectacular and innovative. Perhaps also because Hitler wanted to be remembered by the gas structures he built in the camps as much as by the other monumental buildings he erected, and planned to erect, in German towns."

As Hugo tried to cast doubt on my words, I hastened to finish.

—"I told you that these structures were a matter of pride to him. In case of victory, and nothing but victory has ever existed for him, he was sure that they would be admired by his countrymen and many others in the whole of his vanquished world. That 'Might is always right' is the first fundamental of his creed, which he has often affirmed. And 'who is right is admired', would, to him, logically follow.

"One thing is, however, true, that as regards the human circumstances of the killings, by which I mean the suffering of the victims, the Siller method is the mildest one. To get it done, if done it must be, by a single shot, was the wish of everyone in the ghetto. As for the Siller variations, for example being forced to undress and lie down in a grave one had dug for oneself in a sandpit before receiving the bullet of release - whether this, too, was preferable to gas, we can't fortunately, say, as we haven't yet experienced either."

—"And we had the good fortune not to witness at close quarters one of those methods being applied to our families," concluded Hausdienst.

He was, of course, referring only to Pustkow old-timers like himself.

29 June 1944

Dear Ben Gurion!Forgive my impertinence in writing to you so unceremoniously. Our sages of old, you may know, used to refer to the greatest among them simply by name. You appear to me to tower head and shoulders above the myriad of our exalted leaders who busy themselves all over the world. This is why I have chosen to address this letter to you.

Now, I'll come right to the point. It has come to my hearing that you have recently asked our western Allies to do anything to help us, your enslaved compatriots, in a way that will not be of any advantage to the enemy or prejudice the war effort.

I am frankly perplexed and must ask you - all this hedging and cushioning still in mid-June 1944? Even now, when nothing the Allies do to help us could be of such an advantage to the enemy as to delay the hour of his defeat? Is there anything humanly possible that the Allies could do to help us which might not be claimed to be prejudicing their war effort?

And honestly, this "prejudice", or whatever advantage to the enemy, is it really your overriding concern? I understand very well that your main concerns are different from ours, who are smouldering behind the enemy lines, and yet I can not help asking you, as the question fills my mind - does it require so much courage to tell the Allies straight out that to help the captive Jews accords with their war aims and can not possibly prejudice their war efforts? Privately they might even appreciate such an "unpatriotic" but sincere approach more than requests in the words you've used - which they possibly see as a mere doubtful plea for help. Anyway, how can we expect the Allies to do more than you ask of them?

Of course, I have a notion of what your answer might be - the Allies were not inclined to help, protest was ineffective and pointless, too much agitation could only damage the highest aim, to build a national home in Eretz Israel, while in the end, even if the Allies wished it, they could not deliver us from the Germans.

This last point was probably true in the past. But now? When mere threats could prove a deterrent? Not that the Allies could save us in Pustkow, or our like elsewhere - but those who are not yet past help, the people rushed every day to death in their thousands by train? It is the thought of them that impels me to write to you. Admittedly I do not know if they can be saved. But not to try? The mere thought of this question is hard to bear.

Even were it true, as you say, that rescuing Jews and building the national home are two different concepts - are they contradictory? Regardless of your claim, or shall I say your pretence, that Zionism is responsible for the fate of all the Jewish people - for whom is the Home created? Who will remain to knock at its gates?

And yet, even if we here cannot be saved, certainly not by anything you could undertake, do you know what a comfort it would have been to us to have a word of your sympathy or encouragement? If not from the heart, then from the brain. As future generations may not understand your silence. "Why not?" The question, passing down from the fathers to the sons, joined with a judgement that you may come to regret.

Concepts and symbolic sympathy aside, there is one other question I desire to ask you before I die. Do you really think that we - that is our tormented dead today and tomorrow - preferred the life of a beaten dog? It is true that we die without actively defending ourselves, but do we die like rags? I know that you are too careful to say this yourself. But to pass over the words of your close friends in silence makes me think that you agree - if you agree - with them. Entre nous, are not these accusations an expression of common Zionist, specifically Eretz Israel Zionist patriotism? Or do they just intimate a feeling, cherished by so many people, of personal and collective superiority? In either case it is misguided. What could you know - if you want to know - of the horror and mysteries of protracted death and suffering? What could you know, you who do not "live" our deaths - if it leaves you cold I do not know - of efforts, in the face of ineffable evil, to make a good end? Or of sacrifices made in willing to live on?

To try to explain this, our lives and deaths, is my dearest wish. Alas, I can not in this letter. But let me tell you this - if you will listen - that the strongest hearts are no match for machine-guns. And that in our unusual circumstances, incomprehensible to you, it required great fortitude to acquit ourselves responsibly, to depart silently and in a singular manner, perpetuating with our deaths something more lasting and humane than rebellion or fighting - even under one's own flag - for the good of our people and of all mankind.

And finally a not too modest request: Not that you die a slow death before the "eyes of the world" to awaken its conscience, as our desperate people in the ghettos naively suggested. I know your life is priceless and promising, theirs and mine has been cheap and cheerless. The request I make of you, the survivor of this catastrophe, is not to express false sentimentality over our fate. Please do not make martyrs of us; we are not "sainted dead", we do not qualify for that. Our history is too bright and rich to need to be based on myth and heroism. By all means articulate our loss, fortify with our blood and suffering your holy claim to a Home of our own. But do it wisely, with dignity; do not lay yourself open, as others regrettably have, to the charge of imitating Gogol's scheme for the dead souls.

Accept the assurance of my respect and best wishes for success in your great aim.

CHAPTER TWENTY-TWO

How strange are these days we now live through! So unlike the dull, drab days of our recent past. As time once stood still, so it now flows in long strides. Somehow the air is reminiscent of those equally beautiful, hot summer days a year ago, before the last Aktion. The same anxious waiting and uncertainty of life. And yet there is a difference. These days now also breathe with hope, the tender hope of liberation which is more reasoned and better founded than at any time in the war.

It is now ten days since the Russians resumed their offensive and advance. It is this, rather than the summer, that raises the temperature and fires our hope. "What news from the fronts?" is now the starting point of every conversation. And in this exciting atmosphere more frequent demands are made of me for comment on the meagre news that reaches us. I try to do my best, in pleasant awareness of being wanted and being helpful in lowering the fever, but it stretches the powers of my imagination beyond limits. Inevitably my words are hollow, of little content, but they cheer the hearts. "Three years precisely, almost to the day," I tell my mates. "What a sense of historical timing! Only now the roles are completely reversed. Then the Germans were the attackers, thrusting, conquering, triumphing. Now they are retreating in defeat, the Russians pushing them ever further back. Every day brings them closer to us and the final hour draws nearer."

Osterman, while clearly delighted, also gave vent to his disappointment by asking why the Russians did not strike on "our" front? As if I were privy to the Russians' strategic plans! But as I was expected to answer, I told him: "You're quite right. The Russians were at Kowel farthest to the west on our front, which they call Ukrainian. So your question is quite logical. But where is logic in war?

"When they started their latest offensive, the Russians had already re-conquered virtually all their prewar territory. Shortly before this, they were attacking on the flanks" (what a flashy word, I thought) "of which 'we' form one. Now they have decided to strike on a broad front at the centre, towards the Vistula, further on to Warsaw, on the road to Berlin. But they can't ignore the other fronts and leave all Galizia behind. So they'll extend their offensive in our direction, too. They must!"

But Marek was not so sure. The Russians, he said, may run out of steam, get stuck in a sort of war of attrition, as the Allies did after their landings in the west, before they managed to attack successfully elsewhere. That was just pessimism; what really worries him, as it does all of us, is not Russian strategy or the pace of their advance, but the bearing of this latest tide of war on our lives. It does not matter any longer to us how long it lasts. Time for us has lost all meaning except in relation to our survival. All our present thoughts are condensed into just one question - what will the approaching German debacle bring us: death or liberation? From whichever front they are hammered, I told Marek, the signs are that the end is near. "Yes," he replied seizing upon the imprecision of my talk, "but the end we hope for, or the end we want to escape?" While I am myself not too confident about the answer, I refused to admit it. Deep inside me, I carry the undying belief in our continuity. At the same time I sense the tenuity, if not absurdity of this belief. Far from assenting to fatalism, at least philosophically, I cannot avoid musing about the prankish quality of man's fortune. To survive five years of pain and tears, to endure all the suffering and sorrow of this world, only to perish a day before the end of war. Hm!

19 July 1944

We are counting the days. At least that is something to keep us busy. Not an easy occupation, I can assure you. And even less easy in this state of strained nerves and permanent waiting is maintaining order and the appearance of normality. The days are full of rousing events, though what exactly happens we do not know. The news that reaches us is patchy and, coming from German or western broadcasts about battles in the east, not too revealing. To sum up the significant points of it, as we hear it, what has lately changed is this. The Russian offensive has at last begun at "our" front in Galizia. It started either nine days ago, or perhaps three days later, when the Red Army recorded its first success in breaking through the latest German defence lines. It is very difficult to get an accurate picture of the battle positions, first, because what we regard as "our" front, the Russians apparently sub-divide into several sections, thrusting at each separately; second, because the many familiar places that are mentioned, and which fill us with joy, sometimes do not quite make positional sense and are perhaps deliberately disingenuous, so that a sus-picion intrudes about the veracity of the whole lot. But what seems certain is that yesterday the Russians again broke through the German defences and are advanc-ing rapidly in our direction. This latest break-through coincided with a new attack at (what the Russians call) the Byelorussian front, towards Lublin.

Thus we now suffer abrupt changes of mood every day: sweet euphoria alternating with depressing uncertainty and fear. We are euphoric about the Russians approaching and uncertain about its consequences for us; we are exhilarated about the German retreat and fearful that it is advancing the day of our demise or depar-ture. The whole agonizing suspense came eloquently through today in Maniek Lander's remark: "I wouldn't mind if we had to spend the rest of the war in Pustkow." This drew a rare humorous remark from Marek Rainer: "If the Russians don't free us, what right have they to encroach upon our camp?"

In the workshop, Hugo, trying to put on a brave face, or perhaps to give himself courage, asked: "Isn't it better to die than to live this life of slavery?" The question was certainly an insincere one, for we are all now definitely not satisfied with sim-ply witnessing the German collapse - we want to survive it. That our future depends, as Knepel says, on the speed of the Red Army's advance is one of those wisdoms which are either true or not. Osterman, in a quaint play of words, retorted: "If they don't come in time, the Russians will make us go with their coming."

If only they had come two years earlier, flashes through my mind. Are there now many more Jews, besides us, left to be liberated?

24 July 1944

Tension now extends into the night. The once tranquil nights reverberate in our heads with echoes of battle snatched during the day, and this arouses a strange desire to dream while still awake. An unchanging dream, an unchanging fear, heightened by the sounds ringing in our ears.

On Saturday, the day before yesterday, the Russians reached the San north of the town Jarosław, and have apparently established bridgeheads across the river on "our" side. The electrifying news has set our minds on fire. The San, besides its popular name and historical significance as part of the so-called Curzon-line - which Hitler and Stalin adopted as a provisional border on their partition of Poland in September 1939 - is the last natural obstacle on the road to us. And Jaroslaw is "in a straight line" merely 45 miles away from Pustków. Thus it was not surprising that no one demurred at my comment today in the workshop: "In this age of motorized warfare, 45 miles are hardly a day's ride." Besides, no one could deny the nearness of the front because of the muffled yet audible resonance of heavy gunfire in the air. However dangerous it is, even if we are hidden behind a barracks, we cannot suppress our latest passion to stretch out for a while and press our ears close to the ground to listen to the pounding tremble of the earth. Dear, dumb whispers of the nearing "end" and liberation, we prefer, despite all the doubts, to think.

Yet not one but two days have already passed and nothing has changed. Is it time, or the Red Army, that moves with such agonizing slowness - we ask as the waiting grows ever more oppressive. Waiting, as Marek put it, at the door revolving between death and life. This was before he heard Hugo repeating after Olkowicz, who could only have got the information from Bubi, that there is a standing order from Himmler to finish off all inmates of concentration camps on the approach of enemy forces, so that not one falls into the enemy's hands. The rumour has plunged even me into still greater gloom and prompted others as well as Marek to repeat like a litany "that it is useless to deceive ourselves". The only question is: "Shall we be finished off in Pustkow or out of it?"

Yet the irrational in man lives on even, or just in blackest despair. With us, one of its manifestations is the frequent talk, which has intensified since the rumour spread, of impossible escapes. Though, Osterman today asked: "Suppose they let us free, where could we go before the Russians come?" No one offered an answer. But I think that "escape" just satisfies for many of us the need to dream awake - the real escape from thoughts that are too hard to bear.

And so we are still waiting for a last minute miracle. Is it only an illusion as most of us overtly say, or rather a pious desire? Faith.

25 July 1944

We are in a true race with time. Every hour counts, we like to believe. The earth trembles faster, the pounding grows louder and louder, it seems to be coming from nearby. Perhaps it is still not too late? Our heart beats double. Knepel jokes that it is hypertension that will kill us rather than a bullet. But seriously, everyone is asking: will they have enough time to kill us?

Or, as the hours pass, will they themselves have enough time to flee?

PART FOUR

The Journey

CHAPTER TWENTY-THREE

The sudden noise roused Arush from deep sleep. The door opened. Krel burst in. "Up!" Everyone up, quickly! Roll-call at six."

Sooo... at six - Arush's brain began slowly to work. He descended quickly from the bunk and opened the windows. Another beautiful July morning looked in. The air was fresh, the sky blue, but it did not reveal the hour of the day.

—"A few minutes past five," said Maniek Lander.

There was nearly an hour to go, no need to hurry, thought Arush. And yet everyone was in a hurry and visibly excited. Arush felt slightly shivery.

—"You know, Marek, we should really be calm," he said, more to reassure himself than his friend. "It is not the first, and, perhaps, even not the last morning surprise we've had."

—"It's no surprise at all," protested Marek, "we have been expecting it any time since the good news began to come in."

—"Quite right. Indeed how often have we wondered what the next hour will bring? Moving away? Well - whatever is to happen will not miss us, wherever we may be."

None of this talk gave much relief. Arush looked round. All talk stopped. The tension in the room was so great it seemed as if it would burst the walls.

You should really be ashamed, he told himself. Who else had behaved like that? Mother? Father?...You must pull yourself together. And he ran out of the barracks.

Rebuking himself and recalling his dearest somewhat helped him to calm down. Fresh air and cold water did the rest. In the latrine and washroom, men were already engaged in conversation, fragments of which reached his ears.

—"They'll not move us from here."

—"Oh, surely not," retorted the usually tight-lipped Jakubek, "it'll be just a few yards, up there," pointing with his head to Hill 218, which today was not smoking.

—"So they will burn us, you say?" asked another man.

—"There's no question of moving us, it is too late," threw in Herszkowicz. "The Russians may be ahead of us. Anyway, they move faster than our rotten masters."

—"Rely on the Germans. They'll find a way to get rid of us in the end," insisted Jakubek.

—"Or they'll run," said Biegel quickly.

Outside it was soothingly still. Sheltered by the washroom barracks, Arush quickly stretched out on the earth - "for the last time", he thought. The pounding sounded much nearer than yesterday, and renewed in him a flicker of hope: "Perhaps even now it isn't too late?"

With his spirits improved, he was back in the barracks. There was not much time left. The usual routine still had to be followed. Arush wondered if he might not be praying for the last time in his life? Many words seemed to have a special, solemn meaning today, which was, however, lost in his hurry to finish. Coffee was already being ladled out. Hardly had they started to bite into the bread, when the whistle sounded.

"Los! Everyone out! Leave your bread!" shouted Krel, and turning to Szainowitz: "I'll knock your teeth out!"

Szainowitz did not move, defiantly trying to finish his breakfast.

"You son-of-a-bitch! Didn't you hear me?" and Krel punched him. But amazingly Szainowitz today hit back. Arush ran outside.

Though they were lined up as they were every day, this was no ordinary roll-call. No SS man was present. Bubi, in his usual shrill voice, but with the unfamiliar look of a chastised dog, began to transmit the instructions.

"You'll be leaving this place today. You're to be moved to another camp. For the journey you'll get bread, a whole loaf, and a tin of marmalade, per man. It'll be distributed to you later. You're to take with you a blanket and all your personal belongings. Meanwhile everyone is to stay in his barracks. You'll wait there for further instructions. And now - *abhauen!* (buzz off)!"

"That's it. At least now you know," Arush told himself. But do you? It all sounds so familiar. And the most suspicious thing is this taking of "personal belongings". This was the catchphrase used by the Germans to deceive their victims before each evacuation. After all those years, he reflected, they were no wiser than the others had been years ago.

Arush, like all his mates, felt as if they had tasted another defeat. After the sweet illusion of liberty within their grasp, the bitter reality of unfathomable slavery.

Some hope still remained. In their waking dreams, the prisoners saw the Red Army drawing every day, every hour nearer to them. On the morning of Wednesday 26 July, they calculated that the Russians must be only a few miles away from Pustkow. True, for them, awaiting evacuation any moment, a few miles was very far away. But it was only a few miles, and it was not impossible that the dream that had gone unfulfilled for millions of their brothers and sisters, would come true for them - the last remnants. And so the long hour of waiting was racking everyone's nerves. All their talk turned around the one and only question: what would the Germans do with them.

The opinion of most was that their jailers didn't know themselves yet.

–"Nonsense," shouted Hugo. "They know. They've got the orders. We, too, shall know them soon. One thing is certain, I'm telling you, they won't kill us here."

–"How d'you know?" several voices asked together.

–"Because the Russians are so near. The place must not look like a slaughter-house. And there are witnesses - the Poles."

–"The Poles? They'll force the Poles to erase the traces," said Maniek. And, as to leaving witnesses, what's so sure about the Poles surviving us?"

–"Yes, really," added Knepel eagerly. "They'll wipe them out here, and blame the Russian soldiers for the crime."

–"No," almost everyone protested. "They can't shoot three thousand 'short-term' Poles just like that. There's not even time to move them away, with the Russians on their heels."

–"They don't have the means to transport such a mass of people," said Blatman with the air of a final arbiter.

The prattle of the men irritated Arush. Though what they said reminded him how different their predicament was from that of the Poles, from whom only a one-yard-thick wire formally divided them. The Poles might stay where they were, alive - the Jews must be removed. "Where shall we be when the sun sets?" While he was meditating on these things, Arush as if in a dream, heard Hugo saying: "If I could only pass a word to Brzostek or some other Pole to contact my sister after their liberation."

A word? A message? To whom could he send one? Arush continued musing. He could send only a thought, and for this he didn't need a messenger. On the contrary...He wanted to be alone, and when he was out of earshot of his mates, almost immediately other companions joined him from the blue sky, bringing with them gifts of a tender melody hidden deep in his memory. Like a distant call, the tune carried him back over many years to a happy day one vacation. The sun had shone as it did today. Nili, his sister, sitting on a boulder was humming the melody, her hand protectively around his shoulders. Eli was throwing stones into the rushing stream. Soothing sounds of water beating on rocks...The surrounding birch-trees were like those in the ancestral garden in Jaroslaw - yes, the same Jaroslaw, where the Russians must already be now. Under the tree, two dug-in benches stood on either side of a table, at which grandfather was sitting, narrating one of his mysterious-sounding tales in his spell-binding way. It was there on vacations, that little Dave, scarcely seven years old, had pushed his fist into the mouth of a dog - an identical dog, at least in breed, to Grzimek's..."I only wanted to peep into his throat," he explained...When Empress Elizabeth had died, grandmother -a gentle faced woman of middle age, as Arush had known her from the portrait at home - wore black for a whole year. What a shame, such a damnfool show of affection! For such fellows! In Zakopane, Dave had asked the still cursing Klara, how much she would pay for the head of the little sparrow who had soiled her new hat the night before. What laughter...All the children sitting together in a circle in the sun-bathed glade, chatting loudly, vibrating with life. Poor little Julia G, a year older than Arush, watched in sorrow, her nose pinched between the fence-posts. No playing with Jewish children for her - the girl's father, chosen during the war as a candidate for "Quisling", forbade it. But Kazik and Miecio, two sweet brothers from Poznan, whose parents rented the other wing of the same wooden Skibowki chalet, did play with them undisturbed. It was only 1930. And what fabulous games they had!...Those were happy days. He never wanted them to end. Would they ever come back? Would he ever again enjoy a happy moment?

As if to answer his silent question, he heard the capos shouting: "Roll-call!" There was no need to repeat the order. They had all run to the square and quickly lined up in columns. Everyone sensed the weight of the moment. Everyone was overwhelmed by danger and his personal memories. Arush's own still clung to the images of his beloved ones and to the indomitable charms of childhood, from which he drew new strength to face whatever might come.

They stood to attention in the sun, which had by now grown quite strong, while they were counted, mustered, and surrounded by SS men, some of whom held sub-machine guns, others dogs on the leash. All the guards were there, including, unexpectedly, Hauptscharführer Saar who, after Bubi had reported to Ruf, and Ruf to Bruchkraut, stepped forward and with feigned solemnity - there had always been something theatrical in his demeanour - began his farewell speech.

"You have worked well." What a lie, Arush thought. Perhaps for him personally. "But your work here is finished. There's plenty of work for you in another camp. You'll go there now. There, your work is needed."

A faint sound of sadness was in his voice. Arush watched him closely. His face was pale, his eyes expressionless. He spoke quietly, pausing between his words, which made him look a little moved. Was this only a mask? A skilfully designed false face to arouse confidence? Or did his look truly reflect a whit of pity for the poor creatures, who, he must know, were soon to die? Or was he merely sad at the loss of his workshop, of his slaves - the source of his "riches"?

-"I expect you," Saar went on, "to do your work properly, as you have done here. You won't be hungry! The *Verpflegung* (victuals) you have received will suffice until you arrive at your destination."

A glimpse of the other SS men showed them standing as if rooted to the spot, a grave sense of duty on their brutish faces, while their eyes flashed aggression mixed with gloom. They, too, were lucky to have been in Pustkow. Did they now fear transfer to the front? Probably not - they belonged to the elite that serves on the battle-front of concentration camps, the noblest of a national socialist's assignments. Have no illusions, Arush concluded, for all the rapport they had established with the prisoners, they were still their deadly enemies, bound, perhaps even eager to finish them off.

Saar was quickly his usual self again. He spoke briskly, flailing his arms, with froth appearing at the corners of his mouth.

-"Be sure to make no noise! The journey won't take long. You're well equipped. If you run short of something...if there is something the matter with you, tell the guards who will be with you on the train." So, by train, Arush quickly noted. "Everything will be taken care of. Only be reasonable! Make no *Dummheiten* (stupidities)! If anyone makes a *Dummheit*, then he will..." His voice faltered. He could not bring himself to say what he meant. He searched for softer words. The SS guards were growing visibly restless. Their looks seemed to ask: where would this lead? Though Saar's weakness was probably a sign of the times. Meanwhile he had found a way out, and mumbled: "Eh, well, you know what'll happen. Trouble, unnecessary trouble. By your own fault. Let no one try to escape...No reason...Make no *Dummheiten!*"

He continued to harp on about the victuals, the journey, the stupidities, until his words were drowned by whirring sounds from outside the camp. Trucks had arrived. The men started moving in columns, and hardly had they climbed onto the lorries, then they drove off. What a hurry! "The Russians are probably nearer than we think," Arush heard his neighbours whispering.

Soon the barracks disappeared from sight, and then the watchtowers. Nothing but hill ridges, mingled with tree tops, now stretched out into the distance. It may seem fanciful for Arush to feel disappointed because they were not made to march on foot to the train. But no one who has ever tasted prison for long, could fail to feel the same magic touch of even a short walk in open, sunny space, within reach, as it were, of trees and flowers.

The train was waiting at Kochanowka, the single-track rail extension to the Pustkow SS base. No sooner had the men taken their places on the bare floor of a wooden goods truck, than the door was slammed and bolted from the outside. The shock of the experience seemed too great for words. To Arush it was like the proverbial closing of portals of the nether world. "We are buried alive," was his instant thought. Distance shrank. Darkness descended. A black darkness, reduced to deep grey by rays of daylight, which slipped through cracks in the sides of the truck. But the light was hardly enough to make nearby faces glimmer or bodily shapes distinctive. And yet, however great was the change in the men's physical surroundings, the mental impact it had on them was still greater.

They were about eighty to a truck, crammed into a space of twenty square yards, between windowless walls three yards high. In this oppressive crowd Arush felt very lonely. Not only because of his distress, but because many of his fellow passengers were not known personally to him. They were mostly cobblers who in Pustkow had lived in the other barracks. It was merciful at least, he felt, that with the exception of the master-cobbler, Prater - a decent, elderly man - none of the elite prisoners shared his cage. And so there were no orders, no favours, no giving way to anyone - all were equal inside the truck. Thanks to that, and by the chance of boarding the truck among the first, Arush's place was privileged - close to a wall. But thoughtless as he had been, he failed to position himself near an outer wall, where, hidden between its planks, were tiny, hardly visible cracks - the only life-giving "substance" in that altogether death-filled pit. Thus with his back against the wall and legs bent on the floor, Arush settled for the journey, which, as a neighbour of his whispered, seemed by all the signs on the forgotten earth and heaven to be their last one. In this trying situation, the men in his death-truck none the less had the prudence and dignity to behave calmly. Solemn and anxious, they talked only in whispers.

–"I didn't expect it to be so bad," Arush heard someone saying.

–"Bad?" asked another voice, "it hasn't begun to be bad yet."

–"It certainly could have been much worse. We're only eighty," yet another voice sounded.

321

–"Only?" asked an inquisitive whisper.

–"Yes," said Arush, "sometimes they pack twice as many people into a truck. On the route to Belžec in 1942 one hundred and fifty was the norm."

–"But was that possible?" asked the anxious man. "How could they survive?"

–"They didn't. That is, not all. Many arrived dead. Others half-dead."

–"What was the difference?"

There was - and what a difference! But Arush ducked the question, merely saying: "In cool weather even a hundred and fifty could live for a day or two in a truck like ours."

This, in the circumstances, comforting statement, was a deduction that just rushed into his mind. Dave, Gila, oh Heavens - Arush shuddered as he recalled his brother and sister - had travelled to Belžec in November, and had sent a card from half-way, posted in Przeworsk.

–"D'you feel cool?" snarled his questioner, who turned out to be Breitel, the Pustkow plumber. He did not need to spell out what he meant to say.

–"Still, we're only eighty. Without real bundles. And the truck was clean and empty."

–"Empty," repeated Breitel with scorn. "D'you think that the other trains had benches or beds?"

–"No, but some trucks had floors covered with lime."

–"Lime? What for?"

–"I don't know. Perhaps to cover the filth, or to kill the stench. But, more likely, to speed up suffocation."

All fell silent, as if by secret understanding.

In the stillness, Arush could not help thinking that his mother and Eli had made this same journey - perhaps in this same truck - sitting in lime. How did they endure? he asked himself despairingly. Even in his present conditions the question was too trying to dwell on for long.

Despite all the earlier rush, and the closed doors, the train did not move. Neither at once, nor for the next two hours. And so gradually dejection rose in the dark cage. The only thought that sustained the men's hope of coming out alive from this train had been that the journey would not last long. Not knowing its destination, that same hope required of them to opt for a nearby target. The nearest camp to the west they had heard of was Plaszow, a suburb of Cracow, only eighty miles away. Hadn't Saar said that the journey would not take long? They would seize on anything seemingly hopeful. But when Prater, the head cobbler, remarked: "Plaszów was too near, and the Germans may be evacuating it as well," all agreed. There was logic in his words. The Russians would advance at this round at least to the Vistula. Cracow was too near.

The second nearest camp they knew of was Auschwitz. Thirty miles west of Cracow. Even if their train travelled slowly, they reasoned, it should without stops - and why should it stop, who was to get off or to get on this train? - reach Auschwitz in a matter of five to six hours. This, they calculated, was still within limits of survival. So they all agreed upon Auschwitz. And from then on the train was, in their minds, bound for Auschwitz. Nothing nearer, nothing farther than Auschwitz.

They had heard a great deal about Auschwitz, even if not in definite terms, but somehow no one seemed now to remember what it was. This train was not the proper place to worry about the future. It would have been a luxury. Men who have another chance and are not too tired worry about their future. Arush, for once, certainly saw no point in torturing his mind with such things as Auschwitz, or the fate that might await him there.

Not that he did not know that Auschwitz was a horrid place, a camp of no return, as people used to call it. But it was a camp...He immediately started recalling the horrifying stories he had heard about Pustkow, and what it had turned out to be like there in reality. Pustkow was, admittedly, unique. It would be worse, even much worse, in Auschwitz. But Auschwitz was a place that was fixed on earth - not a dark, walled, stifling cage on dead wheels. He shook off all thoughts of Auschwitz.

The summer of 1944 was hotter than is usual in Poland, and in the last days of July the heat reached the climax of the year. Hitherto, especially at camp, spring and summer had been their only allies. But now, in the train, the summer passed onto the enemy's side. In the glowing sun about noon, the temperature rose to forty degrees centigrade. In their pent-up truck, it must have been much hotter. And they knew that it would become worse, that they would have to face the coming hours without air, without water, without release from the damp heat - the nauseous dampness reeking from their bodily ordure.

Naturally the environmental conditions, and how to adapt to them, had become the men's prime concern. But what could they do? They took off their clothes - not everything at once, as their innate modesty did not vanish as quickly as that. They tried to spare their fading energy, to hold back their excrement, to squeeze their noses in one of the cracks, whose owners - that is, prisoners who monopolized them - so far gave free access to anyone for a short breath. But that was all they could do to adapt physically - while the heat was simply choking. They were reduced to a state in which a man's body wants only air and water. At first, a "glutton" or two tore off a chunk of his bread, but the rest left their loaves, let alone their marmalade, untouched. But for a drink of water every one of them would give all he had.

Thirst and thoughts of stilling it became a major subject of the low-voiced conversation. Memories of filling one's mouth with drinks whenever you wanted, the delights of ice-cold soda water on a hot day, were coming alive. One could not banish them - though later even this changed. One gets used to everything. The mechanism of a man's body can endure more than its owners think.

–"Water, ordinary water. There must be a tap at the station," argued someone plaintively.

–"What station?" asked Cetel contentiously. "We're in the middle of a heath. But if they would only open the door..."

–"And it would also relieve the thirst," added another man.

–"Perhaps if we ask, they'll open the door. Let's bang on it, when the guards come near, and ask them to open it."

This seemingly rational suggestion provoked a jumbled discussion. Some were in favour - "there was nothing to lose," said Schimek, who having his seat at the centre of the truck was leaning back to back with Doler. Some argued that it was too risky - instead of opening the door, the SS men might start shooting into the truck - while still others considered the whole idea crazy.

But when Prater, the eldest and perhaps most comfortably seated man in the truck, said: "Don't bang. Knock - gently, and if they respond, let one man ask them politely to open the door," his advice was followed. For several minutes, the men who had been sitting near the door knocked on it - ever less gently. But no one responded.

It was silent again - a deep, more despondent silence than before. You can knock only on the door of heaven, thought Arush. You can call only for God's help, and this you can do in silence. Will He listen? Will He respond?

This question was probably on everyone's mind while they waited, parched by the fire that was racing through their bodies, for the train's departure for Auschwitz.

In this sultry silence, while marking the hours that seemed certain to be their last, yet still at an early stage of their stationary journey, Dichter, the ex-cantor-cobbler, crawled close to Arush. He sat down on his right, gazing at him entreatingly with eyes wide and filled with fear. He seemed anxious to unburden himself, but held back from uttering a word. At last, leaning yet closer to Arush, he faintly whispered into his ear: "I want to say *Vidui* (prayer of confession). I don't know the words. You must know them."

While it came to him unexpectedly, Arush was not in the least surprised by this strange communist's wish to confess. Not that the men in his truck were particularly devout, or even knew much about religion. But in situations like theirs, looking into the eyes of death, many a man's heart, and a Jew's heart in particular, turns to God. And within the walls of their little universe, the horizon reduced to a few yards, His presence seemed, at least to Arush, as evident as if it were felt physically.

Dichter's assessment of Arush was only partly correct. The prayer of confession consists of two parts. One that is said only in the imminent expectation of death, is only printed in very special prayer books. The other is part of weekday-morning prayers, and this Arush knew by heart. Yet, without hesitation, Arush refused. Shaking his head, he uttered, "No!"

The surprise on Dichter's face, his reproachful eyes, demanded to know why.

In truth, Arush had himself started to think of saying the confession prayer almost as soon as the doors closed on them. The darkness on a bright sunny day, bore the vision of death. Plain reason led him to conclude that he was unlikely to come out of this truck alive. It seemed to him only sensible to prepare in spirit for parting from his temporal life. The ultimate question of the meaning of life and death, the border between them being perceptible, had nowhere appeared to him so urgent as in the truck he had just been shut in. But a silent inner voice was obstinately telling him: No! You will live! You will survive!

The inner voice made Arush wonder. Was it, he kept asking himself, just his belief in individual providence, the mighty invisible Power which guides and guards man, and which had saved him, against all hope, times and again from the lowest depth of the abyss? Or, was it his disbelief - disguised as presentiment - in his own death - a disbelief common to all men, especially at the age of twenty. But it was more than that. He had actually felt the impulsion of that invisible Power, and hence it must have marked him out to live. Others in his truck might possibly die, but not he. There was still a refuge for him.

Where? How? Oh, the Russians might overtake and seize the train. Or, a sudden deluge might turn their truck into a sort of Noah's ark. A miracle? Yes, or just another reprieve. In Auschwitz? Yes, if they were bound for Auschwitz.

Then there was the argument of quite a different nature. In this truck, does one need to confess? Was not their present predicament, on top of all they had experienced during their brief lives, a sufficient expiation for their sins?

Instinctively, Arush had resisted confessing for one other reason. But to Dichter his reply was short: "We're going to live! You and I, and the rest of us!"

Dichter stared at him incredulously, yet thankfully - all rancour had vanished from his eyes, which suddenly welled with tears. He spoke quickly and incoherently.

–"Is it possible? How? Are you serious? Let us face up to it. We can't escape. No hope. I wish to confess, as long as it is time...Why not?"

–"You're penitent, that's enough - here. We're going through Hell, being purged from our sins. We're cleansed. From this truck, and after all the suffering, the road leads straight into Paradise. For every one of us."

Dichter listened intently, his eyes opened even wider, to express both scepticism and enchantment.

–"The important thing is not to lose heart," Arush went on, and a little grandiloquently added, "We must rise above this hell. We must not give in! To give in, just in the last moments, would be revolting."

Dichter only asked: "What would it matter?"

–"We may soon be meeting our beloved ones. How will you face them, if you give in? Be strong and hopeful, Dichter!" Arush made the effort to tap him on the shoulder.

He was too absorbed in his thoughts to give much care to what precisely he was saying to Dichter. Careful words you must not expect from a man under stress, bathed in streams of sweat and dirt. But the words he had spoken were genuine sound-flashes of his inner thoughts. Still, in a situation like theirs, what did he mean by telling Dichter "not to give in"? Did he speak to him or to himself? Was it fear of dying, or fear that he might have to live with the memory of having surrendered? Surrendered? To whom? What? His soul, his will, life itself. There was this hidden force - the energy of faith and one's inner conviction - that gives a man the will to live. This indomitable will to survive was his last personal freedom and made him master of himself. Many had died when they started asking, like Dichter, "Is it possible?" "Why go on?" In circumstances like his you needed the whole animating power of your spirit to keep your body alive. And why should a man like Dichter give in? Was it his first appointment with death? Why should he, who had seen his wife and six children led away to the slaughter, who had lost his home and all his possessions, who had slaved in camps for years, and all that time had retained his strength and will to live - why should he lose it now, just after he had repented? True, it was more desperate here than before. So what? The more desperate he was, the stronger should his hope be. There is as much hope, as you tell yourself there is.

Arush, of course, knew that he was theorizing, but theorizing in a way that was brave and lofty. And he went on - if for them, in this truck, still to have hope was unreasonable, to lose it was simply absurd. The first step on the road to surrender was to say, as Dichter did, "There's no escape." Even if he was right. There's no escape? Then bear it with dignity, and prepare yourself for the future life. What, anyway, was the alternative? To tell Dichter, this despairing man on the brink of collapse, to give in? To languish without any hope in this hell?

He had said to him hell, indeed Hell. But what did he mean? This truck is not the place in which sinners are condemned to live after death - even if it was more tormenting here than in all the mythical visions of the hell. He meant perhaps a place for the purging of sins. Sinners they all are. Who is not? "There is no righteous man on earth, who will not sin." But they, in this truck, submit and repent. To confess was another thing. In this truck to confess was to destroy the will, to break down resistance, it might even look like mocking the poor. And because the suffering is expiatory - he could feel it - that was another reason why it should be borne gladly, and why, when the hour of their release from pain and sorrow came, they would be assured of a place in Heaven.

Submerged in his thoughts and the emotions aroused by his conversation with Dichter, he heard him asking; "D'you, Freund, really believe in meeting your beloved ones?"

Arush was prepared for this.

-"Look, if you believe in saying the Vidui, this means that you believe that your confession would purge you from your sins. And if you believe that you may be relieved of your sins through confession, this implies your acceptance of a life after your death, where you will be called to account. And if this is so, if you believe that there is existence beyond this life, why should you doubt that in this other world you will be spiritually re-united with your dear ones?"

Silently he also asked himself: what on earth, especially on this forsaken scrap of it, was more desirable than such a re-union? What greater solace could lighten up the darkness of this truck?

Dichter digested what Arush had said, and then half in irony and half in resignation he drawled: "You, Freund, can never lose. If you survive, you will have won life itself; if you don't survive, you will embrace your loved ones in happy re-union."

As if to bear witness to his words, the train gave a terrific bump, the floor seemed to sway for a while, and then the train started to move. Slowly, lazily, but it was moving. A sudden vitality swept through the truck, as if a lash had whipped its passengers back to life. Immediately the silence was broken, as everyone began to talk at once.

–"Now that it has started to move, the train will roll on all the way."

–"The start is always slow. The engine must pick up speed." And when Breitel said that it would soon become cooler inside, they all agreed.

–"D'you think of escaping?"

The questioner was Ruben Blonder, Arush's neighbour pressed against his left arm. As he did not address Arush directly, he said nothing. But others who had heard the question subsequently started a long and at times excited discussion about escaping from the train. To Arush the talk sounded familiar. He recalled in particular the debates with Teper; the arguments for and against escaping were the same then as they were now.

–"Only a few could get away from the train. We're hostages for each other. They have our exact number. This must tally on arrival in Auschwitz, otherwise..."

Seibald, the overseer-cobbler, cut in vehemently.

–"How d'you know? D'you think that in Auschwitz they care about numbers? And if they do? Once you have got away, they can whistle. They carry a trainload of slaves for hard labour. Because a few have disappeared, they would have to be mad to kill the rest - after all that costly journey."

–"And," someone added, "how do we know that they won't finish us off whether we all arrive or not? It's essential that at least a few, even only one witness survives."

–"All right! You say at least one should survive! But how? It's nonsense!" Frey, a sham saddler from Szebnie, almost shouted. "They halt, they chase, they shoot! A hundred may be tortured to death for one man's failed attempt."

–"At night," Seibald argued less confidently, "it's possible, it could be done. They can't take a sight, point, and find you in the dark."

To keep the discussion going, Arush threw in one of his friend Knepel's sophistries. "Nothing is impossible, as long as one is daring enough."

–"That's it. Sink or swim!" Seibald echoed with a heroic bravado which even in their circumstances sounded funny.

–"Well said," a man called from the far end, "but how can you slip away?"

The plans that were now unfolded from all sides were copies of stories, true or invented, that had circulated in the camp about escapes from similar train transports.

Some would lift the roof, others would cut a hole through the floor. Some would wait until night, others would not wait a second after the exit hole was finished. There was even a little haggling about who would jump first, and about the order of queuing up after him.

So loud and absorbing was the dispute about when and how to escape, that it escaped the notice of its main participants that the train had come to a stop.

–"A short stop," remarked Seibald. "Trains do often halt. It'll be moving again soon."

No one was inclined to oppose him, nor was there reason for immediate concern. But the train's coming to a halt lowered the tone and intensity of the discussion.

The focus of interest changed, and almost everyone now began asking where they were.

–"At a station," reported Cetel from a spy-hole.

To see with his own eyes seemed to Arush worth the effort of squeezing to the nearest slit. Through it he could see several tracks but all were deserted of trains. Obliquely on the right, the lower part of a brick-built house was visible. "This must be the Dębica railway station," he decided. "Our train has at last been turned on to the main rail line."

–"From Dębica," Arush heard a voice behind him declaring gladly, "it leads straight forward to Cracow and further down to Silesia."

Back in his seat Arush was resting from his excursion, when in a moment of silence in the truck, the distant clatter of footsteps became audible. Soon they could also hear men's voices near their truck. Feeling there was nothing more to lose, prisoners who were sitting close to the wall started banging and clamouring for water.

–"Open! Open!"

To no avail.

–"Are you stone deaf?" shouted someone defiantly.

–"No," answered Prater. "They're our escorts. They walk on and off, they yell and roar with laughter."

CHAPTER TWENTY-FOUR

The men's cries, like their recent change of mood, seemed to mark the end of the first, and the beginning of the second, far more trying, stage of their journey. The tension and excitement which followed the train's short period of movement had reduced their sensation of thirst, pain and heat. Now that the train was stationary again, it returned, and with increased strength. As the day wore on it grew steadily hotter. In the afternoon, when the blazing sun beat down hardest, it inflamed the roof and walls of the truck. The air was unbreathable, the thirst delirious. The men's bodies were shrinking, and they could expect worse. In the growing gloom and agony, it seemed that only death, madness, or a miracle could set them free from their thirst and pain.

"A death train," men could be heard saying as the train continued to stand. "We're trapped! They tricked us in, Saar and his speech." "They never intended to open up." This seemed not unreasonable; for what was reasonable in that last resort of cruelty?

By mid-afternoon, all the earlier fancy talk of escape was forgotten. It was never to be taken seriously, Arush perceived from the start. Apart from other difficulties, well known to him from the past, his co-passengers had neither the necessary tools, nor the strength - superhuman strength required of weary men drowsing in fever and sweat - to escape.

To Arush, the only interesting point about the short episode was how the sudden motion of the train had aroused wild plans and hopes, which betrayed the men's will to live. This was equally true of Dichter, who as soon as the train began to move, had crouched back to his seat.

But his words lingered in Arush's mind throughout the din of the rumbling train and all the spirited talk that followed. It set him thinking that Dichter was not at all a fool. He seemed to disprove the general dictum, rhyming so nicely in Yiddish, that all chazanim, synagogical cantors, are simpletons. A cobbler, unlike a cantor, who revels in the clouds, does not see above his shoes. But a singing cobbler is said to be wise in the ways of the world, if not a man of ideas.

The thoughts that come into a man's mind are a discourse with oneself. To make it more attractive Arush brought Dichter into his silent conversation, saying anything he liked to him. So Arush began by telling of his doubt that Dichter had given full consideration to what he had said. For he, too, could win, if he so willed.

To be a winner, you must choose the winning side. If you don't wish to win, why

329

have you let yourself be tortured? And whatever you may answer, your suffering, your acceptance of it, belies your pretended disbelief in the possibility of winning - surviving.

As for the other dimension of winning, this is again a matter of your own will. Why do you think men believe in an after-life? Well, because they share a need to believe in the significance of their lives, to make their lives answer to a purpose. Purposeless existence is merely another sort of torture, a mental one. What is the meaning of a life full of frustration, suffering and grief, without hope, without a bright, radiant future? If what we call death terminates our miserable lives once for all, what is its purpose?

On the other hand, to a man who believes in the extension of this life he knows into another, mysterious one beyond the grave, death is neither the end of everything, nor is it terrible. You may remember having once heard me explain the theory - if I may call it so - of Proz-dor, of the tunnel of life between two ends of one perennial stream - a tunnel, short as the wink of an eye in terms of eternity, which by the way you live, act, and comply with God's will, serves as the training ground for the Other World.

You shake your head Dichter, and want to ask me something, so let me tell you in advance that existence beyond this life is not a matter of knowledge or proof, though neither is it a myth or an illusion; it is a matter of faith. Proof is not necessary once you live in this faith, then it becomes a personal conviction, a certitude - and whether you have this faith or not depends entirely on you. An act of your will! If you refuse to win, you will lose. It is your choice - to be or not to be!

So, you see, it all boils down to preparing yourself for death and the life after. Purity and equity within the intimacy of faith in God. Even that ambivalent historian of antiquity, Flavius Josephus, noted that for a Jew the crux of his existence is the way he lives. It is in this way that death differs from death and spirit differs from spirit. Proz-dor, its system of preparedness, is spirit at its highest. The opposites of it are our present masters, whose system is kill and kiln, and whose superiority derives from the guns in which they glory. The opposites of spirit are guns; and guns are the ultimate ideal of mechanical life!

Don't jump to your feet, Dichter. It is not worth the trouble to tell the seemingly obvious, particularly in the context of our situation. Long before you, from times immemorial, people have said that spirit is of no avail against guns. But it only seems so; it is only true in this imperfect, transient world; and even in this imperfect world, its validity is limited to times like ours. Wars are exceptions.

Of course, the power of the gun can only be defeated by more power of more guns. Yet in pursuit of what aim? If, admittedly, not exactly to establish the reign of spirit, as past experience suggests, then at least to introduce and preserve a system that is not based on the gun, but one that is founded on a human code derived from the realm of spirit. In a deeper sense, that's what this war is all about. The stakes are very high - devouring millions of people. The alternative to the civilized, human, let alone divine code of living, Dichter, is the code of the master race, our superiors who have invented trains like this. Can their code triumph, to drag everyone into the grave, and turn spirit into phantom? Even now, in the throes of death, I do not believe it can. And I must tell you again that the fact that you submit to suffering gives a lie to the supposed belief of yours that guns will conquer spirit. Were this to happen, why should we want to live? Would it be worthwhile?

Tell me honestly, would you even now change places with our masters? For nothing in the world would I. I am not lying to you. A heart which may soon stop beating could not spell out falsehood. But we are lucky that we are not being put to this brutal test.

Jewish luck, you might say. Yet we are lucky - to be rather the victims than the killers. I definitely refuse to kill, in revenge or hate, even our masters. It may surprise you, but I even feel no hatred of them. One cannot hate something that one loathes.

So you, Freund, want to remain a victim?

What I want to remain is a man, and, if it comes to it, to die becomingly as a man and a Jew. If I succeed, as I hope I will, this will be my final victory over our masters.

Do you understand, Dichter, that to hate and kill would be our self-defeat? Can't you see that to kill would be to affirm the new world order they proclaim? Don't you agree that we must not degenerate to these moral standards? Dig deeper in your mind and you will grasp that every killing is a brick in the edifice of the new world order which they are building. For nothing in the world shall I put a hand to it. We, Dichter, must show that man is and shall be human.

In this truck?

Yes, in this truck Dichter. But the only way to be genuinely human in this truck is to die in dignity. You ask me what does it matter how one dies? It does matter, Dichter, at least to me. It is my ultimate spiritual need. You shake your head in disbelief. You think perhaps I am crazy. You ask, what is dignifying about dying in this abject car?

There is dignity - if you could sense it. I pity you if you can't. For what counts is not where you die or the manner in which you die, but what you feel in your heart at death. The dignity I speak of is the last inner feeling of being a man and a Jew. To remain human and Jewish in this truck is my acceptance of the yoke of divine rule - the Providence of my ancestors, their guide through our long history of suffering and pride.

You now know what I meant by telling you that it all comes down to preparing yourself, to reach the end of the tunnel in good order. Yet, while I say to you, Dichter, be prepared to die, at the same time, fight on to live. If we are to die, it is important, indeed imperative, that we die as men determined to live.

For heaven's sake, you ask, why is this important? Once you have died, you are dead. Who will ever know, how I or you have died?

You seem irritated, but it is important - and I have already explained to you why. If our ordeal in this truck is to have a meaning, at least one of us, our destiny being collective, must come out of it alive. So you, I, any one of us must struggle to survive, and to do what is right, until his last breath. And the right thing, in the first place, is to live - because it is a divine commandment and, in our situation, a human duty.

Do you really want to live only because you feel bound by duty?

To be honest with you, I crave to live regardless of any obligation. It often amazes me that, for all the horror and disgust with which the outside world fills me, when I think of it, I still treasure life greatly. Because what can I expect to win from my present wrestling with death? At best, days and nights of lonely sorrow, everywhere the immutable company of grief and bereavement. And yet I cherish the thought of prolonged life. It could be because my attachment to conscious life is stronger than all anguish and reason, as it is for every man. It could be the strength of the hidden force which impels man to fight for his actual existence. Perhaps we are also expecting to come to terms with the days ahead. More likely it is the resolution to face up to adversity and danger - besides a kind of dedication to the memory of our dearest and of what we have passed through.

Arush hesitated to mention his other reason, his urge "to tell", to record for history the happenings of those days, as a sufficient justification to go on living. He had spoken of it so many times before and now, in the twilight of death, this argument seemed pale and difficult to put convincingly. Though this was perhaps the most potent reason for enduring their tortuous lives. Ordinary truth requires testimony, let alone the story of this truck, the kind of story which no fairy tale writer had ever imagined. Oh my Lord, sighed Arush, if only I could survive and be able to describe this journey! If I were blessed with the talent of a Sienkievicz, who took us on those fascinating journeys through exotic lands and desolate wildernesses, which so exercised my boyhood imagination. Men lost in the desert, like them exhausted, straggling through blinding sand-storms in the torrid heat of the midday sun, and amidst howling ghosts of moonlit nights. At last, a dazzling light in the distance, a lake of cool water, shining green palms - only another mile or so, a last effort, a little more endurance, and you are saved. Alas! *Fata morgana!* The captivating words of his youth. Was it, Arush, all an illusion?

He looked around at his silent, drowsy comrades. They seemed to have by sheer necessity reconciled themselves to their situation. The best, arguably, one could do: keep motionless, save your energy, and await whatever will come. Without any hope? Without memories? Of what are they thinking? Though, if Dichter's request was an example of their thoughts, it intimated spiritual concern.

–"Ruben, where are you?"

–"In heaven," said his neighbour, exhaling a fetid breath of air.

–"Fine! Blessed you are."

–"Of all blessings, celestial or else, I wish I had a little water."

Water, of all celestial blessings! No wish for inspiration, Arush reflected sadly, no nourishing hopes and memories, no dying with dignity - only water. Since he was himself going crazy with thirst, he could well understand Ruben. Yet nothing but water means void. Void in water.

–"No water in heaven?" he inquired.

–"No, all taps turned off. A drought the like of which the world has not seen before. You could find out for yourself."

–"How!"

–"Just think of it."

–"What else d'you think of?"

–"Nothing else, only heaven and water. In heaven we need no water. On earth we need it, but have none. You can see the advantage of heaven, and the sooner we get there the better."

–"Don't speak like that, Ruben!" An air of mystery lay in Ruben's words. Did he really want to die? Was there no will left in him to want anything but water? Not long ago he had tears in his eyes. He who cries wants to live. He can't fool me, Arush concluded.

–"Think of life, of liberation. To make it happen, Ruben, you must stick to it."

–"To what?"

–"To life."

–"Leave me! My head is bursting. I can't..." He didn't finish, only shifted his head listlessly.

Ruben Blonder was a gentle fellow in spite of a hard upbringing at his father's small-town tinsmith's workshop, without a mother from the age of ten. His words moved Arush, who was himself terribly unhappy at the prospect of dying in this truck. A peculiar, hidden away, death, like that of a man going alive to the sea-bottom in a corked up cask. To wither away in this darkness and silence, while outside bombs thunder, canons spit fire, guns crackle, men run, shout, shoot - and everything only a step from liberation.

If how you die is not significant, Dichter, what the hell is significant in this truck?

I could ask you many more such questions, Arush silently continued. But the one that occupies me now is, what all this means in terms of life in heaven?

I expected you to find fault with it, for there was an inconsistency in what I told you. You might have asked me: "If you, Freund, keep saying that the all important end is to reach the palatial throne-room, why do you insist on staying in the antechamber, your Proz-dor? Aren't you by this lowering the significance of eternal life as opposed to the transient one? You will now invoke history again, your duty to tell posterity. But why tell those living on earth, whose ultimate personal destiny is, sooner or later, to reach heaven,rather than those who have already reached it?"

To be sure, it was an inconsistency, but not a deceitful one - a truth expressed in words but not believed at heart. My slavery to the powers of my conscious life really annoys me. But I can't help it. I am, like any living person conditioned to think in terms of the life I know. And this life is full of cross-roads that are shrouded in clouds, and lead in directions mostly at variance with the spiritual life of piety. Often one is not even confronted with a choice of ways. I, for instance, grew up, from my earliest days, in two worlds, combining Jewish and other cultures. And think of the harsh claims of our everyday lives. The crisis of man in the modern era. The questions you face do not leave you unaffected. Simple, rock-firm, faith of childhood was the ideal. The perfectly pious, such as the fabulous pilgrims of

Klasno, did not desire to prolong their passing lives surrounded by SS guards. They marched joyously to embrace death like children departing for home - the home of their beloved Father.

This was the way you, my dear father, instructed me - in words and, in the end, in the example of your own death. When the SS man ordered you to follow him, though you were in no doubt what came next, you went like a man summoned before the court of a judge.

And you my mother? Arush went on brooding. How did you encounter God? Praying, I am sure. It was so elevating to the spirit, and such an enormous relief in these circumstances. I do not doubt for a second that you faced the end of the tunnel courageously and with that tranquility of yours which was so astonishing in moments of danger. And that while you were tracing the same thorny track on which I am trailing now, you anticipated dying proudly as a Jewess. So it is, so it has to be! A faithful daughter trusts her beloved, omniscient Father; she does not question his inscrutable judgements.

And if you came out of this macabre train, mother, and they led you deceitfully on the dismal path to the deadly bath, you walked dazed, bewildered, savagely exhausted, but you preserved your noble bearing, your head held high. Mother, they took away all your material possessions, even your hair, but they did not succeed in robbing you of the riches treasured in your heart - your humanity, integrity, the strength of your spirit. I can see you there mother, amid the multitude of mothers like you, waiting naked in the open, outside the bath - your tired, pale face, your lips drained of blood, your eyes veiled by mist - how you struggled to keep the thin body erect, confident in your inner strength. Everywhere the barbarians walked about, howling, jeering, laughing. You were terrified but not humiliated, your lovely face looked proud as ever. No need to hide your body, no grounds for feeling shame, all you naked women. The Germans wanted you to be naked. You were not. You didn't feel naked, mother. They disrobed you, but your body was covered by your faith and purity, your charity and love.

And later in the bare, grim bath-hall, crammed beyond limits with hundreds of martyred women clinging together in eternal sisterhood, inhaling the gas - deeply, yes, let it come quickly - the bowels already distend with cyclone, the face contorted, the eyes bulging, the lips frozen, yet still whispering the last prayers, remembering, as in all your motherly years, your children, praying perhaps for me, merciful God spare him, my last one - and the final admonition, your last will: "Don't forget, don't forget!"

I shall not, mother.

And, therefore, I want to live. If there were only a reasonable chance of surviving, this could be justified - perhaps winning today the battle that tomorrow could be victory - yours too, mother. But as a matter of fact, there is hardly any chance, and I refuse this unique opportunity to share your death, mother, while I had always thought that I really wanted to die like you, or Eli, or Gila, or...Now my wish could be easily fulfilled, but, against all the odds, all filial and moral bonds, I want to live. What should I think of myself?

334

Something abruptly interrupted Arush's thoughts. In a moment he realized what it was. The truck was alive again, with living men inside. He heard them speaking with their muffled voices, and this aroused in him the feeling that their agony was losing, even if temporarily, something of its poignancy.

What had brought about this change was plain - the heat had been slowly diminishing. While the train was standing still at the Debica station for all those exhausting hours, evening had crept in. The awareness that night would soon bring even cooler air had slightly changed the mood. Hence the faint motion and talk of the men.

It had always been easy to speak, but, Arush wondered, was it now? Anyway, to sit speechless for so long was not healthy. He turned again to Ruben.

–"How d'you feel?"

–"Fine. It won't be long...either way, it won't be long."

–"It'll be all right. It's getting cooler. And in the morning we will come out."

–"In Auschwitz?"

–"Don't grumble. Just keep on. Don't give up!"

–"You're silly..."

Ruben's words were drowned by someone speaking in a normal voice. Arush traced it to the wall, noting in silence that the guardians of the cracks showed all along more energy than others. It turned out to be the voice of Cetel, expressing a strange criticism.

–"It's sheer madness to keep a train motionless for a whole day."

–"D'you worry for them?"

–"I'm not worrying, but I can't understand it."

–"Cetel is right," said Prater. "They're short of trains. Don't you remember the slogan 'All the wheels roll for victory'? For years it has been shouting from every corner - and here they stand, and stand, and stand...it's beyond all comprehension."

–"Yes, and these carriages are, no doubt, diverted from the army's rolling-stock."

This made Arush think that even in their forlorn trap, they were contributing something to the German's defeat. He marvelled over the inefficiency of their masters, who were world-famous for good organization. While the cracks in the walls of a train like this could be nothing less than sabotage. If knowledge of them had reached the command in Berlin, not a few heads of the responsible, banal bureaucrats would have rolled.

The train's immobility sparked off memories of other train journeys in Arush's mind. The journey by train in his childhood was the most fascinating part of his annual summer holidays. To reach Rabka or Zakopane it took about five hours - that was without the unscheduled, but routine stops that always occurred on these trips. When the engine, luckily, failed at a beautiful spot, and in the summer everything was in leaf or blossom, they would sit down to a family picnic in a nearby meadow, at the foot of the beautiful Carpathian mountains. He always wished that the train would stand still for hours.

Oh yes, trains do stop. Seibald was right. But there are stops and stops. Which only proves that everything is relative. If this is so, why shouldn't it be possible to turn the present stop of their death-train into one of those of years ago? In his imagination everything seemed always possible. After all, men live by the creation, if not of their own genius, then by that of their ancestors. Just picture yourself, Arush, he told himself, to be on one of those other journeys and you might still see the end of the present one - and meanwhile you will feel much less lonely.

Suddenly his rambling reflections were disrupted first by the sound of a whistle, then by the clatter of wheels, growing to a deafening roar. A train rushed by. The dream that this evoked in him was soon shattered by gruff German voices from the platform.

–"Is this the first train like this you have seen?"

–"It's *schrecklich* (terrible). One man had his head in a bandage, covered with blood."

–"Ja, ja (yes), the war is coming nearer to us."

The two men moved away - and so did Arush, in his thoughts, from the other train.

Time was moving as well. After the prostrating hours of the long summer day, night finally set in, renewing some faint hope. It seemed as if the still flickering flame of life in the men, rekindled in the darkness inside the truck. They were talking again, though in undertones, as if afraid to disturb the uncanny stillness of night. Escape was hardly mentioned. Nobody was really capable of trying it, or of wanting anything but deliverance from immediate pain. Talk centred around the familiar question: "What is going to happen?" Either the Germans intended to finish them off under cover of night, or the train must move in the end. They are afraid of running trains during daylight, someone argued. What better proof than that no train had passed Debica until the evening. Others ascribed their train's immobility to a bottleneck on the railways. During the night this would clear away. Meanwhile there was some respite, and in the morning, before it gets hot again, they would, after all, have arrived in Auschwitz, or wherever it would be.

Arush peered at the men he could make out in the darkness. Their eyes shone, but there was none of the mid-day excitement in their voices or movements. They spoke quietly, apathetically, which however was not to be mistaken for indifference to their fate. There was no strength left to plague their minds with secondary questions. They were trying to stretch out their aching limbs, as a way of adapting themselves for the night, to fall into sleep - a long, pain-drowning sleep.

He was probably as tired as anyone of the brotherhood. But as soon as night had fallen, a strange, you might say extravagant, yet irresistible desire seized him. He must catch sight of the stars. Perhaps to feed his eyes with the vision for the last time. Through the tiny cracks, the sky was out of reach. Merely rewarded with a breath of fresh air, Arush crouched back to his seat disappointed.

It was time to take stock of the situation. This day was enough for a million days. Scores of generations had passed away without having ever experienced a day like this. And yet at the end of it, they were twelve hours nearer liberation, should they survive. Survive they must, otherwise all the suffering until now had no meaning in this world. Though "this world" what was it? Wasn't it just an illusion? For what he saw, or rather sensed, was a thick darkness filled with stench and lethargy. And he, like every one of them, was part of that darkness. No, to sit and think like this was no good.

–"Sleep Ruben," Arush turned to him. "You must be tired after this long day - in heaven," he added.

Ruben had apparently liked it, for he snapped back mildly: "You're not tired, you may even be freezing here."

–"Yes, like on a cold Chanukkah night. Can you remember?" Arush tried to stir him, to awaken in him the faint hue of life that memory gives, knowing that every one of them cherished some memories of Chanukkah.

–"Remember nothing. Better let us sleep as long as we're alive. And switch off the light!"

Sleep as long as we are alive, repeated Arush as if in disbelief. To be alive solely in sleep? Yet, he knew what Ruben had meant. All the same he must fight sleep. He must stay awake. This night here was charged with danger. Who knew what lay in wait for them. If he fell asleep, he might never regain consciousness. He must not die in his sleep, or be so easily murdered. This might well be their last day, and it must be prolonged for as long as possible. He must stay vigilant - a vigilance that must not be relaxed.

CHAPTER TWENTY-FIVE

When Arush woke up, it was already day. The message was ushered in by slender rays of light which filtered through the slits in the walls. And, strange thing, the train was moving. But the rumble of the train, Arush noted crossly, had not the usual, pleasantly soothing sound. The wheels were rather tapping out the plaintive melody of sorrow. Nor were they conveying the train's speed.

So his first question was for how long had the train been running? Though this he asked more to reassure himself that his brain was working than out of curiosity. Schimek insisted that the train had moved during the night. No one would corroborate it. Was he telling the truth, Arush wondered, or only showing off childish pride that he had not slept? Several men said that at whatever time they were awake, the train was standing still. This seemed to be nearer the truth; and before long the wheels of the train were motionless again.

Contemplating the scene around him, Arush got the impression, fortified by his own feeling of weariness, that by this second day, marking a new phase of their journey, nobody was perturbed by the train's standstill. The passengers, their bodies hunched with pain, seemed resigned to conditions they could not change. Besides, little strength was left in them to worry about anything.

What in this listless mood still induced in them a sense of annoyance, was their inability to find out where they were. The slits merely revealed the usual local landscape - grassy meadows, fields awaiting harvesting, here and there clumps of trees. Everything was terribly silent, with no human creature to be seen; not even a dog barked.

The immodest dissatisfaction of man with the bare fact of his existence, however flimsy this might be, his reluctance to relinquish his curiosity about where he was led in their little cage to a harmful strife which was sapping the last shreds of vigour left in the wasting antagonists. They were divided between those who maintained that they had not yet reached Cracow, and those who said they had passed it. Arush felt very weak and his tongue had so hardened that he merely listened to those husky exchanges - uncomfortably reminding him of their partially lost capacity of speech. But several minutes after the train had stopped, all this talk stopped as well.

Ruben uttered a sigh, indicating that he was not asleep. But Arush had no desire to speak to him. Surprisingly, Ruben had.

338

–"Another day, what? And still here...You said we would be out in the morning."
–"Sorry."
–"The night, the cooler air, were to bring relief, strengthen us," he had become gentler, reproaching Arush only indirectly, "but I feel more exhausted today than yesterday. I can't lift my head or arm after that night."
–"Sleep wasn't good," Arush felt obliged to say something to him, however hard it was for him to do so.
–"I thought it would be good to sleep, to be unconscious, at least until we reach Auschwitz - death comes too slowly."
Ruben was lying crooked, not moving, in the self-same position, the self-same contraction, the self-same stench, for the second day. And Arush had thought, he reproved himself, that they could not live here for six hours.
–"Don't think it's so easy to die," he turned to Ruben. "Thirst and exhaustion bide their time."
Though, even if they did not die yet, they were half-dead-men, lost in langour, their bodies cramped to dwarfish forms, the limbs refusing obedience. Arush's own legs would not move an inch, every bone was aching, to try to move was agony.
As their senses had become blunted today, thirst tormented them less, but the air was more unbreathable, the sickly smell filled the puckered mouth, pierced the lungs, while the accumulated, now augmenting heat, seemed to burn out the dehydrated bodies like a searing fire.
How could they face it for another day? How could they get used to it? How could anyone? Living was never easy, and these past years it had been very hard, but on that day it seemed to Arush utterly impossible.
His present neighbour to the right, Mandel, was a relatively robust-built man of thirty, and he looked less tired than most. But he was exceptionally raucous today, and kept moaning that he was getting mad with thirst. "If not now, then certainly at liberty," he repeated. Perhaps he was already mad, if he worried now about his life after liberation.
Arush scarcely worried at all. His mind that early morning was slow, lazy, hardly capable of imagining anything. Gone were the brave thoughts of yesterday, the concern with eternity, admonition of others; today it all seemed a distant, fairy dream. Was the heat, the inner fire, blowing up his brain? he asked himself. Had he lost his sensory faculties, and with them all his will-power? To think about it had become a nightmare.
What increased his feeling of anguish was the inner call of irremissible duty of worship - probably the compline prayer of his life - and his want of strength to follow it; the feeling of losing the battle of the will against energy, of the spirit against the body. Not to soil himself, to keep the body clean for the solemn service, he held back both bladder and bowel, by then for nearly a whole day. It was not too difficult, for he had been equally long without food or drink. Then a doubt - or perhaps a relief, if not an excuse - entered his mind: was it right to utter holy words in such a veritable dung-hole?
For the night, in the intimacy of complete darkness, most of the men had taken

off the rest of their clothes. They lay naked, relieving themselves where they sat. There were no vessels, and no room to allot a special corner. Urine at least dried up quickly, soaking into the planks, though sometimes not before an irritated man had sponged it up to rub his itching skin.

Well, in the circumstances he could pray without too much compunction, in his mind only. But to put on phylacteries required a superhuman effort. It may sound incredible, but Arush could not stir a toe. Had he lost his bodily feeling? Rather, he thought, his will-power. While he was thus sitting semi-delirious, temporizing, continually weakening, sunk in thoughts not thoughts, doubting the purpose of anything, something happened that seemed to signal to Arush his internal dissolution. His muscles loosened, refused to obey him, his bowels took charge of him. The thing terrified him - the horror of feeling himself incapable of exerting control over his body. He took it as his final defeat. In the panic that seized him, he saw the darkness getting darker around him, the floor of the carriage slipping from under his bottom, his memory vanishing - he, Arush, melting away into nothingness, only his ordure remaining real.

Yet this shocking incident also galvanized within him a current of resistance, which ignited all his remaining energy of faith for the decisive psychic battle against death. Either you collect your wits and brace yourself up, he told himself, or you will unquestionably decay in this filth. If you want to survive you must desire it, and you must deserve it; you must do something! You are what you think of yourself, what you honestly believe that you are. You soiled yourself, so what? Deep in this dirty, shrinking, perhaps even rotting body of yours, there is a spirit which is clean and sound. Refuse to be defeated: lift up your body and your spirit will rise as well.

Time went by. The train moved, the engine hissed, and halted, moved and halted, halting for much longer than moving. And so was Arush - brooding and swaying, yet not moving. The self-prodding was, however, not in vain.

The final push came from a most unexpected quarter. As if it were a signal from heaven, the engine hooter, as is the way of hooters, suddenly trilled a deep roar. In response, with almost his last breath, Arush cried out merciful Father, and made the superhuman effort of dragging himself from his seat. Leaning on his trembling arms, he slowly tried to raise his writhing body. However willing he was, his strength failed him. After a rest, he started again, becoming used to the pain, moving his limbs gently about to firm them, while his heart-beat quickened, and blood rose to his brain - and so at last he stood up on his two numb, clog-like legs. A heroic effort you might think. He felt exhausted beyond description. His head was moving in circles, his ears were humming, he staggered about dizzily. But he fought tooth and nail, leaning on the wall, to keep standing. A pleasant surprise awaited him.

His pain began to ease, and though still giddy and weak, the lifeless corpse that he had been only minutes before, appeared now to be a human being with arms, legs and a head on its neck. He had also regained hope, reawakening the instinct to live, all of which touched off a different train of thoughts. He even felt real satisfaction at his recovered capacity for mental anguish. As his memory returned, he recalled from the deepest recess of the brain, a rare teaching (and one that he misinterpreted) about phylacteries requiring a body clean like that of "Elisha the master of wings".

The magic power of wings, as enigmatic as life itself, as miraculous as the forces behind his recovery. Imagine - wings that could pierce through the walls of their cage as the lightning breaks through the clouds.

With his eyes closed, Arush removed himself to speak entreatingly with "the master of wings". "Oh Elisha, carry me away, please take me on your wings. Not to follow the birds, to scorn the horse and its rider or to tour the world - not even, as yet, to raise me into heaven. No, I beg the help of your wings to reach the remotest regions of the universe to proclaim aloud among its denizens, among friend and stranger, the secret and iniquity of this train; how in the darkness of a cramped truck eighty captive souls are slowly suffocating, how they are struck dumb with thirst, how they are dying without tears or comfort, how..." Arush, he collected himself, you are losing your senses. Don't let yourself be carried away. There are no wings, only dead limbs, in this place...But why don't they bomb it?

A distant, grunting drone of an aeroplane vibrated in the silence of the truck. It seemed as if they were all waiting with bated breath for the thunderous flash of light from the invisible sky.

—"Just one bomb, if they would only drop just one," Prater, his voice choking with hoarseness, started a husky discussion.

—"It's Russian," contended Seibald. "They wouldn't let the English or Americans come here. Their planes can't fly this far, anyway."

—"A decent, blaring explosion," groaned Mandel in excitement. "Damn them!" Cetel, still relatively clear-voiced thanks to his guarding the largest chink, objected: "All right if you get killed, but you may be only maimed."

—"This isn't a time to worry. Oh that only something would happen," answered Prater.

—"Yes, anything is better than this slow, sticking, stinking death," Seibald agreed eagerly.

Convicts desirous of self-immolation. Nothing spectacular, commented Arush in silence. But, however genuine their sense of despair may be, they long rather for a miracle than a bomb. But nothing happened.

—"Are you waiting for the bomb?" Ruben turned to Arush. He was so near to him, that Ruben would hear his whisper, reducing the pain of speaking. So he answered.

—"Funny, but the Germans may still have a plane or two left."

—"But the bomb...would you want it?" reiterated Ruben.

—"Who knows, it might be German. Who else would bomb this train?"

—"Does it matter whose bomb?"

—"It does. Didn't I tell you that death differs from death?"

Ruben pondered Arush's words in amazement.

Disappointed by the skies - no sound of an explosion, no deliverance, no hint of an

event that would make their death easier, some of the men gave vent to the frustration that was rankling in their hearts. "What interest are we to them." "They don't
want to know it." "They have all forgotten us." "Our own brothers...Damn them
all!"

Ruben protested, spuriously as it turned out. "My father's two brothers in
America certainly think of the family they left behind. They were very close to
each other. I can almost hear them asking: 'But can I, or you bring them back to
life? Have another beer, Zalman, for our poor dear Itche, as they called my father,
for the privation he and his children must have suffered'."

—"What an imagination! Cold beer, right now. Ruben, I don't recognize you. You
must feel much better today."

—"Not really. Yesterday I was certain that the end was just around the corner
here, any minute. But today, I still live. I can't think of death all the time. Talking
makes it easier."

—"Yes, in deepest despair. a few words can bring a man relief. But do not become
bitter, Ruben. D'you want your relatives or the 'world' to pity you? What would it
give you?"

Arush reasoned with Ruben, but was himself bitter. It was almost impossible not
to be. Yet he was conscious that to look at the world, including its section of free-
Jews, through the roof of their truck was like viewing art or nature with the eyes of
a dying man. And although he was equally aware of the hollowness of talk about
"conscience of the world" or of exemplary Jewish charity, he was no less mindful of
the self-pity trap.

—"You know how it feels. Sometimes I crave for a word of comfort," answered
Ruben sadly.

—"Yes, not only you. But to pity yourself is very dangerous. Especially here, in this
truck."

—"I don't understand what you mean."

—"We must hope, believe in our endurance, and will it. Self-pity destroys a man's
will and hope."

—"D'you still believe that we'll survive, if only this journey?"

—"Divine succour comes in the wink of an eye'."

Ruben fell silent - for a while. At first his face showed a pleasant surprise at the
spontaneity and resolution of Arush's answer. But then his face changed, sounding,
as if one could hear it, thoughts which must have been worrying him over the past
few hours or perhaps years.

—"Tell me, how can I be saved?" he asked melodramatically. "For you see," he
went on, "I have never prayed since my bar-mitzvah day, and even then I only pretended to. Today I would."

—"It isn't too late. On the other hand, since you have waited for so long, nothing
much will happen if...I mean, this is not the ideal place to pray. Perhaps without
words. To Eternity one can turn in silence. Sometimes even mere intention may
suffice. Don't misunderstand me, what I wanted to say is that this place is quite
exceptional. Pray when you come out.

"We share a common destiny. Our lives are united. Jointly all of us may even become sanctified...Mercifully, the Jews have no saints."

–"Why not, really?" Ruben interrupted Arush's sudden sermon.

–"A long question...In short, as long as a man lives he's fallible. And afterwards - there's the danger of idolatry."

"What is the mortal, that thou rememberest him, and the son of man, that thou thinkest of him," had swept through Arush's mind, and it pleased him as a sign of his improved mental state.

–"But you said that we might be sanctified?"

–"That's something different. A matter of status - awarding to certain dead a loftier status. You must die to become sanctified. No martyrdom for the living. And quite right!"

Ruben had raised his eyes, apparently wishing to ask something, but Arush went on, as if he had guessed his question.

–"Martyrs, you know, must remain a rare species, if they are to retain their high value. But just as demand for them was rising, supply fell off. Nowadays truly faithful men are few. And in the modern age martyrs are in greater demand than in the past. In our times of rising nationalism, with new national states being formed, martyrs are needed more than ever. So they will put up memorials for us, make rousing speeches, establish days of mourning, perhaps even a new fast, a day on which people will say special prayers for the 'saintly and pure like the shining sky'. But nothing for the living, should you, by Heaven's grace, remain alive."

Arush was aware that he had let his tongue run away. But in his circumstances to be fair and self-possessed required even greater strength than usual. He was reproved by his neighbour.

–"You sound as if you expected some sort of monument after the war, at least a medal, for being on this train and in Pustkow. I expect nothing," added Ruben with humble resignation.

–"Neither do I. But we may become a constant reproach, and have to hide the facts. Worst of all, there may be no one willing to listen to you. And heavens, what will be said of the few who might, after all, see liberation. This is how life is. The best die, they don't survive."

–"How d'you know who are the best?"

–"Those who die."

As he said this, Arush recalled Rabbi Maleachi's quotation of the ancient sage Rabbi Akiba, about the unfavourable sign to him who remains alive in times of "heavenly decree". From the day Arush had heard this solemn saying, it had never ceased to lie at the back of his mind. Now he said to himself that he need not worry about that unfavourable sign. For all its horrors, this truck would at least release him from that torment.

As if in reply to this, he heard Dichter sniggering into his ear: "You always win."

But did he know what a consolation it was, in these dire circumstances to win? Anywhere, it wasn't a crime. To kill is a crime.

–"Curse them," Arush cried out loudly.

–"Whom?" asked Ruben as if he were frightened.

Though Arush had meant their oppressors, and all their fiendish kind, who had sanctified homicide, he did not answer Ruben's question. He felt remorse and shuddered slightly. He was cursing at the door of death. Would he repeat what he had said at the Last Judgement? "Suffer not your mouth to cause your flesh to sin." Yes indeed, flesh! Even in this truck, and at this late hour, invariably flesh - a man with emotions, ambitions and wants. But did they have to bless them for this train journey? It wasn't the first time he had asked such a question. It couldn't be avoided.

Arush wished to sort out his thoughts. But he could not tell Ruben to hold his tongue. He had no one to talk to, except Arush. His other neighbour was dozing, the men in front of them sat with their backs turned. But a little rest might be good for Ruben as well. He would talk to him later, Arush compromised, but sparsely - whereas Ruben had now become truly loquacious.

–"You're angry. Does that make sense? When I asked you about the bomb, you seemed to be against it."

–"Look Ruben, you speak about sense. Could you tell me what is sensible about wishing to be hit by a bomb, when the only thing that we may not be able to avoid here is losing our lives?"

–"Just so! Isn't it, then, natural to wish for a quick end to this dreadful, hopeless existence?"

–"Natural? No, quite the contrary. By nature our souls induce us to believe and to hope against all reason. It would be easier for you to go on, if you would believe and had hope of something. The one follows the other; hope is the reward of faith."

–"Don't be angry with me, Freund, but I don't quite believe you. You probably think of death, and are in terror of it, as much as I am. But once we are dead, there will be no more fear of dying."

–"Of course, if the Marquis de la Palisse was alive fifteen minutes before he died, as every French child knows, our present anxieties will cease fifteen minutes after we are dead. True, I'm not expressing myself exactly, in carefully chosen words; it's impossible here, when I don't even know if I, and you, are still in our right minds? You're obsessed with your wish to die, I'm obsessed with my wish to live - and I won't let anything, even you, break me. Though, I'm very sorry if life here is too much for you - if it really is?

"I don't believe that you're really devoid of all hope."

–"Hope no, I haven't. Doubt, yes! I'm not capable of imagining living. Everything, death itself, seems unreal - and doubtful. In this state of constant death, I mean, constantly meditating on the idea that I am to die in the next hour or so, a doubt enters, a silly sort of question, what will happen after death? 'You never know', something tells you. This doubt disturbs me, but you can't banish it...What d'you think will come?"

–"Well...This is a time of testing. Keep all your strength, Ruben, to bear it well. Don't meditate...Death is unreal, as you say, if you believe in life after it. The hardest thing is to look into the void, to expect nothing."

344

He didn't know how to end this talk. He argued inwardly, that though they were convicts, inside a death-truck, they were still left with some freedom from the oppression of human chatter. He was determined to free himself, to take refuge in his memories and contemplation, which alone could give him some comfort. But Ruben protested.

–"It isn't emptiness to wish to know what comes after death. Whether there is, or is not, existence?" He was stuttering and then sobbed out: "Hell, d'you think there is a hell, where we're all bound to go?"

–"This is what you're afraid of - hell? However horrible the thing may be, does it frighten you now? That other hell is paradise compared with the one we're passing through. Think of felicity in Paradise, Ruben!" Arush concluded firmly, closed his eyes, and turned his head away from Ruben. So he began to meditate.

Tormented by fear of hell after twenty-four hours in this truck? Hard to imagine. Yet he may be genuinely worried. Hell is an aspect imprinted on man's mind from childhood. Later he grows up with it, hell becoming inseparable from our preoccupation with physical death, on the one hand, and from our uttermost desire of eternal life, on the other. It's probably because hell puts before man's eyes the sheer vanity of the passing, material world, that hell has attracted from the earliest days of civilization the greatest masters of the word, who have described it in the boldest, most colourful terms: a sea of fire, a dominion of demons and beasts, men driven by tempestuous winds, burning out their sins in sweeping flames. Against such cruelties of hell, how could the calm and radiancy of Paradise contend for man's imagination?

No wonder that the Inferno stamped your popular image, Maestro Dante.

This sudden appearance of the great poet was not so unexpected or mysterious as it might seem at first sight. With the onset of the worst oppression, the people in the ghettos had evolved a new, almost irresistible, desire to compare their agony with striking examples from history and literature - Dante Alighieri's Inferno taking pride of place. In Pustkow, it was above all Hugo Bester, who continued this practice. His critical remarks and the reactions of other mates had stuck in Arush's mind and partly contributed to his monologue with Dante. With his usual sarcasm, Hugo had noted that for all his love of the immense and magnificent, the main terror of Dante's house was a worm with three crushing mouths. "Oi vai (Woe to) me," Knepel had cried out mockingly when Hugo had mentioned that the sight of serpents curdled the great Italian's blood.

But in these days - Arush continued his silent speech - Maestro, the Germans have reduced your titanic creation to a little, dark hutch on wheels. They have smashed your story. How fortunate that they cannot kill your poetry! But you have in them formidable competitors - not in poetry, heaven forbid; here, with us, everything is very prosaic. But in reality, and in horror, they have surpassed your fantastic capacity to invent new forms of torment and cruelty - which was perhaps why they claim your genius for their own people. Yes, my great Maestro, crimes and savageries unsurpassed and unheard of in the whole history of mankind are being committed before my eyes. Forgive me, therefore, if I, and my mates, can't help laughing at your antiquated system of hell.

What is an underworld city of flames against a Reich, a realm, of darkness? What is seething pitch against a reeking dung-car deserted even by vermin? What is the stab of a fork compared with an airless breath? Don't you know that thirst can be more torturing than scalding steam, and heat, ordinary heat, more fiendish than boiling blood? Can't you see that a hell such as yours, pardon the slight, would afford a shelter to us?

You, Maestro, following the demands of art, were bound to display the natural fear that ordinary man would experience, descending into such a terrifying place as your Inferno. That fear, the shuddering, deterring fear of punishment, is, I dare say, incompatible with conditions such as we are now in. Overcome, as we are, by inhuman weariness, and dulled of ordinary human emotions, one can feel no fear. Neither of death nor of what comes next. Today both seem incomprehensible to me.

That is the difference. Yours is a comedy, a creation of your superb imagination. I speak of real-life drama, and real life occasionally produces scenarios that even the fanciest dreams of a genius could not conceive. How could you have imagined hell on rail tracks? In a truck without light, without movement, without breathing space, without life itself - the air inside turned into a solid mass, and its inmates transformed into mummies.

As a spokesman of your age, you certainly regarded, and with justice, the geography, structure, and instruments of your hell as the last word in subterranean planning and cruelty. But since your days, I can tell you, the world has enormously progressed, and in nothing has its progress been so great as in the invention of new forms of killing. Have you heard in your times, of bombs, planes, cyclone? Of course not. How could you? And we are still progressing, and do not even know what new forms of torture and killing are under way.

And so crimes and cruelties that only a few years ago seemed incredible, crimes that the maddest mind could not have dreamt of, are being committed before our eyes. But you, centuries back, must have foreseen all that. Not only thanks to the penetrating vision that an imagination as powerful as yours brings with it. But also because you, Maestro, understood evil and vileness, and the glorious history of man, better than almost anyone else. And neither evil nor man have basically changed.

Nor have killing and torture changed essentially since your days. Only its means and dimensions have.

Your poetry, however, the words with which you strive to achieve your ambitious aim of changing man, survived as a lasting monument to your genius.

I know, it is funny to talk of poetry now in this place. But it is not a sham. I am convinced that even inside the gas chambers, some victims recite, or think of, poetry. It is such a relief. Distracting from mental anguish. Keeps your thoughts miles away from death, which is in reality only an inch or less away. A marvellous theme to think in order to exist, to forget that you are soon to non-exist. A little bit of poetry, living sparks of timeless fantasy of the spirit, uplifts your longing for hope. Hope that normally arises from memories. I said normally, for to remember is to feel. And we, in this truck, have mostly lost the capacity of normal feeling.

No more aural gifts from days past and gone. Even your voice, mother, does not reach me any more. No calls to survive, never to bend, your "I'm with you". Not even sounds of grief, cries of eternal human pain - just you, man alone, in the bare solitude of death.

Not that I am rebelling. So it must be, even though it is past my understanding why. I accept that it is all for the good of us, setting thus the Lord before my eyes. Father, your teachings have not been entirely in vain. All that descends from Heaven is good. You are not His only son. A father punishes the child he loves. We must prove worthy of this love, to accept our sufferings with grace. And you, mother? You had instilled into us, your children, human dignity and endurance. There is a limit to everything. "It's too much" your glowing heart must be telling you. Too great a sacrifice to ask of him now to struggle on, to continue for the sake of the rest. He is, isn't he, no longer alive. But mother, I'm not dead yet.

Or are we all actually dead and only think that we are still alive? There is life in the realm of death; a state in which the distinction between the two is unreal. Shades virtually released from the ephemeral bonds of flesh and bone - but we are not lost. None of us - innocent, blameless souls - is lost.

Something quite different from your audience, my Maestro. Yours is an enormously interesting gallery of characters, who are more alive than they were before they died. Ours is a boring, lifeless sort of brotherhood, and would need a man of your powers to give us telling words. And, unlike yours, we're an innocent lot. This makes quite a difference when it comes to sociability and merriment. Not that we, here, are not sinners. Man is sinful. But none of us is persisting in sin. Nor are we damned. Doomed yes, but damned? They are, the Minotaurs of our phlegeton. They are not on guard now, as the train is moving. They travel comfortably in the last, open carriage.

They are murderers goaded by satanic man and doctrine, but not by satans or Lucifer chained in thick-ribbed ice. I wonder if Lucifer could breathe in our little, fiendish pit? And you, Maestro, who claimed to have descended into hell, could you breathe here? Would you like to try? But I warn you. The walls burn, the floor emits smoke, though without flame. Nor does light from the sun come in; the only glow that I can see comes from Dichter's tear-filled eyes. No devils, no animals or reptiles. Only tortured human bodies, wallowing in mess and manure, soaked with parching rain of sweat, and swallowed up by a storm of sorrow and torment. Forgive me, but will you - the most critical of men - ever understand how it really feels in hell? Or, that there is no greater joy in misery than recollecting happy, even less than happy, bygone days?

Will you, who spoke dire truths to the living and the dead, admit that tombs, coffins, however gruesome, look strange in hell? Simply inconceivable. Such a luxury! Such a ruin! Doubtless a financial ruin of the kingdom of darkness. A coffin, a simple box, for only every other one of its victims would undermine the Reich's entire war effort. You can't ask this much. But a simple grave, just a hole in mother earth to hold our mortal dusts? Thousands of my brothers, I can tell you honour

347

bright, had asked, raising their eyes to Heaven, for little else. A Jewish dream, you might think. The grace of place in barren soil.

In vain!

If I am inviting you, Maestro, to our limbo-train, it is not out of spite, or because the place inspires envy. No signore - but you would understand that I am ineffably unhappy at the thought that we, here, will vanish without a trace, without a single word to survive us in the memory of others. Ours may be the first major Jewish tragedy to pass without a poem, even without a dirge in prose. Not for us a Jeremiah to sound a lament that would blow far away the ashes of desolation, the eternal sigh of grief. Not a Kallir to extol the pang and pride of martyred souls. Not a lyric to eternalize death from a Crusader's dart or a Cossack's lance. Just so - to die without a verse. From the free but remote don't expect a rhyme. The dead only inspire dread. Forget what has passed and cannot be helped. The living and their demands come first. To remember in verse, there is love, liberating, intoxicating love, a fragrant rose on a night in May, the vanity of a world passing away. Besides, too great is this vale, a tragedy of epic scale, to be absorbed in mind, let alone befitting words to find.

But it can be done. For all its vastness it can be told. In words chiselled in fire by someone of your inspiration and talent. This is why I invited you, a sort of brother, who preceded us in imagination to this chamber of terror and tears. For just a short visit. To re-emerge, of course. To see the stars again. To carry away our memories, our lives, all that has passed before our eyes. To put them down in rhymes, for ever, for all times. A poem, a song, will escape safe and sound, even while its maker, a mere man, vanishes into the thin air.

The mystery of the written word's power of survival!

I wouldn't have disturbed your unapproachable, majestic rest, if I could command rhymes of any kind. But though a man of so little worth, I confess to a passion tormenting my soul. To leave but a spark of this fiery tale for generations alive and yet to come. To translate into simple human words the horror of the present days. Alas, it is not enough to see, to remember, to have a frantic will. It still needs inspiration and skill. The loftier the theme, the greater the inspiration required. Oh, have mercy, my Lord! Support me in this intention and desire. "Would that were written my words, would that in a book engraved, for ever in stone carved." Oh, give ear unto my prayer to preserve me strong and able to lift but a little the lid from this greatest of all tragedies.

But this is sheer vanity, Arush. You are incorrigible. It's not enough for you to stay alive, you pray for inspiration. In this truck!

Vanity it was - so what? What if not vanity is our, every man's eagerness to survive? And vanity being part of our earthly existence, one should aim high. If you ask for little, you'll get little, if you ask for much, you'll get much - your words father - for He is good our Creator, and He grants what one asks for. And I, even in my last sigh shall pray for inspiration and light.

Delusions Arush, control yourself! Even now you seem to feel a very important person. You lose the thread. Be silent! What was that noise?

CHAPTER TWENTY-SIX

There were once again murmurs inside the truck. Someone was moaning, causing a little commotion around him. His nearest neighbours were trying to lay the moaning man on the floor.

–"He's dying," Arush heard a voice saying.

–"Who is it?"

There was no answer.

After a while, the groans grew weaker, partly deafened by the clatter of men and wheels. This made Arush more conscious of the noise. The rhythmic rattle of the wheels, which had lulled him into reflection for the past hour, had unobtrusively passed away.

–"It's Goldman," reached Arush's ears.

–"Poor old Goldman," repeated Ruben. Age, perhaps also the memory of the exceptional death of the old man's son on their arrival at Pustkow, apparently still commanded respect and sympathy with the expiring mates.

Meanwhile, after travelling continuously for more than an hour, the train had started shuffling and bumping over points and switches. It must be nearing a station, Arush inferred. The end station?

Ruben, as if he had read Arush's thoughts, said: "After so much rattle and shuttle, this must be an important station." Was it the unknown destination?

All the mates were probably asking themselves the same question, raising tension to new heights. It was somewhat eased by a man who declared: "He has had a heart attack."

Dammit, a heart attack, Arush thought. This was all they needed!

But trains move on, heart attack or not. While the same man went on to say: "What can we do? He's had a heart attack!"

–"How d'you know?" asked another voice.

–"I'm telling you. He's dying. Perhaps already dead."

–"A heart attack at a time like this," muttered Ruben under his breath.

–"Yes, as if a heart attack was permitted here," Arush joined him willingly. "It'll be sabotage, if he dies of it. And ingratitude. A man is offered the favour of suffocation and he goes for a heart attack."

–"Oh really. It's unfair," Ruben grinned approvingly.

–"You'll see, they'll do something about it. This is not a lawless world."

In reply to Goldman's neighbour, a man shouted; "Rub his heart!"

–"No! Don't rub it!" opposed a friend near him. "It will make him worse in this heat. The heart needs cooling!"

–"Where can we find coolness here?" the man who was in favour of rubbing asked despairingly.

The cursed train had finally drawn into the station, and halted. Instantly, strain stopped the breath of the men inside the truck. "My heart is beating again," murmured Ruben.

A din of loud, sturdy voices and of stamping boots was heard from the platform. "Is this the end of the journey? Will the door open?" Arush's spellbound neighbours were asking. Yet long minutes went by without anything happening.

Then suddenly the men sitting near the outer wall, who must have heard familiar voices, all at once started calling: "Herr Oberscharführer, please open. Open! A little air. A heart attack. Open! Help! Goldman, heart attack!"

A voice seemed to have answered. Arush would not believe his ears. But the men near the wall confirmed the thing. "'Yes. Wait!' he had said. It was Ruf," agreed several men in excitement.

Amidst the expectation of what was to come next, men began bustling inside the truck. Goldman groaned more loudly, as if pleading: "Have pity on my body. A heart is not a stone." But the excitement soon subsided, and as doubt mounted, the men fell back into silence. The world seemed to vanish again.

After they had almost abandoned hope, the men heard the click of an unbolting padlock, and then the truck's sliding door opened.

The thunderous impression this made was beyond all imagination. At first, Arush thought that he was dreaming, a capriciously delusive dream. He rubbed his eyes - though more perhaps because of the dazzling daylight that suddenly flooded the truck. It was, likely enough, midday. The sun's full glare they were, mercifully, spared by the platform's grey-washed glass roof.

Surrounded by armed guards, Ruf and Zapke, both looking spruce yet grim, stood outside the open door. They were accompanied by Bubi and Dr Vadovitzer, stripped down to his trousers and carrying a little portmanteau with a physician's paraphernalia inside.

Arush looked out of the door rather impassively. He was overcome by a strange feeling. A real railway station, and normal, freely moving people. Quite a different world. He could sense how Columbus must have felt on sighting the new continent. Arush was also uncertain where they were. Yet no, this couldn't be anywhere but Cracow. No other station in this part of Poland had so many sidings and such an imposing building. True, he could see only a part of it, no more than the section directly outside the truck's door. But it looked to be a fairly big structure.

And beyond it lay Cracow - echoes of home, childhood, adolescence, all merging into one nostalgic memory. The familiar streets and houses must still be there, stretching along the delightful Planty, parks and gardens. What a jump from that quiet, ordered, cheerful life to the present slavery and death! No - parks and buildings they did not destroy, only people. Without our people, was it the same town? Would he recognize it? What really makes a town, its streets and houses, or its people? A difficult question. He must leave it for more serene days.

Meanwhile crowds of people were darting from the hidden sides and walking as silently as shadows past the truck. They aroused in Arush the illusion of a procession marching before them, taking their salute. The women and girls were cheaply but neatly dressed, all alike in the style, and hardly less in the colour, of their blouses and skirts. The men wore bright trousers and open-necked shirts with mostly rolled up sleeves. They all moved in a hurry. Hurrying people - how fantastic, how incredible! For whom the sun shines time is moving, Arush recalled something from school. Indeed it seemed that none of these people had a moment's time to stop. Certainly not to pass a drop of water. It was forbidden, of course. Those fresh and spry guards, for whom this journey had been a happy excursion, kept a sharp eye and a finger on the trigger. Fear might indeed partly explain why all these Polish men and women were in such a hurry. Some did not even turn, or move their eyelids. What was the good of looking at a forbidden sight? And what was so extraordinary about a truckload of naked skeletons, in this fifth year of war? What serious man wants to be a gaper? And who wants to gape at a spectacle that is bound to leave a trace in the memory for the rest of your life.

Yet some did peep from the corner of their eyes and moved on indifferently. Others walked by looking straight at the scorching men, their eyes filled with horror. What a ghastly scene they, in the truck, must have presented, Arush pictured a sort of charnel-house on wheels. Still others, a majority of those who stared rather longer than the rest, seemed, by the expression of their eyes and faces, to be thinking: "Oh, how the Yids are frying themselves!"

While Arush was watching the seemingly endless crowd, Dr Vadovitzer had climbed onto the truck and taken a syringe from his case and an ampoule to inject its contents into Goldman's arm. Such was the temperature inside the truck that the needle had bent. Goldman cried out loudly. Vadovitzer put back his instrument, advised them to let the patient rest on the floor and dashed out of the raging furnace.

Less than five minutes after it had opened, the door of the truck slid back. Once more the picture changed entirely. Airless darkness resumed its reign. Death crept back again.

Arush only then realized that he had not drawn a deep breath to fill his lungs with air for the rest of the journey. "I don't know why," he reproached himself. Was he perhaps reluctant to waste a moment of daylight with breathing? Or was it because of the smarting tightness of his throat? Or because the air in the truck had not improved, remaining stagnant and unbreathable? Surely the day was windless, sultry, tropically hot.

Yet if in terms of breathing space, if one may say so, this short episode was meaningless, it would be wrong to deny it any significance at all. Psychologically it was quite a treat, as all the mates must have thought shortly after. At least Arush was intent on thinking it out to the end. But Ruben was flattering him in order to resume conversation.

-"You're right. But how did you know that they would have a prick at Goldman?"

–"You don't understand the rules. This here is a death-machine, and like every machine it has its own logic. In this place you may die of asphyxia, eventually dehydration, or of another conveyancing hazard. But not of a heart attack, or a stroke, the cholera, or any of the thousand and one similar infirmities. This is discipline, this is logic, this is care."

In his mind there was another reason. Arush had recalled how about a week after the first Aktion in Tarnow, during which twenty thousand people were either murdered locally or "evacuated", a Jew had been run over by a lorry and killed in the Lwowska Street, just outside the future ghetto. German police had arrived in cars. Traffic was halted for at least half an hour. The German driver of the lorry involved was detained. His vehicle examined. Precise measurements on the road carried out, and testimonies from witnesses taken down. But to make a point of what he had said, Arush continued telling Ruben: "You know what is happening outside now. The most savage war. Thousands are killed daily. But, heaven forbid, if a soldier gets ill. If only he can prove it with his temperature or his furred tongue, he will get the best care on earth."

–"That isn't the same."

–"Quite right! It isn't the same. But the logic is much the same.

"Besides, if the orders say that so and so many livestock were entrained, then so and so many livestock are to be detrained at the destination, even if that's the incinerator."

–"This may be. But still - we had quite a ride, and may soon be driving off again. And they opened the door! What on earth for? Only to make fools of us? Of us to make fools? And whatever their orders, they might have let Goldman die. No one would have reprimanded Ruf, or any of the other footpads, for that. And if they opened the truck to let Vadovitzer treat a heart attack, then they are not carrying us to the slaughter. What d'you think?"

But without waiting for an answer, Ruben continued: "Rules are rules, but you know, they aren't always lived by. And for the sake of just a rule, all that exposure under the Poles' eyes? For all the world to see?"

Always the same, Arush thought. What a naive boy! His mood, his entire outlook, had changed. So must that of the others, too. And all because of that five minute marvel! Suffocating dried bones, perishing of thirst, without energy even to breathe, and they seem to think that their destinies had taken on a new appearance! As if the course of their journey had altered. While there was actually no end to it in sight. And the conditions, despite the open-door interval, are ever more killing. It apparently needs no more than a flimsy ray of light in the darkest blackness of one's existence to make all the difference between hope and despair, between belief and doubt, between resistance and surrender. At least here, this borderline crossing was not dangerous, was indeed pointless. Yet it was a good, however unconvincing, motive to struggle on. He must not weaken Ruben. Arush picked up his last point.

–"What does it interest the world what happens to us? For all the world cares, the Jews could bust themselves.

"Who of all those men and women whose salute we took, will weep at the sight of us? What are we to them? Men? Jews! Sinners! 'All their own fault', have you never heard them saying?"

–"I did. But what did you expect of them? Would any of our distant, affectionate Jewish brothers have cried if he were among that hovering throng?"

–"Hardly any. I also didn't mean it literally - to weep. I couldn't bear that; or any manifestations of pity. And it's improbable anyway - for a sight such as ours occasions not tears but fears.

"Besides bullets, there's typhus, and the melting heart. These days everyone is worldly-wise and knows that his life is worth as much as yours. Fear makes people callous."

–"And what about me and you? All of us? Aren't we, too, saying 'my life is worth as much as yours'? Our free brothers also tell themselves, 'keep yourself out of danger', as they are not in the enemy's grip.

"But tell me, what could those noon platform strollers really do to help us? A gulp of water? Rascals or no rascals, they wouldn't grudge a glass of water. And it wouldn't have made a shade of difference to us? Would it?"

–"Who could tell? It might. Water besides being wet and fluid, possesses mysterious life-giving powers."

–"I'm not familiar with mysterious powers. But when I saw the crowd swarming down the platform I had a strange feeling that I was watching the endless lines of our men and women pouring out of the ghetto on their way to some terrifying destiny, then gradually rising on a band of clouds to heaven."

–"You need some sleep, Ruben. Don't think about such things. Enough of that. Sleep a bit Ruben!"

Nothing novel, Arush commented in silence. Whatever one sees these days brings the same images. They are passing through time, never to be forgotten, even if one wished to rid one's mind of them.

Ruben still mumbled something, at least so it seemed to Arush, for he was no longer with him, but back in his silent monologue.

It was so convenient telling Ruben to sleep. And he may have wished to disperse his thoughts of death, to keep from going mad. Like the men outside, he had washed his hands and turned away. And why? To keep himself to himself - even in this insanely tight squeeze. What a selfish person he was!

But one cannot talk all the time. It really hurts - even to breathe. To face up to the constant challenge of death, one must let one's mind wander off from the insane, insufferable reality to a reverie of things eternal and delightful, to flee from the melancholy of extinction to the brightness of hope and fancy.

The train surprisingly hurried out of the station. For a few solemn moments their little world seemed to hang in suspense. Ruben re-opened his eyes, dim with goodness knows what, and announced with that air of gravity which was normally preserved for something that could decisively affect man's continued existence: "We're moving again!"

–"Yes, moving. So it seems. Heaven grant it."

–"And at what a speed! Have you noticed?"

–"Yes. Everything about this train is so uniquely strange that it even drives off at an abnormal speed."

–"Let it only be like that - abnormal. What, anyway, is normal?"

To answer him was not necessary. The wheels rattled underneath, carrying the sounds of hope, filling the stillness which no one wished to disturb. They counted the minutes and seconds which were bringing them nearer to the end of their journey - thus renewing their sense of a race against death.

But the rejoicing did not last long. Ten minutes. Ten minutes, and the train came to a stop. It had apparently been cleared out of Cracow railway station to a side-track some three miles away, where it would not impede the passage of more important trains.

Whatever the reason was, their train was now standing under the open sky, the blazing sun directly above them. Inside the truck, the heat began rising, and with it, doubts rose in their harrowed minds. They soon realized that for them time was now running out more quickly than they had felt before.

In what could he take refuge? Arush asked himself. Where had his hope gone? His sense of not dying, his passion to survive? Had he lost the capacity to retrieve them? His feeling of providence calling to lift him from the brink of the abyss? It was terrifying to admit, but he was no longer receptive to any calls. Not even from the world within him. It was not hurting him; nothing, it seemed, could hurt him any more.

Was he demented? Perhaps. Which of us could honestly tell if he was in his mind or out of it? Though Arush could not think of anyone in their truck having gone really mad, except perhaps Mandel, who, like a wound-up organ-barrel kept on saying that he could not hold out and would become insane - after liberation, he now added less frequently.

No doubt, it's the weather. Tammuz! The hottest month, and the god of fertility. Fertility as heat, barenness as cold. The wives of Babylon weeping for heat. He could understand the animating quality of warmth. In the biting cold at Szebnie, he had wished to die, only not to suffer. The heat he was now experiencing - however dreadful, and potentially far more deadly than the cold had been then - was rather encouraging his will to live, and to keep sane. Actually in most normal times, people had gone crazy in Tammuz days. The right question to ask was not if they were mad, but, if they were not, how had they not yet become so? What was that hidden and uncontrolled force that drives a normal person out of his mind? That makes a man's thoughts race as if he were set on by a beast of prey? Or was it a mere longing to escape reality?

But if he was still conscious of reality, as it seemed to him he certainly was, he couldn't have lost his senses. Yet, for all that, it was the reality that was unreal. Future chroniclers of these years will never get even the touch of them. They might think, as he occasionally does, that one could explain everything on earth, or even in heaven. But how wrong they would be! They would first have to get their minds unhinged before they could explain these days, which, he could tell them, are more insane than a man could ever hope to become.

Yet he must stay sane. And still. Calm, tranquility, open up the mysteries of death and thereafter.

The truck was again full of noise. He could even hear wheezy screams mixed with puny arguments coming from what in normal circumstances would be termed near-by.

Another heart attack? This time opinions were divided. Some said that the screaming man was dying, others that he was feigning - "wants to be coddled"; some even told him to shut up. "We're all weak and thirsty."

–"Leave him," said another man in a tone, the true quality of which Arush couldn't make out.

–"What does he think? Wants to lie stretched out? And where are we to go?"

–"Put him close to a crack, he needs a breath."

–"Such men get along in any situation," said one of those who considered the screams a fake.

–"Oh, can't you see that he's at his last gasp," pleaded Schimek for the poor screamer.

–"Then take him to lie on you," replied Doler.

At this point, Arush joined the exchanges. "Give him here," he said. "To me."

The end was inevitable this way or that way, he reasoned, and he had recalled the saying that "Whoever saves a single soul of Israel is assured the future life". His offering might be of no help either to him or to the screaming man, in this world. But what a bargain for the future!

–"Give him to me," Arush repeated with determination.

There were dissenting voices. "How will he get through? Impossible!" "He can't move." "You come and take him."

–"Get up! You must help us," Schimek told the man concerned, "if you want to pass by."

Mandel was raging. "He'll take away the tiny bit of air left. What have I done to you?" he asked Arush. "He'll crush me. The wall."

Arush could not tell if Mandel really feared that the wall would be crushed, or only himself. And although his shrill voice was menacing, Arush concluded that he was not dangerous, and would almost certainly do nothing, if only because the slightest move was so exhausting.

Ruben, on Arush's other side, was also muttering, but not unfriendly: "What a thing to fuss about - at this place."

As if fuss could be shut out of any place.

Pushed, shuffled, jostled and dragged, the man managed to creep the yardlong distance on his back, and Arush, gathering all his remaining will power and physical strength, took hold of him with an almost unbelievable effort.

It was Zundel. A tailor. In Pustkow they had worked in the same workshop, but at its two, diagonally opposite ends; while their bunks were in different barracks. Arush could not remember their ever having talked to one another. A trouser-tailor-assistant from Berlin, Zundel was one of those numerous men with whom fate threw one together in a camp, but with whom one had otherwise little in common.

Zundel was a rather short and reticent man in his forties with already greying hair. What always drew Arush's attention to him was his sharp-pointed cranium and sickly-pale face, adorned by shining grey eyes. Now Arush could only imagine how pale with exhaustion Zundel must be, as he continued to groan like a man in agony. He lay on the floor, his legs crooked, his head resting on Arush's lap. He was nursing him. That is, Arush wiped with his shirt the sweat which was running down Zundel's face, fanning him with his hand, alternated with a caress - and he talked to him.

–"Don't worry! You'll be all right. We'll soon be out," and the like.

Ruben, who apparently had watched them, warned Arush: "Don't pamper him so much. You may spoil him. He may not wish to get out!"

Zundel did not utter a word, but he gradually groaned less pathetically, and he grew less restless. It seemed to Arush that he could see an expression of gratitude in his face.

While thus physically occupied with Zundel, Arush's thoughts were far away from him. How did he come to do this? he asked himself. He felt so little for the man personally - no more than doctors feel for most of their patients. Surely his concern was more for himself than for Zundel. True, the sages of old had ruled that a man who says: "This coin for charity, so that I reach eternity, is a perfectly righteous man". But he was not satisfied. What, anyhow, precisely does to be "perfectly righteous" mean? Can anyone be perfectly righteous, even when, unlike the men in this truck, he is still susceptible to sinful temptation? He certainly did not feel righteous. Regrettably, but undoubtedly not. With that scorn for a fellow man! If not now, would he ever be capable of doing something disinterestedly? That cursed self-love! Would he ever free himself of its tyranny, if he could not do so even in this place?

On the other hand, this place itself destroys almost all human faculties, be it for good or evil. A place of diminished responsibility - yes, but of human responsibility nonetheless. And whether a man takes it up or not, depends solely on himself. If he was unable to be perfectly, or less than perfectly righteous - at least he could refuse to be indifferent, conceited, selfish, and similar refinements of the enemy within one's self, against whom a real man's fight never and nowhere ends.

Perfectly righteous might possibly mean to embrace genuinely your enemy without. As a token of complete submission to God's will. Can a man incarcerated in a sheath of flesh and bone accomplish this? He had said before that he did not hate them. But to embrace them? These master torturers, who keep them, for hours on end, slowly suffocating to death? To embrace these super-murderers, who have robbed them of their mothers and children, of their homes and possessions, of everything he treasured and that would make life worth living, were he to survive?

And yet, were they not the Almighty Lord's messengers? If it were not by His sanction, could all this have happened to him? There can be no existence or event, except by His will - so how could they be his enemies? Can he accept the Message but not the messenger who delivers it?

But were they really messengers of God? Did not man's actions proceed from his own free will and motive? The same source that speaks of hidden divine will, or the predestination of human action, teaches that man was given free choice to act, even to the extent of defying the will of Divinity. There was the law, father used to say, that governs the predetermined order of life, and there was the law by which human action freely takes place. Both laws were of divine origin, running concurrently, side by side, and, above the limits of human cognition, independently of each other. No, definitely nobody was forced to do evil - or good for that matter - and there could be no escaping responsibility for one's deeds before celestial justice in Heaven.

For all that, it might be prudent and worth trying to embrace his enemies as the ultimate act of repentance, and the final victory over his self. Oh, what a task! Holy Creator, thou knowest the secrets of a man's heart. It would be absurd pretending before Thee that he did embrace them. He was unable. It was not defiance. He simply could not rise to such heights, or rather humble himself to such depths, even while bodily he was more downtrodden than the lowest of Thy creatures. It would require a much higher spirit, one loftier than the clouds, a saintly man of Rabbi Israel Baalshemtov's calibre, to embrace an oppressor such as his Germans.

Yet, the simple truth that follows from this admission is that in the final moments of his life, by which he would be judged, he was not truly repentant.

Why was he not? A question made in search of self-justification. If a man's will is free, if his actions are of his own volition, if he is responsible for them before Deity - to embrace, or not, these Germans could have nothing to do with being, or not being repentant before God. Still, at the same time that an event in life on earth is, as of the will of man, humanly autonomous, it is divinely predestined and inevitable. Oh Heavens, how intractable this appears to be! How confusing even to a man with a full ration of air and blood! But it is only because his mind is so little that those laws and ideas come to blows. By humility he could perhaps find a way to their solution. Instead, man is proud. And where does that lead him?

While superior on earth, he slights the immense distance from heaven. His belief in himself, his pursuit of power, his desire to be superman, daring ascent to demiurge, the rival of God, or even to make of himself a god. This is both the origin and consequence of evil.

Show at last humility, Arush - he told himself once again. Burn out your pride in this flaming heat. Cast away your disgusting passion to penetrate the mysterious. Humble your mind and everything will become clear and simple. Enough for you!

And yet it would be untruthful to deny that just then, at that place, to be thinking was a singular blessing. What other proof, he pondered, did he have that he was still aware, that death had not taken possession of his body? Breathing - there was no way of telling that he still was. And so little feeling of other senses. Life was practically reduced to thinking. I think, so I live. Perhaps, that French arch-doubter was, after all, reasonable. Who knows?

Meanwhile, Zundel had ceased moaning. He lay quietly, and Arush seemed to see a peaceful expression hovering over his face. He did not ask him how he felt in order not to provoke a grunt in reply. But he kept on nursing him, cradling his head in his lap. Quite clearly, it had worked wonders. How? For all this nursing was a psychic bubble, no more than a friendly gesture. Perhaps it was just this that he had screamed for - a little human warmth, a token of affection in the solitude of death? For he knew something, Arush told himself, how utterly lost one could feel in the midst of that crowded, to the point of choking, heap of human bodies.

It was possibly the same, familiar dread of dying alone that made a sister and brother, two loving hearts, choose to die together, when only one was given the chance to live. The intense longing not to be separated from each other on the last march down the road to the deadly bath - husbands and wives, with their mothers and children, closely nestling, walking abreast, hands clasped, fearing more to die separately, than death itself. The same agonizing fear that urged families to stick together, rather than to persuade the young, strong members to try to flee the ineluctably vanishing ghettos. The horror of having to carry the load of the unfolding tragedy on one's lone back, the prospect of remaining alone in this vast and cruel world seemed unbearable. Better take together the path of death, the heart had counselled, than the route of single escape.

Hours passed. The train still stood where it was, and it didn't think to move. It was afternoon, the sun at its highest point, striking them with its mighty flames. Outside, the man recording this day would put down in his diary that the sky was blue, the sun golden, the fields basking in its splendour. Life looked brighter, yet it seemed to have stopped in the afternoon hours, when the sun shone most "vivaciously".

They, in their den, were entirely at the mercy of this mighty sun. Sky-high above, what did it care about what was happening to the lowly creatures herded inside a forsaken railway truck? What is, anyway, man to the sun? How insignificant is he with the days of his life a few tens of years compared with a sun which since that memorable day at Givon over three thousand years ago had never ceased to shine. Today, Arush reflected, it glitters with all its resplendent energy, a little too much for even the toughest among them. You plainly feel how it roasts your skin, how it grabs you by the throat, drying out the last drop of fluid from your guts. Quite distinctly he could hear death marching, its steps ringing in his ears. He could scent its nauseating smell which spins the head and turns the eyeballs round. He had no means of defending himself - be it from the darkness of death or from the brightness of sun.

Those feelings were certainly common in their truck. But, characteristically, the roaming ghost of death had elicited from the damned men a last spurt of the will to live. The truck was once more noisy with whispers and curious sounds; some probably began to pray, others to blubber. Certainly something was seething all over the place. Though drawing all his attention, Arush could not initially make out what it was. But soon the turmoil burst out with the ferocity of desperate lambs.

What happened was that the impulse to live had suddenly drawn to the surface a lasting, discordant issue in their truck. The issue was the cracks in the wall. They were seen by most of the inmates, who by then felt their lives running out before their eyes, as the last remaining refuge. So that a number of the men had tried, using up all their remaining vitality, to take a turn at a crack, if only for a few seconds. But for the same "life conserving" reason, the individuals who had been "holding" the cracks, were at the present critical hour more determined to keep them for themselves than at any time before. And this gave rise, unbelievable as it might sound, to a struggle for a little chink in a wall, or more accurately, for lying-space near a chink. And however physically soft, it was a struggle for survival of man against man in the most direct way that one could imagine.

The defenders were fitter than their assailants. While Seibald was holding to his tiny slit, the two largest ones on the outside wall nearer to Arush were firmly guarded by Cetel and Pelz. Cetel had a robust constitution and looked the fittest of all in the truck. Pelz was thin and shortish. In Pustkow, where he was a cobbler, Arush had always avoided him. There was something in his appearance which had scared and repelled him. He was one of those few prisoners who had consistently exchanged their bread rations for smoke. He was apparently a very strong man.

Now there in the dark truck, it appeared to Arush as if Pelz had leapt to his feet and taken up a pose with the look of a man, who was ready to pull out a knife to defend his skin or property from attackers.

–"You stir, my good brother, and I'll make you regret it," he shouted.

Cetel, less aggressively but not less categorically, kept on calling: "No one will come up to the crack. Only try, and you'll see!"

There were, of course, more voices claiming that the cracks were common to all, that access to them should be in turns, that they only wanted to catch a breath or two, and so on.

–"Over my dead body," howled back Pelz. "This has been my seat from the beginning, and no one will grab it from me as long as I'm in one piece."

Some minor scuffles broke out, but in the main the struggle was, mercifully, confined to shouts and threats. Most men were too weak for a serious fight, and even at this late hour they retained the good sense to understand that access to the cracks being possible to only three or four men at a time, a crack-free-for-all struggle could only result in a murderous pandemonium.

Five years of this lovely war had passed him, so Arush knew what men were capable of doing one to another. Nevertheless the latest scene of men who were bound to die together, pitted one against another in a fight for a whiffle of air, saddened him deeply. How good, he thought, that there were no cracks in the walls of the gas chambers.

In all that turmoil Arush took no part. Not that he was indifferent to what was going on, but he had chosen to watch and keep silent. Ruben, who like Arush, had remained quietly seated, told him what he thought. "Let them keep the cracks, but it makes me a little angry that they may survive owing to aggressive behaviour towards their fellows." This reflected Arush's own thoughts. But he also tried to rationalize in his mind. Even if he were of different make, a fighter by nature, and not so feeble as he was, it would not have been worth making the effort. The cracks cannot make that much difference. It was one's power of endurance that counted. Indeed, to concentrate too much on aspiration could even be perilous, reducing one's vigilance to other dangers.

He would do better to hold on to his pet; it was a much safer bet. He gave Zundel a caress, and told him: "We'll manage. You'll see."

Arush seemed to discern a faint smile right under his nose.

The dust had settled. The last hope, however dim, had vanished. It was quiet again. There was nothing to be done about the situation. Ruben had dozed off. Everything had returned to the heartrending apathy of silence. Yet the darkness was full of alarmingly mysterious sounds. He was too exhausted by then to grasp their meaning.

After thirty hours in this fabulous truck, he was getting weaker every minute. The slight attention he had shown to Zundel might have been too much for him. When you are as weak as he was, when you are smothered by blasting heat, when, as a result, your life hangs on a thread, every gesture is a risk, the slightest movement could snap the thread. Anyway, he had had enough of it.

Indifference, at first unobtrusive, was steadily gaining on him. Though he had the curious feeling of life slipping out of his body, he was too tired to understand what was happening to him. He was too wearied to realize that in a few moments the adventure of his life would draw to its end.

Arush was no longer capable of mobilizing the power of faith to fight back and defend himself. He was not capable of thinking clearly. He could see no connection between one thing and another. Everything was losing sense. Was he still alive? He did not know. He had no will and no means of knowing. He knew nothing. He feared nothing - not even the losing of his consciousness.

And then there was light and peace - Arush's soul signalled from heaven.

PART FIVE

Arrival and Departure

CHAPTER TWENTY-SEVEN

Back on earth, Arush felt someone pulling his shoulder. He heard human speech. Was someone talking to him?

Another pull. He opened his eyes and stared in helpless amazement. Where was he? At long last he perceived the early light of day and that the doors on both sides of the truck were wide open. Was he awake? he asked himself. Had he got his breath back? Was he living? Again?

Yet another pull. This one shook his whole body. A man was telling him firmly, yet quite softly, in German: "Get up! You must get off the train! Dress and take all your things with you!"

Who was he? Arush could not figure it out. A stranger, he concluded. He looked around. The truck was empty. Some burly characters in civilian clothes were moving about inside it. One of them turned again to Arush.

–"Get off the truck, for heaven's sake! You can't stay here, on pain of death." He now spoke Yiddish.

Arush only had a vague realization of what the man was saying. Anyway he was without any inherent power of movement and could not get up. The man lifted him and again ordered, "Pick up all your belongings!"

Leaning on the wall, Arush now stood on his feet, but still in an utterly dazed condition. With untold effort he managed to struggle into his short coat, which the man had handed to him, but he was too weak to put on the shirt. He was fortunate to be wearing his trousers.

–"Your shoes?" asked the man.

Arush nodded.

–"Take them!"

The strangers on the truck must have noticed that Arush was tottering and on the point of tumbling, because one of them took Arush in his arms and carried him down to the ground.

–"Go forward," he said. "Follow the others. Hurry up!"

Weary and numb, Arush found himself somehow trudging along the road in dead silence, like the rest. The narrow path was laid with little, spiky stones, sharp enough to make even Arush feel the pain. His shoes, like his shirt, he carried in his hands.

Arush walked, Arush breathed, Arush could hear words, but he could not reason them out. He was neither thinking nor responding to the surroundings. Clearly something had seized up in his head. And, consequently, his recollections of those first steps on that Friday morning were also numb, as were those of most of his companions.

But as with almost everything in life, this mental stupor had its good side as well. It spared them the first impressions of the new place: the peculiar smell in the air, the scent of burnt human bodies from which there was no escape, and the agonizing tension, while their immediate fate hung by a thread.

What Arush clearly remembered of that early morning was that they waited - quietly waited in the middle of a patch of earth which bore no particular name and suffered no description. Occasionally someone, breaking orders, disturbed the silence with a sigh or query.

–"What are we waiting for?"

–"Admission to camp," answered a fellow behind Arush.

–"We're inside a camp, aren't we?" insisted the questioner.

–"No! Not yet."

–"What camp?" asked a sleepy voice nearby.

–"Auschwitz."

Auschwitz after all, Arush commented in silence. If he had heard then the name of any other camp, or that they were waiting to be sent home, it could not have left him more indifferent.

–"And we didn't die immediately," added the fellow who had said Auschwitz.

"Immediately" was not yet over, but this they were only to learn later.

Meanwhile, they continued waiting, crowded together, without visible attention from any authority. Only at a distance they could see Unterscharführer Ruf and one or other of his Pustkow colleagues bustling in and out of a massive building, which stood out among the countless, unvarying barracks. The whole vast area was surrounded by long stretches of barbed wire fences, which were only interspersed every furlong or so, by watch-towers shooting against the sky.

Why were their former Pustkow guards fussing about so much? The question was asked by Arush's companions not so much out of idle curiosity, as from deep anxiety. The answers they offered were curious. "They're pleading for us at the local command." "They're demanding a decision from Berlin." But Berlin is still sunk in sleep. This, incidentally, explained their long wait.

While they remained like this for hours, impassively awaiting their sentence, another transport of Jewish prisoners arrived in a similar train at the same platform. Situated at the edge of a little birch-wood, this camp platform had been only recently built as an extension of the Auschwitz station, to shorten the distance from the train to eternity. The reception accorded to the new arrivals was not so quiet as their own had been. They were greeted by shrill shouts and whistles, cries and screams, by SS men and dogs. Nearly as many dogs as SS men, barking, howling, pouncing and jumping.

Driven out of the trucks, the terrified newcomers were set on the same path Arush and his mates had followed earlier that morning. Proceeding under close guard, they eventually passed by a doctor in SS uniform, who with a movement of his finger directed a few of the young and fit among them towards the side the Pustkow group had taken. The rest, upwards of a thousand men, women and children, continued straight on their very last walk to the "bath".

At that time Arush and his companions did not know that admission to the camp was itself a pronouncement of sentence, granting the captives a temporary reprieve. Older prisoners enlightened them later that although this was the rule, there had been numerous exceptions to it in the recent past. If the queue to the gas chambers was too long, the doomed men were admitted to the camp "on deposit" - in official, presumably humorous SS jargon - and kept waiting before being driven back to their deaths. At the time when Arush and his friends arrived, the old-timers explained, murder was at its highest in Auschwitz, and possibly the highest it had ever been in the whole history of mankind.

Whatever was the reason for the Pustkovians' delay, some senior prisoners finally arrived to take charge of them. SS men did not need to attend to such minor business themselves; they could rely on the "function-prisoners" - those assigned to special duties - to carry out their orders.

–"Follow me!" Forward march!" commanded one of these.

After a short walk they reached a solid brick building, the so-called Sauna. The place of holy disinfection, without which no new arrival could be admitted to camp.

–"Undress!" was the next order. "Leave everything where you stand!" the man pointed to the ground.

–"Clean yourself properly! Do not try to dodge! Dirt is the prisoner's enemy." Soap was handed out to everyone.

Then began another round of waiting, but with a difference: they were now standing naked, soap in hand, facing an ugly building.

The morning was warm, without a breeze, the sun again the prisoner's friend and ally.

Many of them were suspicious of the building. Arush was happily unconcerned. He did not hear the frightful noise of groans and shrieks, which faintly reached their lines. Nor did he see the roof with the smoke-puffing chimney which lurked behind the Sauna building. He stood sucking in all the air his lungs could absorb. Oh, he sighed, if only he could grasp the air with his hand and store it away! And water! Never mind the wash, but drink, drink...His body knew but one cry - water! His thirst was even more piercing than yesterday in the truck. "Quickly, what are we waiting for?"

–"You don't know?" Arush heard a neighbour whispering. "And you know where you are?"

They were at the entrance to the showers and in his feverish fancy Arush heard a roaring, intoxicating gurgle of water. And he was only a yard or two away from it. What a promise! What a dream!

Was he aware of the peculiar impression his first acquaintance with Auschwitz made on him? His arrival in Szebnie had been a most depressing experience. It was difficult to imagine a more decisive change in living conditions than the transition from urban surroundings into a new world of barracks, bunks, towers, barbed wire, and muddy earth - on a bleak autumnal day at that. By contrast, the admission to Auschwitz was for him, and his entire group, an enlivening occasion. They had come from a camp and outwardly all camps looked much the same and had a similar frame of life. Far more important was the jump from the pitch black darkness of the truck and the throes of death into a new lease of life on a beaming, sunny day. The light was simply exhilarating. And, on top of everything, the quaint sensation of relief a man, falling slowly down the precipice, feels on reaching the bottom. He could fall no further. He was at the anus mundi germaniae. From now on he could only move up. The possibility that he could remain at the bottom, was a prospect blurred by his renewed will to live.

Who could really think about such a contingency at that time? A man's instinct takes him under its wings; it tells him that the great thing is to stop worrying and that he must rise above all adversity. And his senses rush in with more support, carried by the feeling of chilling comfort that comes with total deprivation.

Surely it is strange to feel a sense of relief in being freed of one's last possessions. But it was common in their circumstances. Every time they had been moved, they had grieved to leave some things behind. First, house and home, then books, beds and rugs, later still crocks and pots. But till the last they had been left with a bundle of rags. Now, everything that was their own had at last gone. Not even a belt or bowl, a blanket or trinket, no pants or socks. Try to understand - as Hugo Bester had once sardonically observed - a civilization without pants and socks. A new reality based on non-possession and simplicity; imagine the harmonious simplicity of existence without material goods. Naked among the naked, like Adam and Eve. They were in Paradise!

Down on earth, you are a slave. You live all your days a prisoner of your acquisitive passion, and your carnal passion, and your intellectual passion, and your passion for power. Is it not this fever to get as much out of life as possible during the brief span of your mortal years, that breeds most human crimes, culminating in Auschwitz? But the moment you possess nothing the world takes on another aspect. There remains only the Word.

Arush Freund was slowly recovering his spirit. For most of the time since his arrival at Auschwitz he had been dazed, and his thoughts chaotic. It would be more truthful to say that he was not thinking at all, somehow delighting in the idleness of his mind, which had brought him peace, harmony and escape from agonizing uncertainty. The brilliant sunshine, the outward absurdity of waiting naked in the open, and the vague realization that there was so little to lose, combined to put him into rather good spirits. But perhaps more than anything else, it was the piercing cry for water which had been instrumental in setting his brain slowly back to work. And after another hour of waiting in front of the Sauna, he had already revived enough to resume gradually his inward conversation.

What goofs his new guardians were, if they thought that by stripping him naked they could break him. The only effect was just to make him determined to adapt himself and draw fresh strength from this nakedness. There was a creative force in it. Highest spiritual values could originate from it. When one is as naked as he actually was, all that divides innocence from sin, right from wrong, is just the leaf of a fig. Put it on and don't moan about it! Lift yourself from the cheerless dust of matter to the real riches of spirit. "Oh God," he declaimed in self-justification, "because for thy word I long, I pant for breath and I lust for water." This cursed lust for drink! This raging thirst! The ancients were right: all human desires derive from the element of water. If only he could get rid of this passion! He did not care about food. Only water. "A little water," he cried out loud.

A neighbour rapped him with his elbow. "What's with you? He may hear," the man whispered, pointing in the direction of a senior, red-cheeked prisoner, with an equally red triangle, above the letter P, sewn to his smart shirt. Arush looked at the senior closely, though from the very first glance he had reminded him of Bera.

In the good old days every family of not too modest means had stocked up with coal for the winter. A cart or two would pull up before the house to carry the coal down into the cellar that belonged to every flat in a decent but not so new building. It was as useless to mount guards as it was to use shouts, threats, the cover of night, or the presence of police. In no time some of the coal would be gone, carried away by a gang of youths. Their leader was Bera, a young man, very handsome - if he had been cleaned up a bit - whose looks, however, witnessed that no decent crime was strange to him.

The senior prisoner to whom Arush's neighbour had pointed was, but for his meaner stature, as like Bera as two drops of water are alike. He must have heard Arush's cry, but pretended not to. Thus in almost undisturbed stillness the men he watched continued to wait, stripped, strained and consumed by their raging thirst.

But everything comes to an end, and after two more hours, by which time the men were sufficiently tired and resigned to put their heads even into the lion's mouth, the doors of the Sauna opened like the gates of a castle in a fairy tale. Shortly, his turn would come, Arush delighted in his fantasy. As soon as the water flowed, he would drink. If only there would be enough water. As for washing - he did not care a tinker's curse.

Inside the washroom, it was very crowded, a hundred men squeezed to a dozen taps. They looked like any other shower sprays. Let them only not stay dry! But they did, and the men waited for the water to come, counting seconds for hours.

At last, as if to whet their appetites, a few single drops dripped down. One could count them. Arush managed to catch one drop in his open mouth. Oh, what a cheat! This was never water. Liquefied iron-rust. At least that's what it tasted like to him. A second drop, oh no! No matter how dry a man were, he could not swallow this stuff. Well, at least have a decent wash, Arush told himself. "When will the water come?" the mates were demanding loudly, emboldened by the fact that the place looked like a real bathhouse. But there was no one who could tell them.

Four minutes more and the farce was over.

—"*Genug!* Enough! Everyone out this side!" came the orders, leading them into another room outside. Arush was too distracted to recall that their reception was basically the same as in Szebnie.

No one had managed to wet as much as the palm of his hand. Yet woe to him who tried to come near anyone who had not yet passed through the showers.

Next, to the coiffeur's salon. One by one, in a queue, they had to pass a prisoner who with a few turns of the clipper plucked their hair from wherever it grew. The clipper was no blunter than in Pustkow, but the skin was softer in those parts which had not been touched before. Another function-prisoner, dipping a brush in dark, petrol-stinking liquid, moved it over the shaved parts of the body. They were now officially deloused.

−"Everyone move along! This side!" But where you were to go you did not know, until you had walked across a long corridor, and queued up again before the desk of a camp bureaucrat, who wrote down your answers to his brief questions.

−"Hurry up! Wear this!"

They were thrown a bundle or rags. What dirt! Sickening merely to look at it. Put a louse for every spot on what had once been a man's shirt and you would know the number of their casualties. The clogs they were given had a procrustean fit. To shuffle along in them, you had to shrink the toes of one foot and stretch those of the other.

−"Form fives! Quickly!"

Marched off in the direction of barracks, or blocks as they were called in Auschwitz, they were greeted at the entrance to one by little Bera. Actually he was called "krwawy Józek", Józek being his Christian name, while *krwawy*, which translates into English somewhat equivocally as bloody, was an appellation neither undeserved nor demeaning and certainly not arbitrary. It was simply derived from Jozek's habit of occasionally beating a prisoner until, in his own words "blood gushes from your arse". Nevertheless, the epithet *krwawy* was not entirely fair. For, as Arush learned later, Jozek had not personally battered ordinary, little-folk, since the time he had been invested with the insignia of his present office. Jozek was the "eldest" - the second highest rank in prisoners' seniority - of the block to which the Pustkow men were allocated. It was truly remarkable what wonders this war had produced, Arush brooded; who would have guessed that such an illiterate Warsaw cut-throat, in his early twenties, had learned not only to address men, but in a foreign language at that - though Jozek's German sounded like the speech of a perverse, parochial parrot.

−"You are now in my block. I'm the block-eldest. This is your home for as long as you remain in quarantine. Keep your home clean. Respect your seniors. Be obedient, listen to orders, and you'll be happy to live in Block Two. You can do everything that's allowed. You'll be told what that is. Just take my word for it!" At this he struck himself on the chest.

Minutes later, Jozek's aides-de-camp told the men some of the rules, the most important of which was that no ordinary prisoner was allowed, under pain of severe punishment, to be in the block during the "day" - that was from morning roll-call till evening roll-call, except during lunch-time. The "quarantinee" must stand around his block; literally stand, for to sit was against the rules.

−"What's quarantine?" almost every one of the newcomers asked.

To an outsider this may sound a stupid question. But the exclusive world of German concentration camps had its own vocabulary, and one which often differed from camp to camp. Anyway, Jozek's aides-de-camp had no time for such questions.

–"*Anstellen!* All in line!"

It was about noon when the men from Pustkow entered the camp's barracks-compound, and soon lunch, that most important event in the long day of a prisoner's life, was to be served. They were lined up for soup together with the older inmates of block two, providing the newcomers with their first opportunity to make acquaintance with other prisoners. But to talk in the queue was forbidden and, under the capos' eyes, dangerous. Two orderlies handed out bowls, but no spoons. The men held the red enamel bowls with the awe of ancient priests holding holy goblets. Their hands trembled with impatience, while they waited for the soup. Let it be watery and cold today, Arush said to himself. To volunteer was, however, against the prudent prisoner's manual, and even in this case it had seemed too daring a thought. At last two huge cauldrons arrived, and when the lids were lifted steam shot up, despite the heat of the day. While the functionaries were holding a council on the side, excitement, particularly among the old-time prisoners in the queue, rose to boiling point. The men in the first lines were nervously thrusting forward their bowls. "Why don't they start ladling it out?" ran through everyone's mind. "Oh now, at last! They're coming."

–"Newcomers, hand back your bowls!" A block functionary explained: "You're late. You are not on the kitchen's service list yet."

Well, supper was only six hours away.

The contact with other prisoners caused a mental diversion, and time seemed to pass more quickly. It was, of course, the newcomers who were the centre of interest. "Where have you come from?" "And before that?" "Have you perhaps heard of my brother?" "Are there still any Jews in Poland?" and many other familiar questions.

Hard as he tried to retain all that was said around him, Arush could not remember very much. So many different thoughts were crowding his mind, making everything he heard sound a little distant. The first question that he asked was, "Where can one get water?"

–"Water? You can buy a glass for a watch or a chain of gold," explained a young man who had apparently been there long enough to know about these things.

Where could one get such precious things, the newcomers wondered. They had not come straight from home. They were camp evacuees. There was not much booty to be found on them. It was their good fortune - though of this they were unaware at the time - for this was why no SS men or any of their close aides had bothered to be present on their arrival at the ramp. Even in Auschwitz no one was interested in paupers.

Next to water, the thing most of the newcomers were anxious to find out was where precisely they were and what quarantine meant.

–"You're in Birkenau, in quarantine," a prisoner assured them, a man who had himself arrived there two weeks earlier from Transylvania, a fact which he mentioned almost apologetically.

–"So not in Auschwitz?"

–"Yes in Auschwitz. But you see, Auschwitz," the man stretched his arms out over his mates' heads, "is the whole huge complex, extending over several miles and enclosed by barbed wire and watch-towers. This part where we are, is called Birkenau. This is where the trains arrive, unload their passengers, and where, you know," he stopped for a while, "the chimneys are." He pointed discreetly towards them. "You're lucky," he went on, "that all of you have come in. From the whole of my train of more than a thousand men, women and children, only about eighty were allowed to live."

He had to take a deep breath, so that another prisoner, who had arrived with him on the same train broke in quickly.

–"The new arrivals," he explained, "as long as they are in Birkenau, are said to be in quarantine. That's what the Germans call it."

–"How long?"

–"It varies," threw in the first of their friendly initiators into Birkenau mysteries. "Some are still here after six months. Others are moved after a week."

–"Where to?" the newcomers wanted to know.

–"To the main Auschwitz camp, or to another of its innumerable branches. There they start to work. In quarantine you don't work. You just stand around the block the whole day long. And so one day looks like another, just as one prisoner looks like another. But don't think," he added, "that this is a rest-house. Oh no, quarantine isn't a sanatorium. The great thing is to get out of Birkenau, and the sooner the better. Even for hard work."

That's good to know, Arush thought, but, meanwhile they were lodged in Birkenau. Hesitantly, like a child tasting a new delicacy, he entered the block.

It was a well-built wooden barracks, bright inside, with daylight coming through normal sized windows - a mixed blessing this, as they were to learn at night. The furniture consisted of three-tiered wooden bunks, ranged in three lines and separated by not too narrow gangways. Counting one man to a single bunk, the barracks could house 400-500 people. At midday the bunks looked vacant, free of straw-sacks, blankets, or anything else. The planks were clean, and the whole structure seemed only a couple of weeks old.

At the centre of the barracks, a few of the men who waited inside, were queuing to put on phylacteries. Arush joined them.

The treasure belonged to a teenage boy, whose pale, almost childish face was lit up by large shining eyes and a tranquil smile. He had arrived the same week from Hungary. Though deeply intrigued how he had managed to get such a bulky and dangerous thing through "disinfection", it seemed to Arush pointless to ask him. Time was short and the recess-time running out quickly. Indeed, only a few minutes later, two orderlies burst into the block, shouting wildly and incomprehensibly.

Arush left quickly, but not before he had managed to catch a glimpse of the solemn writing above the door: "The block is your home..." Bloody Jozek was perhaps not such a wit, as Arush had been first inclined to think.

Outside everyone had gathered around the barracks, the less privileged prisoners, such as the Pustkow arrivals, along the wall facing the glaring sun. As to sit down was against the rules, and to remain standing, and thereby conspicuous, seemed imprudent, Arush, Marek and a new acquaintance, settled down squatting - like most others - by the wall. Lolek Kwas, their new colleague, came with a group of Jewish prisoners from a camp near Budzyń, a town which, in the good old days, had been his home. He was about the same age as Arush and Marek, fairly tall and dark-eyed. When he turned his face, it looked long and lean, his whole figure suggesting that he had not exactly overeaten these past weeks. He had a pleasant, sonorous voice, and was keen to display to the newcomers the experience of nearly twenty days seniority in Birkenau.

–"Uncomfortable? Don't grumble," he spoke quickly, not allowing anyone to interrupt him. "Conditions in quarantine are now much better. Everyone says so. Once they used to send the Muselmans - those are the emaciated, the beaten and the wasted bodies of men no longer fit to work - for gassing. There are practically no Muselmans in quarantine at present, and for some months now it's only Jews who are being gassed. Aryans are left in peace, as long as one of them is not caught red-handed doing something truly bad."

–"So it seems, Auschwitz is only half as bad as we thought it would be. At least if one is Aryan," said Marek.

Lolek noticed Marek's irony, and tried to correct himself.

–"I didn't mean it that way. What I meant to say is that, given the conditions, there's now a chance to survive, if one isn't sent to the gas. Every day is a day gained, every day the end of war is nearer. Now it's really only a matter of weeks. At most. Why did they evacuate us, d'you think? Isn't it because the Russians are treading on their heels? The whole week before we left our last camp we could hear gun fire at nights. Now, here, everyone says, and there are some chaps who listen to the radio and even get hold of German newpapers - that's not here in Birkenau, but in the main camp - they say that Lublin is Polish. The Germans have retreated. That is, they never retreat..."

–"What news is Lublin," Marek cut in, "when this week the Russians were close to Pustkow, which lies far more to the west?"

–"Well, you know, the bastards don't move in a straight line. They took Lwow only this week, and Lwow, I understand, is upwards of 150 kilometres to the east of your Pustkow."

–"That's just the grape-vine," Marek contradicted.

–"But I swear to you that I got it, quite confidentially, from a man whose previous information has always proved true. He also said that the Germans are 'straightening their lines', on the river Bug, among other places. That's what I meant, that they never retreat. You perhaps remember how they used to laugh at the English, in those bleak days after Dunkirk, saying the more they retreated the less they were defeated. So the Germans do not retreat, they only straighten up their lines, and shorten the front."

–"And what about in the west?" asked Arush.

370

–"Still no change. Quiet. Our English and American allies have caught a cold from crossing the waters. Sneezing, you know. So they are taking a rest. But you wait, it'll soon start rolling from the west, too.

"And you can see some pretty consequences of the changing military situation here, in Birkenau. The Germans, well, they were killing in victory, and they go on killing in defeat, and they are in a hurry to finish the job as completely as possible; and so the killings have now reached unprecedented dimensions. But their flunkeys have stopped killing, and are even thrashing far less now than they used to. Take Jozek. No one around remembers him to have ever seriously hit an ordinary prisoner. He only mangles his future aides - every single one of them. Right at the start of their damned careers. The head in the stove's little door, feet in the band, arse up on the log, and the rod down on the arse. After such an initiation the new appointees beat their commonplace victims for any reason, and for no reason, just to make sure that they never again attract Jozek's displeasure. What a method! They must have a special academy in Berlin for this kind of discipline. But lately all ranks of senior prisoners, even some who are German, have lost their nerve. They beat less frequently and less furiously. One of our block orderlies, you know that lanky fellow, Franek, who in happier days used to come to my father's workshop, he recognized me. And you know what he said to me? That he's doing only what he's required to do. 'I'm a prisoner like you,' he told me. Would a peace-time tearaway like him have said such a thing in 1942, or even a year ago? Deny his own superiority? Compare himself with an ordinary prisoner, and a Jew at that? Unthinkable. But nowadays even the most fanatical of the German collaborators, whether he's Polish, French, or Hungarian - and not just here, but outside, at liberty, too - have lost their faith in a German future. That Franek, and fellows like him, must already sense that what they may face at liberty is another 'Auschwitz'."

–"Ah, that's foolish," Marek again objected. "What fellows like him now think of is, how to capitalize after liberation on their 'evident' patriotism and martyrdom, as former prisoners of Auschwitz. And as for their words being signs that the war is nearly over, we had plenty of those in Pustkow, and they were more telling, because they came from SS men themselves. All those signs aren't worth a groschen, for in relation to us the Germans' will, and power, of destruction is as strong as ever."

Yet there was no doubt that Lolek's observation was correct, and they had instant proof of it. For, feeling pins and needles in his legs, Arush stretched them out and sat down on the ground. Almost immediately shouts and yells came in his direction, but, after he had lifted himself quickly back into a squatting position, nothing worse followed.

–"Your good luck," muttered Lolek, turning to Arush."Fortune favours fools! Forgive me...We're all fortunate...I mean that we didn't come here earlier. Life in Auschwitz is now a paradise, compared with the horrors of the past, as any of the few veteran-survivors will tell you."

Lolek was in a talkative mood and there was nothing to stop him.

–"You look at me as if you don't believe me. I don't blame you. No one, let alone newcomers of only a few hours standing, can believe everything that's going on here. It simply doesn't enter your head. You're like little children. And that's why you don't realize how fortunate you are - all of you, young and old, strong and frail, a whole trainload, to be let in. These days many of the Hungarian transports are directed straight to the oven without selection, and your transport was sent straight into quarantine without selection. And this at a time when the crematoriums are working continuously, three shifts round the clock to cope with a dozen trains unloading every day. The poor arrivals, hunched with fright and pain, have to queue up to six hours, the crowd is so great. And in what conditions they wait! Merely to think of it makes your hair stand on end. Never before were the gleanings of death as large as they have been in the past two months. A thousand people every hour, seventeen per minute...and you don't even seem to appreciate..."

–"Babble, gabble," Marek interrupted him angrily. "You're prodigal with figures. Where did you get them? You can tell they're nonsense, without being here for any length of time. How many killers do they have on the job? How many chambers do they have to take in that many people in one day?"

–"Five chambers. And killers - ever so many." Lolek was unruffled by Marek's objections, and went on: "The figures are real and genuine, like gold. No exaggeration on my part, or on anyone else's. Sheer brutality does the job. It's a matter of time, not of chambers. The bottleneck starts with disposal of the bodies. So people in the know say. And they also say that that's what causes the horrible smell. Never before this summer was the stench so sickening. Just now you don't get the full strength of it. The wind is carrying the scent in the other direction, towards the place where you arrived, and where you got your call-numbers.

–"What are you talking about?" Marek asked insolently, as if he now had proof that Lolek had been merely blathering all along. "What numbers?"

–"So that you don't get lost. A nice blue tattoo as a souvenir. Haven't you got one?"

–"No! We can do without it," said Marek defiantly, while Arush admired his posture. Yet, for all his passivity, the mention of "tattoo" had stirred him, though rather light-heartedly. Aha, Arush thought, they want to brand us as criminals, and regardless of what they do with us ultimately, to give us yet another humiliation. In his mind tattoos were associated, apart from sailors, with hard-core criminals. For a moment he strangely fancied himself with a heart pierced by an arrow painted on the skin of his arm or chest. He only grasped the seriousness of Lolek's question when he showed them his left arm on which a short, prosaic, yet mystifying number was engraved. "Don't you have one of these?" he asked.

Marek and Arush only shook their heads, with probably equally felt incredulity.

–"Ah, you didn't get a call-number?" Lolek repeated his question with the air of a man seeing, Arush could not say what, a rare bird, a ghost, or a man led to the gallows - perhaps all three at once. Lolek mumbled out a few more words and slipped away from them.

They gazed at each other a little confused and surprised at their companion's behaviour, but otherwise showed no particular concern. Arush at least was still unable to collect his thoughts properly, though by then, perhaps no more than the other men of his transport. All of them were that day in a mood which discouraged too much thinking, let alone worrying. And this thoughtless inward tranquillity was beguiling them. Danger, immediate or future, seemed unreal. Only later did he understand Lolek's strange behaviour. The hierarchical order did not cease to exist even in quarantine in Birkenau. Men without a tattoo were in more immediate danger of being killed than men with one. This made them relatively inferior to Lolek, as indeed all Jewish prisoners were inferior compared with Aryan prisoners, who were no longer being gassed at all. Lolek must also have been afraid that he would have to explain to them their uniquely uncertain position. For in those days no one cared to explain such a thing, as if to do so were inhuman or immoral.

Accepted wisdom or compassion, in addition to strict orders, required camp new-comers to be greeted with silence. "Never tell a man about to die what awaits him," was an old, if unwritten rule. You would only increase his agony of anticipating the inevitable. He, and me and you, will die anyway. And this self-excuse absolved one, as it were, from rendering the ultimate service to a fellow man and brother.

Arush broke the silence first, asking: "Have you noticed the air of mystery about him?"

–"Yes. I did."

–"Why did he run away from us?"

–"I don't know. Perhaps quarantine, you know, avoiding the plague. We may look infectious."

–"It isn't that, I think. There's a secret he wouldn't tell us."

–"What secret? That we haven't got a number? Don't we know that?"

–"Yes, but there is apparently more to it than you think. He didn't want to give it away."

–"You think it is serious?"

–"Perhaps without that skin-stamped passport, there's no entry visa?"

–"Will they send us back?"

–"Who knows? They may."

–"Where to? To Pustkow?"

–"No. To the station."

–"And then?"

–"Up the chimney, perhaps," said Arush.

Marek remained silent, probably indicating agreement, so Arush continued.

–"But why not tell us?"

–"What for? Whether you know it or not, it comes to the same thing."

–"Suppose it were your father who was sent there on his last walk, wouldn't you tell him?"

Arush could not prevent himself from posing this question. For two years it had been deeply in his mind, and he had asked himself over and over again: "If I had been standing there on the landing when they drove father down the stairs, what would I have said to him?"

–"No," answered Marek categorically. "Why should you increase his agony in the last minutes of his life? The only time ever known that someone told the people

373

standing outside the chambers what they were waiting for was when a German guard did it. Certainly for no other reason but to increase their suffering.

"The only right thing to do is what they say that one function-prisoner did who suddenly found his mother walking to the 'bath'. When she asked him what was going to happen, he said nothing but gave her a piece of soap and a towel, took the same himself and joined her silently in the queue to take the 'bath'."

–"A fine chap. I suppose that I would have done the same. But suppose they didn't let him join her? And suppose it wasn't your mother, but a stranger; whether you knew him before or not, would it not be your duty to tell him, particularly if he asked you?"

–"What the hell kind of duty is that?"

–"Well...say a moral obligation - if not courage - to tell the truth, and to a man in his last hour at that."

–"I see nothing moral nor any obligation to tell him the truth in these circumstances. To increase his suffering? So that he will curse me? He certainly wouldn't bless me for it. At best, he wouldn't believe me. But I can't see what good the bitter truth would be to him?"

–"Good or not, every human being has a right to know the truth, to die knowingly, and with as much dignity as possible."

–"Oh, you and your high-flown twaddle. Dignity, or indignity, where is it here, in these circumstances? What choice is left?"

–"To resist - even if only in one's heart. Just to defy the killer, however ineffectively."

–"And with what consequences? You know, as I do - more suffering, more cruel death, more trouble."

–"Yes, but for the killers as well." Arush was unaware that, under the impact of Birkenau, he had taken on the basic attitude of Eltes and his fellows in Tarnow, whom at the time he had opposed. Nor did he realize the difference in this respect between conditions in the ghetto and in Auschwitz.

–"Would it be worth while?" asked Marek.

–"Who knows? If not just one person, but a whole transport were to resist, it would at least cause a delay; they could not kill a thousand people every hour, as Lolek said. Killing would cease to be a mere routine, a child's game performed willingly, merrily, exultantly, even, for a prize of extra meat, wine, and women; they would have to work hard at a dirty job, even by SS standards; and perhaps they would even have to ease off, to retrain, to find new ways of mass killing."

–"It would change nothing. They would bring more dogs and more killers to the job, and there's no shortage of either. The only difference that resistance would make to the victims is that they would die in still greater pain and horror.

"Suppose you told a man the truth," Marek had now warmed to his subject and was visibly excited, "and suppose he resisted, and you then saw him, as a result, slashed, chopped, writhing in pain, dying much more dreadfully than the rest who did not resist. You would, if I know you, tear your hair out, wouldn't you?

"Look, in the whole wide world there's no one who loves another human being more than mothers love their children. And what do they do? Suspecting the worst, that's the 'truth', they talk away to their little ones - 'look my heart how your dolly smiles, will you bath her as well?' - but they do not tell the truth. Believe me, these are the most courageous mothers in the world. And so it's much neater and easier for both, mother and child."

–"Perhaps. It's so hard...Don't you think that these Hungarian children are strangers to the game? It all came on them so suddenly. A matter of weeks at most. Many were still moving about freely only days before they arrived here. Our kids from Poland, with their long experience of life in the ghettos and of almost daily killings, know what is happening better than their parents and could tell them."

–"But they don't. They, too, say nothing. You see! Even these pure, innocent souls do not tell the bitter truth."

–"No, they say nothing. Hunched with horror, exhausted from the journey, chilled to their bones in the winter, and breathless with the heat in summer, these little children never complain. They keep silent, anxious only to stay with their mothers. Isn't it surprising, Marek, how calmly we all die? Normally people have a traumatic fear of death, but these, blood-engraved days, everyone, children and grown-ups alike, face their ends stoically. Have our people conquered the fear of death?"

–"Don't ask me such questions. This is not the proper place."

–"Not the proper place? What d'you mean? Would you like to remove the subject into a funeral parlour? Or, perhaps into the grave, after gaining, so to say, personal experience? What better place than quarantine? Where else shall we have so much time to talk? Heaven only knows how many days we are going to spend like this one."

–"Don't grumble! We might have been squatting in cold and rain. Thank God for the fine weather and sit quiet, if it does you good!"

–"All this would be very nice, if people were not being burnt right under our noses."

As Marek and Arush were infringing the rules by talking almost ceaselessly, they attracted the attention of their neighbours, and Hugo Bester sneaked through in the most circumspect manner to join them. With a baggy cap on his small head, Hugo looked particularly funny. At first he kept silent, so that the other two continued to chat on undisturbed. But soon he burst out with his usual ferocious criticism.

Arush and Marek were debating whether this conveyor-belt murder in Birkenau was or was not something radically different from the kind of murder they had known before. In support of his view that the difference was only a matter of degree and familiarity, Marek suggested: "Look at the old-timers how they have become used to what's happening here. It's only the first day or two that people feel concern."

It was at this point that Hugo joined in to say: "And feel only concerned for their own death."

This charge, at least coming from Hugo, was not new to Arush, but the way he said it was nonetheless resentful, and prompted Marek to counter spitefully: "All the same they'll burn us, one like the other."

His remark, especially since it was not wide of the mark, must have got under Hugo's skin, because he accused both Marek and Arush of deriving pleasure from speaking of burning. This was an absurd accusation; the only reason they were able to talk about burning and the like at all was because, in the circumstances of constantly impending danger of death, even if they were not always so spectacular as in Birkenau, one could not speak about death seriously.

Hugo moved to ask another question: "A chap I spoke to earlier, said that there's an unwritten law in Auschwitz 'Kill or be killed!' Would you kill other prisoners to win your match?"

A little angered by the question, Arush replied hastily.

–"First, this law is an ass. All the killers are sooner or later killed themselves. Second, the question is hard, but the answer isn't difficult. Never kill others!"

–"As long as you're not put to the test," replied Hugo as quickly. "Haven't you said yourself that you pray you will never be put to the test?"

Marek took sides with Hugo, saying: "We're all saying the same as you, Arush, but when it comes to the test, however painful it is to admit it, one fails like the other. We're simply not made to be heroes."

In their circumstances, it was not easy to refute what Marek and Hugo said, even though they were largely mistaken. Provided one was constantly on guard, one could evade the test. Failing was usually either a matter of deliberate decision, or the consequence of initial and compounding errors of judgement. In addition, what made the trial very stringent was the inequality between the stress and helplessness of the tested and the ease and power of the tester, whose cunning was only surpassed by his brutality. These testers were also masters of torture and deceit. They knew how to appeal to a man's basic instincts, and with the promise of a little more life, to make him face the hardest choice one could imagine. The testers did this partly as a studied, sophisticated method of torture, and partly to reduce their own physical load. The problem was, then, not one of heroism, as Marek implied, or of courage, or even of unwillingness to die, which anyway had lately diminished among the victims, but mainly that the tested was no match for the tester.

Marek was also mistaken because although by nature man was no hero, he was capable of performing admirable deeds; and even in the most inhuman conditions of the German-created ghettos and camps, men of great heroic spirit were not rare. Only their brave acts remain, by force of circumstances, mostly unknown, as, with a few exceptions, neither the performers - who themselves mostly did not feel that they were doing something unusual - nor the witnesses, survive.

When Arush had replied to Hugo's question: "Will you pass the test?" and Marek added sarcastically: "He will, because he doesn't want to live," Hugo became very angry. "Yes," he said, "unlike you, I don't want to live, if that means the death of others." This was the freedom of every man, to die at his own behest.

At this, Marek began to scoff slightly, saying, in short, that if Hugo wanted to exercise his freedom, and so do the Germans a favour, he had an excellent opportunity here to show it. But Hugo's "humanity" and "inner freedom", could not worry him now.

This made Hugo still more eager to accuse Marek that his lust to live had blinded him to every other aspect of their cursed existences. When his outburst was over, Hugo waved his arm, as if saying "a pity to waste more words on you", and he pointedly moved a few inches away from Marek and Arush.

Marek, who did not know Hugo well, dismissed his invective as little more than posturing. "Humanity, morality," he said, "it sounds noble but not at their interment. Here, at this place, you can find them only in death. A man who is exposed to death every minute of the day, must think of how to avoid it. What else can we do to prevent the Germans from killing us, except try to dodge them?

"Do I care that others are dying while I'm still alive? Of course I do, as much as any one of us. But it can't make me despair. I don't believe that it makes Hugo. In this endless murderous mess, death no longer rouses emotion. Today, it simply doesn't reach our senses. How could it - barely a few hours ago we ourselves escaped with our lives by a hairsbreadth.

–"Did we?" asked Arush.

Though glad of the change of theme, Marek stared at Arush curiously, expressing surprise. This moved Arush to add: "Some may have not escaped. Not entirely."

–"What d'you mean? Did someone die in your waggon?"

Ever since the morning Arush had felt an impelling need to tell of his precious experience in the train. It was this experience which was at the root of his initial, strange query. But Marek was not the man he would have chosen to share it with. By then, however, it seemed too late to withdraw completely. He, therefore, replied to Marek's question cryptically: "It seems so," hoping that this would end the matter. But his reply only increased Marek's curiosity.

–"Who was it?" Marek sounded aghast.

Taking a deep breath, Arush drawled out timidly: "I."

Marek's face brightened and, smiling, he said:

–"What a wag you are! You took me in completely. But what's the hochme?" he finished with the Yiddish word meaning "being wise".

–"I'm not being wise. What I said is the simple and solemn truth."

–"Ah, drop it! This is no joking matter."

–"But I'm not joking. I know that it's hard to believe, but I did die."

Marek was chuckling, trying hard not to burst into loud laughter.

–"How did you do it?" he asked. "Tell me, perhaps I'll do the same."

Arush started telling Marek what had happened to him, speaking as seriously and as accurately as he could. He explained to Marek briefly the atmosphere in his truck, his personal feelings, the experience with Zundel, and the last moments he could remember.

–"Then all at once there was light, weak, melancholic electric light. Oh, how good it was to stop living! It seemed as if I suddenly felt a joyous lightness of existence. 'Where have I gone?' I seemed to be asking. Then, to make it all the more mysterious, I found myself in a huge, dimly lit room. The room was slowly circling.

In the middle of it, lying on the floor, seemingly alive, there were the bodies of young female dancers, dressed in greyish-white, flounced organza costumes, with black slippers on their feet. They lay close to each other, hands at their sides, heads tight together at the centre, but I didn't see their faces. Everything, the dancers, the room, myself, was moving round - with one exception. In a corner of the room a grand piano stood firm and still. Strangely familiar - I mean the grand piano.

"From the earliest days that I remember, there was a mahogany-brown grand piano at home, in the corner of the so-called salon. The instrument needed re-tuning from top to toe, but it was a large, impressive piece of furniture. Now, this grand piano re-appeared in that mysterious, whirling room.

"All this I perceived as if it were not happening to me, but as if I was watching from afar through the eyes of someone else. Then everything disappeared, together with me. There was absolute peace and oblivion. Non-existence! Vanished from the world!"

–"You're back," remarked Marek drily, trying to stifle the irony in his remark.

–"Yes I am, but in the meantime...When does it get light now? At four? Then for twelve hours I was dead."

–"You didn't die. If you are still alive now, then it must be that you weren't dead, at least not wholly, consummately dead."

–"You speak almost like a doctor. But death, or life for that matter, is much too serious a problem to leave for the rotating staff of Aesculapius to define. Wholly or not wholly - and perhaps you could tell what the difference is - I know that I died. I know that, for twelve hours, I stopped thinking, I ceased breathing, I wasn't receptive or responsive to anything in the world - in short, I had lost all connection with the living. And if this isn't death, what is, consummate or not consummate, according to you?"

There evolved between them a long, in part irate discussion about man's own "self", whether its retention was sufficient proof of his viability, about the current definition of death, its neuro-psychic criteria, leading Arush to say that people had been dying for thousands of years before the new-fangled idea of cerebral death was invented. Then he asked: "If one can live without consciousness, who really needs to die?"

Marek, after urging Arush not to play the resurrected, countered with a no less teasing question: "Did any of your relatives have similar experiences?" Adding that in ancient Greece, resurrection was a hereditable vocation.

Annoyed by Marek's insulting question and refusal to admit he had actually died, Arush retorted that with his stark rationality and theory of terrestrial life in aerial unsconciousness, the first thing Marek should do if he survived the war should be to make a will providing against premature burial. And he turned away from Marek.

His friend's attitude made Arush a little angry, indeed. For he was defending an experience that was precious to him, a pleasant sensation of strange, mysterious reality, a longing after some other world, tender and lost - altogether mixed with the feeling of senseless sacrifice in returning to a world of cruelty and suffering.

378

But what did it mean to Marek? Arush asked himself. It was unlikely to be envy of his unique experience, nor pique because it looked as if he were trying to be one up on him. Arush rather thought that his tale had unsettled Marek. Death, though it has been for centuries the greatest mystery in life, is the one certainty of all doubters, and Arush's description of his experience had shaken Marek's certitude about it. Nothing was sacred to a disbeliever, Arush sadly concluded, but to question the accuracy of the prevailing definition of death is blasphemy.

CHAPTER TWENTY-EIGHT

Squatting solitarily in the midst of his fellows, Arush began to collect his thoughts and to scan the scene before him.

If you looked around, as he did, this Birkenau camp seemed almost a bay of peace. The tranquillity of that quarantine-afternoon was so casual, so indolent, as if to give the lie to what the place really was. To think that all this slothful time people were dying there - a macabre death that no one had heard of before - seemed unreal. Of all places, Birkenau never appeared as unreal as it did on that afternoon in Birkenau itself. Yet, for all the serenity, the air was somehow filled, besides the acrid smell of burning bones, with the muted cries of their owners.

On his left-hand-side, which was not screened by barracks, the so-called Lagerpromenade spread out widely. This was a rugged road of dried-up mud in the summer, here and there covered by sparse tufts of grass, which was growing stealthily in defiance of camp regulations. To the right and left of the road, bordering at each end thick wire fences, numberless, light-brown, barracks stretched monotonously away into the dim distance. No other buildings were visible, the crematoria being well hidden from the prisoners' sight behind fine-leaved birch-trees and clumps of shrubby bushes. Only the tops of chimneys could be seen, if you stood up.

At the moment Arush was looking, there was no one in sight on the promenade, but from time to time, some flat, frail figures, dressed in blue and white stripes crossed the path quickly. Indeed they would normally run, in groups of two, always either carrying something in their hands - a barrel, a cask, a pole - or pushing a cart. For they were on duty - otherwise moving about during quarantine hours was strictly forbidden. Now and then, the men would stop, after a short while resuming their hurried, yet so distinctly clumsy walk, then they would disappear from sight. Occasionally, a man would walk self-assuredly, almost leisurely, to emphasize his rank and status of a more or less senior prisoner. But during all those long hours of the afternoon, your eyes could not catch sight of a man in SS uniform. They had no time for what was happening inside the camp. They were busy at the ramps with the unendingly arriving transports.

Not far away was another group of squatting men, hunching their shoulders and mostly leaning, like Arush, on the wall of the barracks opposite to his. And yet another small group of ordinary, but apparently privileged prisoners was doing quarantine to the right of the space between the two barracks. This group included a

Russian general, whose relaxed, imposing bearing had already caught Arush's attention during the lunch break. He spoke little but he knew how to impart to the few words he did say a commanding gravity. The apparent resolution and dignity of his countenance was somewhat increased by his short fringe of hair, which, given the setting, Arush found truly exotic. The man was even allowed to sit on a low stool, such as Jews use on mourning days. The Russian was surrounded by a few prisoners, who were all standing and talking openly in the most blatantly irregular way of doing quarantine.

Hugo, in squatting position, had sidled back to Arush and, having seen his gaze fixed on the general's group of men, turned his head in the same direction. After a while, he started talking slowly yet engagingly.

–"He thrills his audience."

–"You can't deny that there's something unusual about him. Impressive even."

–"Yes, he holds his head up and spreads some fancy ideas which he is trying to plant in the minds of his simple listeners. He's ranting that Auschwitz forges a new brotherhood of men, uniting all the various nationalities and creeds. As a result, after the war a solidarity of men transcending all ethnical and national boundaries will arise. People will live at maximum liberty, and will fulfil their spiritual and cultural heritages in brotherhood.

–"Oh, how nice," said Arush. "The day he comes out, if he sees liberation, he'll forget all this pretty talk, and will start ordering, warring, ruling, extolling might and rank, groups and troops. We know this sort of man. They're the ones who direct wars and thrive on them."

–"Do you know who he really is, then?"

–"That puzzles me, too. If he's a general, what is he doing here? They don't send prisoners of war to Auschwitz."

–"Perhaps an Askari?"

–"Indeed. Vlasov's general, who turned his coat again. For his devoted services in the past, they now reward him with the mourning-stool and peep-frisette."

Hugo must have liked Arush's off-hand comment, for he seized upon it to expand the theme.

–"There must now be," he said, "millions of people all over Europe, who are moulting their brownish wolf's skins and returning to their natural colour."

–"And they'll argue, not unlike this screamer of a general, no punishment please, this kills the sense of humanity."

–"It really does; and anyhow they'll get away with it. 'Magnanimity' because of the sheer weight of numbers who are changing colours.

–"With the Russians it's different. They're so numerous, so endless, and they have a giant country. Siberia...for a short quarantine."

Hugo nodded understandingly, and after a moment's reflection, he said:

–"Say what you like, it's a strange company here. It's not just a Russian general, but all that Babel of tongues and people. Outside they kept the Jews hermetically separated from other people. A bullet for making contact. But here they let everyone mix together. A fraternity of people as that poser calls it."

381

—"Incredible indeed," Arush agreed. "A colossal blunder from the Germans' point of view. Not a mistake like the cracks in the walls of human freight carriers. But an error of judgement of historically unpredictable dimensions."

—"What's so portentous about it?" Hugo was curious.

—"If Auschwitz were a camp for Jews only, as exclusive as their gassing is, the earth might cover the secret for ever. Fences within which crimes are committed remain silent. Even if some word did filter through, the Germans and their friends could easily deny it."

—"Who could believe what's happening here, anyway," interrupted Hugo. "They could say, it's just another Jewish plot against the German nation."

—"That's the blunder. With so many people of different nationalities around here, it won't be possible to hide the facts entirely."

—"On the other hand, keeping us together with so many other people means anyone (not just Germans) can deny that Auschwitz and the murders committed there was a basically Jewish affair."

Here Marek, who had re-joined them, threw in with a hint to Arush.

—"The question is would they wish to deny the facts? Haven't I heard you saying that they are proud of it? So much of their passion and pride is in that fire, why d'you suspect they wish to scatter the ashes silently away?"

—"I'm speaking now of after the war, when their might will no longer make them always right."

Hugo seized on Arush's reply to Marek, to add:

—"Sure, the defeated are always wrong. The experiment has failed, but the idea was magnificent. Look at those chimney tops."

—"No, no, it's not as simple as that," countered Arush vigorously. "This isn't a matter of an experiment that went wrong, or of blown off chimneys. You seem to have little sense of history. A tiny blot it may seem to be, but one with all the makings of a Cain's brand. History will nail them to a pillar of shame."

—"Perhaps? Men like to pillory the crimes of others and to bask in their shame. But I doubt it. Nothing in the world is as quickly forgotten as the bestiality of men. The dead can't speak, and new structures - cultures they call them - grow up on their graves."

Hugo warmed to the subject, and whether because it interested him, or because he regretted his earlier outburst, he was now honey-sweet, even giving the impression that he was trying to wheedle himself into Arush's favour.

—"You bank so much on history. But what is history? Isn't it a continuous cycle of wars and mutual killings? Peace and amity are exceptional states - intervals between the epics of war. There's victory and defeat - depending on which side you stand - so many dead, so many wounded, so many homeless. But there are no crimes, not in war. In war, death, violence, the vilest acts directed at your enemy are art and virtue."

Arush objected that they were not in a battle-field; the enemy held not a spear, or even a sling; the killings were of defenceless men, women and children. Hugo agreed grudgingly. But Marek interrupted him.

–"Of course that is so. But war, total war as they call it now, knows no laws. Nothing is sacrosanct, they say."

Ignoring what Marek said, Hugo continued with his own line.

–"If we speak of history, you should know that from the dawn of civilization war has been the climax of human accomplishment. Manhood and gallantry have been measured by the number of men you killed. The greater the devastation, the greater the achievement. It was above all the gods of war that the ancestors of the people fighting now idolized - a fire sweeping through the universe was to them the most magnificent manifestation of power and destruction. Next in their esteem were Homer's demi-god warriors, the most cruel characters that the human mind ever conceived. But the ones who were killed? They belong to their killers. What does a dead man count for? Good to mend a fence, or to make soap.

"Haven't those monster-warriors been the heroes of what is called western civilization - which our murderers say they're defending? Has their example not set the seed of fire alight over the ages?"

As if this question was directed at him, Arush said,

–"Perhaps, but their example would not have carried significant weight, had not this glorious heritage been enriched with the progress of time by other ideals, embodying above all LOVE - love of your (dead) neighbour, the true creed, the fatherland, honour and chivalry, and presently love of blood and race."

Something had happened to Hugo. As he continued to talk, the feeling in his words struck Arush, who realized the impact Auschwitz had apparently had on Hugo but the abruptness of the change was striking.

–"You speak of history, so tell me how many wars have there been in Europe in the past fifteen hundred years, that is since the time Christianity, ostensibly the religion of love and non-violence, has held sway over its people? Countless. They have been almost continuously waging their wars, and for the most part they've been fighting fellow Christians. When the devout Poles fought the no less devout Russians, or when the pious French and Spaniards were cutting each other's throats, both sides were, funnily enough, claiming to be fighting a just war. And in their long ancestral tradition they go on warring and killing ever more efficiently, ever more extensively. And I'm telling you," Hugo concluded his long speech, "that as long as men devour men, as long as they don't cast aside all the ideals, beliefs and pursuits, for the sake of which they kill one another, the name and fame of the Führer and of his torch-bearers will shine bright and high in the chaotic darkness of man's historical despondency."

Even though Arush disagreed with much of what Hugo was saying, he kept silent in order not to increase Hugo's flood of words. Arush was, of course, well aware that they were all used to seeing matters in sharp colours and to using strong words. This was one of the unquestioned privileges of prisoners and the damned. In Arush's view, the right thing for Hugo to ask was what sense does a killer's life make? At long range, the killer loses more than his victims. That the victims do not belong to their killers - as the Hellenes had maintained - and that the dead bodies of the victims bear witness to the futility of killing, was just what the survivors must try hard to prove. Equally they must try to keep alive the human side of their deaths - the suffering, the thoughts and sighs preceding their last breath. Certainly it could not be unjust, as Hugo might have implied, to oppose their aggressors and mass murderers. Peace under Nazi skies would have been a greater evil than war. That wars appear as almost the single reality of history is largely due to its scribblers. The Jews had not waged a war for one thousand eight hundred and twelve years. This was not a matter of religion or a sign of a "lamb-like" disposition. It was the peculiar enforced prize of having been landless, even if the reward was often simple dispatch and similar charitable attentions from the pious victors. Whatever the main cause of wars had been, it was incontrovertible that while other people had needed land to exist and preserve their national lives and pride, the Jews had survived as an historical people, without land of their own and without staging wars, but through attachment to their heritage, the bond of religion, and the unbending spirit of its peoples. Whose darkness, or chaos?

Arush could feel, as it were, from a distance the scoffing glance of Hausdienst (who at the lunch break had already made the first moves towards a position as a function prisoner) suggesting that the Jews' plight and landless existence were just because, unlike their neighbours, they did not kill. They must start to kill like the others, to live well and safely. But he had failed in his attempt to silence Hugo, who turned directly to Arush.

–"I know what you're thinking. A drink wouldn't come amiss? Or that one should spare one's brain to keep the body alive? Certainly you must be thinking that I was wrong - wrong to imply that the present war is merely the latest link in the ancient Aryan cult of the sword. But what is the worship of power, which the present - combatant or non-combatant - societies idolize, if not a modern version of the cult of the sword? Everything is based on power, they think - individual welfare, destiny of peoples, supremacy of nations. And, infatuated with power, they revere the men to whom they have transferred it. For, where does the Führer's power come from if not from his people? A war like this one, requires a collective will and effort, and a shared responsibility. He's as much solely responsible for the killings as this is a one man's war. He only justifies to them all the falsehoods and crimes. In return, they adore him, they venerate him, they serve him, they are blinded by his grandeur and might."

Glad that Hugo had come completely around to the view he had long held, Arush refrained from remarking that Hugo's observation had lately lost its validity, at least partially. But it was likely that he was referring mainly to the past, as the sequence of his discourse also suggested.

–"Now they can't free themselves from their original infatuation, even if they wished to. Now the Führer holds them captive, ruthlessly exercising the power with which they have invested him. Now they can't stop. They persist in terror, rather than risk the terror of restraint or thought."

Marek objected, not quite to the point, that not everyone in the world was evil. And from the present destruction a new generation of humble men and women might arise who would recognize the senselessness of killing one another.

—"I wish it were so," replied Hugo. "But it's a dream, as fanciful and absurd as dreams usually are. It strikes reality in the face. War and killing have become almost a law of necessity to which men are hopelessly enslaved. They can't find a way back to liberty. Why only after this war? Why didn't they retract before? How was it that millions of people down the ages have died so easily, so willingly, and so senselessly? What makes millions still obediently die?"

—"What makes millions obediently murder?" Arush blurted out.

—"D'you ask how an ordinarily sensible man turns into a killer?" Though this was not precisely what he had meant, Arush remained silent. So Hugo continued. "It's simpler than you think. Take the concrete case before us. They feel there's nothing wrong in what they're doing. Quite the contrary. It's a supremely right thing. To feel like this, you have commonly been given the motives of your moral conduct from society and you have been individually coached and conditioned by experts for long enough. Several months or more, depending on the individual candidate, and you'll be committing crimes for the sake of some symbols which you're made to believe have the greatest national, or even cosmic, significance. Love your own people, your honour, your country. Admire the gun - symbol of glory and power - and him who commands it.

"Along with love for your own kind, you're encouraged to hate the alien kind - the prospective victim, who's a harmful insect to you, to your nation, to humanity at large. You're a soldier, Auschwitz your supreme battlefield. You get your food, your pay, your medal, the gratitude of the whole nation, which defends your actions. You can't have any scruples; how could you? If you ever had, you were wisely instructed how to project them on to your commanders. The super-man suzerain. He absolves you of all responsibility. You feel assured and proud. But once a man sheds all his responsibility, he acquiesces in the crimes of his kind. You see how simple it is?"

At this instant the gong sounded. Through the blare, Arush still heard Hugo shouting, "Endless fame and glory for him who kills most!" Then came a loud cry - SOUP!

Today's quarantine was over. They stood up, stretched their limbs, and hurried to queue up for supper. What a taste or smell had the greyish broth, which Arush gulped down his constricted throat, he could not tell - but it was watery. And this was what mattered. Only that the liquid rather increased his thirst, which it seemed would never be quenched.

Inside their camp enclosure, everyone could now go where he liked, and it was in the hope of perhaps finding a hidden tap of water that, instead of going straight to sleep, Arush decided to take a stroll along the Lagerpromenade.

This was more easily said than done, with such things as he had on his feet. As he shambled along, one of his feet was falling out of the shoe, the other remained continuously cramped. Oh, feel your bones, Arush told himself, and thank heavens for it. And be thankful, too, that at night you will be able to take off the boots, without worrying that anyone will steal such treasures as yours.

385

To walk was certainly an effort, but one, Arush felt, not to be regretted. By getting acquainted with the camp, he could perceive the wonderland quality of the surroundings.

–"Are you going to the latrine?" asked Ruben who had suddenly joined Arush. "There may be water."

No, there wasn't, but there were plenty of other wares; men were transacting, and talking, and smoking - a mixture of camp emporium and club-room.

Ruben was not communicative today, perhaps because he was, like Arush, absorbed by the changing scenery. Most interesting were the people, who spoke many languages, and provided a cross-section of nationalities from every corner of Europe. They were mostly wandering about aimlessly, lean, haggard figures, staring at one another with gloomy, morbid eyes. Though nearly all of them were dressed identically, from close to, every prisoner looked different. Proceeding into the interior of the camp, Arush had already learned to distinguish from external appearance between the various groups of prisoners. The healthy looking faces, not yet pinched by hunger, were those of newcomers to camp life. From their bodies, their clinging together, and their peculiar movements, the brightness of home, which they had lost only days ago still shone out. They had nearly all come from Hungary.

The drawn, bloodless faces of men lost in their striped garments and listlessly dragging their feet, were the unmistakable features of camp wear and tear. That evening, a small group of shaky, shadow-like men, sat cross-legged by the wall of a barracks. Unfit for further work, they had arrived last night from a nearby camp, awaiting you can guess what. (But do *they* guess it?) Clearly recognizable by their clownish rags were the Pustkovians. Many passers-by stopped to enquire where they had come from. On hearing Pustkow, some enquired about acquaintances.

Penetrating deeper into Birkenau, Arush also saw its various extensions, and reached a point from which, beyond the wires, the outlines of other camps were visible, with their long rows of barracks. While looking around, Arush heard his name called, then saw a slender, yet upright and neat looking man, standing almost in front of him. Samek Gesang, a playmate of childhood and early school years! After four such eventful years, they were both pleased to meet, and Samek proved his pleasure by deciding to keep company with a man dressed like a circus performer. Casting a glance at Arush, Samek's sad, glistening eyes seemed to say, "I haven't forgotten my first day here." A duffer at school, Samek was clever in worldly matters, and at the age of sixteen had become a local ping-pong champion. Handsome as well, it was no wonder that he had married, as he told Arush, the daughter of the vice-chairman of the Cracow Judenrat and thus survived till the last "evacuation". On arrival in Birkenau last autumn, he had been parted from his wife, and had become a barber, presently attending to ladies and important officers. In other words, a distinguished function-prisoner with the official, awe inspiring title of Lagerfriseur. There was no need in Birkenau for brush makers or photographers, metiers he had performed in the ghetto, so he had changed to his present calling. While he was doing time in gaol on the Russian side, before crossing back over the San in 1940, he had tried his luck with a clipper, which incidentally had helped him to escape.

The obvious initial questions over, he asked Arush why he looked so confused? Arush had no wish to explain his re-birth that morning, or that he was still half-choked, so he only said, pointing to his feet, "aching". Samek offered to get him decent shoes, and asked "What's your number?"

People say "number" in Polish to mean "size". But the number Samek asked for was not the "number" of shoes, and he was genuinely sympathetic, perhaps even worried, when he heard Arush's answer. "It's nothing." And to prevent Samek from taking to his heels, as Lolek Kwas had done, Arush added quickly: "We'll get it tomorrow." To his relief, another smart-looking prisoner with a "P" above his red triangle then approached Samek. After being introduced, Bolek, their new companion, started telling them the latest news he had just heard from an official at camp headquarters. "Break-through from Calais. Beating them in Belgium. The Fritzes have no defences there. The English landed from gliders, upon my word - they've only to cross the Rhine, and it's all over." Ruben remarked that the Rhine was too far away from them, and asked where the Russians were. "The deuce take them," replied Bolek, "resting in some uncouth pygmy holes. But one Blitz-thrust, and they'll surprise us."

–"First come, first blessed," said Samek with ill-concealed irony. Arush felt a little more optimistic, and began to like Bolek, who just then said that it was a bit risky to walk four together, and bade them farewell. "God willing we shall meet again."

–"Not a real Pole. His mother is Jewish," Samek lowered his voice conspiratorially. Bolek had been on Aryan papers in Warsaw, where he had been arrested at the time of Stalingrad, when the Germans, furious over their military misfortunes and the visible delight of a part of the Polish population, had staged a big round-up of people in all parts of the city. Bolek was glad, as he had once confessed to Samek, who shaved him regularly, to have come to Auschwitz where he was much more hopeful of surviving than in blackmailer-infested Warsaw. It also raised his mother's chance of escaping detection. In camp, Bolek was "well off", he worked in the personnel office, and received parcels from his father. He shared the food, in great secrecy, with some Jewish mates (if Samek was included, he didn't say so) parting even with an onion or a patty. "A very good fellow, but a liar. As he lives permanently in a lie," commented Samek, "it has become a habit with him to tell wildly invented stories unblushingly."

Poor Belgium, Arush sighed inwardly.

Their attention was distracted by the noise of human voices, which, as they proceeded, became louder and, a surprise, sounded distinctly female. After a moment or two they reached a spot where, a few yards to their right, was the women's camp, separated from the men's by only plain, not very thick barbed wire. What a strange sight! Young women in kerchiefs knotted mostly at the front, dressed in grey, loosely hanging wrappers, resembling countrywomen's russets. Some women had bared their shaven head, and if they had not been segregated, it would have been impossible to tell these from a man. How much more hair means to a woman, thought

Arush. All the women naturally looked flat and chaste, and, it seemed to Arush, even more piteous and grotesque than their male companions-of-woe. Yet, it's not the cowl that makes the monk, as the proverb has it.

One would have liked to shake their hands, but it was too dangerous even to be seen assembling near the other camp. This was why men who wished to communicate with the women were moving back and forth along the stretch of the promenade which ran parallel to their camp. The women inside were bolder, defiantly standing by the fence, their faces almost thrust between the uncharged wires, talking blatantly.

Tens of clamouring voices. They were speaking Hungarian, most seemed not to know any other language. All were asking about their male relatives, or from where they, the men, had come; some were telling who they were. One woman with imploring eyes fixed on Arush, recognizing in him a novice like herself, asked in German with a shrill, begging voice: "You my friend, my brother, tell me, please tell me what happened to our fathers, our boys..." Arush must have stared at her with eyes no less fixed than hers, while he wondered silently if he was a friend or a rival? A rival for life. Not likely, he concluded, between men and women. Does it bring them, therefore, nearer or farther? Poor Jewish sister! She did not know yet what had happened to her father, or what help she could count on here. In another day or two she would learn.

A stranger, walking beside Arush, was saying to his neighbour in Polish: "No one resists because of hope, yet without hope there's no life."

–"All the same. The rebellious and the passive all end alike," replied his companion.

Beyond the wires, a young woman held the eyes of the men who stood watching her, as if they were nailed to the ground. The woman, her head shaved of all hair, her eyes petrified, was moving, at varying pace, in a circle, dangling her arms as if doing callisthenic exercises. Arush felt curiously terrified. But then, he thought, to be still frightened by such sights is rather a good sign.

–"She's lost her senses," explained Samek. "At noon she was still shouting no one grasped what, except 'viz', 'viz' (water). Oh, I remember how, on my first day, I pressed the air to my mouth deluding myself that it was reducing thirst."

–"How long did it last?" asked Arush.

–"Over a week. It's fairly hard to stay normal here, but once you have passed the first day safely, you'll get away with it."

That was comforting to know, Arush thought, as his first day was near its end. But then Poldek, a neighbour who had earlier despaired of the predictability of human conduct, overheard Samek, and joined in a voice of protest.

–"It's not thirst that has made her mad. She was crying before, the Hungarians heard her crying 'give back my child'. She arrived last night and the child was taken away from her. It was, the women say, still a fairly little child. Literally torn away from his mother's breast."

But Poldek's companion whose name Arush did not learn, demurred.

–"Others say that she threw him away. Having apparently got wind of what's

388

brewing, she gave the baby to her old mother."

A hum of excited voices asked all at once: "How d'you know?"

–"What women say of one another," remarked Ruben censoriously. "People always try to find something to blame others with. You shouldn't repeat such things."

Samek asked more calmly: "And if she did pass the child to her mother, how can we know what she intended? Perhaps her arm was hurting, and she would have taken back the baby after a while?"

–"Indeed," added Arush, "How can one pass judgement on such a case? Perhaps she gave the child away, because she couldn't bear to watch his death?" Arush recalled a story from the ghetto about a woman who had thus explained why she had abandoned a little girl. When, a minute later she had second thoughts and reached out to take her back, it was too late.

–"Who knows? Who could see into a person's heart at such moments? People just break down. The strain is too great. And then to think that you live in the smoke of your child, requires indeed a brain of stone."

–"For you these cries are a novelty," said Poldek turning to Arush, as if to say "You aren't yet a full member of this neighbourbood." "But the cries have not ceased for weeks now. Not a day passes without new people arriving, each with his, or her new-born tragedy. And don't think that only Jewish women cry.

"The other day, a Polish woman was moaning and tearing her stubble of hair, because she had perhaps forever deprived her little son of a mother. As if, she said, childless women couldn't distribute underground papers. 'I did it with my own hands. It was my own heart's decision.'"

Next door, so to speak, or a few hatches in the fence farther on, another woman at her wits' end was grievously shouting - as far as Arush could make out -"come back mother," while close to her a tall, very lean woman was laughing hysterically.

–"Is madness infectious?" inquired Ruben seriously.

–"How d'you know?" asked Arush in reply, "that they're mad, and we're normal? If we can walk and talk calmly in the face of this horror, aren't we crazy?"

"What a sight!" exclaimed Poldek's companion mournfully. "I wonder, how people will look at La Gioconda after they have seen this?"

What a fool! Arush said in silence, though he knew that to speak light-heartedly was one of their defences. Indeed he, too, wished that Leonardo were with them to paint one of those mad Lisas.

Aloud he asked Samek: "What will happen to her?" pointing to the first clearly insane woman.

–"They'll take her away at night." Samek must know. He was an old-timer. "You'll get used to it," he added. "When you stay longer it's like facing the picture that hangs on the wall of your living room. Only here you can't change houses, or run away."

Poldek once more wished to impress them with Arush did not know what - courage, free-thought, banality? - by asking: "What are they waiting for? A miracle? Why do they leave her in torture until the squad comes to pick her up?"

It seemed to Arush that the woman's madness might have relieved her of all the suffering, including thirst, and of the will to live as well. But he was not sure and remained silent. Then Ruben asked in turn: "What can the women do? Kill her?"

–"How can you call it killing? In these circumstances?" replied Poldek. "To lead her onto the wires...It could be done, at least as soon as night has fallen."

–"But that would be murder," remarked Samek.

–"Quite so," concurred Poldek's companion. "Indeed, doing the Germans' job. Our own life isn't ours to dispose of, let alone the life of a fellow human, even if it is that of a fatally demented woman."

–"A life! Not worth the candle," Poldek persisted in his opinion. "It's everyone's last free choice. If the poor woman can no longer exercise it of her own volition, she should be helped out. It's this freedom to terminate our lives which differentiates us from other animals."

His words roused Arush to protest with anger rising within him.

–"Perhaps because they commit no suicides, other living species don't butcher wholesale members of their own kind, as we 'humans' do. It's not the freedom to take one's life that is the difference between men and animals, but the freedom of men to hate life."

–"I won't argue with you," Poldek waved Arush aside. "I know chaps like you. A little more, and you'll start talking of invisible forces, new existence, and goodness knows what else. And as for the future, if you aren't keen on joining the 'Himmelskommando'," he pointed to the pillar of smoke gushing from the chimney, "take my advice - use your brain, have no bad conscience, and lie low but play high!"   The sun was about to set, the light was less bright and the women's camp's boundary behind Arush and his companions. Ahead, the end of the road seemed too far a target for a man with his aching legs. Arush turned back alone walking now, strangely, more quickly than on the way there.

When Arush entered the barracks it was still day and inside all was quiet. Men, wedged together on the bunks, lay fast asleep. He must not disturb anyone in his rest or dreams, Arush told himself. Only the sound of rattling throats broke the uneasy stillness of the huge barracks. Yet Arush felt "at home" in the midst of the sleeping strangers. The most important thing was that he would lie down, Arush kept telling himself, as he removed his shoes at last. His place was on the upper bunk, about the middle of the barracks, near the outer wall. He hardly exchanged a word with his drowsy neighbour, who lay stretched rigidly on the bare planks. He turned on his side, his back to Arush, and fell asleep again. Indeed with two to a bunk, one could only lie sideways, and a hand under the chin had to serve as a pillow. A sigh from his neighbour below seemed to let Arush know that he had wakened him too.

Curiously, in spite of what he had thought earlier, Arush was a little apprehensive for the safety of his shoes. Oh, hang it! He would not worry. He began reflecting. Could he already tick off this day? And what a day! A thousand years when it was past. His head split from merely thinking of it. Still some bunks have only single occupants; the block was not full to capacity, so they might not be removed at night to make room for others. With no number on his arm? What did this portend? And he didn't know what it was to be hungry, after three days without food. Well, apart from the little sop down the leather-like gullet. They had put them on the kitchen's service list. No, he must recall the happenings of this long day. And the days before in the train.

Yet in spite of his resolve, Arush dozed off.

In his sleep, Arush dreamt that he was in the room he had been in before. Now it was unlit, completely dark. On the floor of the room lay the white-clad dancers, their lifeless faces inexorably frozen. Then, mysteriously, they were hanging as if on hooks from the ceiling, clothed only in their flesh and pain - naked, breastless torsos, swollen bellies from which half-alive embryos climbed, bone to bone, skull to skull, up to the ceiling to get out of the house, which a growing crowd of stern, motionless, black-unifomed men were surrounding. There was commotion in the room, as the embryos, fluttering like birds, gradually slipped away in smoke through the chimney of the railway truck.

Arush must have escaped with them, for next he found himself in a fallow field on a misty, frosty afternoon, with only, some distance away, a woman wrapped up in a shawl and holding a bundle in both arms. She was walking towards Arush from the other side of the field. When she stood beside him, gasping for breath, she unwrapped the blanket and with great effort, almost falling to the ground, handed him the hidden child, saying in a faltering voice: "I can't do any more. You take him, and save him! Hurry up, because they are waiting..." Where and who, Arush did not know. He took hold of the boy, who was about seven, tall and slenderly built, with dark-golden hair. Arush loved him. His beautiful, thoughtful eyes, set in a pale, subtle face, showed perfect understanding of the situation. Arush, holding the child's hand, felt him trembling. Arush had to comfort him, while they ran as fast as their feet would carry them. Inside a large room, resembling the interior of a barracks, there were many people. They were telling how the gendarmes were searching house by house, and room by room. Arush was overwhelmed with fear for the child. He was conscious of nothing but the single task of saving the boy. He put him to bed under the cover of an eiderdown, imploring him to lie motionless. What if he moves, squeaks, or breathes just when the gendarmes are in? "If we don't get him out quickly, he'll suffocate to death," Arush shouted loudly, but no one heard him. Outside, beyond the barbed wire fence, a woman was waiting. She looked like Frania, his nannie. Arush tried to run to her to tell her that she must take the child out of Auschwitz, but his legs refused to move. Quickly, hurry up, she won't wait, but he was as if paralysed. In that state, he became aware that he was dreaming, and upon this awoke. Bathed in perspiration.

Oh, another of those dreams, he told himself. How these silly things return at night! Awake, he did not want to think of them; they took their revenge on him, and came in sleep.

Arush remained lying without stirring, his eyes closed. The stillness said it was yet night. What bliss! More time to sleep. But as he became more fully awake, a

391

strange, swishing whisper reached his ears. He was immediately alert, listening with bated breath. For a moment he even opened his eyelids slightly. He saw nothing but dark night. Yet its secret sounds disturbed his mind. He cocked his ears and, propping his head on his arm, he forced his eyes wide open.

O God, what am I seeing! Arush issued a silent cry. Flames! They lit up the night, casting a ghastly gleam through the window into the barracks. This is no hallucination, he assured himself; what he had heard was the rustle of fire. Only yards away, it seemed. Terrifying! He was frightened to look at the window, yet he also feared to take his eyes off it. The scarlet flames which flared into the vault of night gripped his gaze and mind. There was no need to tell him what was happening. It was people who were burning. Was he still dreaming? As if to satisfy himself, he gave a loud sigh, almost a shriek, to wake his nearest neighbour at least.

–"It's burning, can you hear?" Arush asked in German.

–"Sleep" D'you want to change places?" was the man's considerate answer in a curious Hungarian accent.

–"No!" said Arush curtly.

–"Don't look at the window. Close your eyes!" The neighbour spoke without turning over, or raising his head. Soon he was snoring again.

–"What was the use of closing your eyes," Arush reflected. Even if he kept them tightly closed, he would see the fire, he would hear the ripple behind the wall, he would smell the fumes that carried the taste of blood. To sleep - in the midst of a fire? With flowing lava as his feather-bed? Others did sleep. The whole barrack was snoring, men slumbering away while their brothers and sisters burnt in their thousands. Every night was like this...He was more unfeeling than they were: he watched it in a state of awareness - the first night? He was lying quietly awake and was unable even to emit a sound. The hush, the very way everyone in the barracks was silent was oppressive. Oh, if they would only yell! Why don't you shout? a voice within him asked. He was struck dumb. Simply petrified. How heartless! Disgusting! Brr! he shuddered. Why doesn't the earth swallow it all up, together with him? This animal insensitivity was more horrifying than the horror itself; to feel incapable of any gnawing anguish, untainted despair, of tears makes him a beast. Why was he making all this fuss? Didn't he know all about this? Hadn't he felt like this before? But now he was actually seeing it. People burning like faggots, worse - like refuse. Just burning...*Und morgen die ganze Welt.* And tomorrow the whole world, sing SS men at the end of a day's or night's shift. You may believe them, given enough time and power, they would set the whole world on fire. And the world did not perhaps deserve anything better. Believe me, Arush was addressing the "world", that for all that he had disclosed about his present feelings, that he was sick at heart and deeply unhappy - as unhappy as a man could be. True despair was dumb. He would scream, he would weep his fill for all those burnt lives - but not now. Now he cannot, even if he wished it with all his strength. Now he had not even the strength to roll over onto the other side, or to close his eyes. He was completely helpless, divested of all thoughts other than of this conflagration. It seemed to him before that he had already experienced everything, every possible terror, pain and grief. But the fires that swirled nearby, their shadows - long and short dancing shades of human lives, were unique. Uniquely terrifying. Lying there, and watching them gave Arush the idea that the dark shapes endlessly mounting in the glow of the bursting flames formed the underworld, whilst the sky had buried its face beneath the surface of earth. Close your eyes, Arush urged himself, force yourself, and you may see other things. What things? Visions of the past, salutary memories, which had often come back in the gloomiest moments of his life. Today he could see nothing. He could do nothing in the world in this night of fire, smoke and shades of death. "I know, mother, you burnt like this. Was it painful?" No more. But he could not really recall her tonight, to bring her, or any other memory back to Birkenau. Yesterday in the truck it was different - dark, tight, suffocating, making everything intimate. His mother was so close, and so were death, and God, and all the images he had loved. The big barracks, bright with flames, and the space beyond the window, made everything distant. And distant also was his feeling of personal death, though the fire raged round the corner. Round the corner - and they lie or sleep calmly as if they were wooden clogs. "Sleep today for tomorrow you may burn!" Nobody in this large barracks gave as much as a groan, a murmur, not even a sigh at what was happening. How he wished he could sense, could recollect, all those things he had been brooding over and over and sermonizing to others. Faith and hope, loyalty and dignity, death and eternal life. Tonight he himself needed to be reminded of them. People were burning unceasingly at his elbow, but he sensed no foretaste of death. He got it into his head that one feels death's coming. "Oh my Lord," Arush prayed silently, "who hath led me through darkest days and alleys, watch over me this night. And the coming days. Thou who hast shown me so many wonders, abandon me not now." Praying for himself. But do the dead need a display of wonders? Relief from sorrow? Protection from the dust? Perhaps they do? He must start thinking of something else! Nothing comes of this brooding. In vain, the same thoughts return. He could not escape them.

Cries were coming from beyond the wall. He could clearly hear them - human cries. They were burning them alive. Oh dear, what horror! Poor little babies. No bullets for them in the ghettos, no gas for them in the chambers. Roasted alive, in their nappies. The one exemption from *Werterfassung*. He could not take any more of this. Can anyone imagine how terrifying this experience was? Does anyone know how battered a man can feel? He did now close his eyes - only to see images rising, familiar faces moving through the clouds of flames. He was now even more frightened. Those images were more terrifying, more shattering, than the shades of unseen lives. The Prophet promised Moab that it shall die with tumult because it had burned bones into lime. But the Moabites burned dead bones...The curse of the present fire was greater, it would endure longer. In the same way as life was eternally preserved in some part of heaven, so must be this fire. Not a single tremor of these flames will be lost. They will be felt and told about centuries from now. The bush that burns in fire, and is not consumed. And Thou lookest from heaven on this? Did this drain his faith? Not really. Only a horrifying incomprehension. His fear of God was actually greater. In the face of such evil, he felt the need of His presence more than ever. "Shall cling to Thy name more firmly. Oh Lord, fortify me in my belief in miracles." Nothing short of a miracle could save them. "It's such a small thing for Thee. Deliver me from my fears. Help me not to worry." What sense did it make to worry? Some day he would die anyway. Die again. Arush Freund, the "extra" man, would die twice. He was losing his senses and tried to sustain himself. Close your ears as well! Thrust it all out of your mind! It's Sabbath. "The sheep of the slaughter-house are fatter than me." Three times, repeat! And be still! What had to come, would come. He could not prevent it. "Don't have a bad conscience" - that bastard counsel. Sleep! Was one stupid life worth so much fear? To die, so much better. Giving up in the end? No, he didn't feel like giving up, only his fear was shrinking. Becoming coarser. Always the same thoughts, the same, the same...Ad nauseam. He felt giddy. Those raving dark figures! The promise of coming days. But tonight sleep! And them that sleep in the dust...

CHAPTER TWENTY-NINE

Shouts and the distant baying of the gong awakened Arush. The world is still there, was his first thought, and the same killing thirst. He was mercilessly awake.

The sun must have long been out. His neighbour, having apparently clambered over him, was already down. At camp, a man's inner alarm-clock gets set very quickly. Arush had remained lying on the bunk, calculating that he was dressed, had only shoes to put on, and no "bed" to make.

–"What's the hurry?" Arush answered his bunk-fellow, who, while pulling up his trousers, had urged him gently to get up. He had also asked his name. His own was Miklos.

–"It's hard, I know," he said, "the first minutes and of the first day."

–"Why? One's gone."

–"Yet another begins."

He was right, the first full day in quarantine. It needed courage to start. But in truth Arush did not feel any specific terror of the day ahead, merely a diffuse apprehension of the unknown. For immediately the most pressing questions of yesterday returned to his mind. The chimneys, the fires (the thought mechanically excited him to take a deep sniff); would they get a number or not? Or the question which Poldek's wisdom had summarized: "one day you die of thirst, the next day of madness." Arush tried to resist those thoughts by persuading himself that this was a day like every other day and his early morning worries were nothing but idleness. "Arush, you just have it too good."

Miklos, who had already managed to return with an emptied bladder, looked scandalized when he saw Arush still tossing about on the bunk.

–"Get off, there'll soon be coffee," he said smartly.

Arush climbed down quickly, shivering slightly. A chill? He must take hold of himself. "Oh, my Lord, that Thou has put me through this endless, macabre night!"

Outside the sky was still cloudless, radiating even upon Birkenau its usual morning tranquillity. Just what, it seemed to Arush, they needed most.

On the way to the latrines, he met Marek.

–"Hurry up! There's a long queue."

Arush had contemplated perhaps watering a lonely flower in a dark corner, but he was afraid to shock Marek with such a confession, so he only stammered out, "How are you feeling?"

–"Tolerably well. When I woke up, everything looked so menacing..."

Arush did not let him finish.

–"Where are the wash-rooms?" he asked.

–"Forget about it. There's no water. They won't let you pinch a drop."

Arush nodded knowingly and ran off.

"Be quick! It'll soon be breakfast," Marek shouted after him.

In the queue, the first words Arush heard were the usual "still a long way before you," which one chap was saying to another. No one spoke of the night. Most men looked rested, and full of fresh strength to "carry on". Water was on every lip and seemed almost the only aspiration.

With the so-called coffee, which everyone drained to the last drop, the daily bread-ration was dealt out. But no one of the Pustkow transport had so much as a bite of it. For some time now, Arush reflected, he had known that almost anything could be eaten by human beings, but that fresh, good bread would not go down the gullet of healthy men, he would have never believed.

–"Abnormal! Incredible!" commented a man nearby in ecstasy.

–"Messianic times," Arush said to Marek.

–"Think about the times later on," rejoined Marek in a friendly tone. "The days of starving are not yet over."

They were no less surprised on hearing that there would be no roll-call, which everyone in Arush's group had awaited with trepidation. It was the common opinion among them that their immediate destiny would be announced at the roll-call this morning. And now such a disappointment. "A day in camp without a roll-call is like a bath without water," remarked Maniek, whose metaphor had, in the circumstances, grisly connotations.

–"I'm damned if I understand this," exclaimed Biegel, their former cook. But Miklos explained with the superior knowledge of his two weeks stay in Birkenau, that this was not unusual in quarantine.

And only yesterday, Arush pondered, he had heard near the fence of the women's camp an old-timer recalling how he was made to stand for long hours in severest weather at roll-calls. It seemed, Arush concluded, that an air of mystery hovered over their stay at Birkenau.

–"Well, let's find a good seat and start squatting," suggested Arush. But Marek preferred to wait for the camp elders' orders.

But no one was giving orders or even seemed to pay the slightest attention to their existence. So they stood around in small groups wondering - quietly wondering like men used to uncertainty. Here and there a rumour made the rounds - they were to be moved to other barracks; Auschwitz refused to admit them; partisans were lurking nearby in the woods. But on the whole there was little talking. Each man looked lost in his own thoughts, which were apparently not different from one another, and hence not worth communicating. The lives they had lived before seemed as if they had taken place in a previous incarnation. Even the train journey of only one day ago was already fading into a remote, forgotten past. Man thinks and speaks of what is necessary to his existence. And what could they think of except water or such a brain-numbing wisdom as "what has to be will be"?

396

Thus the call *Anstellen!* (form lines) came at once as a relief and a fluster. At first they drew up in the usual fives, but then the order was to march in single line. Quite extraordinary, it seemed to Arush. Surely they were not arrayed to raid enemy lines? The only time he could remember walking in single line at camp was out of Pustkow. Inevitably an association with trains came into his mind.

Though short, the march was tense and seemed very slow. The seniors, who were deputizing for Jozek, walked alongside them as guards. The men in line were led on the same route they had come in yesterday. Were they sending them back? Arush wondered in silence. His last march? How many times had he asked himself this question? To die once more in a train? Yesterday out, today in. Quite mad - but was he regretting the ejection from Birkenau? It is hardly possible to believe, yet this was what he felt. This was what to "have your life hang before thee" means.

And then once more they were standing silently before the ugly Sauna building, and after another spell of waiting that strained every nerve, they were once again walking naked across the long corridor of the *Zugangsbarracke* (admission barracks) to queue up before the desk of a camp official - but with a difference. This time the official, will, in addition to the prisoner's name and age, register the number, which only seconds earlier, another prisoner, evidently highly experienced in his job, has engraved with a few pricks of a sort of pen on the underside of their left arm. Some men had uttered muffled screams, but Arush was apparently, animal-like, immune to pain.

Thank goodness, he was a number; a real citizen of Auschwitz like others. Entering a new phase of life. From now on until the grave, or until the Reich's burial, whichever came first, this number would be his only official name. No more visas and passports, no more identity cards and permits, only a little, tiny tattoo. The pinnacle of one long band of progress!

It all happened in a flash, as if the thing had dropped from heaven. The men could smell the thrill, though there was no time to breathe in relief. They were handed new clothes. Literally new - straight from the factory, a celluloid made, blue-and-white striped uniform, and clean, good quality shirt and pants. A close-fitting prisoner's beret for the head, a piece of cloth to wrap round the feet, rather like a soldier, and shoes. Real leather lace-up shoes. Would you believe it? "What is your size?" the prisoner working in the store-house was asking each man politely. "Try them on and see if they fit you. You won't be able to exchange later."

And there was no shop in the whole world that could offer a larger assortment. "Your good luck," another storeman explained curtly, "the last transport for Germany left twelve days ago." So all this wealth of shoes was only eleven days' Werterfassung. But who had time now to think of such things, or to wonder about the person whose shoes he was putting on? Now each of them felt like the gambler whose very last stake had struck the jack-pot, and as a result was drunk with joy.

—"Thank goodness, elegance lives on in Auschwitz. And it makes demands on you as well. Elegance, I mean."

—"Oh certainly," Marek seized on this and thus prevented Arush from continuing. "We must improve our manners. Above all, we must not use bad language. But

397

don't become a bore."

Meanwhile it was being whispered all around that they were to leave Birkenau. That very day, some were saying. The rumour seemed to have gained credence from the store-house workers remarking that such clothes as they had been given were not distributed to ordinary prisoners in quarantine. Though they remained sceptical, the rumour fortified the men's change of heart since the morning. And it had all happened so suddenly.

—"Fate strikes like lightning," Marek was philosophical.

—"Haven't I always told you that heavenly succour comes in the twinkling of an eye," Arush corrected him. In their present hopeful mood he could not stand this heathenish attribution to fate. But Marek went on straightening the sleeves of his shirt and showed no inclination to argue.

Could he, indeed, expect to pick a decent quarrel in the present circumstances? Were they not like men flitting about in mid-air? And from the moment they had been given the skinpricks everything had happened so quickly around them, as if time were moving faster than usual. Hardly had they returned to their barracks compound, than the gong sounded. *Appel!*

Nothing seemed to Arush any longer unduly unusual. Though it turned out later that this was not to be a usual, "everyday" roll-call, but one of the greatest importance in Birkenau.

As always, Arush took care not to stand in the first row at the Appel-Platz - the square which at other times of the day formed part of the so-called promenade. Once they had lined up, sobriety returned and every single man became well aware of the pith and moment of the occasion. Standing to attention, while everyone tried to make himself as tall as possible, only increased their tension. The passing minutes were as long as hours. In this suspense, fear contended with the eloquence of that morning's omens - the tattoo, the new clothes, the lace-up leather shoes. But had the Germans not played similar jokes before? Arush suddenly recalled the story of the little boy found "illegally" living in the ghetto "A". When he fell on his knees imploring von Malotky to spare his life, von Malotky told him gently to get up, then asked his name and age, ordered the commander of the OD accompanying him to get the child a decent suit, and finally told the boy: "And now *mach dass du wegkommst!* (make yourself scarce). As the boy moved round and started running, von Malotky shot him in the head. Perhaps the shoes and the rest of the day's package were a sort of catch to reduce their vigilance, now that they had learned the secrets of the place? Why evacuate just them? And consider the haste with which this roll-call was ordered! The bravest mind would have begun to doubt, after what they had seen and experienced. Doubt and hope, the two immemorial antagonists, and the latter often bows to the former for fear of disillusionment.

At last they saw several uniformed men approaching, some with bamboo sticks in their hands. They walked at a slow pace, and with an air of careless indifference, resembling men about to enter an exhibition of sick birds in cages. Behind the uniformed men trailed a pack of assistant senior prisoners.

Though it was dangerous, Arush risked a glance at the men. They were rather

398

slimly built, and in their uniforms and fashionable boots looked amazingly buoyant, springy one might say, and yet very official. Even from a distance their eyes gleamed with ferocity, and the coarseness in their faces no doubt projected their inner selves.

A single SS man was taking the roll-call, standing at only an arm's length from the front row of prisoners. Tall, handsome, perfectly casual, everything about him was cool and commanding. His well-groomed face betrayed sharpness, cruelty and intelligence. Though wearing a simple grey-green uniform, a cloth peaked cap, and no badge to indicate rank or merit, he looked elegant, superior, suavely affected as if he had come straight from a medical-social gathering. He must be Viennese, thought Arush, so much polish, nonchalance, exquisite co-ordination of movement, could hardly be of Dusseldorf or Berlin breeding. But why gloves, though immaculately bright gloves, on such a hot day? A *faux pas,* a blemish! perhaps he fancied himself in an operating theatre? Perhaps he was like that secretary who put on gloves each time she had to type an unpleasant letter? Or perhaps he wore them for the same reason that Goeth immediately threw away the gloves in which he had hit a Jew? Rather, Arush inclined to believe, because it must feel more exciting to hand out death and life with a move of a finger muffled in a glove.

As he paced slowly along inspecting the lines, his eyes glanced carelessly, yet he took stock of the prisoners' general appearance. Then the selection started in earnest. And at such speed that you were bound to ask: was it really happening? He scrutinized each man individually and asked him about his age and calling, though some about the latter only. After a while, he would give only a slight nod of the head, as much as to say: "And you?", and the prisoner would shout his occupation. *Tischler* or *Schlosser* (joiner or locksmith), for the most part. The selector would then point with his gloved finger in a barely perceptible manner either to the left or to the rear. About one in three went to the back, in general the older and physically less fit-looking prisoners, including most of the master craftsmen of Pustkow. They were drawn up a hundred steps behind the longer lines.

For those who were awaiting their turn, tension rose with every man selected. The shorter the distance, the longer the road. Why am I standing so far down the line? Arush asked himself. Had he chosen, consciously or not, a place that would delay decision? What should he say? Twenty years. Not a year more. It was nowadays dangerous to be more than twenty. Less? He must be mad. Nineteen is a nonage. Look tall and strong, that's what counted. But what was he? What a curse this want of a trade! Now was not the time for regrets. But he must say something. The agonizing question - *Tischler* or *Schlosser?* It drove him mad. Joiner would not be a complete lie. He had made mouse-traps. But locksmith was so much better, more in demand and more men were shouting joiner. Don't be a fool - whether your answer was true or not did not matter in the slightest. But it did matter. Most of the "locksmiths" were sent to the left. You could not say for sure. And how did he know which group was better? Dark horses - highest stakes. Eh, came the silent reply, you staked your life long ago. But there was still everything to gain. He might succeed in driving a straight track. But what if he had to bend a wire? You idiot! You became a furrier without knowing what tacking means, and it saved your life. Oh, Holy Father, help me again! What shall I say? It's all the same, whatever the craft. Live by your wits, not by sweat! Have courage, lie! Work, toil can only kill, not save, you. Joiner, locksmith, could be just a fix. But this time it looked serious. He could not take this lightly; even if the end did not seem to be coming today. He had sensed no such forebodings. And so, standing tensely waiting, one worrying thought followed another, while all the time the men continued to be directed this way and that, bringing the decisive moment nearer and nearer.

At last he was face to face with the selector. He had not the demonic eyes of Goeth. Not even of a hypnotist. Screwed up lips, scornful contempt, he looked uneasy at being restrained, this time from taking lives (as it turned out later, the men grouped in the rear were not selected for the gas chambers). A nod of his head, and Arush cried out *Tischler*. Another nod, as if to say, "I know your tricks. But you won't escape me. First work yourself to death," and a twitch with the fore-finger to the left.

Sentence passed. "Temporary reprieve," commented Arush silently.

Who could tell his relief! The experience weighed him down, almost knocked him off his feet. Yet he stood still.

The selection was over, but not the roll-call. The tension surrounding it had, however, clearly eased. There was movement, human voices were heard, feigned activity perceptible, as the selector's assistants stepped forward and imitated their immaculate master. Even he had come out of his artificial shell - pacing more quickly, displaying a forced smile, a point to a colleague. In a few words, they are to leave today for another *Arbeitsplatz* (working place), he said. "Anyone for *Lagerälteste*? Raise his hand!"

Now something unexpected and most astonishing happened. After seconds of suspense, a spontaneous burst of cries - a loud chorus of rhythmic cries: "Bubi! Bubi!"

Not since his school days had Arush witnessed such a public expression of collec-tive will. Election by acclamation. Democracy affirmed at Auschwitz. Could you believe it?

"An event without parallel in the whole history of German concentration camps," was Hugo Bester's exultant comment. Maniek Lander made a more sober one: "The whimsical fancy of an arch-murderer." Indeed, who could tell all the whims of SS men registered during the past four years? Nevertheless the "election" made a point.

For what made the mates spontaneously suggest Bubi for their most immediate lashing whip was their knowledge of a cruelly simple fact, namely, that a Lageraelteste they must have, whether they liked it or not, and that, unless a pris-oner was very tired of his life, he must formally submit to the camps' hierarchical order and unwritten laws. The men also knew that to be a KZ eldest demanded cer-tain qualities, the least of which were feebleness, chivalry, or delicacy. The job called for a man who was capable of exerting control over his subordinates and enforcing camp discipline, but who ideally, from the prisoners' point of view, would not willingly exceed the amount of force necessary to perform his duty. And the overwhelming majority of former inmates of Pustkow apparently considered Bubi to be the man to meet these requirements.

Arush abstained from voting. Not because of a fanatical dedication to secret ballot, or abhorrence of public display of feelings, but because he doubted the general soundness of the "never-pray-for-a-new-ruler" Jewish wisdom.

Under the watchful eyes of the SS, Bubi immediately took up his office, earmarking, with the assistance of other functionaries, his new-old-herd. An instruction or two, a warning not to stray, and the rows were dispersed.

It was noon, the square was bathed in brilliant sunshine, and bread distributed for the journey. With two spare rations of bread in Birkenau, you begin to feel like a millionaire in the midst of dearth.

–"Real capitalists," remarked Ruben pointedly.

–"What shall I do with it?" is the standard question a man starts to ask the moment he has scraped together some savings. Though Arush had asked the question lightly, he genuinely wondered what to do with the bread.

–"Keep it! Who knows what a hunger cure they'll make us take at the new resort. At best, you could always turn it into something else."

Bread was indeed cash in all camps, but all the bread that he and his mates could pool together was not enough to pay for one glass of water. Mercifully, this morning's tension and turmoil had eased the craving for water a little. Like every sensation, thirst has its degrees. But bread - what did he need bread for? He was not hungry, and still felt an aversion to even a scrap of solid food. To take bread out of Birkenau, he thought, would be a triumph of greed. A sacrilege. A plan had developed in his mind. He would distribute his bread. Not everything to one man and only to one from among those starving shadows he had seen yesterday, for whom this would be the very last opportunity to eat bread on earth. And, conscious of stories about SS men throwing bread onto lorries carrying men to death in order to watch them fighting for a morsel, he would do it discreetly. Let this at least be his thanksgiving. At the same time he mocked his own generosity. "Arush, the Birkenau philanthropist."

Do not be surprised by this altogether light-hearted thinking. In the moments after the selection, they were all literally bubbling with excitement. There was cheering and laughter - the blueish sky itself seemed to smile.

But before long the hilarity began slowly to wear off and a more down-to-earth mood prevailed. Arush noticed Marek sitting by the wall of a barracks, sunk in thought, an expression of vague wonderment on his face. Yet when he joined him, Marek proved more eager to talk than ever.

–"Why so pensive?" asked Arush for a start.

–"It all came like a flash, it was like magic, and after all, it might be one damn big illusion.

"Meanwhile, some of our fellows are whirling among the stars. It only arouses envy, and tomorrow everything might be over."

Is he afraid of the evil eye, Arush asked himself, while to Marek he said: "But

401

these prisoners around here know better than to envy us. Except for our bread."

–"I gave my bread away. It's not that. Sooner or later they too will leave. But they think us a lucky lot, and nothing arouses more envy than good luck."

–"Whom have you given your bread to?"

–"Last night's neighbour. A good boy, and very sad. Father, mother, younger brother 'went', he alone from the whole family came through. And he mentioned in passing, that I might have to get the bread disinfected at the new place."

–"I won't be trapped by such talk," said Arush, and he told Marek of his own plan.

Marek argued that Arush was not doing the right thing, because a man in this condition has not the strength to swallow bread. Arush disagreed and, to change the subject, he asked: "Doesn't it feel strange to make gifts of bread?"

–"No more strange than to make gifts of gold in your last will. For a lifetime of several hours we have been rich. Tomorrow, who knows what hell of a cage we'll be in?"

–"What matters is that you're alive, and so there's still hope of winning the game. Thank God for it!"

–"You have always something to thank for. I would keep my thanks until we see the new place. We may yet be jumping from the rain into the sump."

–"But this, here, is the deepest sump. I smell sunshine in the air. Now that the long chain of horror and despair has been broken, a decisive change for the better is coming."

–"Where was the chain broken? Whether Auschwitz, I, Auschwitz II, or Auschwitz III, it's still Auschwitz. All one stage. For heaven's sake, what has changed?"

–"Don't you really know? We're about to leave the largest scene of murder in the history of mankind, and only half a moment ago we feared immediate departure for the other world. From the sickening rags of yesterday to this morning's neat camp outfit. And only a few hours earlier, from the dark, strangling train into the open air of a sunny day. That's where the chain has broken."

–"What chain? It's all just chance. We reached the end of the journey still alive, so we got out. Chance, like all the rest."

–"Couldn't it be more than chance? Don't you really feel that 'chance-event' of yours was a turning point? Don't you sense that, whatever awaits us, our life since that journey has been an anti-climax, and will remain so to the end of our days?"

–"My bones don't feel so acutely as yours. I can't see any turning point. It's an event like any other event that has been pushing us around till now."

–"If you can't see the sky is blue, it doesn't mean that it isn't."

There was no point in continuing with this talk. Arush was walking straight ahead, and he hardly noticed that the sky was now covered with light fluffy clouds, and turning a little grey. Similarly unaware of his surroundings, he found himself on the meadow. Don't be startled. This was yesterday's promenade, but was only given that name after official quarantine hours had passed. Quarantine was not yet over and, therefore, it occurred to Arush that discipline had somehow eased. Certainly, the news of their fabulous selection and impending departure had spread through the length and breadth of Auschwitz with the speed of a hurricane. But whether this was the reason for the milder climate of that afternoon, was less certain. For in addition to the Pustkovians who were fidgeting about in small groups, so as not to miss hearing the call to leave, Arush saw other prisoners prowling on the meadow in unusually large numbers for that time of day.

Mere chance, as Marek had said, it may have been, but as he stood contemplating the scene around him, Arush could hardly believe the change he saw. Men, who only hours ago, had turned their faces away when the Pustkow fellows crossed their path now gazed straight into their eyes; some were even glad to stop in front of Arush or another of his mates and say a friendly word. It could be that it was not them in person, but the bread they possessed, that attracted the interest. One way or the other, he felt a little embarrassed and tried to appear as humble as possible; and to dampen his spirits, he recalled the visions of last night.

Preoccupied with his inner feelings and his quest for water, Arush was slightly startled to notice a man walking beside him who immediately put his arm around his shoulder, and said: "You have no idea, how glad I am." Arush recognized the voice of Lolek Kwas. He was speaking quickly but gently, and looked even thinner than yesterday.

—"Where is your friend Marek?"

—"Over there, not far away," Arush gestured backwards with his head.

—"He too may have misunderstood me. You can't imagine how it distressed me yesterday to hear that you had no number; and you didn't even seem to understand its significance. How was I to explain it?"

—"Ah, we told you that there was no cause to worry. How is it that you're promenading at this time of the day?"

—"I was picked out with three other fellows to fetch some plumbing materials from the main camp. It was actually there that I first heard of your good luck and sensational escape."

—"What news d'you bring from main camp?"

—"None this time. Nothing particular is happening on the war fronts. Your departure is the greatest news. It signifies important changes. You don't know how much even the Poles are welcoming it. They take it as a sign of the times. Soon everyone will be leaving, they say. Transport after transport. Auschwitz is to disappear."

—"Not sorry for our good turn?"

At this moment Bolek joined them. He introduced himself to Lolek by his full name of Bolek Wróbel.

—"You look smart," he said, eyeing Arush from head to toe. "A pity that Samek can't see you like this. He's shaving the guards. Saturday, you know. At night a raut. Escorting the dames of the Puff..."

Arush began to explain to Lolek who Samek was, but Lolek did not allow him to finish, eager to reply to his last question.

—"Perhaps a little envious, but not grudging," he said, speaking even faster than before. "They aren't like that now. Not those who stay here. No question of delighting in our tribulations. They have changed. A Jew, they say now, is a human being, even if he's a Jew. Without denying the irony..."

–"Wait a minute," Bolek cut in sharply, " you speak as if you had swallowed a *szczekaczka* (literally a barking instrument, figuratively, the loudspeakers which the occupant had installed in major streets of towns.) Are you speaking of Polish prisoners? You are, and you are talking a lot of nonsense."

Bolek was resolute and went on. "True enough, the Poles keep themselves apart from our Jews. But you can't blame them for that. Where separation is not enforced, where Poles and Jews work together, no matter the job or place, they form a tight pack and stand up like one man. I hope, you weren't suggesting any sort of rejoicing here by Poles at Jewish misfortunes. It would be mean of you."

–"I certainly didn't mean you," replied Lolek spitefully, his eyes on Bolek's badge.

–"Me? Why? In a sense we're all Polish. But as he," referring to Arush, "already knows, I am also a Jew - of the New Testament. But, then what's the irony you started blathering about?"

–"Well, how shall I say, a curious blend of circumstances...the ironical situation that the men who keep the Poles here, deprive them of their families and country, these same men have 'cleansed', as they used to say, Poland of Jews. And this was something the Poles didn't expect only a few years ago, even in their wildest imagination."

–"Dirt!" Bolek protested indignantly. "Dragging sheep and goats, the pure and the corrupt, through the mud together. You're unfair to so many who, moved by highest motives and pity, endanger their lives to help Jews, even here. Yes, even the fanatics of yesterday. Only the other day, I saw a Polish woman, a very nationalistic lady - one of those who not so long ago was saying that after the war, true Poles would place flowers on Hitler's grave because he spared them from doing themselves the dreadful job he did with the Jews - I saw her pushing bread and water into the hands of a newly arrived Jewish child, almost under the eyes of the SS. Have a cigarette," and he held one out to Arush.

He nodded at once thanking and refusing, and also wondered if this wasn't a subtle bid for his bread. Who could tell?

–"I accept that," said Lolek with increased animation. "No doubt, living here together for months, sharing the suffering, and witnessing all that horror, makes people less intolerant of one another. And no doubt, the attitude that 'to pity a Jew is to censure God' is much less common here than outside. But why don't you accept that as far as Jews are concerned the heart of every decent Polish man and woman is, even here in Auschwitz, torn between feelings of humanity and patriotism?"

–"No! That's not true." To make his point, Bolek was now not only waving his arms about, but also standing still, which in the circumstances was even more conspicuous and potentially dangerous. "I admit that there aren't many pious women here, and even fewer men. The majority locked in here are the flower of the nation - progressive, politically conscious people, imbued with both patriotism and humanity. They feel no conflict between the two, and the help they give to Jews is disinterested."

–"No doubt. What interest could there still be in our destruction? We have nothing, only our naked lives - and the very way in which life is taken away from us is too barbaric not to arouse revulsion. It requires superhuman effort not to feel pity at the sight of a little child waiting to burn. Besides, killing is infectious, like typhoid: one can never be sure where it will stop."

This made Bolek resentful. He spoke angrily, telling Lolek that he had a wayward imagination and that he imputed to others what was on his own sick mind. No Pole in Auschwitz thinks like that, he said. They earnestly hope, and say so, that after the war a new Poland will arise, free of all prejudices and hatreds, a just, loving mother to all its faithful sons. And, whether he intended to change the subject, or, rather, to go over to the offensive, he went on: "But what the Polish prisoners do wonder is what happened to the renowned inter-Jewish solidarity and compassion in this war? Other people get on the air to send a message of comfort to their captive brothers - and you know what a life-saving tonic every hopeful word that reaches us from abroad can be. But it's just the Jews, normally so vocal and meddlesome, who keep silent. Not a sound..."

–"It hurts them so much," Arush interrupted him, succeeding in hiding his irony, "and anguish makes people dumb."

–"They aren't dumb when it comes to accusing others."

–"How d'you know?"

–"I can imagine from what I have heard your friend saying. What were they saying or doing, I ask you, those free fellows of yours in the West, while their compatriots here, in Poland, have been massacred wholesale? Who knows what those brothers of yours want of you? What comes to mind is too awful to say..."

He could not say it anyway, because Lolek would not let him, robustly asking: "Why haven't your friends rebelled then? They do get comfort from their brothers abroad, and money, and, most important, weapons. And they even have a government to direct them, though it is on alien soil. Yet we've not heard much these five years past, of them putting up a fight. Have we?"

–"You hear the hard way. But for this I don't blame you. How could you hear? Only this week prisoners at the Pawiak rebelled. And elsewhere in Warsaw, boys of the A.K. rescued scores of prisoners from a hospital. That's the latest news!

"As for a large-scale rising, the time has not yet come. They must await orders. This, I mean the Underground, is a real army, with strict discipline. Not a herd of sheep to be led to slaughter."

The allusion was transparent enough to make Lolek now lose his temper. It did not provoke Arush, partly because he had yesterday had a foretaste of the man, so that he did not take Bolek seriously, and partly because he had grown philosophical about what people said, in particular camp inmates with their pugnacious way of debating. Arush, too, had not forgotten that in relation to Jews even the *Christian-Untermenschen* actually considered themselves a superior race, and that this could not have changed in Auschwitz.

–"I know what you're getting at," Lolek fumed. "I've heard this before, 'why d'you let yourself be killed?' 'Why don't you fight?' whereas to fight, to defend ourselves, is the last thing your dear friends wish us to do - let alone helping us with the means to fight. And I've heard that same sneering reproach, the same sanctimonious pretence even here. 'They couldn't be tricked like the Jews.' 'They wouldn't let themselves be slaughtered like sheep.' Oh, not them. They would throw themselves on their killers, grab their arms, put their eyes out.

"How many Poles have died here? I'll tell you - perhaps a million. How many of them have resisted? Not even one. If there were acts of resistance, if there were cases, though very few, of men jumping at the hangmen's throats, they involved Jews. Why don't *you* rebel? Kill? Wait, till when?"

–"Calm down," Bolek tried to cool the argument. "You get too excited and therefore say much that is irresponsible and not to the point. The reproaches and the pretences are of your friends, the 'mighty' and the 'fearless' ones. Mine don't say such things (meaning 'as herds of sheep to the slaughter'). To cheer you up, I'll tell you what I heard just before I met you. The Russians are in Praga (district of Warsaw on the right bank of the Vistula). They have cannons which are so big that their barrels bridge the Vistula. You can see them from the Saska Kempa with the naked eye. It's the truth, in all conscience! Would you have us fight now, here, when the Russians are so near? To make things worse?"

It was not clear for whom things would be made worse, but it became unnecessary to ask, for Bolek went on, "To provoke reprisals? A bloodbath? Human life is a sacred thing. And thus God willing we'll be free in a matter of weeks. At most. Come to see me in Warsaw. You'll be my guest," he was addressing only Arush. "The valiant Fritzes are fleeing head over heels. Orders come from the rear. Backwards is onwards. Wheels uppermost. 'The wicked flee as no one pursueth them', as the proverb has it. But I must go now. You'll leave by lorry."

He shook Arush's hand, but as Bolek went away Lolek joined him.

This Bolek is insanely contradictory, Arush thought as he walked on slowly down the meadow. But how smartly he altered the course of conversation and eased the tension. He, Arush, might be underestimating him. In his blabbing, he was at once attractive and repulsive. But Arush liked him. The good news he brought evoked dreams of home. After all, perhaps it was not Bolek who was contradictory, only the respective Polish-Jewish positions. Incredible, he thought, how difficult they are to reconcile even now, even behind barbed wire. A wider range of sentiments than Arush would have thought were involved. The Poles can afford to bide their time, and show unconcern. To us Jews every minute counts, every minute means precious lives lost. How often had he himself said, it was wrong not to avoid death? Anyway, how would it help us if the Poles started fighting now? How would this favourably alter the course of events for Jews? Had not our actual and would-be rebels in the ghettos also been planning to fight only at the "end of all ends"? Bolek's arguments are, none the less, a sham. At least you can answer him back; to a real Pole, without a Jewish scab under his cap, prudence forces you to bite your lips, whatever he may say. Bolek had only meant to justify, as everyone justifies, the case he supports. "Going by lorry." How does he know? Why didn't he ask Bolek where they were going to? Eh, he's just wagging his tongue. Hitler escaped another assassination; or, the British escapade into Belgium. People who make up stories like that are just frivolous. If you still feel strong, with no hunger, and there is a dim chance of surviving, the skies take a bluish tint. And dignity returns. He must resist guilt. And to think that it was all about nothing more than moving from one death camp to another. Not exactly. But it's a strange thing, no one gives a thought - where to?

He could, however, not be diverted for long from the indolently suppliant faces of his fellow wanderers, or their talk. Some would only express their feelings with a look, others had a question or a piece of good advice. A few openly asked for the bread which they could see sticking out from under the jacket or out of the pockets of the leavers. One young man stopped to say, as a gesture of good will to Arush, that others would also soon be leaving.

The well-wishers' voices followed him until he found himself opposite the women's camp. At first it seemed to him as if the women lined up beyond the wire fence had been standing there without a break since yesterday. The same shapeless, still figures one could not tell apart from this distance, the same bereaved, anxiously questioning faces - today beaming still warmer looks mingled with scarcely perceptible farewell gestures.

A young, round-faced girl with a smile about her eyes and one hand stretched half-way through the strands of wire, asked loudly: "Where are you leaving for?"

Arush shrugged his arms in reply. She understood, and went on to say: "I watched your selection through the wires with my fingers crossed and prayed for you. If by chance you meet a boy of your age, Shiku Brumlik," here her voice sank with emotion, "his sister, Tuzi, is here...Don't forget to tell the world!"

Arush nodded in promise, as if he were quite sure of fulfilling her request, and sent her back a parting kiss.

And so he had a new mission, to deliver regards from Tuzi. But would he ever be able to carry it out? The weakness of character that he felt he displayed minutes later made him even more doubtful.

As Arush had noticed before, the saunterers on the Birkenau meadow looked nearly all alike in outward appearance. But in mind and body, they represented a medley of distinct nationalities, creeds, and cultures, and each of those groups showed a preference for its own members. That the languages the men spoke did not necessarily coincide with the religion or nationality they shared with other inmates was not a striking revelation, nor that it was language rather than religion or nationality, which kept the citizens of this milling city apart. This was in particular true of the Jewish prisoners. For there were in Birkenau Polish Jews, Hungarian Jews, Greek Jews, western Jews, eastern Jews, Ashkenasi Jews and Sephardi Jews. Many of them had no common language, both literally and figuratively, and consequently the community ties, which normally hold Jews together, were not too strong between certain sections; while relations between them inasmuch as they existed, were despite the infernal experience they had all endured, cultivated highly selec-

407

tively.

So that when a passing fellow asked for their spare bread, he did it mostly in Yiddish, adding "brother", "bread", or another word in Polish if he knew it. Or, he would make his request in Polish and say "I'm hungry", or something like that in Yiddish. Yet however moved he was, Arush resisted all these heart rending entreaties, determined as he was to stick to his plan. This made him, on his way back, search more intensely for someone who did not have the strength to stretch out his hand, while at the same time he hoped faintly that the man might also happen to be a Polish Jew.

But when a young, healthy looking boy of about seventeen, with a humble expression in his sun-darkened face began to plead with him, gesticulating and crying, *"Lechem"* (bread), *"Corfu"*, *"Israel"*, and again, *"Lechem"*, *"Israel"*, *"Corfu"*, *"Lechem"* (apparently his entire Hebrew vocabulary), and then, in support of his sectarian claim, pulled down his trousers, flaunting the private evidence of his Jewish distinction - Arush threw him his bread. And both rations at that.

Why did he do it? Arush asked himself, as he continued to walk down the meadow. Was he so astounded by the boy's act? Or was he subconsciously recalling his friend Abe Flacher?

Then he began to wonder how his tailor mates of Pustkow would have felt about this episode. That the age-old custom, of which the boy made such a successful exhibition, would not have been too near to their hearts was beyond any doubt. And as for the boy's touching exploit itself, they would have had little sympathy for an exposure that could be interpreted, however obscurely, as dissociating Jewish identity from Yiddish (unspoken in Corfu). The case would have certainly promoted a lively debate about the broader question it raised, namely, what was the stronger: ties of a common language, or ties of a common nationality, let alone religion?

The boy's action could even have proved that Tacitus, usually so wrong-headed about the Jews, was right when he complained that the rite of circumcision had no other purpose than to provide a recognizable mark of Jewish otherness. Unreckoned generations apart, his disciple in aspersion and venom, Father Trzeciak of Poland, had improved on Tacitus by saying that the rite of circumcision, like keeping a full beard, was intended purely as a means of forging exclusive commercial links.

"Oh," sighed Arush, "my dear brother from remote exotic Corfu, how you have proved everything by your bold, extraordinary coup! How could I ever forget you? Will you live to remember?"

CHAPTER THIRTY

On that afternoon, life in Birkenau seemed quite relaxed to Arush. While quarantine was still in force for less fortunate prisoners, in front of the barracks - his home of one day - the Pustkow men were standing unmolested and chatting like provincials assembled in the town square to discuss current affairs. They impressed Arush as men who had somehow managed to forget their thirst and weariness, and who, though instantly expecting a call to line up, were not impatient. They seemed to be absorbed in interpreting the day's eccentric events. Views differed of course, and some of the fellows were still suspicious, still doubting that they would soon leave Birkenau. Marek Rainer sounded almost cynical in his distrust. When Arush came up to him, Marek told him: "As always they keep us guessing, and we, as always, are waiting - waiting to be sent up the chimney in the end." When, to rouse him a little, Arush had said that there would be water at the new place, Marek replied in the same mournful tone: "Hanging gardens with flowing fountains."

Arush suspected that besides instinctive fear of a disappointment, there was some posturing in this pessimism of Marek's, and instead of listening to his gloomy thoughts, he moved away from him. He squatted down close to two young men, who in the midst of "doing" quarantine were engaged in a lively discussion. Arush had earlier heard about the two. Both were natives of Warsaw and had been students at the local university before the war. Both had survived the Jewish ghetto uprising in Warsaw, to be subsequently evacuated into the Poniatowa concentration camp, from where they had arrived lately in Birkenau. One of them, called Baruch, was said to be the faithful son of a rabbi, the other, Felek, the son of Polish artists of Jewish birth.

As Arush had sat down, he heard Baruch quoting, curiously in German, a familiar saying of Goethe's, that "High up there in heaven care is taken that a tree doesn't overgrow."

–"Inasmuch as any care at all is taken whether it grows or not," snapped Felek. "The whole thing is unintelligible to me. Why let it shoot up in the first place?"

–"What a silly question! In the germ of a tree the limit of its growth is already inscribed. Besides, this is the way poets talk. And this view isn't fairyland, it's historically proven. From Pharaoh to Nebuchadnezzar, from Vespasian to Napoleon, from Hannibal to Schickelgruber. What better signals the futility of might, of conquest, of hero worship than the continued existence of Jews, compared to the fate of all those world conquerors? All have shared, or will share, Haman's end. A wit like you should know that this is just the law, how things are ordered in this world."

–"You're a man of such vivid convictions, that I fear I may offend you by asking if this bloody war and butchery are also part of that same Law and its world order?"

Baruch was clearly angered when he replied.

–"You can't offend me with such questions. It merely shows your own vivid mis-apprehension, my dear unbeliever. The law is divine, but not Divinity itself. Nor is everything that happens on earth divine. Your hollow rationalism, grown on alien soil, I'm afraid, would prevent you from understanding such things."

–D'you understand them?"

–"What?"

–"Well, where shall I start? Why is all this happening to us?"

Baruch interrupted him indignantly, apparently irritated by the common and to some provocative question.

–"All right, I know all of you rationalists are feasting in this great tragedy of ours, and choose it as the favourite ground to declare war not so much on God as on Jewish religion. I say Jewish, for by the same token you certainly regard what has happened to Jews as a triumph of the Germans' religion. They must indeed be blar-ing songs of praise, offering thanksgiving prayers for their outstanding achieve-ments."

–"They have no religion, they're godless."

–"True. But all of them? Even among the SS every other man is said to be a member of one church or another. You may have heard that the SS commander of Auschwitz - if he's still with us I don't know - is a priest manqué.

"But if they're godless, and we're, as I have often heard people like you saying, Godforsaken, then you aren't, after all, so much a terrific atheist, as a fuddled athe-ist, full of contradictions. All right, if this place here, Auschwitz, is your favourite battlefield against God, and you have no better argument than to say that in view of the present state of human, particularly Jewish, affairs, He has apparently taken leave of absence - as you go on claiming with undisguised joy - then your bigotry is only surpassed by your irrationality. Why attack something that's not there? But if He is, if He does exist, then He fills the air and sky of Auschwitz as much as of any other corner of the universe."

–"You're putting words into my mouth. But, still, tell me what separates the things that happen here, or elsewhere, from the Law, as you seem to prefer to call Providence?"

–"If you mean to say that Auschwitz is your battlefield merely against religion, then bring your own here and let us see how it stands up to comparison. Your thrust of rationality and humanism, your gods of art, your religion of progress - for those chimneys undoubtedly are the pinnacle of progress - your adopted adoration of Love, from the preaching of which partly proceed the little sentiments we're chari-tably allowed to relish."

When Felek interrupted him to ask if the "charity" wasn't the will of the Law? Baruch didn't allow him to continue, but continued himself.

–"At least, I'm glad to say, you aren't as bad as many of your kind, who are shedding crocodile tears over their allegedly lost faith, or ability to believe, because of what is happening here. But why are you so vexed that others should still believe?"

—"Not in the least," denied Felek vigorously. "There's nothing I respect more than a man who earnestly believes in God and acts up to his belief. But that isn't the case, only...why should you deny that it isn't God's will? Then what is it - the purpose, the higher sense of all that happens to us here?"

Arush felt that the question was more provocative than insincere; so, apparently, did Baruch but in any case, it released another flow of words from him.

—"Aren't you too pretentious? Here on the canvas of Auschwitz you want to discern the purpose of things?" While Baruch was now using a milder tone, Arush could hardly restrain himself from interrupting, as he was inwardly ranting at the "shameless heathens" who proclaimed day and night that life was mechanical and purposeless, yet still sought just the purpose of Auschwitz.

—"You don't understand," continued Baruch, "the motives of your own deeds, but you aspire to understand the motives of divine action. If your brain could grasp what an Einstein's brain does, if the infant Spinoza could explain what the mature master did, if an ass understood what things a man does, you wouldn't sound so presumptuous. An ass at least has the humility not to concern himself with human affairs, but you wish to penetrate the inaccessible nature and workings of God."

—"Very nice rhetoric, an old device, for dodging a question. But you can't escape. The more you try, the more it thrusts you into a maze of confusion. So, you say, there's no purpose, no meaning in this calamity that has befallen us? God has just, so to speak, retired from the rule of the world, stopped intervening in its affairs? Strange coming from you."

—"Now you're not only misunderstanding, but also twisting my words. I'm not trying to escape anything, there's no need for me to do so. No single event in this world, be it as ponderous as the present tragedy - or let us say, no historical process has a discernible ultimate meaning. It certainly acquires a different meaning in time. To Columbus, America meant something different from what it means to us. Look at Christianity - the powerful, universal religion of today, appeared to Tacitus as just another Jewish quarrel. Everything that is meaningful must surely have a purpose. But we don't know what it is. This is no proof of confusion, or reason for shame. That there're some peculiar media to reason out the purpose of contemporary historical events is a pagan belief. Besides, purpose for whom? For the Germans, Auschwitz serves very well the purpose for which it was built. For the Poles, it has, indirectly, the purpose, as far as we're concerned, of realizing a national dream. For the Jews? It's rather nice, if not surprising - considering your background - for you to insist on a specific Jewish purpose. I believe there is one, but I don't know what it is. You, who believe there is no purpose in anything that exists in this world, but want to know what is the purpose of Auschwitz, it may interest you to hear that the Greeks believed that their gods devised Auschwitz-like earthquakes, so that posterity would have something to narrate."

Once more Arush held back from telling Baruch that the idea was borrowed from Exodus to explain the plagues: "And that you may narrate in the ears of your son

411

and of your son's son what things I have wrought in Egypt." Or from telling him of the Psalmist's mystifying sentence: "For this is God, our Lord, for ever and ever, He will lead us onto death." Actually the last two words, *al mut* in Hebrew, probably convey a musical term, and with different punctuation, which replaces vowels in Hebrew, it would also mean soprano, maidens, youthfulness; and if a single, interchangeable letter of it is transmuted - eternity. Thus the great Rabbi Israel commented: This our good Lord leads us by the hand like little children onto death, to make us eternal. A formidable idea, but not for Felek, who resumed his questioning.

–"So it's just a little plot - neither punishment nor divine intervention in history, but a pastime of the Creator of the World? And Auschwitz is His playground? Are you serious?"

–"Ask Homer. I was only repeating what he said.

"But why d'you lose your temper so easily? Is it because you can't accept any idea which is out of your way of thinking? Because divine purpose is beyond the rational categories of your understanding? Or is it because you can't explain to yourself why you are here? Well, you must get used to these humiliating realities, otherwise you'll worry the life out of yourself.

"And please do understand that this 'Auschwitz' is not a punishment. Punishment by whom? D'you realize how stupid it is of you to speak of superhuman punishment? I could understand it, if you were a believing Christian. But then I would have had to ask you to which Christian prayers the Almighty had listened? Apparently not to the devout Poles - who have been punished all right - nor to the prayers of Frenchmen, or of the people in the Low Countries. It would seem that at the moment the British and Americans have the ear of Heaven, though in the end the main beneficiary may turn out to be the godless Soviet state. But you're a Jew, albeit one without religion, and indeed your stricture about 'Auschwitz' being a punishment for Jews - and as a logical corollary, a reward for Germans - reminds me of the ancient pagan belief that the gods direct the will of men for divine ends. For a believing Jew this catastrophe is not a punishment."

–"So what is it?" interrupted Felek impatiently.

–"I don't know. Perhaps a sort of enlarged national cleansing once in a thousand years. Though it could be a lesson - not just to Jews - a last warning."

–"Warning to whom?"

–"To all the people in the world, a warning that if they don't come to their senses, they'll disappear next time they indulge in their little martial games."

–"Now I can see - the chosen Jewish people selected as the warning sign to the nations of the globe; the eternal survivors who must suffer for the sins of mankind desecrating the world that was created for them. The longer I listen to you, the more absurd your theological explanations sound to me. Can't you see that this time the cleansing winds will sweep away the eternal survivor along with the warning sign?"

–"No, that's either exaggerating or disparaging things. Where do you get your hostility to almost anything linked with Jewish religion? Do you really not know that the very qualities which you impute to Jews were contrived and then

412

attributed to them by others?"

–"That's new to me. Can you explain?"

–"First, the idea that world history centres around the Jews and so is graced with a peculiar meaning. This view, like the one that history in its empirical course was of supernatural construction, was not something the Jews conceived."

–"By whom then?"

–"It has been attributed to Jews by self-interested people from without, using selective quotations from, and controversial interpretations of, the Jewish prophets. The focus on the ancient history of the people of Israel, and reference to its prophets was necessary to stress the universal significance of Christianity's entering into history. Christianity - the superseding religion, has since then fulfilled the purpose for which Providence had initially chosen its precursors."

–"But did not in fact the Hebrew prophets originate the concept of a world history focused on Jews?"

–"No, that's not so. And the curious thing about the Hebrew prophets is that they were neither historians, nor philosophers of history, nor did they view its course as being due to a final purpose; and history apparently didn't much interest them. Inasmuch as it did, and the fate of empires had crossed their vision of the universe, it was solely as the background to their prime concern."

–"What's this concern, particularly if everything that you have mentioned were merely fallacious allegations?"

–"The condition of man, as he stands, individually, before the Court of Supreme Justice.

"What eventually the prophets intimated was that, because of the Jews' relatively higher perception of God, they had been charged with the task of spreading this perception among the people of the world; and this had obligated them to higher moral standards and stricter observance of divine commandments. Hence, you see, the 'warning sign' post."

–"Indeed I see - the assignment is divine, the warning comes from heaven. How does this square with what you said before, that virtually nothing that happens on earth is divine?"

–"There's no flaw, except in your logic. Let me tell you again that the view that events on earth *merely* reflect the will of God, or that He is co-operating, let alone merging, with men in the process of history, is no part of the Jewish religion. History, and in particular its major subject - war, are, as I was taught, made by man; it's his freedom to determine the course of his action; and consequently it's he who is responsible for his deeds before God and his fellow men. These are the principles which stand at the centre of Jewish religious and world experience. This should teach you not to make Heaven responsible for 'Auschwitz'."

–"It's never too late to learn. But leaving responsibility where it belongs," continued Felek in his scornful way, "I'm immensely surprised at your 'teaching'. To hear you suggesting, there's no Kingdom of God on earth? History a distortion of divine will?"

–"I know the rest. But let me finish!" Baruch cut in quickly. "The role of divine

413

will in any historical event, why it has taken place, let alone what its ultimate purpose is, is beyond the grasp of human intelligence. Actually, the higher a man's intellect rises to discern these things, the more it proves to be beyond its comprehension. Your mind is filled with false notions and your thinking is, perhaps unconsciously, affected by strange teachings, which, by their different perception and apprehension of God, vary fundamentally from our Jewish ones. Following the latter, it's senseless to speak of the distortion of divine will. What concerns Divinity, all movement of mankind is foreseen and, over the long, unending course of history, directed by the Maker who is independent of all and everything. And so, as a corollary and by divine order, the world is independent. Hence at best it's a kind of republic, not a kingdom, and, like man, has its freedom of development. Every historical event occurs, simultaneously, in two different, almost infinitely distant, spheres each with its own, different kind of perception and pre-ordained divine laws. In the earthly sphere the events are determined by man, in the other, transcendental one, they're predetermined by God. This is the meaning of the classic sentence: 'All is foreseen, but freedom of choice is granted'. To human reason this is an antinomy, the greatest of the Jewish religion, and perhaps of all humanity - but antinomies are a part of our experiences and thinking, and we must live with them. This was a question which has occupied the best human minds for hundreds of years, but the answer God has reserved to Himself. By His will we may know it in the 'latter days' envisaged by the prophets."

–"In the meantime?" asked Felek, as if despondently.

–"We can only hope. But, as in history the two spheres have already combined, we need not concern ourselves with foresight and necessity, but should concentrate on freedom of choice."

–"But isn't it all an illusion?"

–"I know that you disbelieve all I have said, not just concerning foresight or free will of man, which you regard to be an illusion. But free will I won't discuss with you, because its presence is felt at almost every step of life, and nowhere more urgently than here with us in Auschwitz, where the agony of moral decisions has reached its pitch. You can either follow your impulses, as the Germans do, committing the vilest possible crimes, or you can rise above your inclinations, overcoming them with the power of your will and thus showing that, though imprisoned, you're a free man."

Arush who had been listening carefully to this debate had some reservations about its central points. In his view there was no uniformity in Jewish traditional teaching on such weighty questions as the interplay between free will and predestination, the degree of man's freedom of choice, providential participation in human affairs, or even concerning the question of a divinely appointed mission of Jews in history. The vastly mysterious contrast of the little man able to defy the omnipotent Deity by the power of his will had produced over the ages varying, sometimes compromising, if not contradictory, interpretations. But Baruch's version tallied, to the best of Arush's understanding, and as far as he could remember, with what he had been told by his forefather. Arush had, therefore, decided that it would make no sense to tell Baruch of his reservations and even less so Felek, who now started to demolish Baruch's structure.

–"A poor consolation. Faced with cruel reality, men produce all kinds of theories, doctrines, dogmas to justify what they can not explain and seek comfort in what they can imagine, even if it is an insoluble contradiction. Men crying out for mercy, hands outstretched to the heavens, which, you say, are not involved in the hard facts. The earth that burns is of His creation, but the fires are of human making. 'Emperors are in the hands of Providence', but as men they're free and masters of their deeds. Aren't you desperately trying to shield Jewish religion from the shattering defeat it has suffered in recent days? If everything was foreseen, then surely what we're witnessing must be part of a comprehensive providential plan of history. If so, it must also have providential purpose. I'm not asking what this is, for what we have been learning at our own cost resists not only religious explanation, but a rational one as well. Yet, shouldn't we seek one? Are we to abandon any attempt to understand what is happening before our eyes?"

–"I have never suggested that we quench our desire to discern the mysterious ways by which humanity moves, even if we're bound to fail, for the passion of discovering them is deeply implanted in our hearts. The sheer vanity of man. Yet, it also is, and I say this from my own heart's experience, the perpetual grappling with the mystery of human existence, the desperate quest for its meaning, that moves our lives and makes it appear worth enduring. At the same time I'm also aware that there are matters which it is unhealthy for all but a few selected minds to dive into, and he who probes into such awe-inspiring questions as divine purpose or the meaning of history, must be prepared to face the prospect of chronic disappointment. Just because you exclude irrational explanations doesn't make you wise. Is only the rational true? How can you rationalize about earthly human matter in terms of a purpose that transcends the subject? It's a question of faith. Our lives, I firmly believe, are formed with an intention, and, as I have already told you, whatever happens in this world has a purpose, which a posteriori forms part of what you call 'the plan'. It's only because you're still yoked to the parochial idea of an absolute celestial kingdom upon the earth we're treading on that you can make preposterous claims such as that 'Auschwitz' is a cause of despair for believers in God. What a primitive suggestion!

"'Auschwitz', inasmuch as religion and ethics are concerned, is not a Jewish crisis. If 'Auschwitz', and this war in general, makes a religious crisis at all, then it's one of the Christian religion alone."

–"The makers of Auschwitz, as I already told you, have no religion. They're against it. You can't make Christianity responsible for what they do."

–"And I already told you that I agree, even though there're many people who say that the present massacres of Jews merely brings to a climax centuries of Christian persecution of Jews.

"But if, as you say, the makers of 'Auschwitz' aren't real Christians, they're nominal ones. Are they not? Were they not baptized as such? Anti-Christs - all right, but how did Christianity produce them?

"Anyway, the question is not relevant now, the massacres are secular, not religious, and whatever happens to Jews, or to any other people for that matter, is no impeachment, forgive the expression, of Divinity. And for all its immensity, 'Auschwitz' is, against the background of the long drama of Jewish history, but a little episode."

–"A little episode you call the extinction of half a nation? What would a large episode be to you? You baffle me more than ever with your historiosophy and religionizing. Tell me if this city of woe does not speak against Jewish religion, what place does religion have in your life? What does it mean to you? What sense does religion make at all in Auschwitz?"

–"You continue to ascribe to the massacres a religious meaning. Just the ungodliness of its perpetrators is the best answer to what we owe to God, and to His significance in human lives. We need to believe in God to make our lives tolerable and meaningful. We need faith to preserve our humanity, here more urgently than ever. God is, at least for me, the source of support and endurance in this bitter trial; we need faith in Him to live on, to believe that this is not the end, that even death is not the end of our existence, that 'Auschwitz' is only a limited, passing reality. This is what I meant by saying 'little episode'. What, indeed, is 'Auschwitz' in the totality of our history?"

–"Indeed nothing, if you look at Jewish history as one massacre after another, a continuous chain of suffering and humiliation. All the rhetoric of yours is a smokescreen behind which you desperately seek to reduce the significance, the enormity of 'Auschwitz', because of its bearing upon your faith, which is founded on supernatural realities."

–"How should I describe your insistence on a religious explanation to our history. Rhetorical? No. Earnest? No. Assuming? Rather - or worse, if you who admit to no religion, unless anti-religion, can ascribe religious meaning to 'Auschwitz'."

–"You may call it what you like, for the reason I'm trying to get a religious explanation from you is only because you're denying there is one - which I find inconsistent with your usual declarations of faith. Wouldn't you expect the almighty God, watching what's going on, to intervene on behalf of His chosen flock? Don't you see that the murdered are by far its most devout lambs? Not vice, but virtue, not blasphemy, but the slightest manifestation of faith, is punished with particular brutality."

–"At least one of your questions was put down not so long ago, if you aren't stingy with time, by the men who watched the Romans chopping the living body of Rabbi Akiba with iron sticks: 'Lord of the universe is this Torah and this its reward?' According to the tradition, a Voice from Heaven replied: 'Be silent! This came upon my mind!' Whether or not you accept that this was the only possible answer, you must admit that since the time it was given, the Roman empire and other kingdoms, powerful and famous in their own time, have disappeared, some leaving no trace at all, while the Jews live on, to the unspeakable anguish of their changing enemies, right up to this day. Amazingly, the persecutions and killings over the ages have rather strengthened us and raised Jewish attachment to God.

Therein perhaps you could find a religious explanation to Jewish secular history. And just as today we understand many events of the past that were incomprehensible to our ancestors, so the present happenings will probably be understood by future generations."

–"Does that comfort you?"

–"Yes, definitely - even if only for lack of any alternative. To see the disappearance of the present empire, the one-thousand-year-Reich, there's no need to gaze through the prism of time, even if we do not live to attend its interment. If, against this, it comes true once more that the Jewish people, in harmony with its long experience, recover from 'Auschwitz' to retake its place in history, our surviving brothers and posterity, along with the nations of the world, will have to ask by what powers this happened? What is its meaning? We ourselves might not know the answer until 'the latter days'."

–"Between now and then, as you're so generous with time, is there any hope?" asked Felek apathetically.

–"Between now and then, we must have faith in God to derive and retain hope. If we lose hope and faith, we shall become merely living ghosts. And 'Auschwitz' is merely an episode. Even you, against all the odds, may one day realize this and, having reached 'the latter days', also understand that everything that happened was right and necessary."

–"This, I understand, is your profession of belief? I can't imagine that you really believe what you have just said. And in the same way, your earlier avowal of faith in God, is rather a belief in the idea of God. Isn't it?"

–"Oh no! Faith in God is a silent whisper of the heart that can not be heard. It can only be felt. To feel God, you must live Him, and will to feel Him. You, who speak so much of God, must not be, I suspect, entirely unaware of this. And as to the idea..."

In the sudden clamour, Baruch's concluding words were lost to Arush. He stood up quickly to follow the summons for his Pustkovian group to assemble.

At first relieved that they were at last marched out of the camp, when later they were standing in columns ready to climb onto the waiting lorries beyond the gate, Arush was seized with a vague fear of something obscurely horrid looming in the air. Is it tension? he asked himself. A surge of emotion blended with self-pity? "Setting out on a new pilgrimage through goodness only knows what hell." Or, the simple pain of parting? No matter what it was, or what one had thought, it felt strange to be leaving Birkenau. The place, despite itself, somehow overawes a man by the sway death and evil hold over it. Until the last moment no one knows if his departure will, or will not be followed by life. Turn back, a voice within him told Arush, and take a last look at the barracks and chimneys exposed to open sight, and at the invisible ashes, at somebody dear who didn't come to see you off. A hallucination - there was no one in the world who could be missing you, and in this mammoth jug of a city no one remembers anyone, anyway. Soon new, fortunate entrants from one of the unending transports will fill the space vacated by his

417

group. With whom will Miklos share his bunk tonight?

As if bidding farewell all alone, a thin trail of smoke was meandering like a ser-pent up the shy sky. And now this mystery trip. To ask the SS guards assigned to the voyage, even though they do not look the worst gallow-birds, is to risk a sound drubbing with the butt-end on the ribs; at best they would not admit to knowing the destination. So better ask, yourself of course, what if they get ambushed on the way - fall back on faith!

Mounted already on the lorry covered by tarpaulin on top and sides, and seated on the floor between the legs of Gur and the back of an unknown companion, with his face towards the half-open rear, and once more waiting in silence, Arush was asked by Marek in a whisper: "Is it another joke of fate? On the edge of freedom, moving from a giant death-trap only to be done in at a lesser one?"

–"No! It isn't a joke, my dear. It can't be a joke to get out of here on the most tragic day in the Jewish calendar. You know what Tisha B'Ab is?"

As Marek gave no answer, Arush went on to explain. "This is the day long said to be destined for Jewish suffering and disaster. The day on which the greatest mis-fortunes in history have befallen us. The day set aside throughout the centuries for weeping and wailing." While he was explaining, his father suddenly sprang before Arush's eyes, tears running down his cheeks like a stream as he recited on Tisha B'Ab the martyrdom "the Cedars of Lebanon, the Titans of Torah" met at the Romans' hands; whereas his own eyes, Arush reproved himself, had failed to shed a single tear over what they had seen the night before. But he went on to tell Marek: "The day, to quote Jeremiah from memory, 'of the Lord's anger, which none escaped nor remained'. If on this very day we escape this site of greatest 'anger' on earth, which even the genius of a prophet could not imagine, then it is to 'remain'! All of us to remain alive!"

Marek looked dubiously amused, probably thinking it was just a coincidence, but he held his tongue. It must have seemed to him too ungracious to demur this time. Ominous or not, the significance of the moment was overwhelming, and one could not help but surrender to it.

Like Arush, they were all rendered speechless by emotion. They looked around in the gathering twilight, dazzled by the changed scenery, dazzled by the dim-dense, gently moist tones of a summer evening. They listened breathlessly to the cool-quiet, soothingly exciting sounds in the motionless air. Their hearts quivered as they took in the damp-grassy, delicately fresh smell of earth.

Slowly everything was flying past, faster, ever faster, the ghastly outlines of Birkenau vanishing in the distance. On both sides of the black bedewed, asphalt-laid road, a pine forest reared proudly against the horizon. The deep green foliage of the trees, their dark trunks, which looked closely bound in the thickening dusk, together formed as it were a tall, inscrutable wall, which was softly swaying at its crest. From time to time, the tender murmur of the trees changed into loud splatter-ing of leaves brutally struck by the canvas of the dashing truck.

Arush felt sorry, almost grieved. This lovely forest! What a strange happiness breathes from it! How strange the desire to reach into its depth! Oh, to be able

418

once more to walk between the trees, and listen to the forest's blowing wind! A real, free world stared through the black enticing thicket. He could only imagine this world, feel it yearningly when he closed his eyes, see it in dreams of timeless pain. He was barred from it, watched by armed guards, he was heading toward another, terrifyingly cramped, obscure world, to be shut within walls of a different kind from the moving green ones on either side. If only this journey would last for a long time, enduringly long, endlessly - if only to be lost in the night!

It was easy to escape into dreams. Try not to, if you could in the wondrous warmth of stillness, vibrant with harmonious sounds. If you could, in the declining hours of day, stripped of every shield, drown the rhythms of the heart, of rustling trees, and rolling wheels, which merged into one lulling, melodious song. Oh, how delightful is this song! It makes you drowsy, shuts your eyes, balms your bleeding soul. He felt he was rocking backwards and forwards, lulled by darkness, as in the long gone cradle days. He kept thinking he heard echoes ringing from the reaches of that happy past, inaudible sounds of soothing murmurings, intimate whispers from glowing lips, which like the murmur of a mountain-brook were drowning every sorrow on earth. How mighty was a loving voice! He clung to it, he opened his eyes, fought for awareness to retain every precious tone.

He was too weak, conceded defeat. He was no more conscious of his stark bones, no more conscious of his whereabouts, his mumbling thoughts, the depths of his tired mind. Peace descended. For a while - peace.

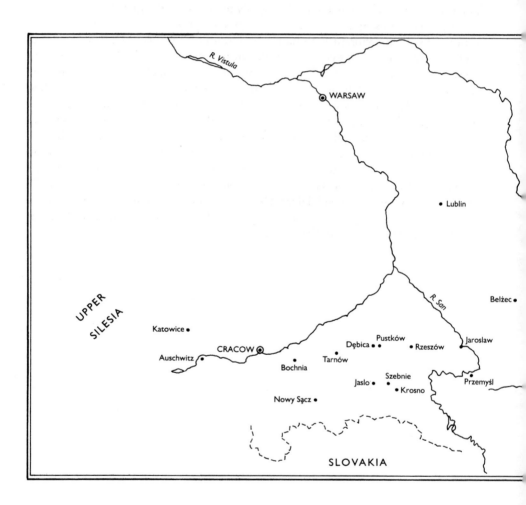

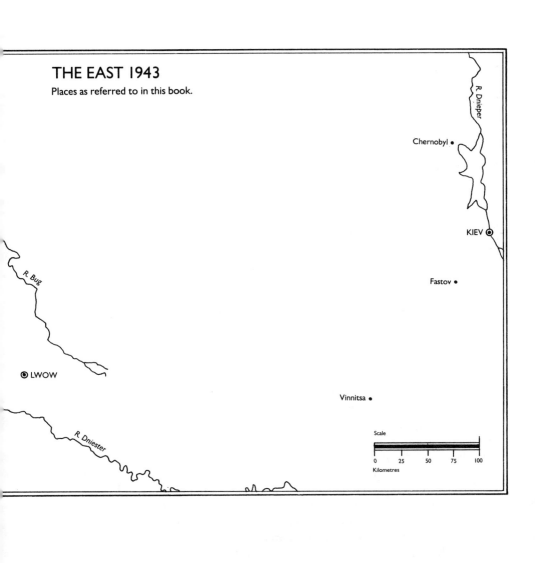

THE EAST 1943

Places as referred to in this book.

R. Dnieper

Chernobyl •

KIEV ◉

R. Bug

Fastov •

◉ LWOW

Vinnitsa •

R. Dniester

Scale

| 0 | 25 | 50 | 75 | 100 |

Kilometres

BIBLIOGRAPHY

The following selection of books, articles and periodicals tries to give some idea of the extent and diversity of the sources. While the bibliography refers primarily to Jewish experience in Nazi occupied Poland, it also includes published matter not directly related to the contents of this book, or indeed considered in its preparation. Where possible, preference is given to the English translation of foreign texts, even if most are significantly revised. In these cases, the original title of the work is occasionally cited. A list of Periodicals and their abbreviations is at the end.

Books and articles

Abel, T. "The Sociology of Concentration Camps". Social Forces, no. 30, 1951.
Abramsky, C. and others, eds. The Jews in Poland. Oxford, 1986.
Adelsberger, L. "Psychologie in Auschwitz". Schweizerische Zeitschrift für Psychologie, vol. VI, 1947.
———. Auschwitz: Ein Tatsachenbericht. Berlin, 1956.
Adler, H.G. Der Kampf gegen die "Endlösung der Judenfrage". Bonn, 1958.
———., and others. Auschwitz: Zeugnisse und Berichte. Frankfurt a.M., 1962.
Agatstein-Dormontowa, D. "Żydzi w Krakowie w okresie okupacji niemieckiej". Rocznik Krakowski, tome XXXI. Cracow, 1949.
Ainsztein, R. Jewish Resistance in Nazi-Occupied Eastern Europe. London, 1974.
Ajzensztajn, B., ed. Ruch podziemny w ghettach i obozach: Materiały i Dokumenty. Warsaw, 1946.
Aleksander, Edward. The Resonance of Dust: essays on holocaust literature and Jewish fate. Columbus, 1979.
Aleksandrowicz, J. Kartki z dziennika doktora Twardego. Cracow, 1962
.———. "Służba zdrowia w podziemnym i okupowanym Krakowie". Przegląd Lekarski-Oświęcim, 1963.
Anatoli (Kuznetsov), A. Babi Yar. London, 1967.
Apfelbaum, E., ed. Maladie de famine. Polish: Choroba głodowa (clinical research of famine in the ghetto of Warsaw in 1942). Warsaw, 1946.
Arad, Y., and others., eds. Documents on the Holocaust: selected sources on the destruction of the Jews of Germany and Austria, Poland, and the Soviet Union. Yad Vashem, Jerusalem, 1981.
Armstrong, J.A. "Collaboration in World War II: The Integral Nationalist Variant in Eastern Europe". Journal of Modern History, no. 40, 1968.
Assmann, K. "The Battle for Moscow: The Turning Point in the War". Foreign Affairs, no. 28, 1950.
Auschwitz Prozess, Der. Eine Dokumentation. 2 vols. Frankfurt a M., 1965.
Avriel, E. Open the Gates. New York, 1975.
Barkley, A. Atrocities and Other Conditions in Concentration Camps in

Germany. Washington, 1945.

Barthel, G. Krakau, Hauptstadt des deutschen Generalgouvernements Polen. Gestalt und künstlerische Leistung einer deutschen Stadt im Osten. Cracow, 1940.

———., and Krause, A. Sichergestellte Kunstwerke im Generalgouvernement. Precise date and place of publication not available.

Bartoszewski, W. The Blood Shed Unites Us. (Transl. from the Polish.) Warsaw, 1970.

———., and Lewin, Z. Righteous Among the Nations: How Poles Helped the Jews, 1939-1945. (Transl. from the Polish.) London, 1969.

Bauer, Y. They Chose Life: Jewish Resistance in the Holocaust. New York, 1973.

———. The Holocaust in Historical Perspective. Seattle, 1978.

Baumgart, W. "Zur Ansprache Hitlers vor den Führern der Wehrmacht am 22. August 1939: Eine Quellenkritische Untersuchung". VfZ 16, 1968.

Bauminger, R. Przy pikrynie i trotylu: Obóz pracy przymusowej w Skarżysku-Kamiennej. Cracow, 1946.

Baynes, N.H., ed. The Speeches of Adolf Hitler, April 1922-August 1939. 2 vols. London, 1942.

Bednarz, W. "Obóz zagłady Chełmno". Biuletyn GKBZHwP, no. 1, 1946.

Berenstein, T. "Hitlerowska dyskryminacja gospodarcza wobec Żydow". BŻIH, nos. 2-4, 1952.

———. "Martyrologia, opór i zaglada ludności żydowskiej w dystrykcie lubelskim". BŻIH, no. 21, 1957.

———. "Eksterminacja ludnosci żydowskiej w dystrykcie Galicja". BŻIH, no. 61, 1967.

Berenstein, T., and Rutkowski, A. "Prześladowania ludności żydowskiej w okresie hitlerowskiej administracji wojskowej na ziemiach polskich (1.9.1939-25.10.1939)". BŻIH, no. 39, 196l.

———., "Vegen ratoven Yiden durch Polaken beeys der Hitler-okupatje". (Also in Polish and English, "revised" versions.) Bleter far geschichte, no. 14, 1961.

———. "Grabieżcza polityka gospodarcza hitlerowskiej administracji wojskowej". BŻIH, no. 42, 1962.

———. "Hitlerowskie sprawozdanie statystyczne o zagladzie Żydów w Europie". BŻIH, no. 49, 1964.

———. "Żydzi w obozie koncentracyjnym Majdanek (1941-1944)". BŻIH, no. 58, 1966.

———., and others., eds. Eksterminacja Żydów na ziemiach polskich w okresie oku pacji hitlerowskiej: zbiór dokumentów. (In German: Faschismus-Ghetto-Massenmord. Berlin, 1961.) Warsaw, 1957.

Berg, M. Warsaw Ghetto: A Diary. New York, 1945.

Berman, A. "O losie dzieci żydowskich w getcie warszawskim". BŻIH, no. 28, 1958.

Bettelheim, B. The Informed Heart. London, 1961.

Beylis. The Ritual Murder Accusation and the Beilis Case. London, 1913.

Beylis, M. The Story of my Sufferings. New York, 1926.

Bezwińska, J., and Czech, D., eds. Człowiek staje się numerem. Cracow, 1958.

————., eds. "Rękopisy członków Sonderkommando". Zeszyty Oświęcimskie, special no. 2, 1971.

Biegański, W., ed. Encyklopedia II wojny światowej. Warsaw, 1975.

Billig, J. Les Camps de Concentration dans L'economie du Reich Hitlérienne. Paris, 1973.

Binion, R. Hitler Among the Germans. New York, 1976.

Blumental, N., ed. Dokumenty i materiały z czasów okupacji niemieckiej w Polsce. Lodz, 1947.

Bór-Komorowski, T. The Secret Army. London, 1950.

Borwicz, M. Uniwersytet Zbirów. Cracow, 1946.

————. Organizowanie wściekłości. Warsaw, 1947.

————. L'insurrection du ghetto de Varsovie. Paris, 1966.

————., ed. Oczyma dwunastoletniej dziewczyny (Janka Hescheles). Cracow, 1946.

————. Ze śmiercią na ty: wiersze z obozu i partyzantki. Warsaw, 1946.

————. Pieśń ujdzie cało: antologia poezji ghett i obozów. Cracow, 1947.

————., and others. W trzecią rocznicę zagłady ghetta w Krakowie. Cracow, 1946.

————., Dokumenty zbrodni i męczeństwa. Cracow, 1947.

Bracher, K.D. The German Dictatorship: The Origins, Structure and Effects of National Socialism. (Transl. from the German.) New York, 1970.

Brand, J., and Brand, H. Satan and the Soul (Hebrew). Tel Aviv, 1960.

Brendel, G. Der Führer über die Juden (composed of Hitler's speeches and writings). Munich, 1942.

Broad, P. "Wspomnienia Perry Broada SS-mana oddziału politycznego w obozie koncentracyjnym Oświęcim". (Transl. from the German.) Zeszyty Oświęcimskie, no. 9, 1965.

Broszat, M. Nationalsozialistische Polenpolitik, 1939-1945. Frankfurt a M., 1965.

————. "Hitler und die Genesis der Endlösung. Aus Anlass der Thesen von David Irving". (English transl. in Yad Vashem Studies 13, 1979.) VfZ 25, 1975.

————., ed. Hoess Rudolf. Kommandant in Auschwitz: Autobiographische Aufzeichnungen. Stuttgart, 1958.

————., and others. Nationalsozialistische Konzentrationslager - Kommissarbefehl und Massenexekutionen sowjetischer Kriegsgefangener - Judenverfolgungen. (Vol. 2 of Buchheim, H. Anatomie des SS-Staates, q.v.) Munich, 1979 ed.

Bryskier, H. "Żydzi pod swastyką, czyli getto w Warszawie". BŻIH, no. 67, 1968.

Buchheim, Ch. "Die besetzten Länder im Dienste der deutschen Kriegswirtschaft während des zweiten Weltkrieges". VfZ 34, 1986.

Buchheim, H., and others. Anatomie des SS-Staates. Frankfurt a M., 1967.

Bühler, J., ed. Das Generalgouvernement - seine Verwaltung und seine Wirtschaft. Cracow, 1943.

Bund. Di geschichte fun Bund (Yiddish). Ed. J.S. Hertz and others. Vol. 4, New York, 1972.

Camus, A. The Plague. London, 1948.

Chomet, A., ed. Turne: Kiyum un churben fun a yidisher shtut (Yiddish). Tel

Aviv, 1954.

Ciołkosz, A. "Broń dla getta Warszawy". Zeszyty Historyczne. Paris, 1969.

Cohen, E.A. Human Behaviour in the Concentration Camp. London, 1954.

Cohn, N. Warrant for Genocide: The Myth of Jewish World-Conspiracy and the Protocols of the Elders of Zion. London, 1967.

Cracow. Die jüdische Gemeinde in Krakau in der Zeit vom 13. September 1939 bis 30. September 1940 und ihre Tätigkeit. (Report published by the Cracow Judenrat.) Mimeographed, Lodz, 1946.

Cygański, M. Z dziejów okupacji hitlerowskiej w Łodzi 1939-1945. Lodz, 1965.

Cyprian, T., and others., eds. Proces ludobójcy Amona Goetha: Dokładny stenogram procesu. Warsaw, 1947.

Cyprian T., and Sawicki, J. Materiały norymberskie. Warsaw, 1948.

Czech, D. Kalendarium der Ereignisse im Konzentrationslager Auschwitz-Birkenau 1939-1945. Hamburg, 1989. Revised English translation: Auschwitz Chronicle 1939-1945. London, 1990.

Czerniakow, A. Dziennik getta warszawskiego 6.9.1939-23.7.1942. Ed. M. Fuks Warsaw, 1983.

Dąbrowska, D. "Zagłada Skupisk Żydowskich w 'Kraju Warty' w okresie okupacji hitlerowskiej". BŻIH, no. 13, 1955.

———. "Struktura i funkcje administracji żydowskiej w getcie łódzkim (1941)". 2 parts. BŻIH nos. 51-52, 1964.

———. (Dombrowska), and Dobroszycki, L. eds. Chronicle of the Lodz Ghetto 1941-1944. (Transl. from the German.) London, 1984.

Dąbrowski, J., and others. Cracow Under Enemy Rule. (Condensed transl. from the Polish.) Cracow, 1946.

Dallin, A. German Rule in Russia: A Study of Occupation Policies. London, 1957.

Dante Alighieri. The Divine Comedy. London, 1932 ed.

Datner, S. Walka i zagłada białostockiego getta. Lodz, 1946.

———. 55 dni Wehrmachtu w Polsce. Warsaw, 1967.

Dawidowicz, L. The War Against the Jews, 1933-1945. New York, 1975.

———. The Holocaust and the Historians. Boston, 1981.

Dawidsohn-Draengerowa, G. Pamiętnik Justyny. Cracow, 1946.

Des Pres, T. The Survivor: An Anatomy of Life in the Death Camps. New York, 1970.

Dicks, H.V. Licensed Mass Murder: A Socio-psychological Study of Some SS Killers. London, 1972.

Dobroszycki, L., and others. Okupacja i ruch oporu w dzienniku Hansa Franka. 2 vols. Warsaw, 1970.

Dolata, B. Walki zbrojne na ziemiach polskich. Warsaw, 1977.

Domarus, M., ed. Hitler. Reden und Proklamationen, 1932-1945. 2 vols. Würzburg, 1962-63.

Dornberger, W. V2. (Transl. from the German.) London, 1954.

Dorré, R.W. Neuadel aus Blut und Boden. Munich, 1930.

Dunin-Wąsowicz, K. "Polski Ruch Socjalistyczny wobec walki i zagłady warszawskiego getta". BŻIH. nos. 86-87, 1973.

———. Resistance in the Nazi Concentration Camps 1933-1945. (Transl. from the Polish.) Warsaw, 1982.

Du Prel, M.F., ed. Das Generalgouvernement. Würzburg, 1942.

Eckardt, A.R., and Eckardt, A.L. Long Night's Journey into Day: Life and Faith After the Holocaust. Detroit, 1982.

Eichhorn, L., ed. Szebnie (collection of testimonies, mimeographed). Cracow, 1946.

Eisenbach, A. Hitlerowska polityka zagłady Żydów. Warsaw, 1961.

———. Operation Reinhard: Mass Extermination of the Jewish Population in Poland. Offprint from Polish Western Affairs 3, 1962, no.1.

———. Ringelblum Emanuel: Kronika getta warszawskiego, wrzesień 1939-styczeń 1943. Warsaw 1983.

Fackenheim, E. The Jewish Return into History: Reflections in the Age of Auschwitz and a New Jerusalem. New York, 1978.

Falstein, L., ed. The Martyrdom of Jewish Physicians in Poland. New York, 1963.

Feifel, H., ed. The Meaning of Death. New York, 1959.

Feingold, H. The Politics of Rescue. New Jersey, 1970.

Fejkiel, W. "Eksperymenty dokonywane przez personel sanitarny SS w głównym obozie koncentracyjnym w Oświęcimiu". Przegląd Lekarski-Oświęcim. 1964.

Fenelon, F. The Musicians of Auschwitz. (Transl. from the French.) London, 1977.

Fest, J.C. The Face of the Third Reich: Portraits of the Nazi Leadership. New York, 1970.

Fiderkiewicz, A. Brzezinki: Wspomnienia z obozu. Cracow, 1954.

Fischer, F. Griff nach der Weltmacht: Kriegszielpolitik des kaiserlichen Deutschland 1914/18. Düsseldorf, 1967 ed.

Fiszman-Kamińska, K. "Zachód, Emigracyjny Rząd Polski oraz Delegatura wobec sprawy żydowskiej podczas II wojny światowej". BŻIH, no. 62, 1967.

Fleming, G. Hitler und die Endlösung. Munich, 1982.

Flinker, M. Young Moshe's Diary. (Transl. from the Yiddish.) New York, 1965.

Frank, H. Das Diensttagebuch. Eds. W. Präg, and W. Jacobmeyer., q.v.

———. Hans Frank's Diary. Ed. S. Piotrowski (q.v.)

Frankl, V. "Higiena psychiczna w sytuacji przymusowej: Doświadczenia z zakresu psychoterapii w obozie koncentracyjnym". (Revised and enlarged transl. of Ein Psycholog erlebt das Konzentrationslager. Vienna, 1947.) Przegląd Lekarski-Oświęcim, 1965.

———. Man's Search for Meaning. (Transl. from the German.) London, 1964.

Friedman, F. (Ph.) Zagłada Żydów lwowskich. Lodz, 1945.

———. This was Oświęcim. (Transl. from the Yiddish.) London, 1946.

———. Zagłada Żydów polskich w okresie okupacji niemieckiej 1939-1945. Munich, 1947.

———. "The Lublin Reservation and the Madagascar Plan". Yivo Annual of Jewish Social Science, VII, 1953.

———. Their Brothers' Keepers. New York, 1957.

———., and others, eds. Martyrs and Fighters: The Epic of the Warsaw Ghetto. London, 1954.

———. Roads to Extinction: Essays on the Holocaust. Ed. Ada J. Friedman. Philadelphia, 1980.

Garliński, J. Fighting Auschwitz: The Resistance Movement in the Concentration Camp. London, 1975.

Gebirtig, M. Es brent (Yiddish). Cracow, 1946.

Gelber, Y. "Zionist Policy & The Fate of European Jewry". Yad Vashem Studies, no. 13, 1979.

Generalgouvernement, Das. Ed. M. du Prel, q.v.

———. 1940-1944. Cracow, 1944.

———., Ed. J. Bühler, q.v.

———. Amtlicher Anzeiger für das Generalgouvernement. Cracow 1939-1945.

———. Verordnungsblatt für das Generalgouvernement (German, Polish). Cracow-Warsaw, 1939-1943.

———. Das Recht des Generalgouvernements. Ed. A. Weh, q.v.

Gerstein, K. "Augenzeugenbericht zu den Massenvergasungen". VfZ., 1953.

Gilbert, M. The Holocaust: The Jewish Tragedy. London, 1986.

———. Auschwitz and the Allies. London, 1981.

———. "The Question of Bombing Auschwitz". The Nazi Concentration Camp. Eds. Y. Gutman and A. Saf, q.v.

Gilman, S. Jewish Self-Hatred. London, 1986.

Goeth, A. Proces ludobójcy (Trial of). Ed. T. Cyprian and others, q.v.

Goldmann, N. "Al Gvurat Netzurim". Bitfutzot Hagola, no. 2, 1963.

Gorbatow, B. Obóz w Majdanku. Lódz, 1945.

Grabstein, M., ed. Jewish Resistance during the Holocaust: Proceedings of the Conference on Manifestations of Jewish Resistance, Jerusalem, 7-11 April 1968. Jerusalem, 1971.

Gross, J.T. Polish Society under German Occupation: The Generalgouvernement 1939-1944. Princeton, 1979.

Grossman, K. Die unbesungenen Helden: Menschen in Deutschlands dunklen Tagen. Berlin, 1952.

Grossmann, W. Piekło Treblinki. Katowice, 1945.

Grünbaum, I. Milchamot Yehudei Polania 1913-1940 (Hebrew). Tel Aviv, 1941.

———. Introduction to M. Prager's Yeven Metzula Hechadash, q.v.

Grunberger, R. A Social History of the Third Reich. London, 1971.

Gumkowski, J. Eksterminacja ludności w Polsce w czasie okupacji niemieckiej 1939-1945. Poznan, 1962.

———., and Leszczyński, K., eds. "Raport J. Stroopa o likwidacji getta warszawskiego w 1943 roku". (Transl. from the German.) Biuletyn GKBZHwP. No. 11, 1960.

———. Poland under Nazi Occupation. (Transl. from the Polish.) Warsaw, 1961.

———., and Rutkowski, A. Treblinka. Warsaw, 1962.

Gutman, Y. Anashim Va-efer (Hebrew). Tel Aviv, 1957.

———. "The Concept of Labour in Judenrat Policy". Patterns of Jewish Leadership in Nazi Europe 1933-1945. Ed. Y. Gutman and C. Haft, q.v.

———., and Rothkirchen, L., eds. The Catastrophe of European Jewry: antecedents - history - reflections: selected papers. Jerusalem, 1976.

———., and Greif, G., eds. The Historiography of the Holocaust Period: Proceedings of the Fifth Yad Vashem International Historical Conference, 1983. Jerusalem, 1988.

———., and Haft, C., eds. Patterns of Jewish Leadership in Nazi Europe 1933-1945: Proceedings of the Third Yad Vashem International Historical Conference, April 1977. Jerusalem, 1979.

———., and Saf, A., eds. The Nazi Concentration Camp: Proceedings of the Fourth Yad Vashem International Historical Conference, 1980. Jerusalem, 1984.

———., and Zuroff, E., eds. Rescue Attempts during the Holocaust. Jerusalem, 1977.

Haffner, S. The Meaning of Hitler. (Transl. from the German.) London, 1979.

Hallie, P. Lest innocent blood be shed. London, 1979.

Hart, K. I am alive. London, 1961.

Hausner, G. Justice in Jerusalem. New York, 1977.

Hawes, S., White, R., eds. Resistance in Europe 1939-1945. London, 1975.

Hilberg, R. The Destruction of the European Jews. London, 1961.

———. "The Judenräte: Conscious or Unconscious 'Tool'". Patterns of Jewish Leadership in Nazi Europe 1933-1945. Ed. Y. Gutman and C. Haft, q.v.

Hirszfeld, L. Historia jednego życia. Warsaw, 1957 ed.

Hitler, A. Mein Kampf. (English transl.). London, 1939.

———. Speeches, April 1922-August 1933. Ed. N. Baynes, q.v.

———. Der Führer über die Juden. By G. Brendel, q.v.

———. Reden und Proklamationen. Ed. M. Domarus, q.v.

Hochberg-Mariańska, M., and Grüss, N., eds. Dzieci oskarżają. Cracow, 1947.

Hoess, R. Autobiographische Aufzeichnungen. Ed. M. Broszat, q.v.

Hoffmann, S. "Collaborationism in France". Journal of Modern History. No. 40, 1968.

Höhne, H. Der Orden unter dem Totenkopf: Die Geschichte der SS. Frankfurt a M, 1967.

Homze, E.L. Foreign Labour in Nazi Germany. Princeton, 1967.

Huberband, S. Kidush Hashem (Hebrew). Tel Aviv, 1969.

Iranek-Osmecki, K. He Who Saves One Life. (Transl. from the Polish.) New York, 1971.

Jaspers, K. The Question of German Guilt. New York, 1947.

Jaworski, M. Janusz Korczak. Warsaw, 1978.

Kacherginski, S. Lider fun getos und lagern (Yiddish). New York, 1948.

Kamenetsky, I. Secret Nazi Plans for Eastern Europe: A Study of Lebensraum Policies. New York, 1961.

Kamiński, A. Hitlerowskie obozy koncentracyjne i ośrodki masowej zagłady w poli tyce imperializmu niemieckiego. Poznan, 1964.

Kaplan, C. The Scroll of Agony. (A Diary from the Warsaw Ghetto. Transl. from the Yiddish). London, 1966.

Karski, J. Story of a Secret State. Boston, 1944.

Katzenelson, I. Das Lied vom letzten Juden. (Transl. from the Yiddish: Dus lid funem oisgehargeten yidishen folk.) Zurich, 1951.

Katzetnik 135633. (Yehiel Dinur). House of Dolls. (Transl. from the Hebrew.) London, 1956.

——. Piepel. (Transl. from the Hebrew.) London, 1961.

——. House of Love. (Transl. from the Hebrew.) London, 1971.

Kaul, F. Zweiter Auschwitz-Prozess-Schlussvortrag. Berlin, 1966.

——. Ärzte in Auschwitz. Berlin, 1968.

Kermisz, J. Powstanie w ghetcie warszawskim. Warsaw, 1946.

——., ed. Dokumenty i materiały z czasów okupacji niemieckiej w Polsce. Vol. II. "Akcje", "Wysiedlenia". Warsaw, 1948.

Kershaw, I. Der Hitler-Mythos: Volksmeinung und Propaganda im Dritten Reich. Stuttgart, 1980.

Kersten, K., and Szarota, T., eds. Wieś Polska 1939-1948. 2 vols. Warsaw, 1968.

Kiedrzyńska, W. Ravensbrück: kobiecy obóz koncentracyjny. Warsaw, 1961.

——. Materiały do bibliografii hitlerowskich obozów koncentracyjnych: literatura międzynarodowa 1934-1962. Warsaw, 1964.

Kiełkowski, R. "Obóz pracy przymusowej i koncentracyjny w Płaszowie". Przegląd Lekarski-Oświęcim. 1971.

Klukowski, Z. "Niedola i zagłada Żydów w Szczebrzeżynie". BŻIH. Nos. 19-20, 1956.

——., Dziennik z lat okupacji Zamojszczyzny 1939-1944. Lublin, 1958.

Koch, H., ed. Aspects of the Third Reich. New York, 1985.

Kogon, E. The Theory and Practice of Hell. (Transl. from the German.) New York, 1950.

——., and others, eds. Nationalsozialistische Massentötungen durch Giftgas: Eine Dokumentation. Frankfurt a M, 1983.

Kolb, E. Bergen-Belsen. Hannover, 1962.

Korbonski, S. The Polish Underground State: A Guide to the Underground 1939-1945. East European Quarterly, Monograph 39, 1978.

Kossak, Z. Z otchłani: wspomnienia z lagru. Rome, 1946.

Kowalski, T. Obozy hitlerowskie w Polsce południowo-wschodniej. Warsaw, 1973.

Kraus, O., and Kulka, E. Massenmord und Profit: Die faschistische Ausrottung und ihre ökonomische Hintergründe. Berlin, 1963.

——. The Death Factory: Document on Auschwitz. (Transl. from the Czech.) Oxford, 1966.

Krausnick, H. Der Beginn des Zweiten Weltkrieges. Bonn, 1960.

——., and Wilhelm, H. Die Truppe des Weltanschauungskrieges: die Einsatzgruppen der Sicherheitspolizei und des Sicherheitsdienstes 1938-1942. Stuttgart, 1981.

Krzepicki, A. "Treblinka". BŻIH. Nos. 43-44, 1962.

Kubiak, A. "Dzieciobójstwo podczas okupacji hitlerowskiej". BŻIH. No. 18, 1956.

Kubiak, Z. Półmrok ludzkiego świata. Warsaw, 1963.

Kubowitzki, A. Survey of the Resistance Activities of the World Jewish Congress 1940-1944. New York, 1944.

Kühnrich, H. Der KZ-Staat: Rolle und Entwicklung der faschistischen Konzentrationslager 1933 bis 1945. Berlin, 1960.

Kulski, J. Zarząd miejski Warszawy 1939-1944. Warsaw, 1964.

Kwiet, K. From the Emancipation to the Holocaust. (Transl. from the German.) New York, 1986.

Lacquer, W. The Terrible Secret: Suppression of the Truth about Hitler's "Final Solution". Boston, 1980.

Laks, S. Gry oświęcimskie. London, 1979.

Landau, L. Kronika lat wojny i okupacji. 3 vols. Warsaw, 1962, 1963.

Lang, J. von., ed. Das Eichmann Protokoll. Eichmann interrogated: transcripts from the archives of the Israeli police. New York, 1983.

——. Die Gestapo: Instrument des Terrors. Hamburg, 1990.

Langbein, H. Menschen in Auschwitz. Vienna, 1972.

Leszczyński, K. "Działalność Einsatzgruppen policji bezpieczeństwa na ziemiach polskich w 1939 r. w świetle dokumentów". Biuletyn GKBZHwP. Vol. 22, 1971.

——. "Z dziejów zagłady Żydów w Kraju Warty". BŻIH. no. 82, 1972.

Levi, P. If this is a man. (Transl. from the Italian.) London, 1960.

Levin, N. The Holocaust. New York, 1968.

Lewin, E. "Z lwowskiego getta". BŻIH. no. 18, 1956.

Levy, G. The Catholic Church and Nazi Germany. London, 1964.

Lichtenstein, H. Warum Auschwitz nicht bombardiert wurde. Cologne, 1980.

Littel, F. The Crucification of the Jews. New York, 1975.

Lowrie, D. The Hunted Children. New York, 1963.

Łukowski, J. Bibliografia obozu koncentracyjnego Oświęcim-Brzezinka 1945-1965. Parts I-III. Warsaw, 1968.

Madajczyk, C. Generalne Gubernatorstwo w planach hitlerowskich. Warsaw, 1961.

——. Polityka III Rzeszy w okupowanej Polsce. 2 vols. Warsaw, 1970.

Małcużyński, K. Norymberga, Niemcy,1946. Warsaw, 1946.

Malinowski, M. "Stanowisko PPR w kwestii żydowskiej w latach wojny wyzwoleńczej". BŻIH. nos. 86-87, 1973.

Manvell, R. and Fraenkel, H. The Incomparable Crime. Mass Extermination in the Twentieth Century: The Legacy of Guilt. New York, 1967.

Marcus, J. Social and Political History of the Jews in Poland 1919-1939. Berlin, 1983.

Mark, B. Życie i walka młodzieży w gettach w okresie okupacji hitlerowskiej 1939-1944. Warsaw, 1961.

——. "Statut Żydowskiej Organizacji Bojowej". BŻIH. no. 39, 1961.

——. "Ruch oporu i powstanie w getcie warszawskim". BŻIH. nos. 45-46, 1963.

Maszlanka, B. Druga wojna światowa. Warsaw, 1969.

McGovern, W. From Luther to Hitler: The History of Fascist-Nazi Political Philosophy. New York, 1973.

Meisels, Z. Mekadshei ha-Shem. Chicago, 1955.

Michel, H. The Shadow War: Resistance in Europe 1939-1945. (Transl. from the French.) London, 1970.

——. "Jewish Resistance and the European Resistance Movement". Jewish Resistance during the Holocaust. Ed. M. Grabstein, q.v.

——. The Second World War. (Transl. from the French.) New York, 1975.

Michel, J. Dora. (Transl. from the French.) London, 1979.

Milward, A. The German Economy at War. London, 1965.

Mitscherlich, A., and Mielke, F. Medizin ohne Menschlichkeit. Frankfurt a M, 1960

Morse, A. While Six Million Died. London, 1968.

Müller, F. Auschwitz Inferno: The Testimony of a Sonderkommando. London, 1979.

Musioł, J. Przesłuchanie. (Concerning medical experiments in concentration camps.) Warsaw, 1978.

Naumann, B. Auschwitz: A Report on the Proceedings against Mulka and Others Before the Court at Frankfurt. (Transl. from the German.) London, 1966.

Nirenstein, A. "Widerstand fun Yidn in Kruke". Bleter far Geschichte. No. 5, 1952.

Oshry, E. Responsa from the Holocaust. (Abridgment of his five-volume Sheilot u-Tshuvot mi-Maamakim (Hebrew). Brookline, Mass., 1984.

Oświęcim: Hitlerowski obóz masowej zagłady. Warsaw, 1977.

Pankiewicz, T. Apteka w getcie krakowskim. Cracow, 1947.

Pawelczynska, Anna. Values and Violence: a sociological analysis. Berkeley, 1979.

Penkower, M. The Jews Were Expendable: Free World Diplomacy and the Holocaust. Chicago, 1983.

——. "American Jewry and the Holocaust: From Biltmore to the American Jewish Conference". Jewish Social Studies. Vol. 47, 1985.

Phelps, R.H. "Hitler's 'Grundlegende Rede' über den Anti Semitismus". VfZ, No.16, 1968.

Philippi, A., and Heim, F. Der Feldzug gegen Sowjetrussland 1941-1945. Stuttgart, 1962.

Pilichowski, C., ed. Obozy hitlerowskie na ziemiach polskich 1939-1945: Informator Encyklopedyczny. Warsaw, 1975.

Piotrowski, S. Misja Odyla Globocnika: Sprawozdanie o wynikach finansowych zagłady Żydów w Polsce. Warsaw, 1949.

——., ed. Hans Frank's Diary. (Abridged transl. from the German.) Warsaw, 1961.

Plodeck, R. "Die Treuhandstelle im Generalgouvernement". Das Generalgouvernement. Ed. M. du Prel, q.v.

Pobóg-Malinowski, W. Najnowsza historia polityczna Polski. Vol. 2. London, 1960.

Poliakov, L. The Harvest of Hate. (Transl. from the French.) New York, 1954.

——. "The Weapon of Antisemitism". The Third Reich. London, 1955.

——., and Wulf, J. Das Dritte Reich und die Juden: Dokumente und Aufsätze. Berlin, 1955.

Poradowski, S. "Zagłada Żydów rzeszowskich". 3 Parts. BŻIH. Nos. 126, 129-30, 135-36. 1983, 1984, 1985.

Porat, D. An Entangled Leadership: The Yishuv & the Holocaust 1942-1945

(Hebrew). Tel Aviv, 1986.

Pospieszalski, K. "Niemiecka Lista Narodowa". Polskie Sprawy Zachodnie. Nos. 4, 5, 6. 1949, 1952, 1958.

———. "Nazi Terror in Poland 1939-1945". Polish Western Affairs. No. 5, 1964.

Präg, W., and Jacobmeyer, W., eds. Das Diensttagebuch des deutschen Generalgouverneurs in Polen 1939-1945. Stuttgart, 1975.

Prager, M. Yeven Metzula Hechadash (Hebrew). Tel Aviv, 1941.

———., ed. Ani Maamin (Hebrew). Tel Aviv, 1962.

Prekerowa, T. Konspiracyjna Rada Pomocy Żydom w Warszawie 1942-1945. Warsaw, 1982.

Pülzer, P. The Rise of Political Anti Semitism in Germany and Austria. New York, 1964.

Rawicz, J. and others, eds. Okupacja i medycyna: wybór artykułów z "Przeglądu Lekarskiego - Oświęcim" z lat 1961-1970. Warsaw, 1971.

Rawicz, P. Blood from the Sky. (Transl. from the French.) New York, 1964.

Reder, R. Bełżec. Cracow, 1946.

Reitlinger, G. The Final Solution: The Attempt to Exterminate the Jews of Europe 1939-1945. New York, 1953.

Rich, N. Hitler's War Aims: Ideology, the Nazi State, and the Course of Expansion. Vol. 1. New York, 1973.

———. Hitler's War Aims: The Establishment of the New Order. Vol. 2. London, 1974.

Ringelblum, E. Notes from the Warsaw Ghetto. (Edited transl. from the Yiddish.) New York, 1958.

———. Ksuvim fun ghetto (Yiddish). 2 vols. Warsaw, 1961, 1963.

———. Polish Jewish Relations during the Second World War. (Transl. from the Polish.) Ed. J. Kermish and S. Krakowski. Jerusalem, 1974.

Robinson, J. And the Crooked Shall be Made Straight. New York, 1965.

———., and Friedman, F. Guide to Jewish History under Nazi Impact. New York, 1960.

Rothfels, H. "Zur 'Umsiedlung' der Juden im Generalgouvernement". VfZ. 7, 1959.

Różański, Z. Mützen ab (Polish text). Hannover, 1948.

Rubinowicz, D. Pamiętnik. Warsaw, 1960.

Rubinszteinowa. "Pamiętnik ze Lwowa." BŻIH. No. 61, 1967.

Rudashevski, Y. The Diary of the Vilna Ghetto: June 1941-April 1943. (Transl. from the original Yiddish and revised on the basis of the Hebrew edition.) Tel Aviv, 1973.

Sakowska, R., ed. Archiwum Ringelbluma. Warsaw, 1960.

Schade, H. Ein Engel war mit mir: Ein Tatsachenroman. Zurich, 1949.

Schechter, F. "Ucieczka przed śmiercią: pamiętnik z czasów okupacji hitlerowskiej w Krakowie". BŻIH. No. 55, 1965.

Schindler, P. Response of Hassidic Leaders and Hassidim During the Holocaust in Europe 1933-1945. New York, 1972.

Schwarz, J, and Goldstein, Y., eds. Hashoa (Hebrew). Jerusalem, 1987.

Schwartzbart, A. The Last of the Just. (Transl. from the French.) London, 1961.

Sehn, J. Oświęcim-Brzezinka. Warsaw, 1964.

Seraphim, P. Bevölkerungs-und wirtschaftspolitische Probleme einer europäischen Gesamtlösung der Judenfrage. Munich, 1943.

Serwański, E. Obóz zagłady w Chełmnie nad Nerem 1941-1945. Poznan, 1964.

Sierakowiak, D. Dziennik Davida Sierakowiaka. Warsaw, 1960.

Smólski, W. Zaklęte lata. Warsaw, 1964.

Snyder, L. German Nationalism: the tragedy of a people: Extremism contra liberalism in modern German history. Harrisburg, 1952.

———. The Idea of Racialism: its meaning and history. Princeton, 1962.

Solzhenitsyn, A. One Day in the Life of Ivan Denisovitch. (Transl. from the Russian.) London, 1963.

Sosnowski, K. The Tragedy of Children under Nazi Rule. (Transl, from the Polish.) Poznan, 1962.

Staff, I. Justiz im Dritten Reich: Eine Dokumentation. Frankfurt a M, 1964.

Stendig, J. Płaszów. Cracow, 1946.

Streit, C. Keine Kameraden: die Wehrmacht und die sowjetischen Kriegsgefangenen 1941-1945. Bonn, 1977.

Streng, H. von. Die Landwirtschaft im Generalgouvernement. Tübingen, 1955.

Stroop Report. Ed. J. Gumkowski, and K. Leszczyński, q.v.

Szajewicz, S. Lech-L'cha (Yiddish, poems). Lodz, 1946.

Szarota, T. Okupowanej Warszawy dzień powszedni: studium historyczne. Warsaw, 1973.

Szewczyk, R. Z dziejów Majdanka. Lublin, 1945.

Szmaglewska, S. Smoke Over Birkenau. (Transl. from the Polish.) New York, 1947.

Szpilman, W. Śmierć miasta. Warsaw, 1946.

Szrojt, E. "Obóz zagłady Bełżec". Biuletyn GKBZHwP. No. 2, 1946.

Szternfinkiel, N. Zagłada Żydów Sosnowca. Warsaw, 1946.

Szyfman, A. Moja tułaczka wojenna. Warsaw, 1960.

Timpke, H., and others. Studien zur Geschichte der Konzentrationslager. Stuttgart, 1970.

Treblinka. Das Menschenschlachthaus Treblinka. Vienna, 1964.

Trunk, I. Judenrat: The Jewish Councils in Eastern Europe under Nazi Occupation. New York, 1972.

———. Jewish Responses to Nazi Persecution. New York, 1979.

Waite, R. Hitler and Nazi Germany. New York, 1965.

———. The Mind of Adolf Hitler. London, 1973.

Waxman, M. A History of Jewish Literature. Vol. 4. New York, 1960.

Wdowinski, D. And we are not saved. New York, 1963.

Weh, A., ed. Das Recht des Generalgouvernements. Cracow, 1941.

Wein, A. "Die anti-yidishe tetigkeit fun 'Antik'". Bleter far Geschichte. No. 12, 1959.

Weinberg, G.L. "Der deutsche Entschluss zum Angriff auf die Sowjetunion". VfZ. No. 1, 1953.

Weinreich, M. Hitler's Professors. New York, 1946.
Weisberg, A. Advocate for the Dead. London, 1958.
Weiss, A. "Jewish Leadership in Occupied Poland: Postures and Attitudes". Yad Vashem Studies. Vol 12, 1977.
Weissmandel, M.D. Min Hameitzar (Hebrew, family edited). Jerusalem, 1960.
Weliczker, L. Brygada śmierci. Lodz, 1946.
Werth, A. Russia at War, 1941-1945. New York, 1964.
Wieliczko, M. "Obóz wyniszczenia w Szebniach w latach 1941-1944. Rocznik Przemyski. Nos. 13-14, 1970.
Wiesel, E. Night. New York, 1969 ed.
Wolken, O. "Z zagadnień losu Żydów w Oświęcimiu". Przegląd Lekarski-Oświęcim. 1964.
Wroński, T. Kronika okupowanego Krakowa. Cracow, 1974.
Wylężyńska, A. "Z notatek pamiętnikarskich, 1942-3". BŻIH. Nos. 45-6, 1963.
Yad Vashem. Documents on the Holocaust. Eds. Y. Arad and others, q.v.
——. The Catastrophe of European Jewry. Eds. Y. Gutman and L. Rothkirchen, q.v.
——. Jewish Resistance during the Holocaust: Conference Proceedings. Ed. M. Grabstein, q.v.
——. Patterns of Jewish Leadership in Nazi Europe 1933-1945. Eds. Y. Gutman and A. Saf, q.v.
——. The Nazi Concentration Camp: Conference Proceedings. Eds. Y. Gutman and A. Saf, q.v.
——. The Historiography of the Holocaust Period: Conference Proceedings. Eds. Y. Gutman and G. Greif, q.v.
Zaderecki, T. Gdy swastyka Lwowem władała. (Mimeographed.) Warsaw, ca. 1957.
Zelechower, N. "Siedem obozów". BŻIH. No. 68, 1968.
Zygielboim Buch (Yiddish). New York, 1947.
Żywulska, K. I Came Back. (Ed. transl. from the Polish.) London, 1951.
Ziemian, J. The Cigarette Sellers of Three Crosses Square. (Transl. from the Polish.) London, 1970.
Zimmels, H. The Echo of the Nazi Holocaust in Rabbinic Literature. New York, 1977.

Periodical Publications

Abbreviations used in bibliography*

Biuletyn Głównej Komisji Badania Zbrodni Hitlerowskich w Polsce (GKBZHwP*).
Biuletyn Informacyjny dla Spraw Żydostwa Polskiego. (London, 1941, 1942.)
Biuletyn Żydowskiego Instytutu Historycznego (BŻIH*).
Bleter far geschichte. (Yiddish, Warsaw).
East European Quarterly. (1978.)
Foreign Affairs. (1950.)

Holocaust and Genocide Studies. (International.)
Jewish Social Studies. (1985.)
Journal of Modern History. (1968.)
Najnowsze Dzieje Polski 1939-1945. (1966.)
Polish Western Affairs. (1964.)
Polskie Sprawy Zachodnie.
Przegląd Lekarski - Oświęcim. (Separate January issues devoted to medical
    problems under Nazi occupation of Poland. Cracow, starting 1961.)
Przegląd Zachodni. (Poznan.)
Rocznik Krakowski.
Rocznik Przemyski. (1970.)
Rocznik Sądecki. (1965.)
Schweizerische Zeitschrift für Psychologie. (1947.)
Social Forces. (1951.)
Vierteljahreshefte für Zeitgeschichte (VfZ*).
Yad Vashem Studies on the European Jewish Catastrophe and Resistance.
Yivo Annual of Jewish Social Science. (1953.)
Yivo Bleter. (New York.)
Zeitschrift für Geschichtswissenschaft.
Zeszyty Historyczne. (Paris.)
Zeszyty Majdanka. (1967, 1969.)
Zeszyty Oświęcimskie.

Trial records (incl. testimonies) in evidence of criminals mostly related to text of
this book. In particular:Willy Bernhard; Hermann Blache; Amon Goeth; Artur
Greiser; Franz Grün; Josef Grzimek; Willi v. Haase; Heinrich Hamann; Kurt
Heinemeyer; Rudolf Höss; Kurt Klipp; Paul v. Malotky; Karl Oppermann; Hanns
Proshinsky; Wilhelm Rommelmann; Hubert Schachner; Johann Unterhuber.
Copies of most of the records (often only excerpts) are kept at the Yad Vashem
Archives in Jerusalem, where the date and place of trials and their original refer-
ence numbers (Aktenzeichen) can be found.

Index